Praise for *Master Planning and Scheduling*—the Book, the Process, the Results!

Past and Present

Be at your best when your best is needed!

"The overarching driver for supply planning and supply scheduling is the master planning and scheduling set of processes. This is covered in depth in the best book ever written on the subject, *Master Scheduling* (Proud 2013). Suffice to say that the term *master* says it all—it is the master of all other detailed supply plans and schedules. *Master Planning and Scheduling* is the fourth edition of the very successful *Master Scheduling* book (originally released in 1994)."

— Rod Hozack, Stuart Harman, Todd Ferguson, and Dawn Howarth, authors of *Integrated Tactical Planning*, Oliver Wight International, Inc.

"In *Master Planning and Scheduling*, authors Proud and Deutsch bring us both the science and the art of integrated planning and day-to-day execution—application based on sound theory—written in a clear and straightforward way. The vital role of master planning and scheduling in a holistic, effective, and efficient planning and execution environment is brought to life in a real-world and compelling fashion. This book is a comprehensive resource for the education, design, implementation, and measurement of best-practice supply chain processes to support sustainable value creation and enduring competitive advantage."

— Bob Hirschey, president, Oliver Wight Americas, Inc. and former vice president, strategic planning, cellulose fibers, Weyerhaeuser Company

"Planning together, as one team . . . a novel concept that is too frequently overlooked. The work here by Proud and Deutsch reinforces the fact that *planning together* is imperative to the success of any organization embarking on a journey of becoming Best in Class. While executing or implementing this plan may be daunting, *Master Planning and Scheduling* provides a roadmap to linking the day-to-day operations with the strategic vision of the company."

—Kris Morgan, director of Planning & Third Party Manufacturing, Curation Foods, Inc.

"Proud's third edition of *Master Scheduling* has been on my desk for the past 15 years. The front and back covers are missing, and the binding barely holds the pages any longer. I've referenced this book at least monthly irrespective of the company/ industry I was working for (consumer products, electronics, capital equipment, pharmaceutics, biotech). In each experience we reaped the rewards a great master planning and scheduling process delivers, and each MPS improvement had its origin in John's (and now Eric's and John's) book."

—Paul McGuire, former planning manager, materials manager, supply chain director

"*Master Planning and Scheduling: An Essential Guide to Competitive Manufacturing* is a comprehensive road map to managing a business in this competitive world. Proud (and Deutsch) teach the value of a disciplined approach to balancing supply and demand, while reducing manufacturing cost via transparency and timely diagnostics."

—Shaker Chandrasekaran, former vice president, Cellulose Fibers Manufacturing, Weyerhaeuser Company

"This latest edition of *Master Planning and Scheduling* further refines the definitive body of knowledge on the topic. A valid master (planning and) scheduling process has been and remains one of the most effective tools to manage the complexities of a manufacturing business and will provide the practitioner as well as the executive with valid insight and support to direct the critical activities of their enterprise."

—Michael L. Bales, former president, Delta/Unibus Corporation

"Proud (and Deutsch) clearly outline, define, and explain the process of master (planning and) scheduling. The book is an excellent read for both the beginner and practitioner, giving either one an understanding of how to apply the concepts and tools for the best results in any manufacturing environment."

—Jimmie White, materials and logistics manager, RGM Products

"Proud (and Deutsch) help the reader understand the application of master planning and scheduling principles and describe what works in great detail. *Master (Planning and) Scheduling* will become the text for any course on master (planning and) scheduling and the standard resource for all manufacturing companies."

—Richard C. Ling, president, Richard C. Ling, Inc.

"Master planning and scheduling, the complex integration of all management planning activities, is presented in Proud (and Deutsch's) effective style. A tremendously broad undertaking, *Master (Planning and) Scheduling* is sensitive to the need of the practitioner to know how and the executive to know why."

—Richard Pugliese, former executive, Monitor Labs, Systech, and Xerox

MASTER PLANNING AND SCHEDULING

OLIVER WIGHT

MASTER PLANNING AND SCHEDULING

An Essential Guide to Competitive Manufacturing

FOURTH EDITION

JOHN F. PROUD | ERIC DEUTSCH

WILEY

Published by John Wiley & Sons, Inc., Hoboken, New Jersey.
Published simultaneously in Canada.

For general information on our other products and services or for technical support, please contact our Customer Care Department within the United States at (800) 762-2974, outside the United States at (317) 572-3993 or fax (317) 572-4002.

Wiley publishes in a variety of print and electronic formats and by print-on-demand. Some material included with standard print versions of this book may not be included in e-books or in print-on-demand. If this book refers to media such as a CD or DVD that is not included in the version you purchased, you may download this material at http://booksupport.wiley.com. For more information about Wiley products, visit www.wiley.com.

Library of Congress Cataloging-in-Publication Data is Available:

ISBN 9781119809418 (Hardcover)
ISBN 9781119809432 (ePDF)
ISBN 9781119809425 (ePub)

COVER DESIGN: PAUL MCCARTHY
COVER ART: © GETTY IMAGES | NANOSTOCKK

SKY10030651_102721

This book was originally (and still is today) dedicated to manufacturing professionals worldwide, especially those who chose or have chosen master planning and scheduling as a career for the past 50 years and beyond.

John and Eric, 2021
Oliver Wight Principals

Additionally, this enhanced and updated master planning and scheduling book is dedicated to my late wife Darlene, who I lost in the final month of 2014. She was always the *wind beneath my wings*. I only regret that I did not recognize enough her contributions to my life, career, and this book during her living years!

John F. Proud, 2021
Oliver Wight Principal

Additionally, this book is dedicated to my amazing wife Claudia, my partner in life's adventures. She keeps my inner curmudgeon in check and makes me laugh when I need it most. You're the best, Babe. I love you!

Eric Deutsch, 2021
Oliver Wight Principal

Oliver Wight Supply Chain Management Book Series

Master Planning and Scheduling: An Essential Guide to Competitive Manufacturing, Fourth Edition
John F. Proud and Eric Deutsch

Supercharged Supply Chain: Discover Unparalleled Business Planning and Execution Practices
James G. Correll, Lloyd C. Snowden, and James Bentzley

Integrated Tactical Planning
Rod Hozack, Todd Ferguson, Stuart Harman, and Dawn Howarth

The Oliver Wight Class A Standard for Business Excellence, Seventh Edition
Oliver Wight International

The Oliver Wight Proven Path, Second Edition
Oliver Wight International

An Executive's Guide to Achieving Class A Business Excellence
Dennis Groves, Kevin Herbert, and Jim Correll

Achieving Class A Business Excellence: An Executive's Perspective
Dennis Groves, Kevin Herbert, and Jim Correll

Demand Management Best Practices: Process, Principles, and Collaboration
Colleen Crum with George E. Palmatier

Supply Chain Colloration: How to Implement CPFR and Other Best Collaborative Practices
Ronald K. Ireland with Colleen Crum

The Transition from Sales and Operations Planning to Integrated Business Planning
George E. Palmatier with Colleen Crum

Enterprise Sales and Operations Planning: Synchronizing Demand, Supply and Resources for Peak Performance
George E. Palmatier with Colleen Crum

The Marketing Edge: The New Leadership Role of Sales & Marketing in Manufacturing
George E. Palmatier and Joseph S. Shull

Gaining Control: Managing Capacity and Priorities, Third Edition
James G. Correll and Kevin Herbert

Purchasing in the 21st Century: A Guide to State-of-the-Art Techniques and Strategies, Second Edition
John E. Schorr

High Performance Purchasing
John E. Schorr and Thomas F. Wallace

Manufacturing Data Structures
Jerry Clement, Andy Coldrick, and John Sari

Distribution Resource Planning
Andre J. Martin

Inventory Record Accuracy, Second Edition
Roger Brooks and Larry Wilson

Orchestrating Success
Richard C. Ling and Walter E. Goddard

World Class Production and Inventory Management, Second Edition
Darryl V. Landvater

Just-in-Time: Surviving by Breaking Tradition
Walter E. Goddard

Just-in-Time: Making It Happen
William A. Sandras, Jr.

The Executive's Guide to MRP II
Oliver Wight

Master Scheduling: A Practical Guide to Competitive Manufacturing, First through Third Editions
John F. Proud

Contents

6
Where and What to Master Plan and Master Schedule 203

7
Scheduling in a Flow Environment 227

8
Planning Bills 255

9
Two-Level MPS Coupled with Other Advanced Techniques 277

10

Using MPS Output for Make-to-Order Products 313

11

Master Planning and Scheduling in Custom-Product Environments 355

17

Demand Management and Aggregate Master Planning 603

18

The Proven Path to a Successful MPS Implementation (Phase 1) 669

19

The Proven Path to a Successful MPS Implementation (Phase 2) 705

20

The Proven Path to a Successful MPS Implementation (Phase 3) 743

Epilogue
Order from Chaos 779

Final Thoughts – People and Process and Profession 783

Acknowledgments

You're never too old to set another goal or to dream a new dream!

We are jointly grateful to a number of people who have shaped as well as enhanced our professional careers through education, coaching, and idea sharing. Many of these people are current and past members of Oliver Wight International, of which we have been members for 33 years (John) and 10 years (Eric). One person in particular, George Palmatier, has had more influence in our combined careers than the many others.

George Palmatier, former Oliver Wight associate, was not only a great thought leader but a great simplifier, a quality that Oliver Wight (the man) held with high esteem. George was the man who could stand up in a room full of passionate (and opinionated) Oliver Wight principals, engage in a heated debate on one topic or another, and speak simple truths and principles that would cut right to the heart of the matter. Simply put, when George stood up, we listened. He brought the same gravitas and unique perspective to his clients. We have had the pleasure in our careers, both as clients of Oliver Wight while in industry and as Oliver Wight principals, to listen to and absorb George's wisdom. We will be forever grateful for his influence, guidance, and friendship.

Additionally, we would like to thank our book reviewers, who spent many hours working their way through parts of this book (the entire book might have been too much for each reviewer in the time allotted in our master plan and schedule!). Those book reviewers are David Goddard, Oliver Wight Americas (OWA); Paul McGuire, OWA; Kris Morgan, Curation Foods, Inc.; Pam Lindsey, OWA; and Ben Sellers, OWA. The book's original reviewers should *not* be forgotten. Those reviewers were Darryl Landvater, OWA and the late Mike Bales, Dick Pugliese, John Sari, and Larry Wilson.

John F. Proud's Personal Acknowledgments

I continue to find myself in a place surrounded by people who care about doing things right and doing the right things. My career has covered 50-plus years from being a naval officer to a co-author of this master planning and scheduling book. Without the navy in my background, I'm not sure what type of person I might have turned out to be. Without Oliver Wight in my past and present, I again don't have any idea where I might have wound up. However, I do know one thing: this book and its preceding three editions might never have been written, or, if they were, I would not be one of the co-authors.

Besides the people already mentioned in my present and past acknowledgments, I want to highlight what a pleasure it was to work with Walt Goddard, Tom Gillen, Al Stevens, Dick Ling, Roger Brooks, Jim Correll, Jerry Clement, Marv Jensen, Bill Pendleton, Tom Allen, Eric Deutsch, and so many others. When I was in learning mode, they taught me. When I was in listening mode, they talked to me. When I was in teaching mode, they listened to me. When I was in troubled mode, they comforted me. And the story goes on!

Now in 2021, I once again find myself in a very privileged situation. Working for the past couple of years with my colleague, Eric Deutsch, we are proud to release this first and only definitive book covering the complete subject of master planning and scheduling.

Original Acknowledgments for *Master Scheduling—A Practical Guide to Competitive Manufacturing*, First (1994), Second (1999), and Third (2007) Editions

I am deeply grateful to a number of people who have shaped as well as enhanced my professional career through education and idea sharing. Many of these people are current and past members of the Association for Operations Management (APICS), which I have been a member of for over 25 years. However, two people have had more influence in that career than the many others.

Dick Ling, former Oliver Wight associate and former president of Arista Education and Consulting, exposed me to the real profession of master scheduling. Had I not crossed paths with Dick Ling and several other Oliver Wight associates, I would not have been able to write this book. I learned my master scheduling skills from the best in the industry— Dick Ling, Oliver Wight associates, and professional master schedulers working in Class A companies worldwide.

Dick Pugliese, while serving as general manager of a Xerox plant, gave me the opportunity to be part of a Class A Manufacturing Resource Planning system implementation. It was during this time that I learned how a manufacturing company should work if it is to be successful and achieve Class A results.

Other colleagues and associates have also taught me much about this complex subject. John Dougherty literally spent hours with me discussing and developing concepts that we hope furthered the industry's understanding of how important master scheduling is to the manufacturing environment. Walt Goddard, John Sari, and Al Stevens also developed numerous master scheduling concepts over the years and were kind enough to share them with me. Oliver Wight associates Tom Gillen, who helped me with the engineering issues, and George Palmatier, who made sure I did justice to the demand side of the business, also deserve recognition.

Several other people who I would like to thank and acknowledge are: Dick Luecke, who was instrumental in taking my thoughts and structuring them into sentences and phrases that actually make sense; Lori Stacey, who spent hours upon hours typing, correcting, retyping, and recorrecting the lengthy manuscript; the Oliver Wight Publications staff, who have been effective, cooperative, patient, and understanding throughout this book's entire process; and the John Wiley & Sons staff, who added the professional flavor.

Once the manuscript draft was available, Mike Bales, former vice-president operations, G & W Electric; Dick Pugliese, retired executive; John Sari, Oliver Wight Alliance; and Larry Wilson, Oliver Wight Americas principal worked their way through the many pages, challenging my thoughts and recommending changes as appropriate. Without their critical input, this book would be less than the book it is today. My "severest and best critic" was former Oliver Wight associate Darryl Landvater, who challenged not only content but organization. A special thank you goes to Darryl for his effort, time, and patience.

Another special thank you goes to my original editor and publisher, Jim Childs, as well as my current editor, Matt Holt, who I am sure I caused great grief when I missed several milestones along the way—What? The person who wrote the book on valid master schedules was "past due"? If you ever doubt how important it is for a manufacturing company to create valid schedules and then perform to these schedules in order to satisfy its customers, just give my publisher a call. In addition to Jim Childs, Dana Scannell was the first to give me the chance to write this book and encouraged me to keep going when my frustrations were high and my stamina was low.

My final thank you goes to my lovely (late) wife, Darlene, who gave me the time necessary and seldom complained about being left alone while I worked in the office. Darlene was truly my best friend, and without her understanding and encouragement, I would never have found myself in a position to write these acknowledgments for what I still believe was the first and only definitive book covering the subject of master scheduling.

Eric Deutsch Personal Acknowledgments

I am deeply grateful for those who had faith in me and enabled me to grow and learn throughout my career. Their companionship, coaching, and inspiration was, and is, invaluable to me.

I began my career at Novagen, Inc., a growing biotech company in Madison, Wisconsin. Tom Foti hired me as a dish scrubber and lab assistant while I was working to attain my Bachelor of Science degree in Bacteriology from the University of Wisconsin–Madison. When I graduated, he hired me as a laboratory production scientist, but soon I took on other supervisory and operational responsibilities outside of the lab under his guidance. Tom and I worked on many projects (scientific, operational, software implementations, etc.) and had many adventures over the ensuing years. It was then that I learned, largely through the school of hard knocks and a little scientific problem solving, how to plan and schedule for manufacturing in a growing company. I owe Tom a huge debt of gratitude.

Tim Moser seemed to appear at just the right time in my career. Tim was an intern at Novagen via the University of Madison School of Business and was hired full time after attaining his MBA in Supply Chain Management. Tim opened my eyes to the true profession of supply chain management. It was through Tim and his network of supply chain professionals that I took my "subsistence understanding" of manufacturing management to a true appreciation of the science behind operations and supply chain management. I must also thank Pete Lukszys for bringing Tim into the Novagen organization and providing his own guidance and leadership to me over the years.

Novagen was the target of several acquisitions over time, ultimately by Merck KGaA. There are many people I would like to thank: Bob Mierendorf and Lisa Johnson for showing executive leadership with heart, compassion, and integrity; Tom Van Oosbree for his leadership, scientific guidance, and being such an all-around great human being; Aditya Sobti (now an Oliver Wight principal) for his faith and guidance through lots of changes and trying times. And all of the friends and colleagues that put up with my mistakes, grew with me, and provided companionship along the way.

I had the privilege of leading the IBP/S&OP implementation in the North American divisions of Merck KGaA and we partnered with Oliver Wight in that endeavor. As a client of Oliver Wight and since joining Oliver Wight Americas, several Oliver Wight principals have been enormously generous in their guidance, mentorship, and friendship. In addition to George Palmatier, who was acknowledged earlier, Donald McNaughton and David Goddard provided valuable guidance and friendship during the Merck IBP/S&OP implementation as our coaches and as my colleagues through the present day—class A guys all the way. I thank Coco Crum for her leadership, guidance, and friendship and for teaching me the principles of demand management. It is a great honor to be working alongside all of my Oliver Wight colleagues and to continue to learn from each of them.

John Proud, my generous and patient colleague and co-author for this fourth edition, has given me an immeasurable gift. His generosity in sharing his decades of experience and knowledge with me, both as a client and an Oliver Wight principal, is beyond compare. The faith and generosity that he has shown to include me in the writing of this fourth edition is also beyond compare. I am deeply humbled and grateful for this opportunity.

Finally, to my wife Claudia, for her love, support, and patience while I was writing the fourth edition of this book. I'm a lucky man!

Foreword

I am honored to provide this forward to the latest edition of the definitive work on master planning and scheduling. I have known John Proud for 17 years and Eric Deutsch for nearly 10. I admire their dedication to the science and art of best-practice master planning and scheduling, and their passion for advancing understanding and application of the subject.

John has impacted me professionally and personally in several ways: as an educator who taught me the basics on best-practice planning beyond just master planning and scheduling, as a coach and mentor who guided me to lead an initiative that achieved over a dozen Class A certifications, as a colleague who I had the privilege of working with side by side to support successful business process transformations at clients, and as a friend who unselfishly offers his wisdom on being an effective part of a business team, whether in support or leadership roles.

Likewise, with Eric I have had the privilege of learning from him, teaching with him, creating with him, and sharing memorable personal and professional experiences with him. I respect both of them deeply for their knowledge, wisdom, expertise, and character.

As with the first three editions of this book, this is not a theoretical treatment of the subject, but is much more practical, application-oriented, and comprehensive. John and Eric bring a rare combination of real-world experience across a wide range of industries, understanding how master planning and scheduling should and really does work and how it interacts with other fundamental planning processes and the software tools to enable effectiveness and efficiency. They have brought all this together in a common-sense and very readable format.

Given its comprehensive treatment, the reader might be overwhelmed by simply reading it cover to cover. I recommend that this book be used in pieces to practically inform and guide process transformations that are most applicable to the most pressing issues and opportunities, reserving other chapters to create general awareness and understanding. On my own transformational journey to Class A, I carried this book around with me as an implementation companion to plants, sales offices, warehouses, and so on to reinforce my own understanding of what good should look like.

This latest edition not only updates the subject matter of early editions, but tenders additional topics—for example, inventory governance planning and data integrity requirements supporting master planning and scheduling. Via this book, John and Eric offer a comprehensive guide that should be used and required reading not only in the manufacturing community, but in business in general as well as academia, and professional organizations and societies.

John and Eric, my sincere appreciation and congratulations for writing such a definitive book on master planning and scheduling: the why, the what, the how, the when, and the who.

Robert Hirschey
President, Oliver Wight Americas, Inc.

Introduction

The Master of All Detailed Supply Plans and Schedules (Below-the-Line)

I seek not to know all the answers, but to understand the questions.

The 1960s were times of radical change in America; the youth of the country challenged almost every traditional value, rebelling in ways unheard of in previous generations. In manufacturing, a much quieter, though no less dramatic, revolution also was taking place.

Traditional means of production and inventory control went by the wayside as companies like Twin Disc and J. I. Case made effective use of material requirements planning (MRP) a reality. Though crude by today's standards, these early attempts at MRP gave manufacturing professionals their first real weapons in the war on production inefficiencies.

When companies first began using MRP, they drove it with a sales forecast and/or customer orders (demand). In other words, to calculate material requirements, computers multiplied the latest demand numbers by the quantities required in the bills-of-material (BOM). The problem with this approach was that it blindly assumed that the resources would be available to manufacture products in sufficient quantities just as it was sold. In fact, in an effort to gain economies of scale and level-load resources, manufacturing companies rarely produced each product in the quantities in which it was sold, though this would be rightfully and continuously challenged by the lean manufacturing school of thought in the coming decades.

Furthermore, as demand numbers inevitably changed over time, material requirements changed with them. With the emerging software tools, it was very possible to generate overwhelming change to schedules that plants and suppliers could *not* handle. This meant that the information in the software system was often in chaos. And so was the production line. The frequent result was an overloaded schedule, underutilized resources, or both.

Some of the MRP pioneers quickly realized that their formal software systems were of little value if they failed to predict and control the resources needed to support the way production was actually scheduled. They also realized that they had left the computer too much decision-making power; nowhere in the process was there a human being who ensured a true balance between demand (customers) and supply (manufacturing and supplier resources). These insights led to the development of a *master schedule* that controlled all other schedules: plant, factory, mill, suppliers, and so forth.

Equally important, a new position was created: that of the master scheduler. These developments really marked the birth of *master production scheduling (MPS)*, or, to use the term originally favored in this book, *master scheduling* and now *master planning and scheduling (MPS)*. (The acronym *MPS* is used throughout the book when referring to master planning and scheduling and/or master scheduling.)

Master planning and scheduling is the pivotal point in a manufacturing business when demand from the marketplace is balanced with the capabilities and capacities of the company and its suppliers in real-time terms. As the modern manufacturing environment has grown more complex in terms of products and product options, and more demanding in terms of the competitive requirements for quality, fast and on-time delivery, low prices, quality service, and technology enhancements, this balancing mechanism has been a vital tool for management at many levels.

At the executive-team level, integrated business planning (IBP) has become the integrator of all top-level plans: product and portfolio, sales, marketing, engineering, manufacturing, quality, logistics, and financials. At middle-management levels, and on the plant, factory or mill floor, master planning and scheduling spells out in detail what needs to be produced so that the company can ensure that capacity will be available, that materials will be on hand when needed, transportation requirements are known, and that customer requirements will be satisfied on dates specified by the customers and agreed to by the manufacturer and/or service entity.

Master Planning and Scheduling as Part of Enterprise Planning Systems

Like all other enterprise planning systems, master planning and scheduling is geared to satisfying market demand while safely making money and a profit. It coordinates that demand with resources in a company to schedule optimal manufacturing and service rates.

To help leadership and management make decisions about aggregate supply rates, the Oliver Wight Companies developed a process called integrated business planning (IBP), formerly known as (advanced) sales and operations planning (S&OP). In the IBP process, the leaders of each major business function meet once a month to review operational and financial plans, make necessary decisions, and approve a holistic company game plan that aligns and synchronizes planned marketplace *demand* with manufacturing's *supply* output.

The integrated business planning team considers products and services by aggregate families. It is the responsibility of the supply manager, master (supply) planner, and/or master (supply) scheduler to break down those aggregate build rates into detailed, weekly and/or daily production schedules for each item within the families. In this way, IBP drives and guides the master (supply) plan and master (supply) schedule.[1]

The expansion of the original material requirements planning technique into a set of functions encompassing strategic management, integrated business planning, product management, demand management, supply management, financial management, master planning and scheduling, material planning and control, capacity planning and control, and supplier and operational scheduling has become known as supply chain management (SCM) supported by enterprise resource planning (ERP).[2] It's fair to say that the addition

---

[1] For a complete discussion of sales and operations planning (now referred to as integrated business planning), see George E. Palmatier with Colleen Crum, *Enterprise Sales and Operations Planning* (Boca Raton, FL: J. Ross Publishing, 2003) and Richard C. Ling and Walter E. Goddard, *Orchestrating Success* (New York: John Wiley & Sons, 1988).

[2] For an up-to-date discussion of supply chain management and enterprise resource planning, see Jim Correll, Lloyd Snowden, and Jim Bentzley, *Supercharged Supply Chains* (Hoboken, NJ: John Wiley & Sons, 2021). Additionally, for another complete discussion of manufacturing resource planning and enterprise resource planning, see Darryl V. Landvater, *World Class Production and Inventory Management* (New York: John Wiley & Sons, 1993), and *Manufacturing Resource Planning: MRPII, Unlocking America's Productivity Potential* (New York: John Wiley & Sons, 1981), Appendix 1, pp. 403–417.

of MPS was a key ingredient in the evolution of MRP to MRPII to ERP, IBP, and SCM (see Chapter 2 in this book for schematics of the MRPII, ERP, and SCM processes and Chapter 14 for more detail on IBP).

Just having a master plan and/or master schedule does *not* ensure success. As with all processes and tools, the master plan and/or master schedule must be managed. Failure to manage the master plan and/or master schedule results in the company's manufacturing and supplier resources being poorly deployed. This in turn means that the company may be unresponsive to customer needs or wasteful in its use of resources. Ultimately, the company risks losing its competitive position. Moreover, if the master plan and/or master schedule is improperly managed, many of the benefits from the integrated business planning or sales and operations planning process will be lost.

Managed well, the master plan and/or master schedule provides the basis for good customer order promising and good resource utilization. By maintaining an up-to-date picture of the balance between demand and supply, master planning and scheduling allows each customer to get the best service possible within the constraints of inventory, resources, and time. And by providing updated information about the current status of company master plans and schedules and their ability to support customer commitments, the master plan and/or master schedule focuses the company's leaders' and management's attention where it is needed. In short, master planning and scheduling plays a major role in helping companies stay responsive, competitive, and profitable.

Who Should Understand Master Planning and Scheduling?

This book is *not* intended solely for master planners and/or master schedulers, but also for those who should participate in designing their company's approach to master planning and scheduling. For master planners and master schedulers—both new to the job and those who have been doing it for years—this book can help them to do their jobs more effectively.

Beginners will find a complete framework for understanding the MPS process and how it connects with the rest of the business. Seasoned professionals will be challenged into rethinking master planning and scheduling at their companies. And all readers will benefit from numerous tricks of the trade, drawn from years of practice/user management, coaching/consulting, and educating/teaching experience.

Leaders and managers in sales, marketing, design, engineering, operations, logistics, quality, information technology, and finance will also benefit from knowledge of master planning and scheduling, which is, after all, the integration point for other planning, analysis, prioritizing, scheduling, data gathering, and performance measurement. They will find the chapters that cover the general principles of the MPS process useful reading.

Executive team members should familiarize themselves with the basic concepts of this book and should understand the later chapters, which cover data integrity (Chapter 13), integrated business planning (Chapter 14), rough cut capacity planning (Chapter 15), supply management and aggregate master planning (Chapter 16), demand management and aggregate master planning (Chapter 17), and the proven path to a successful MPS implementation (Chapters 18–20). This is because master planning and scheduling balances customer satisfaction and resource utilization while supporting the company's strategic as well as tactical directions determined in the integrated business planning process.

As one manufacturing manager put it, "No one ever got to Class A without doing MPS well."[3] It therefore behooves everyone of authority in the company to understand what goes into and comes out of the master plan and/or master schedule.

The master planner and/or master scheduler and people in special environments will benefit from the middle chapters, which cover specific environments and advanced techniques. Overall, the book has been designed to have something for just about everyone connected with today's as well as tomorrow's changing and competitive manufacturing world.

How This Book Is Organized

Master planning and scheduling involves many functions of business and crosses most departmental lines. This is the first and only book designed to pull together a comprehensive body of knowledge about master planning and scheduling and to discuss the

---

[3] The term *Class A* refers to the top rating a manufacturing and/or service company can achieve, based on the Oliver Wight Class A Standard for Business Excellence (formerly titled the Oliver Wight Class A Checklist for Business Excellence, Oliver Wight ABCD Checklist for Operational Excellence, and Oliver Wight ABCD Checklist). The original checklist was developed by Oliver Wight in 1977 and has been updated since to reflect the evolving standards of performance achieved by world-class manufacturing and service companies. (See Appendix A, page 817.)

MPS process within the context of various manufacturing environments. It not only paints a broad perspective across the whole canvas of service and manufacturing operations but provides the fine details needed to understand MPS in specific types of businesses. Whether you make finished goods to stock, manufacturer or assemble or finish to customer order, package/repackage or kit to customer specification/order, or design and build products to customer specifications, you will find information and tools relevant to your business.

Chapters 1 through 6 define the master planning and scheduling process by explaining why and what to master plan and/or master schedule, the basic terminology, calculations, formats, mechanics, and how to manage change using master planning and scheduling. Chapters 7 through 12 cover specific tools and techniques used in various manufacturing environments (make-to-stock, make-to-order, design-to-order, engineer-to-order, make-to-contract, finish-to-order, kit-to-order, package-to-order). Chapter 13 is devoted to data integrity requirements in order to support an effective and efficient master planning and scheduling process. Chapters 14 through 17 describe process supporting functions of MPS, such as integrated business planning, resource requirements planning/rough cut capacity planning, supply management, and demand management. The book's chapters conclude with Chapters 18 through 20, which provide guidelines for implementing and operating successful master planning and scheduling processes across the supply chain and entire enterprise.

Following the 20th and final chapter, the Epilogue describes that fictional chaotic company introduced at the beginning of the book as a company that now has its master planning and scheduling act together and is behaving as a true Class A company as described in *The Oliver Wight Class A Standard for Business Excellence*. Additionally, the authors have included some Final Thoughts regarding master planning and scheduling people, process, and profession.

The reader may think that the authors have provided enough information on successfully running an effective, best-practice master planning and scheduling environment, but no, the authors have more for the reader. The book concludes with helpful appendices full of examples, a glossary defining new as well as well-known terms, and a carefully thought-out index to make it easy to find master planning and scheduling topics and discussions quickly.

Master Planning and Scheduling is not intended to be read cover to cover in one sitting. Rather, the general sections should be covered first, followed by those chapters that address the reader's service and/or manufacturing environment.

This book is intended to impart a thorough understanding of the master planning and scheduling process, how it interfaces with other service and/or manufacturing processes, the roles various people play, and the technology as well as other tools necessary to support it. It aims to arm the reader with the knowledge required to fine-tune the master planning and scheduling process to the needs of his or her own company with the goal of improving customer satisfaction and enhancing competitiveness while safely making money and a profit for the company.

No company ever gets to Class A without managing the master planning and scheduling processes well, nor does anyone ever perform master planning and scheduling well without having a firm grasp of the basic concepts and principles underlying the process. In the service and manufacturing arena, knowledge is truly power. Use that knowledge well, and you and your company will prosper.

Initial Thoughts

People and Process and Profession

Not everything that is faced can be changed,
but nothing can be changed until it is faced.
The time is always right to do what is right!

To open the somewhat lengthy master planning and scheduling discussion, the authors would like to highlight a few initial thoughts regarding supply chain management (SCM) as a complete planning, control, and execution function that includes master planning and scheduling (MPS) as a subprocess of that SCM function. These discussions will center around *behaviors* (as in **people** *behaviors* within a SCM/MPS environment), *break-throughs* (as in *breakthrough* **processes** within a SCM/MPS environment), and *business* (as in *business* **professional** within a SCM/MPS environment).

There have been many changes in the supply chain management and master planning and scheduling world over the past 50 or so years. For instance, people were originally left out of the equation when material requirements planning (MRP) hit manufacturing support and the manufacturing floor; inventory and production control people were told to just buy this MRP system and then sit back and watch all their material shortage problems disappear. Well, that didn't happen! Over the next 10 years, production scheduling professionals were told to just buy this shop dispatching software, sit back, and watch all those missed production due dates disappear. Well, that didn't happen, either! And so, the story goes for many years thereafter.

Best-practice supply chain management along with master planning and scheduling require four forces to be working together to guarantee success regarding planning and scheduling in the competitive manufacturing world. Those four forces are: (1) proper people behaviors, (2) well-designed business processes, (3) technology and tools to support

Master Planning and Scheduling
Is the Clock Ticking for the 3Ps of MPS?

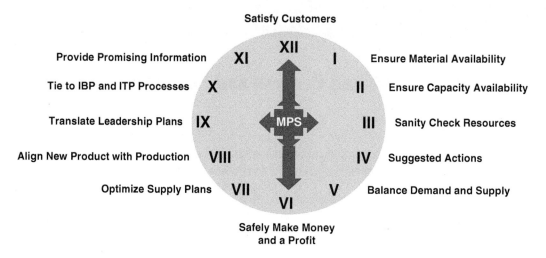

the people and/or processes, and (4) data integrity that is accurate and trustworthy, all the time! Master Planning and Scheduling—Is the Clock Ticking?

Planning and scheduling has been done in some manner as far back as the caveman days. To provide service to a customer or to build a product for a customer requires some type of a plan to gather the needed materials and resources, define *when and what* needs to be done, and then do that *what by the when*!

Some 50 years ago, manufacturing professionals decided that manufacturing operations could no longer be planned by using the ever-changing sales forecast and the profession of master production scheduling, later called master scheduling and now referred to as master planning and scheduling, was born. This was truly a major breakthrough in supply chain management, called inventory and production control at that time.

Master planning and scheduling (MPS) has several basic objectives that are highlighted throughout this book. However, to get us all on the same page before moving into the details of master planning and scheduling, let's take a look at a clock face, on which key MPS objectives have been attached to the numbers.

So, here are the all-important questions that all leadership and management personnel should be asking every day: Does the company have educated and trained master planners and/or master schedulers on the payroll? Does the company have a best-practice master planning and scheduling process in place? Does the company support the notion that master planning and scheduling at a best-practice level is a well-respected profession?

These are the 3Ps (people, process, profession) of MPS and it's because of these 3Ps that this book was originally written before the turn of the century and why it's now being updated for the third time after its initial release in 1994! It should be noted that this fourth edition goes beyond just updating the previous three editions of master scheduling; this update and new edition includes not only master scheduling but describes the all-important master planning part of supply chain management.

The A's to Z's of *Master Planning and Scheduling*, Fourth Edition, 2021

Quoting Steve Jobs (movie version), co-founder of Apple Computer, Inc., "Boards don't run companies; people who build the product run the companies!" Well, if the reader believes that Jobs (as well as this book's authors) got it right, then companies that wish to operate as one of the best in their industry need to embrace the 3Ps cited in the previous section and concentrate on implementing the four force fields (people behaviors, integrated processes, technology and tools, and data integrity) highlighted in these initial thoughts.

As a summary that is now being discussed at the beginning of this book, let's take a look at the A's to Z's of a best-practice master planning and scheduling (MPS) implementation using this MPS book as an essential guide.

A. *Additions* (making additions to the MPS process and system when required)

B. *Benchmarks* (comparison to what works and what doesn't)

C. *Changes* (making changes to the MPS process and system when required)

D. *Deletions* (making deletions to the MPS process and system when required)

E. *Enhancements* (adding, changing, and deleting to make MPS better)

F. *Futures* (guidelines for planning future MPS involvement and the environment)

G. *Gotchas* (watch-outs to be aware of that can disrupt a smooth-running MPS system)

H. *How* to do it (guidelines regarding implementation)

I. *Information* (screens highlighting history and future projections)

J. *Just-in-case* (scenarios and what-if analysis)

K. *Knowing* what should be done (step-by-step approach to success)

L. *Learning* throughout (education and training requirements)

M. *Metrics* definitions (listing and one-pagers as examples)

N. *Numbers/numbers* (time-phased matrices)

O. *Open* and honest (principles to follow when communicating)

P. *Proven Path* (version 2, 1989/1990; version 3, 2007/2021)

Q. *Questions*/answers (asked and replies)

R. *Right way* vs. wrong way (success vs. failure)

S. *Standards* (7th edition, 2017—supported by the 6th and 5th editions)

T. *Task list* for MPS (micro project plan for MPS implementation)

U. *Uniform* and consistent (message is basically the same for 50 years)

V. *Value* of MPS (benefits vs. investment, tangible vs. nontangible)

W. *Workbook* of integrated planning and control including MPS (revision 4, 2017)

X. *X-ray* of MPS (people, process, profession)

Y. *Yardstick* for success (Class A as an objective)

Z. *Zealous/zealots* to MPS success (Yes, we can! and Because we can!)

Time to get started! The authors hope you all enjoy reading this fourth edition of *Master Planning and Scheduling: An Essential Guide to Competitive Manufacturing* as much as they had in creating, updating, and enhancing it.

Chaos in Manufacturing

Don't mistake activity for accomplishment.

A TYPICAL SITUATION IN TODAY'S MANUFACTURING WORLD

The Place: A typical world-wide manufacturing company
The Time: 10:00 a.m.
The Date: Friday, the last day of the month

What had been a quiet and sporadically busy area three weeks ago has turned into a three-ring circus. Lift trucks career through the stockrooms at full tilt, barely avoiding head-on collisions. Every inch of the shipping department is piled with partially completed products waiting for missing materials and components. Normally neat and orderly work areas now resemble obstacle courses as excess materials clog the aisles.

Outside the supervisor's office, an angry manager berates an expediter, demanding to know why the night shift had run the wrong size product. The expediter shifts his weight from foot to foot as he explains that the required product had been at the top of the hot list—and maybe, just maybe, the night supervisor did not get that revision of this week's list (of which there had already been three).

Over in one of the assembly areas, a worker complains that she has gone as far as she can without the next skid from the processing department. A supervisor moves from worker to worker, asking people to sign up for weekend overtime. A chart on the wall shows that 30 percent of the month's shipments still need to be made.

The cost variance reports that were the burning issue of the manufacturing meetings just two short weeks ago are now buried under a stack of quality control reject reports. Management has temporarily waived the rejects so that needed materials and components can be used to meet this month's numbers.

Off in a corner by the coffee machine, a gray-haired foreman shakes his head and mumbles: *"So this is the manufacturing of the future that the folks in corporate promised. It looks like the manufacturing of the past to me."*

This scene continues to play itself out in many manufacturing companies today. Worse, like a recurring nightmare, it returns to haunt companies month after month after month. It happens, in part, because many companies still operate in a reactive mode, in which all decisions, priorities, and schedules are driven by the day-to-day fluctuations of the marketplace, momentary changes in the plant, and the performance of individual suppliers. It is a cycle of action and reaction, and until companies break the cycle, they will never rid themselves of the end-of-the-month crunch and nightmare.

Breaking the cycle entails four steps:

1. Admitting that problems, some serious, exist, and that the current situation is not healthy for the company or the people who work in it;

2. Identifying the specific problems—not just the symptoms;

3. Determining the cause of the problems;

4. Creating and acting on efficient and effective solutions.

Problems in Manufacturing

Consider again the scenario depicted above, this time through the eyes of the managing director, supply manager, and/or plant manager, who sees that although everyone is attempting to do a conscientious job, the efforts are often misdirected. The use of hot lists to establish and direct production priorities in getting products out the door causes major disruptions and confusion in manufacturing. Schedule changes prompted by these hot lists satisfy some short-term requirements but throw a monkey wrench into others. Shipment dates are missed, the customers complain to the sales force, and the sales manager vents his anger onto the production manager.

Although there appears to be much work in process, the reality is that most of the work is sitting in queues. In addition, a staggering amount of unplanned overtime and quality problems are mounting. After inventorying the problems, the plant manager begins to look for their underlying causes. The hot lists, he finds, are used because of frequent material and/or part shortages, some of which result from late deliveries from engineering (specifications) and suppliers (materials), late ordering by the company (poor planning), and nonconforming quality of materials actually delivered by manufacturing (inside supplier) or outside suppliers in general. Other material and part shortages result from inaccurate bills-of-material (missing items or duplicate items, wrong quantities per, incorrect unit of measure) and inventory record inaccuracies showing materials in stock when they are not.

Schedule change problems often stem from the lack of a priority mechanism, or from following the wrong priorities—such as keeping a machine busy rather than satisfying a customer. *(It is not unusual for a company that has just purchased a new piece of expensive equipment to believe that its first priority is to keep the machine running, even if there are no customer orders for the machine's output.)*

Missed shipment dates may result from material and part shortages or problems with capacity (undefined or incorrectly defined as well as overloaded and/or underloaded conditions). Some companies are not ever sure what their capacity is, nor do they have a process in place to measure it. In other companies, measuring processes may be available, but capacity plans are not trusted due to suspected accuracy issues.

Additionally, incomplete product builds and materials can sit in queues on the manufacturing floor because of material and/or part shortages, because of the capacity issues just described, or because plant priorities and work flows are driven by an overly-optimistic demand or sales forecast that is used to communicate priorities to people on the manufacturing floor *(driving manufacturing priorities and material purchases with a demand or sales forecast was identified as a bad idea 45 years ago)*.

Why do so many manufacturing companies today insist on driving their supply chain planning (and execution) with a certain to be inaccurate and constantly changing demand or sales forecast? These forecasts (*if the company lets them*) can and do instruct the plant to build either too much or too little.

Unplanned schedule changes, missed shipments, material shortages, past-due supply orders, and so on might not highlight the real problem or problems. These shortcomings might only be the symptoms of the real problems. Figure 1.1 lists a key dozen-plus symptoms that might cause problems in master planning and scheduling as well as in a company's entire supply chain management function.

Symptoms of Master Planning and Scheduling Problems

Uncontrollable costs	Hot lists
Disruptions on the shop floor	Frequent schedule changes
Late deliveries to customers	Many full-time expediters
Late deliveries from suppliers	Customer complaints
Unplanned overtime/off-loading	Many "past due" orders and plans
High work-in-process	Long queues
Mismatched inventories	End-of-month crunch
Over/underutilized resources	Finger pointing/low morale

**Figure 1.1   Symptoms of Master Planning
and Scheduling Problems**

Does solving the symptoms of a problem or problems solve the problem or problems? In most cases, probably *not*! However, people in supply chain management and master planning and scheduling try every day to do just that—solve the symptom and expect the problem to go away. This entire book is directed at identifying and providing solutions to problems, not solutions to symptoms of problems. There are a few cases within the pages of this book (e.g., safety stocking) where the authors do suggest techniques used to deal with problem symptoms while the company works on solving the real problem or problems.

THE INACCURATE FORECAST

It seems to happen all the time. Marketing forecasts customer demand at one level, while actual demand turns out to be something different—sometimes more, sometimes less.

The difficulty of planning and scheduling production in the face of forecast inaccuracies should be obvious: Materials and capacities are planned for one level of demand, but the demand that actually finds its way to the production facility is something different. Consider the simple case in Figure 1.2. This company's quarterly forecast was off the mark by 25 units (about 8 percent). Not bad, you say! However, its forecast for individual monthly periods was greatly off target. This is typical, as forecasting aggregate demand (such as quarterly) is always easier and tends to be more accurate than forecasting more detailed demand (such as monthly or weekly) or even shorter time periods.

Periods	April	May	June	Quarterly Total
Forecast	100	100	100	300
Actual Demand	140	65	120	325
Variance	+40	−35	+20	+25

Figure 1.2   Case Example of Forecast Accuracy

Unfortunately, most production is scheduled in these shortened (or even smaller) time periods, where grousing about inaccurate forecasts is commonplace but does little to alter the fact that forecasting the future will never have the precision of rocket science. Demand forecasts may be improved, but never guaranteed. Besides, any forecaster who could really see the future clearly would be in the next limousine headed toward Wall Street or Las Vegas or Monaco, where rewards for accurate forecasting are mind-boggling!

Management Issues

People in the day-to-day business of manufacturing must learn to live with the variances between anticipated (forecasted) and actual customer demand, and with the problems they create. For company leaders and managers, forecast inaccuracies create a number of important issues. First among these is the fact that when someone creates a forecast, real things happen: Materials and components are ordered or canceled. If current capacity isn't up to the forecast, people start thinking about increasing it with new equipment and new personnel. If current capacity is greater than the forecasted requirements, people start thinking about decreasing it by shutting down production centers, laying off employees, or even closing entire manufacturing operations. In other words, forecasting demand is not an intellectual exercise done for its own sake, but an activity that triggers a number of other costly actions within the company.

Unfortunately, forecasts are not always taken seriously. Salespeople may be tempted to overstate the demand forecast as insurance against possible stock-outs. The demand forecast itself is generally uncritical of the estimates submitted by each salesperson and contains no rewards and penalties for accuracy. The task of management is getting all parties involved in the forecasting process to work together and take accountability for its accuracy. Production and finance need to understand the concern of sales personnel about stock-outs and lost commissions. Sales and marketing need to understand the cost of excess inventory to the profitability and survival of the company.

There is now a large body of knowledge and experience indicating the heights of customer satisfaction and profitability that result when teamwork replaces hostility among research, design, engineering, marketing, sales, production, procurement/purchasing, receiving, shipping, quality, and financial personnel. Management can and should act as the catalyst in team-building efforts.

While building a cohesive and energized team may be the greatest contribution of the executive team, other issues merit executive and leadership concern:

- *What about inventory?* If a plant is scheduled to build 100 units and orders for 140 appear, is there enough inventory to satisfy the unexpected demand? In the reverse case, when demand fails to appear, should the plant keep running and building inventory?

- *What alternatives exist on the manufacturing floor?* When forecasted orders fail to appear, equipment and trained people are idled—unless alternative work is found. Moving up an order might keep some hands busy that day; maintenance or training might occupy others. When demand exceeds scheduled supply, can more supply be created through overtime or outsourcing of part of the workload?

- *What are some of the real costs of forecast inaccuracy?* An overloaded schedule creates overtime expenses. The production floor and its personnel are stressed and, perhaps, made less productive. Over-forecasted demand creates idle hands and capacity, and inventories of unused materials.

- *How are customers affected?* When actual demand is underestimated, management becomes a traffic cop, directing the company's limited output to certain customers and withholding it from others. This is known in industry to be placing the customer on allocation (such a nasty word). If allocation of product is necessary (the company will not have enough product to satisfy all its customer demand), how should the product be allocated to customers when there simply isn't enough to go around? Which customers get product and when do they get it? *Remember, all customers are equal; it's just that some are more equal than others.*

It should also be noted here that placing a customer on allocation is done when the company does not or will not have enough product to satisfy its demand. This is different from identifying a customer's priority or which customers get their product first, second, third, and so on when product is available.

As management ponders these issues, the fallout of forecast inaccuracies has other minds working. Marketing observes the discrepancies between its forecasts and actual demand and wonders if these mark a trend. If the forecast is usually on the high side, manufacturing thinks about discounting the forecast as a matter of policy. The corporate controller jokes about just tossing the manufacturing budget out the window. Out in the field, the individual salesperson grows apprehensive about guaranteeing delivery on firm orders; when push comes to shove, another sales representative's customer may have priority.

Knowing that forecasts will never match actual demand, except on rare occasions, experienced master planners and schedulers understand that they must be flexible in shifting capacity and materials from one time period to another. They must know whom to call about splitting a customer's delivery over two or more time periods. And they must have the courage to look beyond the forecasted numbers as they plan production. Indeed, many top managers would be stunned to know that the solution to many of their production headaches is in the hands of the master supply planner and/or master scheduler, who either solves them with skill and ingenuity or allows them to fester out of inexperience or indifference. So, what can be done?

And the Solutions

The search for solutions to these problems should begin with a fundamental question: *Why is this company in business? The answer should be: To satisfy customers while safely making money and a profit*. This answer entails ensuring an adequate product supply to meet the demand for the company's products. If a product is not in inventory to satisfy demand, the company must have the material, labor, equipment, capital, and time to produce it. This is where master planning and scheduling (MPS), enterprise resource planning (ERP), supply chain management (SCM), and integrated tactical planning (ITP) play such a critical role in the purpose of the business.

Integrated tactical planning, supply chain management, enterprise resource planning, and master planning and scheduling processes are integrated as well as being demand-driven supply planning processes. This demand can consist of a demand forecast, booked customer orders (which may or may not be part of that forecast), customer contracts or long-term agreements, engineering prototypes, branch warehouse requirements (i.e., replenishing a distribution center), or orders from another division within the company if the product in question is, in turn, a component of that division's products. Demand can also originate in the need for specials (industry shows, samples), service parts or spares, increase in safety stock requirements, or lot sizes.

To satisfy these demands, the master planner and/or master scheduler needs to consider the availability of materials and capacity resources. These materials include those being produced internally as well as those being procured from outside sources. Besides the item itself, quantities, dates, and lead times must be taken into account. Capacity can involve people, equipment, floor space, supplier capability, and so on—all of one's own company and of its multiple suppliers. Time, storage areas, and money are also important considerations.

As mentioned in the Introduction, the challenge the master planner and/or master scheduler faces is to effectively balance product supply with product demand. One way to envision the situation is to imagine a seesaw like the one shown in Figure 1.3 on page 9. In a perfect world, the seesaw is parallel with the ground; supply is always an equal counterweight to demand. When demand changes, supply instantly adjusts in a way that keeps the system in perfect balance. In the real world, however, demand rises or falls in unpredictable ways, and imbalances occur. These occasions require a master planner and/or master scheduler to make adjustments to the system in order to get the demand and supply back into balance.

When a company has more demand for its products than it has supply, it has three options for returning to a balanced condition:

1. Increase the supply of product—get more material and resources.

2. Decrease the demand—turn away or reschedule some demand orders.

3. Some combination of the above.

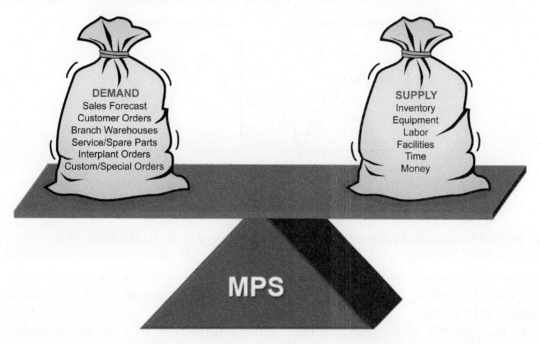

Figure 1.3   Balancing Supply and Demand

The situation in which there is more supply of the product than demand also suggests three choices:

1. Increase demand—energize the sales force, run a promotion, discount the price, and so on.

2. Decrease the supply of the product or the material/capacity needed to produce it—cut back on production, people, and equipment.

3. Again, some combination of the above.

Even though these situations can be solved only by one of the choices described or, as stated, some combination of the noted choices, some companies nevertheless believe that if they ignore the situation, it will just go away—an approach to problem solving called *ostrich management*.

The periodic imbalances between demand and supply are represented in Figure 1.4 on page 10, which shows inventory's constant fluctuations over time between high, medium, and low demand as well as high, medium, and low supply, resulting in a *sawtooth curve*.

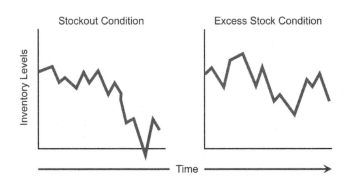

Figure 1.4   The Sawtooth Curves

In profitable manufacturing companies, the goal is generally to stabilize production by level-loading the plant while smoothing out the demand. The situation shown—stock-outs as well as excess inventory—is certainly not the objective; the objective is to have just enough inventory to satisfy demand, thereby satisfying customers and safely making money and a profit.

In the presence of sawtooth demand, manufacturing will be a seesaw in constant motion, with all the stock-outs, hot lists, and confusion that characterize the company profiled at the beginning of this chapter. If the company is not experiencing stock-outs, it is experiencing excess inventories. What is known for sure about this environment is that it continually goes back and forth. Companies that try to smooth out sawtooth demand through artificial contrivances usually fail. Tactics like schedule freezes and placing limits on the volume of orders salespeople can take cause more problems than they solve. Telling a sales force to limit its sales for a particular time period (due to poor planning of the supply constraints), for example, is a sure way to torpedo the important relationship that must exist between the demand organization (sales and marketing) and the supply organization (manufacturing and procurement) if a company is to grow and prosper.

Using these types of approaches is like installing welded struts onto the bottom of the seesaw: nothing moves. A better approach may be to install "shock absorbers" under the seesaw, to dampen expected fluctuations in demand and supply (see Figure 1.5).

Inventory in the form of finished goods, for example, is one traditional type of shock absorber. Inventory helps the company to accommodate changes in both demand and supply. Another type of shock absorber is flexibility in the supply chain, which allows the company to alter the activity rate on the production floor in order to satisfy demand fluctuations without severe disruption. Flexibility can also be extended to sales and

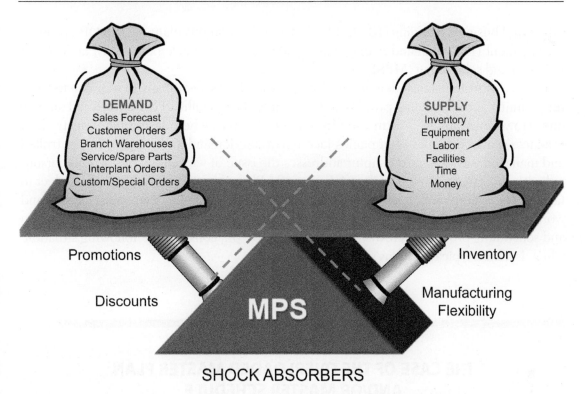

Figure 1.5   Dampening Supply and Demand Fluctuations

marketing. If the customer orders a red item, will a blue one work? If the customer requests the product for a next month or week delivery, would that delivery better suit the customer's business purpose if it arrives in this month or week or in two months or weeks? If the customer cannot be so swayed, discounts or other sales inducements may give the customer reasons to assist you with your demand and supply balancing problem.

The point is, don't be afraid to ask. In any case, the company should identify whether it wants its greater flexibility in demand (sales and marketing) or supply (manufacturing and procurement or possibly engineering). It should decide whether it wants to "sell the products manufacturing makes" or "build the products that sales sells." (Further discussion regarding these choices is done in Chapter 4, "Managing the Supply Chain with Master Planning and Scheduling.") Once that determination is made, the company can move on to the task of balancing product supply with market demand. This effort takes place in integrated business planning (IBP) and/or sales and operations planning (S&OP), product management (PM), demand management (DM), supply management (SM), and master planning and scheduling (MPS).

It's this effort to balance demand and supply that drives a company to improve its master planning and scheduling process and capability. The job ahead certainly is not an easy one. However, Class A (a term used by some companies when describing industry best practices) and world-class companies face uncertain demand and supply in a controlled and managed way. The next chapter addresses the issue of why companies whose personnel wish to formally establish Class A Integrated Planning and Control processes elect to tackle the master planning and scheduling function right from the start. Most Class A and world-class companies believe it's never too early to start to improve their master planning and scheduling processes. However, before we move on, consider the following situation, which is all too typical of today's manufacturers.

THE CASE OF THE OVERLOADED MASTER PLAN AND/OR MASTER SCHEDULE

Some companies are always behind schedule on production and shipment. If Friday afternoons are a hellish race to whittle down the mountain of late manufacturing orders, Monday mornings are even worse. On Monday morning, the manufacturing manager and master scheduler face the dismal prospect of starting the new week under a load of past-due orders. It is tough enough to run a smooth operation when each week begins with a clean slate, but when you are faced with the normal scheduled orders *plus* all the work that failed to get done the previous week, the outlook is far from rosy. Yet, this is how many companies operate today—many on a continuing basis. Like a football or soccer team that starts the second half three touchdowns or goals behind its opponent, the manufacturer that carries past-due orders into the next time period plays a desperate game of "catch up."

Let's look at a typical scenario (see Figure 1.6 on page 13). Spectrumatic Paint Company, which has a weekly capacity of 300 units, begins the current week with 500 units to produce—the result of inept planning and scheduling as well as arm-twisting by salespeople to accept orders, and so forth. To compound its current problem, Spectrumatic ended the previous week sitting on 200 units of past-due orders.

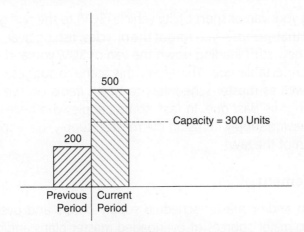

**Figure 1.6   The Overloaded Master Plan and/or Master Schedule
with Past-Due Orders**

There is one unfortunate principle about past time periods and it is *inalterable*: Time that passes is gone forever! Once a current production time period expires, there is no retrieving it, and any orders left undone must either be done in a future period or dropped entirely. Many companies simply move them into the current period. In the case of Spectrumatic Paint Company, its inexperienced scheduler simply piled the 200 past-due units on top of the 500 units currently scheduled, resulting in a total burden of 700 units in a period with 300 units of capacity. As Figure 1.7 shows, this is what the company was faced with on Monday morning.

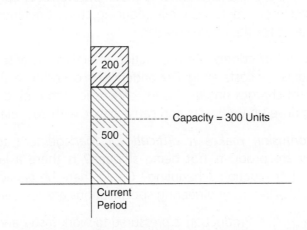

**Figure 1.7   The Overloaded Master Plan and/or Master Schedule with Orders
Rolled into Current Period**

This is like packing your van or sport utility vehicle (SUV) to the rain gutters for a summer vacation, only to find that—*oops*—you forgot the bicycles, fishing gear, and canoe. Chances are that with all this new stuff loading down the van or SUV, you and your passengers are destined for an uncomfortable ride. Therefore, this scenario suggests an ironclad law for master planners as well as master schedulers to obey: *Items on the master plan and/or master schedule cannot be past due.* In fact, some people who believe and live MPS best practices think that having supply items on the master (supply) plan and/or master (supply) schedule is a violation of the law!

Issues for Management

Past-due master plan and/or master schedule supply orders and overscheduling current work periods are two major sources of overloaded master plans and/or master schedules that plague so many companies. And these overloaded plans and/or schedules create a host of *internal* problems for management.

- *Production efficiency decreases.* "Drop what you're doing and start order 247. We have to get this customer taken care of or we'll lose their whole account!" Poorly timed line changeovers, downtime due to material shortages, and stress take a toll on the effectiveness and efficiency within the manufacturing facility. Production supervisors and cell leaders also get mixed signals as to real priorities.

- *Products do not get shipped.* An overloaded master plan and/or master schedule can result in material stock-outs; partially built products are taken offline, where they sit as work-in-process until missing materials are received. Products built, but not shipped, increase inventories while reducing current revenues, thereby creating financing problems for the entire company.

- *Costs go up or out of control.* As production effectiveness and efficiency decrease, financial managers see costs rising. Dependence on overtime, expedited material purchases, air freight charges on late orders, concessions to irate customers, and other compensations drive up unit costs and cause havoc with cost planning and budgets.

- *Widespread confusion makes it difficult for management to identify the real problems.* Why are products not being shipped? Is there a lack of coordination of materials and production scheduling? Could there be capacity problems? How about credit holds? What, engineering specifications are not available?

- *Product quality suffers.* Production is pressured to work faster and faster to complete work in less than planned lead time, possibly causing quality to drop.

Given all of these negatives, the authors have to ask: Why would anyone allow the master plan and/or the master schedule to be overloaded? *Very often, the answer comes down to some basic human behaviors in situations where trust and confidence are absent.*

Consider the sales representative who must ensure delivery of 100 units of Model 5B3 refrigerators to an appliance distributor on the 15th of October. If the company's history is such that production is *always* late, or *always* short, or the stockroom *never* has enough components to complete an order, this sales representative has every incentive to inflate the size of the order and to ask that the order be available earlier in the schedule. "One hundred twenty units delivered to the customer on the first of October" becomes his or her entry to the order book. Discounting production's capabilities is a natural response to past lack of performance, and deliberately overloading the schedule is seen as a way of ensuring that enough materials will be on hand and that enough units will be built. Naturally, production schedulers also learn to play this game and begin discounting orders as they appear. In no time at all, no one can trust anyone else's numbers.

The unfortunate part of this dysfunctional charade is that all the players are motivated to do the right thing: for the sales representative, to fill the customer order with the right quantity at the right time; for the purchasing department, to have just enough materials on hand; for the production facility, to meet *real* demand in an efficient and timely manner.

The net result of all these fine intentions in an atmosphere of distrust, however, is an overloaded master plan and/or master schedule and profit- and energy-sapping people problems, the deadliest being the *blame game*. Sales blames manufacturing for lost orders due to shipment delays. Manufacturing points the finger at the sales representatives, who promise anything to get an order. Everything is a crisis! Finance yells that costs are out of control because of overtime charges as well as air freight expenses. In this atmosphere, the refusal to recognize the seriousness of the problem naturally becomes a survival trait. Why admit that there *is* a problem? You can only be blamed for it and, maybe, fired ("If you can't get the job done, we'll find someone who can!"). Avoidance or denial of the problem becomes the course of least resistance. Sweep it under the rug. Park it at someone else's door.

Ultimately, all the people problems come to rest at the doorstep of the management team. Management must create an environment in which all concerned can be honest about their numbers. Sales and production must be motivated to be frank with one another and to operate in a mutually beneficial partnership. Very often, the key to developing this environment of cooperation is, as W. Edwards Deming noted, to "drive out fear."[1]

---

[1] From W. Edward Deming's "Fourteen Points," in *Out of Crisis* (Cambridge: Massachusetts Institute of Technology/Center for Advanced Engineering Study, 1982), p. 23.

Management must end the blame game and create a climate in which people can admit to problems and past mistakes without fear of blame or retribution. Lacking this climate, problems will simply continue being swept under the carpet.

With fear driven from the workplace, the next step toward dealing with an overloaded master plan and/or master schedule is a top-down analysis that:

- Lists sales and production priorities;

- Seeks practical remedies to production constraints;

- Prioritizes and allocates production to customer demands;

- Establishes a strategy to get out of—and stay out of—the overscheduled condition;

- Implements and communicates the chosen strategy; and

- Monitors and measures the strategy's success.

The ultimate goal of this analysis, of course, is to give leadership and management the knowledge and the tools to shake off the oppressive burden of the overloaded master plan and/or master schedule and to reschedule production with completion dates that are both realistic and that satisfy customer needs to the company's best ability.

Getting Out of the Overloaded Master Plan and/or Master Schedule

One of the primary responsibilities of the master planner and master scheduler is to create a realistic, valid, and doable master plan and master schedule. A valid master plan and/or master schedule is one in which the material due dates equal the material need dates, and the planned capacity equals the required capacity. Look at Figure 1.8 on page 17. As you can see, a master plan and/or master schedule item has gone past due. This MPS item is used to drive the material requirements for all lower-level items as well as the capacity requirements for all manufacturing and engineering resources. If the MPS item is past due, what does that say about all the material that still needs to become part of the scheduled item? All this material is also past due. If we start with a past-due master plan and/or

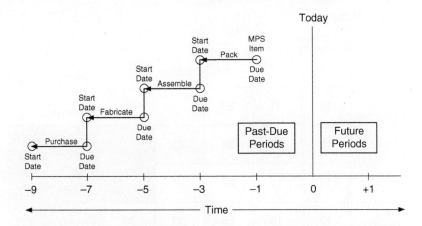

Figure 1.8   Past-Due Master Plan and/or Master Schedule

master schedule due date, all the material and capacity still required, by definition, is past due. And how valid is a past-due date? How do you answer manufacturing, suppliers, or engineering when they ask, "Which past due do you want me to work on today?"

The job of creating a *valid and doable* master plan and/or master schedule is *not* an easy one. It certainly is harder to do than to create an *invalid and unrealistic* plan or schedule. In fact, it is not difficult at all to create an *invalid* plan or schedule! Just about anyone can do that! The real challenge is to create a plan and/or schedule that balances supply of resources and materials with the demand for those resources and materials. So, when in an overloaded condition, how does a master planner and/or master scheduler successfully orchestrate getting out of this inevitable situation?

The first step is to admit that the master plan and/or master schedule is overloaded. With this question answered, an assessment of the situation and identifying the constraints facing the company become necessary. Can overtime be used? Can work be subcontracted? Can more people be hired? Can material be expedited? Can premium air or ground freight be used? Knowing these opportunities and constraints, a rescheduling strategy needs to be identified.

Other approaches to the rescheduling strategy have been tried, most of which have been unsuccessful. Look at the example presented in Figure 1.9 on page 18, which illustrates a situation in which 42 orders have been scheduled over a seven-period (current plus six periods) horizon. As the figure shows, six of these scheduled orders are past due, while five others have been committed over the planned capacity. Clearly, this represents an overloaded master plan and/or master schedule. Over the years, three approaches have been tried to correct this situation. The first approach might be referred to as ostrich

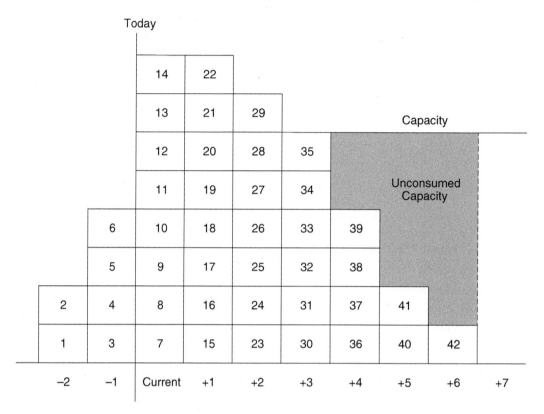

Figure 1.9   Overloaded Master Schedule

management—ignore the situation and it will simply go away. History has shown that this approach has never worked and probably never will.

The second approach is to *freeze the plan and/or schedule*; no more orders are taken until a time period well into the future—this will allow the company to work its way out of the overloaded condition. Refer to Figure 1.10 on page 19 for a visual of this approach. What management or the master planner and/or master scheduler has done in this example is to inform everyone that no orders can be committed for delivery inside of seven periods. By doing this, the master planner and/or master scheduler expects to use the unconsumed capacity in time periods current plus four through time periods current plus six (see Figures 1.9 and 1.10) to work off the overload. In other words, the supply orders keep their same priority and just shift to the right, as seen in Figure 1.10.

How long do you think this directive will last? Maybe about 17 seconds—or until the next customer order that must be committed within the seven-period freeze zone! Another issue with this approach is to recognize that these orders are not shipping because of

Today

	Capacity							
	6	12	18	24	30	36	42	
	5	11	17	23	29	35	41	
	4	10	16	22	28	34	40	
Past Due	3	9	15	21	27	33	39	First New Order Placed Here
	2	8	14	10	26	32	38	
	1	7	13	19	25	31	37	★
	Current	+1	+2	+3	+4	+5	+6	+7

Figure 1.10   A Poor Strategy to Correct the Overloaded Master Plan and/or Master Schedule

some problem (material, capacity, quality, credit hold, missing engineering specification, etc.). This approach somewhat ignores the fact that these problems may exist, and the product cannot be completed as scheduled, or cannot be completed even in the first or second periods, no matter how much pressure is put on the people or the facility. *A better approach, although requiring more work initially, is to reschedule the entire workload into time periods that best satisfy the customer while addressing the supply constraints causing the problem(s) in the first place.*

Rescheduling the Overloaded Master Plan and/or Master Schedule

Using the reschedule strategy requires that the right mix of people—people who have the authority to make decisions—participate in an exercise to put achievable and realistic dates on all orders needing rescheduling. This process may require properly scheduled products to be moved out (or in some cases moved in) due to another product being rescheduled into its committed time slot. Using Figures 1.9 (page 18) and 1.11 (page 21), let's review how this rescheduling process takes place.

Caution! Before beginning the actual rescheduling process, the company should be sure to identify a more realistic approach to booking customer orders in the future. This is important so that when the rescheduling exercise is complete, the company will not find itself right back in the same overloaded condition. Not only does the company need to identify how it will book orders in the future (using available-to-promise and realistic lead times), it must also implement the changes necessary to ensure that this more realistic approach is followed.

To start the rescheduling effort, a few key people must be available. The first and probably most important players are sales and marketing. In fact, when it comes to determining customer priorities, sales and marketing, working with the facts as known at the time as well as within the identified constraints, should have the final say. Manufacturing and materials management also should be included in the session to answer questions on capacities, capabilities, and materials.

Other requested functions may include finance, quality, engineering, and general management. For obvious reasons the president, general manager, or managing director should speak last: it's called "people empowerment" and getting the people close to the situation to solve the problem. Of course, general management always has the right to make the final call. General management is also responsible for breaking ties when sales, marketing, manufacturing, procurement/purchasing, engineering, quality, and finance cannot agree.

Figure 1.9 on page 18 identifies an overloaded condition. Before starting the exercise, the status of each order (why it is past due or scheduled beyond the capacity limits) needs to be known. Once this information is on the table, the painful process of deciding a realistic and valid promise date begins. Looking at order number 1 and reviewing the problems associated with it, the group determines the new, realistic date. In the example, order numbers 1 and 2 remain as the highest priority. Order number 3 has been rescheduled into the current time period plus four, while order numbers 4 and 5 have been rescheduled for a time period 2 (current plus one) delivery. Order number 6 is designated as the number-three priority and rescheduled into the current period. The rescheduling process continues until all orders have new expected delivery dates.

Now, that looks like a lot of work, and it certainly is that! However, as stated earlier, implementing a rescheduling strategy along with a redefined order promising strategy is one that works and works well! But this is the third decade of the twenty-first century and technology has come a long way since a man first walked on the moon. How can

Today

Capacity						
13	22	29	35	38	41	40
9	17	25	34	28	19	42
7	14	24	33	26	11	20
6	5	23	30	32	39	37
2	8	21	28	31	27	16
1	4	15	12	3	26	10

Past Due

Current +1 +2 +3 +4 +5 +6 +7

Figure 1.11 An Acceptable Strategy to Correct the Overloaded Master Plan and/or Master Schedule

the required rescheduling process be a joint venture between man and machine? Let's take a look!

Technology Assistance in the Rescheduling Process

Master planning and scheduling has always, and will always, required technology assistance. People's brains have always been, and will always be, required (in some capacity) as well. However, our human brains will be required to process information at a pace not demanded of them today. In addition to working at an acceptable pace, people's brain storage, as well as recall ability, simply needs technology assistance. With that thought in mind, let's turn our attention back to rescheduling the overloaded master plan and/or master schedule.

First of all, the computer and its related software have most of the pieces needed already as part of the company's enterprise resource planning system. Second, computer hardware and its associated electronic components continue to add new capabilities at lightning speed. Third, and maybe most importantly, is that the technology people will use in the next few decades will integrate directly with people's bodies, from wearable tech to assimilation directly into people's brains. Perhaps, in the future, a master planner and/or master scheduler will create, validate, and approve the master plan and/or master schedule just by thinking it!

Looking inside the company's enterprise resource planning (ERP) system, we see the master plan and/or master schedule (work orders, firm planned orders, computer planned orders—past dues as well as future builds/purchases) displayed as numbers in a matrix format or as a stacked graph based on a priority driven by due dates. Along with the master plan and/or master schedule is the aligned, synchronized, and integrated rough cut capacity planning data displayed in a matrix format or as a stacked graph based on date (time periods in which the master plan and/or master schedule driven resource requirements fall). Using these two pieces of data (or information), the ERP system can balance the required workload using infinite (supported today by people) and/or finite (supported by computer) scheduling software. Therefore, the ERP system is a big plus to the rescheduling effort.

What additional data might be available in the company's ERP system that can be used during the rescheduling exercise? Well, all booked demand—that is, customer orders (past due as well as future requirements)—are noted by customer, product, unit of measure, quantity, and due date. Additionally, all supplier agreements, supplier schedules, purchase orders, firm planned orders for buy items, and computer planned orders for buy items are stored in the company's ERP system. The ERP system can (and does in a Class A company) use this data to calculate the item's available-to-promise (ATP) that can be used by the demand organization to commit and protect the booking of customer orders. Coupled with this ATP knowledge, many companies (most Class A companies) have the ability to identify, in their ERP system, whether a customer order represents *normal* demand or *abnormal* demand.

Normal demand is orders that were expected and included as anticipated (i.e., forecasted) demand when the demand plan was developed. Abnormal demand is orders that were not expected and therefore were not included in the development of the demand plan. In summary, the company can see current obligations, planned obligations, what is available to sell, and which orders may need special consideration when rescheduling.

So, the reader can see that most of the needed pieces to carry out the rescheduling effort are already in the company's enterprise resource planning system. What's missing are a few parameters, such as customer priorities, acceptable customer delivery policies (full delivery required, partial deliveries accepted, split deliveries accepted), acceptable marketing lead times, maximum inventory levels, maximum capacity levels, and supply order requirements regarding rescheduling dates, splitting supply lots, and so on. This list does not look overpowering, nor is it unreasonable to expect that securing the data and loading it into the ERP system is out of reach. Of course, if the ERP system has all the data mentioned in the prior paragraph along with the missing scheduling parameters just mentioned, most of the rescheduling effort can be machine based.

Machine and/or technology based? Yes, the master planning and scheduling rescheduling effort that needed to be done mostly manually just one decade ago can now be done almost completely by the technology. The operative word in the previous sentence is *almost*. As we move into the third decade of the twenty-first century, there still are tasks that people can and will do, such as reviewing, analyzing, tweaking, and finalizing the computer's decisions. However, these tasks will decline as people-intensive tasks and will become increasingly machine-intensive tasks.

For now, touchscreen technology that allows the user to drag and drop data from one place to another can be used during the rescheduling process. If the master scheduler wants to move an item from one time period to another time period, he or she just needs to use the curser or fingers on the screen to drag that item, along with its quantity, due date, specification, and so on, to the other time period. And when the item is dropped into its new location, the rough cut capacity planning graphs are instantly updated. If the master planner and/or master scheduler wants to look deeper into the rescheduling situation, he or she can use technology, like zooming in and out of a satellite photo, to assist in reprioritizing supply orders.

Computers have, and will continue to, become increasingly important and increasingly powerful *technology assistants*. To assist the technology assistant in assisting the master planner and/or master scheduler (that's a mouthful!), sales needs to do their homework each time a rescheduling effort takes place within a company. Sales is responsible for reviewing all customer orders and identifying the priority for each customer order (or group of orders), ranking these orders from high to low. Supply must note why supply orders are past due, including material, quality, capacity, and capability reasons. The leadership of the company must establish the priority for demand and supply based on the manufacturing strategy being used for the items under rescheduling analysis. And, the target inventory (maximum, minimum, and range of asset management) and desired backlog position (acceptable marketplace and customer lead time), must not be overlooked during the overloaded master plan and/or master schedule rescheduling effort.

Let's summarize what was just discussed relating to using the computer and its associated hardware and software as a technology assistant in rescheduling the overloaded master plan and/or master schedule. The computer does the initial rescheduling based on parameters set by the demand organization (sales and marketing), the supply organization (material and production), and the finance organization (financial planning and cost accounting).

Following this initial rescheduling by the computer, the people with the responsibility review, analyze, tweak, and finalize the reschedule draft. Master planned and/or master scheduled orders are moved around in the plan and/or schedule by using the planner's and/or scheduler's fingers on a touchscreen or the curser integrated with the computer. As the master planner and/or master scheduler moves the orders around on the computer screen, the company's rough cut capacity planning charts and graphs are instantly updated. Finally, the revised master plan and/or master schedule is forwarded (with supporting explanations) to management and/or leadership for approval prior to releasing it to the people with a need to know.

What a world master planners and master schedulers live in today. Tomorrow will be even more interesting for the profession of master planning and scheduling!

Implementing the Revised Master Plan and/or Master Schedule

The next step in the process is to secure approval for the new plan from product, demand, supply, and finance general management and leadership. Once this is done, it is time to implement the reschedule and make it happen. This is when the sales and marketing people really earn their money. Someone (with sales and marketing responsibility) must tactfully notify the customer of the anticipated delay and reschedule—generally not a pleasant task. Remember, many of these orders are already late and the customer is now being told that the expected delivery may have been pushed out even further. No, it's not a pleasant task, but someone needs to do it (it's called *open and honest communication*). The challenge now is to ensure that the new delivery dates are met; that means that the company must implement a strict monitoring process. Although implementing a rescheduling strategy may seem difficult (and it is), when coupled with the implementation of the new promising strategy, it works and the benefits are many.

As you can see in the scenario, guarding against an overloaded master schedule is one reason why companies need to pay attention to how they master plan and master schedule. The next chapter discusses the whys of master planning and scheduling and the framework into which this master planning and scheduling process must fit.

2

Why Master Planning and Scheduling

Success in business is easy if you do two things well: plan your work and work your plan.

The Four Cornerstones of a Manufacturing Business

All manufacturing entities have a set of cornerstones—markers that define who they are, whom they serve, and the resources they draw upon. If they have been in operation for any length of time, they have customers, products, internal resources, and a set of suppliers. These are their cornerstones and getting these cornerstones to fit together profitably is one of the challenges of manufacturing.

This view of the manufacturing business is represented in Figure 2.1 on page 26. Here, each of the cornerstones is disconnected, and in the center are the two qualities that must bring them together: vision and competence. Vision is the creative element that sees new and effective ways to combine the resources of the organization (human, material, equipment, and financial) with those provided by suppliers to create products that serve customer needs. Competence is the sum total of organizational and technical skills that transform the intangible vision into tangible plans and the activities that make the vision a reality. These competencies include research and innovation, sales and marketing, design and engineering, manufacturing and procurement, and so forth.

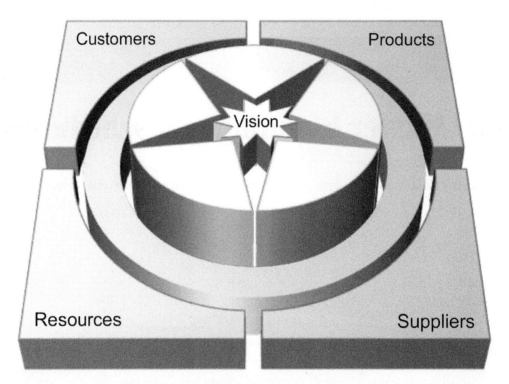

Figure 2.1   Using Vision and Competence to Connect the Cornerstones

Both the vision and the competencies that exist to fulfill the vision express themselves through plans. All businesses have plans. Planning is first among the four essential functions of management, along with organizing, motivating, and controlling. Without a plan there will be no control. Vision expresses itself through strategic plans determined by the executive team, painted in broad strokes, and addressed to the fundamental goals of the company. Strategic plans inevitably speak in the language of finance: revenues of $800 million, pretax earnings of $90 million, and a return on shareholders' equity of 15 percent. At other times they present a market share goal.

But strategic plans cannot, by themselves, accomplish anything. To be fulfilled, they must be broken down into tactical operating plans—*plans that define what must be done*. These plans focus on business problems at operational levels and include:

- *The sales plan:* The number of units the sales team will sell;

- *The marketing plan:* Markets to target; product, pricing, promotion, and distribution schemes used;

- *The design or engineering plan:* Programs and projects on the drawing board;

- *The manufacturing plan:* How much the plant or mill will make, when it will be made, and at what rate;

- *The financial plan:* Target revenues, expense budgets, and profit margins.

These operating plans must be linked with one another and with the strategic plans of the company. The financial plan, for example, establishes target revenues, but this target is meaningful only when plans to make and sell the product are considered. Likewise, manufacturing cannot independently determine what it will make and in what quantities: Manufacturing quantities must be determined in consultation with sales, which has its thumb on market demand; with engineering, which knows what is on the drawing boards; with material planning and procurement, which knows the supplier base and their capabilities; with logistics, which knows transportation availability; and with the financial department, which must pay for materials, labor, and carrying inventory.

Between Strategy and Execution

The broad area between strategic plans and their execution at the tactical level is the domain of middle management. Middle managers or key influencers of the company are charged with the development of lower-level plans and their execution. In this sense, middle management couples the broad strategies of the company to the details of execution. As detail execution takes place, middle management is responsible to ensure linkage of the detail work to the executive's or top management's aggregate plans. Figure 2.2 on page 28 represents the integration between top-management plans and execution.

The master planner and/or master scheduler are, or certainly should be, one or two of these important mid-level management members. This individual (or individuals) operates as a buffer between one set of activities in the company—demand (sales and marketing)—and another—supply (engineering, manufacturing, logistics, and procurement). Customer demand for the company's products can vary from time period to time period, and that variation is difficult to forecast with anything resembling certainty. Suffice it to say here that variation can be greater than manufacturing's ability to respond. Nor is it generally in the company's best interest to have production fluctuate in lockstep with incoming sales.

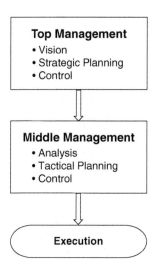

Figure 2.2   Middle Management as a Decoupler

The frequent result of direct linkage between demand from customers and supply from the production floor is the kind of manufacturing chaos and the sawtooth production rates described in Chapter 1. What's needed is a way to decouple the direct input of incoming demand from the company's valued resources until the analysis process required can be completed. The decoupling capability in master planning and scheduling gives a company the opportunity to avoid chaos on the manufacturing floor, uneven production rates, ups and downs in logistic planning/commitments, and stress in the procurement function.

Figure 2.3 on page 29 shows two different planning environments. Company A, on the left, has no (middle management) buffer (master planning and scheduling) function between its demand (sales) forecast and the manufacturing floor or procurement. Its demand forecast drives supply planning, production scheduling, logistics planning, material planning, and procurement directly; there is no intermediate gearing, no decoupler, to keep the demand forecast from causing gyrations in production, logistics, and procurement. Company B, on the right, has interposed a middle management (master planning and scheduling) function between the demand forecast and supply of production, logistics, and procurement.

The master planning and scheduling function has the intelligence and experience to interpret the signals it gets from sales and the forecast, to think of alternative means of satisfying anticipated customer needs, and to make the adjustments necessary in capacity, inventories, transportation, and so forth that allow the company to serve the customer without causing demand and supply imbalance. In so doing, it helps the company avoid

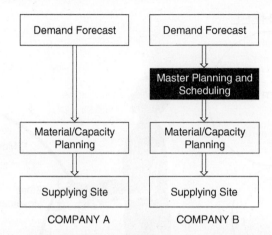

Figure 2.3   Master Planning and Scheduling as a Buffer Between Demand Forecast and Supply of Production, Logistics, and Procurement

manufacturing chaos and fulfills the overarching strategy of profitability while satisfying customer needs.

Both sides of Figure 2.3 show material/capacity planning perched atop the production, logistics, and procurement functions. Material/capacity planning is shown here for a simple reason: Without the buffer provided by master planning and scheduling, material/capacity planning takes the full shock of every fluctuation in the demand forecast. It, in turn, causes production, logistic, and procurement fluctuations, sometimes two, three, even ten times faster than the initial change in the demand forecast.

Figure 2.4 on page 30 presents a couple of analogies to this situation. In the first (left side), a big wheel makes a half turn to the left; its movements cause the small wheel geared below it to make a full turn in the opposite direction. The still smaller wheel attached to it makes two full turns . . . and so it goes, in escalating fashion down to the very smallest wheel, which spins at high speed in response to the slightest movement of the first, largest wheel. In the second, a small movement of the whip's handle causes the end of the whip to move a considerable distance.

Early practitioners of material requirements planning (MRP) discovered how disastrous the unbuffered linkage between production activities and the demand forecast could be, and developed master production scheduling followed quickly by master scheduling (master of all schedules) followed by master planning and scheduling (master of all detailed supply plans and schedules below the aggregate integrated business planning approved supply plan) as the solution. This development allowed MRP to work very effectively. In fact, it was not until the advent of the initial master scheduling computer

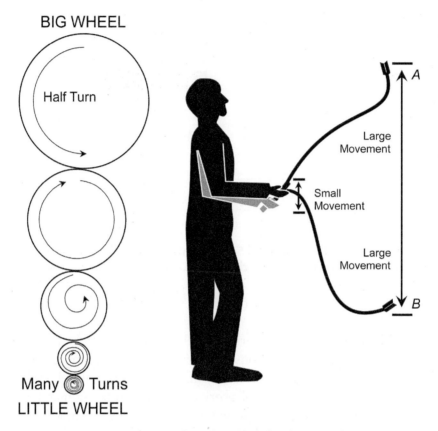

Figure 2.4   Big-Little Wheel and Whip Analogies

software in the mid-1970s and the practical implementation of the master scheduling process that material requirements planning (MRP), enterprise resource planning (ERP), supply chain management (SCM), and now integrated tactical planning (ITP) and master planning and scheduling (MPS) started to achieve their full potential.[1]

Material requirements planning (MRP) users in the early 1970s were unsuccessful because of the missing link of the master schedule (originally referred to as master production schedule and now known as the master plan, master supply plan, master schedule, and/or master supply schedule; the various supply planning levels are described later in this chapter).

---

[1] Oliver Wight could not have defined Class A performance (which first appeared in 1977) without the master scheduling function, now known as master planning and scheduling.

What Is a Master Plan versus a Master Schedule?

The master (supply) schedule is an operational plan, a subset of the larger master (supply) plan that is a subset of the larger aggregate (approved) supply plan (ASP) created in integrated business planning (IBP) or sales and operations planning (S&OP). And like any plan, it is integral to the plans of other functional areas within the company. It must be linked to sales, marketing, design, engineering, finance, materials, manufacturing, logistics, and in some sense, it is in a pivotal position between these and other important functions. As shown in the following list, according to the *APICS Dictionary*,[2] the master (supply) schedule (1), master schedule (2), master scheduling (3), and master (supply) planning (4) is defined as:[3]

1. **Master (Supply) Schedule:** A line on the master schedule grid that reflects the anticipated build schedule for those items assigned to the master scheduler. The master scheduler maintains this schedule, and, in turn, it becomes a set of planning numbers that drives material requirements planning. It represents what the company plans to produce, expressed in specific configurations, quantities, and dates. The MPS is not a sales item forecast that represents a statement of demand. It must take into account the forecast, the production plan, and other important considerations such as backlog, availability of material, availability of capacity, and management policies and goals.

2. **Master Schedule:** A format that includes time periods (dates), the forecast, customer orders, projected available balance, available-to-promise, and the master production schedule. It takes into account the forecast; the production plan; and other important considerations such as backlog, availability of material, availability of capacity, and management policies and goals.

3. **Master Scheduling:** The process where the master schedule is generated and reviewed and adjustments are made to the master production schedule to ensure consistency with the production plan. The master production schedule (the line on

---

[2] Paul H. Pittman and J. Brian Atwater (eds.), *APICS Dictionary*, 16th ed. (American Production and Inventory Control Society [d/b/a ASCM], 2019).

[3] The authors have taken some liberties in the master planning definition by redefining it to only be master supply planning.

the grid) is the primary input to the material requirements plan. The sum of the master production schedules for the items within the product family must equal the production plan for that family.

4. **Master (Supply) Planning:** A group of business processes that include the following activities: supply management (which includes aggregate production and resource requirements planning) and master (supply) scheduling (which includes the master schedule itself, rough cut capacity plan, and available-to-promise).

The key words in the master (supply) schedule definition are *anticipated build schedule*. The master schedule is a statement of supply that drives the detailed material and capacity processes, and that statement is based upon expectations of demand—present and future— and of the company's own as well as outside estimated resources.

Other key points are *specific configurations*, *quantities*, and *dates*, all of which are specified in the master schedule. Finally, the master schedule (as well as the master plan) is *not* a sales forecast; rather, it takes the demand forecast into account, along with the approved supply plan (again, created in the integrated business planning or sales and operations planning process), master (supply) plan if used by company at the corporate level, backlog position (orders booked, but not shipped), desired inventory levels (current and future), availability of material and capacity, and logistic support (transportation availability and associated costs).

Maximizing, Minimizing, and Optimizing

Many books tell us that manufacturing companies should have these objectives: maximize customer service, minimize inventory, and maximize the utilization of company resources as well as the entire supply chain. Ideally, this means running the plant, mill, or factory at or near capacity at all times while keeping inventory levels at or near zero. When the customer calls to order a company-produced product, that product should be just coming off the line for shipment.

Practical considerations of the real world, however, tend to obscure this perfect world of manufacturing. Fast customer response usually requires some inventory, and most manufacturing plants cannot be run at constant, level rates when demand for the product goes up and down on an irregular basis. So instead of being "maximizers" on customer service and plant utilization and "minimizers" on inventory and other supply costs, master planners and/or master schedulers must be "optimizers"—finding the best middle course, the one that best satisfies conflicting goals in demand and supply as well as the tactics and strategies of the company.

Ultimately, master planning and scheduling is an important part of the competence that, along with vision, unifies the four cornerstones of the manufacturing business. Taking its cue from customer demand, master planning and scheduling sets the pace at which internal and external resources are drawn upon. In other words, master planning and scheduling touches all the cornerstones in a manufacturing company.

Objectives of Master Planning and Scheduling
(If You Don't Know Where You're Going, Any Road Will Get You There)

Master planning and scheduling (MPS), coupled with integrated tactical planning (ITP), is the supply chain management (SCM) process that translates the integrated business planning (IBP) approved, aggregate demand and supply plans into understandable and executable, detailed demand and supply plans. Even though the previous sentence is a mouthful, it's only one master planning and scheduling objective. There are probably a hundred or more MPS objectives (one reason this master planning and scheduling book has so many pages), but the authors have boiled that hundred or so into a list of 20 objectives over and beyond the aggregate to detail translation just noted.

The master planning and scheduling process sits right between leadership's (including middle management support) integrated business planning monthly process and supervision's (including key influencers and those who get the work done) production, logistics, and procurement processes. Let's take a look at those objectives that reside in the master planning and scheduling function:

1. Disaggregate aggregate demand and supply plans into detailed plans and schedules;

2. Create a valid and realistic master (supply) plan at the product subfamily level by weeks and months;

3. Create a valid and realistic master (supply) schedule at a grouping and/or stock-keeping unit level by days and weeks;

4. Ensure that the capacity (including tooling) is available when production commences the building process;

5. Ensure that the material is available when production commences the building process;

6. Align new product releases (also new product production testing) with production needs;

7. Ensure that material due dates equal material need dates;

8. Ensure that planned capacity equals required capacity;

9. Optimize the master (supply) plan as well as master (supply) schedule stability, order creation, rescheduling, and load leveling;

10. Implement action as suggested by system-generated exception-driven action messages;

11. Balance customer demand with the company's supply capabilities;

12. Continue to challenge and reduce customer delivery lead times;

13. Provide the demand organization (sales and customer service) with available-to-promise information, which is used in customer order promising and booking;

14. Test supply capabilities to meet demand needs before releasing the master plan and/or master schedule;

15. Ensure that detailed supply plans are synchronized, aligned, and integrated with aggregate supply plans;

16. Identify, negotiate, and resolve conflicts in demand needs and supply capabilities;

17. Create a master plan and/or master schedule that satisfies customer demand utilizing optimal inventory and resource levels and enhances the company's chances to safely make money and a profit;

18. Create the driver for detailed material and capacity planning;

19. Assist demand management in setting priorities when demand outstrips the company's supply capabilities;

20. Establish a working line of communications with all company functions.

It's important for master planners and master schedulers to understand these objectives as well as their responsibilities, which are detailed in Chapter 20. Now that we have discussed the master planning and scheduling objectives, let's take a look at the challenges that a master planner and/or master scheduler face each and every day.

Challenges for the Master Planner and Master Scheduler

Ask someone in the sales function what the demand for digital televisions is and the likely answer will be something like, "$10,000,000 this year or 4,800 units per year—about 400 each month." This way of thinking about sales—in broad terms—suits the sales department just fine. Its planning is most likely done in monthly, quarterly, and annual terms; sales forecasts, commission structures, and sales quotas are usually expressed in monthly, quarterly, and annual figures; marketing budgets are expressed in annual spending. If sales in some months are 300 and others are 500, this may be just fine for the sales department, as they average out to 400 a month, or 4,800 a year.

Down on the production floor, demand painted in broad, *average* strokes will *not* do. The production floor needs disaggregated information: The questions asked by production personnel are, How many should we build today? . . . This week? . . . This month? In this sense, the production floor is more on the customer's wavelength than is the sales department. The customer does not want 1,000 *this year*. The customer wants 100 this week, 125 the next week, 90 the following week. Take a look at Figure 2.5 on page 36.

Customer demand is just as the sales department would likely express it: 4,800 per year, an *average* of 400 per time period. On a period-by-period basis, however, the production department sees volatile demand: 400 in time period 1, 500 in time period 2, 200 in time period 3, and so forth. This kind of volatility is difficult to manage in a manufacturing facility.

For a master planner and/or master scheduler, the challenge is to plan production to approximate the stable master plan and/or master schedule shown at the bottom of Figure 2.5. In a nutshell, the challenge the master planner and/or master scheduler faces to take the chaos out of manufacturing is to balance needs with capabilities in the real world. In other words, the master planner's and/or master scheduler's responsibility is to balance demand requirements (actual customer orders and anticipated customer orders) with the supply build schedule (released production orders, firm planned orders, computer planned orders).

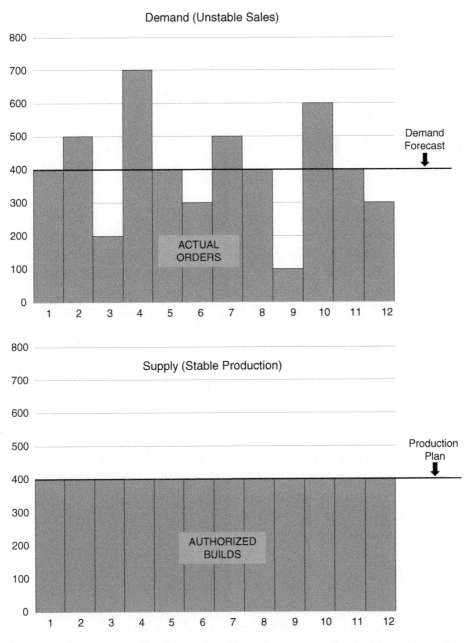

Figure 2.5 The Real World—Varying Demand versus Desired Supply

Principles of Master Planning and Scheduling

But how does the master planner and/or master scheduler (and his or her company) smooth out the peaks and valleys of demand while stabilizing the master plan and/or master schedule? Before we look at some of the choices, let's review some master scheduling principles:

- Today you can't do something yesterday—*no past dues* on the master plan and/or master schedule.

- You can't put 15 pounds in a 10-pound sack—valid, realistic, and doable plans and schedules.

- Bad news early is better than bad news late—communicate (good news also should be communicated).

- Something will always change—firm the plan and schedule in the near-time zone, but do *not* freeze it.

- Demand and supply should be equal over the long term—balance is the name of the game.

- Change is *not* always bad—change can be good if there is time to respond.

- Measurement of changes is critical—it's hard to improve that which is *not* measured.

- Separate external from internal change causes—understand both environments:

  - External: Must respond to customer needs (key business objective is to satisfy the customer).

  - Internal: We have met the enemy and it is us (key business objective is to make money and a profit).

- Understand when a change is costly or impractical—remember, a company objective is to safely make money as well as a profit.

- Management approval must be timely—be careful *not* to overmanage the master plan and/or the master schedule.

- Understand why the supply organization wants to lock down the plan and schedule (no changes).

- Understand why the demand organization wants total freedom regarding the supply plan and/or schedule (multiple changes to satisfy all customer product requirements).

- The master plan and/or master schedule is the balancing point between demand and supply.

- Frozen schedules don't support the customer while ever-changing schedules don't always support the company's business objectives (satisfying customers while safely making money and a profit).

- The master plan and/or master schedule and master planning and scheduling process must act as a shock absorber (eliminate any and all radical swings in demand from making it to the manufacturing floor as well as the procurement function).

- Although today's computing technology improvements and enhancements are happening at the speed of light, people's rationalization remains a key to master planning and master scheduling success.

Keeping these master planning and scheduling principles in mind, here are several choices that the master planner and/or master scheduler can use when smoothing out the peaks and valleys of the master plan and/or master schedule:

- Use inventory and safety stock strategies;

- Manage the supply through the use of overtime, offloading work to other facilities, adding a shift, using an additional or alternate production line, and so on;

- Manage demand by running promotions, offering extras for customers who take early delivery, price breaks for customers willing to delay delivery, and so on;

- Vary the lead time when quoting delivery dates to customers or vary internal lead times by prioritizing orders;

- Use some combination of the above choices—manage demand, supply, and lead time;

- Step up to a modern heresy: turning away customer orders that cannot be delivered as requested; put another way, *choosing the business you want*;

- Design for manufacturability—a longer-term method for coping with demand/supply imbalances in MPS, MRPII, ERP, and SCM.

While most of these choices are people-related, it would be very difficult in today's world for a master planner and/or master scheduler (no matter how gifted) to sort out the right choices from the wrong ones without the use of an effective master planning and scheduling (MPS), manufacturing resource planning (MRPII), enterprise resource planning (ERP), and/or supply chain management (SCM) system(s). The popular system choice over the past several decades has been the ERP system, including MPS and MRP capabilities.

MPS, MRPII, ERP, SCM, and ITP

In essence, four important functions must be fulfilled if the company expects to operate effectively: (1) planning priorities (quantities and dates), (2) planning capacity (internal and external resources), (3) controlling priorities (execution of function 1), and (4) controlling capacity (execution of function 2). To help manufacturing companies perform these functions, a formal integrated process, supported by technology (computer hardware and software) in a variety of capabilities and configurations, is available. Some readers may recognize this process and software as manufacturing resource planning (MRPII) while others may refer to it as supply chain management (SCM) or enterprise resource planning (ERP).

Master planning and scheduling (MPS) is an important element of that process and the system or systems that support it. To understand just where master planning and scheduling fits, see Figure 2.6 for MRPII (page 40) and 2.7 for ERP (page 41). Here master planning and scheduling is one of the four (MRPII) or five (ERP) central boxes—along with integrated business planning or sales and operations planning, resource requirements planning or rough cut capacity planning at the IBP or S&OP level, demand management, supply management, and rough cut capacity planning at the MPS level—which, collectively, form the basic content of this book.

Within the *closed loops* of MRPII, ERP, and SCM, master planning and scheduling is a vital link to these processes as well as the rest of the supply chain management processes. For those who are not familiar with an MRPII, ERP, or SCM system, it may be useful here to discuss some of the main system parts.[4]

---

[4] Here we rely on the description of the MRPII loop provided by Thomas F. Wallace in *Customer-Driven Strategy* (New York: John Wiley & Sons, 1993), pp. 131–135, and the authors' interpretation of enterprise resource planning (ERP).

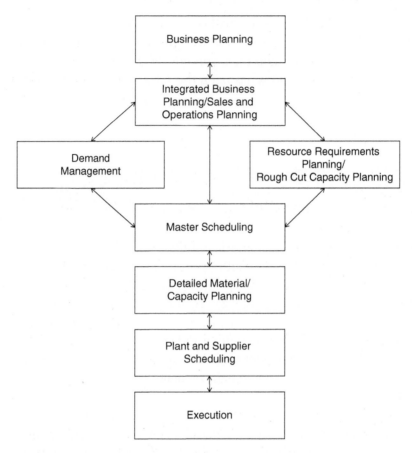

Figure 2.6 Manufacturing Resource Planning (MRPII)

Business Planning

Business planning acts as the brains of this ERP system. As a function of top-level strategic planning, middle-level tactical planning, and company financial planning, business planning is the driver of all other activities. Business planning communicates through both annual, quarterly, and monthly operational and financial budgets that project revenues and expenses for all major elements of the business. Being a top-level function, business planning is done by the chief executive officer (CEO), managing director, or president and other executives of the company and their staffs.

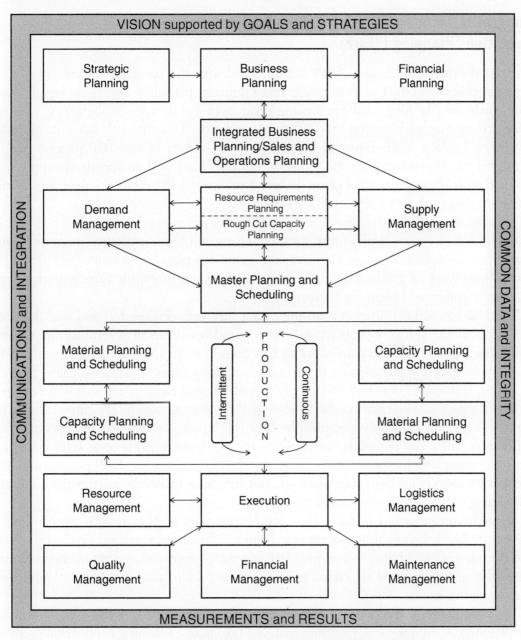

Figure 2.7   Enterprise Resource Planning (ERP)

Integrated Business Planning (IBP)—Formerly Sales and Operations Planning (S&OP)

Integrated business planning (IBP) is concerned with the company's vision, strategies, aggregate (new) product planning, aggregate demand planning, aggregate supply planning, financial planning, and reconciling product/demand/supply imbalances, whereas sales and operations planning (S&OP) was/is concerned mostly with sales, production, inventory, backlog, and shipment balancing. The outputs of the IBP process are an approved (new) product plan, an approved demand plan, and an approved supply plan coupled with aligned financial plans designed to execute the strategic objectives represented in the company's vision and business plan.

The resulting product, demand, and supply plans are generally expressed in financial as well as nonmonetary terms: units, tons, hours, and similar quantitative measures. Integrated business planning as well as sales and operations planning is conducted within the broad framework of product families, rates, volumes, and monthly time periods over a 24-month (minimum) planning horizon.

The IBP (or S&OP) process is an important link between the top and middle levels of management. The process is typically conducted by means of several formal reviews that bring together the company's various functions in order to create a single game plan. In these forums, the participants thrash out conflicting expectations about new product launches, anticipated demand, and supply's capability and capacity to meet that demand.

Other topics covered during the various IBP reviews are opening comments by IBP process owners (e.g., supply vice president for the supply review), performance metrics, action plan items completed, actions needed for this review, and process critique. There is a more complete discussion of the integrated business planning (IBP) process and how the IBP process is aligned, synchronized, and integrated with the master planning and scheduling (MPS) process in Chapter 14.

Once the business functional leaders reach consensus on the various approved plans (aggregate level; i.e., volumes of expected sales, volumes of required production, etc.) and the management business review (MBR) owner concurs and accepts these integrated plans, the aggregate plans are communicated to the middle management level personnel with a need to know.

These high-level approved plans are then disaggregated into the detail required for planning customer sales, planning material purchases, planning production capacity, planning production activities, planning inventory needs, planning backlogs deliveries, planning transportation needs, and so forth. These planning activities are done at the product mix level, for weeks as well as months, and generally for a planning horizon shorter than the 24-month minimum used at the integrated business planning level (e.g., 12-month planning horizon).

Planning and more planning are considered a good thing! Remember, you can't control what you haven't planned. However, planning is only half of the business game and/or business requirement. The other half is that of execution and control. Recognizing this as a fundamental fact in business, a company using Class A processes like master planning and scheduling most likely has a middle-management level of integrated business planning, execution, and control; it's called integrated tactical planning (ITP). Let's take a look at the ITP weekly process, its participants, activities by time period, and expected output.

Integrated Tactical Planning (ITP) with Emphasis on Master Planning and Scheduling—A Brief Discussion

Integrated tactical planning is a near-to-intermediate-term process for optimizing and synchronizing changes in the product portfolio, demand plans, supply plans, and associated financial implications. The ITP time frame is *within the master planning and scheduling planning time fence* as opposed to the integrated business planning process, which *focuses on the planning periods beyond the planning time fence*. Figure 2.8 displays a typical business's time phasing of planning across the entire planning horizon.

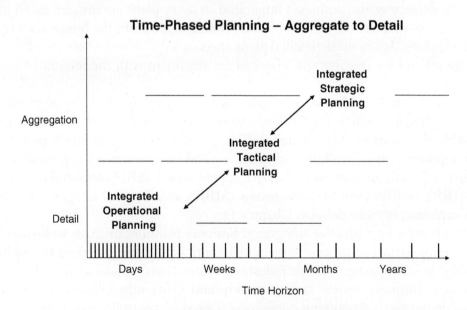

**Figure 2.8   Integrating the Business
(Top to Bottom, Bottom to Top, Side to Side)**

The overall planning process starts at both the bottom (detail subfamily/group-level data and plans/schedules) and the top (aggregated family-level data and plans). Over the near-term horizon (generally three to six months; see Chapters 3 and 4 for more detail on how to define this horizon using policy and tools such as the planning time fence), the detail plans are summarized into semi-aggregate plans, the semi-aggregate plans are rolled into aggregate product subfamilies and product families.

Over the intermediate-to-long-term horizon, the data begins with the aggregate plans supported by higher-level assumptions, including new products that may or may not be present yet in the detail data. The "bottom-up" aggregated detail plans were once "top-down" intermediate-to-long-term plans that were translated into details for execution purposes as the plans moved closer to today.

An important part of the integrated business planning process (IBP; more on IBP in Chapter 14) is to ensure that the detailed bottom-up plans are being executed in accordance with top-down executive direction; therefore the near-term aggregations are checked against previously approved top-down plans for alignment. Once developed, bottom-up *and* top-down, the product subfamilies and product families are reviewed by the leadership team to gain consensus on one-integrated-company game plan, and the one-company game plan is approved and communicated to those with the responsibility for detailed planning, execution, and control.

Stated another way, the business's integrated strategic plans are disaggregated into the business's integrated tactical plans, which are disaggregated into the business's integrated operational plans. Again, these detailed plans are coupled with execution as well as control requirements and are continuously checked for alignment with the integrated company game plan.

When the business leaders review, gain consensus, and approve the aggregate company game plan, a direction for the business to travel is established and communicated to all within the company. The elements of integrated business planning depicted in Figure 2.9, supporting integrated strategic planning and execution, are the product management review (PMR), demand review (DR), supply review (SR), integrated reconciliation review (IRR), management business review (MBR), and financial integration with all of these is explained in more detail in Chapter 14.

Besides using a best-practice integrated business planning process, well-run companies also implement the process known as integrated tactical planning to ensure that leadership direction (coupled with milestone destinations) established during the IBP management business review are effectively and efficiently followed during execution. Integrated tactical planning encompasses product/portfolio management (P/PM),

Integrated Tactical Planning – Business Process

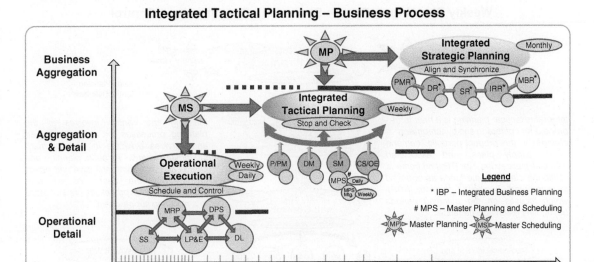

Figure 2.9 Tying Master Planning and Scheduling (MPS) to Integrated Tactical Planning (ITP)

demand management (DM), supply management (SM), customer service (CS), customer order entry (OE), and financial management (see Figure 2.9). Each week, *stop and check* reviews are held to discuss various aspects of the company's ability to satisfy customers while safely making money and a profit (two bookend business reasons why the company is in business).

As Figure 2.9 shows, integrated tactical planning sits in the middle of the planning horizon. Its function is to plan the near-to-intermediate time frames and then couple those detailed plans with execution and control. The integrated business planning process feeds the integrated tactical planning process its intermediate-to-long-term input data, and information is via the company's *master (supply) planning* process. The integrated operational planning process feeds the integrated tactical planning process its near-to-intermediate term input data, and information is via the company's *master (supply) scheduling* process.

Master planning and scheduling is part of detailed supply management, which is part of integrated tactical planning. During the master planning and scheduling process, weekly master scheduling meetings are conducted at Class A companies. The agenda of the master scheduling weekly meeting includes what happened the prior week, what's expected to

Weekly Planning to Ensure Successful Execution and Control

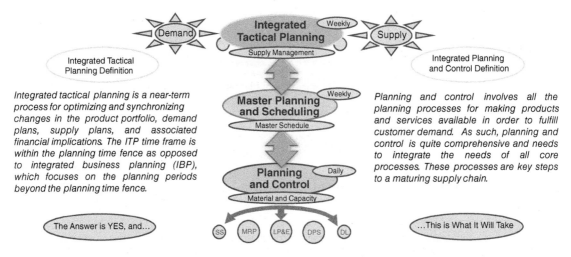

Figure 2.10   You Can't Control the Detail If You Haven't Planned the Detail

happen in the current week, and what needs to be done to ensure that the following week will be a successful week when it comes to master scheduling performance and on-time-in-full shipments. Integrated operational planning, execution, and control is supported by time-phased material requirements planning (MRP), time-phased detailed production scheduling (DPS), supplier scheduling (SS), work dispatch lists (DLs), and logistics planning and execution (LP&E).

Coupled with integrated tactical planning is integrated planning and control. Integrated planning and control involves all the planning processes for making products and services available in order to fulfill customer demand. As such, planning and control is quite comprehensive and needs to integrate the needs of all core processes. These processes are key steps to a maturing supply chain.

As highlighted in Figure 2.10, master planning and scheduling is an integral part of not only integrated tactical planning, but also material and capacity planning along with material and capacity execution along with material and capacity control. Without a master planning and scheduling process, *there is no integrated tactical planning process.* Supply management's key role in integrated tactical planning is to always say "yes" to demand coupled with what it will take to make it happen. Again, this is the detailed planning required so that effective execution can happen with effective control.

The detailed planning associated with master scheduling and tactical planning is a must if the company is to implement and use an effective and efficient control process.

Figure 2.11 is an example of what happens during a week of master scheduling, including the weekly master scheduling meeting. The first thing on the weekly master scheduling agenda is to discuss the past:

1. What was the master schedule performance last week?
2. What is the performance for this month-to-date?
3. What customer orders were shipped last week?
4. What customer orders did *not* ship last week?
5. How well did production run?
6. How were identified production issues and problems handled?
7. Did the suppliers perform?
8. Did logistics get the job done?
9. Were the data record audits within defined guidelines?
10. Were all supply issues handled effectively and efficiently?

Efficient companies do not spend a lot of time on the past, but the master scheduling meeting participants need to know how well their piece of the business performed. Once the discussion concerning the past has effectively and efficiently occurred, near-term future planning commences (refer to Figure 2.11 on page 48). The master scheduling weekly meeting participants turn their attention to what has to be done to be successful during the current and following week. Discussions regarding the first couple of time periods center around the following:

1. What is scheduled to ship this week?
2. What is available to ship this week?
3. Are there any supply concerns about hitting the shipping target for the current week?
4. How does the following week look regarding on-time shipments?
5. Are sales and customer service following the company's customer order booking policy?
6. What actions need to be taken today to ensure success during the next couple of weeks?

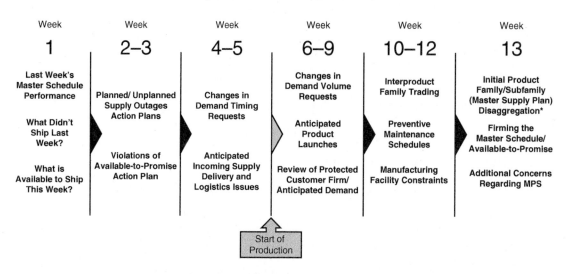

Figure 2.11 Master Planning and Scheduling the Near-to-Intermediate Time Frame

Reviewing Figure 2.11 in a little more detail, the reader observes the layout of a 13-week planning horizon for the master scheduling weekly review. The figure lays out an example of activities and events that might occur during each weekly session. As the master scheduling meeting participants look and discuss the current month (it's a rolling horizon by week—as a week passes, it is dropped into the past time period and replaced by another week on the horizon). What this says is that planning weeks 1 through 5 consist of the current week and the next three to four weeks (five weeks total in Figure 2.11, as an example).

Figure 2.11 next breaks the 13-week planning horizon into five additional pieces or time periods composed of two to four weeks each (it's an example—the reader's master scheduling planning horizon and time period groupings could certainly be different than the example's horizon and/or time period groupings). This example reviews a dozen additional activities and events plus a closing open discussion forum. These key dozen (recommended) activities consist of the following:

1. Planned/unplanned supply outages action plans;

2. Violations of available-to-promise action plans;

3. Changes in demand timing requests;

4. Anticipated incoming supply delivery and logistics issues;

5. Changes in demand volume requests;

6. Anticipated product launches;

7. Review of protected customer firm and anticipated demand;

8. Interproduct family trading;

9. Preventive or productive maintenance schedules;

10. Manufacturing facility constraints;

11. Initial product family and subfamily (master supply plan) disaggregation;

12. Firming the master schedule and available-to-promise.

Note: Additionally, concern regarding the master (supply) plan and/or master (supply) schedule execution probabilities should be addressed.

Also, it should be noted that compliance aggregation is taking place on a regular basis to ensure that the lower-level plan(s) are within the defined tolerance of the higher-level plan(s). What this means is that the weekly master (supply) schedule is summarized for the month and is compared to the monthly master (supply) plan to ensure that the master (supply) schedule is within a defined and approved tolerance (tolerances generally exist for quantities and dates). Again, Figure 2.11 on page 48 and the associated discussion is only an example of what goes on during the near-to-intermediate master scheduling time period planning, scheduling, execution, and control.

As stated earlier and shown in Figure 2.10 on page 46, master scheduling is part of the integrated tactical process. In most cases, the master scheduling weekly meeting precedes the weekly integrated tactical planning review. For this reason, the weekly format and discussion points that occur during an integrated tactical planning review looks much the same as the weekly master scheduling meeting.

Figure 2.12 on page 50 identifies a couple of timing boundaries: (1) what decisions need to be made during the week's review and (2) what decisions can be made at next week's

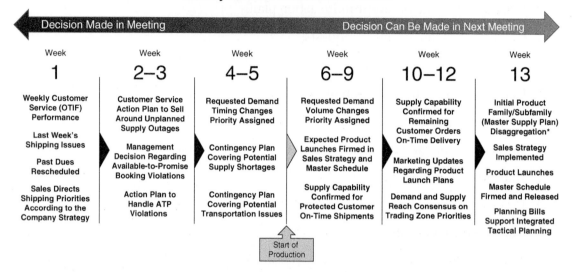

*Compliance aggregation is done weekly, monthly, and quarterly.
Figure assumes a 13-week planning time fence boundary as well as a five-week manufacturing lead time (example only).

Figure 2.12 Integrated Tactical Planning the Near-to-Intermediate Time Frame

review. Additionally, there are six breakouts (the same as the master scheduling template) of the 13-week planning horizon in the example displayed in Figure 2.12. Example formats in Figures 2.11 (page 48) and 2.12 and initial thoughts are derived from the Oliver Wight white paper entitled "What Are You Doing in the Next 13 Weeks?" written by David Goddard[5] (plus the authors' experience).

Here the reader can see that there are four activities that occur during the current or first week in the 13-week planning horizon. The four activities on which the integrated tactical planning participants concentrate their short-term efforts are:

1. Weekly customer service/on-time-in-full performance in the prior week;

2. Last week's shipping issues;

[5] David Goddard, "What Are You Doing in the Next Thirteen Weeks?," Oliver Wight White Paper (New London, NH, 2020).

3. Past dues that are to be rescheduled;

4. Sales directing shipping priorities according to the company strategy.

Once the discussion about the past and current week finishes (again, efficient companies do not spend a lot of time on the past, but the ITP participants do need to know how well *each* of their piece of the business performed during the past week), the near-to-intermediate-term planning horizon is discussed (refer back to Figure 2.12 on page 50). Following the discussion regarding the current week, the integrated tactical planning participants focus their attention on the following activities:

1. Customer service action plan to sell around unplanned supply outages;

2. Management decisions regarding available-to-promise booking violations;

3. Action plan to handle available-to-promise (ATP) violations;

4. Requested demand *timing* changes priority assigned;

5. Contingency plan covering potential supply shortages;

6. Contingency plan covering potential transportation issues;

7. Requested demand *volume* changes priority assigned;

8. Expected product launches firmed in sales strategy and master plan and schedule;

9. Supply capability confirmed for protected customers' on-time shipments;

10. Supply capability confirmed for remaining customers' on-time shipment orders;

11. Marketing updates regarding product launch plans;

12. Demand and supply reach consensus on trading zone priorities;

13. Initial product family/subfamily (master supply plan) disaggregation;

14. Sales strategy planned and implemented;

15. Product launches according to plan;

16. Master schedule firmed and released;

17. Planning bills are used to support integrated tactical planning.

Again, it should be noted that aggregation is taking place on a regular basis to ensure that all lower-level plans are within the defined tolerance of the higher-level plans (e.g., the detailed sales plan is within the approved demand plan as well as the defined demand organization's strategy). Figure 2.12 and this associated discussion is only an example of what goes on during the near-to-intermediate ITP time period planning, scheduling, execution, and control.

As stated early on in this book, the master (supply) plan as well as the master (supply) schedule are the masters of all detailed supply plans. These detailed supply plans can include, but are not limited to, time-phased material plans, time-phased production capacity plans, time-phased production schedules, time-phased supplier schedules, time-phased transportation plans/schedules, time-phased inventory projections, time-phased backlog delivery plans, time-phased discrepant material review schedules, time-phased preventive maintenance schedules, time-phased new product production testing, time-phased first article testing, time-phased quality sample testing, and general plant shutdowns. With all that said, it's the master (supply) planner's and master (supply) scheduler's responsibility to always say *yes to all those requesting supply facility's time* along with *what it will take to make the requested time available.*

There's a lot to the master planning and scheduling process and its tie to integrated tactical planning as well as supply chain management as a whole. The authors recognize that, on first review, the reader may feel a bit overwhelmed with the processes, activities, and reviews that must be executed effectively in order for a company to ultimately achieve its strategic aspirations. It is precisely the *lack* of this level of discipline that leads many companies to fail in executing their strategy.

Championship-level sports teams do not skip practice! They review their past games ("the tapes"), find and rectify their faults, adapt and modify their plans in the face of competition, run the corresponding practice drills, and ruthlessly follow the game plan to best their opponents. They also ensure that they have the resources available to do it all effectively. It is simply this level of discipline that is required to compete and win at a high level. This is what is required for Class A performance.

The following section dives a little deeper into master planning and scheduling. Supporting the integrated tactical planning process is another reason why a company needs to implement an effective master planning and schedule process.

Master Planning and Scheduling

Master planning and scheduling as part of a closed-loop manufacturing resource planning or supply chain management system have already been discussed. The master planner and/or master scheduler must develop a master plan and/or schedule that makes it possible, given the resources available to the company, to meet the requirements articulated through integrated business planning. This plan and/or schedule takes the form of groups of items (or individual items), quantities, and specific dates.

But here, the level of planning is *not* within the broad context of product families, but of product subfamilies or individual product family members; here, quantities and dates are generally not expressed in months, but in days and weeks (master schedule level) except for the end of the master (supply) planning horizon, where months are sometimes used. Furthermore, master planning and scheduling must meet those requirements with a plan and/or schedule that makes optimal use of the company's valued productive resources and time. This is the balancing act described earlier.

In developing this master plan and/or master schedule, four other disciplines are brought to bear:

1. **Demand Management** is the function of recognizing and managing all demands for products to ensure that the master planner and/or master scheduler is aware of them. It encompasses the activities of supporting the demand review in the monthly integrated business planning process, disaggregating the approved aggregate demand plan from the integrated business planning process, aggregate and detailed demand forecasting, customer order entry, customer order promising, identifying branch warehouse demand requirements, processing interplant orders, managing service parts demand requirements, and demand control. Many companies do not pay sufficient attention to this important part of the process. That's a big mistake! Manufacturing resource planning, enterprise resource planning, supply chain management, and integrated tactical planning are all demand-driven processes during planning (which may be demand-driven or supply-driven during execution) and, therefore, the demand aspect of these processes needs full attention.

2. **Supply Management** is the function of pulling together the company's overall supply planning efforts as well as the successful execution of the aggregate as well as the detailed supply plans and schedules. Replenishment quantities are created in response to anticipated and firm demands for product. Supply management encompasses supply planning in preparation for the integrated business planning process, rationing out the supply plan to the company's manufacturing facility or facilities, coordinating finished goods or option inventory levels, planning and managing manufacturing and production to satisfy customer demand, establishing and honoring competitive lead times, and counseling with manufacturing facilities' master

planners and/or master schedulers. This supply management process is called master planning or master supply planning in many companies.

3. **Resource Requirements Planning (RRP)** addresses the question "Do we or will we have the right resources (critical and key groups of assets, labor pools, materials, money, space, and other aggregate resources) to meet the product, demand, and supply plan volumes as currently written, within the strategic direction and financial constraints?" It's a sanity check on the quantities and timing developed in the IBP process (more in Chapters 14 and 15). If the answer is "no" to any of those questions, some rethinking is required.

4. **Rough Cut Capacity Planning (RCCP)** addresses the question "Do we or will we have enough equipment, enough people, enough materials, and enough time to meet the mix-level demand and supply plans as currently written?" It's a sanity check on the quantities and dates developed in the master planning and/or master scheduling process (more in Chapter 15). If the answer is "no" to any of those questions, some rethinking is required.

Many companies do not have the aforementioned supply management function formalized and aligned with the demand management function. Ignoring this critical function in a multiple plant, multiple business, or global business supply chain could be an error. As Figures 2.6 and 2.7 on pages 40 and 41, respectively suggest, manufacturing resource planning, enterprise resource planning, supply chain management, and integrated tactical planning require that demand and supply be in balance at all levels within the global supply chain.

The remainder of the closed loop, detailed material/capacity planning, detailed operations/logistics scheduling, and material/capacity execution and control is very much a part of the MRPII, ERP, SCM, and ITP processes and systems. Full discussion of these important interfaces with master planning and scheduling is, however, beyond the scope of this book. Suffice it to say that once the master plan and/or master schedule is created by groups of items (or individual items), quantity, and time, its groups or items are "exploded" using planning bills (see Chapter 8 for a detailed discussion on planning bills and their usage in master planning and scheduling), bills-of-material, recipes, and formulations to determine the gross requirements for all lower items. Master planning and scheduling (MPS) coupled with material planning, capacity planning, plant scheduling, supplier scheduling, logistics planning, and execution ensure that the materials and the capacity to build all of the items planned by the master planner and/or master scheduler are available at the right time, in the right place, and in the right quantities.

Not shown in Figure 2.6 or Figure 2.7 are other important functions that make master planning and scheduling (MPS), MRPII, ERP, SCM, and ITP possible. For example, inventory records with a high degree of accuracy (95 percent minimum and, in some cases, as high as 99.5 percent) are required to support the master planner's and/or master scheduler's most basic decisions along with bills-of-material that define the contents of products in detail must be at least 98 percent (in some cases, as high as 99.5 percent) accurate. The process routings that identify the sequences of events that a product goes through to become the desired product must be at least 95 percent (in some cases, as high as 99.5 percent) accurate in regard to structure, sequence, manufacturing centers, and times (within tolerance) for setup and run. Besides the routing data, a manufacturing center database identifying available, demonstrated, planned, and maximum capacities must be available to support the overall MRPII, ERP, SCM, and ITP processes for many (if not all) manufacturing environments.

Enterprise Resource Planning (ERP)

Through the years, manufacturing resource planning has expanded its scope. When industry integrated the operational plans with the financial plans, it was called *manufacturing resource planning II* or MRPII. Twenty (maybe even 25) years ago, it was time to start thinking about the next iteration of that development cycle. Driven by hardware and software advancements, MRPII was renamed *enterprise resource planning* (ERP). Unfortunately, there have been several definitions of ERP throughout industry. For example, 20 years ago the Association for Supply Chain Management (ASCM), formerly known as American Production and Inventory Control Society (APICS), defined ERP as an accounting-oriented information system for identifying and planning the enterprise-wide resources needed to take, make, ship, and account for customer orders.

The definition went on to say that an ERP system differs from the typical MRPII system in technical requirements such as graphical user interface, relationship database, fourth-generation language and computer-aided software engineering tools in development, client/server architecture, and open-system portability. Based on this definition, one could certainly reason that ERP 20 years ago was (and still is) nothing more than a technology enhancement (don't lose this thought).

Another source at the time defined ERP as an integrated application software suite that balanced manufacturing, distribution, and financial business functions. The noted source stated that ERP was the technological evolution of MRPII through the introduction of relational database management systems (RDBMSs), computer-aided software engineering (CASE), fourth-generation languages (4GLs), and client/server architecture.

The definition went on to state that when fully implemented, ERP could enable enterprises to optimize their business processes, and it could allow for necessary management analysis and appropriate decision-making in a quick and efficient manner. Furthermore, as more robust technology is implemented, ERP improves an enterprise's ability to react to market changes.[6]

According to the Piper Sandler Companies, ERP is any software application that automates and synchronizes the day-to-day operations of medium to large organizations.[7] This includes cross-industry operations, such as financial management and human resource management, as well as industry-specific operations, such as manufacturing, distribution, and merchandise management.

These three definitions supported the notion that ERP was (and still is) a technological evolution of MRPII (remember, we are holding the thought from above). However, advancements in the areas of human resources, quality, finance, maintenance, logistics, and transportation management provide today's enterprise with processes to better plan and control the business. So, the authors believe that ERP is a term given to what might have been called "*advanced* manufacturing resource planning" or "supply chain management" or "integrated tactical planning" (refer back to Figure 2.7 on page 41).

Reviewing the figure, the reader will note the addition of strategic planning, financial planning, supply management, human resource management, quality management, financial management, maintenance management, and logistics management to the manufacturing resource planning diagram shown earlier in Figure 2.6 on page 40. These additions are not to imply that companies using MRPII or ERP failed to do these activities; they certainly did, especially in Class A integrated planning and control companies. The intention of Figure 2.7 is to highlight the emphasis on other business processes that affect or are affected by the master planning and scheduling process. It also can be seen in the figure that the manufacturing environment quite often affects the sequence in which business activities are performed. (For instance, planning intermittent production usually does material planning and scheduling before capacity planning and scheduling, while planning continuous production does capacity planning and scheduling before material planning and scheduling.)

The last thing to note about Figure 2.7 is that it all starts with the company's vision, which is supported by the company's goals and strategies (see Figure 14.2 on page 458 for a graphic showing company activity ultimately driven by the business vision). To achieve Class A recognition in Managing Internal Supply (according to *The Oliver Wight Class A*

---

[6] "Computer Integrated Manufacturing," The Gartner Group.

[7] "Supply and Demand Management," Piper Jaffray brokerage firm (now Piper Sandler Companies).

Standard for Business Excellence, 7th edition), a company must demonstrate clear lines of communications and integration, use a single set of numbers of the highest integrity, measure accuracy and performance for improvement purposes, and achieve defined and approved results. Put it all together and the company becomes a best-practice enterprise based on criteria that have been (and are) accepted throughout industry as the supply chain management standard for the last 40+ years. From this point on, enterprise resource planning (ERP), supply chain management (SCM), and integrated tactical planning (ITP) will be used when referring to various processes that integrate with the master planning and scheduling (MPS) process.

Supply Chain Management (SCM)

Supply chain management (SCM) is defined as a process that brings together the design, planning, execution, control, and monitoring of supply chain activities with the objective of creating net value, building a competitive infrastructure, leveraging worldwide logistics, synchronizing supply with demand, and measuring performance globally. In other words, supply chain management is the process that brings together the internal and/or external links in a product management, demand management, supply management, and financial management environment for a single company or multiple companies. This SCM process works to form a team or linked chain for the purpose of making products and providing these products and services to the customer (see Figure 2.13).

An integrated supply chain is characterized by a smooth, continual product flow that is matched to consumer consumption. Additionally, information is exchanged in a timely, paperless flow. Supply chain management interfaces with all business and management

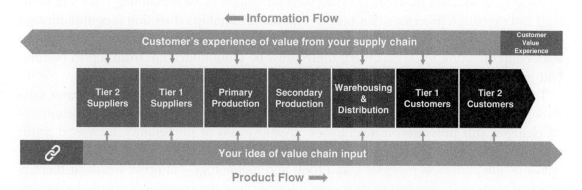

Figure 2.13   Supply Chain Management (SCM)

processes that involve planning and scheduling in the supply chain. Companies involved in SCM seek to get better product to the customer, faster and for less money. If this is done properly, a win-win situation is created and maintained. SCM is also known as customer/supplier collaboration and partnerships. It should be noted here that customer/supplier collaboration and partnerships could exist internally within a company (a machine operator at manufacturing operation 20 with a machine operator at manufacturing operation 30) as well as externally outside of the company (with the company's customers and suppliers).

Master planning and scheduling occupies a critical point in the MRPII, ERP, SCM, and ITP processes—midway between the planning functions of top management and the detailed tactical and operational levels that turn those plans into products that satisfy customers. To better appreciate *why* master planning and scheduling is such an important part of the entire process, consider the following scenario, which the authors refer to as the *Diamond*.

Finding the Diamond in the Rough—Why It's Important

Companies have for a long time struggled with leadership planning as well as sales and production planning at too detailed a level. The leadership team generally works hard to set the direction for the company. However, many times this direction is not communicated well enough to the people within the company who have the responsibility to execute the plans in order to move the company in the desired direction.

Integrated business planning coupled with integrated tactical planning is a set of planning and execution processes that ensure that the leadership's direction is communicated and executed. The operative word in the last sentence is *integrated*. In order for the leadership direction to be executed, there must be communication from top to bottom, bottom to top, and side to side. This is why the *Diamond* is so important.

Today, businesses have many challenges. Some of these challenges are greater customer expectations, fierce competition, shorter product life cycles, forced environmental changes, stiff pressure on inventories, greater levels of uncertainty, increased profit pressures, and higher shareholder expectations. If there are disconnects among the company's people, business processes, and tools and technology—in other words, if there is a lack of alignment, synchronization, and integration of the company's people behaviors, planning and control processes, and computer hardware/software coupled with work instructions—it becomes difficult to face these challenges and operate a successful enterprise. And it can be worse if there is a lack of data integrity, that is, the people who should be using the data just don't trust any of it!

What's needed is a company-wide, integrated set of business guidelines operated by people with best-practice knowledge and know-how (supported by Class A business workflows), business processes that are formalized (supported by the computer and functioning software), and technology and tools that are used by people who have defined and approved roles/responsibilities/relationships/accountabilities. Of course, these people behaviors, business processes, technology/tools, and data integrity come along with the requirement of solid communications among the company's departments/suppliers/customers. This aligned, synchronized, and integrated approach can avoid frustration, alienation, and automated chaos.

The next question is, "What does a company need to integrate?" Enter the Diamond. The elements of the Diamond are integrated business planning (formerly known as sales and operations planning), demand management, supply management, resource requirements planning, and master planning and scheduling. These processes need to be linked up and down as well as side to side. To get us started, let's take a brief look at each of the Diamond's five pieces (see Figure 2.14 on page 60).

Integrated business planning (sales and operations planning) is the first piece of the Diamond. Integrated business planning is a process led by senior management that, on a monthly basis, evaluates and revises time-phased projections for new product, demand, supply, logistics, and the resulting financials. Sometimes referred to as sales and operations planning, it is a decision-making process that drives the tactical plans for all business functions into alignment with the business plan and company vision. A primary objective of integrated business planning is to reach consensus on a single operating plan that allocates the critical resources of people, equipment, materials, time, and money to most effectively satisfy customers in a profitable way. The planning horizon is typically a rolling 24 months.

Integrated business planning concentrates its effort on intermediate- to long-range planning (typically month 4 and out). The focus is on strategies and tactics, such as what the company is going to manage (inventory, lead time, capacity, demand), where the company is going to meet the customer (manufacturing strategy such as make-to-stock, make-to-order, etc.), and who in the company is going to manage changes to the approved and/or released plans (preparation for anticipated demand, consensus tactics to handle demand variation and uncertainty, etc.). Regarding integrated business planning, the Diamond is really about achieving an integrated set of numbers and running the business with integrated plans with common shared tactics.

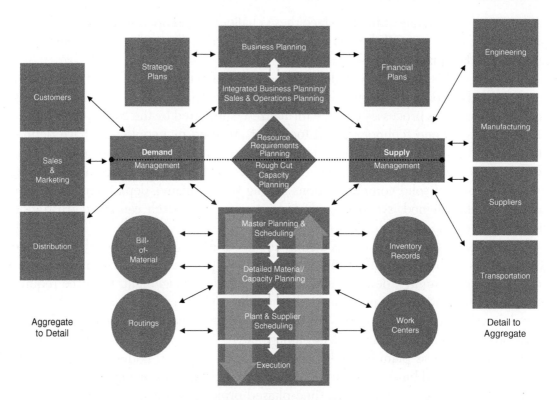

Figure 2.14   Integrating the Functions of the Diamond

The second piece of the Diamond is demand management. According to Philip Kotler, a respected thought leader on marketing management, the purpose of demand management is to influence the level, timing, and composition of demand (composition of demand is the mix breakdown of the noted volume).[8] In order to do this, there are four parts of demand management. The first part is to predict (forecast the customer requirements). Once this is done, the anticipated demand, as well as firm demand, must be communicated (the second part) to the people with a *need to know*. The third part is to influence (get the customer to buy the company's products) followed by the fourth part, that of prioritizing and managing (sell what the company makes versus make what the company sells).

The initial element in demand management is demand planning or assumption-based predictions of demand. Several process steps are included in demand planning—marketing input, statistical analysis, sales input, business plan and strategy, product/brand management input, and customer input. Using this information, a demand plan is created.

---

[8] Philip T. Kotler and Kevin Lane Keller, *Marketing Management*, 14th edition (Pearson, 2011).

The demand plan is a projection of *unconstrained demand* for product. Unconstrained demand means that the initial demand plan is *not* constrained by production capacity to manufacture the product (i.e., supply), but *is* constrained by the company's strategy. The demand plan is the company's ability to get business if supply capacity was never an issue.

Once consensus is reached on an unconstrained demand plan, it becomes a formal request from the demand organization (sales and marketing) to the supply organization (supply planning, manufacturing, procurement, and logistics) to make the relevant materials, capacity, and transportation available at the time that sales and marketing anticipate customers will require them. The demand management part of the Diamond is the mechanism for reaching this consensus and communicating the formal *request for product* to the supply organization.

Effective demand management communicates initial demand as well as changes in demand to the supply organization in sufficient time with sufficient detail for supply to economically respond. Benefits of good demand management include improved customer service, proactive customer management, improved margins, reduced inventory, reduced firefighting costs, better understanding of the business, and improved marketing and sales plans (improved market share) as well as dramatic improvement in cash flow.

Coupled closely with demand management is supply management, the third piece of the Diamond. The purpose of supply management is to put a supply plan together that satisfies customers while safely making money and a business profit. Dependent upon the manufacturing strategy for the product being planned, the supply plan is equal to the demand plan plus the desired ending inventory minus the beginning inventory (make-to-stock strategy) or it is equal to the demand plan plus the beginning order book minus the desired ending order book (make-to-order strategy). In other words, the supply plan is equal to the demand plan plus or minus desired inventory and/or order book adjustments.

Once the desired supply plan is created, it is sanity-checked using the fourth piece of the Diamond, that of resource requirements planning or what is often called rough cut capacity planning. The purpose of resource requirements planning (rough cut capacity planning) is to test the validity of the supply plan and to initiate action to make intermediate-/long-range capacity adjustments. (Note: Rough cut capacity planning logic is also used to test the validity of the master plan and/or master schedule after they are created.)

A company's capacity must be planned for make-to-stock products, make-to-order products, design-to-order products, new product development, article one runs, scrap and rework, emergency changes, production line updates, tooling changes, and productive/preventive maintenance. Successful resource/capacity planning and control suggests that there is a balance between the company's required capacity and the manufacturing facilities' planned capacity, which is based on demonstrated output plus or minus any planned changes to the resource or intended work location.

The final piece of the Diamond is master planning and scheduling. The approved supply plan (through the integrated business planning process or IBP) is the *budget* for master planning and scheduling. The master (supply) plan and/or master schedule is the anticipated build plan by specific items or group of items, specific quantities, and specific dates. Whereas the approved IBP supply plan is by product family, the master (supply) plan may be by product subfamily, and the master schedule is by members of the product subfamily. Whereas the approved IBP supply plan is noted by volume, the master (supply) plan and/or master schedule is noted by mix. Whereas the approved IBP supply plan is displayed in monthly time periods, the master (supply) plan is displayed in weeks and months while the master schedule is displayed in weeks and sometimes days.

The focus of the master schedule is months 1–3 using a planning horizon of 6–12 months. The focus of the master (supply) plan (as part of supply chain management) is months 4–6 with a planning horizon of 9–18 months, which is different from the approved IBP supply plan where the focus is months 4 and out using a planning horizon of 24 months.

The goals and/or objectives of master planning and scheduling are to translate leadership's approved aggregate demand and supply plans into detailed demand and supply plans for middle management, support sales and customers, execute the aggregate IBP supply plan, balance demand and supply at a detailed level, regulate response to suggested demand and supply changes, manage the valuable resources of the company's manufacturing facilities, and provide visibility to the company's suppliers of what is needed to support the company's build schedule.

The master (supply) plan and/or master schedule is a balancing act between demand and supply. Additionally, the master (supply) plan and/or master schedule is a projector of required material to purchase, people required to build, cash needs for spending, equipment capacity requirements to use in building process, logistics/transportation needs for storing and moving product, and the necessary tooling, again to support the building process.

The master planning and scheduling process uses computer hardware and software to create and maintain an integrated plan and/or projection for demand, supply, inventory, backlog, and lead times. The master planning and scheduling process provides available-to-promise information that is used by the demand organization to promise, commit, and protect booked customer orders. Finally, the master planning and scheduling process assists management in resolving issues that arise during the near-to-intermediate time periods.

To make it all go, the master plan and/or master schedule is aligned with the approved IBP supply plan and becomes the *request for supply* to the manufacturing facilities. If the Diamond remains "lost in the rough" (i.e., *not* properly implemented), the direction set by the leadership team drops into a *black hole* (see Figure 2.15 on page 63).

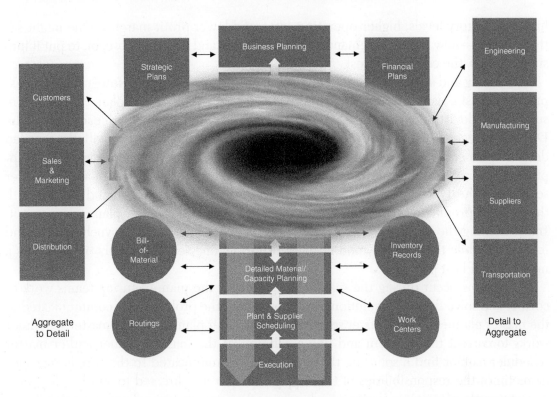

Figure 2.15 Lose the Diamond in the Rough—Drop into a Big Black Hole

Now, how does a company make the Diamond work to its advantage? The trick is to operate the business using one set of integrated plans linking leadership's direction to the demand and supply functions, at both an aggregate level and a detailed level. Companies generally have most of the elements of the Diamond but have often *not* developed them into an integrated management process. Sometimes what the demand organization wants is in conflict with what the supply organization wants, which may be in conflict with what the financial organization wants or what the leadership team wants.

Therefore, the approved new product plan, the approved demand plan, the approved supply plan including the logistics plan, and the approved financial plan must be communicated to the people with a *need to know*. Breakdowns in this integration effort can occur if the people do *not* trust the plans, or there are constant last-minute changes, or there is a lack of communication as problems occur, or a consensus is *not* reached on a balanced demand and supply plan. If a breakdown occurs, the consequences may be poor on-time delivery, product can't be delivered, dissatisfied customers, lost sales revenue, higher inventory levels, higher operating costs, and lower profit margins. One might say that all sides—new product, demand, supply, logistics, and finance—lose, or, to put it into simple terms, the company loses!

The linking and alignment of the Diamond is a must! The output of integrated business planning must ensure that the approved new product development plan, demand plan, supply plan, logistics plan, and financial plan are linked and aligned with each other. The Diamond suggests that the approved demand plan be linked and aligned with the detailed demand plan (sales and marketing plan). The Diamond suggests that the approved supply plan be linked and aligned with the detailed supply plan (master plan and/or master schedule). The Diamond suggests that the master schedule be linked and aligned with the detailed production schedule as well as the material and capacity plans to support it. Implementing the Diamond means that all plans are linked, aligned, synchronized, and integrated while the company and business are using one set of numbers (now, there's a mouth full of best practice).

If problems occur during the manufacturing cycle, the manufacturing teams work to correct and solve them. If a solution cannot be found, the problem(s) is communicated to the master planner and/or master scheduler. The master planner and/or master scheduler works to correct the problem and find a solution. If the master planner and/or master scheduler cannot find a solution, the problem is communicated to the supply manager (sometimes the responsibilities of the supply manager are directed to and handled by a master supply planner or senior supply planner). Again, the supply manager works on finding a solution and if this cannot be done, the problem is communicated to the demand manager (sometimes the responsibilities of the demand manager are directed to and handled by a master demand planner or senior demand planner).

The process of looking for the solution continues until a solution is found, or the problem is communicated to demand/supply management and/or leadership team. As one can see, the successful implementation of the Diamond ensures linkage and alignment top to bottom (leaders to machine operators and buyers), bottom to top (operators and buyers to leaders), and side to side (demand to supply and supply to demand).

In summary, the Diamond is customer focused, drives the delivery of the business plan, ensures that plans are integrated and realistic, creates the company game plan, welcomes and anticipates external change, drives internal change through continuous improvement, and deploys the strategic plan. Alignment of the Diamond is all about customers needing products, products that have demand plans, demand plans that have supply plans, operational plans that have financial plans, results with expectations, resources with needs, and desires with capabilities. A company and business can have all this if it implements the Diamond to a Class A certified level!

WHERE HAVE ALL THE ORDERS GONE?

"We really missed it this time," the marketing vice president sighed as the chief executive officer (CEO) and other managers stared glumly at his revised forecast. "Frankly, we were as surprised as everybody else that interest rates would spike upwards as they have. And that single fact accounts for the dismal outlook for orders over the next few time periods. The financing costs for the customers are just too unfavorable right now."

"So, when do you expect things to pick up again?" the manufacturing vice president asked.

"When interest rates come back to earth—and please don't ask me when that will happen. I don't know, and I doubt that any of the so-called experts know either."

Original Forecast	10	10	10	10
Actual Demand	7	4	3	1
Master Schedule	10	10	10	10

Indeed, the current outlook for the next four time periods was dreadful. Almost as bad was the uncertainty. As a producer of expensive machine tool equipment, sales were extremely sensitive to interest rates, and uncertainty as to future rates created a puzzle for production planners and schedulers. If rates came back down, demand for the company's products would quickly bounce back. As for correctly forecasting those rates, the firm's treasurer liked to say that "those who tell don't know, and those who know don't tell."

The current master schedule has undoubtedly already triggered the purchase of materials and components and building other components of various lead times, which are either in the stockroom or somewhere in the pipeline. The production capacity is there; the skilled personnel are there; the fixed costs of the plant are there. All that's missing are the customer orders. What to do?

Lots of head scratching takes place in times like these. The marketing people wonder: "Why was our forecast so far off target?" The sales force beat the bushes for opportunities to fill the gaping hole in its revenue forecast. Manufacturing evaluates other ways to utilize unused capacity, fearing layoffs of experienced people who might never come back when business improves. The people in finance start having nightmares in which production keeps "humming along" and keeps piling up expensive and unsold inventory.

Management Issues

The situation just described raises a number of management issues—both with respect to the current situation and with respect to a company's whole approach to the problem of operating in environments of unstable demand. In terms of the immediate situation, some would advocate pulling up three of the orders from the second time period into the first time period. Perhaps some customers could be induced to take early delivery. This would keep all activities on course through the first time period but would create a worse situation for the second time period.

An optimist would hope that a sudden uptick in demand would rescue the master schedule and might build inventory in the expectation of an order turnaround. Someone once said that the definition of an optimist is "a person who has no experience." A pessimist would begin reducing capacity and laying off labor. Someone also once said, "I'd be a pessimist, but it wouldn't work anyway." A pragmatist would think through alternatives for preserving the company's financial, productive, and human resources through a hostile period: building common items or parts for use in a variety of company products; rescheduling material purchases to later dates; redeploying personnel to other useful work.

What Kind of Company Are We?

The situation of slack demand provokes a larger question introduced earlier about a company's sense of itself: Are we in business to sell what we make or to make what we sell? A production-oriented company sells what it makes; it usually listens more closely to technical capabilities than to the voice of the customer and relies heavily on sales and marketing to move its steady output. In the face of slack demand, it may slow down, but it rarely stops. Instead, it invests heavily in a tool set that sales and marketing can use to clear its inventory and/or reduce its backlog—price flexibility, attractive financing terms, warranty extensions, and so forth. A sales-and-marketing-oriented company makes what it sells. When sales are brisk, production responds; when order volume withers, its production responds accordingly—it is not in the business of just pushing product.

Which orientation is best? It probably depends on the product, the industry, and the time period (more discussion in Chapter 4, "Managing the Supply Chain with Master Planning and Scheduling"). But one thing is certain: both require flexibility. The company that sells what it makes needs flexibility in the ability to move finished goods and/or options. The company that makes what it sells needs greater flexibility in production; for it, the model of *lean production*—the capability to produce at low cost in small batches, and to economically switch production to other items—may be an important key to getting through periods of slack demand like that in our example.

The Four Cornerstones of Manufacturing Revisited

The first part of this chapter conceptualized the manufacturing business as four cornerstones—customers, products, resources, and suppliers—integrated by the unifying power of vision and competence. As the following chapters will make clear, master planning and scheduling is a competency like engineering, logistics, and finance. It represents a capability to get the job done and to fulfill the larger vision and mission of the company.

To see the core of vision and competence in more tangible terms, refer to Figure 2.16. Here the core of the company is represented by five people-based technologies that, when linked together, integrate the four cornerstones of the business. Starting at the top and moving clockwise, these pieces are: (1) customer-driven strategy, (2) new-product development, (3) total quality management, (4) people and teams, and (5) planning and control.

Each of these people-based technologies is critical to the success of a manufacturing company, and each is worthy of study. It is also a matter of convenience that each

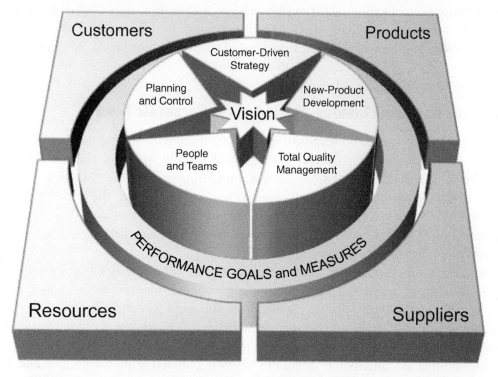

Figure 2.16   Integrating Elements of the Manufacturing Business

is represented separately, as if there were no links between them, or that somehow one piece—new product development, for example—did not have its own requirements for planning and control, or total quality management in the development process, and so on. Master planning and scheduling, the subject of this book, resides in the planning and control wedge of the figure.

Four Levels of Planning (Sometimes Use Only Three)

It has long been said that you can't control what you haven't planned! Companies that choose to implement Class A supply chain management processes, including master planning and scheduling, traditionally do planning at four levels (possibly some companies use only three planning levels) within their business organization: (1) integrated business planning/sales and operations planning, (2) master planning/master supply planning/supply management, (3) master scheduling/master supply scheduling, and (4) detailed production scheduling/shop floor dispatching. Let's take a look at each of these planning levels and how each level is integrated with the other levels (see Figures 2.17a and 2.17b on pages 69 and 72, respectively).

Integrated Business Planning—Level 1 at the Corporate Level

The company's executives are responsible and accountable for setting the direction for the business as it moves into the future. If we go back roughly 40 years, this was done solely using the popular, but somewhat ineffective, budgeting process. Let's make sure that we start this discussion on the right foot—we are not suggesting that the budgeting process (still used today) is a bad thing. What we are suggesting is that this annual event (referred to as budgeting) should be accompanied with a more dynamic process called integrated business planning (see the top of Figure 2.17a).

Integrated business planning (IBP) is the latest and most effective advancement in executive leadership, direction setting, communication alignment, executive management, and proactive replanning of the enterprise's business. This aggregate executive planning process is a monthly series of executive management reviews centered on the company's various product families. The key discussions taking place during the IBP reviews discuss volumes of business, that is, anticipated demand volumes, planned supply volumes, and so on.

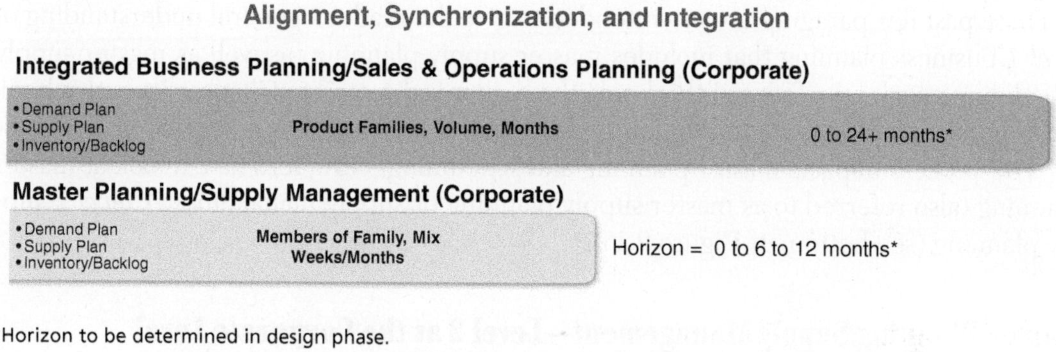

Alignment, Synchronization, and Integration

Integrated Business Planning/Sales & Operations Planning (Corporate)

- Demand Plan
- Supply Plan   **Product Families, Volume, Months**   0 to 24+ months*
- Inventory/Backlog

Master Planning/Supply Management (Corporate)

- Demand Plan
- Supply Plan   **Members of Family, Mix**   Horizon = 0 to 6 to 12 months*
- Inventory/Backlog   **Weeks/Months**

*Horizon to be determined in design phase.

Figure 2.17a   Supply Planning at the Aggregate Levels

Additionally, anticipated resultant volumes of inventory for each product family using a make-to-stock strategy and resultant volumes of backlog remaining to be shipped for each product family using a make-to-order strategy are reviewed.

This monthly balancing of demand and supply is done at the product family level (this is an executive process and therefore needs to deal in volumes and units of measure that are meaningful to the executive—executives need to stay out of the weeds). The one unit of measure that all executives are familiar with is the financial unit of measure, that is, dollars in the United States, pounds in the United Kingdom, euros in European countries, and so on.

The integrated business planning horizon is a minimum of 24 months, with each period of time being equal to one month. The executives' focus during the series of reviews is generally month 4 through month 24 (other more detailed processes, such as integrated tactical planning and master planning and scheduling, are focused on months 1 through 3—again, executives need to stay out of the weeds). In most companies the IBP process is composed of five (sometimes six) steps: (1) product management review, (2) demand review, (3) supply review, (4) integrated reconciliation review, and (5) management business review. Not to be forgotten is that all-important executive unit of measure, the financial number.

To incorporate financials, some companies add a formal financial appraisal review (i.e., standing monthly meeting, established agenda and participants, action items, etc.) just prior to the integrated reconciliation review, while other companies prefer to do the *financial appraisal* more as a *preparatory process* derived from each of five steps previously noted, and feeding into the integrated reconciliation review where the financials will be assessed (either way, the financials are a critical part of the IBP process).

These past few paragraphs were intended to give the reader a general understanding of *level 1* business planning that includes master supply planning (as well as master supply scheduling), again, the focus of this book; the reader is directed to Chapter 14 in this book for a more in-depth understanding of the integrated business planning process and how the IBP process impacts master planning and scheduling. Now, let's take a look at master planning (also referred to as master supply planning or supply management), *level 2* supply planning (see bottom of Figure 2.17a).

Master Planning/Supply Management—Level 2 at the Corporate Level

The master (supply) planning portion of the master planning and scheduling process starts the disaggregation of the aggregate product family (level of planning done at the IBP process level). During this level 2 planning process, the aggregate planning done in level 1 is broken down into a vocabulary that middle management and key business influencers (regarding plans execution) understand, or, said a different way, a language that adds some detail to the aggregated volume plans.

Each product family is divided into members of that product family, product family volumes are broken down into the mix of products offered within each product family, the monthly time periods at the beginning of the 24-month planning horizon are divided into weeks while further out in the horizon, monthly time periods may remain, and the supply planning horizon is shortened to, say, 9–18 months (a general statement for this book's discussion is that horizon depends on the company's business and the manufacturing strategies used).

Master (supply) planning for large companies is traditionally done at the business's corporate headquarters, regional offices, or a manufacturing/distribution site with multiple supply operation sites reporting to it. The aggregate, approved supply plan is most likely for the entire business; that aggregate, approved supply plan by product family must be disaggregated into members of the product family and supply requirements distributed to the various supply (manufacturing) facilities as a *request for product* or *request for supply*.

In the year 2022 the supplying site (manufacturing facility) still *should have* the *right of refusal* when it receives the request for product or request for supply. The reason for having the right of refusal is that the receiving manufacturing site may *not* have the capacity or capability to do the work (even if an IBP-level resource requirements plan indicated no issues, the mix can uncover constraints that were not visible in aggregate) or there is not enough time to secure the materials required (even if the request for supply is communicated to the plant at or beyond cumulative material lead time, unforeseen issues may occur in material supply).

Letting the requesting entity know that there is an issue early in the game gives the higher-level entity a chance to place the request for product or request for supply on another supplying site that does have the capacity, capability, and material needed or they (the alternate manufacturing site) can secure the capacity, capability, and material needed to satisfy the request for product or request for supply.

Another Class A principle is to only hold people (or things, such as computers—see the authors' final thoughts following this book's Epilogue) accountable for things that they (or it) can control. It doesn't matter how good the manufacturing site's master planning and scheduling process is, or how good the master planner(s) and/or master scheduler(s) is/are, or how good the manufacturing operation is, without materials and capacity, product will *not* be built!

The issue here is one of accountability! So, here's a thought for the reader: It has long been known how to hold people accountable, but how do you hold technology or a computer and its software accountable? The authors share some of their vision regarding people and machine accountability in this book's Final Thoughts.

All right, with an understanding of level 1 and level 2 planning behind us, let's drop down a level to the manufacturing site planning known as master scheduling, master supply scheduling, or master production scheduling (the authors prefer the term *master scheduling* or *master supply scheduling* since the plant's master scheduler plans more than just production).

Master Scheduling/Master Supply Scheduling—Level 3 at the Plant Level

As the planning process continues, we turn our attention to the disaggregation and planning done at the manufacturing site (i.e., plant, mill, factory, or production shop). During this level 3 planning, the portion of the master (supply) plan assigned to the manufacturing site via the request for product or request for supply is disaggregated into more detail (see the top of Figure 2.17b).

The members of the product family assigned to the manufacturing site are now broken down into specific items/products or groups of items/products. The weekly time periods at the beginning of the 9- to 18-month planning horizon used at the master planning level are divided into days while further out in the horizon weekly time periods may remain (there never is a time period on the master schedule that is greater than a week). Lastly, the supply planning horizon is shortened to say, three to six months (a general statement

Alignment, Synchronization, and Integration

Master Scheduling (Plants)

| • Demand Plan • Supply Plan • Inventory/Backlog | **Units, Mix Days/Weeks** | Horizon = 0 to 3 to 6 months* |

Detailed Production Scheduling (Plants)

| • Inventory • Production • Capacity | **Units Timing Hours/Days** | Horizon = 0 to 1 to 2 weeks* |

*Planning horizon to be determined in detailed design phase.

Figure 2.17b Supply Planning at the Detailed Levels

for this book's discussion is that the planning horizon depends on the company's business and various product manufacturing strategies used).

As we enter this new decade of planning, most manufacturing companies employ master schedulers at their manufacturing sites. These master schedulers use enterprise resource planning systems (e.g., Oracle, SAP, JD Edwards, to name a few), that include master planning and scheduling modules to assist in planning and scheduling their manufacturing operations. What this means is that the supply chain management software manages large amounts of data and uses this data to make recommendations and suggestions as to what the master (supply) scheduler should do in preparing the manufacturing site for building the products being demanded by the customer.

Again, as we discussed earlier in this chapter and will discuss further in the next few chapters, a couple objectives of master (supply) scheduling are to ensure that material and capacity are available when production commences the building cycle (there are more master scheduling objectives, but these two lead us to the next level of supply planning, that of material requirements planning and detailed production scheduling).

Another point that needs to be made here is that the master scheduler does not release the master schedule without doing a sanity check on the capacity requirements using the process known as rough cut capacity planning (see Chapter 15 for a complete discussion of rough cut capacity planning for supply planning, levels 1 through 3). Remember, one of the objectives of master scheduling is to ensure that the required capacity is available when manufacturing operations and/or production is ready to build the scheduled item or product.

Detailed Production Scheduling/Shop Floor Dispatching—Level 4 at the Plant Level

Planning is necessary if we are to expect good control and execution! Again, one cannot control what one hasn't planned. Let's say that again, one *cannot* control what one hasn't planned! During level 4 planning (see the bottom of Figure 2.17b), the plant's master schedule is now broken down into more detail. Specific items on the master schedule are driven through the material requirements planning process to create time-phased material requirements as well as lower-level build item requirements.

Groups of items on the master schedule are converted to specific items that manufacturing can build (or purchasing can buy); the daily time periods at the beginning of the three- to six-month planning horizon used at the master scheduling level are divided into hours (and sometimes minutes) while further out in the horizon daily time periods may remain (there never is a time period on the detailed production schedule or shop dispatch list that is greater than a day); and the supply planning horizon is shortened to say, one to two weeks (a general statement for this book's discussion is that, again, the planning horizon depends on the company's business and various product manufacturing strategies used).

Most manufacturing companies employ detail production schedulers although it is not uncommon that the role of the master scheduler and detail production scheduler are combined and filled by the same person at small- to medium-sized manufacturing sites. These detail production schedulers use enterprise resource planning systems that include production authorizing capabilities such as work order preparation, production scheduling, and capabilities that include authorization for manufacturing to take materials and use the facility's capacity to build needed product.

So there you have it, the *four levels of supply planning* (combine Figures 2.17a and 2.17b into Figure 2.18 on page 74 with the *request for product or request for supply*) tying corporate planning (leadership's direction) to manufacturing site planning for those with a need to know (schedulers, planners, operations, logistics, etc.—those who get it done).

At the beginning of this section, the authors mentioned that some businesses only use three of the four supply planning levels. What these companies do is to combine level 2 planning with level 3 planning. This combined planning has traditionally been done at the manufacturing site, using the output of the IBP process as the driver of the middle management planning process.

However, due to the somewhat recent technological advancements in computer hardware and software, more companies today are doing master planning and scheduling at the corporate or regional level. In the authors' opinion all the various approaches work well if the company operates at Class A standards for business excellence.

Integration, Alignment, and Synchronization

Figure 2.18   Supply Planning at the Aggregate Levels as Well
as the Detailed Levels

Why Master Planning and Scheduling Is a Must in Business Excellence

Let's take a few minutes to discuss how planning (remember, you cannot control what you haven't planned) is or would be done without the master planning and scheduling process in place. Figure 2.19 on page 75 suggests that the business and/or company being discussed would either use their annual budgeting process coupled with some form of demand forecasting and/or firm customer order demand along with some form of integrated business planning (IBP)/sales and operations planning (S&OP) process to communicate the company's leadership direction. The remainder of this section's discussion is based on a business or company using some form of IBP or S&OP.

So, Does a Manufacturing Business Need Master Planning and Scheduling?

Integrated Business Planning / Sales & Operations Planning (Corporate)

• Demand Plan • Supply Plan • Inventory/Backlog	Product Families, Volume, Months	0 to 24 to 36+ months*

Detailed Production Scheduling (Plants)	**Detailed Material Planning Procurement and Purchasing**	**Detailed Logistics Planning and Execution**	**Detailed Demand Planning and Control**
• Inventory Units • Schedule Timing • Capacity Hours/Days	• Have it Units • Need it Timing • Get it Days/Weeks	• Receive Units • Store Timing • Ship Hours/Days	• Sell Units • Promise Timing • Book Days/Weeks

Horizon = 0 to 1 to 2 weeks*   Horizon = 0 to 13 to 26 to 52 weeks*   Horizon 0 to 2 to 4 weeks*

*Planning horizon to be determined in detailed design phase.

Figure 2.19   Planning Without Master Planning and Scheduling

Note: If the reader's company is *not* using either IBP or S&OP, it is suggested that the reader carefully read Chapter 14 in this book as well as *Enterprise Sales and Operations Planning: Synchronizing Demand, Supply and Resources for Peak Performance* by George E. Palmatier and Colleen Crum, former Oliver Wight principals.[9]

The company's leadership team has most likely worked quite hard to create and maintain valid, realistic, and doable product plans, demand plans, supply plans, logistics plans, and financial plans during the integrated business planning or sales and operations planning monthly cycle. However, these level 1 plans are at a very high level, certainly *not* in enough detail for the people and/or machines with the execution responsibility. These aggregate plans need to be disaggregated into the detail needed by the executing functions, that of material planning, procurement, purchasing, receiving, receiving inspection, production scheduling, shop dispatching, operations, packaging, quality, logistics, shipping, and so forth.

Figure 2.19 suggests that this is or would be done using several people armed with today's advanced technology. So, a few of the questions that might be asked here are:

1. How does the system disaggregate the aggregate plans directly into the detailed production schedule, detail material plan, detailed logistics plan, and detailed customer promising plan?

---

[9] George E. Palmatier and Colleen Crum, *Enterprise Sales and Operations Planning: Synchronizing Demand, Supply and Resources for Peak Performance* (Boca Raton, FL: J. Ross Publishing, 2003).

2. How many people are needed to respond to any machine aggregation and disaggregation that is done?

3. Does the company have the latest technology to do the required aggregation as well as the disaggregation, and if it doesn't, how are these to be done?

4. Is there or will there be enough time to secure the required raw materials and packaging needed to build the product?

5. Is there or will there be enough time to secure the required capacity and tooling needed to build the product?

6. Does the company have enough inventory or material on order to satisfy anticipated demand?

7. Does the company have the right machines, tooling, and people skills to satisfy all anticipated and expected demand?

8. Is the company satisfying enough of their customers' product requests within the customers' desired lead time to be competitive?

9. Is manufacturing prepared for and ready to process all new product production trials and first article production?

10. Does customer service and/or the sales organization have the information that they need to make good promises to the customer regarding the booking of customer sales orders?

11. Are all the detailed plans and schedules aligned and synchronized with the approved aggregate plans?

12. Are responsibilities and accountabilities clearly laid out and all functional parties (people and machines) educated and trained on their respective roles?

This is only a partial list that could be created by manufacturing and manufacturing support professionals. Although machine technology advancements are occurring at the speed of light in today's world, well-run businesses and companies continue to use one or two interim steps between leadership planning and operational planning.

At this point we can summarize many (there are more) reasons why master planning and scheduling is a required process for a company to operate in an effective and efficient (or what might be referred to as a Class A) manner. Let's take a look:

1. To ensure integration and implementation of the business, sales, marketing, design, engineering, manufacturing, procurement, logistics, and financial plans;

2. To manage inventory and backlog to a position desired by the company's executive team;

3. To promise product deliveries and feel confident about the company's ability to keep these promises;

4. To plan and commit the necessary resources to satisfy customer demands;

5. To drive detailed material requirements, capacity requirements, detailed production scheduling, logistics, supplier scheduling, procurement, and purchasing;

6. To create a foundation for accountability within the business and company to customers, to suppliers, and to ourselves.

The details of how a company goes about master planning and scheduling are treated in this book's remaining chapters. In those chapters the reader will learn the basic mechanics of the master planning and scheduling (MPS) process. Initially, these master planning and scheduling mechanics will appear to be a process better relegated to a computer than to a human being (the authors believe that this is where the MPS process is going, but let's not be too hasty).

Computers have proven to be excellent helpmates in the business of storing, displaying, predicting, calculating, and underscoring the numerical data that is essential to master planning and scheduling. Indeed, the availability and improvement of master scheduling software introduced in the mid- to late 1970s has done much to advance the implementation of master planning and scheduling (MPS) in the ranks of manufacturing, and in so doing has helped make enterprise resource planning (ERP) and supply chain management (SCM) the powerful processes that they are today.

As a moderate-level *expert system* with built-in decision rules, modern master planning and scheduling software can detect potential demand/supply imbalances and alert the master planner and/or master scheduler to their presence; the software can even recommend what action should be taken. As time continues to pass, the diagnostic, simulation, and actual scheduling abilities of master planning and scheduling software are bound to increase.

However, as we moved through the early days of the twenty-first century and continue to move through the current decade, this incredible computing power has *not* (yet) eliminated the need for the human judgments or the insights and decision-making capabilities that a master planner and/or master scheduler brings to the job. Master planning and scheduling is *not* (yet) a cut-and-dried numbers game.

The numbers are there in abundance, but understanding the assumptions behind them, how to use those numbers, and making decisions in an atmosphere of uncertainty is at least 50 percent of the master planner's and/or master scheduler's job. No one said that this job was easy! In the authors' opinion, today master planning and scheduling is *just as much art as it is science* (that's a change from the first decade of the twenty-first century, where master scheduling was *more art than science*.

If we fast-forward to the middle of the third decade of the twenty-first century, master planning and scheduling will be *more science than art*! By the end of the third decade of the twenty-first century, master planning and scheduling will be *ALL science, no art to it at all*! The big breakthrough during the third decade of the twenty-first century will be the acquired knowledge of how to hold a computer and its decision-making capabilities accountable! (This paragraph is the authors' opinion—please see this book's Final Thoughts for an expansion of these opinions.)

This chapter has explained the *why* of master planning and scheduling in today's environment. The following chapter explains the *how*, or the mechanics of the master planning and scheduling subject. Once the mechanics of basic master planning and scheduling (inventory plus supply minus demand) are understood, discussion will move on to *what* the master (supply) planner and/or master (supply) scheduler does with the numbers and information available.

3

The Mechanics of Master Planning and Scheduling

You can definitely make mistakes, but you can't make mistakes indefinitely.

The Importance of Master Planning and Scheduling

One of the objectives of master planning and scheduling (MPS) is to plan the impact of demand on materials and capacity. This is a vital function because every company must deploy its people, equipment, material, and capital in the most efficient way possible. Master planning and scheduling does this by ensuring that enough product is available for customers, while costly and unneeded inventories as well as unacceptable lead times are avoided. This is the process of balancing demand and supply.

In addition, master planning and scheduling lays out product-mix plans/schedules along with detailed build schedules in support of the aggregate volume plans developed during the integrated business planning (or sales and operations planning) process. By ensuring that the product-mix and detail plans are within the constraints of the overall aggregate volume plans, the master planner along with the master scheduler implements the leadership team's directives.

Finally, the master plan and/or master schedule is/are used to establish some degree of control and accountability: Who is accountable for the different inventory levels the company maintains? Who is accountable for managing capacity? Who is accountable for bringing the needed materials in-house? Who is accountable for managing the lead times that are used to buy and produce the product? Accountability is very important if a company is to successfully use the processes of supply chain management (SCM), enterprise resource planning (ERP), integrated tactical planning (ITP), and/or master planning and scheduling (MPS).

The Master Planning and Scheduling Matrices

One of the bottom-line goals of master planning and scheduling is to balance demand and supply *by time period*. That means looking at all demands—from all sources—in discrete time segments and understanding the resources that will be necessary to satisfy that demand—again, in terms of time segments. This business of matching up demand and supply in time segments creates the need for a matrix that immediately reveals when demand and supply are in or out of balance. There are several different MPS matrix formats available, and the actual design is a matter of software choice. For purposes of illustration, this book uses the one shown in Figure 3.1 shown on page 81.

The MPS matrix in the figure is a series of columns and rows that define scheduled activities in terms of time and type (demand or supply). The time elements are arrayed across the top, and the activities (or data elements) are listed along the side. Each column contains the master planning and/or master scheduling activity expected to take place within a specific time period (typically a week/day on the master schedule—*planning level 3* as noted in Chapter 2, Figure 2.18 on page 74, or month/week on the master plan—*planning level 2* as noted in Chapter 2, Figure 2.18). The nature of the activity or data element—either demand or supply—is determined by the row in which it appears.

Time Segments

The matrix displayed in Figure 3.1 shows time periods 1 through 8 across the top. The number of periods is dependent upon the software and the company's choice of planning horizon. Each period could represent a day, a few days, or a week on the master schedule or a week, a few weeks, or a month on the master (supply) plan. In practice, the array is usually dated: for example, time period starting 10/1 (month/day), 10/8 (month/day), 10/15 (month/day), and so forth.

The format of the master (supply) plan is basically the same as the format of the master (supply) schedule; therefore, the remainder of this chapter will only refer to the master schedule matrix (done to simplify matrix explanation), thereby asking the reader to visualize a similar matrix for the company's master plan.

By convention, time period 1 is the *current* time period—the *present*—and remains so as time passes. Thus, in week 1, period 1 would read 10/1 (month/day); a week later it would read 10/8 (month/day) and so forth through the planning horizon. The data in each column shifts to the left as time passes. The column just to the left of the current time period is labeled *past due* (an explanation of this will come later). The columns to the right represent future time periods and are used to display data and information by identified activities. The cells in the master schedule matrix are for convenience of display when using a horizontal MPS format. Inside the computer software, the quantities are stored by real dates—for example, April 11th, October 15th—and, therefore, can be displayed using any time period arrangement that the master (supply) planner and/or master (supply) scheduler requires.

Demand Section

The top four rows of the MPS matrix show the component elements of the demand plan for a master scheduled item: the *item forecast* of independent demand, the *option forecast*

Master Schedule: 12345		Periods							
LT: 1 OQ: 20	Past Due	1	2	3	4	5	6	7	8
Item Forecast		10	10	10	10	10	10	10	10
Option Forecast									
Actual Demand									
Total Demand		10	10	10	10	10	10	10	10
Projected Available Balance	12	2	12	2	12	2	12	2	–8
Available-to-Promise									
Master Schedule			20		20		20		

Note: The matrix used for master planning is basically the same format used for master scheduling.

Figure 3.1   The Master Schedule Matrix

of dependent demand, the *actual demand* or customer orders, and the *total demand*, which is *some combination* of the above-mentioned demands. (The total demand calculation is explained in Chapter 17, "Demand Management and Aggregate Master Planning.") Now, let's take a little deeper dive into these MPS matrix rows:

Item Forecast: The forecast row identifies the *independent demand* for the master scheduled item. An example of this would be an item such as a table saw motor sold directly to the customer. Besides selling the table saw to customers, the motor used in the table saw could be sold by itself and would appear on the motor's *independent forecast* line if the motor is an MPS item.

Generally, demand of this type is to satisfy a service or spare part requirement. An item can, of course, have both *independent demand* and *dependent demand* (the motor is also be required to build table saws). This situation explains why we have a *dependent demand* line or *option forecast* line in the MPS matrix.

Option Forecast: The *option forecast* row reflects the anticipated demand for an item that will be sold as part of something else. For example, suppose that the production of electric motors is master scheduled. Sale of the motor outright, as a service or spare part, would constitute *independent* demand. The same motor may also be used as a component in other products produced by the company, such as drill presses.

Demand for these motors will therefore be *dependent* upon the volume of drill presses the company expects to sell as well as the *independent* demand for motors to be used as service parts. Consequently, demand for these motors will appear on *both the service or item forecast row as well as the dependent demand or option forecast row.*[1]

Actual Demand: Actual demand is concerned with customer orders that are booked or sold, but not yet shipped (the actual demand row is also known as the order book or backlog row). A customer has placed an order for a quantity of motors. Because of the customer's desired delivery date(s), company strategies, current schedules, material

---

[1] The scheduling literature has for years used the term *production forecast* for what is here called *option forecast*. The former is not an appropriate term in this case since the forecast is not of production, but of demand. The master scheduling line represents supply, that is, production. Thus, "option forecast" is used in place of the original production forecast term throughout this book; the option forecast term has become the standard term over time.

Naturally, when scheduling products that contain no option element, this line of the MPS matrix remains blank. Sometimes in make-to-stock products (products produced for inventory in anticipation of customer orders), the option forecast line is used to display the requested inventory replenishment by time period.

availability, plant capacities, or other customer desires, these motors might not have shipped or be ready for shipment for several weeks.

These motors constitute actual demand, and the master (supply) scheduler (supported by the master planning and scheduling computer software) must keep track of each order by customer, quantity, and promised delivery dates to ensure that the customer will receive the desired products as promised.

Total Demand: This row in the MPS matrix reflects the combined demand for the item by time period. Total demand is calculated in various ways. Normally, it is the sum of the item forecast, option forecast, and actual demand.

If the respective forecast row is reduced whenever orders are booked, then the total demand remains unchanged as demand is recorded. If, however, the forecast is not replaced with booked customer orders, then the logic used in the master planning and scheduling system must take this into account when calculating the total demand. The process we are talking about is called *forecast consumption*, which is addressed in Chapter 17 covering demand management.

For the purposes of this chapter, as demand orders are received, the forecasted quantity will be reduced by the quantity ordered. On the surface, this seems logical. Since the forecast is really an expectation of future demand orders, customer orders that are booked by the sales force may be seen as the fulfillment of that earlier demand forecast. However, what if the customer order was *not* thought of when the forecast was created? In this case the customer order would *not* be part of the forecast and should be treated as incremental demand. This type of demand is known as *abnormal demand* and will be covered later in this book (see Chapter 17, "Demand Management and Aggregate Master Planning"). Until then, all demand in the examples will be treated as normal or expected demand.

Supply Section

Look again at Figure 3.1 on page 81. The rows in the matrix that indicate the level of demand for each time period have already been explained. It now remains to interpret the rows within which the level of supply along with the balancing of the demand and supply will appear.

First, look at the bottom line, the *master schedule* row, or the total supply line for the referenced master scheduled (or master planned) item (remember, if our discussion was focused on a *master planning* matrix, this row would display the total supply for a product family, product subfamily, or group of master planned items).

Master Schedule: This is the row in which the master scheduler (supply manager and/ or master planner if this discussion was focused on aggregate master planning) and the computer's ERP software place supply orders to meet the demand for each time period. Each quantity on the master schedule row represents the amount of supply for the master scheduled item (released work orders, unreleased work orders, or computer-generated planned orders) aligned with the item's due date.

Master schedule supply orders appear in the matrix in three different forms: released orders, firm planned orders, and computer planned orders. These various replenishment orders are identified on the master schedule row by time period. The sequence in which we would expect to see these orders as we move further out on the timeline would be released orders first, firm planned orders second, and computer planned orders last. The nature of these orders, explained next, will make it clear why that sequence makes sense.

Released Orders: If the item is a *make* item, these orders initiate the production process by authorizing material, labor, and equipment to be used to manufacture the item. If the item is a *buy* item (*a buy item can be master scheduled*), the released order initiates the procurement process for that item.

A released order has many aliases; some of the names used are scheduled receipt, campaign, batch, manufacturing order, production order, shop order, work order, and purchase order (if the item is purchased, not made).

Firm Planned Orders (FPO): An FPO is an order that the master scheduler places to take control away from the computer software. It is a *place holder* that allows the master scheduler to firm a computer planned order in quantity and time. The computer software is restricted from changing an FPO; it is the responsibility of the master scheduler to change it.

This technique can aid schedulers in planning materials and capacity by firming selected computer planned orders. Firm planned orders are the normal way of stating the master schedule. In effect, the master scheduler says, "I'm planning to produce (or purchase) so many units of this product, which will be due on this date, but I am not yet ready to authorize the work to begin or ready to issue a released order."

Generally, firm planned orders explode through the bills-of-material using the ERP system to plan materials and capacities (*notice that the master schedule, not the sales forecast, is used to drive material and capacity requirements*). This explosion process is the same as the one used on computer planned orders (*again, the master schedule, not the sales forecast, is used to drive material and capacity requirements forecast*). Released orders are not exploded through the bills-of-material via ERP because these orders create lower-level allocations for materials when they are placed, which are then treated as demand on the materials contained in the FPO's bill-of-material until that material is issued in accordance with the build plan.

Computer Planned Orders (CPO): A CPO is an order created by the computer software rather than by the master scheduler. It is not a green light to manufacturing or purchasing to start producing or buying product, but it is a suggestion to the person doing the master planning and scheduling that a firm planned order of the indicated size will be needed if demand and supply is to be in balance.

Generally, for a computer planned order to have a lasting effect on a master scheduled item, the master scheduler must convert the CPO into either a released order, unreleased order, or firm planned order. As stated previously, the firm planned order takes control of the order away from the computer software and firms the due date and required quantity. Chapters 4 and 5 discuss in detail when this action needs to take place.

The ERP software bases its creation of CPOs on demand need dates, predetermined lot sizes, and lead times to ensure that the release and production or procurement of material will satisfy the demand quantity and need date. Computer planned order creation rules are generally built into the MPS system's software and controlled by a *planning time fence* (a more detailed explanation of the *planning time fence* and how it is used in master planning and scheduling is presented later in this chapter).

This *planning time fence* boundary allows the computer ERP software to only generate CPOs with due dates *after* a predefined boundary date (the planning time fence), and not before. Inside the *planning time fence*, the master scheduler (supported by the ERP and MPS software) must control all the supply orders. By operating within the boundaries of the *planning time fence*, the computer SCM, ERP, and/or MPS software *knows* when it may or may not generate computer planned orders.

Each type of supply order plays a unique role in the master planning and scheduling process. A released order (an unreleased supply order operates the same way as the released supply order when it comes to charging material, labor, overhead, cash, and other resources) is a manufacturing or purchasing order against which material, labor, overhead, cash and other resources can be charged.

Firm planned orders are also essential; without them, the computer software logic would assume responsibility for balancing demand with supply and would then attempt to rectify the situation by launching CPOs where needed, regardless of the actual material or capacity availability. Computer planned orders in effect represent the computer software's own version of a firm planned order. Once the master scheduler creates firm planned orders and balances supply to demand, the computer software will not attempt to create additional supply orders because they will not be needed.

Note that there can be many variations on the preceding supply order scheme; the movement from computer planned to firm planned to unreleased to released order is only a generic approach. In fact, it is possible for the master scheduler to take a computer planned order (CPO) and convert it directly into a released (or unreleased) supply order without ever going through the firm planned order phase. Additionally, a computer planned order can be converted to a firm planned order that authorizes production (this is known as producing to a run rate).

Regardless of how supply orders are used, each contributes to the master schedule row in the computer matrix format, which is the underpinning for an *anticipated build plan*— what the master scheduler and supplying company intend to produce or purchase. It's the combination of the stated supply orders (released orders, firm planned orders, computer planned orders) that drive lower level requirements within an ERP system.

Projected Available Balance: This row predicts what will be in inventory at a specific point in time. It is also the basis for the computer's critique of demand-and-supply balance. The outcome of the critique determines what action will be recommended. Action recommendations are sent to the master scheduler by the software in the form of *action* or *exception* messages.[2] Unless a company uses safety stock, the perfect demand-and-supply balance will be a projected inventory balance of zero (the supply of the product perfectly matches the demand for the product so that there is no projected inventory remaining). If a company uses safety stock (e.g., 100 items), then the perfect balance of demand and supply is at the defined safety stock level or an inventory of 100 units as noted in this sentence example.

Rarely do we have a perfect balance in an imperfect world of manufacturing. Assuming that a company is not using any safety stock, a positive balance for any period of time in the projected available balance row suggests a potential surplus or excess stock condition. If there is a negative projected available balance, the system is projecting a potential shortage.

In the case of a potential surplus, the computer software system may recommend that the master scheduler move supply orders out or even cancel supply orders altogether. In the case of a potential shortfall, the master scheduler will receive recommendations from the computer system to release new supply orders or move future supply orders in (generally, the computer software suggests move-ins prior to suggesting the releasing of new supply orders) to cover the projected deficit.

In summary, the projected available balance line is used for scheduling and causes the main exception-driven action messages (reschedule-out, reschedule-in, order, cancel) to be generated. Again, exception-driven action messages are recommendations for the

---

[2] Exception-driven action messages are notes to the master scheduler made by the computer software based on data in the system. These typically appear beneath the formatted demand-and-supply information or on a separate screen or report. Chapter 4 explains exception-driven action messages in detail.

master (supply) scheduler (master supply planner) to consider during the supply planning processes.

Available-to-Promise (ATP): This row is used for customer order promising and displays the projected supply of product less actual demand commitments. The result of this calculation informs sales, customer service, and customer order entry personnel of the products that can still be sold without modifying the current master schedule (or customer commitments). *This is an extremely useful piece of information because it identifies what can honestly be promised to a customer in terms of delivery.*

If available-to-promise indicates that a total of 10 units are or planned to be available by a particular time period and the company makes a promise to deliver 12 units to a customer by that period, then that company has most likely made a *bad* promise. Anyone who books demand orders should be aware of ATP, how the computer system calculations are done, and what the company's policy is regarding the commitment of product to customers. Available-to-promise (ATP) is discussed in depth in Chapters 9, 10, and 17.

Master Scheduling in Action

Now that the matrix for organizing master scheduling data and information has been presented, we need to understand how to use it as a scheduling tool for a simple product (in this book's example). The product we will be looking at is a standard flashlight, with a bill-of-material consisting of the following: one head subassembly, one light subassembly, and one body subassembly (see Figure 3.2). While each of these subassemblies might in reality contain other subassemblies, fabricated items, and components, for simplicity's sake, we will ignore any secondary product structures at this time.

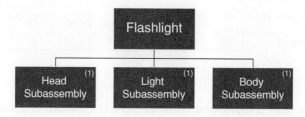

Figure 3.2 Flashlight Product Structure

In Figure 3.2 on page 87, it is important to note that the numbers in parentheses indicate the number of items needed to build the *parent* item, the finished flashlight. In addition to knowing the specific product structure, several other pieces of information regarding the flashlight must be known before master scheduling can begin. We make the assumption here that the flashlight is being made-to-stock, that is, completed flashlights are placed in a finished-goods inventory. With that assumption in mind, consider the current status of flashlights:

On-hand inventory balance: 12

Planning lead time: 1 time period

Minimum order quantity:[3] 20 units

Thus, 12 flashlight units already exist in inventory, a lead time of one time period is required to complete the flashlight final assembly process, and the company has determined that flashlights should be built in order quantities, or lot sizes, of 20 units; this means that whenever the decision is made to build more flashlights, the *minimum* order quantity should be 20 units. In Figure 3.3, we see how this data finds its way into the MPS matrix.

Computing the Projected Available Balance

For the purpose of this example, we assume a flashlight forecast of 10 units every time period, and these appear in the flashlight's forecast cells in each of the eight time periods considered. No actual demand is present because the flashlights are being built to stock

Master Schedule: Flashlight		Periods							
LT: 1 OQ: 20	Past Due	1	2	3	4	5	6	7	8
Item Forecast		10	10	10	10	10	10	10	10
Option Forecast									
Actual Demand									
Total Demand		10	10	10	10	10	10	10	10
Projected Available Balance	12	2	12	2	12	2	12	2	−8
Available-to-Promise									
Master Schedule			20		20		20		

Figure 3.3   Flashlight Master Schedule Matrix Example

---

[3] *Order quantity* and *lot size* are used interchangeably in this book. In the process industry, *lot size* is sometimes used in reference to a quality sample.

using the flashlight forecast of independent demand as the only demand input (make-to-stock strategy treats finished goods inventory as the customer).

In reality, actual demand and the consumed forecast would likely be displayed in the planning matrix for make-to-stock items, but for the sake of simplicity at this time, we omitted actual demand. Of course, customer orders or actual demand for a product where a make-to-stock manufacturing strategy is being used would most likely be limited to the near term, generally no more than a few days or maybe a week into the future; by definition, the make-to-stock manufacturing strategy plans to satisfy *all* customer orders and actual demand off of a finished goods shelf. With this in mind, the total demand for each time period is 10 units.

Notice that the column labeled *past due* of the forecast row is blank—this indicates that there is no past due demand or unconsumed forecast. *A past due forecast is a forecast that was not consumed or satisfied. All unconsumed forecasts should be analyzed and either rolled forward or dropped, depending upon company policy and the forecast consumption rules being used* (more detail on forecast consumption is available in Chapter 17).

Besides the demand, we know we have 12 flashlight units on hand, which have been placed where the past-due column and the projected available balance row intersect. This does not imply that the on-hand balance is past due; it is merely a convenient place to put the on-hand balance so that the MPS software can begin its calculation of the projected available balance line. Knowing the on-hand quantity (12), the forecasted quantities in the future (10 per period), and the expected supply orders (20 in time periods 2, 4, and 6), the MPS module of the ERP computer system can project the expected quantity on hand for future time periods.

Once this is done, the MPS software system will be in a position to critique the balance of demand and supply (potential surplus or excess stock, potential shortage, and/or potential *perfect* balance where the projected inventory balance is equal to zero units on hand or equal to the predetermined safety stock quantity of units on hand).

Time Period 1: There are no supply orders (*master schedule* row) due in time period 1, so we have 12 flashlight units available to satisfy time period 1's demand of 10 flashlight units. Therefore, our *projected-available-balance* at the end of time period 1 will be 2 flashlight units (calculated by taking the 12 flashlight units available – 10 flashlight units of demand), a surplus reflected as *projected available balance*. This becomes, in effect, the projected beginning on-hand balance for the next time period.

Time Period 2: Again, demand exists for 10 flashlight units. What about supply? There is a supply order or scheduled receipt of 20 flashlight units due in time period 2. This scheduled receipt is a result of the master scheduler having placed a supply order for flashlights prior to now. If this scheduled receipt is received as scheduled (MPS quantities are shown by due date), the 20 flashlight units can be added to the 2 flashlights already projected to be on hand and will equal 22 flashlight units available to satisfy time period 2's demand. Since the total demand in time period 2 is 10 flashlight units, a projected available balance of 12 flashlight units will be left at the end of time period 2 (calculated by taking the 2 flashlight units projected to be in inventory + the 20 flashlight units scheduled to be received in time period 2 by the master scheduler – the 10 flashlight units of expected demand in time period 2).

Time Periods 3 through 7: The master scheduling system has projected a positive balance of 12 flashlight units at the end of time period 2. Demand again stands at 10 flashlight units in time period 3, and no scheduled receipts are identified in the master scheduling row. In case the reader has not recognized this situation, it is the exact duplicate of time period 1. Looking ahead, we can see that the same pattern of demand, projected available balance, and anticipated scheduled receipts repeats every other time period through time period 7. The reader may want to work through each period in turn to gain added practice in the projected available balance calculation, going back to the beginning on-hand-balance column and time period 1 if he or she gets stuck.

Time Period 8: In time period 8 the situation changes. Time period 7 ended with a projected available balance of 2 flashlight units. Again, this constitutes a projected beginning on-hand balance for the next period. Demand in time period 8 is again at 10 flashlight units. No additional flashlights are scheduled for receipt in time period 8 (see master schedule row, period 8 cell). Given this situation, the system will correctly project a negative balance of 8 flashlight units (2 – 10) in time period 8 if the master scheduler does not take corrective action and the anticipated demand occurs as planned.

Nature abhors a vacuum, cats hate water, and MPS software cannot stand the sight of a negative projected available balance. The computer software will spot the potential shortage in time period 8 and will automatically place a computer planned order (CPO) to be received in time period 8 to restore the projected available balance to zero or a positive number. Its (the computer's software logic) CPO will be for 20 flashlight units (the minimum lot size or supply order quantity).

If in the future the master scheduler chooses to accept the computer software's recommendation, the computer planned order will be converted into a firm planned order, unreleased supply order, or a released supply order and the projected negative available balance of 8 flashlight units will shift to a positive 12 flashlight units (the 2 flashlight units available from time period 7 added to the expected receipt of 20 flashlight units less the total demand of 10 flashlight units). The result of the adjustment is displayed in the MPS matrix in Figure 3.4 on page 91.

Master Schedule: Flashlight	Periods								
LT: 1 OQ: 20	Past Due	1	2	3	4	5	6	7	8
Item Forecast		10	10	10	10	10	10	10	10
Option Forecast									
Actual Demand									
Total Demand		10	10	10	10	10	10	10	10
Projected Available Balance	12	2	12	2	12	2	12	2	$^{-8}$12
Available-to-Promise									
Master Schedule			20		20		20		(20)

Released Order									
Firm Planned Order			★		★		★		
Computer-Planned Order									★

(For purposes of illustration, the entries in the master schedule line have been specified as to the *types* of orders they are. Thus, the supply orders in time periods 2, 4, and 6 are firm planned orders and the final supply order in time period 8 (*circled*) is a computer planned order).

Figure 3.4   Flashlight Master Schedule Matrix with CPO

In addition to determining where and for what quantity CPOs should be generated, the computer software system also critiques the timing of the receipts in time periods 2, 4, and 6, provided they are scheduled release (supply) orders, scheduled unreleased (supply) orders, or firm planned (supply) orders, to determine if the orders are scheduled properly.

The system will start its critique by going back to time period 2 and asking, "Is this MPS order of 20 flashlight units scheduled properly?" In this case, the answer is *yes*. This is so, because without the 20 flashlight units arriving as scheduled, the projected available balance will be negative (2 flashlight units – 10 flashlight units).

The same logic is used in testing the supply orders on the *master schedule* row in time periods 4 and 6. The answer to the question will be *yes* in both cases since each MPS lot of 20 flashlight units is properly scheduled and needed in the defined periods.

Analysis

This example not only illustrates how the projected available balance is calculated, but underscores the fact that the computer's recommendations are just that—recommendations. The master scheduler ultimately determines whether the computer's recommendations are valid for the particular situation at hand. This is still true as we enter the third decade of the twenty-first century, but as we move through that third decade, more and more decision power is being turned over to the computer hardware and software—yes, machines will continue to perform and replace tasks that master planners and schedulers currently do (authors' opinion).

There is a long-standing universal principle in master planning and scheduling, enterprise resource planning, and supply chain management: *Machines make recommendations; people make decisions*. Well, that long-standing universal principle is being challenged in today's environment and will continue to be challenged in tomorrow's environment. Accountability remains the underlying issue.

The MPS software system supports the master scheduler in creating a valid master schedule based on the availability of material and capacity. With respect to the availability of material, the issue is whether material *due* dates (dates placed by the master scheduler) match the true *need* dates (dates calculated by the computer software). With respect to capacity, it (capacity) must be available in sufficient quantity to satisfy the resource requirements by specific time periods. This is a balancing activity, and how well or how poorly a master planner and/or master scheduler does that activity determines the real worth of that master planner and/or master scheduler and the particular MPS system.

The question now is what to do with time period 8's computer planned order. To balance the demand and supply at the master schedule level, this order for 20 flashlights is necessary. (Actually, only 8 are needed, but 20 flashlight units is the minimum order quantity.) Therefore, the system will assume that the master scheduler will convert this computer planned order into a firm planned order (or unreleased supply order or released supply order) when it is necessary (based on the lead time of the product).

The next step in the process is to communicate this expected build plan to the detailed production schedulers and material planners and/or supplier schedulers for lower-level materials to ensure that the required materials and capacities will be available when needed. Let's look at the integration between master scheduling and material requirements planning.

Why and How Master Scheduling Drives Material Requirements Planning and Detailed Scheduling

The *why* of master scheduling (discussed in Chapter 2), including the basics of the MPS matrix and *how* the computer software system and master scheduler together ensure a balance between demand and supply, should now be clear for the simple case just discussed. So far, we have been dealing at the level of completed flashlights, ignoring the flashlight's underlying components. Yet we know that other scheduling issues may lie beneath the surface of the master scheduled item.

The need to deal with the underlying components—and the materials, capacity, and build-time issues that each entail—requires an interface between master scheduling and material requirements planning (time-phased material planning). That interface is made via the flashlight's bill-of-material. To fully understand that interface, let's look a little deeper into the flashlight example.

Given that it takes one time period (planned lead time) to build the flashlight once the head, light, and body subassemblies are available, and since some flashlights are scheduled for completion in time period 2, then there must be sufficient head, light, and body subassemblies on hand in period 1 to start building the flashlights required for completion in time period 2. If the master scheduler expects to have 20 flashlights as scheduled receipts in time period 2, then 20 head subassemblies, 20 light subassemblies, and 20 body subassemblies had better be available in time period 1. Therefore, a *gross requirement* for 20 of each of these subassemblies exists in time period 1.

In other words, it's the master schedule row that drives requirements down to MRP (time-phased material planning) for lower-level assemblies, manufactured items, components, and raw materials. It also should be noted that detailed production requirements, detailed capacity requirements, and logistics requirements can be driven by the output of MRP or, in many cases, directly driven by the master schedule.

Using the same logic, 20 head, light, and body subassemblies are needed in time period 3 coming from the MPS lot due for completion in time period 4, and 20 more in time period 5 coming from the MPS lot in time period 6. The computer planned order in time period 8 also generates a gross requirement for 20 head, light, and body subassemblies, this time in time period 7. Each of these subassemblies, then, needs its own MRP plan and schedule. Figure 3.5 on page 94 represents the linkage of these schedules graphically.

To understand how MRP accommodates each of these subassemblies (and *their* various subassemblies, manufactured parts, components, and raw materials if they exist) and links them to the master schedule, we will follow just one of those subassemblies—the light subassembly—from the master schedule down to its own MRP matrix.

To get started on planning the light subassembly, some basic information about the subassembly is required.

On-hand inventory balance: 3

Planning lead time: 2 time periods

Minimum order quantity: 25 units

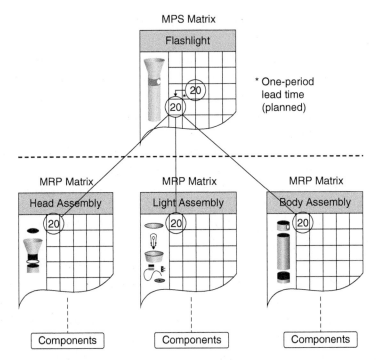

Figure 3.5 Master Schedule Linked to Material Requirements Planning

For illustration purposes and to show just how the MPS and MRP matrices are linked via the computer software, the bottom row(s) of the MPS matrix (master schedule by due date and master schedule by start date) is/are shown in Figure 3.6 on page 95. The various orders for 20 *completed* flashlights in time periods 2, 4, 6, and 8 of the *master schedule* line are shown to trigger respective gross requirements for the same quantity one time period earlier in the MRP matrix (MPS quantities by due date and offset by planning lead time to the start date).

The projected gross requirements row of the MRP matrix represents demand for the identified item, not from the final customer, but from the master schedule—specifically, from the MPS (master schedule) start date row. For instance, when the master scheduler places a supply order for 20 completed flashlights in time period 2 on the master schedule, that information is translated into a projected gross requirement of 20 light subassemblies in time period 1 on the MRP matrix. Taking the lead time into account, the computer software system places this requirement of 20 light subassembly units in time period 1 in

MPS Matric: Flashlight		Periods								
LT: 1 OQ: 20	Past Due	1	2	3	4	5	6	7	8
Other rows of MPS matrix not shown									
Master Schedule (Due Date)			20		20		20		(20)
Master Schedule (Start Date)		20		20		20		(20)	

MRP Matrix: Light Subassembly		Periods								
LT: 2 OQ: 25	Past Due	1	2	3	4	5	6	7	8
Projected Gross Requirements		20		20		20		20	
Scheduled Receipts		25		25					
Projected Available Balance	3	8	8	13	13	$^{-7}$18	$^{-7}$18	$^{-27}$23	$^{-27}$23
Planned Order Release				(25)		(25)			

Note: Circled values are computer planned orders (CPOs)—Negative notations in the PAB (time periods 5–8) show PAB before CPOs are taken into account.

Figure 3.6   The MRP Matrix—Light Subassemblies

the MRP matrix.[4] The same process repeats itself whenever a supply order appears on the MPS row of the master schedule.

Projected gross requirements are the sum of all the demands over time for this item. In our simple example, the light subassembly is used only in the flashlight that's master scheduled. In a more complex environment, that same light subassembly might be used in other products manufactured by the company, in which case the demand for the light subassembly from many different master schedules would accumulate in the various projected gross requirements time periods of the light subassembly's MRP matrix.

The scheduled receipts shown in the MRP matrix are supply orders that either MRP planners or schedulers have placed. (There are no computer planned orders here.) These scheduled receipts can go by many possible names: work orders, shop orders, production orders, manufacturing orders, campaigns, or run rates, to name a few, and are used for parts and items that the company builds or produces. Purchase orders or confirmed supplier schedules are used for parts, materials, or items that the company buys. It is important to understand that a scheduled receipt is expected to be received in the time period

[4] Remember, the stated lead time to take the head, light, and body subassemblies and produce a flashlight is one period, which is not to be confused with the lead time of two periods that it takes to build the light subassembly itself.

shown and will be used in calculating the projected available balance, the next row in the MRP matrix.

Just as in the MPS matrix row of the same name, the projected available balance is where the projected inventory balance is reflected. The past-due column in this row contains the starting on-hand balance, but from that point forward, the projected available balance is the sum of on-hand balance for the prior period and scheduled receipts for the period being calculated less the projected gross requirements for that period. That figure, in effect, becomes the projected beginning on-hand balance for the next period. For example, in Figure 3.6 we see an on-hand balance of 3 light subassemblies; added to the 25 scheduled to be received in time period 1, which represents an available supply of 28 in time period 1; since demand in that period (projected gross requirements) is 20, the projected available balance for the period is 8 (3 + 25 − 20).

The MRP system calculates the projected available balance quantity in much the same way as does the MPS system. The basic calculation in both systems is to take the projected ending available balance from the prior period and add scheduled receipts from the period being evaluated, then subtract the anticipated demand for that period. This yields the projected available balance for the period being calculated.

The planned order release row contains the equivalents of the computer planned orders found in the master schedule. It is the row in which the computer software attempts to deal with any potential supply shortages that appear in the projected available balance row. For example, the MRP matrix for the light subassembly projects a negative available balance (the top row of numbers in time periods 5 through 8) unless some action is taken. Anticipated demand from the master schedule outstrips the expected supply of light assemblies by a cumulative 7 units in time periods 5 and 6, and by a total cumulative 27 units in time periods 7 and 8.

To avoid a deficit situation from developing in time period 5, a computer planned order is needed to arrive in time period 5, and therefore must be released in period 3 (remember, the lead time for light subassemblies is two periods). What should be the size of the order? Ideally, the computer software would place an order for 7 units (assuming no minimum order quantity) in time period 3 to cover the 7-unit deficit expected in time period 5. However, the minimum order quantity (set by the master scheduler with input from supply chain management, operations, and finance) for this item has been specified as 25, and that is what shows up in the planned order release row of time period 3.

If the MRP planner or scheduler accepts the computer software's recommendation, he or she will convert the computer planned order into a scheduled receipt when time period 3 becomes the current period (time period 1), and a surplus of 18 units will be available in time period 5, as reflected in the bottom half of the cell (13 + 25 − 20).

An important point is now being made. In order for a computer planned order to be recognized as a scheduled receipt, the scheduler or planner must take affirmative action. Remember, only supply orders placed by a scheduler or planner appear in the scheduled receipt row. It follows that once the computer planned order is converted into a scheduled receipt, the CPO will be deleted when MRP is next run. Lower-level requirements are maintained when the system creates an allocation for each lower-level part or item required to support the scheduled receipt. These time-phased allocations are maintained automatically by the ERP software and generally stored in a requirements file.

Looking ahead to future time periods, no activity takes place in time period 6, so the projected available balance remains at 18 units. In time period 7 a demand for 20 units creates a projected negative balance of 2 units (18 + 0 scheduled receipts – 20 units of demand). The origin of this demand is the computer planned order for 20 flashlights in time period 8 of the master schedule. Using the planned lead time of one period for the flashlight has resulted in this CPO generating a projected gross requirement in time period 7 in the MRP matrix.

The computer software cannot abide a negative balance for the light subassembly, so another planned order must be released, this time in time period 5 (taking into account the light subassembly's two-period lead time) to ensure sufficient supply of the light subassembly in time period 7. If the computer software's recommendation is followed and the computer planned order is converted into a scheduled receipt to be received in time period 7, a projected surplus balance of 23 units will be available at the end of time period 7 (18 + 25 – 20).

In time period 8, the projected available balance will either remain at minus 27 units if no action is taken, or at a positive 23 units if the CPO releases are converted to scheduled receipts when appropriate. The CPO scheduled for release in time period 3 should be converted to a scheduled receipt in time period 5 while the CPO scheduled for release in time period 5 should be converted to a scheduled receipt in time period 7.

The projected gross requirements (demand), projected available balance, and planned order release (supply) rows are automatically calculated by the MRP software system. The scheduled receipt row is the only row on the MRP matrix maintained by MRP schedulers and planners.

Analysis

Using the on-hand balance, projected gross requirements, and scheduled receipts, the MRP system will project the available balance over each planning period, making it possible for the system to determine the true material need dates. If the projected available balance goes negative and then returns to positive, the system recognizes that a timing problem exists—that is, there is enough on order, but some of the orders are scheduled too late. If the projected available balance goes negative and stays negative, the system recognizes a volume problem exists and calls for additional supply orders.

Reviewing the MRP matrix for the light subassembly we observed in time periods 5 through 8, the projected available balance went negative and remained negative (top set of numbers)—evidence of a volume problem. Some type of order action has to take place, and the computer software has suggested that two releases be made to put the demand and supply for light subassemblies back into balance. The scheduled receipts of 25 units in time periods 1 and 3 are both necessary and scheduled properly to prevent the close-in projected available balance from becoming negative, which would have otherwise signified a timing problem.

Each time that MRP is run, this kind of analysis takes place within the computer software, and exception-driven action messages are generated as appropriate. Based on the analysis just completed, the MRP system would not recommend that any action be taken until time period 3 becomes the current period.

The flashlight example just discussed has explained the basics of the MPS and the MRP logic, how internal calculations are made, and how the system (with the input of the scheduler or planner) maintains a balance of demand and supply. Just as important, the example showed the connection between the master schedule for the flashlight and how it is supported by time-phased material planning for each of the flashlight's components, examining one of those components—the light subassembly—in detail.

Experienced supply chain management people will be quick to recognize this as a very simplified case. Few manufactured products are as simple as the one just shown, and even a flashlight is more complex in its component makeup than this illustration has portrayed. In fact, each of the flashlight components used in the example (head subassembly, light subassembly, and body subassembly) can be exploded into its components and their sub-components. This complexity of detail, even for a simple flashlight, is more typical of the multilevel product structure that most planners and schedulers experience.

This added detail is brought in here to make the point that MRP will continue to explode requirements through the defined bills-of-material in order to generate a time-phased material plan for every one of the items identified as part of the final flashlight. The reader can readily see that the ERP system and its bill-of-material explosion capability is counting on the company's bills-of-material, stored in the company's ERP database, being accurate, and we do mean accurate (the data integrity required to support master planning and scheduling, material requirements planning, supplier scheduling, capacity planning, detailed production scheduling, logistics planning, etc. is further discussed in Chapter 13).

The What, Why, and How of Safety Stock

Master planners, master schedulers, material planners, production schedulers, supplier schedulers, and logistics planners must understand safety stocks, why they are used, and their impacts on master planning and scheduling, material requirements planning, detailed production scheduling, supplier scheduling, and logistics scheduling. In developing illustrations of a fairly simple master schedule and showing how it explodes down through the MRP system, we have, thus far, made some convenient assumptions. We have assumed that the inventory records are accurate—for example, if the on-hand balance says 12 units are on hand and in the inventory, we assumed that the inventory balance noted reflected reality. We also assumed the demand at the MPS level, bills-of-material, and the projected gross requirements at the MRP level were valid and accurate. Based on these assumptions, we constructed a master schedule, supported by lower-level schedules, and assumed that production as well as our suppliers would perform to a high standard of timely completions relative to those schedules.

However, forecasted demand is *not* always accurate, and non–Class A companies' inventory records are notoriously inaccurate,[5] meaning that items we assumed to be on hand were not. Even if the inventory records are accurate, other problems could occur. The production floor may run the number of items scheduled, but some of these may be found to be defective. Suppliers sometimes fill a purchase order for 100 parts, but 97 are found to be in the box; and sometimes these parts arrive late.

A system in which one set of assumptions is layered upon others is bound to contain surprises. Often, surprises do not work in the company's favor. Companies and the people who work in those companies must implement Class A data integrity processes to ensure that the ERP planning data base is and remains accurate (this is the reason that the authors decided to include a data integrity chapter in this fourth edition of the master planning and scheduling book; see Chapter 13 for a somewhat detailed discussion on data integrity).

Safety Stocks as a Hedge

Safety stock inventory can be used as a hedge against unanticipated variations in both demand and supply. If the supplier delivers fewer items than requisitioned, if the

---

[5] Class A companies have inventory record accuracy that exceeds minimum standards of 95 percent or, in some cases, 99.5 percent.

production floor builds items that fail to meet quality specifications, or if the demand forecast is for 10 and orders come in for 12, safety stock inventory, used with caution, can be strategically planned to fill out the difference.

What to Safety Stock

In a world in which inventory had no carrying costs for the company, virtually every finished item, every parent part, and every component could be safety stocked as long as there was room to store it. But why stop there? Why not have extra personnel on hand, just in case someone has to go home early? In the real world, however, this is impractical and expensive, so management teams may have to determine what is important to safety stock from a strategic standpoint. The immediate choices that come to mind are finished goods, subassemblies, intermediates, components, and raw materials. However, there are several other candidates for safety stocking, some of which are discussed in greater detail later in this book. Here, our concern is the mechanics of how MPS and MRP software accommodate safety stocks.

In the flashlight example, the company could decide to always maintain an inventory of 10, 20, or 40 finished flashlights. Additionally, it could also consider safety stocking certain components, like flashlight bulbs or even the raw materials used to make the components. Whichever level a company chooses to safety stock, there should be a strategic purpose to offset the extra cost of inventory. Here are a few strategic purposes:

- Items with long lead times can add to the cumulative time needed to build the product. By strategic or safety stocking those items with the longest lead times, the cumulative lead time to build the product may be reduced.

- If a family of finished product is available in many options (colors, trim pieces, etc.), the forecast for the entire family is likely to be more accurate than the forecast for the specific configured product. Thus, the surprises in demand are likely to be most pronounced among the options; therefore, these semi-finished options would be candidates for strategic stocking.

- For many businesses, customers expect that the producer will have certain items on hand *all of the time*, other items *some of the time*, and other items *occasionally*. Consider the analogy of the automotive service station. Its customers expect that gasoline and certain select auto parts (fan belts, oil, oil filters, etc.) will *always* be available. It would be unacceptable for an auto service station to be out of these for any length of time.

Customers would expect replacement batteries and spark plugs to be available, but they would not be shocked or terribly disappointed if the station was temporarily out of stock. They might be willing to wait a day or two for their replacement batteries or spark plugs (many companies have a one- or two-day restocking policy for items like these).

These same customers, however, would *not* expect the service station to have a replacement transmission for a 2010 Ford, and would be prepared to wait for a special order on this part to come in. In this example, gasoline-like items are candidates for safety stock inventory if there is a reasonable chance for unexpected demand or a shortfall. This analogy applies to manufacturers who place a high premium on customer service for their basic, core products or service parts business.

The Mechanics of Using Safety Stocks

With modern MPS software, the desired stocking level for a master scheduled item is entered into the system, and the system flags any situation in which the projected on-hand balance falls below the safety stock level. Consider the example in Figure 3.7. This company desires, as a matter of policy, a safety stock of 50 units. Here, forecasted demand is also for 50 units per period. Seventy units are shown to be on hand; all but 20 of these on-hand units represent safety stock (70 – 50).

In the MPS line, the master scheduler has laid in four separate orders of supply to meet the anticipated demand. A quick glance at the projected available balance line reveals that in time periods 1, 3, and 4, the projected number of units on hand is expected to fall below the safety stock level or turn negative.

Master Schedule: 12345 Safety Stock: 50 OQ: 125	Past Due	1	2	3	4	5	6	7	8
Item Forecast		50	50	50	50	50	50	50	50
Option Forecast									
Actual Demand									
Total Demand		50	50	50	50	50	50	50	50
Projected Available Balance	70	20	95	45	–5	70	145	95	170
Available-to-Promise									
Master Schedule		← 125		←	125	125			125

Figure 3.7   Safety Stock Example

		50	50	50	50	50	50	50	50
Total Demand		50	50	50	50	50	50	50	50
Projected Available Balance	70	145	95	170	120	70	145	95	170
Available-to-Promise									
Master Schedule		125		125			125		125

Figure 3.8   Same Example After Shifting Supply Orders

For example, with 70 as a starting on-hand balance, less the 50 needed in time period 1, only 20 will remain—less than the safety stock policy requirement. Here the master scheduler would receive an action message to shift the time period 2 supply order in the MPS line to time period 1, as indicated by the arrow in Figure 3.7 on page 101.

Following the same logic, the master scheduler would receive an exception-driven action message to shift the 125 scheduled in time period 5 to time period 3 because the projected available balance falls below the safety stock policy of 50. If time period 5's supply order is moved to time period 3 or 4, the projected shortage in time period 4 will not occur.

These shifts would keep the projected available balances above 50 in all time periods.[6] After these shifts in the timing of supply, the matrix for this master scheduled item would appear as shown in Figure 3.8. In this instance, none of the time periods have a projected available balance less than the safety stock level.

Alternative Safety Stock Display Format

Some MPS and MRP computer software handles safety stock by not reflecting the safety stock in the projected available balance line. The inventory is there, but the computer software does not show it. This means that the master scheduler can take those balances down to zero without violating safety stock policy.

As previously discussed, projected gross requirements, scheduled receipts, on-hand balances, lot sizes, and safety stocks affect the placement of computer planned orders. Also, each item's lead time is used to offset the placement (release date) of computer planned orders from the need date. In the flashlight example, we saw lead times of one

---

[6] The computer software would recommend these changes by means of exception-driven action messages, which are detailed later in Chapter 4.

period for flashlights and two periods for the light subassembly. But what would happen if the lead time for flashlights or light subassemblies is five or more periods?

By definition, the planned order release for light subassemblies would be past due. Another way to say this is that there would be inadequate lead time for the proper placement of the light subassembly supply order. Of course, this is not a desired condition.

Fortunately, there is a way in master planning and scheduling to control lead time issues. Modern software links master planning and scheduling to material requirements planning, which schedules descending levels of materials whether manufactured or purchased. Material requirements planning efficiently performs the required calculations and recommends actions, freeing the master planner and/or master scheduler from the drudge work and allowing him or her to focus on critical decision making.

However, MRP software makes the assumption that the on-hand balances, bills-of-material, lead times, lot sizes, safety stock levels, and so on are accurate and the best planning information available at the time. To say it a different way, MRP does not function well if data integrity is missing from the ERP database (see Chapter 13 on data integrity).

Additional Material Planning Techniques

Once the master plan and/or master schedule is put into place by the master planner and/or master scheduler, it is vital that the required capacity and material be made available when needed so that production can successfully meet the product quantities and due dates as noted in the plan/schedule. Before releasing the master plan and/or master schedule, a sanity check against the planned capacity (demonstrated capacity plus or minus planned changes to future capacity) must be done using a technique called rough cut capacity planning (see Chapter 15 for a detailed explanation of resource requirements planning and rough cut capacity planning).

Over the past seven decades or so (using the computer in planning manufacturing operations), material and capacity have been planned using various techniques. We just completed a somewhat detailed discussion on using a time-phased approach known in supply chain management as material requirements planning (MRP).

Although MRP is one of the preferred techniques in material planning, there are other ways to plan and secure materials to support the master plan and/or master schedule. Let's take a look at four other material planning techniques that a company may use to support the supply process:

1. *Order Point* or *Reorder Point* is a material planning technique that sets an inventory level where, if the total stock on hand falls to or below that point, action is taken to replenish the stock. The order point or reorder point is normally calculated based on forecasted usage during the replenishment lead time plus safety stock.

2. *Two-Bin* is a type of fixed-order system in which inventory is carried in two bins. A replenishment quantity is ordered when the first bin (working) is empty. During the replenishment lead time, material is used from the second bin. When the material is received, the second bin (which contains a quantity to cover demand during lead time plus safety stock) is refilled and the excess is put into the working bin. At this time, stock is drawn from the first bin until it is again exhausted.

3. *Kanban* is a method of just-in-time production that uses standard containers or lot sizes with a single card attached to each. It is a pull system in which work centers signal with a card that they wish to withdraw materials or parts from feeding operations or suppliers. The Japanese word *kanban*, loosely translated, means card, billboard, or sign, but other signaling devices such as colored golf balls have also been used. The term is often used synonymously for the specific scheduling system developed and used by the Toyota Corporation in Japan.

4. *Vendor or Supplier Managed Inventory (VMI)* is a means of optimizing supply chain performance in which the supplier has access to the customer's inventory data and is responsible for maintaining the inventory level required by the customer. This activity is accomplished by a process in which resupply is done by the vendor or supplier through regularly scheduled reviews of the on-site inventory. The on-site inventory is counted, damaged or outdated goods are removed, and the inventory is restocked to predefined levels. The vendor or supplier obtains a receipt for the restocked inventory and accordingly invoices the customer.

Our closing message regarding material planning is that the master planning and scheduling process is alive and well and is needed in a Class A service and manufacturing company. Capacity and logistics planning as well as lower-level material planning should be integrated, aligned, and synchronized with the business's master plan and master schedule (some businesses combine master planning and master scheduling into one supply planning function and the master plan and master schedule into one supply planning document).

Creating and maintaining the business's master (supply) plan can be done by people and/or technology/machines/computers (see authors' Final Thoughts, pages 783–808, for more discussion regarding master planning and scheduling in the next decade). These days (and certainly in future days), master planning and scheduling process supporting technology continues to be developed and released to the supply chain management community at lighting speeds.

The Planning Time Fence

One of the truly valuable features of MPS software is the *planning time fence*. A planning time fence (PTF) restricts the master planning and scheduling software system from automatically adding to or changing the master plan and/or schedule within specified time zones (PTF is set by item or groups of items).

If, for example, the master planner and/or master scheduler wants to maintain complete control of all flashlight supply orders within time periods 1 through 6, a planning time fence can be placed at the end of time period 6 (Figure 3.9), forming a boundary within which only the master scheduler can place supply orders (by definition these orders then must be released supply orders, unreleased supply orders, or firm planned orders—no computer planned orders, which are created by the master planning and scheduling software, being permitted inside the planning time fence).

Additionally, since all supply orders within the PTF are release orders, unreleased orders, or firm planned orders, the computer software is restricted from making changes to any and all supply orders within the planning time fence (the master scheduler has control of this part of the horizon). Outside the planning time fence, the computer can continue to place and move around CPOs.

					Periods			PTF	
Master Schedule: 12345 LT: 1 OQ: 130	Past Due	1	2	3	4	5	6	7	8
Item Forecast		70	70	70	70	70	70	70	70
Option Forecast									
Actual Demand									
Total Demand		70	70	70	70	70	70	70	70
Projected Available Balance	135	65	125	55	115	45	−25	−95 35	−165 95
Available-to-Promise									
Master Schedule			130		130			130	130

Figure 3.9   Planning Time Fence Example

The planning time fence can be used to implement management policies and guidelines. For example, management may determine that changes to the master schedule can be accomplished easily beyond the cumulative lead time (i.e., the total time needed to build the product from scratch), whereas making supply changes at points inside the cumulative lead time become progressively more difficult as they take on the characteristics of last-minute changes. The planning time fence can create a boundary between these areas.

The planning time fence also satisfies the master planner's and/or master scheduler's need to restrict the master planning and scheduling software so that only released supply orders, unreleased supply orders, and firm planned orders can be created within close-in time periods. These are time periods within which the master planner's and/or master scheduler's attention must be focused and within which the planner and/or scheduler—not the computer and its ERP software—must make the decisions.

Areas of Control

To better understand how the planning time fence functions, look back at Figure 3.9 on page 105. Let's assume that the cumulative lead time of this MPS item is six periods. The master scheduler has decided to place a planning time fence[7] at the end of time period 6. The PTF indicates that the master scheduler controls all the supply orders up through time period 6, while the computer software can add or make changes in time periods 7 and 8 in this book's simple example (master planning and scheduling best practice is to authorize the computer software to add or make changes to the master plan and/or master schedule from the planning time fence through the remainder of the planning horizon). With a cumulative lead time of six periods, the master planner and/or master scheduler may want these periods "firmed up" and not subject to any mindless changes made by the computer software to balance out a deficiency in some period without careful analysis.

As of the publishing of this fourth edition of the master planning and scheduling book, the authors still believe there are master planning and scheduling tasks that need to be performed by a person, the master planner and/or master scheduler. However, we stated earlier that computer hardware and software continue to erase people-dependent tasks from the master planning and scheduling *to-do* list!

To understand the utilization of the planning time fence, consider again the problem represented in Figure 3.9. In this case, forecasted demand for the master scheduled item

---

[7] Where to place the time fences for various master schedule items is discussed in Chapters 4 and 16.

is 70 per period. The starting on-hand balance is 135 units. The on-hand balance plus the scheduled receipt of 130 units in time period 2 is sufficient to cover the demand through that period and leaves a projected available balance of 125. That surplus supply is enough to meet the next period's demand, but not enough to meet the demand of time period 4.

However, a firm planned order of 130 units is scheduled and due to be received in time period 4, thereby leaving a projected balance of 115. Taking this supply order into account, the projected inventory is sufficient to meet demand through time period 5, but, as we observe, a potential shortage appears in time period 6. Here the projected available balance at the end of time period 6 is 25 units short of meeting the anticipated demand of 70 units in the period.

In the absence of a released order or firm planned order on the MPS row of time period 6, the MPS display shows a projected available balance of negative 25 units. That deficit would increase by 70 units per period through the horizon if no additional supply orders were placed, which is indicated by the negative projected available balances in time periods 7 and 8 (–95 units and –165 units, respectively).

Maintaining Demand/Supply Balance Inside the Planning Time Fence

Since master planning and scheduling software cannot tolerate a potential supply shortage (its circuits get upset when a negative available balance appears), it would normally place a computer planned order (CPO) in the MPS row of time period 6 to cover the projected available balance of negative 25 units. However, the planning time fence restricts the computer software from any CPO activity through time period 6.

If the reader reviews this paragraph in the previous edition, the author made the following statement, "If it [technology in the form of a computer] could *think and* speak (it speaks now and it probably will think someday in the near future), the computer software would shout to the master scheduler, -*"Wake up and fix that deficit in time period 6!"* Well, it has been a decade since the third edition of this book was released and computers do speak, so perhaps we will soon see ERP systems shouting to the master scheduler, "Wake up and fix that deficit in time period 6!"

Until the master planner and/or master scheduler listens and takes some action, the computer software settles for piling enough CPOs into time period 7 (the first period outside the planning time fence) to create a positive projected available balance and informs the master planner and/or master scheduler by means of an action (or exception) message that a negative availability condition exists inside the planning time fence. With this action or exception message, the decision today of what to do is dropped directly into the master planner's and/or master scheduler's lap. (It is the authors' expectation that this paragraph will need to be rewritten in the next edition of this book due to most, if not all, of the current master planning and scheduling *people tasks [due to technology advancements]* having been replaced *by machine [computer and/or robot] tasks*.)

Converting a Computer Planned Order (CPO) to a Firm Planned Order (FPO)

The master scheduler must take some sort of action in time period 6 if the potential supply deficit in that period is to be avoided. It would appear that the computer planned order of 130 units in time period 7 must be converted into a firm planned order with a due date in time period 6. First, though, the master scheduler should be sure that this action is in the best interest of the company. Several questions must be answered:

- Will the sales forecast of 70 units really turn into customer orders? In other words, does the master scheduler want to respond?

- Can we get the material to produce these items in time? In other words, can the master scheduler ask production to build the product and be certain that the necessary material will be available?

- Does the capacity to produce these items exist? In other words, can the master scheduler ask production to build the product and be certain that the necessary capacity will be available?

- What will it cost to make this change? In other words, this is a decision point—four-decimal accuracy is not required to answer this question (roughly right is better than precisely wrong)!

- Does authorization exist to make this change? In other words, if the master scheduler makes the required change, will the master schedule for the item still be within the constraints of the approved supply plan?

- What is the business impact if the change isn't made? In other words, what is the consequence if the master scheduler does not make the change in question?

Determining the answers to these questions takes master scheduling beyond the straightforward job of juggling numbers to keep demand and supply in balance. This is an area in which the computer software can provide assistance, but not a final judgment—at least not yet (this will change in the third decade in the twenty-first century). What we are now talking about is the current, real job of the master scheduler.

The Demand Time Fence

The challenge of master planning and scheduling is balancing demand and supply. We have just concluded a discussion on the use of planning time fences to control the behavior of the computer and its ERP software. This begs the question: How about the demand side of the business?

Some master planning and scheduling software has the capability to accept user defined rules on how the total demand is to be calculated. One of these capabilities is the use of a demand time fence, which is not to be confused with the demand management time fence described later in this book.

The use of a planning time fence in the master planning and scheduling software is only a mechanical means of controlling where the computer software can place computer planned orders. Some master planning and scheduling software has another time fence capability: that of a demand time fence.

Like its supply-control planning time fence counterpart, the demand-control demand time fence (DTF) has basically one purpose, and it is strictly mechanical. Inside the DTF, the total demand will consist only of customer orders (actual demand). In other words, the forecast will be ignored between the current date and the DTF (Figure 3.10).

Master Schedule: 12345		Periods			DTF			PTF	
LT: 1 OQ: 130	Past Due	1	2	3	4	5	6	7	8
Item Forecast		0	20	40	60	70	70	70	70
Option Forecast									
Actual Demand		70	50	30	10				
Total Demand		70	50	30	70	70	70	70	70
Projected Available Balance	135	65	145	115	175	105	35	−35 95	−105 25
Available-to-Promise									
Master Schedule			130		130			130	

Figure 3.10   Demand Time Fence Example

The forecast for this master scheduled (MPS) item has been time-phased across time periods 1 to 8. The actual demand line on the matrix shows committed customer orders (promised deliveries) in time period 1 for 70 units, time period 2 for 50 units, time period 3 for 30 units, and time period 4 for 10 units.

A DTF has been established between time periods 3 and 4 using the DTF definition. The total demand for this item is calculated using only the actual demand line in time periods 1 to 3, and a combination of forecast and actual demand from time period 4 through the planning horizon.

Using the logic previously explained in this chapter, the projected available balance for time period 1 is the sum of the on-hand inventory balance (135 units) plus the MPS in time period 1 (zero units scheduled), minus the total demand in time period 1 (70 units). This calculation creates an ending projected available balance for time period 1 of 65 units. Time period 2's and 3's projected available balance is calculated basically the same way. Take the projected ending available balance (65 units) from time period 1, add it to the MPS in time period 2 (130 units), and subtract the total demand for 50 units (this represents actual demand only since time period 2 is inside the DTF—the remaining forecast of 20 units in time period 2 is ignored), leaving a projected available balance of 145 units. Using the same calculation generates an ending projected available balance of 115 units in time period 3 (145 units projected to be on hand at the end of period 2 + 0 units scheduled in time period 3 – 30 units demand in period 3).

As we move into time period 4, we are crossing the DTF. Therefore, the total demand calculation will take the forecast into account. The total demand in time period 4 is the sum of the 60 units forecasted and 10 units of actual demand equal to 70 total units. That total demand is subtracted from the ending projected available balance of 115 units from time period 3 plus the MPS of 130 units scheduled for completion in time period 4, carrying the calculation to its completion. We see a projected available balance of 175 units in time period 4 [115 + 130 – (60 + 10)]. This mechanical calculation continues throughout the planning horizon. These calculations are why we have and need computers in master planning and scheduling.

Before using the DTF, a company should understand how it works and its impact on total demand and scheduling. A policy should be in place defining the setting of the DTF by MPS item, maintenance of the demand time fence, and its use in master planning and scheduling. Since this demand time fence affects the calculation of total demand, it needs to be under the control of the demand side of the business, perhaps by the demand manager/demand planner. A detailed description covering the role of demand management and its demand manager is given in Chapter 17.

This chapter has described what the master planning and scheduling system mechanics do to support the master planner and/or master scheduler. The next chapter begins the discussion of how the master planners and/or master schedulers use this data and information in order to manage the production (as well as purchases, although indirectly involved in the material procurement part of the supply chain) at his or her plant, mill, or manufacturing site. But before this discussion begins, we must conclude this chapter with a discussion on some of the design or redesign criteria of the master planning and scheduling process.

Time Fences (Demand vs. Supply, People Behaviors vs. Computer Behaviors)

A manufacturing business has two primary objectives (there are more, but these are the *Big 2*), that of satisfying customers at an economical cost (not at any cost) and safely making money (and a profit). When it comes to achieving these two primary objectives, businesses using master planning and scheduling have two definitive advantages over businesses using other planning, execution, and control techniques. Those two advantages are: (1) the capability to decouple demand and supply—a manufacturing operation can build at a different rate than sales sells the product and sales can sell product at a different rate than manufacturing builds the product and (2) the capability to inform sales when and how much of a product can be promised to the customer.

The technique used to decouple demand and supply is referred to as time fencing or boundary setting (time when decisions need to be made). These time fences or boundaries affect how people as well as machines (computers and related software) need to or do behave. Figure 3.11 discusses people behaviors as well as computer/software behaviors for the demand side of the business as well as the supply side of the business.

Time fences and/or decision points are tactical ways to implement Class A and the business strategy. Time fences are *not barriers* to prohibit action, but rather boundaries where and when decisions need to be made. Manufacturing schedules should *never be frozen; firming the schedule* at some point makes sense to ensure an efficient and effective build process.

It must also be remembered that when a promise is made to a customer, it must be kept: *A promise made is a debt unpaid* and *Doing what you said you were going to do* are a couple of principles Class A companies and businesses respect and live by! Making and keeping promises to a customer while running an efficient and effective manufacturing operation sometimes leads to conflicting objectives between the demand and supply organizations; this fact should not surprise the reader!

Demand Side of the Business

People Behavior – Demand Time Fence (DTF)

Demand matches supply inside DTF using available-to-promise information;

Supply matches demand outside demand time fence using projected available balance information;

Policy or policies along with action procedures are required;

Education is needed for all with a need to know to ensure business strategy understanding.

Computer/Software Behavior – Demand Time Fence (DTF)

Only customer orders used in PAB calculation inside DTF;

Some combination of forecast and customer orders are used in projected available balance calculation outside DTF (depends on forecast consumption rules and option selected);

Education and training are needed to ensure understanding of mechanics.

Supply Side of the Business

People Behavior – Supply Time Fence is referred to as the Planning Time Fence (PTF)

Three change zones (firm, trading, free);

Changes are more difficult, disruptive, and costly to make in the firm zone versus trading or free zones;

Careful analysis done in firm zone before changes are made, demand and supply trading done in trading zone, changes in free zone are allowed if within approved supply plan constraints;

Change policy required and respected/enforced (who approves changes in what zone);

Six (possibly seven) questions to answer before seeking change approval;

Education is needed for all with a need to know to ensure business strategy understanding.

Computer/Software Behavior – Supply Time Fence / Planning Time Fence (PTF)

Use of planning time fence (PTF) to decouple demand and supply (the selling rate can be different than the building rate);

No computer-planned orders inside the PTF (master scheduler has manual control);

Action-driven exception messages are generated as needed (inadequate lead time);

Computer-planned orders placed outside PTF (computer software has automatic control).

Figure 3.11   Time Fencing Impacts in Master Planning and Scheduling

Enter master planning and scheduling to assist in the decision making as well as getting everyone in demand and supply on the same page. Missed customer deliveries can result from poor demand as well as poor supply performance. What we mean here is that missing a customer delivery could result from demand making a bad promise in the first place and/or supply not building a quality product in the right quantity by the due date on the master supply plan and promised to the customer.

Using time fencing in master planning and scheduling can prompt planners and schedulers to do some analysis before a decision needs to be made. Master planning and scheduling is a process that moves everyone to consensus-based decision making and gets all parties on the same page. The business itself needs to determine the strategy it will use in dealing with customers when problems occur, but the business certainly should tell itself the truth regarding any and all somewhat awkward situations.

Finally, let's take a look at the benefits of using time fences in a Class A manner. Time fences in master planning and scheduling enable people to tell the truth as it's known at the time, highlight potential problems before they happen, establish guidelines for booking and satisfying customer orders, and prevent bad promises from being made.

Additionally, time fencing in master planning and scheduling can prevent the business from overloading manufacturing and suppliers while reducing non-value-adding expediting (all levels). When a manufacturing company is running well, it can focus its attention on satisfying customers and safely making money (and a profit).

Master planning and scheduling using the MPS time fencing capabilities ensures that decisions are made by the right people, ensures that the whole picture is known while making decisions, informs all with a need to know of the rules of the game, and reduces stress due to bad decisions by relying on good planners and schedulers, *not* good expediters! Besides the above-noted benefits of using time fencing and the master planning and scheduling process, Class A companies realize customer service improvement along with inventory reductions as well as productivity improvements while material expenses are decreased. Now, that's a process worth understanding, implementing, and using to achieve the business's goals and vision!

Master Plan and Schedule Design Criteria

In order to make supply chain management (SCM) and enterprise resource planning (ERP) function properly, the integrated business planning, master planning and scheduling, capacity planning, material planning, and logistics planning functions and systems must be carefully linked. This linkage is done via bills-of-material and process routings along with integrated computer software modules. Besides tying the noted processes together, the MPS process and system should adhere to a set of design criteria.

While there is some flexibility in the design of any MPS process, certain guidelines should be observed. These guidelines reflect the cumulative experience of many companies in many different industries. The following design areas need to be addressed.

Time Criteria

Basically, all MPS software now on the market manages all demand and supply-by dates. If the real dates are known, master planning and scheduling data can be displayed in any variety of ways. It is recommended that the maximum length of a master plan display period be no greater than one month while a master schedule display period be no greater than one week. In fact, there are many cases where weekly time periods are preferred in the beginning time periods on the master plan while daily time periods are preferred in the beginning time periods on the master schedule.

Monthly increments at the master scheduling level (referred to as *level 3 planning* in this book; the reader may want to refer back to Figure 2.18 on page 74 for a refresher on the four different planning levels associated with supply chain management) *are simply unsatisfactory*; attempting to manage master scheduling time blocks of this size increases the chances that the master scheduler will miss the details necessary to convert production rates into specific item or material numbers, quantities, and due dates. The result: completion dates *not* met and *missed* deliveries.

It's a different story when the discussion turns to *master planning* (referred to in this book as *level 2 planning*). Generally, *master planning display periods are weekly in the short term into the intermediate term and monthly in the intermediate term to long term* (the time periods suggested here are just that, suggestions). It should also be noted that the authors frown on quarterly increments at the master planning level (referred to as level 2 planning in this book; refer to Figure 2.18 on page 74).

Time period displays are identified and defined during the detailed design in the Transform Phase on Oliver Wight's Proven Path to successful master planning and scheduling implementation (see Chapter 19 for a more detailed explanation regarding The Proven Path's Transform Phase).

Planning Horizon

At the master planning and scheduling levels, it is necessary to deal with two different types of lead times. One is the lead time required to produce the master planned and/or master scheduled item itself when all items one level down in the MPS item's bill-of-material are available. The second is the cumulative lead time—the longest planned length of time required to produce the master planned and/or master scheduled item from scratch. This takes into account *all* the lead times of *all* the items that go into the master planned and/or master scheduled item. In short, it is the critical path that recognizes some processes that can be done in parallel.

Many companies find it necessary to extend the planning horizon beyond the cumulative lead time if they need additional visibility for supplier planning and establishing supplier agreements. Extension of the planning horizon may also be required to properly assess capacity requirements. Thus, while some companies have a short material lead time, they may need to extend the overall planning horizon because of heavy equipment or other capacity needs.

Frequency of Review

Ideally, the master plan and/or master schedule is reviewed continuously or daily using an online computer system. At a minimum, each item on the master plan should be reviewed monthly while the master schedule should be reviewed weekly. With today's technology it is possible to keep the master plan and/or master schedule constantly online, where changes can be seen on the MPS screen as they are made. As Chapter 17 on demand management and available-to-promise (ATP) will make clear, the ATP row of the master plan and master schedule screens need to be analyzed in a real-time environment if customer orders are received on a regular basis.

So, What's Next?

This chapter covered the basic MPS matrix and the calculations used in the master planning and scheduling process. Some basic guidelines on the design of the MPS process have also been addressed. The fact is, however, that we have only described how to get information into a format that the master planner and/or master scheduler as well as the master planning and scheduling computer software system can effectively use. The next step is to understand how to manage with the information provided by the MPS system. This is discussed in the following chapters.

4

Managing the Supply Chain with Master Planning and Scheduling

If you don't have time to do it right the first time, when are you going to find time to do it again?

On Wednesday morning, just as they were preparing to go off to lunch, Judy Wilson, master planner and Mark Owens, master scheduler for Criterion Electric Controls Company, received a call from the vice president of sales.

"Judy, I just got a call from our sales representative in Philadelphia. He has a chance of making an important sale of an A3 control system to a big company out there if we can beat Drumlin Electronics in making delivery."

"Well, that's good news," Wilson replied. "An A3 is a $120,000 unit."

"Right," said the sales vice president, "and this would be a new and important account for us—one that Drumlin has always controlled. Once we get our foot in the door, other business should follow."

Wilson knew that the sales vice president had not called just to announce some good news. The phrase "if we can beat Drumlin Electronics in making delivery" was to be the real reason for this conversation. The master planner and master scheduler braced themselves for what was surely coming next.

"Here's the deal, Judy. Delivery is the big issue in the sale. Drumlin has promised to expedite the order and deliver in just four weeks—not their usual five." The sales vice president paused for just a moment, preparing to drop his bomb on Wilson. "We have to do better to get the business. Could we have an A3 unit for this customer in three weeks?"

Wilson and Owens had just looked at the master plan and master schedule for A3s that morning and knew that the production line was totally committed through the period in question. They also knew that the cumulative lead time for a finished A3 was six weeks. "Is that three weeks to ship?" Mark asked.

"I'm afraid not," the vice president responded. "That's three weeks to the customer's loading dock."

All three knew that the product was too heavy to air freight, and that express trucking would take a full two days.

"Let us work on it," Wilson said. "I'll call you back in a couple of hours. We need to check the master plan and master schedule and talk with some other people."

While the sales vice president was off to a business lunch, the master planner and master scheduler went to work on the problem. They would spend the next hour or more reexamining the master plan and master schedule for A3s, several of which were on order and in various stages of production for other customers. They would consider current capacity and materials. And they would do whatever they could to make it possible for Criterion to deliver its A3 for the sales representative to open this important new account, and to ensure that all other customer commitments would be satisfied. It was their job to make these things happen when they could.

By 1:30 that afternoon, Wilson was on the phone to the sales vice president. "Tell your sales representative in Philadelphia that he'll get his A3 three weeks from today . . . on the customer's loading dock."

"Great, Judy! How did you manage it?"

"Well, Mark found that we had an A2 already in production. We had your assistant call the account representative for the A2's customer to determine if he could live with a two-week delay. We worked out a deal with that customer offering a free extension on his warranty if he would take it two weeks later. The customer had no problem with it, and finance has approved the deal. Mark can upgrade that A2 to an A3 with available materials and capacity and deliver as promised. Tell your sales representative that he has a green light on this one, if we can solve one problem."

"What's that?" the vice president asked apprehensively.

"Your Michigan representative has an A3 on order that will be delayed by three to four days if we make these changes. Is that all right with you?"

The ball was back in the sales vice president's court. But he was used to this give and take with Wilson and Owens, who had educated everyone to the fact that when the production system was carefully scheduled, even the most creative rescheduling to satisfy customers usually carried some sort of penalty. "Yes, I can deal with the customer on that delay," the vice president ended. "We'll forward the order to you in an hour."

Wilson made a note for the upcoming cycle of Criterion's integrated business planning process (more on this process in Chapter 14) to analyze whether there was a significant impact of this unanticipated demand on the product-family-level (i.e., aggregate) plans in which the A3 belonged, and collaborate with the Criterion's demand manager and include this unanticipated demand and supply in the performance appraisal. Furthermore, they needed to collaborate, review, and update the assumptions supporting future plans for the A3 product family if needed. While unanticipated demand is often a welcome surprise, it must be managed like any other variability.

As this story makes clear, there is much more to master planning and scheduling (MPS) than knowing how to move numbers around on the MPS matrix. Proficiency with the mechanics of scheduling is essential, but other skills are equally important: a sense of the company's overall business and its customers, knowledge of its products and production processes, and understanding of the reliability of its suppliers, to name just a few. These are areas in which judgment combined with a good business sense are critical, and they relate closely with the ability to use the mechanics of the MPS system to manage production operations.

In this story, the master planner and master scheduler used their MPS software tool to get a picture of current A3 production, capacity, and materials. But they went beyond this, thinking creatively about how the picture could be tactically rearranged to meet the interests of their company and its customers. Their collective knowledge of the company's products and how they are manufactured allowed them to see how an A2 could be converted into an A3 on short order. And they had the organizational skills to work through other parts of the company—sales, marketing, engineering, finance, manufacturing, procurement, logistics, and general management—to create a solution in a way that would be supported by all affected parties.

The mechanics of master planning and scheduling (described in Chapter 3) provide an important management tool, but the master planner and/or master scheduler must know how to use that tool, which is the focus of this chapter.

The Master Planner's and Master Scheduler's Job

One way to understand how to manage the supply chain with the master planning and scheduling system is to consider the job requirements of the master planner and master scheduler. (A detailed job description is supplied in Chapter 20). Basically, the master (supply) planner is responsible for creating a weekly/monthly realistic and valid master (supply) plan by product subfamily and/or grouping and the supplying manufacturing facility that satisfies current and anticipated demand. The master (supply) scheduler is responsible for creating and maintaining a daily/weekly doable master (supply) schedule by product grouping and/or stock-keeping unit (SKU) and manufacturing facility that satisfies all demands, booked orders as well as planned bookings. These are not tasks restricted to the factory, mill, or plant floor, but ones that need to be coordinated with other important functions within the company and its constituency of customers and suppliers:

- **Sales:** Sales personnel live to secure orders on which a profit can be made and commissions earned. Their task is made easier when a quality product can be delivered on the date the customer wants it and in the correct quantities.

  In today's competitive world, stockouts, missed delivery dates, and the inability of the manufacturing facility to fill rush orders or orders with a short delivery lead time make the lives of sales personnel more difficult. Conversely, the ability to avoid stockouts, meet promised delivery dates, and accommodate special customers with rapid delivery helps secure both sales success and the overall success of the company.

- **Marketing:** Marketing personnel are skilled in bringing product into the marketplace and communicating its features and benefits to potential customers. They work on product branding, forecasting issues, pricing strategies, distribution systems, product promotions, and so forth.

  Untimely production delays, stockouts, and unreliable service to distributors and dealers are issues that require regular interaction with the master planner and/or master scheduler. The better they can work together, the more effective their marketing and manufacturing programs will be in the future.

- **Engineering:** Design engineers live for the day when development projects, which for months and years had been merely ideas or drawings, emerge from the plant as finished new products. Anything that reduces manufacturing and material complications or failures ranks high on their list of important issues.

- **Finance:** Financial managers measure the world in monetary terms. Inventory requires costly capital. Surpluses of materials and finished goods are nonproductive assets that create expense and no income.

  On the other hand, shortages of deliverable products and the materials from which they are made can result in expensive unplanned air freight, overtime pay, performance penalties, and lost sales. Finance wants the manufacturing facility to walk a fine line between too much inventory and stockout situations.

- *Manufacturing:* Plant managers like to maintain an orderly flow of production—one that levels the load on the manufacturing facility over extended periods. An orderly flow facilitates optimal plant usage, steers a course between layoffs and overtime, and eliminates the stresses that create the end-of-the-month nightmares described at the beginning of Chapter 1.

- *Logistics:* Logistics strives to optimize the loading of trucks, railcars, and marine vessels to reduce the total unit shipping costs. The objective is to secure the best use of the transportation vehicle by loading it with the proper mix of products needed by the customer or distribution center.

   It should be remembered that in many companies, transportation makes up a large portion of the total product cost or cost of getting the product to the customer (sometimes, transportation accounts for the largest portion of the logistics cost). The better a company plans its transportation needs, the better its customer satisfaction and profits will be (fact, not fiction).

- *Top Management:* The role of the executive team is to harness the capital and human resources of the company to a strategy that will result in economic prosperity for the organization and its owners. Top management has to steer the company into the future, and that is possible only when all the machinery of the organization is working together.

   The ability of management to lead and control is compromised with shipping delays, confusion on the manufacturing floor, excessive expenses in production, poor quality, and other internal emergencies. Let's say it again: All company supply chain management activities need to be aligned, synchronized, and integrated if a service and/or manufacturing company is to reach the lofty goal of being considered a Class A enterprise.

The activities of the master planner and/or master scheduler are important to each of these functions of the company. Sales and marketing must be accommodated to the greatest extent possible to win orders, but undisciplined demands for large inventories and expedited production need to be balanced against other concerns. The desire of finance to reduce inventory expenses must be balanced against the requirements of the competitive marketplace and the needs of production to keep the plant running in a sensible way. The desire of manufacturing to produce steady runs and level the load on the plant must be judged in the context of foreseeable customer demand for the plant's output. And, of course, the product must get to the customer in the most effective way.

In some respects, the master planner and/or master scheduler attempts to do from the middle-management level of the organization what the executive team attempts to do from the top, namely, optimize the cooperation of the company's many functions in serving the needs of the customer. This is a job for which master planning and scheduling software is clearly just one tool; a job for which an acute sense of manufacturing dynamics as well as negotiating and communication skills are critical. The following case illustrates how master planning and scheduling is more than a mindless numbers tool, but one that requires finesse on the part of the master planner and/or master scheduler.

MOVING A CUSTOMER ORDER TO AN EARLIER DATE

"We'd like to *reschedule* our order."

This is *not* the worst kind of message to get from a customer. It's certainly preferable to "We'd like to *cancel* our order." Still, it can present problems for manufacturing and challenge the ability of management to run the business in a way that delivers a profit to stakeholders and satisfies customers—which are the two bases for *being*, and *staying*, in business.

Consider the case of Acme Glassworks, a producer of plate glass. One of its major customers, a manufacturer of commercial windows and glass sheathing for buildings, has called to request a change in its scheduled orders, from 10 pallets in each of the next four weeks (40 pallets in all) to 10 this week, 14 next week, 6 the following week, and 10 the following week (again, 40 in all).

The master scheduler at Acme Glassworks recognizes this as a straightforward timing change, one that will require some shifting from week to week. If capacity and materials were no issue, this could be accomplished as follows:

On the surface, a request to move up an order would seem like a clear-cut opportunity for the manufacturer to please and satisfy the customer. But is it, really? This move-up request may actually have some source other than the customer. The order might have

PERIODS	WK 1	WK 2	WK 3	WK 4	MONTH
Customer Orders (pallets)	10	14 ~~10~~	6 ~~10~~	10	40
Master Schedule	10	10	10	10	40

been triggered by one of the company's own sales representatives. With the sales contest for the trip to Hawaii coming into the final stretch, the representative in Omaha might have pleaded with a customer to place the order early, thereby pushing his sales numbers up in the contest period.

In another situation, the order might originate on a clerk's computer screen. The *customer* in this case might be a clerk in the company's inventory control group whose computer software flagged the item, indicating a demand change due to arbitrary safety stock requirement.

If a great fuss is to be made in moving an order in, then we need to be sure that all the pain and suffering will have a positive result, that of profitably serving a paying customer.

Issues of Management

Even the simple Acme Glassworks situation raises a host of important issues for managers and supervisors.

- *Can we get the capacity?* Sure, you want to satisfy the customer's request to move up an order! But it's often easier said than done. Will this gesture of customer satisfaction overload the manufacturing schedule and throw a monkey wrench into the production facility?

- *Can we get the materials?* Even if the capacity problem is solved, a manufacturer might *not* be able to move up his own order for materials. With so many companies operating on razor-thin parts and materials inventories, the materials might *not* be obtainable.

- *How much will it cost?* If overtime is part of the capacity solution, and if expedited purchases and air freight of materials are part of the materials problem, then this order change may squeeze any profit out of the order that so many people will be scrambling to accommodate.

- *What will this change do to morale and teamwork on the floor?* Personnel close to the action may be working diligently to create a stable and smooth-running operation for management. Will this order change and disrupt the efficient routines and undercut the progress personnel has made in creating an orderly workplace?

These are important issues that need management's attention. Others in the organization will have their own issues of concern. Marketing may see the order change as important for market penetration. In the absence of any explanation, manufacturing may see the order change as just another headache. Finance may see a revenue opportunity.

Of course, they may also recognize a cash-flow problem—namely, how will the company pay for the material and manufacturing costs that are now being moved up and out of its budget?

Typically, requests to move up an order in the schedule come from someone in sales, and they usually want an answer right away—while they are still on the telephone or waiting for a quick reply test. "Well, can you do it or not?" We all like to please, but moving an order usually requires some checking: with the current manufacturing schedule, the stockroom, and sometimes with suppliers. There is nothing wrong with saying, "I'll need to do some checking and call or text you back. It may take a day or two to get you an answer, depending on which suppliers we need to check with to see if we can get the materials." *To imply otherwise is to send the signal that schedules are of no great importance and can be changed at will.*

Sometimes, we simply have to say *no* to change requests. But instead of an absolute *no*, we should say something like this: "I can't move that order up because the production schedule is currently booked. However, if you would be willing to move one of your other orders to a later date, I might be able to use that capacity to satisfy your current request. Do you want me to look into that?" This response helps the salesperson understand the limits of schedule flexibility, and the important idea that tradeoffs are often the answer.

For companies whose traditions have been to reflexively accept order changes, the greater care and study suggested above may not be agreeable to everyone—especially at first. Sales representatives who routinely telephone, e-mail, or text order changes and get an instant answer will not like being told "we'll get back to you after we do some checking." One of management's challenges is to help these people see that *a more thoughtful way of handling order changes is in the company's best interests.*

Of course, tools and technology, including computer hardware and software, continue to get better and better in their support of product (portfolio) management, demand management, supply management, and financial management and the all-important balancing of these business elements. However, management is not just about computer software. The company must have solid processes that approach Class A to make use of the hardware and software available today and tomorrow. The movement in the twenty-first century is to customer and supplier collaboration and the sharing of information. This is what might be called *real* Class A integrated demand-driven supply chain management.

Exception-Driven Action Messages

The master planning and scheduling (MPS) computer system proposes; the master planner and/or master scheduler disposes. Chapter 3 explained that the computer software looks for imbalances in demand and supply, and places computer planned orders where necessary, taking into account given product lead times, lot sizes, or defined supply order quantities, and safety stock requirements. It should also have been observed how a planning time fence can be used to create a boundary between time periods in which the *computer software proposes* and the *master planner and/or master scheduler disposes*.

One way in which computer software and master planner and/or master scheduler communicate is through action messages (also known as exception messages or exception-driven action messages). Exception-driven action messages are the MPS software's way of getting the master planner and/or master scheduler's attention and directing that attention to areas of potential problems. These exception-driven action messages identify the need for intervention to correct a current problem or to avoid a potential one. Examples of exception-driven action messages are: release an order, reschedule-in a supply order to an earlier date, reschedule-out a supply order to a later date, cancel a supply order that is no longer required, convert a computer planned order into a firm planned order, and so forth.

Figure 4.1a on page 126 provides a master schedule example in which several of these exception-driven action messages appear. Here, the planning time fence is somewhere beyond time period 8; thus, all the numbers in the master schedule row represent released supply orders (say, work orders) or firm planned orders (FPOs).

Demand for the product is stated as 50 units per period. With 70 units on hand, the master schedule logic projects the available balance for each time period. An FPO for 115 is scheduled to be received in time period 2 (the lot size set at 115 units when the firm planned order was created, or the master scheduler had decided to override the lot size specification of 125 when the order was placed, or possibly 10 units have already been received or scrapped, etc.). This could be true if the company manufactures to a rate and expresses this rate using firm planned orders.

It is the master scheduler's job to keep the master schedule line valid in unit of measure, quantity, and due date. Remember, inside the planning time fence only the master scheduler (or master planner if the planning matrix is displaying a master supply plan) can create orders and alter released and firm planned order dates and quantities. Additional FPOs for 125 have previously been placed in time periods 5, 6, and 8.

On Hand: 70 Units
Lead Time (One Level): 1 Period
Cumulative Lead Time: >8 Periods
Lot Size: 125 Units
Safety Stock: 0

PTF ⟶

	Past Due	1	2	3	4	5	6	7	8
Item Forecast		50	50	50	50	50	50	50	50
Option Forecast									
Actual Demand									
Total Demand		50	50	50	50	50	50	50	50
Projected Available Balance	70	20	85	35	−15	60	135	85	160
Available-to-Promise									
Master Schedule		115			←125	125→			125

Release   R/I   R/O   Cancel

EXCEPTION-DRIVEN ACTION MESSAGES:
1. Release FPO in period 2; start building period 1.
2. Reschedule-in FPO in period 5 to period 4.
3. Reschedule-out FPO in period 6 to period 7.
4. Cancel FPO in period 8.

Figure 4.1a   Exception-Driven Action Messages Example

A potential shortage of 15 units is projected for time period 4, but a positive projected available balance reappears in the next period (60 in time period 5). Subsequent periods project additional positive balances (135, 85, and 160). Because the projected available balance goes negative in time period 4 and then returns to positive, the master planning and scheduling system recognizes that a timing, not a volume, problem exists. The master planning and schedule system notes this and looks into future periods for orders that could be moved up. Since an FPO for 125 units is scheduled to be received in time period 5 and really is needed in time period 4, the system generates an action message recommending that the FPO in time period 5 be *rescheduled-in* to time period 4, thus solving the deficit problem.[1]

The computer software would also scan future periods and spot the larger-than-needed available balance of 135 in time period 6. If the scheduled FPO for this period were

---

[1] Only 15 units are needed here, but most MPS and MRP systems recommend bringing in the entire lot. However, the master scheduler has several options: Split the lot of 125 into 15 and 110; increase the planned order in time period 2 to 130; do nothing; and so forth.

not received, the 60 remaining from the previous projected balance would be more than enough to cover time period 6's demand of 50 units; 10 units would, in fact, be left over. This being the case, the master planning and scheduling software would send an exception-driven action message to *reschedule-out* the 125 units from time period 6 to time period 7.

Scanning still further, it would be clear that the FPO of 125 units in period 8 is not needed if the projected demand beyond time period 8 is less than 35 units and a *cancel* message would be sent to the master scheduler for his or her consideration. In addition to the exception-driven action messages discussed earlier, the master planning and scheduling system would notify the master scheduler that the firm planned order due in time period 2 should be *released* (e.g., *convert* the firm planned order to a released order, such as a work order) since the item under evolution has a one-period lead time.

To review, a master planning and scheduling system generally has the capability to analyze the demand/supply balance and to generate the following key exception-driven action messages (see the following list as well as Figure 4.1b on page 128):

- Convert firm planned orders into released supply orders (i.e., work order).

- Convert computer planned orders into firm planned orders.

- Reschedule released supply orders or firm planned orders into a closer time frame.

- Reschedule released supply orders or firm planned orders into a future time frame.

- Cancel or reduce a released supply order or firm planned order.

- A negative projected available balance exists within the planning time fence.

- Demand requirements are past due.

- Scheduled receipts or firm planned orders are past due.

- A planned order release has inadequate lead time to properly order material or secure the necessary capacity (past due release).

- An error has occurred during the product explosion using the bills-of-material (or possibly some other identified event) indicating a potential problem with master data.

Note: Although the exception-driven action messages listed here are considered the key ones, enterprise resource planning and master planning and scheduling systems today have the capability to generate far more exception-driven action messages (too many to list in this book, much less this chapter) than are displayed in Figure 4.1a on the previous page, an exception-driven action messages example.

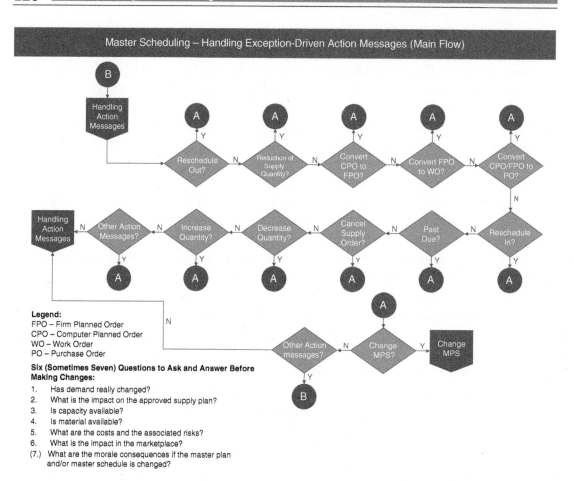

Figure 4.1b   Handling Exception-Driven Action Messages (Main Flow)

Figure 4.1b shows a process flow diagram highlighting activities and decision points for handling exception-driven action messages. The figure displays several key decision point questions that can be answered either *yes* or *no*. Dependent upon the answer to the decision point question, the process flow diagram provides a path to the required activity or another decision point question. Also noted on Figure 4.1b are the six (or seven) questions that should be asked and answered before any changes to the master plan and/or master schedule occurs.

It is recommended that this type of process flow diagram be used by any initiative improvement team after the related policy/policies are created and prior to the creation of any and all related procedures and work instructions. The process flow diagram provides the process designer with a pictorial of the physical flow as well as the information flow; these pictorials can be very helpful to the designers and improvement team in seeing the overall process flow.

Six (Sometimes Seven) Key Questions to Answer

Exception-driven action messages are the recommendations made by the computer software system. These systems range in price from several thousand to a few million dollars (or company's currency) and are terrific for making calculations and linking the required master planning and scheduling calculations horizontally across time periods, and vertically through the planning bills as well as bills-of-material and material requirements planning (MRP) systems. They are practically infallible in the black-and-white area of numeric logic, but even the best systems are not totally capable of dealing with the many gray areas that permeate the complex manufacturing environment in today's world.

It is in these gray areas that today the human master planner and/or master scheduler is superior to the machine, and in which his or her natural skepticism about demand forecasts (but commitment to *communicate* those skepticisms with the demand manager when they arise), intuitions about risk, and so forth are essential. These gray areas may be defined in terms of six (more likely seven) key questions that most computers cannot completely answer but which must be addressed before computer-directed reschedules and order launches are executed.

Question 1: Has Demand Really Changed?

The computer and its software can look up the demand number, compare it to the supply number, and recommend action. However, it rarely challenges the validity of that demand number. If the demand number is seriously in error, the reschedule or order message may be invalid. Maybe a customer has just shifted an order out of one time period and into another; the period demand has changed, but the aggregate demand remains the same. Before making changes in manufacturing, a human being must ask, "How realistic is this demand?" or "What caused the demand change?" or "Should we react to this changed demand?"

Consider a product that normally has demand for 50 units per period. A period with 80 units appears in the total demand row on the planning horizon. The master planner and/or master scheduler must make a decision with respect to creating supply to match this demand. Certain subtle clues may suggest that the high demand is not genuine. For example, if this high demand comes in just prior to the end of the annual sales bonus period, could the sales force be *stuffing* their regular customers with sales, robbing the next period just to enhance this period and reach their bonus requirements? Meeting this abnormally high demand might likely mean paying high overtime rates, costly special freight charges, and general stress on the factory. A telephone call, e-mail, or text might determine how genuine the demand really is and how important it is that the company react to it immediately. Once this question is answered, changes can then be made accordingly.

Question 2: What Is the Impact on the Approved Supply Plan?

A computer-generated action recommendation may put the master planner and/or master scheduler at odds with one or more executive plans. In a Class A supply chain management (SCM) and enterprise resource planning (ERP) environment, aggregate monthly supply (production) rates by product family are reviewed and authorized by executive management; these production rates constitute a supply plan that the master planner and master scheduler must support in aggregate.

This means that master planned groupings and individual line item master schedules can be altered only in a way that preserves the validity of the overall monthly approved supply plan totals. One master plan and/or master schedule change may have to be counterbalanced by an equal but opposite change for another grouping or item in the same product family or product subfamily. If this is not possible, higher-level approval may be needed for a change that would disrupt the monthly supply plan volume.

Question 3: Is Capacity Available?

The desire to make a change to the master plan and/or master schedule may be constrained by available resources. A manufacturing facility is like a piece of rubber: You can stretch it in a number of different directions to accommodate demand and supply level changes (overtime, extra shifts, outsourcing, etc.). However, when action recommendations appear, capacity must be ensured before taking the recommended steps.

Question 4: Is Material Available?

Capacity alone does not manufacture products; availability of the right materials in the right quantities is also essential to making master plan and/or master schedule changes. If the recommendation is for a supply increase, there probably is a need for additional materials. Conversely, if demand is being reduced, it may be necessary to consider added space requirements for materials inventory.

Question 5: What Are the Costs and the Associated Risks?

In many cases, extra capacity can be found, and more materials can be obtained to accommodate changes made within the lead time. Almost everything is possible if given enough time, but at a cost. Express delivery companies have multibillions of dollars (or a company's current currency) in annual revenues, much of it earned from companies and individuals rushing documents and materials around to meet deadlines and schedules. But revenues to express delivery companies are expenses to companies that use their services.

In manufacturing, freeing up capacity, shifting work, and expediting materials delivery and product shipments all raise the cost of producing product. They also increase the risk of producing poor-quality products and damaging important customer relationships due to failure to keep delivery promises.

Question 6: What Is the Impact in the Marketplace?

What if the master planner and/or master scheduler does not reschedule—might the company risk becoming vulnerable to losing an important customer order, getting a reputation in the marketplace for being inflexible, being seen as an arrogant supplier, or worse? Here, the master planner and/or master scheduler wants to know the pain of *not* changing the schedule. Many times, the answer to this question becomes a tiebreaker when deciding whether the master plan and/or master schedule should or should not be changed.

From a management viewpoint, the costs and risks of MPS changes have to be measured and compared to the benefits of these changes. Does management understand the impact on financial performances due to these changes? Will the changes impact support for other customers and products? In the end, management needs to ask the question, "Is it a smart business decision to make this change?"

There are the six all-important questions that need to be asked and answered before the master planner and/or master scheduler makes a change to the master plan and/or master schedule or, if required by policy, requests from management or leadership authorization to make a change to the master plan and/or master schedule. However, many Class A companies have added a seventh question to the list, that of the effect on the morale of company personnel. Let's take a look at this seventh question.

Question 7: What Are the Morale Consequences If the Master Plan and/or Master Schedule Is Changed?

What will be the impact on manufacturing operations personnel and the manufacturing support teams' morale if the change under consideration is made? What about the morale impact within the procurement, purchasing, supplier scheduling, quality, and logistics functions? And, whether the change is made or not made, what is the impact on the customer's (possibly the company's partner or long-time reason for the company to be in business) morale?

This just says that master planners and master schedulers need to be good planners, replanners, schedulers, reschedulers, observers, listeners, analysts, influencers, speakers, mathematicians, geeks, documenters, and the list goes on! The authors believe it is also important that master planners and master schedulers have a somewhat tough skin, with a soft heart and mild temperament under that tough skin.

A manufacturing company measures many things, such as customer delivery, supply plan performance, master plan and schedule performance, production performance, data record accuracy, production efficiency, and so forth. These measurements are quite tangible, and leadership and management can get their hands around the results. Armed with the results and some Pareto analysis,* people in positions of authority can and do make changes leading to improvements in the area under discussion.

*Pareto analysis is a creative way of looking at causes of problems because it helps stimulate thinking and organize thoughts. However, it can be limited by its execution of possibly important problems that may be small initially, but that grow in time (many problem solvers combine a Pareto analysis with other analytical tools). This technique helps to identify the top portion of causes that need to be addressed to resolve the majority of problems.

Once the predominant causes are identified, then tools like fishbone analysis or mind mapping can be used to identify the root causes of the problems. While it is common to refer to Pareto as the "80/20" rule, under the assumption that, in all situations, 20 percent of causes determine 80 percent of problems, this ratio is merely a convenient rule of thumb and is not, nor should it be, considered an immutable law of nature.

However, there are other elements of the business that might be considered quite hard to measure (and even harder to get one's hands around). These measurements are quite intangible, and leadership and management have a hard time getting their hands around the results. Take, for instance, how much stress the people in manufacturing were under during the last round of schedule changes. Does everyone in the supply chain management function have the tools and support to do the job that they are being asked to do?

Answering the Six (or Seven) Questions

Each of the six or seven questions just discussed should be answered before any master plan and/or master schedule change is made. Obviously, in complex environments involving many products, many materials, and many capacity types, answering each question in complete detail would be enormously time consuming. In these cases, time-saving tools like rough cut capacity planning (explained in Chapter 15)—which focuses attention on only critical or key resources and materials—are invaluable. Also, using modern software that can generate simulations in minutes or even seconds is desirable. However, no matter how difficult the task, answers to these questions need to be determined if sound business decisions are to be made.

Equally invaluable is the master planner's and master scheduler's experience and judgment. That experience and judgment will make answers to some of the questions intuitively obvious. In other cases, hours and days of investigation by the master planner and/or master scheduler and other personnel may be required to gather the data on which analysis and an informed decision can be made.

A good master planner and/or master scheduler satisfies demands from forecasts, contracts, customer orders, and other sources, along with the demand variations that inevitably occur, through the use of effective managed plans and schedules, safety stock management, safety capacity management, and selective options or key items overplanning. However, building a good master plan and/or master schedule is just half of the challenge; operating a master plan and/or master schedule within 95–100 percent of plan is the other half. Today, this is as much art as it is science, because the master planner and/or master scheduler must balance materials, capacity, time, and finances against the goals and needs of other parts of the business.

Time Zones as Aids to Decision Making

The example given in Figure 4.1a on page 126 allowed the master planner and/or master scheduler to use judgment in rebalancing the master plan and/or master schedule through change orders. For a number of reasons to be discussed soon, it is beneficial to have a set of guidelines, or *rescheduling time zone rules*, to aid master planners and/or master schedulers and management in making decisions.

These rules are linked to management policies that determine what kinds of changes can be made to the master plan and/or master schedule at certain points in time. Figure 4.2 is a graphical representation of the MPS matrix and shows how the time horizon of periods can be grouped into zones for managing schedule changes.

The meaning of these time zones for management is fairly intuitive. The *firm zone,* sometimes colored red, includes the current period and close-in periods and is one in which the master planner and/or master scheduler and management must carefully investigate all suggested changes. Because these time periods are almost always within the cumulative and possibly the finishing or final assembly lead time of the master planned and/or master scheduled item, any changes will be somewhat disruptive and probably costly. Generally, safety and emergency changes are honored here. All others need high-level approval.

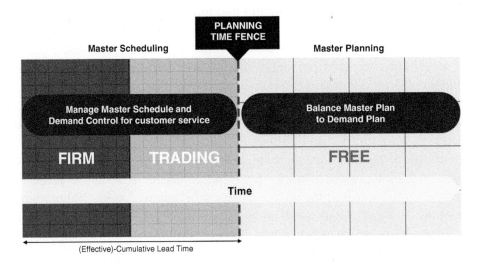

Figure 4.2   Rescheduling Time Zones

The *trading zone*, sometimes colored yellow, is one in which caution should be exercised with respect to changes. Capacity and material availability for changes need scrutiny here, and prioritizing of different orders may be required. Generally, within this zone, material has been ordered, and capacity is firm. Changes that cannot be traded with other demand need some level of approval.

In the *free zone*, sometimes colored green, the master planner and/or master scheduler, and often computer software, are free to make changes as long as the schedule remains within the approved supply plan constraints. This period is by definition far enough into the future that the master planner and/or master scheduler can modify their MPS without affecting the procurement and/or purchasing of material or the process of getting the product to market. Changes in this zone can generally be approved and accomplished by the master planner and/or master scheduler without further management analysis or discussion.

Guidelines for Establishing Zones

There are no hard-and-fast rules for establishing where each zone starts and stops. These are totally dependent upon the nature of the product and the marketing and manufacturing strategies of the company. As a general rule, it is useful to think about the boundary separating the firm and trading zones as a point at which the supply (production) process is highly locked in—where changes will be quite costly and disruptive (firm) and in which a certain amount of careful trading can take place (trading). The boundary between these two zones often coincides with the final assembly or finishing process.

The next step is to determine the boundary between the trading zone and the free zone. When in doubt, the product's cumulative lead time is a logical candidate for this boundary. The logic here is that beyond the cumulative lead time, the master planner and/or master scheduler has the time necessary to obtain the required lower-level materials and move capacity around as required.

In some cases, however, the trading zone could extend beyond the cumulative lead time. This happens when management wants more control over the master plan and/or master schedule and pending plan and/or schedule changes. However, the downside of this is the human effort required to approve and make changes within this zone.

The opposite is also possible; management might make the trading zone smaller, thereby extending the area of the free zone. If a scheduled item had, for example, a cumulative lead time of two months, and fewer approvals and less control were wanted near the end of that period, the boundary could be brought inside the *true* cumulative lead time, making it the *effective* cumulative lead time referred to in Figure 4.2 on the previous page. This provides for needing less people and more computer empowerment in making changes.

However, the risk of not making the time, capacity, materials, and financial resources come together as necessary is certainly there due to changes occurring inside of cumulative lead time. Before leaving this subject, let's consider the following case of an order change.

Moving a Supply Order to an Earlier Date

The new production facility of Bordertown Salsa Company had not only been able to meet its scheduled production load but had actually gotten ahead of the game. It now felt capable of taking on more work. For a new production facility this was an encouraging development. The general manager, however, was cautious and reluctant to push the new plant to the limits. "No sense in giving them so much that they choke themselves," he thought.

Bordertown's production manager told the general manager that he would like to move in two units of scheduled output from time period 3 to time period 2. This would provide a test of the plant's productive capacity in time period 2 and, if that went well, would open up some slack time in time period 3 to do some line adjustments. The general manager agreed.

Pulling work forward is *not* always a bad idea. In this case, it is done for a rational purpose: to test the limits of a new production facility and to create future slack time for line adjustments. Another instance might involve the opportunity to fill unused production capacity.

Likewise, a company may find that its manufactured items or materials inventories are too large and moving orders in can help reduce these inventories and associated carrying costs if the product built can be sold, shipped, and invoiced. The reasons to move a manufacturing order to an earlier date are numerous. However, moving up a supply order involves more than just a change in the due date.

Management Issues

Some orders are moved in because they *must* be moved: a batch of finished product was damaged and must be quickly replaced, preshipment product testing found many

Period	Week 1	Week 2	Week 3
Demand	10	10	10
Supply	10	12 ~~10~~	8 ~~10~~

defective units, a cycle count found an inventory error placing the company out-of-stock on a popular product, a new safety stock level has been approved, and so forth. Other move requests may have less merit, and part of management's job is to create a working environment in which necessary and frivolous change requests can be sorted out on a rational basis.

It takes very little effort to request a supply order change, but implementing the change is often difficult, disruptive, and costly. Management needs to determine whether a change request is frivolous or essential to the goals of the business, and whether it can be justified from a cost standpoint. If the move-up request is simply to satisfy some internal convenience—such as an arbitrary safety stock requirement—that might not represent a genuine business need. If the move is to satisfy an important customer, the company's management should measure the benefit of greater customer satisfaction against the cost of making the change. The company leaders need to ask: "What would happen if we didn't make the change?"

Here are some other issues that the master planner and/or master scheduler along with management must think through:

- *The order movement may be inside the lead time.* One or more components needed for this stage of production may not be available based on the newly scheduled date. This could create a materials problem as well as a credibility problem for the master planner and/or master scheduler (i.e., by asking manufacturing operations to build a product without materials).

- *Is there sufficient capacity?* Whoever approved the move-in supply order may not have checked (or had the experience to determine) that the capacity was available. If the factory cannot respond, what purpose would be served by moving the order?

If an order *must* be moved forward, yet the plant cannot respond, then management must make hard choices. Being between a rock and a hard place is a dilemma that is common in the business world. Management's job is to exercise judgment and creativity in dealing with these dilemmas.

Naturally, management is not the only party concerned when the idea of moving in a supply order is considered. If manufacturing resists, sales and marketing may respond: "You've done it before. Why not now?" Manufacturing may counter with: "We are flexible—to a point—and can handle this one moved-up order. But we cannot handle three, five, or ten such orders."

Manufacturing rightfully wonders why they are seldom notified of opportunities to move *out* orders to make room for the orders in question. Finance, as always, is concerned with the costs of the change and how it will enhance or reduce profits. The master planner and/or master scheduler, whose job it is to satisfy customers within the capabilities and capacities of manufacturing, may rightfully muse that "nothing seems impossible to the person who doesn't have to do it."

Two other time fences are sometimes used by companies to help in managing the business. The capacity time fence (CTF; for example, see Figure 10.7, pages 322–323) reminds the master planner and/or master scheduler that changing capacity within this boundary is difficult. The material time fence (MTF; for example, see Figures 10.8 [pages 332–333] and 10.9 [pages 338–339]) reminds the master planner and/or master scheduler that changing the material requirements inside this boundary is difficult. Both of these time fences or boundaries are warning-type fences and/or boundaries and don't affect the master planning and scheduling (MPS) software or the enterprise resource planning (ERP) logic.

Planning Within Master Planning and Scheduling Policy

Chapter 3 described the use of planning time fences, which is a system technique in which the master scheduler interacts with the computer software. It is not unusual to see the planning time fence (PTF) established at a product's cumulative lead time. In fact, if you do not know where to put the PTF, this is a good starting position.

However, the master planner and/or master scheduler may want to take more control of the horizon. This can be done by putting the PTF further out onto the horizon. This gives the master planner and/or master scheduler more control but also requires more effort since there may be more firm planned orders (FPOs) to control. The master planner and/or master scheduler could also decide to take less control. This can be done by putting the PTF *inside* the cumulative lead time. While this requires *less* effort, the master planner and/or master scheduler is turning over more control of the product to the computer software. Care is needed here since any time the PTF is placed inside the cumulative lead time, some strategic stocking of long-lead-time items should also be taking place in order to ensure material availability.

Company policy needs to define where the planning, material, and capacity time fences are to be placed and which functions within the company are responsible for their maintenance. In addition to the PTF and computer logic, we must also consider the relationship between the managerial decision zones just described and the position of the rescheduling timing zones.

The Hierarchy of Change Approvals

As time passes, a company's ability to make changes to the product becomes increasingly more difficult. Actually, the closer the change is to the product's due date, the more difficult, disruptive, and costly it will be to make that change. Less than Class A companies choose to ignore these simple and important facts. It should be obvious that changes in the firm zone will be more difficult, disruptive, and costly than changes in the trading and free zones (see Figure 4.3). Likewise, changes in the trading zone will be more difficult, disruptive, and costly than changes in the free zone. In fact, as steps in the manufacturing process are completed, a company's flexibility to even change the product diminishes.

Thus, changes that cause minor disruption and cost increase can be made by individuals lower in the hierarchy of authority, while changes that cause major disruptions as well as significant cost increases should be scrutinized and approved at a higher level. This is

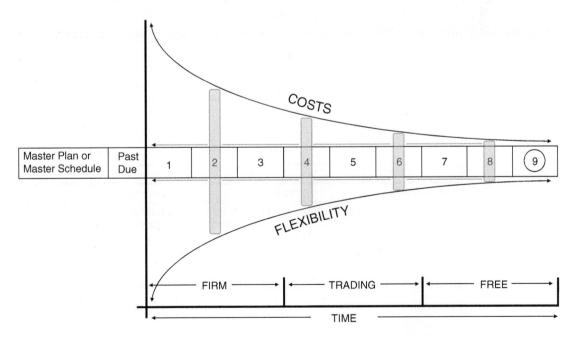

Figure 4.3   Master Planning and Scheduling Change Gap Analysis

the sort of policy that prevails in Class A companies and is analogous to other corporate policies that involve commitments of resources.

A caution in the development of a change-approval policy is that the list of people needed to approve a change should not be so formidable as to make needed changes overly difficult to implement. If a master planner and/or master scheduler has to run around to 17 people to get approval for necessary changes, one of two things will happen: (1) the changes will never be made, or (2) the master planner and/or master scheduler will ignore the policy and make changes arbitrarily. There is a fine line between overburdening the approval process and giving out too much authority to lower-level functions.

Figure 4.4 illustrates this hierarchy of authority to approve changes against the background of the master plan and/or master schedule time horizon and the firm, trading, and free zones previously mentioned. The exact location of the zones in the figure is hypothetical and strictly for illustration purposes. In any Class A organization, however, these demarcations are thoroughly thought out and communicated through written policies.

The Placement of Approval Zones

While approval policies that govern the domain of humans are divided into three or more time zones, the domain of the computer software is generally broken into two by means of the planning time fence (PTF): one in which the computer software has no control (can

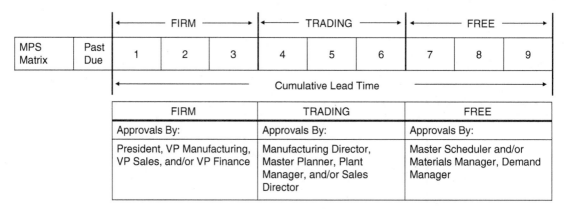

Figure 4.4   Time Zones and Approval Policy Example

recommend changes) and another in which it operates freely. The point has already been made that in the absence of any other guidelines, a good place to put the PTF is at the end of the cumulative lead time.

In the development of a formal policy with respect to the rescheduled approval zones, a good place to put the break between the trading zone and the free zone is also at the end of the cumulative lead time. A logical place for the break between the firm zone and the trading zone is at the end of the finishing or final assembly process. These are not hard-and-fast rules by any means, but they are good rules of thumb when the company has insufficient information to place the decision points elsewhere.

No Past Dues

It should be against the law to permit the master plan and/or master schedule to go past due and remain there. In Chapter 1 we discussed the impact of a past due master plan and/or master schedule. Effective and competitive manufacturing relies on valid scheduling. There simply is *no* other choice. Several things can be done to encourage valid schedules while discouraging invalid past dues when it comes to the master (supply) plan and/or master (supply) schedule.

First of all, an executive policy needs to be written and put into effect that clearly states that there will be no past dues when it comes to the master plan and/or master schedule. Second, there needs to be an understanding of what the policy means and why adherence to it is so important. Third, the people affected by the policy must have the discipline to follow it. Fourth, a performance measurement program that rewards valid schedules while penalizing invalid (past due) schedules needs to be implemented. Fifth, a corrective action process should be put into place just in case any MPS item does go past due and remains past due.

Doing these five things and paying attention to the validity of the master plan and/or master schedule will greatly enhance a company's ability to satisfy their customers while maintaining a profitable business. More detail on past dues and performance to the master plan and/or master schedule is included in Chapters 18 through 20.

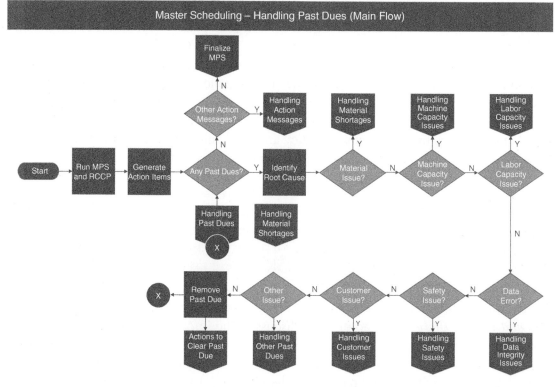

Figure 4.5   Handling Past Dues (Main Flow)

Managing with Planning Time Fences

It is now useful to return to planning time fences to discuss how the master planner and/or master scheduler can use them to more effectively manage production schedules. Consider again the MPS matrix used to introduce the concept of planning time fences, reintroduced here as Figure 4.6 on page 143. Let us consider this to be the master schedule for an A3 unit manufactured by Criterion Electric Controls Company, introduced earlier in the chapter.

Criterion has forecasted level demand at 70 units per period. The master scheduler, Mark Owens, has placed a PTF at the end of time period 6, and, as before, the computer software has spotted the potential deficiencies beginning in time period 6 and generated two CPOs of 130 each to counteract the deficiencies. However, since a PTF has been established between time periods 6 and 7, the first of these CPOs has been placed in time

On Hand: 135 Units
Lead Time (One Level): 2 Period
Cumulative Lead Time: 6 Periods
Lot Size: 130 Units
Multiples: 130 Units

PTF

	Past Due	1	2	3	4	5	6	7	8
Item Forecast		70	70	70	70	70	70	70	70
Option Forecast									
Actual Demand									
Total Demand		70	70	70	70	70	70	70	70
Projected Available Balance	135	65	125	55	115	45	−25	−95 35	−165 95
Available-to-Promise									
Master Schedule			130		130			130	130

Figure 4.6   Managing with Planning Time Fences

period 7 with an action message (negative availability inside the PTF) being sent to the master scheduler. Moving the first of those CPOs into time period 6 as a firm planned order is necessary from the vantage point of the computer software. However, additional analysis must be done before taking action. To learn something new from this situation, consider the following scenario.

The sales group has just returned from a major trade show where customer response to the A3 unit has been extraordinary. Each of the regional sales managers has told the national sales vice president that its sales representatives will be submitting new and higher forecasts for A3 units within the near term. This is truly good news for the company, and the sales vice president is anxious to ensure an adequate supply of A3 units to meet the tremendous demand he expects to materialize soon.

Normally, he would have consulted with the vice president of finance on any major change in the sales forecast, but today he was so excited by future sales prospects, and so uneasy about the company's ability to satisfy orders, that he picked up the telephone and called Judy Wilson first.

"Judy, this is Phil. Good news on the sales front. We have big orders ready to come in on A3s, so we are increasing the forecast in period 4."

"I'm glad to hear about the big sales, Phil, but could you give me a figure for how much higher your forecast will go?"

"Sure," said Phil, proudly. "Right now, it is 70 units in period 4. We plan to knock that up to 270. Wait, on second thought, let's go to 370. No sense in getting caught short, is there?"

Wilson knew immediately that she would earn her paycheck this day. Several things would happen if this forecast change was entered into the enterprise resource planning system. The obedient computer software would place a series of CPOs for 130 units in the MPS row of time period 7, along with an action message to convert three CPOs for 130 units to FPOs and move them into time period 4. Figure 4.7 demonstrates just what Wilson's computer screen would show her.

The large new demand forecasted for time period 4 would create a projected deficit in time periods 4, 5, and 6. The computer software would never dial the sales vice president to ask

On Hand: 135 Units
Lead Time (One Level): 2 Period
Cumulative Lead Time: 6 Periods
Lot Size: 130 Units
Multiples: 130 Units

	Past Due	1	2	3	4	5	6	7	8
Item Forecast		70	70	70	370	70	70	70	70
Option Forecast									
Actual Demand									
Total Demand		70	70	70	370	70	70	70	70
Projected Available Balance	135	65	125	55	−185	−255	−325	−395 / 125	−465 / 55
Available-to-Promise									
Master Schedule			130		130			(520)	

(PTF) ←

Figure 4.7   MPS for A3 Units, with Increased Demand in Time Period 4

how realistic this demand forecast was; the computer would respond in the only way available to it: it would place a very large computer-generated supply order—520 units, four complete lot sizes (multiples of 130 specified)—in time period 7, just outside the planning time fence.

These large CPOs, which have been aggregated to a larger CPO, would solve the volume problem for Wilson, but certainly not the timing problem in time periods 4 through 6. An action message would recommend firming the CPO of 520 units into an FPO and moving the FPO into time period 4 or moving two FPOs of 130 each into time period 4, one of 130 to time period 6, and creating one for 130 in time period 7 (dependent upon the software logic).

Keeping the CPOs outside the planning time fence has the benefit of avoiding unexamined new demand forecasts from automatically exploding downward through the material requirements planning (MRP) system, where materials would be ordered and expected as well as capacity called for on short notice. The planning time fence permits the master (supply) planner, Judy Wilson and master (supply) scheduler, Mark Owens to keep this change in suspension while they consider its consequences on the entire production and materials system.

An experienced master planner, Judy Wilson, and an experienced master scheduler, Mark Owens, knew that they would not be changing the master plan and master schedule on the sales vice president's request alone. A few things were out of order:

1. This change would take place within the trading zone, and Criterion's company policy required the approval of both the sales vice president and the plant manager. The reason for this policy was to avoid the chaos that normally resulted from unauthorized changes made within the cumulative lead time. Wilson and Owens would first check to see if the plant manager had signed off on this proposed schedule change.

2. Wilson's natural suspicion was aroused by both the timing of this request and the sales vice president's initial tentativeness with respect to the number of orders he expected to receive. Saying "on second thought, let's go [from 270] to 370" was not reassuring to Wilson. Also, forecasted demand increases, typically followed the annual trade show attended by the company and, historically, many of these sales failed to materialize in the forecasted period—if at all.

Aside from these two concerns, Wilson and Owens knew intuitively that if they brought the CPOs into time period 4, the magnitude of the increased supply would create material and capacity problems below the level of the master schedule. Completing this volume of A3 units would require evening shifts at double-time wages, rushed materials purchased at premium prices, and expedited shipments to customers—all very costly to the company. "Had anyone even spoken with the vice president of finance?" Wilson wondered aloud.

In the case just described, the master planner and master scheduler earned their pay by being both open- and tough-minded. They had to be open-minded to the possibility of increasing shipments by considering possible alternatives to the computer software–generated action messages, like bringing some of the 520 units into time periods 4 and 6—capacity, materials, and costs permitting. They also had to be tough-minded in observing change policies that support smooth operations and collaboration of different functions of the company. Finally, they needed to answer the six or seven questions with respect to demand, the impact of demand changes on production, materials and capacity availability, costs, risks, and opportunities.

Planning time zones help master planners and master schedulers manage these difficult situations. Planning time fences hold automatic MPS changes outside of the firm zone and trading zone, where unexamined changes invariably cause problems; and they prompt master planners and/or master schedulers with exception-driven action messages to either implement its suggestions or think of better alternatives.

Management is often asked whether the company should *sell what it makes* or *make what it sells*. The answer should always be *yes*. That's a good idea! What the company needs to do is add time to the question. Refer to Figure 4.8. In the close-in time periods, the company should make the demand equal to the supply—sell what's being produced. Beyond a defined timeline, the company's planned supply should be balanced to the planned demand, roughly equal in some cases, offset for seasonal inventory builds in some seasonal businesses, and so on, but without driving inventory or backlog through the roof or negative over time. The reader may be asking where this timeline appears. Again, no hard-and-fast rules, but the finishing or final assembly time is a good starting point.

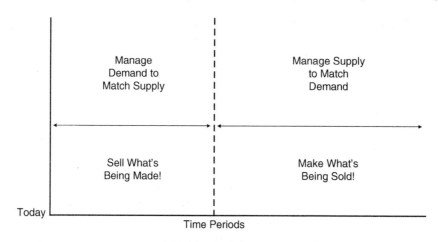

Figure 4.8   Demand and Supply Management Time Fence

Load-Leveling in Manufacturing

Every plant manager's dream is to run the manufacturing facility at a steady pace—that is, with a level-loaded facility. Ideally, this level-loaded facility is very close to peak operating capacity yet provides enough slack for periodic repairs and maintenance. In a perfect world, overtime and expediting costs are eliminated, and workers are spared the scourge of forced periodic plant shutdowns and/or layoffs.

The top half of Figure 4.9 on page 148 represents this idyllic condition. The bottom half, however, represents every plant manager's nightmare and a condition all too common among traditional production plants. In the bottom half, the plant load varies widely: underutilizing capacity in some periods and demanding more than the plant can deliver—except with costly overtime—in others. These variations may be attributed to fluctuating demand, equipment downtime, or just poor scheduling. The master planner and/or master scheduler cannot always make the plant manager's dream come true, but he or she can even out some of the peaks and valleys of production.

Since a major cause of load-level problems is demand fluctuation, consider the following situation. The company forecasts total demand for 400 units at a very uneven rate over the next eight weeks. One approach to leveling production is to plan orders for 400 units at a level rate of 50 per week ($400 \div 8 = 50$).

Figure 4.10 on page 149 demonstrates the result of this naive approach. Assume that the company starts with a zero on-hand balance and that the master planner and/or master scheduler has effectively leveled production at 50 units per week. The resulting projected available balance line indicates that promises to customers may be broken in five of the eight weeks. The first-cut level load just will *not* work.

Several possible solutions present themselves:

1. Anticipating this situation, the master planner and/or master scheduler might build up inventory to a point where the company would start week 1 with an on-hand balance of 40 units. This would render the projected available balance (PAB) positive in all subsequent weeks. The negative side of this approach is inventory costs for certain periods.

2. Work with the sales department to manage demand so that it takes on a more level profile. Discounts or other inducements could be effective in this effort.

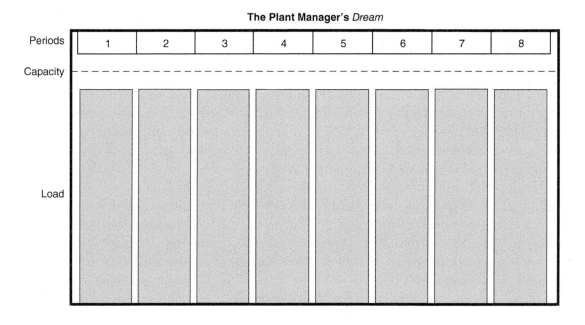

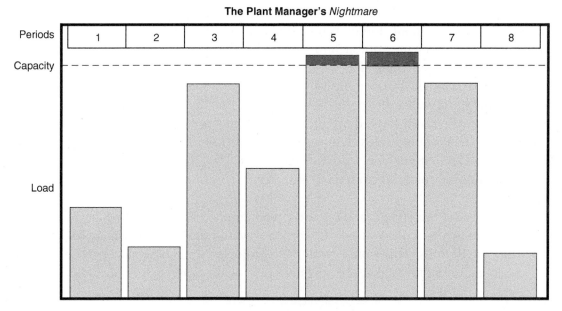

Figure 4.9   Load-Leveling

	Past Due	1	2	3	4	5	6	7	8	Total
Total Demand		30	80	60	70	20	20	80	40	400
Projected Available Balance	0	+20	−10	−20	−40	−10	+20	−10	0	0
Master Schedule		50	50	50	50	50	50	50	50	400

Figure 4.10   A Naive Approach to Load-Leveling

3. Break the eight-week time span into smaller time blocks that can be level-loaded. A quick review of the demand figures indicates that the first four weeks is a block of fairly high demand (30 + 80 + 60 + 70 = 240); weeks 5 through 8 have less demand (20 + 20 + 80 + 40 = 160). By simply scheduling orders for 60 units in each of the first four weeks (240 ÷ 4 = 60), and 40 units in each succeeding week (160 ÷ 4 = 40), as demonstrated in Figure 4.11, two level-loaded blocks of production are created that satisfy all anticipated customer orders with a minimum of excess inventory.

4. This might not be the perfect solution of 50 units per week, but it is close. Of course, the master planner and/or master scheduler must evaluate the impact of the reduction in the MPS between weeks 1–4 and 5–8 (what are we going to do with the people and equipment?).

The company can come closer to the perfect solution if it implements a continuous improvement program with lean manufacturing characteristics that possibly makes use of mixed-model scheduling. Let's take a look!

	Past Due	1	2	3	4	5	6	7	8	Total
Total Demand		30	80	60	70	20	20	80	40	400
Projected Available Balance	0	30	10	10	0	20	40	0	0	0
Master Schedule		60	60	60	60	40	40	40	40	400

Figure 4.11   Load-Leveling by Time Blocks

Lean Manufacturing and Continuous Improvement

Over the past three to four decades much attention has been paid to improving the manufacturing process, largely as a result of the continuous improvement (CI), just-in-time (JIT), and lean manufacturing (LM) movements. As manufacturers learned more about CI/JIT/LM, they came to realize that improving their processes involved more than simply getting material to arrive at the factory every two hours. They began to see CI/JIT/LM in a broader sense—as a continuous improvement program that has as its objective the elimination of waste—where waste is defined as any activity that does not add value to the product.

Consider a three-step process that produces a plastic part (Figure 4.12). In Step 1, the part is formed in a mold; this step adds cost (machine, material, labor, electricity, etc.). This step also adds value. Step 2 moves the molded part some one hundred feet to the packaging line. Again, this step adds cost (material handling equipment, labor, etc.). But does Step 2 add value to the final part? Absolutely not! The customer is no better off for the fact that the part moved one hundred feet across the manufacturing floor. Step 3, part packaging, adds both cost and value.

The principles of lean manufacturing and continuous improvement suggest that the non-value-adding activity of Step 2—physically moving the molded part around the facility—should be minimized or eliminated completely. One way to do this would be to place the packaging line next to the molding machine. Besides this obvious candidate for elimination, there may be other, less obvious non-value-adding activities associated with this molded part: the preparation of schedules, dispatch lists, hot lists, shortage reports, work orders, and so on. The use of these traditional control mechanisms continues to be challenged by many manufacturers today. Those activities that cannot be shown to add value are being eliminated.

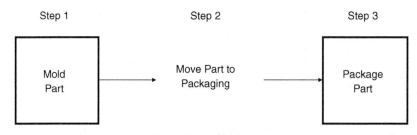

Figure 4.12   Value-Adding and Non-Value-Adding Operations

The same scrutiny is being applied to traditional lot sizes and safety stocks, two factors that produce inventory. Inventory does not directly add value for the customer (unless the product is wine, which gets better with age), even though the company may have reason to maintain it. However, any increments of inventory that can be reduced without impairing customer service and satisfaction may legitimately be viewed as waste.

Lot sizes are generally the result of long setups and/or complex changeovers. Continuous improvement programs suggest that the way to reduce lot sizes is to reduce setup times. Safety stocks are used as protection against demand/supply variation. Continuous improvement programs suggest a way to reduce inventory is to reduce safety stocks, and a way to reduce safety stocks is to reduce or eliminate the demand/supply variations.

As this book intends to demonstrate, careful management of new product launches, demand planning and control, supply planning and control, and financial parts of the business are effective in reducing the need for wasteful inventory, such as safety stocks and safety times. Lean manufacturing professionals taught the master planning and scheduling community a lot and the master planning and scheduling professionals who make up that MPS community need to practice what has been learned over the past three to four decades.

Mixed-Model Scheduling

Traditionally, manufacturers have attempted to build products in large lots to take advantage of cost savings associated with volume. Today, the cost savings associated with volume production continue to be challenged. As companies move closer to the lean manufacturing environment, they are discarding the ideas of large production runs in favor of smaller ones that match incoming customer orders.

Since demand for many different products or models may require shipment of many products on the same day, a growing number of companies continue to implement the technique called *mixed-model scheduling*, which allows/forces them to reduce order quantities, build less of a product at one time, build the product more often, and provide better customer satisfaction and service. Paradoxically, they can do this without increasing costs.

Mixed-model scheduling means building a small volume of each product every day or every week. Consider, for example, a company that produces a five-member family of golf carts—Types 151 through 155—with a mixed-model sequence. For this producer,

50 percent of its unit business is represented by Type 151; the other types normally account for sales as follows: Type 152, 10 percent; Type 153, 10 percent; Type 154, 20 percent; and Type 155, 10 percent. Under traditional methods, the company would produce each type of golf cart in a batch to minimize production costs.

The mixed-model method, however, schedules each type of cart as needed. Figure 4.13 represents the schedule of a company that builds 10 units per week. The top part of the figure is the traditional approach, and the bottom is the mixed-model approach.

In the traditional approach, the customer who orders a Type 154 cart at the beginning of the week must wait until Thursday for shipment (assuming that two golf carts are produced per day). In the mixed-model approach, that cart can be shipped on Monday or in the worst case, on Friday. This method reduces the chance of a stockout and the overbuilding of inventory. As a scheduling method it is not perfect, but manufacturers that use it have reported good results.

One such manufacturer is Tennant Company, which makes industrial floor sweepers. Tennant implemented mixed-model scheduling many years ago to improve delivery times and reduce the need to carry large, finished goods inventory. To accomplish this, Tennant needed to reduce setups, lead times, and cycle times (from four weeks to one week).

The three parts of Figure 4.14 on page 153 show the company's transition from a traditional economic order quantity (EOQ) producer—one that optimizes lot size relative to carrying costs—to a mixed-model producer. Section A of the figure identifies Tennant as an EOQ producer. Looking at the assembly line starts and the "parts kitting" activities supporting those starts, the reader can see an unbalanced load on the people doing the

Traditional Approach

Periods	1	2	3	4	5	6	7	8	9	10
Item	151	151	151	151	151	152	153	154	154	155

Mixed-Model Approach

Periods	1	2	3	4	5	6	7	8	9	10
Item	151	154	151	152	151	153	151	155	151	154

Figure 4.13   Weekly Production Schedule for Golf Carts

A. Economic Order Quantity Producer

| Model | \multicolumn{14}{c}{WEEKS} | Total |
	1	2	3	4	5	6	7	8	9	10	11	12	13	14	
A	21→							21→							42
B		17→							18→						35
C			49——→							49———→					98
D						21→							21→		42
E							11							10	21
Total # of Units Kitted per Week	21	17	49	–	–	21	11	21	18	49	–	–	21	10	238

B. Level-Load Producer

| Model | \multicolumn{14}{c}{WEEKS} | Total |
	1	2	3	4	5	6	7	8	9	10	11	12	13	14	
A	17	4						17	4						42
B		13	4						13	5					35
C			13	17	17	2				12	17	17	3		98
D						15	6						14	7	42
E							11							10	21
Total # of Units Kitted per Week	17	17	17	17	17	17	17	17	17	17	17	17	17	17	238

C. Mixed-Model Producer

| Model | \multicolumn{14}{c}{WEEKS} | Total |
	1	2	3	4	5	6	7	8	9	10	11	12	13	14	
A	3	3	3	3	3	3	3	3	3	3	3	3	3	3	42
B	2	3	2	3	2	3	2	3	2	3	2	3	2	3	35
C	7	7	7	7	7	7	7	7	7	7	7	7	7	7	98
D	3	3	3	3	3	3	3	3	3	3	3	3	3	3	42
E	2	1	2	1	2	1	2	1	2	1	2	1	2	1	21
Total # of Units Kitted per Week	17	17	17	17	17	17	17	17	17	17	17	17	17	17	238

Figure 4.14   Tennant Company Transition from Traditional Economic Order Quantity Producer to Mixed-Model Producer

kitting—21 kits to be pulled in week 1; 17 kits in week 2; 49 kits in week 3; no kits at all in week 4; and so forth. Section B of the figure shows Tennant still as an EOQ-based product producer, but level-loading the kitting area at 17 pulls per week. Section C of the figure indicates that Tennant has completed the transition to a mixed-model producer, building a small amount of everything every week, and level-loading the kitting area. The secret to the company's transition was regular, incremental process improvement.

Mixed-model scheduling and lean manufacturing are important parts of being a Class A company. They require good communication among sales, marketing, engineering, finance, manufacturing support, and manufacturing operations. There is just no substitute for people working together as a focused team to eliminate waste. Companies that have not adopted mixed-model scheduling and lean manufacturing are advised to consider them as methods for improving the customer satisfaction process as well as the master planning and scheduling process.

Planned Plant Shutdowns

In many industries, customer demand is fairly continuous, yet production facilities are shut down periodically for vacations, scheduled maintenance, refitting, and other purposes. Accommodating demand when the plant is idle is a regular and important responsibility of the master planner and/or master scheduler and is usually accomplished by a steady buildup of inventories in the periods prior to the shutdown.

To demonstrate this process, consider Minuteman Electronics Company (MEC). Minuteman has planned a shutdown of its Boston production facility during the weeks beginning 7/12 and 7/19 to accommodate annual maintenance and cleaning. Many of its regular production workers will take those weeks as vacation; those who do not will assist the maintenance and cleaning crews.

Demand from customers and from its two regional distribution centers is forecasted at 3,000 units per week during the period before and during the shutdown, meaning that MEC must go into the shutdown period with a reserve quantity of 6,000 units if it hopes to satisfy all forecasted orders. Thus, MEC's master planner and/or master scheduler must plan to build enough product to cover the regular forecasted demand and build up the reserve quantity during the weeks prior to scheduled plant shutdown.

Reserve Quantity: 0
Cumulative to Date: 0
On-Hand Balance: 5,200 Units
Start Build: 6/8
Stop Build: 7/5
Release Date: 7/12

	Past Due	6/1	6/8	6/15	6/22	6/29	7/5	Shutdown 7/12	7/19
Forecast		3,000	3,000	3,000	3,000	3,000	3,000	3,000	3,000
Projected Available Balance	5,200	2,200	6,700	3,700	8,200	5,200	9,700	6,700	3,700
Master Schedule			7,500		7,500⟩ →		7,500⟩ →		

Reschedule Out

Figure 4.15 Plant Shutdown Planning

Figure 4.15 shows the situation at MEC, where the master scheduler has created three firm planned orders of 7,500 each in time periods 6/8, 6/22, and 7/5 to complete the reserve quantity. By the end of time period 7/5, the projected inventory balance is 9,700, enough to cover the planned shutdown as well as any demand in 7/26, while the plant is coming back up.

However, as the master planning and scheduling software analyzes the projected available balance line, it will notice that the firm planned orders in 6/22 and 7/5 can be rescheduled-out (the projected available balance will remain positive if this is done) and will signal the master scheduler with action messages. Of course, the master scheduler is aware of the reason for the projected surplus inventory and plans to ignore the system's recommendations.

The master scheduler may want to get rid of these correct, though unwanted, action messages. There are three approaches to do this:

1. Use a non-movable firm planned order if the MPS software offers this capability.

2. Create artificial demand by placing a reserve requirement in the system over the course of the buildup period.

3. Modify the software so that it will create artificial demand equal to the amount needed during the planned shutdown period.

Figure 4.16 on page 156 indicates how the artificial demand suggested in the last two alternatives may be implemented. As the figure indicates, an artificial demand equal to

Reserve Quantity: 6,000 Units
Cumulative to Date: 0
On-Hand Balance: 5,200 Units
Start Build: 6/8
Stop Build: 7/5
Release Date: 7/12

	Past Due	6/1	6/8	6/15	6/22	6/29	7/5	Shutdown 7/12	7/19
Forecast		3,000	3,000	3,000	3,000	3,000	3,000	3,000	3,000
Reserve Quantity			1,200	1,200	1,200	1,200	1,200	−6,000	
Projected Available Balance	5,200	2,200	5,500	1,300	4,600	400	3,700	6,700	3,700
Master Schedule			7,500		7,500		7,500		

Figure 4.16   Plant Shutdown Planning with Artificial Demand

the forecasted demand for the shutdown period has been created and placed in the master scheduling matrix under the *reserve quantity* line. As each period's projected available balance is calculated, the planned shutdown demand is taken into account.

This process continues until time period 7/5, when the entire buildup quantity is released (7/12) and recorded in the inventory balance. The projected inventory balance in 7/12 is determined by summing the 3,700 projected to be available in 7/5 and the *reserve quantity* of 6,000 (3,700 + 6,000 = 9,700). From this, the forecast of 3,000 units is subtracted, leaving a projected available balance of 6,700, which will be used to satisfy demand in time periods 7/19, 7/26, and so on.

Of course, plant shutdowns can also result from the termination of a particular product or from a corporation's need to reduce overall manufacturing capacity. Witness, for example, the continuing efforts of a large automobile manufacturer to slash its auto- and part-making capacities. The following case situation speaks to a similar situation, and one that points out the important implications for executive leadership, operating management, and the master planning and scheduling function.

THE PRODUCTION SHUTDOWN

In 1976 a leading medical group announced its conclusion that women below the age of 55 should *not* have regular mammograms. The danger of repeated radiation exposures, in its view, outweighed the benefits of regular mammograms in the detection of breast cancer among younger women.

For Xerox Corporation's Xeroradiography Operations Unit, this announcement struck like a torpedo amidships. Almost overnight, a large chunk of the market for its expensive mammography machines was blown out of the water. Though some of its backlogged orders held firm in the wake of the announcement, many were canceled, and only a few new customers appeared. With its demand forecast sinking quickly, managers and production schedulers in the Xerox unit had to make new estimates of future demand and reflect these in dramatic revisions of the supply plan.

In the fast-paced business environment, when products are quickly undercut by new technology and new competitors, the situation faced by Xerox in 1976 is not uncommon, and just about everyone in the affected business unit—including the master scheduler—is forced to make dramatic course corrections. Consider the following set of numbers for a hypothetical operation.

The original forecast had been for 100 units per period, but new developments have cut deeply into that figure. With future demand slowed to a trickle, and the future of the product clearly in doubt, management sees a shutdown of the production line as its best option. But how should that shutdown be scheduled?

Original Forecast	100	100	100	100
New Forecast	30	10	10	10
Master Schedule	60	0	0	0

In this simple example, management decides to keep the production line open during the next period, building for all demand anticipated over the next four periods. This plan will result in heavy initial inventory, but financial managers determine that the inventory carrying costs will be less than the costs associated with maintaining a low-volume production line over time. Once its inventory of built products is exhausted, the product will be terminated due to insufficient demand.

In the case of Xerox, the Xeroradiography Operations (XRO) Unit determined that the combination of existing finished goods, current production scheduled through the next several months, and machines sent back for refurbishing would be sufficient to satisfy reduced market demand for a period of two years—an estimate that proved to be remarkably accurate. Current work on the production line was completed and then the line was shut down.

Two other developments occurred within two years: Medical opinion on the benefits/risks of mammograms for women under 55 took an about-face and engineering changes at Xerox were successful in reducing the radiation levels of the next generation of mammogram machines. However, due to the reduction in demand, many XRO employees were transferred to other Xerox businesses.

Management Issues

Production shutdowns can result from several causes: a dramatic reduction in market demand (as just described), recall of the product because of safety or sabotage problems (e.g., Johnson & Johnson's recall of Tylenol), and others. Whatever the cause, a number of important issues confront management:

- Should we continue production and simply build inventory until the horizon is clearer, or should we shut down the line?

- If we reduce or halt production, what will we do with materials in inventory and on order, with production personnel, and with the production facility itself?

- Should we fight the issue and rebuild demand by pumping resources into public relations and advertising?

If our leaders and managers are paid to make decisions, they really earn their pay during episodes like these, when the stakes are high, and the future is uncertain. Worse still, the best solutions may only reduce the financial damage to the company. For business leaders and managers, all the choices may be undesirable, but choices nevertheless must be made (sometimes, the decision needs to be the least-worst choice).

Abrupt production shutdowns affect everyone, not just top management. Financial managers analyze the costs of the alternative solutions and project their effects onto the bottom line. Sales and marketing personnel must deal with affected customers and wonder what other products they should be selling. Manufacturing personnel contemplate line changeovers to other products as they await the decision of top management. Engineers and quality people scramble for solutions that will put the product back into the market.

The two preceding chapters should have imparted a general understanding of master planning and scheduling and materials requirements planning mechanics, planning time zones, exception-driven action messages, and what the master planner and/or master scheduler needs to do in order to successfully guide several of the company's valuable resources, that is, operating people, machines and equipment, plant space, and so forth. But there's more to mastering planning and scheduling than just the mechanics.

The next two chapters deal with how to use the master planning and scheduling system output in the make-to-stock environment and *what* to master plan and/or master schedule. The mechanics discussed so far are important, but not nearly as important as how the master planner and/or master scheduler makes decisions using the computer software-generated information.

5

Using the Master Planning and Scheduling Output for Make-to-Stock Products

It requires a very unusual mind to make an analysis of the obvious.

This chapter examines the computer software output—reports or screens—used by master planners and master schedulers in managing demand and supply balancing, timing, as well as quantities. The content in this chapter is deliberately focused on screens supporting the master scheduling process and leaves more in-depth discussion on master planning techniques and supporting software for Chapter 16, "Supply Management and Aggregate Master Planning."

Suffice it to say, the screens supporting the master planning process have similar information to screens supporting master scheduling (e.g., pertinent header information, time-phased planning grids depicting demand, inbound/planned supply, projected available inventory balances, capacity information, etc.) but are geared toward a higher level of aggregate planning. The master plan, derived from and in support of the aggregate supply plan approved in the integrated business planning (IBP) process (see Chapter 14), is not as concerned with actual demand detail and master schedule order detail (although those details do sometimes come into play in aggregate planning, especially when unusually large orders or very influential customers are involved).

The master planning screens' purpose is to support the aggregate balancing of demand, supply, inventory, backlog, and key resource capacity at a specific supply point (e.g., manufacturing plant) and provide direction to the master scheduler as a *request for supply* flowing from the IBP process. They generally deal in product families and/or groups and in monthly buckets translating into weekly buckets. The screens supporting the master scheduling process, on the other hand, deal in product groups and/or individual items/ stock-keeping units (SKUs) in weekly to daily buckets and do take more detailed actual demand and master schedule orders into account.

Understanding the many elements of master scheduling software screens and how they interact with each other is essential in this important management task. Once the master scheduling data and information is introduced, we will see how it can be used in planning and scheduling an actual product—an industrial winch.

The manufacturer of the winch in our example follows a *make-to-stock* manufacturing strategy for this product. This is a fairly common strategy followed by companies that make everything from felt-tipped pens to books like the one you may be holding in your hand. Companies that build products and put those products directly on the shelf—either in their own stockrooms or in those of their distribution centers—are using a make-to-stock strategy.

The relative simplicity of the make-to-stock strategy versus the make-to-order and/or design-to-order (sometimes referred to as engineer-to-order) strategy makes the chore of explaining the master scheduling output for a make-to-stock item somewhat straightforward. Subsequent chapters will discuss how to work the MPS output using other manufacturing strategies, such as package-to-order, kit-to-order, assemble-to-order, make-to-order, engineer-to-order, and design-to-order.

The Master Schedule Screens

Previous chapters have presented matrices for the master planning and scheduling process. It is the authors' hope that these matrices have been useful to the reader in learning the mechanics of the master planning and scheduling process. As planning software providers have proliferated over the past five decades, the screen formats and graphical user interfaces have followed suit. The examples the authors use in this chapter are not meant to represent the *cutting edge* of software development; they do add pertinent, more detailed information to the basic planning grids used as examples in prior chapters, in an attempt to show the reader what is useful to have at one's fingertips when developing and/or adjusting master plans and schedules.

Now, let's take a look at some examples of computer-generated master planning and master scheduling screens in Figure 5.1 on page 162. The screens are divided into three sections:

1. Item Information (data such as master scheduler, lead times, lot sizes, safety stocks);

2. Planning Horizons (data such as demand, supply, projected available balance, available-to-promise);

3. Detail Data (data such as supply order type, supply order quantity, demand identification).

Item Information Section

This section occupies the top portion of the screen and contains information about the product, planning data, and production policy guidelines. Here is a brief description of each data element of this section.

Item Number: The unique identification assigned to the master scheduled item.

Primary Description: Provides a brief description of the master scheduled item and can include name, model number, as well as other data.

Item Status: Describes the item by stocking status (e.g., indicates whether the item or part is a stocked, pseudo, or phantom—pseudo and phantom items will be discussed later in this book).

Product Family: The product family to which the item belongs. For example, lavender bar soap might be part of a product family that includes citrus bar soap, goat milk bar soap, colloidal oatmeal bar soap, and so on.

Master Scheduler: Contains the initials or name of the individual master scheduler responsible for this master scheduled item. The data also allows the master scheduling system to sort reports and/or exception-driven action messages for distribution of secured screens and/or hard copies.

Demand Manager: Contains the initials or name of the individual demand manager responsible for the demand plan (forecast) for the master scheduled item. This information

Item Information Section

Item Number	Primary Description		Item Status	Product Family			Master Scheduler		Demand Manager	
Balance On Hand	Lot Size		Safety Stock		Time Fence			Lead Time	Cuml. Lead Time	Stnd. Cost
	Rule	Factor	Policy	Factor	PTF DTF MTF CTF RTF					

Forecast Consumption	Resource Profile	Critical Resources					
		Resource	Resource	Resource	Resource	Resource	Resource
Selling Price	Special Instructions		Date Run		Actions Recommended		

Planning Horizons Section

Period	Past Due	1	2	3	4	5	6	7...
Item Forecast								
Option Forecast								
Actual Demand								
Total Demand								
Projected Available Balance								
Available to Promise								
Master Schedule*								

* Planned receipts only, including planned orders and released manufacturing and/or purchase orders

Detail Data Section

Master Schedule Detail						
Required Date	Order Number	Lot Number	Order			Recommended Action
			Quantity	Type	Status	

Actual Demand Detail												
Required Date	Order Quantity	Ref. Number	Order Number	T	S	C	Required Date	Order Quantity	Ref. Number	Order Number	T	S C

Figure 5.1   Sample Master Scheduling Screens

gives the master scheduler a point of human contact to ask questions regarding the demand plan and to better understand the source of forecasted demand (i.e., demand from a statistical forecasting system, developed through an explosion using planning bills, or a manually input judgmental number).

Forecast Consumption: Shows the master scheduler how the forecast is consumed when orders are booked.

Resource Profile: Indicates the resource profile to which the master scheduled item is tied (to its own profile, to the product family profile, or to a similar item). This resource profile is used in rough cut capacity planning, which is discussed in detail in Chapter 15.

Critical or Key Resources: Multiple critical or key resources (six in this example) could be displayed for this master scheduled item. The information includes the names of the key resources to allow for quick association (the master scheduler is typically highly attuned to *problem resources* at any given time, so knowing this information can provide quick perspective in decision making), linking to more detailed capacity information within a rough cut capacity planning module.

Balance on Hand: The quantity of the master scheduled items that are in the warehouse as of the date the MPS data was run.

Lot Size: Indicates the preferred ordering practice for the master scheduled item. This category contains two fields. The first field includes the lot-sizing rule used (discrete or lot for lot; a fixed quantity; a period order quantity; etc.). The second field contains the factor attached to whatever lot size rule is used.

For example, if period order quantity is used, a factor of 2 specifies that when the master scheduling computer software generates a supply order (done in the form of a computer planned order), it needs to generate that supply order (CPO) for enough material to cover the next two periods of demand. If a fixed quantity is used, the factor might be, say, 100, indicating that 100 is the minimum order amount.

Safety Stock: This displays two types of information: (1) the policy, which refers to a quantity or time; and (2) a factor, which describes the lower limit (e.g., *never less than 100 units*) or how many periods early the recommended order release and receipt will be specified (e.g., *two periods earlier than required*).

Time Fences: This field shows where the planning time fence (PTF) is set (e.g., between periods 6 and 7). If a demand (DTF), material (MTF), capacity (CTF), or release (RTF) time fence is used, this, too, is indicated.

Lead Time and Cumulative Lead Time: The first data element is the planning lead time for one level of this MPS item. It shows how long it should take to get the product on the shelf once all the subassemblies, intermediates, and materials required one level down are available. The second data element, cumulative lead time, indicates how long it should take to build (or purchase) this MPS item from scratch (the longest leg or critical path of the item).

Standard Cost (cost can be derived by other methods): The target cost of the item (material content, labor content, direct overhead, outside processing, etc.). The information in this field is helpful in determining the impact on cost resulting from changes in the master schedule.

Selling Price: Indicates the list price of the master scheduled item in the marketplace. Selling price is useful in determining operating margins and in quantifying the impact of master schedule changes on total revenues.

Special Instructions: These include reminders such as *see note 11*. Note 11 in turn might instruct the master scheduler to check with engineering before releasing another firm planned order (FPO) because of a planned engineering change.

Date Run: The date on which the master planning and scheduling (enterprise resource planning) computer system refreshed or prepared the screen or report.

Actions Recommended: A summary of recommendations, such as reschedule-in or reschedule-out, release the order, convert a computer planned order to a firm planned order, and so on (refer to Chapter 4 for a discussion of the various exception-driven action messages).

Planning Horizons Section

The planning horizons section describes demand and supply data for a specific time period, typically one day or week. The format in the master scheduling screen is almost identical to the format used in previous chapters. The first period is generally the past-due period, the second is the current period, and each subsequent period extends the timeline into the future. (Note: The number of time periods shown varies from company to company. Also, the master scheduler can often define how many days are in each period; the master scheduler may, for example, define the first five periods in individual days, the next 11 in half weeks, and the six following these in weeks.) Each time period includes the following information:

Item Forecast: Generally *independent* demand. This line is used to display spares or service forecast for the master scheduled item.

Option Forecast: Generally *dependent* demand. The option forecast is the quantity directly forecasted for the master scheduled item as the result of forecasted requirements from a top-level model exploded through a product family planning bill (see Chapters 8 and 9 for an explanation of this process).

Actual Demand: Indicates customer orders already held by the company. For make-to-stock products, the interval between the receipt of a customer order and its ship date is relatively short; therefore, it is *not* uncommon to see little unshipped actual demand reflected on the master schedule screen for make-to-stock products.

Projected Available Balance: The quantity expected to be available at the end of each planning period. This is the balance between demand and supply. A positive projected available balance number identifies potential surplus stock, negative numbers show potential shortages, and zero reflects perfect balance.

(Note: A positive value can also reflect potential perfect balance if safety stock is being used and the positive value equals the desired safety stock level.)

Available-to-Promise (ATP): Shows the amount of product by period that can be committed to customers. ATP is not used extensively for products in make-to-stock environments as the inventory is presumed to be there to support the demand and normal variability in demand and/or supply.

However, ATP is essential in managing abnormal demand (e.g., unusually large orders) and/or supply situations (e.g., running lean due to material or capacity issues). In other words, making good promises and keeping good promises is relatively easy in the normal course of business in an MTS environment, but ATP is vital when things don't materialize as planned outside of normal variability.

Available-to-promise (ATP) is equal to the master scheduled quantity less the actual demand for all time periods, except time period 1, where the quantity on hand is added to the master scheduled quantity less the actual demand (noncumulative in all examples in this chapter—in other words, period-by-period available-to-promise quantities—the reader should be aware that the MPS computer software is certainly capable of summarizing the available-to-promise quantities and displaying a cumulative available-to-promise).

Master Schedule: Shows the anticipated build (or purchase) quantity per time period and consists of scheduled supply receipts, released supply orders, and firm planned supply orders within the planning time fence. Beyond the planning time fence, the computer can place its own orders, which are called computer planned orders (CPOs).

All MPS quantities in this chapter's example are shown in the time period in which they are due (the start period could be displayed by subtracting the master scheduled item's lead time from the period due). Let's continue our discussion by reviewing the detail data section covering supply as well as demand orders.

Detail Data Section

This section of the master schedule screen shows actual data by date and is subdivided into *master schedule detail* on the left side and *actual demand detail* on the right. All data appearing here is linked to the planning horizons data above it and constitutes the supporting detail for the master schedule.

Master Schedule Detail: This portion of the detail section supplies detail information on each expected master scheduled receipt that appears in the master schedule row. Exception-driven action messages are printed for any expected receipt that requires scheduling, rescheduling, cancellation, and so on.

- **Required Date:** Shows the actual date the scheduled supply receipt is expected to be received or available. This date is the one used to place the quantity on the master schedule row of the planning horizon.

- **Order Number:** Shows the supply, manufacturing, production, firm planned, or purchase order number assigned by the master scheduler.

- **Lot Number:** Is a suffix applied to supply, manufacturing, production, firm planned, or purchase orders that further defines the expected supply receipt by lot, run, campaign, or any other unique characteristic.

- *Order Quantity:* Indicates the quantity remaining open on the scheduled supply receipt.

- *Order Type:* Distinguishes between manufacturing and purchase supply receipts and supply orders.

- *Order Status:* Indicates whether the expected receipt is released, firm planned, or computer planned.

- *Recommended Action:* Displays the computer software's recommendation for each supply receipt (e.g., reschedule-in or reschedule-out, release a supply order, cancel a supply order, etc.).

Actual Demand Detail: This portion of the detail section occupies the lower middle and lower right area of the MPS screen. Like the master schedule detail, it provides important details on the demand figures that appear in the planning horizons section. This information is provided in terms of the following categories:

- *Required Date:* Displays the ship date or final assembly start date (depending on which date is being used to synchronize the planning) for the customer order.

- *Order Quantity:* Shows the amount of product remaining open for the customer order.

- *Reference Number:* Is the particular customer name (which, for a make-to-stock product, may just be finished goods).

- *Order Number:* Indicates the actual customer order number for make-to-order products and the manufacturing order or run number for make-to-stock products.

- *Demand Type (T):* Indicates the type of demand, such as assemble-to-order (A), finished goods (F), and so on.

- *Demand Status (S):* Notes whether the demand is a released requirement (R), a customer order in the quotation state (Q), an on-hold customer order (H), a shippable item (S), or demand that has been generated from an upper-level item (F), and so on.

- *Demand Code (C):* Indicates whether the demand is abnormal (A) or normal (blank). If abnormal, it is added to the forecast amount in the time period in which it occurs.

Working Make-to-Stock Master Scheduled Items

Now that the basic components of the master scheduling screen are understood, it can be used in master scheduling an actual manufactured product, in this case an industrial winch.[1] But first, we need to understand this product in terms of its product family, product structure, and cumulative lead time. These are best understood by examining the bill-of-material (see Figure 5.2 on page 169).

The top portion of the figure is a hierarchy representation of the WA01 winch and its underlying components and subassemblies. The winch has four levels: a finished item level (L0) and three lower levels (L1, L2, and L3).

The bottom half of the figure is called an *indented* or *multilevel* bill-of-material (BOM). This bill reveals all the items necessary to produce the WA01 winch from scratch. The various column headings in this indented BOM, however, require some explanation:

LVL: Refers to the level in the BOM. Level 3 items are components of level 2 items, level 2 items are components of level 1 items, and level 1 items are all components of the finished item—the level 0 item.

Item #: Refers to the specific identification number of the item, raw material, component, machined part, subassembly, and so on.

Description: Provides a brief description of the item, raw material, component, intermediate, subassembly, parent assembly, or finished item.

Source: Describes where the item originates. These sources may be any of the following: suppliers, site operations, off-site operations, and so on.

Raw: Raw materials or components, which are used to create machined parts, subassemblies, packaged items, and so on.

Pur: Purchased materials from an outside supplier.

---

[1] The winch product structure example used in this chapter and Chapter 10 was created and published in the *initial* APICS *Bill-of-Material Training Aid* (Falls Church, VA: American Production and Inventory Control Society at the time of publication). The master schedule and material requirements planning examples were originally developed at Arista Manufacturing Systems by a number of people. The intention of these two chapters is *not* to perform mechanics on the numbers, but to discuss what a master planner and master scheduler does with data once it is available. For this purpose, these examples work well.

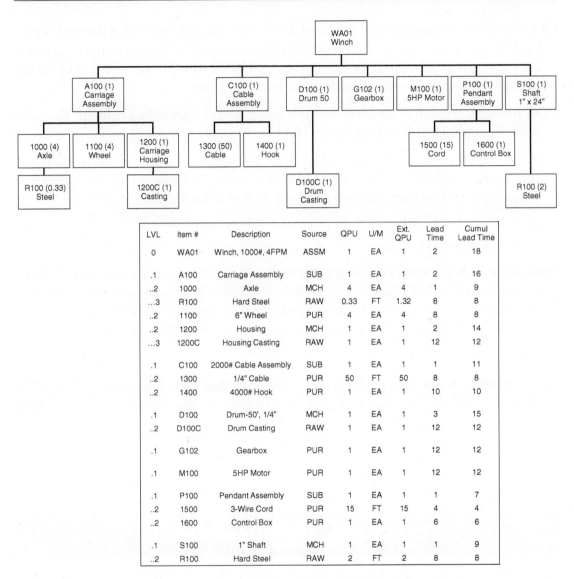

LVL	Item #	Description	Source	QPU	U/M	Ext. QPU	Lead Time	Cumul Lead Time
0	WA01	Winch, 1000#, 4FPM	ASSM	1	EA	1	2	18
.1	A100	Carriage Assembly	SUB	1	EA	1	2	16
..2	1000	Axle	MCH	4	EA	4	1	9
...3	R100	Hard Steel	RAW	0.33	FT	1.32	8	8
..2	1100	6" Wheel	PUR	4	EA	4	8	8
..2	1200	Housing	MCH	1	EA	1	2	14
...3	1200C	Housing Casting	RAW	1	EA	1	12	12
.1	C100	2000# Cable Assembly	SUB	1	EA	1	1	11
..2	1300	1/4" Cable	PUR	50	FT	50	8	8
..2	1400	4000# Hook	PUR	1	EA	1	10	10
.1	D100	Drum-50', 1/4"	MCH	1	EA	1	3	15
..2	D100C	Drum Casting	RAW	1	EA	1	12	12
.1	G102	Gearbox	PUR	1	EA	1	12	12
.1	M100	5HP Motor	PUR	1	EA	1	12	12
.1	P100	Pendant Assembly	SUB	1	EA	1	1	7
..2	1500	3-Wire Cord	PUR	15	FT	15	4	4
..2	1600	Control Box	PUR	1	EA	1	6	6
.1	S100	1" Shaft	MCH	1	EA	1	1	9
..2	R100	Hard Steel	RAW	2	FT	2	8	8

Figure 5.2   WA01 Winch Multilevel Bill-of-Material

Mch: Machined or fabricated items, in which raw materials are converted into other intermediates (in some cases, the machined or fabricated items may be end items in themselves).

Sub: Subassemblies, which consist of a configuration of purchased items and/or parts, components, machined items, or raw materials.

QPU: Stands for "quantities per unit" and defines the quantity needed at the next higher level. Thus, the carriage assembly consists of four axles, which in turn require .33 feet of hard steel (see next column for units), four purchased wheels, one machined housing, and one housing that is machined from a housing casting.

U/M: Indicates the unit of measure for each quantity in the preceding column. The units in this example are feet (FT) and each (EA).

EXT. QPU: Is the extended quantities per unit. For example, as we saw in the QPU column, four axles are needed for each carriage assembly. Each axle in return requires 0.33 feet of hard steel, so four axles will require 1.32 feet of hard steel (4 times 0.33).

Lead Time: Refers to the amount of time it takes to procure or make the individual item (hours, days, weeks).

Cumulative LT: Indicates how long it takes to build the item from scratch. Note that it is *not* the sum of the individual lead times below it; rather, it is based on the critical path—the longest path in time that it takes to produce the referenced item from scratch. The difference is that many of the processes will be done in parallel operations.

In Figure 5.2 on previous page, it can be seen that each intermediate has its own cumulative lead time. In the case of the pendant assembly, that time is seven periods. For the carriage assembly, the lead time is 16 periods. The carriage assembly, in fact, has the longest lead time of any of the intermediates. Since the final winch assembly requires two periods to build once all the intermediates are in place, the cumulative lead time for the WA01 winch is 18 periods.[2]

Time Phasing the Bills-of-Material

With the information contained in the bills-of-material (BOM), the master scheduler knows the items, levels, quantities, and lead times. Using this information, a time-phased bill-of-material is developed that shows the relationship of each item in the winch to each

---

[2] If a winch is to be completed 18 periods from today, a material planner must order the housing casting today, because it requires 12 periods to procure the raw material, two periods to machine the housing, and another two periods to include the housing casting in the carriage assembly, a total of 16 periods. Add the two periods for putting the finished winch together and the total time is 18 periods.

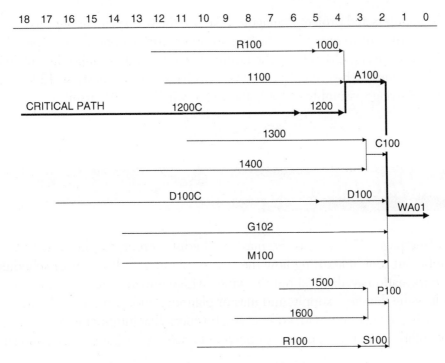

18 17 16 15 14 13 12 11 10 9 8 7 6 5 4 3 2 1 0

R100 1000

1100 A100

CRITICAL PATH 1200C 1200

1300 C100

1400

D100C D100 WA01

G102

M100

1500 P100

1600

R100 S100

Figure 5.3   Time-Phased Bill-of-Material

other in terms of level and in terms of when work on it must be started if the final winch is to be built within the planning lead time—18 periods (see Figure 5.3).

The time-phased BOM in this example makes it visually clear that to produce the WA01 winch, the carriage assembly (A100), cable assembly (C100), drum (D100), pendant assembly (P100), and shaft (S100) must be completed and available two periods before the WA01 winch is scheduled for completion. In addition, the gearbox (G102) and motor (M100) must be received from the supplier. This is true because of the two periods of lead time associated with the WA01 winch.

Looking at just one of the subassemblies for the winch, the A100 carriage assembly, it is easy to see that work on its component items must be initiated still earlier if the carriage assembly is to be ready in time for work on the final WA01 winch to begin. To pick just one of A100's component parts as an example, work on item 1100 (the six-inch wheel) must begin 10 periods before the A100 carriage assembly is due to be finished (eight periods to secure the wheel and two periods to complete the carriage assembly).

Master schedulers and project managers alike use the term *critical path* to describe the longest path in the entire operation. As long as other work can be done in parallel to this critical path, it (critical path) defines the cumulative lead time to build the entire item. In this particular example, the critical path travels from the housing casting (1200C), to housing (1200), to carriage assembly (A100), and to the winch (WA01) itself.

Understanding Exception-Driven Action Messages

Figure 5.4 (see pages 174–175) is the master schedule screen for the WA01 winch. This screen will be our tool in learning how the master planner and/or master scheduler integrates the information available about the winch with company strategies, tactics, and policies as well as the demand, supply, and master planner's and/or master scheduler's strong desire to satisfy the customer with competent, business-like judgments concerning manufacturing stability, inventories, capacity constraints, schedule change costs, and so forth.

Item Information Section

In the WA01 example, 138 units are on hand, and the lot size method chosen is period order quantity (POQ)* for two periods of demands. The safety stock policy is by quantity, and the factor is 100 (the company desires not to drop below 100 winches in stock at any time). The planning time fence (PTF) is set at 20 periods.

 * *The authors recognize that using the period-order-quantity (POQ) lot sizing technique might **not** be the best choice for a master planned and/or master scheduled item (generally, lot-for-lot or fixed quantity is a better choice for a level 0 item). However, the authors chose to use POQ in this chapter's example to demonstrate how POQ lot sizing works and to answer some questions on working the master schedule screen.*

Since the cumulative lead time is 18 periods, one might ask, "Why set a PTF at 20 periods?" In this case, the answer may simply be that the master scheduler has elected to gain an extra two periods of control. Remember, inside the planning time fence, the master scheduler has control of the planning horizon and he or she creates and/or places released supply orders or firm planned (supply) orders on the master schedule line within the master scheduling matrix. Outside the planning time fence, the computer software generates computer planned orders (CPOs).

Finally, the actions recommended in the WA01 example include a reschedule-in, a computer planned order that needs to be converted to a firm planned order, and a firm planned order that needs to be released. Those actions are reflected in the master schedule detail section of the screen, as explained shortly.

Planning Horizons Section

In the past-due column of the planning horizons section, there is an unconsumed forecast of 22 items. This means that the item probably started with a forecast of 100 for the time period, 78 of which were sold and consumed, leaving 22 units unconsumed.[3] The second number in this column is the projected available balance (PAB) of 116 units. The system calculated this as follows: 138 units are on hand and 22 are still forecasted to be sold (the unconsumed forecast). Here the system assumes that the forecasted 22 will in fact be sold (immediately), leaving 116 (138 – 22) as the PAB to start the first time period.

Now consider that first time period (the current period), during which 200 units (on the master schedule line) are scheduled to be received. Combining those 200 units with the 116 opening projected available balance creates a total supply of 316 units. The demand for this time period is 100 units, as shown in the forecast line. Assuming that those will be sold, the system subtracts 100 units from the 316 units available, leaving a projected available balance at the end of the first time period of 216 units. This same logic is used to calculate the projected available balance throughout the entire planning horizon.[4]

The Reflection of Demand and Supply in the Details Section

Supply and demand activities throughout the planning horizon are illuminated in the details section. For example, the 200 units on the master schedule line of time period 1 are reflected as the first entry under master schedule detail. Here, the master scheduler can see that this is more than just a supply of 200 scheduled WA01 units, which is all the planning horizon data reveals. In the master schedule detail section, it is defined as lot number 012. Its required date is time period 1; it is a manufacturing work order (MFG); and it has been released to the manufacturing floor. And if it's on the floor, the assumption

---

[3] Different master planning and scheduling systems would display that 22 in several ways—either as shown here or added to the first time period's demand of 100, making it 122 (refer to Chapter 17 for a discussion of forecast consumption).

[4] Note: If you have trouble understanding the basic calculations and mechanics, refer back to Chapter 3 for a review.

Item Number	Primary Description			Item Status	Product Family		Master Scheduler		Demand Manager
WA01	WINCH			STK	WAXX		PROUD		FERGUSON

Balance on Hand	Lot Size		Safety Stock		Time Fence					Lead Time	Cuml Lead Time	Stnd Cost
	Rule	Factor	Policy	Factor	PTF	DTF	MTF	CTF	RTF			
138	POQ	2	QTY	100	20					2	18	$2,170

Period	Past Due	1	2	3	4	5	6
Item Forecast	22	100	100	100	100	105	105
Option Forecast							
Actual Demand							
Total Demand							
Projected Available Balance	116	216	116	216	116	211	106
Available-to-Promise							
Master Schedule		200		200		200	

Period	13	14	15	16	17	18	19
Item Forecast	115	115	115	115	120	120	120
Option Forecast							
Actual Demand							
Total Demand							
Projected Available Balance	216	101	211	96	226	106	236
Available-to-Promise							
Master Schedule	225		225		250		250

Master Schedule Detail						
Required Date	Order Number	Lot Number	Order			Recommended Action
			Quantity	Type	Status	
1	WA01	012	200	MFG	RSLD	
3	WA01	013	200	MFG	FIRM	RELEASE
5	WA01	014	200	MFG	FIRM	
7	WA01	015	200	MFG	FIRM	
9	WA01	016	225	MFG	FIRM	R/I-01
11	WA01	017	225	MFG	FIRM	
13	WA01	018	225	MFG	FIRM	
15	WA01	019	225	MFG	FIRM	
17	WA01	020	250	MFG	FIRM	R/I-01
19	WA01	021	250	MFG	FIRM	
21			234			PLAN

Figure 5.4 Master Schedule Screen, Winch WA01

(Note: This figure will be referred to several times in the coming text. The reader may wish to bookmark this page for easy reference.)

Forecast Consumption	Resource Profile	Critical Resources					
		Resource	Resource	Resource	Resource	Resource	Resource
ADJUST	WAXX	MCH	SUB	ASSM	PKG	–	–
Selling Price	Special Instructions			Date Run		Actions Recommended	
$3,100	NONE			XX-XX-XX		R/I PLN REL	

7	8	9	10	11	12	Period
105	105	110	110	110	110	Item Forecast
						Option Forecast
						Actual Demand
						Total Demand
201	96	211	101	216	106	Projected Available Balance
						Available-to-Promise
200		225		225		Master Schedule

20	21	22	23	24	25	Period
120	125	125	125	125	125	Item Forecast
						Option Forecast
						Actual Demand
						Total Demand
116	–9	–134	–259	–384	–509	Projected Available Balance
						Available-to-Promise
	234		250		250	Master Schedule

Actual Demand Detail													
Required Date	Order Quantity	Reference Number	Order Number	T	S	C	Required Date	Order Quantity	Reference Number	Order Number	T	S	C

NOTE: All demand in this make-to-stock example is for finished goods inventory

Figure 5.4 *Continued*

is that the material required to make it is likewise on the floor, unless an allocation or shortage shows up on the WA01 components' MRP screens.

In time period 3, 200 units are also shown on the MPS line. In the master schedule detail for time period 3, an action message to release indicates that it's time to convert the firm planned order into a released supply order. The reason for this action is that the winch has a lead time of two time periods, and time period 3 is within one period of that lead time. That means it is time to create a work authorization and send it out to manufacturing.

Further down in the master schedule detail is lot 016, a firm planned order of 225, with a required date of time period 9. Here, the system is recommending a reschedule-in of the supply order by one time period, back to time period 8. To the master scheduler, this message is a cue to examine the demand/supply situation in the planning horizon for time periods 8 and 9. In time period 8, the projected available balance is 96 units, 4 short of the company's desired safety stock requirement of 100.

Therefore, the firm planned order of 225 in the MPS line of time period 9 needs to be moved back into time period 8. The same logic applies to the order in time period 17, where another reschedule-in recommendation appears in the master schedule detail (the same situation: the projected available balance has fallen below the desired safety stock level of 100 units).

To ignore the computer's recommendation on the basis that *we need only 4, not 225, units* would be a legitimate response to the potential safety stock shortfall in time period 8. The experienced master scheduler would understand that the forecasted demand in each time period between 1 and 8 is only a prediction or request for product, and that actual demand may easily fall short by 4 or more units over that period, entirely eliminating the need for an early resupply of WA01 winches.

Additionally, the experienced master scheduler will check the status of the unconsumed forecast discussed at the beginning of the chapter. And even if the demand does materialize, the company would still have an inventory of 96 units.

So, the reader at this time needs to be asked the question, "What action would the computer software take if left to its own devices?" In other words, would the computer software reschedule the firm planned orders in time period 9 and time period 17? The reader's answer is most likely *yes*!

Okay, let's ask the reader another question; "Are *today's* master schedulers and company executives ready to turn this decision over to the computer software without any judgment from the master scheduler being considered?" In the authors' opinion, *not in today's world*, but certainly this is going to happen within the next decade or possibly within the next five years. The technology is basically there; the reason for holding back is accountability (*if the action taken is the wrong action for the company to take,* **who or what is accountable?**). Answer that question and we are good to go![5]

Besides the alternatives of slavishly following the computer software's recommendation to reschedule-in 225 units from time period 9 to time period 8, or simply ignoring the recommendation for action altogether, the master scheduler has at least two other alternatives to choose from:

1. Split the lot of 225 scheduled for time period 9 into two orders: one for 4 units in time period 8, and another for 221 in time period 9; or

2. Simply change the order of 200 in time period 7 to 204.

Either of these options would eliminate the action message. The first, however, might be somewhat costly in that an extra order involves extra paperwork, reporting, material issuing, and possibly changeover costs. In fact, the changeover cost to build just four units may, in itself, be sufficiently high as to disqualify this as a viable solution. The second solution might cause less paperwork, reporting, and changeover, but could still disrupt manufacturing.

Both cases contain other issues that need to be addressed before changing the schedule. Chapter 4 discussed seven important reschedule change questions (remember, there was a seventh question regarding personnel morale; let's not forget this all-important people relationship within the company) that should be answered before any rescheduling is done. It is worth reviewing them here:

1. *Has demand changed?* The screen merely represents a snapshot of the master schedule and does not provide the data necessary to answer this question. However, a working master scheduler in the plant, factory, or mill would be able to secure the information necessary. *We want to know if we should change.*

2. *What is the impact of the change on the approved supply plan volumes?* The supply plan is created and approved during the integrated business planning (formerly known as sales and operations planning or advanced sales and operations planning) process. The master planner and/or master scheduler has a responsibility to work within the constraints of approved supply plan volumes. If a change is made, will the master plan and/or master schedule still summarize up to the approved supply rates? Here *we want to know if we are authorized to make the change.*

---

[5] The authors anticipate that the accountability question will be addressed and answered in this decade and quite possibly in the next five years.

3. *Can the capacity be obtained?* In both reschedule-in cases we need to know if there is enough capacity in time period 7 or time period 8 (depending on choice) to do the work. If the capacity is not available or cannot be made available, then it will do no good to reschedule. *We want to know if we are able to change.*

4. *Can we obtain the material?* In both reschedule-in cases we must know if the required material can be produced or procured in time. To determine what material, we would refer back to the time-phased BOM (Figure 5.3 on page 171). Drawing a line on the WA01 winch BOM, at time periods 7 through 9, we see the material that is affected: hard steel (R100), wheel (1100), housing casting (1200C), cable (1300), hook (1400), drum casting (D100C), gear box (G102), motor (M100), and control box (1600). It may not be easy to cut one or two periods of lead time from these items. Again, *we want to know if we are able to change.*

5. *What is the cost of changing?* Changing schedules generally costs money; in fact, the closer the change comes to the completion date, the greater the cost in overtime, subcontracting, extra shifts, premium payments to suppliers, air freight, expediting, and so on. *We want to know the cost of changing* (four-decimal-place accuracy is not required here, but the master scheduler and possibly executive management need to know the cost impact—Will the cost of changing the master plan and/or master schedule and work associated with the change be $100 or $1,000 or $10,000?). *Here, we are deciding if the change is a good financial choice.*

6. *What is the impact on the marketplace? How painful will it be for the company if the master plan and/or master schedule is not changed?* Questions like: (a) Will the company lose its largest customer? (b) Will the competition get a foot in the door with a current customer? (c) Will the company lose a competitive bid? (d) Will the sales group miss their budget bogie? and so forth need to be answered before a final decision is made regarding the change. *Is the smart decision to make the change or stay the course?*

7. *What are the morale consequences if the master schedule is changed?* What will be the impact on manufacturing operations personnel and the manufacturing support teams' morale if the change under consideration is made? What about morale impact within the procurement, purchasing, supplier scheduling, quality, and logistics

functions? And whether the change is made or not made, *what is the impact on the customer's (possibly the company's partner or long-time reason for the company to be in business) morale?*

As a review, this just says that master planners and master schedulers need to be good planners, replanners, schedulers, reschedulers, observers, listeners, analysts, influencers, speakers, mathematicians, geeks, documenters, and the list goes on! The authors believe it is also important that master planners and master schedulers have a somewhat tough skin with a soft heart and mild temperament under that tough skin.

Getting back to our exception-driven action messages discussion, since the origin of the action message under discussion is only a 4 percent drop below the safety stock level, it is hard to imagine much pain in the marketplace if the master scheduler decides not to take the computer software–recommended action. However, if this MPS item is under a contractual agreement to maintain an inventory balance of 100 units or else penalties would apply, the decision takes on a different perspective.

Only after the master scheduler has the data to answer these reschedule change questions can an informed decision be made. No one ever said master planning and scheduling (MPS) was easy. This is why Class A companies have very creative, organized, and knowledgeable people doing the job.

Finally, time period 21 details a system recommendation to convert a computer planned order to a firm planned order (PLAN). Here's why: The system shows a projected available balance of minus 9 in time period 21. The lot sizing rule tells the master planning and scheduling (MPS) system that any time a computer planned order is placed, it must cover the next two periods of demand. So, in time period 21, nine units are needed, and in time period 22 the demand is 125, leaving a projected deficit of 134 (9 + 125). A total of 134 units will thus cover demand in time periods 21 and 22, but the safety stock rules specify that 100 units should always be in stock, so the MPS system recommends releasing an order for 100 additional units, for a total of 234.

Since in this example we chose a dynamic lot sizing rule (period order quantity), the computer software will recommend that orders be placed outside the planning time fence equal to the requirements for two periods plus safety stock. Remember, the POQ lot sizing rule is used in this example to highlight how POQ lot sizing works and how dynamic it is in choosing its recommended quantity. The authors do not recommend using a dynamic lot sizing rule (with the exception of lot-for-lot) at the master schedule level.

Bridging Data and Judgment

This computer-driven reporting system projects what the plant, factory, or mill will look like in the future. It provides demand and supply information as well as summarizing the company policies regarding lot sizes and safety stocks; additionally, the master planning and scheduling (MPS) system asks the master planner(s) and/or master scheduler(s) to intervene in situations where imbalances and policy violations occur.

This is the mechanical or *scientific* part of master planning and scheduling (MPS); the remainder is *art*—or, more accurately, judgment formed with experience. Armed with the information and recommendations provided by the system, the master planner and/or master scheduler uses judgment in making decisions on a multitude of quantitative *and* qualitative factors.

However, as stated earlier in this chapter, the authors believe that times are changing, computer technology advancements are moving at lightning speed, computer memory continues to drop in cost, billions of operations can be done within seconds using today's technology, and the need for master planners and/or master schedulers is fading and will become a memory in the next decade and possibly in the next five years. This is *not* saying that the process known as master planning and scheduling is going away and being replaced by something else—authors' opinion and belief.

In other words, the master planning and scheduling process is here to stay, but technology/machines/computer hardware/computer software will do it in the *not*-too-distant future! The authors' closing comments in this book discuss the future of the master planning and scheduling process as well as the MPS profession.

Seeing the Big Picture

The computer software's posting of demand data over long periods allows the master scheduler to see patterns in the ebb and flow of demand. In the case of the WA01 winch, for example, demand grows steadily in stepwise fashion (100, 105, 110, 115, etc.) every four time periods. As a percentage of total demand, however, each step is smaller than the one before. From the MPS line of the screen, we observe that the master scheduler has not responded to the steady anticipated growth in demand with an equal increase in supply—at least not at first.

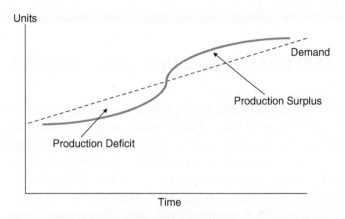

Figure 5.5   Supply Deficit Turns to Supply Surplus

Instead—perhaps to better manage growth in output, perhaps owing to supply and production constraints not revealed here—the master scheduler builds supply gradually, but deliberately. Over the time periods shown in the screen, demand exceeds supply in time periods 5 through 8 and in time periods 13 through 16, but supply exceeds demand in time periods 9 through 12 and time periods 17 through 20. If we were to represent this situation conceptually, ignoring the stepwise changes, it would appear something like Figure 5.5.

Here, a small supply deficit develops in the early periods, but that deficit turns into a surplus in the intermediate periods, which then turns back into a supply deficit in later periods. So how can this be possible? And why would the master scheduler, whose first responsibility is to balance demand and supply, do this?

As to *how,* the answer is safety stock. Safety stock is not there to be worshipped or admired, but to provide some utility to the company. Sometimes this utility takes the form of a supply bank from which the master scheduler can do a little judicious borrowing. In the example, the master scheduler has borrowed a little supply in the early periods, but like any savvy borrower, he or she pays back what he or she owes. Thus, in later periods, any reduction in safety stock is redressed with a supply surplus.

Conceptually, this is how farmers finance their seasonal businesses and how manufacturers maintain manageable loads on their plants, factories, and mills in the face of seasonal demand cycles. While on this topic, let's look at a seasonal business and address some of the management issues involved.

SEASONALITY AND INVENTORY BUILDUP

Bernard Baruch once said that the way to get rich was to "buy straw hats in January"—the presumption being that you could buy them cheaply and resell them at a premium in July and August. Mr. Baruch was a wizard at the investment game of buying low and selling high, but he probably didn't know much about the cost of holding inventory.

For businesses with strong seasonal demand, planning supply to meet anticipated demand while minimizing current inventory and possibly unsold units is a tremendous challenge. Consider the case of Datebook Publishing Company, whose main products are calendars and appointment books. It experiences strong demand during the late fall months and virtually no demand for the rest of the year, as shown below. Any calendars not sold during the period between October and December most likely end up at the paper shredder.

Fortunately, this company has other contract printing and publishing work during other seasons. Still, to meet anticipated demand, it must begin production and start building inventory as early as May.

Management Issues

For companies like Datebook Publishing, seasonality of demand creates a number of management issues to which ingenuity and judgment must be applied.

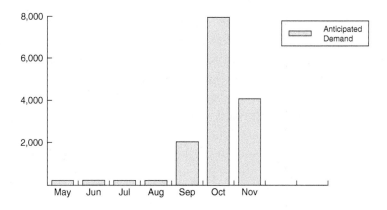

| Forecasted Demand | 0 | 0 | 0 | 0 | 2,000 | 8,000 | 4,000 |
| Master Schedule | 2,000 | 2,000 | 2,000 | 2,000 | 2,000 | 2,000 | 2,000 |

- *Demand forecasting takes on greater importance.* In most businesses, if you are caught short on product availability, the customer might be induced to delay the order while more products are built. In seasonal businesses, you either have product or miss the sale entirely.

  Conversely, building too many products generally leads to obsolete inventory, particularly if a shelf-life or model-year issue is involved. This means that everyone in the organization must understand the importance of accurate forecasting and must have an incentive to provide good numbers and continuous monitoring of anticipated demand.

- *Inventory and fixed capacity are major concerns.* Management faces an important trade-off between building large manufacturing capacity or building large inventories. Large amounts of capacity make it possible to meet the seasonal demand spike without reliance on inventory. It is the difference between handling a make-to-order and a make-to-stock product.

  The problem is using that expensive capacity during the rest of the year. By contrast, keeping fixed capacity low forces the company to build and hold expensive inventory. Finding the optimal condition demands the collective attention of managers in all functions.

- *Can the either/or dilemma of capacity versus inventory be altered through design?* For years, managers subscribed to the idea that you either produced in high volume at low cost or in low volume at high cost. The notion that high quality costs more to build was also universally accepted.

  The experience of the past 20 to 30 years has shown that both of these "iron laws" of manufacturing were wrong. Quality can cost less to produce, and short production runs are not absolutely synonymous with high costs.[6]

  The either/or dilemma of high capacity or high inventory for the seasonal business may be equally antiquated. Managers need to step outside of these constraints and think creatively about alternative ways of producing. They may be able to break out of this dilemma through redesigning products or processes: by creating unique

---

[6] See James P. Womack, Daniel T. Jones, and Daniel Roos, *The Machine That Changed the World: The Story of Lean Production* (New York: Rawson Associates, 1990) and Joseph Pine, *Mass Customization: The New Frontier in Business Competition* (Boston: Harvard Business School Press, 1992).

products from a combination of common and unique parts that are configured after receiving the customer order; and by implementing manufacturing processes with the flexibility to respond to seasonal spikes in demand as they occur.

Executives are not the only ones who should be concerned with these issues. Marketers have to think deeply about the validity of their demand forecasts. Errors are expensive when you have just one shot at the customer. Salespeople are naturally concerned about their booked orders being filled in the event that the company builds too few products. Financial managers are justly concerned with the cost of building and carrying inventory, some of which might never be sold. They need to communicate those concerns to others in the organization and to work with the executive and management teams in creating incentives for all concerned to forecast, build, and inventory only what can be sold.

The Seven Key Questions Revisited

Computer-generated data and the ability of master planning and scheduling (MPS) software to create action recommendations give the master planner and/or master scheduler every opportunity to bring judgment to bear in managing the supply and timing of production as well as procurement and purchasing. Managing change is, in fact, the master planner's and master scheduler's highest responsibility.

Like other managers, the master planner and/or master scheduler must make decisions on the basis of factual information that is often incomplete, ambiguous, or reflective of conflicting goals within the company (reader, remember this when reading the authors' final thoughts in this book). The choice of accepting or rejecting a computer software-generated reschedule-in recommendation to cover a potential supply or safety stock problem is typical of the hard decisions the master planner and/or master scheduler must make.

To the computer software, the answer is clear: A safety stock violation exists, therefore reschedule-in; to the master scheduler, violation of this simple decision rule merely provokes a number of questions for which there may be no simple answers. A good start is to secure the answers to the six (or seven) questions (again, let's not forget personnel morale) previously discussed. Thinking through each of these questions is the first step in reaching an informed scheduling decision.

Scheduling in a World of Many Schedules

The detailed example of winch WA01 should not lull the prospective master planner or master scheduler into the illusion that the real world of manufacturing is this simple. WA01, it should be remembered, is just one of many members of the WAXX winch family, each of which has its own time-phased bill-of-materials, its own ordering policy, its own scheduling requirements, and so on.

Like the game of chess, there are many different types of players on the board at the same time. And like a chess game, we cannot play each item in turn—that is, we cannot deal first exclusively with the pawns, then the bishops, then the knights, and so on—but we must know how to move them about as part of a single game. This makes master planning and scheduling a *dynamic* as opposed to a *linear* process. Thus, in planning and/or scheduling the WA01, we must realize that other product family members may share the same manufacturing floor, the same materials stocking area, and possibly the same production line.

Figures 5.6 and 5.8 (see pages 186–187 and 190–191, respectively) are schedule screens for WA01's cousins: WA04 and WA06 winches, respectively. A quick glance at these screens indicates that they have much in common with WA01: the same family, the same lot size and safety stock policies (but not the same factors), the same lead times and planning time fences. Because WA01 is forecasted to account for two-thirds of all winch sales, all demand and supply figures for WA04 and WA06 are proportionally less.

An experienced master planner and/or master scheduler who knew nothing about these winches—who had in fact just walked in off the street—would nevertheless spot an important relationship among these three different winches. He or she would notice that all MPS quantities for WA01 are due in odd-numbered periods, and MPS quantities for WA04 and WA06 are due in even-numbered periods.

To the veteran planner and/or scheduler, this would suggest that all three winches share an important critical resource: the same production line. This can also be seen by evaluating the critical resources noted on the top of each master schedule under critical resources. Therefore, a master plan or master schedule change for any one winch may affect a resource required by the other two winches. Rough cut capacity planning is one of the useful tools in testing the viability of master schedule changes that impinge upon other more detailed plans and/or schedules.

Working the WA04 Reschedule-in Action Message

Referring to time period 10 master schedule detail in Figure 5.6 on pages 186 and 187, notice a reschedule-in message for lot 306. Reviewing time period 9 of the planning horizons

Item Number	Primary Description		Item Status	Product Family		Master Scheduler	Demand Manager
WA04	WINCH		STK	WAXX		PROUD	FERGUSON

Balance on Hand	Lot Size		Safety Stock		Time Fence					Lead Time	Cuml Lead Time	Stnd Cost
	Rule	Factor	Policy	Factor	PTF	DTF	MTF	CTF	RTF			
82	POQ	2	QTY	30	20					2	18	$2,310

Period	Past Due	1	2	3	4	5	6
Item Forecast	4	30	30	30	30	30	30
Option Forecast							
Actual Demand							
Total Demand							
Projected Available Balance	78	48	68	38	73	43	63
Available-to-Promise							
Master Schedule			50		65		50

Period	13	14	15	16	17	18	19
Item Forecast	34	32	32	32	35	35	35
Option Forecast							
Actual Demand							
Total Demand							
Projected Available Balance	39	82	50	93	58	98	63
Available-to-Promise							
Master Schedule		75		75		75	

Master Schedule Detail						
Required Date	Order Number	Lot Number	Order			Recommended Action
			Quantity	Type	Status	
2	WA04	302	50	MFG	RSLD	
4	WA04	303	65	MFG	FIRM	
6	WA04	304	50	MFG	FIRM	
8	WA04	305	50	MFG	FIRM	
10	WA04	306	75	MFG	FIRM	R/I-01
12	WA04	307	75	MFG	FIRM	
14	WA04	308	75	MFG	FIRM	
16	WA04	309	75	MFG	FIRM	
18	WA04	310	75	MFG	FIRM	
20	WA04	311	75	MFG	FIRM	

Figure 5.6   Master Schedule Screen, Winch WA04
(Note: This figure will be referred to several times in the coming text. The reader may wish to bookmark this page for easy reference.)

Forecast Consumption	Resource Profile	Critical Resources					
		Resource	Resource	Resource	Resource	Resource	Resource
ADJUST	WAXX	MCH	SUB	ASSM	PKG	–	–
Selling Price	Special Instructions		Date Run		Actions Recommended		
$3,300	NONE		XX-XX-XX		R/I		

7	8	9	10	11	12	Period
30	30	34	32	32	32	Item Forecast
						Option Forecast
						Actual Demand
						Total Demand
33	53	19	62	30	73	Projected Available Balance
						Available-to-Promise
	50		75		75	Master Schedule

20	21	22	23	24	25	Period
35	35	35	35	35	35	Item Forecast
						Option Forecast
						Actual Demand
						Total Demand
103	68	33	–2	–37	–72	Projected Available Balance
						Available-to-Promise
75			67		70	Master Schedule

Actual Demand Detail													
Required Date	Order Quantity	Reference Number	Order Number	T	S	C	Required Date	Order Quantity	Reference Number	Order Number	T	S	C

NOTE: All demand in this make-to-stock example is for finished goods inventory

Figure 5.6 *Continued*

data section, the MPS system is recommending that the master scheduler pull in the lot of 75 by one time period to stop the projected inventory balance from falling below the safety stock level (19 units as opposed to the required 30). That is what the system says to do.

However, pulling in the entire lot might overload the production line or critical resources in time period 9, the period the WA01 winch is planned to run. So, here are the master planner's and/or master scheduler's alternatives:

- *Ignore the action message.* By doing this, the master scheduler will use safety stock inventory to satisfy expected demand.

- *Split the lot and pull in only the required 11 units.* Of course, there is nothing sacred about the 11 units except that 11 are needed to bring the projected available balance up to the desired safety stock.

- *Increase the firm planned order in time period 8 to 61 units* (the master scheduler is planning to increase the schedule by 25 units in time period 10 anyway). Again, the only reason for choosing 61 is that this is the quantity required to satisfy the safety stock policy.

- *Some combination of the above.* The master scheduler could choose to pull a few items forward, increase the quantity in time period 8, and still be projected to drop below safety stock policy.

- *Follow the computer software's recommendation.*

In order to determine the best course of action, the master scheduler must first decide whether he or she is comfortable cutting into safety stock by approximately 35 percent. If the answer is *yes*, then the best action would probably be to take *no action*. However, if this cut into safety stock disturbs the master planner's and/or master scheduler's comfort level, a different course of action should be taken.

One of the challenges of master scheduling is to balance demand and supply while maintaining as much stability as possible. Therefore, looking at the example, the master scheduler may not wish to disrupt the production flow of running the WA04 and WA06 across two time periods with completion dates in the even periods.

Figure 5.7 on page 189 shows what the production of WA01, WA04, and WA06 might look like. Let us assume that all winches require four operations to complete the last level of the build process. These operations are equally spread over two periods of planning lead time. As we look at WA01, we see that the first two operations are done in time periods 8, 10, and 12, while the last two are planned for completion in time periods 7, 9, and 11.

		PERIODS											
	...	7		8		9		10		11		12	...
WA01	...	3	4	1	2	3	4	1	2	3	4	1	2	...
WA04	...	1	2	3	4	1	2	3	4	1	2	3	4	...
WA06	...	1	2	3	4	1	2	3	4	1	2	3	4	...

Figure 5.7   Winch Schedule by Operation

Looking at WA04 and WA06 (see Figure 5.8 on pages 190–191 for WA06 master schedule), we observe that the first two operations are being run in time periods 7, 9, and 11, while the last two operations are planned or scheduled in time periods 8, 10, and 12.

Assuming Figure 5.7 is an accurate display of the planned production load, one can see why the master scheduler may be hesitant to change the master plan or master schedule as recommended by the MPS software (reschedule-ins for WA01 in time period 9 and WA04 plus WA06 in time period 10) because of the capacity issues it might cause. If the WA01 lot scheduled for completion in time period 9 is rescheduled to time period 8, an overload of the last two operations would occur in time period 8 while time period 9 most likely would experience a significant drop in production requirements.

If WA04 and WA06 are rescheduled (completion dates change from time period 10 to time period 9), a major drop in production requirement would occur. If this is the case, a change in the quantity for time period 8 seems like the best alternative. However, the six (or seven) important reschedule change questions must be asked—and answered—before making a change.

Since the recommended plan and/or schedule adjustment is for time periods 9 and 10, several items in the WA04's bill-of-materials are affected (refer to Figure 5.3 on page 171) and assume that the WA04 product required materials are similar to WA01's). So, if any change is to be made, a lot of homework must be done to ensure that the change is not only made in the master planning and scheduling system, but also is successfully made on the plant or mill floor and in procurement and/or purchasing.

A Good Master Planning and Scheduling Practice Don't change the schedule any faster than design, engineering, manufacturing support, manufacturing operations, procurement, purchasing, and logistics can economically respond.

One last point on this example: Time period 11 projects an inventory balance of 30 units, exactly the desired safety stock quantity. This is only two periods away from the

Item Number	Primary Description		Item Status	Product Family		Master Scheduler	Demand Manager	
WA06	WINCH		STK	WAXX		PROUD	FERGUSON	
Balance on Hand	Lot Size		Safety Stock		Time Fence						Lead Time	Cuml Lead Time	Stnd Cost

Balance on Hand	Rule	Factor	Policy	Factor	PTF	DTF	MTF	CTF	RTF	Lead Time	Cuml Lead Time	Stnd Cost
74	POQ	2	QTY	25	20					2	18	$2,450

Period	Past Due	1	2	3	4	5	6
Item Forecast	3	25	25	25	25	29	27
Option Forecast							
Actual Demand							
Total Demand							
Projected Available Balance	71	46	71	46	56	27	50
Available-to-Promise							
Master Schedule			50		35		50

Period	13	14	15	16	17	18	19
Item Forecast	34	32	32	32	35	35	35
Option Forecast							
Actual Demand							
Total Demand							
Projected Available Balance	42	85	53	96	61	101	66
Available-to-Promise							
Master Schedule		75		75		75	

Master Schedule Detail					
Required Date	Order Number	Lot Number	Order			Recommended Action
			Quantity	Type	Status	
2	WA06	404	50	MFG	RSLD	
4	WA06	405	35	MFG	FIRM	
6	WA06	406	50	MFG	FIRM	
8	WA06	407	50	MFG	FIRM	R/I-01
10	WA06	408	75	MFG	FIRM	R/I-01
12	WA06	409	75	MFG	FIRM	
14	WA06	410	75	MFG	FIRM	
16	WA06	411	75	MFG	FIRM	
18	WA06	412	75	MFG	FIRM	R/O-01
20	WA06	413	75	MFG	FIRM	R/O-01

Figure 5.8   Master Schedule Screen, Winch WA06

(Note: This figure will be referred to several times in the coming text. The reader may wish to bookmark this page for easy reference.)

Forecast Consumption	Resource Profile	Critical Resources					
		Resource	Resource	Resource	Resource	Resource	Resource
ADJUST	WAXX	MCH	SUB	ASSM	PKG	–	–
Selling Price	Special Instructions			Date Run		Actions Recommended	
$3,500	NONE			XX-XX-XX		R/I	R/O

7	8	9	10	11	12	Period	
27	27	30	30	30	30	Item Forecast	
						Option Forecast	
						Actual Demand	
						Total Demand	
23	46	16	61	31	76	Projected Available Balance	
						Available-to-Promise	
	50		75		75	Master Schedule	

20	21	22	23	24	25	Period	
35	39	37	37	37	40	Item Forecast	
						Option Forecast	
						Actual Demand	
						Total Demand	
106	67	30	–7	–44	–84	Projected Available Balance	
						Available-to-Promise	
75			60		80	Master Schedule	

Actual Demand Detail														
Required Date	Order Quantity	Reference Number	Order Number	T	S	C	Required Date	Order Quantity	Reference Number	Order Number	T	S	C

NOTE: All demand in this make-to-stock example is for finished goods inventory

Figure 5.8 *Continued*

projected problem. This might be another reason for the master scheduler to use some safety stock if necessary and leave the schedule as currently written.

Working the WA06 Reschedule-in Action Messages

Two back-to-back reschedule-in messages appear in time periods 8 and 10 (Figure 5.8 on pages 190–191). Using the same logic as with WA04, there seems to be no point in pulling up the 50 units in time period 8 to time period 7 because of a projected 8 percent dip into safety stock. Why disrupt the production line for two units of safety stock (unless the company is under contractual requirements to maintain a certain level of safety stock or just-in-case inventory)?

Besides, we are halfway through the lead time and any change to the master schedule will affect many material items as well as capacity. And then there is the cost associated with every change at the MPS level within the product's lead time. The best choice seems to be to leave the schedule stand (again, unless the company is under contractual requirements).

Consider the next message. The suggestion of pulling up the 75 units in time period 10 to time period 9 requires more analysis. If we let the plan and/or schedule stand, we anticipate going into planned safety stock by approximately 40 percent. If this is no problem, then the best choice again is to opt for stability by leaving the master schedule alone.

However, if depletion of safety stock threatens our ability to satisfy variable future demand, then raising the quantity in time period 8 to, say, 64 units would take care of the action message and meet management's objective of holding one period's worth of safety stock (demand is increasing from 25 units to 30 units through time period 9). If the master scheduler plans to make this change, the six or seven reschedule change questions (don't forget personnel morale) must again be asked. Again, the only magic about 64 units is that an increase of 14 units is required to bring the company's projected available balance position back in line with safety stock policy.

Given the expected deep cut into safety stock, it would be worth the master scheduler's time to consider the history of the product. A new product might call for greater caution, since demand patterns are unknown. An established product whose demand patterns are stable or more predictable, however, may suggest using safety stock in lieu of plan and/or schedule changes.

These simple examples again demonstrate the need for a knowledgeable master scheduler; left to its own devices, the computer software would initiate the reschedule actions, disrupting the production line and possibly frustrating many. Worse still, the computer software cannot be held accountable for its reschedule decisions. Of course, this is not true when it comes to the master planner and/or master scheduler and his or her decisions. The master planner and/or master scheduler is accountable for creating and maintaining a realistic, valid, and achievable master plan as well as a master schedule.

In the past as well as in today's world (most manufacturing companies), it was and still is believed that an experienced (not always the case in many manufacturing operations) master planner and/or master scheduler made or will make a better decision than the master planning and scheduling software. However, as the master planning and scheduling software technology gets better and better, the notion that master planners and/or master schedulers will always make more informed, correct, and timely decisions is being challenged by supply chain management, master planning and scheduling, and information technology professionals worldwide.

Working the WA06 Reschedule-Out Action Messages

For WA06, the system recommends moving lot 412, a firm planned order of 75 units, out one time period, from time period 18 to 19. It also recommends moving lot 413 from time period 20 to 21. The reason for this message in time period 18 is the projected ending balance of 101 units in that time period.

If the 75 units do not arrive as scheduled, the company would still have a projected inventory balance of 26 units, one more than the current desired safety stock level of 25 units. Thus, it is not necessary to have the lot for 75 units arrive in time period 18. The same logic applies to time period 20; if the 75 units do not come in as scheduled, the company will still end time period 20 with a balance higher than the current desired safety stock.

The cumulative lead time for WA06 is 18 time periods. This means that any action taken by the master scheduler on the FPO in time period 18 will affect procurement and/or purchasing and quite possibly logistics, which will be starting to acquire the long lead time items and arranging needed transportation. If the lot is pushed out to time period 19, the potential overstocking problem will be solved. Of course, another problem may be created by doing this; time period 19 may become capacity constrained.

Another possibility is to not run as many as planned—perhaps 65 units instead of 75 units (the right lot size is, in fact, 67 units or 68 units) starting in time period 10. Therefore, knowing the product, the best approach might be to reduce the firm planned orders (FPOs) in time periods 10, 12, 14, 16, 18, and 20 to some lower amount. This action would stop the projected inventory buildup, thereby freeing up inventory storage space along with eliminating the two action messages.

Now that it is understood how the MPS system recommends actions for individual items, and how the master scheduler must analyze these recommendations, the next step is to test changes to the master schedule using rough cut capacity planning (RCCP). The rough cut capacity planning process and technique is described in Chapter 15. Only when the RCCP step has been completed and the master scheduler is satisfied that changes to the master schedule are reasonable are those changes passed down to the material requirements planning system, where materials are ordered, and capacity and components are earmarked for availability.

From Master Planning and Scheduling to Time-Phased Material Requirements Planning

Material requirements planning (MRP) is defined as a set of techniques that uses bills-of-material, inventory data, and the master schedule to calculate requirements for materials. It makes recommendations to release replenishment orders for materials. Further, since it is time phased, it makes recommendations to reschedule open orders when due dates and need dates are not in phase.

Time-phased MRP begins with the items listed on the master schedule and determines (1) the quantity of all components and materials required to assemble and/or fabricate those items and (2) the date that the components and materials are required. Time-phased MRP is accomplished by exploding the bills-of-materials, adjusting for inventory quantities on hand or on order, and offsetting the net requirements by the appropriate lead times.

Figure 5.9 on pages 196–197 shows the MRP computer-generated screen for the A100 carriage assembly, a common item in the WAXX winch family. Like the master scheduling screen, it has three main sections. The top section contains information about the item itself. The middle section contains planning horizons data. The bottom section contains details: scheduled receipts detail on the left, requirements detail on the right. While many features of the MRP screen are shared with the master scheduling screen already explained, others are unique and in need of explanation here.

Item Information Section

Item Type: Here SUB is *subassembly*.

Commodity Code: A code indicating the basic characteristics of a procurement or purchase order.

Value Class: Refers to a hierarchy of dollar cost among parts in which A items are high cost and C items are low cost. This hierarchy can connote either high unit cost or high total cost (as in the case of a low-priced but high-usage item).

Cumulative LT: Cumulative lead time is calculated as in the master planning and schedule system. In the case of the carriage assembly, this is 16 periods—the time needed to build A100 from scratch. This lead time number is determined from the time-phased BOM. Here cumulative lead time is two periods less than the finished winch, which makes sense in that the final assembly of the winch from A100 and the other required items requires two periods.

Scrap Factor: A bit of information that allows the master scheduler to figure gross production needed to yield an after-scrap net production equal to product demand (sometimes referred to as shrinkage).

Annual Gross Requirements: Strictly memo information.

Total Released Requirements: Summary information computed by aggregating data from the requirements detail section.

Total Scheduled Receipts: Summary information computed by aggregating data from the scheduled receipts detail section.

Planning Horizons Section

This section contains five lines of data for each period. The first two lines reflect requirements; the third, scheduled receipts; the fourth, the projected available balance; and the fifth, the planned order releases. Each is worth examining in some detail.

Service Requirements: If an item is sold as an independent item, and demand orders are taken directly against the item, then these orders show up here. If marketing and sales forecasted that some of the carriage assemblies would be needed as spares, that forecast would also appear here.

Production Requirements: Indicates dependent demand for the item caused by the master schedule or a higher-level MRP item. All dependent requirements for the carriage assembly are summarized and appear on this line.

Item Number	Primary Description		Item Status	U/M	Item Type	Comm. Code	MRP Planner	Value Class
A100	CARRIAGE ASSEMBLY		STK	EA	SUB	–	ARROYO	A

Balance On Hand	Lot Size			Scrap Factor		Annual Gross Requirements		Total Released Requirements
	Policy	Factor						
0	NONE	NONE		NONE		10,400		0

Period	Past Due	1	2	3	4	5	6
Service Requirements							
Production Requirements		200	100	200	100	200	100
Scheduled Receipts		300					
Projected Available Balance	0	100	0	–200	–300	–500	–600
Planned Order Release		300		300		375	

Period	13	14	15	16	17	18	19
Service Requirements							
Production Requirements	225	150	250	150	250	150	234
Scheduled Receipts							
Projected Available Balance	–1950	–2100	–2350	–2500	–2750	–2900	–3134
Planned Order Release	400		400		234		386

Scheduled Receipts Detail								
Required Date	Promised Date	Order Number	Lot Number	Required Quantity	Received	Type	Status	Recommended Action
1		A100	26	300		MFG	RSLD	
3		A100	27	300				ORDER

Figure 5.9   Material Requirements Planning Screen, Carriage Assembly (A100)

Lead Time	Cumul Lead Time	Order		Minimum Order Quantity	Minimum Order Quantity	Multiple Order Quantity
		Policy	Qty./Time			
2	16	POQ	2	100		

Total Scheduled Receipts	Special Instructions	Date Run	Action Recommended
300	NONE	XX-XX-XX	ORDER

7 8	9	10	11	12	Period
					Service Requirements
225	150	225	150	225	150	Production Requirements
					Scheduled Receipts
−825	−975	−1200	−1350	−1575	−1725	Projected Available Balance
375		375		375		Planned Order Release

20	21	22	23	24	25	Period
						Service Requirements
0	386	0	400	0	0	Production Requirements
						Scheduled Receipts
−3134	−3520	−3520	−3920	−3920	−3920	Projected Available Balance
	400					Planned Order Release

Requirements Detail													
Req'd Date	Req'd Qty	Refer. Number	Order Number	Lot	T	S	Req'd Date	Req'dQty	Refer. Number	Order Number	Lot	T	S
1	200	WA01	A100	013	M	F	12	75	WA04	A100	308	M	F
2	65	WA04	A100	303	M	F	12	75	WA06	A100	410	M	F
2	35	WA06	A100	405	M	F	13	225	WA01	A100	019	M	F
3	200	WA01	A100	014	M	F	14	75	WA04	A100	309	M	F
4	50	WA04	A100	304	M	F	14	75	WA06	A100	411	M	F
4	50	WA06	A100	406	M	F	15	250	WA01	A100	020	M	F
5	200	WA01	A100	015	M	F	16	75	WA04	A100	310	M	F
6	50	WA04	A100	305	M	F	16	75	WA06	A100	412	M	F
6	50	WA06	A100	407	M	F	17	250	WA01	A100	021	M	F
7	225	WA01	A100	016	M	F	18	75	WA04	A100	311	M	F
8	75	WA04	A100	306	M	F	18	75	WA06	A100	413	M	F
8	75	WA06	A100	408	M	F	19	234	WA01	A100		P	P
9	225	WA01	A100	017	M	F	21	250	WA01	A100		P	P
10	75	WA04	A100	307	M	F	21	67	WA04	A100		P	P
10	75	WA06	A100	409	M	F	21	69	WA06	A100		P	P
11	225	WA01	A100	018	M	F							

Figure 5.9 *Continued*

Scheduled Receipts: Identifies actions taken by the planner or scheduler for the carriage assembly. When the planner or scheduler creates a job order, work order, manufacturing order, production order, procurement order, purchase order, or run rate, the order quantity appears on this line.

Projected Available Balance (PAB): Displays the projected inventory balance for each period in the item's MRP horizon. The PAB line is used to critique the balance between supply and demand.

Planned Order Release: All computer planned orders are shown on this line. When MRP recognizes an imbalance between demand and supply, and the supply is projected to be short, the computer software places its own orders in the form of CPOs to restore the balance. These orders are placed by the MRP system logic in the time period in which they are scheduled to be released or started. Some MRP systems as well as MPS systems put CPOs in the time period in which they are due, and some may reflect both.

Detail Data Section

The detail data section of the MRP screen, like that of the MPS screen, is divided into two major parts, here called *scheduled receipts detail* and *requirements detail*.

Scheduled Receipts Detail: In the lower left corner of Figure 5.9 (see pages 196–197), the first line indicates that in time period 1, 300 units remain to be received (remaining quantity) for lot 26. Lot 26 is a manufactured item (MFG) that has already been released (RLSD). The next line indicates that a computer planned order (lot 27) for 300 units has been created by the computer software; an action message, prompted by the two-period lead time, recommends that the planner/scheduler convert this CPO into a scheduled receipt.

Looking briefly at the requirements detail, the first date with a requirement is time period 1, which has a demand of 200 carriage assemblies, which we know originates from the WA01 winch. Two quantities totaling 100 units are required for time period 2 (the 65 units necessary to start building WA04s and 35 to start building WA06s). Back in the first line of the scheduled receipts detail is an entry for 300 units, which is scheduled for receipt in time period 1. Since there is no on-hand balance for carriage assemblies, the scheduled receipt of 300 units is expected to be used to satisfy the demand in time period 1 of 200 units, leaving a projected available balance of 100 units. This quantity is expected to be used in time period 2 to satisfy the demand for 100 carriage assemblies needed to support the build plan for the WA04 and WA06 winches.

In time period 3 there is a PAB of –200 units. Recognizing a two-period lead time, MRP logic recommends in time period 1 the releasing of an order for 300 units to be due in time period 3. This amount is 100 units over the requirement for that period, but since the order policy is to order enough to cover two periods of demand, the 300 units are just enough to satisfy the 200 units required in time period 3 and the 100 units required in time period 4.

Requirements Detail: As the requirements detail shows, a quantity of 200 units is needed in time period 1 to satisfy a demand from the WA01 winch. A quick look back at the master schedule for WA01 (Figure 5.4 on pages 174–175) shows an FPO for 200 units in time period 3, lot 013 (remember, the lead time to build the WA01 when all items one level down are available is two periods). This FPO is both the trigger for this 200-unit requirement at the carriage assembly MRP level and the ultimate destination of the completed A100 items. This linking of items requirements to the source of demand is an example of *pegging* and is a very essential part of any MRP system.

The next two lines in the requirements details indicate quantities of 65 units (from WA04), and 35 units (from WA06). The master schedule screens for those two different winches indicate that those quantities are needed at the completed winch level in time period 4, which means that they are required to be started in time period 2—two periods earlier. This is when the carriage assemblies are needed.

From Master Planning to Master Scheduling (It's Called Master Planning and Scheduling)

As this chapter's discussion should make clear, it is important that the master planner, master scheduler, and material planner understand the relationship between what appears on the MPS screens and the underlying MRP system. Less obvious, but just as important, are the productive working relationships among program managers (new product), demand managers, supply managers, master planners, demand planners, master schedulers, customer service, sales forecasters, salespeople, material planners, procurement buyers, purchasing buyers, supplier schedulers, detailed production schedulers, and production personnel.

However, there is another level of understanding that the master planner and/or master scheduler must possess. We have discussed in some detail how master planning and scheduling itself drives requirements down to lower levels.

But where does the master plan and master schedule get its data? We have mentioned the likes of an approved supply plan, which is a volume plan by product family. To be effective, a master planner and/or master scheduler must understand the ins and outs of the integrated business planning (formerly known as advanced sales and operations planning or sales and operations planning) process (discussed in Chapter 14), which is the source of the approved demand and approved supply plans.

However, there are other issues to address before discussing integrated business planning (IBP), one of *where* and *what* to master plan and/or master schedule. Figure 5.10 displays the four (sometimes three) levels of supply within a manufacturing company.

To review, level 1 is where integrated business planning takes place, level 2 is where master planning takes place, level 3 is where master scheduling takes pace, and level 4 is where detailed production scheduling takes place. As stated earlier, some companies only use three levels of planning by combining level 2 with level 3 (master planning and scheduling are done within this one level).

Primary outputs of the IBP process consist of an approved new product plan, approved demand plan, approved supply plan, and approved financial plan. These approved plans (which are by product family and in monthly increments) are the drivers of the company's

Integration, Alignment, and Synchronization

Levels	Integrated Business Planning/Sales & Operations Planning (Corporate)		
1	• Demand Plan • Supply Plan • Inventory/Backlog	**Product Families, Volume, Months**	Horizon = 0 to 24+ months*

Master Planning/Supply Management (Corporate)

Levels			
2	• Demand Plan • Supply Plan • Inventory/Backlog	**Members of Family, Mix Weeks/Months**	Horizon = 0 to 6 to 12 months*

- - - - - - [*Request for Supply (RFS)*] - - - - - -

Master Scheduling (Plants)

Levels			
3	• Demand Plan • Supply Plan • Inventory/Backlog	**Units, Mix Days/Weeks**	Horizon = 0 to 3 to 6 months*

**Principle
Silence is
Acceptance**

Detailed Production Scheduling (Plants)

Levels			
4	• Inventory • Production • Capacity	**Units Timing Hrs/Days**	Horizon = 0 to 1 to 2 weeks*

*Planning horizon to be determined in detailed design phase.

Figure 5.10 Supply Chain Management Levels of Planning

master plan (which is by subproduct family or product grouping and in weekly and/or monthly increments).

Concentrating our efforts in this book on the supply side of the business, this company master plan is the driver of the company's master (supply) schedule (which is by product grouping or finished goods stock-keeping unit and in daily and/or weekly increments). The company's master schedule drives the detailed production schedules along with detailed material planning and logistics planning (which is by stock-keeping unit and in hourly and/or daily increments (there are some companies that actually plan to the minute at this level).

This chapter has reviewed the process of master planning and scheduling in a make-to-stock environment where finished goods are often the items that are master planned and/or master scheduled. But what about products that are design-to-order, engineer-to-order, make-to-order, assemble-to-order, package-to-order, kit-to-order, and make-to-contract? Good question for sure! The answer to this question might lead the supply organization to ask, "What items should we master plan and what items should we master schedule?"

Well, the answer to these questions depends on where the company decides to meet its customer; in other words, what state does the company want its product in when the customer order is received and booked by sales? The answer to this question will lead the supply organization to determine which manufacturing strategy the company should use in supply planning and what, where, and when products will be built in the company's manufacturing facilities. These questions along with the associated answers are the subject of our next chapter.

6

Where and What to Master Plan and Master Schedule

When you think you have all the answers, it may be time to re-ask the question.

Like any tool, master planning and scheduling software is useful only if it is applied in the right way. Here, the right way begins with knowing where and what to master plan and master schedule. In the case of a simple product, like the flashlight in Chapter 3, it may be the flashlight product subfamily by months or weeks that needs master planning and the final assembly of the flashlight that needs master scheduling by weeks or days. In a more complex product, like an automobile, master planning may be done at the automobile subfamily (e.g., two-door models and four-door models) by months/weeks while master scheduling may be done at a number of intermediate steps—engines, transmissions, radios, and so on.

Knowing where and what to master plan and master schedule presupposes a clear understanding of the process by which the product is transformed from either raw materials or purchased components into a shippable configuration. Generally, that process begins with the ordering of the raw materials to be available when the product is to be built. In traditional manufacturing, these materials are inspected by the receiving/inspection department as they arrive to ensure their conformance to order specification and quality standards.

Items that pass muster are then stored and issued to the manufacturing floor as needed. At the point of issue, the conversion of raw materials through the processes of mixing, forming, machining, assembling, and so forth, to final product begins to take place. The item may move into a subassembly or filling area, and then into a final assembly, finishing, or packaging area. The last step typically involves wrapping, boxing, crating, and shipping the finished product either to a warehouse or directly to the customer.[1]

Manufacturing Strategies Defined

The master planner's and master scheduler's company adheres to one or more manufacturing strategies deemed most appropriate for its business and the customer marketplace. Each of these strategies is defined in terms of the point in the supply process (e.g., product design, material procurement, manufacturing operations) at which the customer enters the picture.

Make-to-Stock (MTS) Product Strategy

Company A makes a very simple family of products—plastic wall plates to cover electrical outlet boxes. With just a few exceptions, its products are manufactured by continuous processes of plastic molding, with no assembly except packaging.

This company has determined that it must follow a make-to-stock strategy for most of the plastic wall plates product family—that is, a strategy in which raw materials are ordered and the final product made in advance of any orders by the distribution center and/or final consumer. From the customer's perspective, these are off-the-shelf products. Fasteners, door hinges, batteries, notepads, ballpoint pens, and countless other commodity-like items are typically made on this basis.

Companies follow this make-to-stock strategy when the market dictates that their products be finished and available for immediate purchase and use; in other words, the customer and marketplace demand short lead times to the customer for the company to be competitive.

Design-to-Order (DTO) and Engineer-to-Order (ETO) Product Strategies

Company B designs and builds process equipment for the chemicals industry. Its products are large, complex, and very expensive; most are built on a base of standardized liquid

---

[1] *Finished* is a relative term. In some cases, the finished product of manufacturer X is a component in the finished product of manufacturer Y.

and dry materials, mixing and moving equipment, with computerized monitoring systems. Because each piece of its equipment is expensive and specially tailored to the requirements of the individual customer, work can begin only when a customer order is received and detailed specifications are developed.

Company B follows a design-to-order or engineer-to-order strategy for its products, which is at the opposite end of the spectrum from Company A's products that use the make-to-stock strategy. While make-to-stock products tend to be generic and easily substituted within a product class, design-to-order or engineer-to-order products are, by definition, either unique (as in custom-made) or very complex and produced only in small quantities.

Aircraft, special-purpose machine tools, and other process equipment as well as space vehicles are all design-to-order or engineer-to-order products. In companies that use a design-to-order and/or engineer-to-order manufacturing strategy, no product is designed, engineered, and/or manufactured until the company has at least a letter of intent, an agreement, a contract, or a customer order. At that point the design and engineering process can begin, after which material is ordered and the product is produced and delivered to the customer.

Make-to-Order (MTO) Product Strategy

Between the extremes just cited is the company that chooses to make its products to customer orders, in which some materials may be ordered, some materials may be held in inventory, and some items of the product may even be produced (fabricated or assembled) before receipt of a customer order. With a pure make-to-order strategy, product is designed, but the company does not start final configuration manufacturing until a customer order is received. Highly customized products are generally made in this fashion.

Variations on the make-to-order theme are finish-to-order, assemble-to-order, package-to-order, and true make-to-order. In the case of the first, the company may build product through all but the finishing stage and may proceed to the finishing process only when a customer order has been received. The basic product, a conference room table, for example, may be completed, but the customer's logo etched in the middle of the table is not done until the customer order is received.

Furniture makers often use a finish-to-order strategy, building product up to the point of applying the customer's choice of finishing stain or fabrics as the last step. Assemble-to-order and package-to-order are analogous manufacturing strategies. Automobiles, with their many options, are good examples of assemble-to-order products whereas a ballpoint pen set may be an example of a package-to-order product.

Company C follows an assemble-to-order strategy. It is a leading producer of elevators for commercial buildings. It offers an array of elevator products, featuring dozens of capacities and hundreds of possible car interior decors. Because its customers—architects and building contractors—have long planning schedules, Company C does not need any off-the-shelf items (except for replacement parts), but the economics of its business encourages it to produce most of the components from which its product variety can be fabricated within three weeks.

Kit-to-Order (KTO) Product Strategy

Company D is in a slightly different situation—when the surgeon is ready to do surgery, the instrument kit must be there and there may not be a lot of time to get the kit to the operating room. So, Company D builds all the instruments to stock in advance of receiving the customer order and once Company D does receive the customer order, it quickly prepares the surgeon's kit from completed instruments stored in its finished goods stockroom.

Make-to-Contract (MTC) Product Strategy

Whereas all of the previous strategies generally apply to commercial businesses, another variant of the make-to-order strategy applies to government contractors. Like companies that choose to use a make-to-order strategy for various products they build, companies that choose to wait until a contract is issued before ordering material (many government contracts specify when the company can procure materials) or begin the manufacturing process (many government contracts also specify when the company can commence manufacturing operations) may choose to use the make-to-contract strategy.

The make-to-contract strategy can thus be thought of as a design-to-order, engineer-to-order, or make-to-order approach in which the contract (with progress payments and penalties defined) takes the place of the customer order. The make-to-contract manufacturing strategy has been a popular build strategy in the aerospace industry for many years.

Choosing the Right Manufacturing Strategy

The right strategy for products within a particular company depends on where the supplying company intends to meet the customer (what state the identified product is in when the customer order is received—what materials have been ordered early, what materials are already in stock, what manufacturing operations have been completed, and so on), which is largely dictated by the demands of the marketplace and the company's competitive position within its own marketplace. The strategy chosen determines where in the product structure master planning and scheduling will take place. It should also be noted that where a company chooses to meet the customer within a product family influences the actual structuring of the bills-of-material used in planning for that product and product family.

The choice of where to meet the customer really depends on a company's competitive position, which is determined by a balance of delivery, service, price, quality, and technology. If a company's service, price, technology, and quality are competitive, its delivery performance may be the deciding factor in winning the business or not winning the business. The tremendous impact of master planning and scheduling on meeting schedules and customer delivery dates is therefore an important competitive weapon.

Before thoroughly examining the master planning and scheduling component, we need to reexamine the options for meeting the customer, which are represented in Figure 6.1. The stair step diagram indicates the many points in the manufacturing process at which the actual order may be received—that is, where the company meets the customer. Each

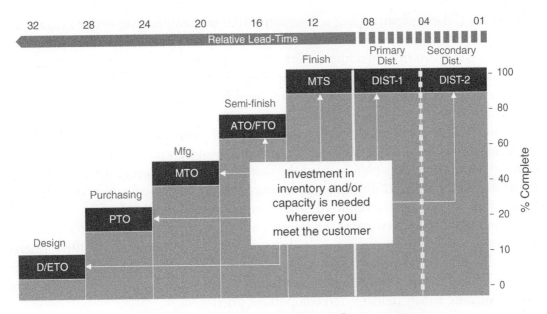

Figure 6.1 Strategies to Meet the Customer

step up the stairway represents a higher degree of product completion or cost/value added and product configuration flexibility lost.

In choosing to ship from finished good inventory, whether direct from the manufacturing plant and/or through a distribution network, a company has, by definition, chosen a make-to-stock strategy for those products. The company that meets its customer at the designing or engineering level has chosen a design-to-order or engineer-to-order strategy for those products. At the purchasing, fabricating, mixing, or intermediate assembly step, it has chosen one of the make-to-order spectrums of approaches for those products. Some examples along that spectrum are purchase-to-order, make-to-order, assemble-to-order, and finish-to-order.

Inventory and Capacity Requirements

In selecting a manufacturing strategy, other factors, such as a willingness to invest in inventory and the capacity required to complete the product from the stocking point within the necessary lead time, should be considered. Any company that chooses to meet the customer at the finished-goods level (using a product make-to-stock strategy) must be willing to make an investment in finished goods inventory. Those companies must be prepared to ship finished goods as customer orders appear (minimal lead time available).

In contrast, the company using a design-to-order and engineer-to-order manufacturing strategy has minimal or zero inventory requirements, since no product building takes place in the absence of a customer order or contract. But the company must have the designing, engineering, supplier, manufacturing, and/or finishing capacity necessary to complete the order within a quoted or promised lead time and most likely by a specified date.

In using the make-to-order manufacturing strategy, particularly finish-to-order, kit-to-order, and assemble-to-order situations, companies must be willing to invest in inventory up to the point where they plan to meet the customer (stocking level), such as intermediates or subassemblies, and must plan and secure the capacity necessary to complete and ship the defined products as required by the marketplace and/or customer.

It is important to understand that wherever a company chooses to meet the customer, its objective must be to provide timely delivery, first-class service, competitive pricing, high-quality products, and leading-edge technology. The next section demonstrates how master planning and scheduling can greatly enhance at least two of those critical components of success: timely delivery and competitive pricing.

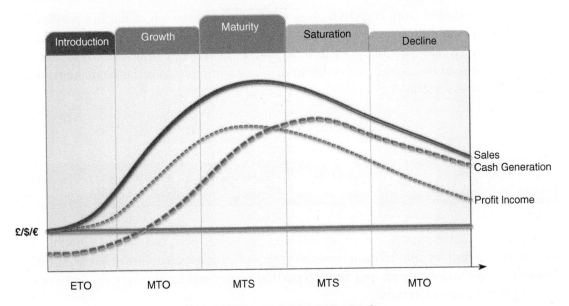

Figure 6.2 Product Life Cycles

Manufacturing Strategy and Product Life Cycles

Like living organisms, products experience life cycles of development, growth, maturity, and decline. Business scholars have described this process as shown in Figure 6.2. Here, the introductory or development stage (measured in sales revenues or units) is fairly flat until such time as the product catches on. At this point it may enter a period of (rapid) growth, followed by a maturity period of sales (large/small but somewhat flat sales), followed by a period of decline (in sales).

Obviously, not every product experiences each of these cycles. Many new products never get beyond the introductory or development stage, and a fortunate few products forestall decline for extended periods through the introduction of product enhancements (new and improved) and long-term growth of their markets.

A company may treat the same product with different manufacturing strategies at various stages of its life cycle. Thus, in the introductory or development stage, when demand is largely unknown, a design-to-order or engineer-to-order manufacturing strategy may be most appropriate (more on this aspect of design-to-order and engineer-to-order follows in Chapter 11). As the product enters its (rapid) growth period, a make-to-order or assemble-to-order or kit-to-order or finish-to-order strategy may be ideal.

Once the period of (rapid) growth gives way to a (long) stretch of flat but predictable demand from established customers, make-to-stock may be the most suitable manufacturing strategy. As the product goes into decline and customer orders become less reliable, going back to finish-to-order or kit-to-order or assemble-to-order or make-to-order may be the most sensible.

Master Planning, Master Scheduling, and Product Structures

In making the determination of where and what to master plan and master schedule, it is necessary to consider the different possible types of product structures (see Figure 6.3). In each of the product structures, the top portion represents finished goods, and the bottom represents raw materials.

Pyramid Structure: Part A of Figure 6.3 represents a business that makes a limited number of finished products from many semi-finished items, components, or raw materials. Small appliances, staplers, ballpoint pens, watches, lamps, and telephones fit this type of product structure.

Inverted Pyramid Structure: Many finished products are made from a limited number of raw materials. Steel, for example, is used to make everything from shopping carts to scaffolding. Nylon thread is the main ingredient in thousands of fabric products. Part B of Figure 6.3 shows this product structure.

Hourglass Structure: Many finished products are made from common, semi-finished items or part/material sets. The automobile is a classic example (see part C of Figure 6.3). At the top level is the car; at the pinch point is the semi-finished product (the engine, the chassis); at the bottom level are the thousands of components or materials used to make the semi-finished parts.

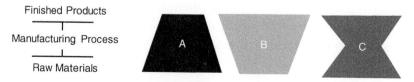

Figure 6.3 Product Structure Shapes

The Optimal Point to Master Plan and/or Master Schedule

In each of the preceding product profiles, the idea would be to master plan and/or master schedule at the narrowest part of the diagram; doing so provides the greatest flexibility and control. The reason for this is that at this narrow point there are the fewest number of items to forecast or project product demand, and desired customer requirements can be configured from this point using the fewest number of *master planned and scheduled* items (a point expanded upon during the discussion of products in make-to-order environments in Chapters 8 and 9). With fewer items to deal with, the narrowest point is also the easiest place to master plan and schedule.

Besides, *master planning and scheduling* at the top level will/would require an investment in inventory at all subsequent levels. Of course, the marketplace, customer, and competition still have a lot to say about what a company master plans and schedules.

If a product has the *pyramid structure*, the top of the pyramid—where the product is finished into a limited number of end items—is probably the place a company would like to master plan and schedule. If, for instance, a company was in the business of selling electric coffeepots off the shelf, it might decide to master plan the entire coffeepot product family by week and master schedule the various standard-colored pots that each manufacturing facility builds by week or day.

The *inverted pyramid structure* presents the opposite situation, and the company's master planner and/or master scheduler may want to focus on or at the bottom, the pinch point. Of course, master planning at this level would mean that master scheduling would be of little assistance in the planning process and master scheduling at this level would mean that material requirements planning would be of little assistance in the planning process. This fact is probably obvious since the master plan and/or master schedule would be for the lowest level in the product structure, leaving little for master scheduling (assuming master planning at this low level) as well as material requirements planning (assuming master scheduling at this low point) to do.

To get more help from the master planning and scheduling computer software, the master planner and/or master scheduler may decide to move up into the product structure and master plan and/or master schedule at some higher level, even though control may be more difficult. In moving to a higher level, common product groupings that use like resources and common base stocks should be considered. By doing so, the master planner and/or master scheduler can plan the common materials, schedule focused resources, and get some help from the material requirements planning computer software logic.

The pinch point in the *hourglass structure* provides a useful master planning and/or master scheduling point. Consider how difficult it would be to master plan and/or master schedule automobiles at the top level: Millions of option permutations are possible at the top (e.g., two doors, four doors, V8, V6, hybrid, manual transmission, automatic transmission, air conditioning, and special interior features, to name just a few).

Two issues immediately surface when discussing the make-to-order and/or assemble-to-order product environment. The first relates to the possible number of bills-of-material for a company that offers several configurations; it would be nearly impossible to structure and maintain all the possible bills-of-material. Without a bills-of-material database, level by level, time-phased material requirements planning is also impossible to implement. The second issue is that of securing a reasonable forecast (statement of demand) for each and every possible detailed configuration.

These suggestions are general guidelines, and the optimal place to master plan and/or master schedule within a product structure ultimately depends on the needs of the company and where it intends to meet the customer (the manufacturing strategy the company plans to use for each product family, product subfamily, product grouping, and specific product itself). Most manufacturing companies today use a combination of the various product manufacturing strategies and therefore master plan and master schedule at different levels within their product structures.

Depending on specific needs, each of the following is a candidate for the status of a master planned and/or master scheduled item:

- End items or finished products;
- Groups of end items or finished products;
- Kits or saleable packages of goods;
- Intermediates, subassemblies, or manufactured items;
- Options or features including assembly/operating instructions;
- Add-ons or attachments including assembly/operating instructions;
- Commonality within product family or product subfamily;
- Purchased raw materials, components, or packaging materials;
- Service, spare parts, or maintenance kits;
- Capacity or resources;
- Activities or events.

The point is this: One can master plan and/or master schedule anything that makes sense to the business. All of the factors and issues discussed above must be taken into consideration when a company is identifying where and what it plans to master plan and/or master schedule. And we're not done.

To say that a company's decision where and what it (the company) eventually plans to MPS is a key to that company's overall success may certainly be an understatement. As stated earlier, to make this decision an even more complex one, a company can elect to master plan and master schedule at multiple and different levels within its product structure.

Multilevel Master Planning and Scheduling

We have seen previously that there are times when it may make sense to master plan and/or master schedule at levels other than the final product. An item that is expensive, difficult to obtain, or difficult to manufacture may need the kind of attention that a master planned and/or master scheduled item deserves and generally gets.

Thus, since there are no hard-and-fast rules for deciding where and what to master plan and/or master schedule, the management team, master planner, and master scheduler may elect to master schedule not only end items, but other items one, two, three, or more levels deep in the company's product structure. This approach is known as *master scheduling at multiple levels*, or sometimes as *master scheduling at two levels*; it is shown at the bottom right-hand side in Figure 6.4.

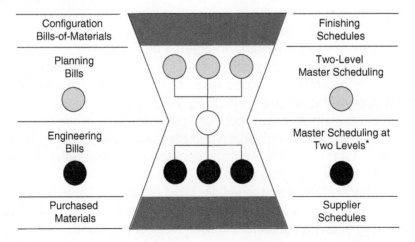

*Master planning and scheduling at two levels (multiple levels) uses engineering bills or bills-of-material for planning.

Figure 6.4   Master Planning and Scheduling Terminology

There are also times when *two-level master scheduling*, which is *technically different from multilevel master planning and scheduling*, is necessary. For example, the first level in two-level master scheduling logic might be at the product family level (shown at the top right-hand side in Figure 6.4 on page 213), as stipulated in the integrated business planning and/or sales and operations planning process. At some point, the discrete demand and due dates for lower-level members that make up that product family need to be determined; one could drive the product family demand through a planning bill in order to forecast demand for the product family members. *When a company uses a planning bill to predict demand at a lower level, it is using a two-level master scheduling approach.*

We will get into two-level master scheduling and planning bills later, but for now, think about the issue raised in the following situation.

TYING MASTER PLANNING AND SCHEDULING TO AGGREGATE SUPPLY PLANNING

No business can operate for long without coordination between its functional parts. All must coordinate their efforts if a company is to survive and prosper. For the manufacturing company, integrated business planning (Chapter 14) serves as an important coordinating function, bringing together product design, customer demand, operational capacity, financial capabilities, and the goals of company leadership and management in a quantitative form, describing—in aggregate—what needs to be purchased, built, and sold in future time periods.

Consider the case of Desk Masters Corporation, a manufacturer of office furniture. As its managers emerge from their monthly integrated business planning review, the manufacturing vice president hands the master planner (master scheduler at smaller companies that combine master planning and scheduling into one middle management function) a copy of the new approved supply plan, which, for simplicity's sake in this chapter and book, we will describe as covering only the month of April (integrated business planning process has a minimum 24-month planning horizon and the leaders are encouraged to spend their time working months 4 through 24). April's leadership-approved supply plan authorizes the supply/production (volume) of 1,200 desks.

Desk Master's master planner and scheduler takes this approved, aggregate supply plan and uses it to create a more specific build plan—breaking it into different types of desks (mix) to be produced in varying quantities in each week of the month covering a 3- to 6- to 9- to 12-month planning horizon on the master schedule and 6- to 9- to 12- to 18-month planning horizon on the master (supply) plan. In this simple example, the desk product family has just two subfamily members: oak and pine.

	April Production Plan = 1,200 Desks				
Weeks	1	2	3	4	Total
MPS Oak	200	200	200	200	800
MPS Pine	100	100	100	100	400
Total	300	300	300	300	1,200

You will notice that the various quantities total 1,200 desks, pointing out an important principle: The sum of the master plan and/or master schedule must equal the approved supply plan plus or minus any approved tolerance understood and approved by the executive team. This principle is discussed in greater detail in Chapter 14, which covers the monthly integrated business planning process.

Management Issues

For management, the supply (operations) or production/procurement/purchasing plan serves as an important control mechanism over manufacturing resources, indicating the authorized level of overall procurement, purchasing, and production. For those who do the work, and who may have more intimate knowledge of current inventories, work in process, plant capacities, and material availabilities at any given moment, the master schedule, supported by the master plan, provides specificity and direction, namely, how many of which products need to be built, and when.

The requirement that master planned and scheduled quantities equal those of the approved supply plan provides an important check against unauthorized and ill-directed activities on the plant, mill, factory, or shop floor. Without this check, the master planner and/or master scheduler would, in effect, be in sole control of the plant or mill or factory or shop floor and its various costs. When product families contain dozens of different members and submembers, the damage done by an uncontrolled master plan and/or master schedule can very quickly get out of hand.

For practical purposes, there may be times when it makes sense to exceed supply or production plan limits in a particular period. Perhaps production wants to build up inventory in advance of a previously unscheduled maintenance shutdown or pending strike. Perhaps the master planner and/or master scheduler desires to overplan unique options and features in some product families because of product mix uncertainty. Management needs to have a clear policy concerning these situations and the link between the master plan, master schedule, and the approved supply plan (also known as the approved production plan).

Ensuring That Supply Plans and Schedules Are Aligned, Synchronized, and Integrated

In Chapter 2, the reader was introduced to the four levels (again, some companies only use three levels) of supply chain planning performed within an organization. Master planning and scheduling (this book's focus) fits directly into level 2 (the *master planning* level) and level 3 (the *master scheduling* level). Between these two planning levels sits the official *request for supply* from the corporate supply manager or master planner to the company's manufacturing sites' master scheduler(s) (see Figure 6.5 as a review of these supply chain planning levels).

It is important to note that planning levels 1, 2, and 3 in the supply chain planning process depicted in Figure 6.5 are directly *demand driven*. The supply chain planning organization develops the optimal supply chain *response* to the demand plan or forecast that is formally communicated to them (while the authors may use both *demand plan* and *demand forecast* throughout the text, they believe that *plan* is a better word in that it

Integration, Alignment, and Synchronization

Levels			
	Integrated Business Planning/Sales & Operations Planning (Corporate)		
1	• Demand Plan • Supply Plan • Inventory/Backlog	**Product Families, Volume, Months**	Horizon = 0 to 24+ months*
	Master Planning/Supply Management (Corporate)		
2	• Demand Plan • Supply Plan • Inventory/Backlog	**Members of Family, Mix Weeks/Months**	Horizon = 0 to 6 to 12 months*

— — — — — — — — — _Request for Supply (RFS)_ — — — — — — — —

Master Scheduling (Plants)

3	• Demand Plan • Supply Plan • Inventory/Backlog	**Units, Mix Days/Weeks**	Horizon = 0 to 3 to 6 months*

Principle
Silence is
Acceptance

Detailed Production Scheduling (Plants)

4	• Inventory • Production • Capacity	**Units Timing Hrs/Days**	Horizon = 0 to 1 to 2 weeks*

* Horizon to be determined in design phase

Figure 6.5   Supply Chain Management Planning Levels

indicates the existence of supporting actions vs. *forecast*, which is more loosely bound to action if at all, e.g., the *weather forecast*).

Level 4 is a mixed bag. Detailed production schedules can be directly driven by demand if using a kanban approach or pull system that is directly responding to customer orders but is more often driven by the master schedule and/or the material requirements plan (also, of course, driven by the master schedule and ultimately the demand plan!). Therefore, when ensuring that supply chain plans are integrated, aligned, and synchronized from top to bottom, one must take into account both the demand plans as well as the corresponding supply plans and schedules.

For the purpose of explaining the top-down disaggregation process from levels 1 through 4, *demand* comes in two basic forms: *bookings* and *shipments*. Bookings are orders taken but not yet shipped. Shipments represent product going out the door to customers. Both bookings and shipments can (and should) be planned.

The demand plan that may come more readily to mind for many readers is really the shipments plan. The demand planning function works to put together a demand plan indicating when the product must be available to ship to customers and the supply planning/scheduling functions do the work to ensure that the product will be there on time, in full, to ship.

In make-to-stock environments, the bookings (i.e., sales orders) and the shipments occur nearly simultaneously from a *planning* perspective in that orders received are shipped directly from inventory (if all goes as planned), often that same day. Of course, some customers buying products from a supplier that is using a make-to-stock strategy may place their orders in advance and really *do not* desire having their product shipped immediately from inventory, but instead shipped at a later date.

Regardless, the *expectation* established by the company is that the inventory will be available at the customer's request, whether immediate or at a later date. We also must recognize that, regardless of how simultaneous bookings (orders) and shipments may seem from a planning perspective, from the order execution perspective, orders that are received throughout the day have to be managed, processed, and shipped in accordance with lead time and order turnaround policies. As a result, inventory is closely managed for products in the make-to-order environment; it is decreased by demand (shipments) and increased by supply (production orders, process orders, purchase orders, etc.), and managed to achieve target levels of customer service and optimal cash outlay to support the inventory.

For products in make-to-order (and finish-to-order, assemble-to-order, etc.) environments, sales orders may be booked days, weeks, even months in advance of when the product actually ships (potentially even longer in design-to-order and engineer-to-order environments). The expectation established between the company and its customers is that there will be a delay (lead time) between when the order is booked and when the order is shipped.

Backlog, or the accumulated order book, is closely managed in make-to-order environments, the desire being to have enough orders on the books to achieve financial and operational objectives while fulfilling customer lead time expectations. Too large a backlog may indicate that some current and future customers may have to wait longer than normal for their product. Too small a backlog may make the company nervous that the lack of booked orders may lead to missed financial objectives and idle facilities.

Again, for products in both make-to-stock and the broader make-to-order environments, it is useful to keep track of bookings and shipments separately for measurements and accountability. If sales and marketing have done what they needed to do to get the bookings (orders) to come in according to plan but the supply chain organization did not provide quality product on time in full for shipment, then supply chain should be held accountable for the poor customer service. Likewise, if supply chain made the product available according to plan (demand and supply), but sales didn't book the orders, then sales should be held accountable for the excess inventory.

Demand plan accuracy (a.k.a. forecast accuracy) should ideally be based on bookings, not shipments, although gathering this data is often difficult (customers may choose not to order if the inventory isn't on hand, so the potential order never gets captured, etc.), so shipments are often used as a proxy for *true demand*. Now that we have defined the two types of demand (bookings and shipments) pertinent to the discussion of translating between levels of planning, let's get into more detail on the levels.

Level 1 planning is the integrated business planning (IBP) process owned and directed by the company's leadership (see Chapter 14 for a discussion of this all-important process, *supporting* and *supported by* master planning and scheduling). The IBP process is conducted monthly with a primary objective of establishing and communicating the company's leadership direction to those within the company with a need to know. As stated in Chapter 14, a key output of this IBP process is the approved leadership plans, one of which is the approved supply plan.

This approved supply plan is used by the supply manager and/or master planner to create the company's master supply plan—level 2 supply chain management planning. This master supply plan consists of the disaggregated approved supply plan (translated through next-level demand/supply balancing) into its next level of detail along with the preliminary assignment of work to the company's various manufacturing facilities (see Chapter 16 for a discussion of this all-important master planning and scheduling process).

Once the master planner has determined the makeup of the company's master supply plan, the *request for supply* or *RFP* is sent to the individual manufacturing sites identifying the requested work generally for the next one to two to three months (the RFP is communicated and sent out monthly following the completion of the current month's IBP cycle). The RFP is a rolling *request for supply* since the master planner each month adds a new future month while dropping the month that has just passed.

Using the RFP, the manufacturing site's master scheduler creates the master schedule (again, through next-level demand/supply balancing)—level 3 supply chain management planning. Once this is done, rough cut capacity planning is run to evaluate whether the manufacturing site can accept the RFP as currently written or if further discussion between the company's corporate master planner and the plant's master scheduler must occur (Class A companies today in the first half of this third decade of the twenty-first century still give their manufacturing sites a *right of refusal* when it comes to responding to the master planner's RFP). Generally, the manufacturing sites are given 24 to 48 hours to respond to the monthly RFP, one way or another (see Chapter 16 for a discussion regarding acceptance or rejection of the *request for supply*).

Once the manufacturing facility has accepted the RFP and created the manufacturing site's master schedule, it is used by the plant's production schedulers to create the daily (generally put out weekly) detailed production schedule or the plant's/shop's dispatch list—level 4 in supply chain management planning. This detailed production schedule is released weekly and identifies what work is to be done each day and in what sequence it is to be done.

These past paragraphs have described how the company's approved supply plan is aligned, synchronized, and integrated with the company's master (supply) plan, which is aligned, synchronized, and integrated with each of the company's manufacturing sites' master (supply) schedules, which are aligned, synchronized, and integrated with the company's manufacturing operations highlighted on the detailed production schedule.

This top-down disaggregation must be coupled with an aggregation process that ensures that the described alignment, synchronization, and integration is truly happening. Now, let's take a more detailed look at the three disaggregation processes as well as the aggregation processes that ensure that these various plans and schedules are tied together during the supply chain management planning process.

Disaggregating the (Approved) Aggregate Supply Plan into the Master Supply Plan

The company's approved supply plan (compiled by the IBP supply review leaders and owners) is expressed in terms of product families and volumes of supply (often across all manufacturing sites) that are anticipated to be available in monthly increments. This aggregated level of detail at level 1 planning is just right for the leadership team to set the direction for the company. However, this aggregated level of detail does not work as the supply chain planning organization moves into planning the company's level 2 master (supply) plan, much less the master (supply) schedule and detailed production schedule.

Disaggregating the approved IBP supply plan into the site-level master (supply) plan means that the product families are broken down into product subfamilies, the volumes of supply that are anticipated to be available are broken down into the anticipated mix of supply, and the monthly increments are broken down into weeks in the near- to mid-term time periods while maintaining monthly increments in the mid- to long-term time periods.

It is important to note that the disaggregation of supply happens *in concert* with the disaggregation of demand. In fact, the disaggregation of demand *precedes* that of disaggregation of supply and then the standard methods of balancing demand and supply (including inventory and/or backlog) occur at each level in the process.

Also important to note is that the *demand plan* that is disaggregated is the *demand shipments plan* (i.e., when product needs to go out the door), not the *demand bookings plan*. The corresponding supply plan recognizes the anticipated demand *shipments* timing and plans supply volume accordingly through multilevel planning with lead time offsets, and so forth.

The *demand bookings plan*, while relevant to sales planning and calculating anticipated backlog levels and the like, is less critical to the planning required to get product produced and/or procured on time in full for shipments. Without this synchronization at all levels, the planning software tool(s) will detect a demand/supply imbalance and send ceaseless signals to the corresponding planner(s) to rectify the situation.

The disaggregation can be done using percentages within a planning bill structure (see Chapter 8 in this book for a discussion on planning bills and their usage in master planning and scheduling), using some other form of disaggregation tool such as an Excel spreadsheet, or just done manually (the authors recommend using the planning bill approach). Regardless of the disaggregation technique the master planner chooses, most (if not all) companies using master planning and scheduling must disaggregate the approved supply plan in support of a disaggregated demand plan.

Depending upon how the company structures its master planning and scheduling process, this disaggregation of the approved supply plan then translates into one of three types of plans: (1) the company's master supply plan (level 2 planning), (2) the company's combined master supply plan/master supply schedule (level 2 planning combined with level 3 planning, forming one planning level), or (3) a RFP for the company's various manufacturing facilities (level 1 planning going directly to level 3 planning—this typically happens when there are single-source manufacturing sites and there is no need to master plan supply across multiple sites for the same product and/or group).

All right, now that the reader has an understanding of disaggregating the approved supply plan into the master (supply) plan, let's take a look at disaggregating the master (supply) plan into each manufacturing site's *request for supply*. During the disaggregation process, the master planners as well as the master schedulers remain conscious of the necessary alignment, synchronization, and integration requirements.

Disaggregating the Master (Supply) Plan into the Master (Supply) Schedule

Disaggregating the master (supply) plan into the master (supply) schedule means that the product subfamilies are broken down into groups of finished goods items, finished goods items by stock-keeping unit (SKU), and/or required options/features, as well as possible add-on options (see Chapter 8 for a discussion on planning bills, Chapter 9 for a discussion on two-level MPS, and Chapter 10 for a discussion on using MPS output for make-to-order products).

Additionally, the volumes of the anticipated-to-be-available aggregated mix of supply is broken down into the anticipated-to-be-available detailed mix of supply. Lastly, weekly increments are broken down into days in the near- and possibly intermediate-term time periods while maintaining weekly increments in the intermediate- to long-term time periods.

Again, this disaggregation can be done using percentages within a planning bill structure (again, see Chapter 8 in this book for a discussion on planning bills and their usage in master planning and scheduling), using some other form of disaggregation tool such as an Excel spreadsheet, or just done manually (again, the authors recommend using the planning bill approach). All right, now that the reader has an understanding of disaggregating the master (supply) plan into each manufacturing site's *request for supply*, let's take a look at disaggregating the master (supply) schedule into each of the operation's production lines, work centers, and/or work locations.

Disaggregating the Master (Supply) Schedule into the Detailed Production Schedule

Disaggregating the master (supply) schedule into the company's detailed production schedule means that groups of finished goods items, finished goods items, and/or required options/features as well as possible add-on options displayed on the manufacturing site's master (supply) schedule are broken down into buildable finished goods items and/or required options, features, and add-on options by stock-keeping unit (SKU). Additionally, the mix of supply is broken down into detailed production schedules identifying each item's manufacturing operation expected start date or time, operation expected completion date or time, location where the work is to be done, machine and/or production line setup time allotted, machine and/or production line operation time allotted, and the item's priority within the work center or work location. Lastly, weekly increments are broken down into days and/or hours (in some cases minutes) in the near-term and possibly mid-term time periods while maintaining weekly increments in the mid- to long-term time periods.

This disaggregation can be done using the company's enterprise resource planning (ERP) system capabilities (note, the aforementioned planning bills can also be used within the ERP system), using some other form of disaggregation tool such as an Excel spreadsheet, or just done manually (the authors recommend using the ERP software). All right, now that the reader has an understanding of disaggregating the master (supply) schedule into each manufacturing site's *detailed production schedule*, let's take a look at the process used to aggregate that detailed production schedule into the company's master (supply) schedule to ensure that these two schedules are aligned and synchronized (we plan/schedule down, make adjustments to the plan/schedule as necessary, ensure that the adjustments to the plan/schedule are within approved guidelines, and continually aggregate up to the next level to be sure that alignment has not been lost).

Aggregating the Detailed Production Schedule and Tying It to the Master Schedule

Aggregating the detailed production schedule into the company's master schedule means that all scheduled finished goods items and/or required options, features, and add-on options by stock-keeping unit (expressed in daily increments) are summarized into groups of finished goods items (for the identified week), finished goods items (for the identified week), and/or required options/features as well as possible add-on options (for the identified week) and compared to the manufacturing site's master schedule by week. All items scheduled to be completed in a particular week are added together for that week. When reporting this comparison and alignment, defined and approved tolerances are taken into account (e.g., the manufacturing site's master scheduler may give the manufacturing site's production scheduler and/or shop dispatcher a tolerance of one week early, no weeks late, along with acceptance of a 5 percent overrun, while stating that any underrun is and will be considered unacceptable).

This aggregation can be done using the company's enterprise resource planning system capabilities, using some other form of aggregation tool such as an Excel spreadsheet, or just done manually (the authors recommend using the ERP software). All right, now that the reader has an understanding of aggregating the detailed production schedule into each manufacturing site's master schedule, let's take a look at the process for aggregating that master schedule into the company's master (supply) plan to ensure that these two *work-to-be-done* schedules/plans are again aligned and synchronized (skilled production schedulers continually aggregate up to the next level to ensure that any and all adjustments made to the detailed production schedule are within approved guidelines as well as to be sure that alignment between the detailed production schedule and the master (supply) schedule has not been lost during translation and communication).

Aggregating the Master (Supply) Schedule and Tying It to the Master (Supply) Plan

Aggregating the master schedule into the company's master supply plan means that all master scheduled finished goods items) and/or required options, features, and add-on options by stock-keeping unit are summarized into product subfamilies of finished goods items and/or required options/features as well as possible add-on options by week and compared to the company's master supply plan by week and/or month. All items master scheduled to be completed in a particular week are added together for that week and compared to the master supply plan for the identified week (weeks for near and intermediate time periods and months further out on the planning horizon). When reporting this comparison and alignment, defined and approved tolerances are taken into account (e.g., the company's master planner may give the plant's master scheduler a tolerance of one week early, no weeks late, along with acceptance of a plus-or-minus 3 percent quantity overrun/underrun; percentages used here are only examples).

This aggregation can be done using the company's enterprise resource planning (ERP) system capabilities, using some other form of aggregation tool such as an Excel spreadsheet, or just done manually (the authors recommend using the ERP software). All right, now that the reader has an understanding of aggregating each manufacturing site's master (supply) schedule and comparing it to the company's master (supply) plan, let's take a look at aggregating that master (supply) plan into the company's approved IBP supply plan to ensure that these two plans are again aligned and synchronized (we continually aggregate up to the next planning level to ensure that any and all adjustments made to each site's master (supply) schedule are within approved guidelines as well as to be sure that alignment between the master (supply) schedule and the master (supply) plan has not been lost during translation and communication.

Aggregating Master (Supply) Plan and Tying It to (Approved) Aggregate Supply Plan

Aggregating the master (supply) plan into the company's approved IBP supply plan means that all master (supply) planned product subfamilies are summarized into product families and compared to the company's leadership-approved IBP supply plan by month (all master planned subfamilies to be completed in a particular month are added together for that month). When reporting this comparison and alignment, defined and approved tolerances are taken into account (e.g., at this high level of aggregation, the company's supply plan owner may give the company's master planner a tolerance of no months early or late along with acceptance of a plus or minus 2 percent quantity over- or underrun). Again, percentages used here are only examples.

This aggregation can be done using the company's enterprise resource planning (ERP) system capabilities, using some other form of aggregation tool such as an Excel spreadsheet, or just done manually (the authors recommend using the ERP software if it has this aggregation capability or, if the ERP system does not have this aggregation capability, then some form of Excel summarization). This final aggregation is necessary to again ensure that these two plans have remained aligned and synchronized (we continually aggregate up to the next planning level to ensure that any and all adjustments made to the master supply plan are within approved leadership guidelines and that alignment between the master supply plan and the approved IBP supply plan has not been lost during translation and communication).

Master Scheduling Capacities, Activities, and Events

Thus far, our discussion has concentrated on master planning and scheduling only one of the productive resources of the company—materials. Equally important to the production process is another resource—capacity.[2] Master planning and scheduling techniques can

---

[2] Here we should not think so narrowly as to construe capacity as applying solely to labor, machine time, and production space on the manufacturing floor. As master planning and scheduling continues to become more broadly applied at a Class A level within companies, capacity can also be construed (and scheduled) in the context of services.

be applied to capacity as well as to material or parts. Understanding this point is especially important for those companies whose business is that of selling capacity.

For example, job or machine shops that make buildings, irrigation, and other large-scale products fall into this category. For such businesses, it is critical to know what machinery will be required so that customer orders can be booked against the uncommitted—or unconsumed—capacity of that machine. Another example is a production line that is constrained by one or more pieces of equipment, such as a mixer. When the next customer places an order, the plant needs to know how much capacity is left or uncommitted on those pieces of equipment so that product completion can be properly quoted and delivered on the promised date. In these cases, a company may choose to master plan and schedule capacity.

Other situations may require a company to master plan and schedule not items or capacity, but activities and events. A testing lab, for example, sells a service that can be broken down into a series of activities. The product that the testing lab sells is capacity, and that capacity is spread among several events that must occur. Chapter 11 details how activities and events can be harnessed within a structure analogous to that of a bill-of-material and shows how points within this structure can be scheduled and capacity can be planned.

This chapter has explained the importance of knowing where and what to master (supply) schedule. It has attempted to show that this *where and what* is not preordained as the last step in the cost/value-adding process, but may focus elsewhere, depending on the product's manufacturing strategy selected by the company.

Manufacturing strategies are largely geared to where a company intends to meet its customers, and this is determined by customer needs, competition, market requirements, lead times, willingness to invest in inventory, and the company's position on employing resources and capacity. Besides these elements, where the company's product is on its product life cycle and what the product structures look like has a good deal of impact when choosing *where and what* to master plan and schedule.

The important point to carry forward from this discussion to succeeding chapters is that the master planner and/or scheduler must be fully versed in the nature of his or her company's products, how they are built, and the competitive constraints under which the company operates. A simplistic default to end-item master scheduling may work in some competitive environments, but in most will be inappropriate, resulting in loss of control of the master plan and master schedule and its underlying levels of materials and capacity management.

In addition, succeeding chapters will help the reader determine *where and what* to master plan and/or master schedule for any given product in any given manufacturing environment. In fact, not until the reader completes reading this entire book will all the decision points and master planning and scheduling techniques be on the table. At that point, answers to the question of *where and what* to master (supply) plan and/or master (supply) schedule can be obtained.

So far, we have discussed why manufacturing companies need to master plan and schedule, the mechanics of master planning and scheduling, managing with the master plan and schedule, and using the master plan and schedule for products where the company has employed a make-to-stock strategy. In the next five chapters we will turn our attention to master planning and scheduling products where different circumstances dictate using a different manufacturing strategy, starting with a flow environment and moving to the assemble-to-order, kit-to-order, finish-to-order, and make-to-order worlds.

In these service and manufacturing environments, upside-down bills-of-material and planning bills are usually necessary to aid the master planning and scheduling process. Planning and scheduling in the process and repetitive manufacturing industries offer additional challenges and opportunities. These flow environments are the subjects of our next chapter's discussion.

7

Scheduling in a Flow Environment

All models are wrong, but some are useful.

Thus far, all of our examples have described products assembled from parts or components such as a flashlight and winches. Many readers, perhaps a majority, may be working in environments that produce these types of products, though their situations may be more complex than those used in our examples. Turbines, aircraft, photocopiers, washing machines, microwave ovens, desktop computers, laptop computers, smartphones, and machine tools are other examples. The list is practically endless. For lack of a better term, we call this *intermittent manufacturing*.

Other readers work in repetitive or process environments: chemicals, food, cosmetics, containers, semiconductors, petroleum distillation, brewing, paint manufacturing, textiles, lumber, glassmaking, and so forth. These readers may be wondering if the principles of master planning and scheduling are applicable in the world of nonassembled products.

The answer to this question is *yes!* As a general statement, everything we've described in earlier chapters applies to the flow manufacturing environment. However, some aspects of master planning and scheduling in this environment are uniquely different, some are much simpler, and others add a new dimension of complexity.

Master planning and scheduling in the world of intermittent manufacturing is primarily concerned with one main objective: getting purchased materials, plant equipment, and people ready to build the product when the customer orders are received by the company. In other words, master planning and scheduling is really a full-fledged planning process. Basically, from that point forward, most everything else is execution and control through plant and supplier scheduling.

With a few exceptions, flow environments shift much of the master planner's and/or master scheduler's work from preparing to build the product to actual execution. The reason for this shift in emphasis is simple: Most intermittent manufacturing operations involve dozens (if not thousands) of components, all with different lead times. Machine tools provide an excellent example. Modern drill presses and lathes are assembled from thousands of parts sourced from hundreds of suppliers. Component parts, labor, and finished goods are expensive, and *optimizing their availability against customer demand* is essential for profitability.

The flow environment, on the other hand, is dominated by the optimization of the manufacturing process. Here, pipes, tanks, and vessels of various sorts are physically arranged to simplify, facilitate, and accelerate the flow of raw materials through the manufacturing process, making the end product in a very short time—a few days or even a few hours. Since many of the products of this environment are commodities or commodity-like items (such as gasoline, paints, industrial chemicals, or processed foods) sold on the basis of price, the *efficiency of the process* has a major impact on profitability.

Thus, the goal of planning and scheduling in the flow environment is less about matching up materials and resources against customer orders than about assuring the efficiency of a manufacturing process that will produce high-quality output at the lowest possible cost. In other words, it's the manufacturing process that matters.

Also, where perishability of raw ingredients is an issue—as it so often is in the flow environment—the planner and/or scheduler may find economic reasons to run the process until all of a newly opened batch of ingredients has been used up, customer orders notwithstanding. In other situations, the matter of government-mandated lot traceability takes on larger significance.

Different Manufacturing Environments

The different manufacturing environments just described are really extreme ends of a continuum of manufacturing practices. One end of that continuum is marked by the traditional job shop. There, the inputs of production are provided by suppliers and follow a route that takes them, by disconnected steps, to several work centers with specialized machines for bending, drilling, assembling, testing, painting, packing, and so on (see Figure 7.1 on page 229).

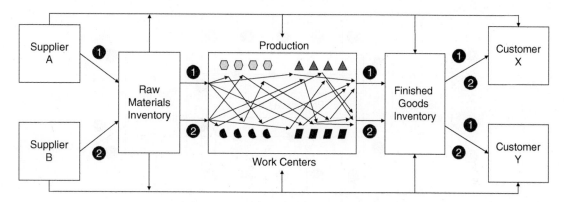

Figure 7.1 The Job Shop Environment

The work *comes to the machine operator or assembler*. And when one machine operator or assembler has completed the task at hand, the work-in-process is transferred to yet another machine operator or assembler, perhaps sitting in production queues along the way. For the planner and/or scheduler, the job shop environment demands a heavy emphasis on:

- Multilevel and often complex bills-of-material and possibly planning bills;

- Detailed routings identifying work to be done by various workstations as well as holding areas;

- Work orders tied to stock replenishments or to satisfying booked customer orders along with authorizing the entire manufacturing process to begin and finish by a noted due date.

On the other end of the manufacturing continuum, we find the pure flow environment, in which raw materials (usually few in number) are fed into a highly automated and continuous process for created finished output. There are *no* intermediate workstations, *no* production queues, and/or *no* handling equipment (intermediate workstations, production queues, and handling equipment don't add any value to the product; these nonoperative steps only add cost). And there are usually fewer people. Machinery and the movement of work-in-process are integrated into a generally seamless, continuous process. Together, these elements reduce manufacturing cost and the amount of time that work remains in the process. In the perfect process, raw materials are dumped into a hopper at one end of the line, and finished goods emerge from a pipe or packaging machine at the other (see Figure 7.2 on page 230).

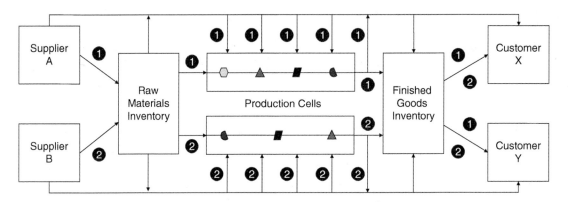

Figure 7.2   The Flow Manufacturing Environment

Few operations, however, fit the ideal image just described. Many are still character-ized by the processing of batches that must be queued from one step of the operation to the next.[1] This makes some manufacturing highly sensitive to the sequencing of work put into the line.

For example, the planner and/or scheduler of salsa would probably want to run a batch of mild salsa through the series of vats and mixers before sending a batch of hot salsa through them. Doing the reverse would require that the equipment be flushed out between batches so that the mild salsa would not pick up any residual spicy ingredients.

Many manufacturing processes, of course, operate in the vast middle ground between the two extremes just described. Some assembly operations, for example—particularly those characterized by moving assembly lines that do rapid, repetitive work—share many characteristics of the flow environment. Indeed, the history of manufacturing of all types of products has followed an evolution from a discrete set of separate operations to a con-tinuous flow of work. In some cases, this has been accomplished by a simple reconfigura-tion of the manufacturing facility, in which machines are arranged to eliminate transfers, queues, and storage areas. In others, process innovations have eliminated and/or com-bined some operational steps.

An excellent example is found in the plate glass industry. A century ago, plate glass was manufactured in batches through an expensive and time-consuming series of discrete steps: (1) mixing and melting ingredients, (2) casting the liquid glass into molds, (3) annealing the glass in a lehr (an oven), (4) grinding, and then (5) polishing. Decades of innovations have converted what was once a job-shop operation to a near-perfect flow operation by reducing the former five steps to a single operation, that of a continuous

---

[1] In food and pharmaceutical industries, regulations often force companies to operate in batch mode as a way of creating identifiable lots.

	Job Shop Environment	Flow Environment
Production Attributes	• Low volume; low speed; short to long runs • Longer lead times • More different inputs (parts)	• High volume; high speed; long runs • Shorter lead times • Fewer different inputs (ingredients)
Schedule Basis	• To meet stock or customer orders • Scheduled to the week or to the day • Schedule materials first, then balance capacity	• Primarily to optimize production utilization • Finer-grained scheduling – often schedule to the hour • Schedule capacity first, then balance materials
Materials Inventory Adjustments Made	• As material issued and product completed	• Via "backflushing" (i.e., materials used deducted by the recipe or formula and the number of finished products)
Terminology	• Factory vs. • Bills-of-material vs. • Routings vs. • Work orders vs. • Fabricate, assemble vs. • Parts, sub-assemblies vs.	• Plant • Recipes or formulas • Process sheets • Campaigns, batches • Fill, pack, or finish • Bulk, intermediates
Level of Scheduling Paperwork	• High	• Low

Figure 7.3 Job Shop versus Continuous Flow

casting of a ribbon of glass that requires neither grinding nor polishing.[2] The parallel development occurred in the steel industry when Nucor built the first plant capable of continuous casting of sheet steel. Readers may recognize similar evolutions in their own industries. Others are bound to follow.

Differences in the job shop and flow environments extend to the language used by company associates, the length of production runs, and other factors. Figure 7.3 itemizes just a few of these differences.

---

[2] See James M. Utterback, "Innovation in Non-Assembled Products," in *Mastering the Dynamics of Innovation* (Boston: Harvard Business School Press, 1994), 103–144.

Similarities Between Intermittent and Flow Environments

Despite the differences just noted in the two manufacturing environments, many of the tasks that involve the planning and scheduling of work remain the same. To identify these, let's revisit the diagram introduced in Chapter 2 as Figure 2.7 (page 41). This is a thumbnail sketch of what must go on in any commercial manufacturing environment (seen here as Figure 7.4 on page 233). Each activity in the figure is essentially the same, down to the level of master planning and scheduling.

Business and Sales and Operations Planning

As before, everything begins with business planning, sales planning, and operations planning, and this is equally true for *both intermittent and flow* manufacturing environment types. Whether a company is making paint or computers, aspects of both planning and scheduling must be addressed.

Demand Management

Demand management is also equally important in both manufacturing environments. Without demand forecasting, no company can hope to put the right mix of material, plant equipment, and human resources into play. *The company that doesn't forecast (and/or master plan and schedule) will either find itself at some state of under- or overloaded capacity; the same is true of its inventories.*

With demand forecasting, however, the job shop or intermittent manufacturer will allocate its resources on the basis of stock and/or customer orders. In contrast, the flow-oriented company, being more inclined to optimize its productive capacity, will tend to produce its products and then use sales inducements to reduce any overstock that occurs.

Rough Cut Capacity Planning

Resource requirements planning (RRP) and rough cut capacity planning (RCCP) were explained briefly in Chapter 2.[3] Those processes are used to answer one question: "Does the company have a chance to meet the approved supply plan (RRP), master (supply) plan (RCCP), and/or master (supply) schedule (RCCP) as currently written?" It (RRP and/or

---

[3] A detailed treatment of RRP and RCCP is found in Chapter 15.

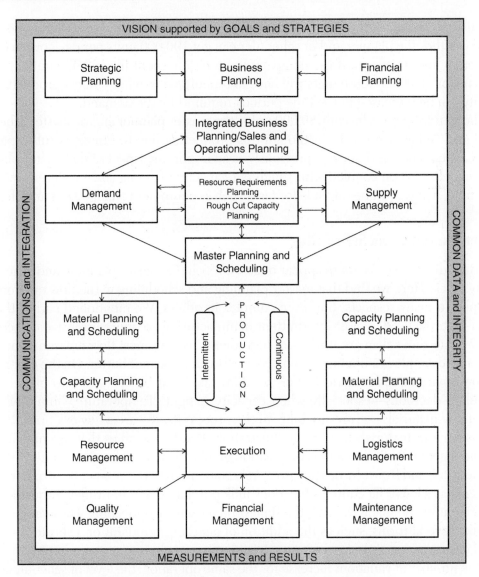

Figure 7.4 The Planning and Control Process

RCCP) answers that question for both modes of production (job shop or intermittent and process flow or repetitive). However, it is even more important in the process flow environment as a basis of planning and scheduling decisions.

The detailed capacity planning boxes shown in Figure 7.4 are often minimized or sometimes bypassed entirely by the planner and/or scheduler of flow type and highly repetitive production. After a rough-cut sanity check is conducted, it can then be determined whether the planner and/or scheduler can get 100,000 units per day down a certain production line. However, if the company has a requirement for 120,000 units, production time for 20,000 of those units will have to be shifted elsewhere unless production line capacity can be increased in the time periods required by the demand.

If the requirement is for only 80,000 units, the master planner and/or master scheduler would ask, "What else can I put though this production line to utilize its full capacity?" Proper sequencing, as described previously, is an important aspect of the master planning and scheduling when coupled with rough cut capacity planning since it determines how much time, if any, must be set aside for tasks such as equipment changeovers and cleaning.

Master Planning and Scheduling

Important differences begin to appear once we reach the master planning and scheduling activity block. Here we find that master planning and scheduling in the flow environment is simpler in many respects, but more complex in others. We mentioned earlier that the bills-of-material used in most intermittent manufacturing are more extensive and complicated by lead times than are the lists of ingredients used in most flow environments.

A prime example is a Boeing 777 compared to a jar of peanut butter. On the other hand, the flow environment contains lots of variables that must be factored into planning and scheduling decisions—especially when capacity is tight. Temperature, humidity, variations in raw materials—even variability in the process itself—are a few examples.

Consider raw materials as just one illustration. Food companies that use milk as a key ingredient generally find that the composition of this raw material varies significantly from batch to batch and from season to season. At certain times of the year, milk purchased from suppliers has a lower fat content than does milk purchased at other times. Adjustments to the recipe must be made to bring the final product into specification. These adjustments may take several forms, such as the addition of another ingredient or a shorter or longer period of processing.

As the number of variations increase for the same operation, the level of scheduling complexity escalates, making the planner and/or scheduler more reliant on sophisticated master planning and scheduling and/or plant scheduling software, such as finite-capacity scheduling and advanced supply-planning software capable of working its way through simultaneous variations and producing an optimized plan for the planner and/or scheduler. These software packages can be loaded with the known data and variations experienced by the company in past operations. Master planning and scheduling parameters also include the time needed to accommodate line changeovers associated with various sequencing situations.

Material and Capacity Planning

Given the relatively few materials used in most or certainly many flow environments, detailed material planning is only needed to translate the master plan and/or master schedule products into raw material supplier schedules. The detailed capacity planning used in the intermittent production environment can often be skipped in the flow environment. In these cases, rough cut capacity planning—sometimes coupled with finite capacity scheduling—is all that's necessary.

Plant and Supplier Scheduling

In the job shop environment, dispatch lists are used to communicate to each work center the order in which it should work on different jobs. Meanwhile, job routings coupled with the dispatch list direct work-in-process from one location on the manufacturing floor to another. The flow environment generally has no dispatch lists and no detailed routings. Instead, plant schedules, which are derived from the master plan and/or master schedule, direct the start of work.

Supplier scheduling, along with procurement and purchasing, is likewise minimal, as fewer suppliers and materials are needed to support the production process. Both the job shop and process flow environments, however, can assure material planning and replenishment through procurement/purchasing, supplier scheduling, and kanban agreements with suppliers.

Execution

A key difference experienced by the master planner and/or master scheduler in this stage between the job shop and flow manufacturing environments is found in the process of adjusting inventories once the products have been finished. As noted in Figure 7.4 on page 233, the job shop environment reduces raw material inventory as parts and components enter production. Work-in-process inventory is increased as these parts and components are issued to the line. The work-in-process inventory is reduced as work is completed and finished goods are increased upon receipt from production.

In contrast, the flow environment is more inclined to use a method called *backflushing*. In this method, the operator knows from the recipe or formula that each finished product requires the consumption of a specified (or average) amount of inventoried material: for example, so many gallons of pureed tomatoes and so many ounces of diced jalapeños per gallon of finished hot salsa. Working back from the final output, the number and makeup of inventoried materials used can be estimated with some accuracy.

In some cases, flow environments actually also produce items for inventory. These are commonly known as by-products and co-products of the production process. For example, the petroleum refining processes or lumber manufacturing that aim to create one product generally produces several others. Many of these by-products and co-products go into inventory as feed stocks for still other petroleum-based or wood final products.

Product Definition

Product definition includes both a description of the materials that constitute the product to be built and the sequence of activities through which it is produced. In the job shop or intermittent manufacturing arenas, a product is defined in terms of a bill-of-materials and detailed routing. The bill-of-material itemizes every one of the components and sub-assemblies that go into the final product; the routing indicates the various steps through which the product will be put together, including operations, description, work center, tooling, setup times, and run times.

Products in the process flow environment are, in contrast, defined in terms of a recipe and a process sheet. The recipe is a list of ingredients or a formula. Like a cook in the kitchen, the manufacturer looks to the recipe book for a definition of the salsa, dog biscuits, latex paint, or whatever product he or she is about to make. The process sheet indicates when and at what stage the ingredients will be added to the product being manufactured.

Once the process starts cooking, the outcome may not, as in job shop or intermittent manufacturing, be a single product. Instead, the flow operation may produce by-products, co-products, or products representing several grades of quality. Some of the output may even be recycled back into the recipe for the next production run. Each of these outcomes has implications for master planning and scheduling.

Structuring Recipes for By-Products and Co-Products

Many chemical processes result in one or more by-products. For example, paper pulping produces calcium lignin sulfonate. Some of these by-products are usable as ingredients in other products made by the company, in which case they go into inventory. Others are marketable either as a final product or as an ingredient for some other company's manufacturing process. The calcium lignin sulfonate just mentioned, for example, is sold as an additive in the making of concrete, tile, and brick, and as a binder for animal foods.

Other operations produce co-products. A meat-packing operation offers a good example. A hog operation produces not just ham, but bacon, tripe, pig knuckles, and a handful of other marketable items. As the saying goes, modern meatpackers sell "everything but the squeal."

If we were to represent by-products or co-products graphically, as we sometimes do with a traditional bill-of-materials, it would look something like Figure 7.5. On the left we see how several raw materials are brought together to produce a single product. On the right-hand side of the figure, we see that a group of several raw materials (the recipe) has produced several unique products—D, E, and F. This situation is sometimes referred to as an *upside-down bill-of-material*.

A petroleum refinery encounters this type of situation, producing several marketable products from the same ingredient. In many cases, by-products or co-products are ingredients for other products manufactured by the company, and the planner and/or scheduler needs to create linkages between the output of one operation and the raw materials used for another.

The several products in the upside-down bill-of-material may also be different *grades* of a single product. Because of variations in the raw materials, in the manufacturing process—or even in the weather—different grades of output may result. For instance, if 1,000 units were produced by the process, 700 units might be grade one, 200 units might be grade two, and the remaining 100 units might be grade three. These must be sorted at the end of the line. In this case, the master planner and/or master scheduler must rely on historical experience and personal insight to hit demand and supply targets. The different grades may also be manufactured by design depending on the grade of the raw materials.

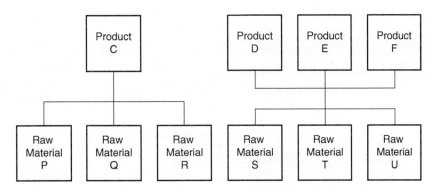

Figure 7.5   Single Product and Upside-Down Bills-of-Material

Recovered Products

Some manufacturing operations that fall within our description of the flow environment actually recover some of the raw materials put into the front end of the process. These are generally counted as an output product and entered into inventory by production, where they constitute part of that on-hand inventory.

A good example of this situation is found in the glass-making business. Broken glass is one of the ingredients of glassmaking. Thus, scrap or breakage that occurs in manufacturing is recycled as inventoried raw materials. Catalysts used in chemical reactions often exhibit the same behavior.

Process Sheets

As mentioned earlier, flow environments generally use process sheets instead of the detailed routings used in job shop and intermittent manufacturing. Both indicate the course that various inputs and outputs will follow during manufacturing.

For example, a routing for a fabricated metal product may say to move the output of work center A to work center D, from there to work center G, and from there to the finished stock room. A planned start-stop date and time for each activity would be stated.

The process sheet is similar to a routing, but it more closely resembles a diagrammatic representation of the manufacturing process itself. It may be (or look like) a one-step routing: start the manufacturing cycle and finish it. This is true since setup for each part of the operation is generally done simultaneously (not sequentially) and the work flows in a continuous stream.

Product specifications are also a part of the flow environment process sheet. Figure 7.6 displays the difference between the multistep routing characteristic of job shop and

Multiple-Step Routing			
Operation	Description	Setup	Run
10	Mix	1.5 hours	0.2 hour/batch
20	Fill	0.5 hour	1 hour/1,000 cases
30	Pack	0.75 hour	1 hour/1,000 cases

Process Sheet (Single-Step Routing)			
Operation	Description	Setup	Run
Line 1	Mix, Fill, Pack	1.5 hours	1.1 hours/1,000 cases

Figure 7.6   Routings versus Process Sheets

intermittent manufacturing and the simpler, single-step routing seen on process sheets used in flow environments.

Accuracy Requirements

Assembly and job shop manufacturers apply a variety of quality controls to assure that finished products meet specification. These include the inspection of items in the bill-of-materials as they come in from suppliers, in-process monitoring, and statistical methods that keep equipment operating within acceptable limits. Flow manufacturers assure the quality of their ingredients and conduct monitoring to verify that in-process activities are within target specifications.

We've already noted how natural variations in raw materials (like the butter fat content of milk, the viscosity of a particular vegetable oil, the sweetness of a patch of peaches, or dye potencies) and environmental factors can create variations in the final product. These can sometimes be reduced by interventions: holding a batch in the cooker for a bit longer, adding more sugar to a processed food or more pigments to a batch of paint, and so forth.

When output is not within acceptable limits, plant personnel, planners, and schedulers need to determine if the problem was in the accuracy of recipe, in the particular batch, or in the production process. Once this analysis is complete, adjustments are made as required.

The Planning Process

In the planning process—in any environment—the master (supply) planner and/or master (supply) scheduler anticipates what will be produced in the future. In the job shop, the master planner and/or master scheduler plans the arrival and storage of the many raw materials and semi-finished parts required for the manufacturing and/or assembly of the final product.

Once the material priority plans are in place, the master planner and/or master scheduler plans the capacity needed to do the job. If capacity is less than required, the master planner and/or master scheduler will look for constraints or bottlenecks, find a way to increase the capacity of particular work centers, offload some of the work to other lines or plants, or find some other way to balance demand with the available capacity or the planned available capacity.

Master planners and/or master schedulers in the flow environment begin by scheduling available capacity, since capacity is usually the dominant constraint. Only then do they turn to scheduling materials. The rationale for this sequence is the fixed nature of most plant capacity and the general availability of raw materials (safety stock inventory is often carried) for the products made in this environment.

Most flow operations are, in fact, capacity constrained. For example, for the past five to six to seven decades the world has been awash in crude oil, but refining assets are limited. If demand for gasoline were to suddenly go through the roof, ExxonMobil Corp could probably pump or purchase all the crude it needed to meet its share of demand but expanding its refining capacity would take years.

Process industries are often characterized by commodity-like materials (like wheat, vegetable oil, sand, lime, or paint pigments).[4] Thus, in many cases, the master planner and/or master scheduler can have all the materials needed within a day or two of a call from the purchasing department. Increasing capacity, on the other hand, requires a major financial commitment and years of design and construction to bring the increased capacity online.

The high cost of most processing plants also dictates that they be run at full capacity. Few companies can afford to idle a multimillion-dollar plant or allow it to operate far below its rated capacity; these generally must run at about 65–70 percent capacity to break even. As a result, utilizing plant capacity is the first order of business for most master planners and/or master schedulers.

Planning Capacity

In the process flow environment, this is the general order of process planning:

1. Understand the anticipated demand.

2. Develop a master plan and/or master schedule using finite-capacity scheduling or advanced supply planning software, if available.

3. Check the feasibility of that master plan and/or master schedule using rough cut capacity planning, if required.

4. Forward the output of the master plan and/or master schedule to detailed plant or mill scheduling to serve as a guideline for production authorization and release of work.

---

[4] Obviously, there are exceptions to this general statement. Some materials are very high-cost and their availability represents a primary constraint on production.

5. Prepare detailed production schedule for the coming periods of time (many times, this is done a week in advance).

If the production process is highly integrated in the flow of activities, there may be no need for detailed capacity planning. Experience will tell the master planner and/or master scheduler (whether this is an actual person or finite-capacity scheduling software) the lower, optimal, and upper limits of a production line's capacity. Because fully utilized capacity is a crucial goal, the master planner and/or master scheduler also looks for underloaded conditions. As these are identified, work may be shifted to correct the problem.

Once the operation begins, changing the detailed production schedule can be difficult and costly, necessitating breaking down the line, cleaning it out, reheating furnaces, and so forth. Urgent customer orders that arrive during production cannot always be accommodated; therefore, careful planning and scheduling of what to run and when to run it is very important. *It is difficult (if not impossible) to control what hasn't been planned!*

The software currently available is an invaluable aid to the master planning and scheduling process. When line capacity data is entered into the scheduling database, the master planning and scheduling software will not recommend a load plan that exceeds or greatly underloads the current or planned capacity. It will instead shift loads around to fit and, perhaps, prioritize orders to accommodate preferred customers.

It is also capable of optimizing the production of different products once all the data for those products are loaded into the database. The software will recommend which sequence of products should be run (as optimized through algorithms such as linear programming, mixed integer programming, artificial intelligence, simulation/heuristics, etc.).[5]

This type of software, then, can handle what we call finite-capacity scheduling. Using a stated level of plant capacity as its starting point, it tells the master planner and/or master scheduler, "Given the stated capacity, this is how you can optimize the master plan and/or master schedule." Some companies can, and do, literally use this software to schedule their production; others prefer to have an override option in the system so that adjustments can be made.[6]

---

[5] This type of software is referred to as a *finite-capacity* planning or scheduling system, since it creates a schedule based upon existing, finite capacity. *Infinite-capacity* planning or scheduling systems begin with the order requirements and tell the operator how much capacity will be needed to produce it.

[6] For an excellent treatment of finite-capacity scheduling, see James Correll and Kevin Herbert, *Gaining Control,* 3rd ed. (Hoboken, NJ: John Wiley & Sons, 2006).

The finite-capacity scheduler described earlier is quite different than the infinite-capacity planning software used in many job shop environments that says, "Given the finished units you need to build by this date, this is the capacity you must have in particular time periods." The chore of finding that capacity or changing the demand is a job left to the master planner and/or master scheduler (in this first/second year of the third decade of the twenty-first century). *This so-called chore of finding needed capacity will certainly be done more and more by machine as each year of this decade passes!*

Planning Materials

Once the process flow environment master planner and/or master scheduler has taken care of capacity issues, he or she shifts attention to plan for the materials used to build the product, as well as materials that will result from building the product (like by-products). Here, two methods are useful: *negative gross requirements* and *special scheduled receipts*.

NEGATIVE GROSS REQUIREMENTS One of the unique aspects of some flow environments is the fact that they can create one or more of the materials used in the process itself. We first observed this in earlier discussion of by-products, co-products, and recovery. Production of these ingredient materials produces what we might call a negative gross requirement. To understand this term, consider our earlier example of glass production.

The glass-making process produces a certain amount of scrap (or *cullet*) that, in effect, is a raw ingredient of the glass-making process, along with sand, lime, and soda. This scrapped glass can be reused and is, therefore, planned as recovery material. Those raw materials are positive gross requirements of the glass-making process.

We need certain quantities to make the product, and we master plan and/or master schedule and material plan accordingly. The scrap produced in making one batch of glass reduces the raw material requirement for making the next batch. (We will need less raw material because we will use the cullet produced during the first batch.) The master planner and/or master scheduler must adjust the recipe and process sheet accordingly.

Negative gross requirements sometimes create an important timing problem for the master planner and/or master scheduler. The material that emerges from the process as a by-product must be time-phased with its availability; that is, we must indicate when this by-product is available for use.

The requirements of the by-product for use in the next batch must also be time-phased. For example, scrap glass can be recycled into the glass-making process, but the master planner and/or master scheduler must know when it will be available, enter that information into the master planning and scheduling (MPS) software, and schedule accordingly.

SPECIAL SCHEDULED RECEIPTS In planning material requirements, the flow environment master planner and/or master scheduler looks to two sources: incoming new materials obtained through purchasing, and the by-products and co-products generated within the manufacturing process itself, as just described. Both represent scheduled receipts. When many by-products, co-products, and different grades result from manufacturing, coordination between master planners and/or master schedulers, operations, customer service, sales, and marketing personnel is extremely important. To appreciate why, consider this example:

> *Y is a by-product of a distillation operation whose main product is X. On average, the production of two barrels of X results in the production of one barrel of Y; the company has developed distribution channels for the sale of both products. Suddenly, the market demand for Y increases, prompting marketing to send the following urgent request to production: "Our customers will need twice as much Y next month as the 1,000 barrels we had projected. Please increase your output of Y to 2,000 barrels in anticipation."*

Of course, complying with this request will have an important consequence: 4,000 barrels of X must be produced to get the 2,000 barrels of Y requested. Will the company be able to move this increased X output? Does it have the capacity to store it until new customer orders can be generated?

In this case, the master planner and/or master scheduler should work closely with customer service, sales, and marketing, reminding its managers that two barrels of X will hit finished goods for every barrel of Y requested. Unless they can develop a plan for offloading that inventory—through discounts, sales promotions, or other means—the company's bottom line may suffer. If the profits generated through by-product Y are low, it may be smart to develop another high-margin product for which Y would be an important ingredient.

The fact that several grades of output may emerge from a production process further complicates the job of scheduling receipts, especially when these must be predicted statistically. For example, a manufacturer knows that natural variability in raw materials, weather, and the production process will result in three grades of output: good, better, and best. These are sorted separately at the end of the production cycle.

Based upon its experience, this manufacturer expects that, *on average,* 20 percent will be good, 30 percent will be better, and 50 percent will meet the standards of *best*. However, every average—by definition—contains some level of variability.[7] For instance, if three men picked at random weighed 120 pounds, 180 pounds, and 270 pounds, we'd have an average weight of 190 pounds. But the high variability around that average (from 120 to 270 pounds) doesn't tell us much about the weight of the next man picked at random.

Likewise, in manufacturing, if variability is high from receipt of one raw material to the next, or from one process batch to the next, averages won't have much predictive value for the person planning scheduled receipts. This is one reason why many flow manufacturers use safety stock or buffer inventory—it protects them from these sources of variability.

Process Company Using Rough Cut Capacity Planning: An Extended Example

Now that the elements of master planning and scheduling in a flow environment have been explained, let's jump into an example, using the kind of planning matrix produced by commercially available master planning and scheduling software.

Jelly Giant is a processed foods company specializing in fruit jams and jellies. Its products are produced in cases using batch operations in which different ingredients are added at different times. (We've altered and simplified this process for demonstration purposes.) One of the company's popular products is grape jelly, which is made from a handful of ingredients: grape mash, sugar, corn syrup, pectin, and citric acid.

The matrix shown in Figure 7.7 on page 245 is representative of the information a master planner and/or master scheduler might see on a computer screen. The top part represents the master plan and/or master schedule for grape jelly; the bottom part is a material plan for one ingredient: grape mash. Other ingredients have their own material plans. Let's start at the top.

---

[7] In statistics, variability of outcomes around the mean (or average) is measured in terms of standard deviations.

Grape Jelly Lot Size: 200 Lead Time: 2 periods	Past Due	1	2	3	4	5	6	7	8
Item Forecast		50			90			200	
Option Forecast									
Actual Demand		110	30	10	40	20	50		
Total Demand		160	30	10	130	20	50	200	0
Projected Available Balance	220	60	30	20	90	70	20	20	20
Available-to-Promise									
Master Schedule (Receipt Date)					200			200	
Master Schedule (Release Date)			200			200			

Grape Mash Lot Size: 1,000 Lead Time: 4 periods Safety Stock: 250	Past Due	1	2	3	4	5	6	7	8
Projected Gross Requirements			1,200			1,200			
Scheduled Receipts		1,000					1,000		
Projected Available Balance	1,300	2,300	1,100	1,100	1,100	−100	900	900	900
Planned Order Release									

Figure 7.7   Master Schedule for Grape Jelly and Material Plan for Grape Mash

The Master Schedule Matrix

As mentioned earlier, the master planner and/or master scheduler in many flow environments uses finite-capacity planning and scheduling software. This software takes all the known data about forecasted demand, expected lead times, desired safety stock or buffer levels, preferred sequencing, and so forth, and indicates how much should be scheduled and when, given customer preferences, inventory objectives, and supply constraints.

Reviewing some of what we learned in Chapters 3 through 5, here is the known data for this example master scheduled item (refer to Figure 7.7 on previous page):

- Item being produced (grape jelly);

- On-hand inventory (220 cases);

- Desired safety stock or buffer (10 cases);

- Batch or lot size (200 cases);

- Lead time, or time required to complete a batch once the material is available (two days);

- Cumulative lead time, or time required to complete a batch from scratch (six days);

- The planning time fence (PTF), which is six periods (days, in this case).[8]

Previous chapters have acquainted the reader with the various elements of data in the left-hand column. Let's review these data elements.

The *Item Forecast* row indicates predicted demand for grape jelly: 200 cases in each of the time periods 1, 4, and 7. *Actual Demand*, however, departs from the forecast. Here we see actual demand, or orders in hand, for 110 cases in time period 1; 30 cases in time period 2; 10 cases in time period 3; and so on. The total actual demand for the first three time periods is 150 cases (110 + 30 + 10).

Since these orders were forecasted, they *consume the forecast* in time period 1, reducing forecasted demand in time period 1 to 50 and in time period 4 to 90.[9] *Total Demand* is then the sum of the unconsumed forecast and actual demand.

---

[8] Everything to the left of the fence is within the control of the scheduler; the computer generates computer planned orders outside the fence, indicating batch sizes it assumes will be produced.

[9] See Chapter 17 for details on forecast consumption.

The next important line of the matrix is the *Projected Available Balance,* which indicates (in this example) the number of finished cases of grape jelly expected to be available at the end of each period. Here, for example, Jelly Giant has 220 cases on hand as it begins time period 1. The available balance satisfies some of the demand in subsequent periods. Ideally, the projected available balance should not fall below the stated safety stock level.

A finite-capacity scheduling system informs the master planner and/or master scheduler what the production process is capable of handling at any given time by creating firm planned orders and computer planned orders on the *Master (Plan and/or) Schedule* line of the matrix. It will not schedule a run or campaign that the process cannot accommodate. Using the information provided by the software, the master planner and/or master scheduler has authorized (in this example) the start of production of a batch of 200 cases of grape jelly in time period 2.

Production of these cases will finish in time period 4 (with two days' lead time), where they appear as a *scheduled receipt*, and just in the nick of time to prevent a stockout. The master planner and/or master scheduler has authorized another release of 200 cases in time period 5, to be completed and received in time period 7.

The Material Plan Matrix

In many flow environments, scheduling is driven by its most critical resource: plant capacity. As a consequence, orders may be arranged for the plant *first*; after the plant is scheduled, the master planner and/or master scheduler turns to the materials or ingredients needed to make the product, getting them when they are needed and in the right quantities.

The bottom section of Figure 7.7 on page 245 is the material plan matrix for the first of several grape jelly ingredients: grape mash. There we see that there are fixed order quantities (1,000 units), safety stock (250 units) for this material, and a planning lead time (four time periods).

There is also an on-hand inventory balance of 1,300 units, which has been put into time period zero, the starting value for the projected available balance calculation. It should also be noted that six units of grape mash (indicated in the recipe) are needed to build one case of grape jelly. Thus, we need 1,200 units of grape mash to produce a batch of 200 cases of grape jelly. This number appears as a projected gross requirement in time period 2 and again in time period 5, at exactly the time—to the day in this example—that orders for 200 cases of grape jelly are to be released to production.

Our materials plan also indicates anticipated scheduled receipts of 1,000 units of grape mash in time periods 1 and 6. These are based on orders placed by Jelly Giant's purchasing group. The master planner and/or master scheduler can see from the

Projected Available Balance line that this second order will have to be moved up to time period 5; otherwise, there will not be enough grape mash on hand to meet the demand for that ingredient in that period. A simple telephone call, text, or e-mail to the supplier may be all that's needed to speed up that scheduled receipt.

Each of the other ingredients of the grape jelly process (not shown here) has its own plan and its own matrix, and each must be periodically checked—and adjustments made when necessary—to ensure that the plant will have all the ingredients it needs to produce the primary product. Some of these ingredients will not be needed until the middle or end of the process; thus, the master planner and/or master scheduler need to time-phase their availability and release.

Planning By-Products and Co-Products

The product definition of by-products was discussed earlier in the chapter. Many flow environments create by-products that are either sold or used as ingredients for other products. A material plan should be created for each of these by-products, especially if they will be recovered for use in other products, or if they will be sold as products in their own right.

In the case of Jelly Giant, the production of 200 cases of grape jelly creates a residue of 180 gallons of grape pulp. For years, Jelly Giant paid thousands of dollars each month to get rid of what it considered worthless sludge. Then one of its marketing geniuses discovered that grape pulp could be sold to nutraceutical processors, who would pay high prices for as much grape pulp as Jelly Giant could produce. To them, Jelly Giant's waste by-product was a highly valued ingredient in a popular naturopathic medicine.

By-products create an interesting problem of signs for the master planner and/or master scheduler (see Figure 7.8 on page 249). If a by-product is expected to be produced, a negative quantity is put on grape pulp within the grape jelly recipe.

When the master plan and/or master schedule of 200 cases of grape jelly is exploded through its recipe, the negative quantity is multiplied by the MPS quantity, which creates a negative gross requirement for grape pulp in time periods 2 and 5. The software must show these gross requirements as negative quantities in the materials plan. When the master planning and scheduling software subtracts these negative quantities, they become positive values and are added to the *Projected Available Balance* line of the planning matrix.[10]

---

[10] Companies that use a by-product as an ingredient in another product will often show additional quantities of material in the *scheduled receipts* line of the matrix. These represent quantities purchased to add to the inventory of the by-product.

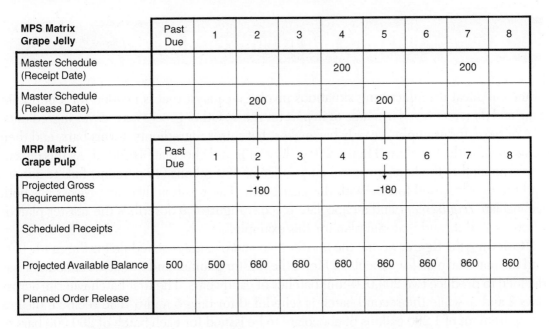

MPS Matrix Grape Jelly	Past Due	1	2	3	4	5	6	7	8
Master Schedule (Receipt Date)					200			200	
Master Schedule (Release Date)			200			200			

MRP Matrix Grape Pulp	Past Due	1	2	3	4	5	6	7	8
Projected Gross Requirements			−180			−180			
Scheduled Receipts									
Projected Available Balance	500	500	680	680	680	860	860	860	860
Planned Order Release									

Figure 7.8   Material Plan for a By-Product or Co-Product

One of the problems with this technique is timing the by-product's receipt into inventory. Most of the time, the by-product will be received on the due date of the main item being produced, in this case, grape jelly. If the lead time of the master planned and/or master scheduled item is short, this problem is not a major concern. If the lead time is long, then the master planner and/or master scheduler needs software capable of exploding selected recipe items by due date, using component/ingredient lead-time offset capability (explained in Chapter 12), or else the master planner and/or master scheduler must use the special scheduled receipt method.

Another problem with the negative gross requirement is the negative quantity on the recipe—this bothers some people because of recipe accuracy issues (refer to Chapter 13 for a discussion on data integrity, including routing or recipe accuracy). Of course, software designed specifically for the process industry should handle these situations.

A similar procedure is applied when a material used in the process is recovered for use in the future. For example, catalysts, broken glass, and chocolate are among the materials recovered for reuse.

Catalysts and Recovered Material

Some chemical manufacturing situations involve a catalyst that is needed for a period of time and then recovered in whole or in part for reuse. Other processes recover ingredients.

Consider, for example, a candy bar maker that mixes ingredients, forms bars, and then coats them with chocolate. Then 1,200 gallons of liquid chocolate is added. As this chocolate is applied to the bars, however, an average of 480 gallons (40 percent) fails to adhere and can be recovered for use with the next batch. The result is that the process has both a chocolate *requirement* and a chocolate *receipt*. Figure 7.9 describes the master plan or master schedule and material plan for this example.

Reviewing the figure, we see the master plan and/or master schedule for the candy bars and the material plan for chocolate. Here, the master planner and/or master scheduler has decided to produce two 200,000-unit batches of candy bars. The first batch will run across days 2 and 3, while the second batch is scheduled for days 5 and 6. The recipe indicates a requirement of 1,200 gallons of chocolate to be issued for each batch of 200,000 bars in

MPS Matrix	Past Due	1	2	3	4	5	6	7	8
Master Schedule (Receipt Date)					200			200	
Master Schedule (Release Date)			200			200			

MRP Matrix	Past Due	1	2	3	4	5	6	7	8
Projected Gross Requirements			1,200			1,200			
Scheduled Receipts		❶ 1,000			❷ 480			❷ 480	
Projected Available Balance	1,300	2,300	1,100	1,100	1,580	380	380	860	860
Planned Order Release									

❶ Purchased Material   ❷ Recovered Material

Figure 7.9   Material Plan for a Catalyst or Recovered Ingredient

time periods 2 and 5. At the end of each campaign, the plan anticipates that 480 gallons of the issued chocolate material will be recovered.

To plan for this recovered material, the master planner and/or master scheduler uses either the negative gross requirement (placing a negative quantity in addition to the positive quantity on the chocolate in the candy bar recipe) or the special scheduled receipt. Both of these techniques were discussed earlier. The figure shows a special scheduled receipt for recovered material in addition to what has been ordered from the supplier.

Production Line Scheduling

The level of fixed overhead represented by process equipment in most flow environments is so high relative to labor, materials, and other costs that every effort is made to keep that equipment fully utilized. That is straightforward when there is only one production line, but it gets more complicated when two or more production lines exist under the same roof. And as we will see in Chapter 16 covering supply management and aggregate master planning, having many roofs in different parts of the country or world increases complexity still further.

Master planners and master schedulers in these highly capitalized plants are responsible for keeping several production lines fully utilized. They generally attempt to do so through finite schedules. They shift products around from line to line where feasible in an attempt to minimize downtime, and they must do so within constraints imposed by equipment adjustments, tank capacities, raw material availability, customer orders, safety stock or buffer replenishments, labor, and so on.

Figure 7.10 on page 252 provides an example of how one plant with two production lines and many products to make might master plan and/or master schedule the flow of work. The top part is a simple table of products and times; the bottom portion is the type of graphic representation that a finite-capacity scheduling system can produce. Here, the dark bars are nonproductive times (changeover, maintenance, crew meetings, and so forth). Both line schedules, top and bottom, come from the same data.[11]

As the reader reviews the information contained on the production line schedule, he or she should note the precision of these plans and/or schedules—products A, B, C, X,

---

[11] Inventory levels, customer demand levels, potential stockouts, and so forth can also be graphically represented.

Line #1				Line #2			
Product	Quantity (cases)	Date	Time	Product	Quantity (cases)	Date	Time
A	10,000	15 Sept	8 a.m.–2 p.m.	X	7,000	15 Sept	9 a.m.–12:30 p.m.
Changeover		15 Sept	2 p.m.–2:30 p.m.	Changeover		15 Sept	12:30 p.m.–2 p.m.
B	20,000	15 Sept	2:30 p.m.–12:15 a.m.	Y	18,000	15 Sept	2 p.m.–3 a.m.
Changeover		16 Sept	12:15 a.m.–1 a.m.	Changeover		16 Sept	3 a.m.–4:45 a.m.
C	12,000	16 Sept	1 a.m.–6 a.m.	Z	6,000	16 Sept	4:45 a.m.–8:30 a.m.

Date	15 SEPTEMBER				16 SEPTEMBER			
Time	6 a.m.	12 p.m.	6 p.m.	12 a.m.	6 a.m.	12 p.m.	6 a.m.	
Line #1	⊙	Ⓐ	Ⓑ		Ⓒ	⊙		
Line #2	⊙	Ⓧ	Ⓨ		Ⓩ		⊙	

Figure 7.10   Line Schedules

Y, and Z are scheduled to fractions of an hour. The production line schedules shown in the figure have been created using a vertical format (top portion) and a horizontal format (bottom portion). Although the graphic display is the most popular, both formats are available using commercially available master planning and scheduling and/or production scheduling software.

Planning Multiplant Workloads

This chapter discussed how master planning and scheduling, material planning, and detailed production scheduling concepts can be used in all manufacturing environments, especially in the flow environments that produce so many goods used in our economy. It should also be recognized that master planning and scheduling concepts and techniques used in repetitive and flow environments apply equally to intermittent manufacturing. Besides being knowledgeable about the various production environments, the master planner and master scheduler must understand how to plan and schedule these environments using the chosen manufacturing strategy (make-to-stock, make-to-order, design-to-order, and so forth).

Chapter 8 covers planning bills, which are most often used to plan make-to-order products. However, there are several applications of planning bills in the make-to-stock and multiple plant supply management worlds as well. Figure 7.11 illustrates a process flow company with three plants (one new). Here the master planner for the company must decide how much of the company's total approved supply plan is to be requested (via a *request for supply*) from each manufacturing site.

To help the reader better understand the loading (of manufacturing facilities), power (of using planning bills), and creation of a *request for supply*, let's take a look at a beverage company and how its master (supply) planner uses the planning bill concept to assist in the workload distribution.

Cranston Beverage Company produces roughly 10,000 cases of bottled water each month (other types of bottled beverages are also produced at Cranston, but for simplicity, this example only concentrates on the bottled water part of the business). At Cranston the company's master (supply) planner resides at corporate while the company's master schedulers reside at each plant (one master scheduler per plant).

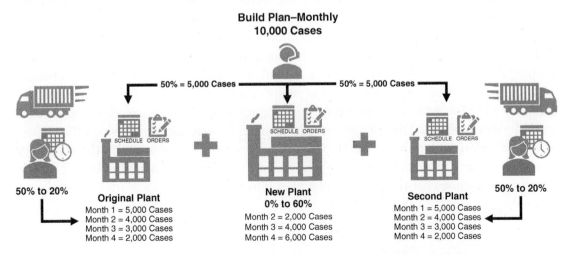

Planning Plant Load – An Approach

**Build Plan–Monthly
10,000 Cases**

50% = 5,000 Cases   50% = 5,000 Cases

50% to 20%

Original Plant
Month 1 = 5,000 Cases
Month 2 = 4,000 Cases
Month 3 = 3,000 Cases
Month 4 = 2,000 Cases

**New Plant
0% to 60%**
Month 2 = 2,000 Cases
Month 3 = 4,000 Cases
Month 4 = 6,000 Cases

Second Plant
Month 1 = 5,000 Cases
Month 2 = 4,000 Cases
Month 3 = 3,000 Cases
Month 4 = 2,000 Cases

50% to 20%

Figure 7.11   Using a Planning Bill to Assist in Plant Selection

The master (supply) planner is responsible for creating a *request for supply* for each plant by the third Friday of each month detailing the number of bottled water cases required for the following month. Cranston's corporate master (supply) planner uses a predefined plant planning structure (resembles a planning bill, which is discussed in detail in the next chapter) to populate each plant's monthly *request for supply* (RFS).

As shown in Figure 7.11 on page 253, the bottled water case approved supply plan (ASP) for the month under discussion is 10,000 cases of bottled water. In the past, Cranston Beverage Company only had two plants, the original plant located in Phoenix, Arizona and a second plant located in Philadelphia, Pennsylvania.

These two plants were built in the last decade of the twentieth century. Well, times have been good in the beverage business in the first two decades of the twenty-first century and Cranston has built a new, larger, and automated filling and bottling plant in Dallas, Texas.

This new plant is now ready to open its doors and accept work directed from corporate headquarters. During the past as well as the current month, Cranston's build demand for bottled water has been evenly split between the Phoenix and Philadelphia plants (50 percent of the total monthly approved supply plan to each plant). That model is now changing to include the Dallas plant, so that the company effectively uses its highly automated bottle filling, capping, sealing, labeling, and packaging production lines.

The phase-in or phase-up (twenty-first-century plant) and phase-out or phase-down (twentieth-century plants) corporate plan is displayed in Figure 7.11 on previous page. Each month starting with next month, the corporate master (supply) planner is increasing the bottled water case RFS for the Dallas plant by 20 percent a month up to a maximum of 60 percent a month while decreasing the bottled water case RFS for Phoenix and Philadelphia by 10 percent a month to a maximum reduction of 30 percent for each plant. The reason for not transferring all the bottled water production to Dallas is to ensure that Cranston has active and ready-to-go production backup bottled water lines as well as keeping a presence for bottled water in the southwest and northeast parts of the country.

Once the ramp-up for Dallas and the ramp-downs for Phoenix and Philadelphia are complete over the next three months, the company plans to maintain this mix for their bottled water business. Discussions are currently under way for transferring other beverages production to the Dallas facility (transfer dates are dependent upon the success of the bottled water production transfer pilot using its version of a planning bill). The next chapter dives somewhat deeper into planning bills and their use in master planning and scheduling.

8

Planning Bills

An assumption is the first step toward a screwup.

Imagine a company that sells conference center chairs off-the-shelf. To remain competitive, the company determines that it must expand its product line—customers want a variety of colors beyond the current black-only model. To accomplish this product expansion, the company must evaluate both its marketing and manufacturing strategies. Under its current make-to-stock (MTS) strategy for conference center chairs, the customer simply asks for a chair, and that item is shipped from finished goods. This system works fine for a product family with a limited number of members.

However, if a company is going to offer greater product variety without a change in its manufacturing strategy, it can and most likely will be very expensive to maintain a finished-goods inventory for all items expected to ship off-the-shelf with minimal lead time. The company's forecasting job will become more difficult, too; if it guesses wrong on demand for its variety of products, it risks having obsolete inventory. As the company continues to offer more options to the customer and marketplace in order to remain competitive, the problem becomes more significant. Therefore, it may be necessary to choose adding additional manufacturing strategies.

Using the MTS manufacturing strategy for make-to-stock products has already been discussed. This chapter deals with an alternative strategy—make-to-order (MTO). First, though, we review the potential strategies at our disposal, using the familiar fast-food industry as a model.

At one extreme, a fast-food restaurant can *make-to-stock* ready-to-eat hamburgers and keep them hot under heat lamps. Some would have ketchup, some mustard, some pickles, others lettuce, and some combinations of the various condiments. The advantage for using this MTS strategy is that the customer gets instant gratification; some of the disadvantages, of course, are the high cost of finished inventory, possible waste due to shelf-life, and the difficulty in forecasting the mix requirements. Some items would move quickly, but others would grow stale and have to be discarded.

At the other extreme, the restaurant could wait for the customer's special order and then do the following: determine the proper wheat to use, bake the buns, run to the grocery store for some ground beef, prepare sliced pickles and other condiments from scratch, and cook and prepare the order as given. Such a *design-to-order* or *engineer-to-order* approach would, of course, be impractical for a fast-food restaurant. The customer would grow tired of waiting.

In between these two extremes, the restaurant could maintain certain items in a finished state—the burgers and the buns. Condiment options could be added on request. This is a form of a *make-to-order, assemble-to-order, or finish-to-order* situation. The customer walks in and says, "I'll have a hamburger with mustard, lettuce, pickles, and tomatoes." The hamburgers are sitting on the grill and the buns are in the warmer; the restaurant simply adds the requested options.

Whether a company makes hamburgers or bolts, the production issues and master planning and scheduling techniques needed are basically the same for products in a make-to-order business. However, these product configurations must be planned prior to receipt of the customer order to avoid high inventory investments and to reduce delivery time to the customer. Additionally, it's just hard to control what you haven't planned!

While make-to-order approaches in master planning and scheduling are considered challenging to most manufacturing operations, they do offer significant advantages in terms of reducing finished-goods inventory costs, giving the customer exactly what they want (within offered options), and (in some cases) shortening customer delivery lead times (certainly, over the design-to-order are true make-to-order strategies). However, they do have the potential disadvantage of creating unwieldy and complex bills-of-material as the number of product options grows (unless the company uses the techniques outlined in this chapter). They also create potential forecasting problems in terms of estimating the right mix of options (again, unless the company uses the techniques outlined in this chapter).

This chapter is concerned primarily with the bills-of-material or list of ingredients aspects of make-to-order product strategies, demonstrating how to set up the product structures in a database so that master planning and scheduling products in a true make-to-order, assemble-to-order, kit-to-order, finish-to-order, and package-to-order environment is feasible. Sometimes, planning bill concepts are *foreign* to readers and *not* understood at first glance, but the concepts presented in this chapter work, and they work well, when set up properly and managed by well-educated, well-trained, well-motivated, and experienced master planners and master schedulers.

The Overly Complex Bill-of-Material

Earlier in this book it was explained that to gain a strategic edge, a company must match or surpass its competitors in terms of delivery time, price, quality, service, and technology. If product quality, technology, service, and price are equal among competitors, then the battle for customer allegiance must be won on the grounds of delivery performance, a factor of competitiveness that falls squarely in the domain of the master planner and/or master scheduler.

With proper master planning and scheduling techniques, it may be possible to meet the customer at a prefinished stage, yet still provide product within a competitive time frame. If so, a competitive advantage will have been gained by offering the same or better delivery times but with substantially lower costs. Since the producer will have the opportunity to carry less inventory, its operating costs will be lower, making it possible either to reduce product price or increase margins or both.

From the master planner's and/or master scheduler's perspective, a company's change to using a make-to-order strategy supported with planning bills means initially *deciding where to meet the customer* (i.e., establishing customer service expectations in regard to configurability and lead time).

"Come in and we will hand you a burger. . . . Give us two minutes and we will put it together for you. . . . Give us two hours and we'll run to the store for the ingredients and prepare it from scratch." The *decision about where to meet the customer impacts the decision of what and where master planning and scheduling* will be done.

Recalling discussions in a previous chapter, any of three types of product structures are possible within a company's framework (Figure 8.1). In the case of the package-to-order, kit-to-order, finish-to-order, assemble-to-order, and make-to-order product environments, the hourglass structure (C) is the relevant shape.

Finished Products
|
Manufacturing Process
|
Raw Materials

Figure 8.1   Standard Manufacturing Configurations

The hourglass structure represents a situation in which the customer buys a certain item from a product family, then selects additional options—like a hamburger, which can be configured in any number of ways. But whether the customer buys a plain hamburger or a cheeseburger with the works, he or she still must buy a hamburger (which, here, is one item represented in the pinch point of the hourglass). The buns, lettuce, tomatoes, and pickles are options added later.

The automobile offers a similar example: No matter which sound system is ordered (satellite radio, AM/FM, MP3 player, Bluetooth®, etc.), or which type of seats (heated, cooled, lumbar, etc.), the customer is still buying a car with bumpers, wheels, chassis, and so forth.

The hourglass is the structure most relevant to the make-to-order, assemble-to-order, finish-to-order, kit-to-order, and package-to-order product environment, and it addresses a key question for the master planner and/or master scheduler: How many bills-of-material (BOM) must be created to accommodate all the possible options? Consider the BOM for a hypothetical product shown in Figure 8.2.

As Figure 8.2 makes clear, the purchaser of one of the products has a choice of 10 different A options. Assuming that all options are mutually compatible, the buyer then needs to select from among eight B options. This equates to 80 possible configurations just among the A and B options. But there are more!

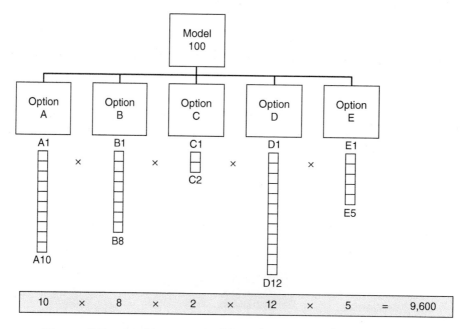

Figure 8.2 Options Availability for Hypothetical Product

Option C lists two choices. A quick calculation of all possible options A through E reveals a staggering 9,600 possible configurations ($10 \times 8 \times 2 \times 12 \times 5$). The job of creating and maintaining separate bills-of-material for each configuration would be staggering. Now, what if a single new option E were added to the list of choices? How many *new* BOMs would need to be created? Answer: 1,920 new bills-of-material ($10 \times 8 \times 2 \times 12 \times 6 = 11,520$ minus the earlier 9,600) each time a change is made to option E.

This situation requires the master planner and/or master scheduler to work with sales and marketing to create the best forecast of demand for the various options—no easy task. Imagine the novice master planner or master scheduler approaching the marketing manager and saying, "I need to know how many Model 100s you're going to sell with the A1, B1, C1, D1, and E1 options next August or, better yet, the first week of August." The marketing manager, a savvy veteran of the manufacturing world, rubs his chin, looks the new master planner and/or master scheduler straight in the eye, and says with great deliberation: "Seventeen!"

Of course, the marketing manager has absolutely *no* idea of how many Model 100s will be sold with those options some months or weeks from now, and perhaps the master planner and/or master scheduler will catch on to his little joke in a short time. The point is, there has to be a better method for getting a handle on products that have a potentially enormous number of BOMs.

One solution is to figure out a way to master schedule one level below the finished product level (say, the master plan level)—at the A1 and A2 and B1 levels, and so forth. How many BOMs would be needed if this approach was followed? Answer: a total of 10 BOMs for A, 8 for B, 2 for C, 12 for D, and 5 for Es. In other words, 37 BOMs would be needed (Figure 8.3 on page 260). This represents quite a difference from the 9,600 BOMs for the full product!

Dropping down a level also could benefit the design engineers in BOM maintenance. If engineering and marketing want to add a *sixth* E option, he or she needs to create *one* new BOM instead of having to gin up 1,920 new ones. The authors believe that the readers who sell and build highly configured products are probably now ready to move to the next part of the make-to-order story.

Of course, it is still necessary to identify how many Model 100s are anticipated to be sold in a given month or week. The rest of this chapter will concentrate on figuring out how many Model 100s will be planned to be sold in a given month (most likely a combination of input from the company's demand owner, demand leader, demand manager(s), demand planner(s), and sales representatives).

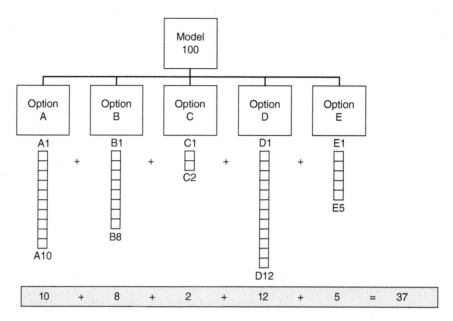

Figure 8.3   Effect of Master Planning and Scheduling One Level Down in the Product Structure

Once the aggregate number is determined, another key question must be answered: For every Model 100 sold, what is the probability that it will be shipped with the A1 option? with the A2 option? and so forth. Sales and marketing can answer these questions by saying something like "Whenever we sell a Model 100, we anticipate that 20 percent of the time we'll sell it with option A1." This is essentially a forecast for the requirement of the option, and being a forecast, it is bound to be inaccurate to some extent. But for the time being, it may be the best number available to the master planner and/or master scheduler and will be used to estimate demand at the product mix level.

After the mix percentage has been determined, the next step is to forecast demand at the lower levels. The following discussion covers a tool for doing just that, the *planning bill*. A *planning bill is an artificial grouping of items or events* in a bill-of-material format (see Figure 8.4 on page 261).

Planning bills are in the category of *pseudo bills*—false or artificial bills. They cannot be used directly to actually build any configuration of the product (they are for planning purposes only). The reason is twofold. First, the product in our example cannot be built with less than 100 percent of a given item. In other words, you cannot take 50 percent of a satellite option, add it to 30 percent of a Bluetooth® option, and then add this to 20 percent of an MP3 option to produce a functional sound system. Second, it takes more than just unique items to build the product—common items are also needed.

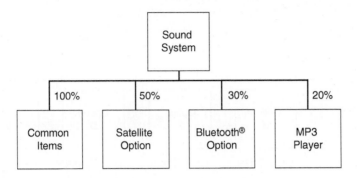

Figure 8.4 Sample Planning Bill

However, a pseudo item with a pseudo bill attached to it can be master planned and master scheduled. Once this is done, the planning bill can then be used to predict what items may need to be planned and/or produced to deliver the product the customer may request. (Note: It is recommended that planning bills be structured only one level down, although there are some instances where more than one level down might be required. This can be referred to as a multilevel planning bill, which is shown in Chapter 16, Figure 16.3 on page 566. This may lead to the need for multilevel master planning and scheduling, an extension of two-level master planning and scheduling detailed in Chapter 10.)

An Example

Consider this simple example. If we know that we plan to sell 1,000 Model 100s, we also know that 1,000 sets of *common* items (those used in *all* Model 100s, no matter which options are selected by the customer) will be needed. Nothing could be simpler. The difficulty comes in determining the mix of the *unique* items.

Suppose that 20 percent of the Model 100s sold in any given month are expected to contain option A1. In this case we would convert the 20 percent to a decimal (.20) and enter that value into the BOM quantity field (some MPS software has a probability field as well as the quantity field—in this case the value is entered in the probability field) for the A1 option, as shown in Figure 8.5 on page 262. The same would be done for each of the other options—say, .15 for the B1 option, indicating that 15 percent of the Model 100s are expected to contain the B1 option.

These numbers are best obtained through a mixture of art and science. The process begins by asking the right people, who in this case happen to be individuals in marketing and sales—who, after all, has more knowledge of the product and its uses, the market

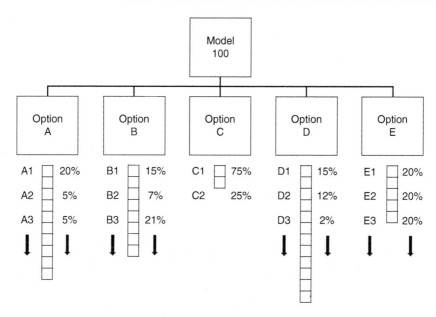

Figure 8.5 Planning Bill with Percentages of Options

appeal of its options, and the intentions of customers? Their information comes through sales and delivery (demand) history and what might be called *future history*—that is, orders booked for future delivery. At some point, *what is booked for future delivery becomes sales history*.

Sales and marketing personnel also keep close tabs on their list of current and prospective accounts, often compiling lists of expected orders months in advance of when those orders are actually received. These lists are used by marketing to focus sales attention on near-term orders that need to be closed, but they can also be used in forecasting. The bottom line in planning bill accuracy is that sales and marketing must be accountable for the determination and maintenance of the planning bill percentages. There may be supporting personnel that are responsible for the keystrokes in the planning system (more on that in Chapter 13, on data integrity).

Once the percentages are obtained, they are entered into the planning bill for the unique options. But should they add up to 100 percent? If the options are required, the answer would be yes. But if the options are add-ons, then the percentages or probabilities of sales may be less than or greater than 100 percent. For example, consider a bicycle with numerous configurations—different frame sizes, a rear derailleur (gear assembly), pedals, and so forth.

No matter what size frame, what gear ratios, or what style of pedals are selected, every bicycle *must* have a frame, a gear assembly, and a pedal set. On the other hand, it is *not* necessary to have a front derailleur (which doubles or triples the number of available gears). The front derailleur is therefore an add-on option, and the total forecast for units with this option could be equal to or less than the number of bicycles to be sold. Another add-on option might be water bottles; the bicycle rider may desire no water bottles, one water bottle, or many water bottles on the bicycle. In this case, the total water bottles forecasted could be equal to, less than, or greater than the number of bicycles anticipated to be sold.

As more options are added, the complexity of the bicycle increases, creating a more difficult situation for manufacturing operations, supply chain management, and the master planner and/or master scheduler. One technique for managing this complexity is to group common items (those that are always needed, such as wheels, brakes, seat stems, wire cables, etc.).

Every bicycle in a given family will have common items, though these may be unique to the product family. One family, for example, might always have an eight-inch seat stem and a standard front axle, regardless of frame size, wheel size, and so forth. Those items would be listed together on a common items bill. The common items bill is also a pseudo, since nothing can be built with just a seat stem and front axle. But the common parts bill can be married with a planning bill-of-material that includes the other options to build the bicycle.

Why do this? Because of the existence of common items, certain probabilities remain constant; the probability that common items will be needed is 100 percent. That fact is very important. If a set of common items for every bicycle is needed, the job of forecasting the mix is certainly reduced. All that is needed then is to get enough sets of common items to match the approved supply plan (generally set to the approved demand plan for MTO environments) generated in the integrated business planning or sales and operations planning process (refer to Chapter 14 for a discussion on integrated business planning or what some call advanced sales and operations planning).

Now consider handlebars. Perhaps option C1 represents dropped bars and C2 represents straight bars. According to marketing, 75 percent of the bicycles sold will have dropped bars, and the remaining 25 percent will have straight bars. In the planning bill C1 would be indicated as .75 and C2 would be listed as .25. Manufacturing cannot produce a handlebar using .75 of a dropped bar and .25 of a straight bar.

Again, for this reason, the bill is called a *pseudo bill-of-material* and is used for planning purposes only. To build the product, manufacturing must use an actual configured bill-of-material and process instructions generally created by product development and/or engineering (see Chapter 12 for a more detailed explanation regarding manufacturing and building processes and documentation used in the make-to-order environment).

So, how does the *pseudo bill* work? Suppose that marketing predicts 1,000 bicycles will be sold in the next month. By exploding 1,000 through the planning bill, and multiplying the aggregate quantity by the projected percentages, one can forecast how many unique and common items will be needed. In this case, if the dropped bars are forecasted at a 75 percent probability, and straight bars at 25 percent, then 750 bikes with dropped bars and 250 with straight bars will be needed. Naturally, the number of common items needed will equal the number of bicycles required—1,000, assuming one set of common items per bicycle.

In the next section, let's consider a familiar product and how the planning bill assists the company and its master planner and/or master scheduler in getting the job done for products that are managed using a true make-to-order, assemble-to-order, finish-to-order, kit-to-order, and/or package-to-order manufacturing strategy.

Soft Seat Listens to Customers, Expands Product Offerings

The Soft Seat Corporation designs and manufactures a successful line of conference center chairs that it sells *off the shelf* throughout North America and parts of Europe and Asia. During a monthly integrated business planning/sales and operations planning management business review, the chief executive officer (CEO) announced that market research indicated that to remain competitive the company must expand its product line to provide models in colors other than its traditional black. "Customers are telling us that they want a variety of colors to coordinate with modern office decors. The increasing success of the one competitor that does provide color choices confirms the research."

Soft Seat had built a successful business on just one product family in just one color. This simple product situation made planning fairly straightforward. Since the company's market forecast was generally reliable, it could satisfy customer orders by keying production to the market forecast. There was no need to guess how many orders there would be for various model options.

The announcement by the CEO would make life more difficult for just about everyone. Marketing would find forecasting more challenging; they would have to estimate demand not just for chairs, but for black chairs, red chairs, and so forth. If estimating demand (volume) for plain black chairs was difficult from month to month, breaking that total forecast into segments (mix) represented by different colors would prove more difficult—and surely less reliable.

The chief financial officer (CFO) would surely find the new conference center chair product family strategy troubling. This was a *get the order and ship it* business. Soft Seat had to have a sizable, finished goods inventory to meet the competitive requirement for fast delivery. Now he feared he would be required to finance not one inventory, but several, one for each color plus the various mixed colors—a red back with a black seat is quite fashionable.

The manufacturing manager was even less thrilled by the announcement because it would greatly complicate what had been a fairly simple and routine manufacturing operation. Nevertheless, he knew that he and his staff were up to the challenge.

The sales force was entirely behind the color idea. Since the other competitive parameters of their business—price, delivery, quality, service, and technology—were closely followed by everyone in the business, this color-option strategy gave them one more piece of selling ammunition. The manufacturing and finance issues were not their concern.

Until now, Soft Seat merely had to secure the customer order and ship from its finished-goods inventory. It followed a classic make-to-stock manufacturing strategy, typical of businesses in which either (1) the competitive environment requires rapid order fulfillment, or (2) simple, low-priced products prevail.

Manufacturers of office supplies, tire companies, and small appliances fit this description. For example, when a customer wants a box of 10 memory sticks, he or she wants them now, not two weeks from now. He or she will not submit an order to the manufacturer to begin production.

The make-to-stock (MTS) manufacturing strategy works well in the environment just cited, but if a company adopts a new go-to-market strategy—as Soft Seat has—then a new manufacturing strategy logically follows.[1] Here we describe a make-to-order strategy.

Recall from Chapter 6 that a make-to-order strategy occupies a middle position between the extremes of make-to-stock and design-to-order or engineer-to-order strategies. A make-to-order product is one that is finished after receipt of a customer order.

In a make-to-order strategy, *some* material may be ordered before receipt of the customer order and *some* materials and/or parts of the product may be produced before

---

[1] Over the past 30 to 40 to 50 years, the business strategy of competing on the basis of rapid introduction of new and varied products has gained many adherents. Furniture companies have introduced configurable furniture: Dell Computers with its "We sell options and will configure them for the customer at no charge" and Apple with its configurable iPhones and iMac computers, to name a few. Business scholars have written extensively on the competitive advantages to be gained by this planning strategy; however, *only a few focused on the supply chain manufacturing along with the master planning and scheduling issues that underlie the use of this planning bill strategy and, in fact, make it possible.*

receipt of a customer order. Within a pure MTO product strategy, the product is designed, but *no* manufacturing occurs until a customer order is received. Highly customized products are generally made in this fashion.

Package-to-order (PTO), finish-to-order (FTO), kit-to-order (KTO), and assemble-to-order (ATO) are variants of this strategy. Here, the company may build product through all but the finishing stage(s), which then is triggered by a customer order.

Anatomy of a Planning Bill

Figure 8.6 shows a *planning bill* for the new Soft Seat chair product family. Here, four different color options are available. (Note: Colors are coded using a significant item number scheme in the form of a suffix. For example, the basic conference center chair is

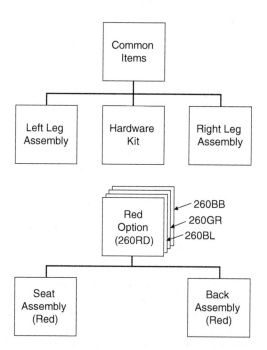

Figure 8.6   Soft Seat Planning Bill for Options and Common Items

model 260; the suffix, BL, indicates black; RD indicates red; GR indicates green; and BB indicates blue.)

Using the make-to-stock manufacturing strategy for the conference center chair product family, all four colored conference center chairs would be built and held as finished goods pending the receipt of customer orders. Looking at the chair one level down (Figure 8.7), we see that the following items are needed: a seat assembly, a back splat assembly, a left leg assembly, a hardware kit, and a right leg assembly. Notice that neither the hardware kit nor the leg assemblies has a color designation. This means that these are common to all chairs, regardless of color, and are *not* unique items within the conference center chair product family.

Time Phasing

At this point we need to *time phase* the conference center chair product family bill-of-material, as shown in Figure 8.7. In a make-to-stock environment, chairs would be stocked at the *zero* timeline. In switching to a make-to-order or assemble-to-order strategy, however, time phasing would become critical, since completed chairs would no longer be stocked. Instead, we may stock seat assemblies (color-sensitive), back splat assemblies (color-sensitive), hardware kits (common), right leg assemblies (common), and left leg assemblies (common).

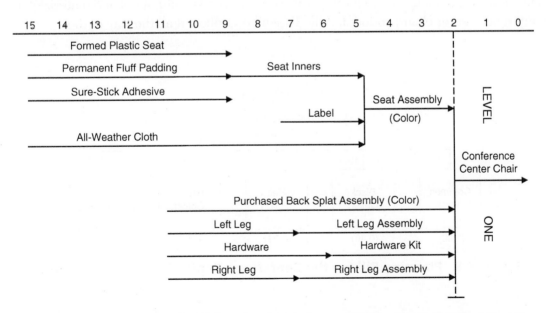

Figure 8.7 Time-Phased Bill for the Conference Center Chair Product Family

The ability and decision to do this depend on where the company intends to *meet its customers*. The capacity to configure these stocked items into customer-defined requirements would also be required within the defined time period. For illustration purposes, let's assume we plan to *meet the customer* with the defined modules, which means that we would need two periods to complete the product once the customer order is placed.

To deploy to an assemble-to-order or finish-to-order strategy, bills-of-material need to be structured for the common components as well as for each offered option. This means that the red option bill will contain a red seat assembly and a red back splat assembly. The black option will likewise contain a black seat assembly and a black back splat assembly.

Figures 8.6 on page 266 and 8.8 below show the planning bills for the entire conference center chair family. The common items planning bill is shown at the top of Figure 8.6, while the lower portion of the figure contains the unique items: red option, black option, and so forth. This bill restructuring makes it possible to greatly reduce the number of bills in the data file.

With this done, another pseudo bill is created for the conference center chair family itself (Figure 8.8). In this planning bill the company structures the common items plus the unique options that it desires to plan. By so doing, the company's master planner and/or master scheduler have made it possible to tie the output of the integrated business planning or sales and operations planning process to the lowest component and material in the conference center chair product family. To see how, follow it all the way to the bottom.

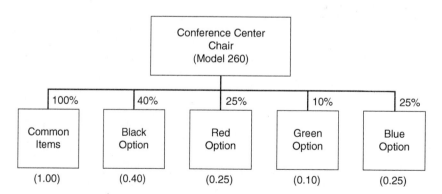

Figure 8.8   Planning Bill for the Conference Center Chair Product Family

The conference center chair calls out the red option, which calls out the red seat assembly, which calls out the seat inners (see Figure 8.7 on page 267), which call out the formed plastic seat, permanent fluff padding, and sure-stick adhesive. The conference center chair also calls out the common items, which call out the left and right leg assemblies, which call out the left and right legs as well as the hardware kit, which call out the hardware.

The key concept here is that the forecasting done during the integrated business planning or sales and operations planning process is done at the product family level (conference center chairs) and the top-level planning bill is also structured at the generic chair level. This provides the vital link needed to tie aggregate planning to detail planning.

During the master planning and scheduling process, the numbers created during the IBP or S&OP process are exploded through the planning bill. Since every conference center chair requires a set of common items, the percentage attached to the common items kit is 100 (or 1.0). Now, according to sales and marketing, every time a conference center chair is demanded, there is a 40 percent chance that it will be black. If you planned to sell 1,000 conference center chairs, you would anticipate needing 1,000 sets of common items (1,000 × 1.0), 400 black seat assemblies (1,000 × 0.4), and 400 black back splat assemblies (1,000 × 0.4).

The other 600 conference center chairs would require red, blue, and green options. In this way the MPS software using planning bill techniques can calculate the expected mix demand at the next-lower level, which is where master planning and scheduling would take place.

What we have done in this example is create *pseudo* (*artificial bills used for planning purposes only*) *bills-of-material*: one for the common items and one for *each* of the unique options. When a customer orders a conference center chair, that customer will indicate a color preference. If the order is for three red conference center chairs, then the company needs to configure a customer order comprised from three sets of red options and three sets of common items.

Knowing that, the company will structure the five pseudo bills into a conference center chair product family (Figure 8.8). The purpose is to tie all the option bills to the integrated business planning or sales and operations planning process output—that is, to the level where the executive management team creates the product family plans that includes the conference center chair family.

The conference center chair family's pseudo bill is also known as a *super bill* or the top-level planning bill. The master planner and/or master scheduler can take the integrated business planning/sales and operations planning output and explode it through the planning bill by time period to determine the expected demand at the MPS mix level (the demand for different color options).

Demand for the common items is determined at the same time. With that demand determined, a master plan and/or master schedule can be created at the common items and option levels, and that master plan and/or master schedule data can be passed down to lower levels via material requirements planning logic (as stated in earlier chapters, there are several techniques that can be used to plan materials in order to support the master plan and/or master schedule, material requirements planning being one of those techniques).

Another way to structure a planning bill is to have the unique items (options) be the components (ingredients) of the common items. This structure is displayed in Figure 8.9 since the common items and the product family are the same or a one-for-one relationship exists. (Common items are planned at 100 percent of the product family.) There is really no need to plan and maintain both.

By doing this, the master scheduler (or supply manager) is saved the effort of maintaining master plans and/or master schedules for both the product family and common items. However, structuring the planning bill this way can cause some problems when *abnormal demand* is introduced into the process (see Chapters 10 and 17).

Deciding how to structure the planning bill for products using a make-to-order, kit-to-order, or package-to-order manufacturing strategy is a matter of choice. Both techniques noted earlier work well in environments when *abnormal demand* is not present.

The opposite is true when *abnormal demand* is present, especially if such demand is significant. An example of *abnormal demand* is discussed in Chapter 10. For now, we need to understand that there are two possible structuring methods.

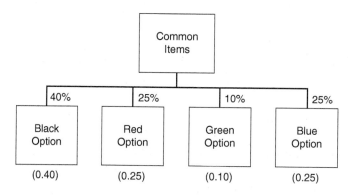

Figure 8.9 Planning Bill with Unique Options Structured into Common Items

Creating Demand at the Master Planning and Scheduling Level

The next step is to calculate demand for the various options. Here our novice master planner and/or master scheduler (who has since been educated on make-to-order scheduling techniques and is now a journeyman), must go back to marketing and sales with some questions. But the questions will now be quite different. Instead of asking how many of a particular configuration (such as red, green, blue, or black chairs) will be sold in future periods, the first question is: "How many conference center chairs are anticipated to be needed to satisfy anticipated demand in August or the first week of August, regardless of color?"

The answer has been determined in the integrated business planning or sales and operations planning management business review (it all started in the demand review or possibly earlier in the new product review). The second question is: "What are the probabilities that conference center chair sales will be red, green, blue, or black?"

To determine the expected option mix demand, the master planner and/or master scheduler takes the estimate for August conference center chair demand (all color options) and explodes it through the planning bill using the probability percentages to determine the expected demand for each option. Thus, if 1,000 conference center chairs are expected to be needed in August, and if the red option has a 25 percent probability, then 250 sets of red option items will be required to satisfy the product family's August demand plan of 1,000 units. With this information the master planner and/or master scheduler is in a position to put together the master plan and/or master schedule for the common items and the various color options, which is a topic covered in the next chapter ("Two-Level Master Planning and Scheduling Coupled with Other Advanced Techniques").

RESTRUCTURING COMPANY BILLS INTO PLANNING BILLS
A CASE STUDY

Dynoline is a major manufacturer of turbine engines used to drive electrical generators in industry and in smaller public utility plants. The company manufactures a variety of engines, each of which can be ordered with one of three different fuel systems: natural gas, liquid, and dual fuel. Because customer preferences for fuel systems are largely dictated by prevailing market prices for different fuels, Dynoline's marketing department has never been successful in forecasting the fuel options ordered by customers. The result is that the company operates on a strictly make-to-order basis, starting the build process once it has the order with the specifications, including the fuel system specification.

The company maintains three different bills-of-material for the fuel system on each engine. It also has a cumulative lead time (CLT) of eight months to complete each engine—from start to ship date. Several years ago, faced with a tougher competitive environment, Dynoline sought a competitive edge in time-to-delivery. If it could deliver a complete turbine engine with the specific product features required by the customer in less time than competing producers, Dynoline would win more business. Thus, reducing lead time was a mandated improvement.

Further, Dynoline's chief executive officer announced that the goal would be to reduce lead time to the point that the customer could have any of the company's turbine engines within three months of placing an order. The CEO also made it clear that solutions to this time compression challenge would have to be made within four weeks.

Walt Webber was vice president of manufacturing for Dynoline. Over lunch, he and the master supply scheduler, Virginia Hall, discussed the problem of slicing five months from their lead times. "Marketing and sales would say that the way to handle this would be to build an inventory of engines with each fuel system," Virginia joked.

"Sure," said Walt, "the finance department would love to keep an inventory of a dozen or so $250,000 engines. They could take the carrying costs out of the soft drink machine fund!"

"Or out of your salary, Walt," she quipped. "I suggest that we take a look at our time-phased bills-of-material as a first step," Virginia offered. "This is probably the best place to start looking for ways to cut lead times. The time-phased bills show us at a glance the time-line for each engine and the cumulative lead times for each component."

Walt agreed, and they went to his office to examine the various products' BOMs (the time-phased versions). For simplicity, they started with the turbine engine with a gas-fuel system, which appears in Figure 8.10 on page 273.

It was clear from this time-phased bill-of-material that the cumulative lead time (the total elapsed time required to acquire or build the entire gas-fuel engine from start to finish) was eight months. Walt took a pencil and drew a dashed line vertically through the time-phased bill-of-material at month 3. "This is it," he said. "We have to be able to ship product in three months from this point. This shows us what we need in stock in order to compress the lead time by five months. So, how can we restructure our engineering bills into planning bills that will allow us to effectively plan these stocked options?" (Authors' note: Of course, another alternative is to reduce lead time for the items within the three-month window.)

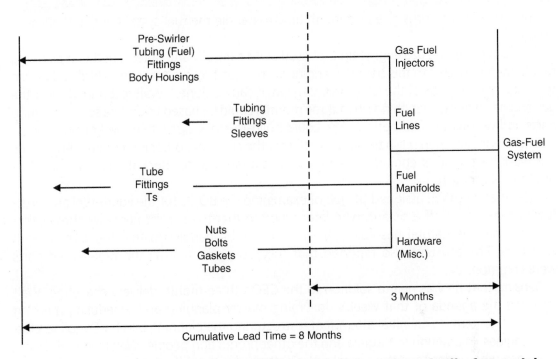

Figure 8.10 Dynoline Gas-Fuel Turbine Engine Time-Phased Bill-of-Material

Both Virginia and Walt knew that they had various options for reducing the cumulative lead time. The most drastic of these was to redesign Dynoline turbine engines to have fewer parts, simpler assembly procedures, and so on, so that they could be built from start to finish in just three months. This was *design for manufacturability (DFM)*, a process used by many companies to improve their products and their lead times. In the long run, this was probably the best solution, but not one that could be accomplished within the four weeks mandated by the CEO.

Another option would be to systematically work on process improvements to reduce the build or order times for a variety of operations. By squeezing these into shorter lead times, the overall lead time for the completed product could be reduced. But there was another way.

"The most obvious way to reduce our lead time," Walt remarked, "without stocking completely built engines, is to work back through the time-phased bills-of-material from expected ship date to three months before expected ship date. Assuming that we cannot compress the lead times for all activities in these three months, we must have everything else in stock and ready to go just as soon as the customer order arrives."

"But will three months give us enough time to handle the fuel-system option?" Virginia asked.

They examined the gas engine time-phased BOM carefully and determined that all of the requirements specific to this being an engine with a gas-fuel system were addressed within the final three months of the CLT. "Yes, Virginia, it can be done," Walt responded. "For the gas engine, at least, everything up to three months could be based upon one set of common parts and various stocked options. We could build-to-stock up to that level of uniqueness and commonality, then finish the engine off after the customer order is received." But would this work for the other engines? The only way to know was to check the time-phased bill-of-material for each.

Later that day, Walt assigned the job of examining the BOMs for the liquid-fuel and dual-fuel systems to a staff assistant, who later reported that the requirements for these other systems, like the natural gas–fuel system, could all be handled within the three-month lead time. The assistant also reported that fully 90 percent of all the fuel-related parts were common.

Sensing that he was near a solution to the CEO's three-month delivery challenge, Walt changed the agenda of that week's upcoming master planning and scheduling meeting from routine items to an initial attempt at restructuring the planning bills for Dynoline's turbine engines. In addition to Virginia and the other production people, Walt invited the sales manager, who understood the typical order patterns for the different fuel-system options.

As the review meeting came to order, Walt's assistant rolled in a whiteboard on which a graphic representation of a fuel system, showing its common and unique parts, had already been sketched out (Figure 8.10 on previous page). Walt explained to the assembled group that their job that morning would be to attempt to cut the time to delivery by sorting out what was common to each of the three engine fuel systems, what was unique to each, and what had to be stocked if the company had only three months to build the product after receipt of a customer order.

"Today we are going to examine the bills-of-material for each of our turbine-engine fuel systems," he explained, "and sort out what is common and what is unique up to a point three months prior to the completion time for a turbine engine. We will go through the BOMs for each of the different fuel systems in turn, and Virginia will lead the discussion of the first one."

Virginia Hall walked up to the front of the room and taped five cards to the wall, as shown in Figure 8.11 on page 275. The words *fuel system, common parts, unique gas, unique liquid,* and *unique dual* were boldly lettered on the cards.

"To get things started, I thought we could *deconstruct* our engine by identifying which of its many parts are common and which are unique. You have the BOMs for the natural

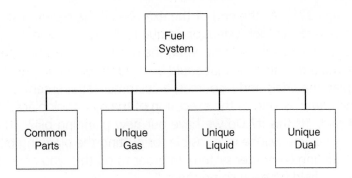

Figure 8.11   Product Family Fuel System

gas-, liquid-, and dual-fuel systems in front of you." (Figure 8.12 is a cut-down version of the product.)

"Let me begin by saying that Level 0 is our finished gas-fuel turbine engine. Level 1 represents all of those items that are required to make one level 0 product, and level 2 represents all of those items required to make one level 1 item. Is everyone with me?" All nodded in agreement.

Over the course of the next 120 minutes, Virginia and other attendees of the review meeting went through the entire bills-of-material for the fuel systems; each part was identified on a *Post-it Note* by item number, description, unit of measure, whether it was a make or buy item, and by lead time, and stuck under one of the five cards taped to the wall

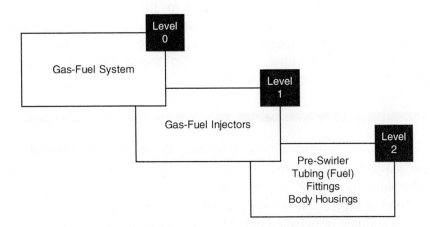

Figure 8.12   Indented Bill for Gas Turbine Engine

(Figure 8.11 on page 275). At the end of the exercise all the required stocked items were identified as common to the fuel system or unique to the gas-, liquid-, or dual-fuel system.

As the group sat back to admire their work, the group knew that it had restructured the engineering bills into a planning bill that could be used for planning purposes. By using this planning bill to plan materials and resources, a customer requirement could be met in the three-month time frame as long as the execution of the plan took place.

"Okay," Walt said, "Is this it? Do we have our new planning bill?" The group nodded its approval. "Virginia, you will be responsible for putting the planning bill into the master planning and scheduling computer system. In order to do this, you need to know what to put into the quantity field for each component."

Walt looked over at the sales manager. "Here's where you come in, Al. We need to know the probabilities of the gas, liquid, and dual systems to be ordered. We will take your probabilities, convert them to decimals [50 percent equals 0.5], and enter the results into the quantity field on the planning bill. By doing this we will be able to take the output of the integrated business planning/sales and operations planning process and determine the expected option requirements. Of course, the common parts are always required and will carry a 100 percent probability [or a quantity of 1.0]. Can you get us those numbers?"

The sales manager indicated that he had done his homework and knew the probabilities or what he called his opening bid (Al indicated that he believed that the probabilities would improve as time goes on and sales worked more with the planning bill). He told the group that he used a combination of order history and future-order forecasts. The numbers were given to Virginia so that she could create the planning bills as directed.

The last thing the group did was to identify who in the organization was going to be responsible for the planning bill database. It was decided that the master planning and scheduling would be responsible and accountable for the planning bill structure (ensuring compatibility with engineering design and proper maintenance of the planning bill), and sales and marketing would be responsible and accountable for the quantities that contained the probability numbers. At this time, the members of the group patted one another on the back and gave compliments for a job well done.

In complex environments that deploy make-to-order manufacturing strategies, the creation and use of planning bills is an effective way to plan and control materials and capacities. Once the planning bills are in place, the master planning and scheduling system can use the structures and probabilities to generate option forecasts for each master planned and/or master scheduled item called out. This logic, plus the actual creation of the master plan and/or master schedule, is the topic covered in the next chapter.

Two-Level Master Planning and Scheduling Coupled with Other Advanced Techniques

Without data, you are just another person with an opinion.

The previous chapter introduced the conference center chair product family of the Soft Seat Corporation, posing a key question: For every chair sold, how many are anticipated to be sold with the black option? Red option? Black-and-red option? The answers to these questions are necessary to complete the planning process, which in turn is essential to creating a master plan and/or master schedule. Before continuing our discussion of master planning, master scheduling, and the forecasting process, another component of the master planning and scheduling process must be examined—the *backlog*, sometimes referred to as the *order book* curve.

The Backlog Curve

Backlog is defined as customer orders booked but not shipped. This definition does not say that the customer orders are past due, which would be referred to as *back orders*; many, and sometimes all, customer orders in the backlog curve (order book)—are *expected* to ship in the future. The backlog curve is a profile of those booked customer orders but not shipped orders in the framework of the company's anticipated demand planning. Virtually all companies that use a make-to-order (MTO) and/or design/engineer-to-order (ETO) manufacturing strategy have customer order backlogs, and each must understand the nature and shape of that backlog in planning and scheduling current and future production.

Figure 9.1 is a conceptualized view of the customer order backlog curve. In the earliest time periods of the planning horizon (the leftmost extreme) the demand pipeline is filled with booked but unshipped customer orders. These customer orders may be demands where production has yet to begin work, others in some stage of work-in-process, and still others ready to be crated for shipment.

The opposite extreme (the rightmost portion of the planning horizon) generally contains no customer orders; the only demand here is *forecasted* or *anticipated* customer orders. Between these two extremes are a number of planning time periods containing both firm (booked) and forecasted customer orders.

Master planners and schedulers segment the backlog curve into zones that define the status of orders in each zone. These zones are referred to as the *sold-out zone*, in which all expected demand is backed by an actual customer order; the *partially sold-out zone*, in which the demand is supported by a combination of actual customer orders and the remainder, which is supported strictly by a demand forecast of anticipated customer

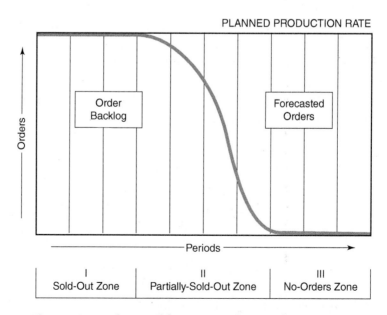

Figure 9.1 The Backlog Curve by Product Family

orders; and the *no-orders zone*, which extends beyond the customer order backlog, in which all production, material planning, and capacity planning is geared to forecasted sales (whereas in the first two zones, some or all production, material planning, and capacity planning is geared to satisfy firm customer or stocked orders).

To understand how master planners and schedulers deal with the customer order backlog curve, we return to the Soft Seat Corporation where, following the integrated business planning (IBP) or sales and operations planning (S&OP) monthly review, executive management has approved a product demand plan and corresponding production rate (assuming a make-to-order product) of 40 conference center chairs per month. (Remember that since this is a make-to-order product example, deliveries are promised into the future after the customer order is booked.)

Figure 9.2 shows a two-month demand plan and production rate of 40 chairs per month (which assumes four periods in each month), and these have been broken down into 20 chairs in every other time period.

Thus, product demand plan and the corresponding production rate are set at 20 units in time periods 2, 4, 6, and 8, for a total of 80 units for the two-month or eight-week horizon. The demand rate is the same as the production rate because Soft Seat Corporation plans the conference chair line as a make-to-order product—that is, the production rate equals the expected shipment rate, which is keyed to the customers' expected product receipt minus transportation time.

It is easy to see from Figure 9.2 that Soft Seat's backlog curve has the three zones just mentioned. In time period 2 it has customer orders equaling its current production rate of 20 chairs every two periods. This, then, is the *sold-out zone* in which there are zero chairs available-to-sell or available-to-promise (ATP).

	Past Due	1	2	3	4	5	6	7	8
Demand Plan			20		20		20		20
Production Rate			20		20		20		20
Actual Demand			20		16		8		0
Available-to-Promise (ATP)	0	0			4		12		20
		0		0	4	4	16	16	36

Figure 9.2   Backlog for the Conference Center Chair Product Family

However, time period 4 contains customer orders for only 16 chairs that have consumed 16 of the 20 units scheduled to be sold and built by production, leaving four chairs available-to-promise to any customer who happens to call. Available-to-promise (ATP) increases to 12 chairs in time period 6 and to 20 chairs in time period 8 as fewer customer orders are booked relative to the planned production rate. Notice that in the ATP line, the top set of numbers is the number available-to-promise for that particular time period (as in time period 6, where 20 chairs are expected to be produced less 8 chairs of actual demand, leaving 12 chairs available-to-promise to future customers orders). The bottom set of numbers is the *cumulative* ATP—that is, the total number of chairs available-to-promise, which is the ATP in that time period *plus* all the previous ATP quantities, which are units or chairs still unsold.

Figure 9.3 displays the current customer order backlog curve for the Soft Seat conference center chair and the position of its various planning and scheduling zones. Time periods 1 through 3 are *sold out*; time periods 4 through 7 are *partially sold out*; and time period 8 is in the zone containing *no customer orders*. The shape of the backlog curve and duration of the planning and scheduling zones will differ for each company and industry.

For products that use a design/engineer-to-order manufacturing strategy, the reader might expect the *sold-out zone* to be quite lengthy, stretching far out into the future. For products that are strictly make-to-stock, the sold-out zone may be very short.

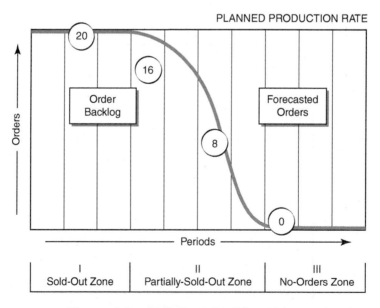

Figure 9.3 Soft Seat Backlog Curve

For products that are finished-to-order or assembled-to-order, the sold-out zone generally is somewhere between the lengthy sold-out zone for products designed/engineered-to-order and the shorter sold-out zone for products made-to-stock.

Planning and Scheduling the Backlog Curve Zones

From the perspective of master planning and scheduling in the package-to-order, kit-to-order, finish-to-order, assemble-to-order, and make-to-order environments, the *sold-out zone* is relatively easy to deal with—the customer requirements and the specifications for each in the form of customer orders are already in hand. Therefore, in the *sold-out zone,* the master (supply) plan and/or master (supply) schedule for any pseudo items (see Chapter 8) should be made to equal the customer orders (demand). No forecasting required.

Furthermore, the *no orders zone* is likewise easy for the master planner and/or master scheduler to plan out. With no customer orders in hand, sales and marketing plans (forecasted demand) provide the guidance. And barring products with short lead times, time is on the side of the master planner and/or master scheduler; one would expect the accuracy of the anticipated demand to improve as time passes and forecasted sales are turned into customer orders.

It is generally the middle area—the *partially sold-out zone*—that can give master planners and/or master schedulers fits. Here, time is slipping away, and there is still forecasted demand for which neither quantities nor configuration specifications have been established. As discussion of the configure-to-order environment continues, keep this thought in mind.

Identifying Demand

Since the demand and production rates for product families over the planning horizon have been determined during the integrated business planning or sales and operations process, the next step is to determine the demand for each master planned and/or master scheduled grouping or item—for example, the demand for every grouping (like-product subfamily) of items that goes into the conference center chair or every detailed item that goes into the conference center chair family. This is done by taking the integrated business planning or sales and operations planning output and converting it into some defined groupings and/or discrete item numbers, quantities, and due dates (*grouping might be sounding like a good thought at this time—read on*).

In the previous chapter we created a series of planning bills that identified common items along with red, blue, green, and black options. In order to simplify the example, this chapter will deal with only two of those option choices, red and black, each of which has a 50 percent probability of sale. For the sake of discussion, sales and marketing have pulled the green, blue, and mixed options from the company's offerings.

The focus in this section will be on the red option, which contains a red seat assembly and a red back splat assembly. The red option bill has already been described as a pseudo bill or artificial bill used only for planning in that manufacturing cannot create a finished conference center chair from a red seat assembly and back splat assembly; only when these are united with a set of common items does a red conference center chair become a real, shippable product. But remember, *even though true pseudo items cannot be built, they can be master planned and scheduled.*

Figure 9.4 on page 283 presents the MPS matrix for the red option components. (Note the item forecast line.) If the red option was a real item (remember, it's a pseudo or artificial item) and if there was any independent demand for the red option, it would show up on this line. But since this item has been identified as a pseudo item (which means it can't be built), there can be no service demand in our example. If, for some reason, the seat and back are sold as a kit, independent demand could then appear.

The Actual Demand Line

When the planning bill for the conference center chair product family was set up, the red option was given a probability of 50 percent—that is, if 20 units were planned to be sold and then committed, Soft Seat expects 10 units of those 20 sold units to be red conference center chairs. Again, when the 20 conference center chairs were sold and promised in time period 2 (of course, the final configuration and transportation lead times would need to be added to the time period 2 due date to determine the customer expected delivery date), the company would have expected 10 units to be red.

However, in the case of time period 2, 12 of the 20 conference center chairs of *actual* demand for the chair family (Figure 9.4) turned out to be red chairs requiring the red option (the example displays when option items are required to be delivered to the finishing or final configuration line). In time period 4, a total of 16 chairs were sold. Here, Soft

	Past Due	1	2	3	4	5	6	7	8
Item Forecast		0	0	0	0	0	0	0	0
Option Forecast			0		2		6		10
Actual Demand			12		7		5		0
Total Demand			12		9		11		10
Projected Available Balance	0	0	0	0	2	2	2	2	2
Available-to-Promise			0		4		6		10
		0	0	0	4	4	10	10	20
Master Schedule			12		11		11		10

Figure 9.4   MPS Matrix, Red Option Items (50 percent probability)

Scat would have expected 8 chairs to be red, but out of the 16 sold, only 7 were for red conference center chairs.

While the predicted sales were wrong, they were nevertheless close; many companies, in fact, would be glad to come this close to the product mix forecast. In time period 6, 8 conference center chairs were sold, of which 5 were red, as shown in the *actual demand* line in time period 6 of Figure 9.4. Again, the *actual demand* did not match the expected demand, but the forecaster was *not* far from the mark. Since *no* customer or stock/distribution center orders are committed for time period 8, the *actual demand* for the red option in time period 8 is zero.

The Option Forecast Line

Now that the master planner and/or master scheduler knows the expected service demand (zero has been forecasted in this example) and the actual demand supported by firm customer orders, the piece of the total demand picture that remains unknown is the option forecast (sometimes referred to as the production forecast)—how many red conference center chair orders are still anticipated to be received over the eight-period planning horizon in this chapter's example? To answer this question, we need to revisit the customer order backlog curve and the conference center chair product family data contained in Figure 9.2 (see page 279).

The Sold-Out Zone (Periods 1 Through 3 in Example)

The data in the matrix tells the master planner and/or master scheduler a good deal about the planned and scheduled group of items or an item itself. Time period 2 is in the *sold-out zone*. The master planner and/or master scheduler knows that 12 red options are required in this time period (see actual demand line, period 2, Figure 9.4 on page 283). The master planner and/or master scheduler also knows that no red options are required in time period 2 to support expected service demand (see forecast line, time period 2, Figure 9.4).

So, the only open question is: How many additional red options will be required in time period 2 to support any additional expected sales? The answer is straightforward: *zero*! Since time period 2 is in the sold-out zone, the master planner and/or master scheduler should not expect sales to book any additional customer orders requiring a time period 2 availability (remember, configuration and transportation lead times must be added to the availability due date to determine the expected customer delivery date). Now, can the reader ever imagine telling sales that they cannot commit any deliveries until time period 4 (the first period in which product is available-to-promise)? But that's exactly what must be done—to a point.

This is a very key point in our discussion of two-level (multilevel) master planning and scheduling. When executive management determines a production rate for products using a make-to-order manufacturing strategy, it is in a sense communicating to the master planner and/or master scheduler how many sets of common items will be required, since there is a one-for-one relationship between a product family and common items.

If the production rate for the conference center chair family is 20 units in time period 2 and all 20 units have customer orders attached, there are no more common items available in time period 2 to satisfy additional orders. Therefore, any booked customer order (or stocked order for that matter) that promises a time period 2 availability may be (and probably is) a *bad promise* unless something can be done to reschedule the already booked and promised demand or to change the master plan and/or master schedule at this late date.

Upon hearing that the company cannot take any more orders for delivery in time period 2 over the 20 product orders already authorized and accepted, sales may suggest that the master planner and/or master scheduler get 22 or 24 sets of common items—*a few extra just in case*. If demand (sales) wants supply to secure more than 20 sets of common items, it must either get the participants in the integrated business planning (IBP) or sales and operations planning (S&OP) process to agree upon a demand rate that translates into a higher production rate, or else have them authorize the extra sets of common items. The master planner and/or master scheduler will then make preparations to have those extra sets of common items ready to satisfy customer demand as booked by sales.

However, if the reader thinks about it, there is little value in the master planner and/or master scheduler hedging any bets or second-guessing the need for common items. *Common items are not the planning problem when using the make-to-order manufacturing strategy; the planning problem is the unique items (red and black option items).*

A company need not put an absolute freeze on customer orders. It may be good business sense to take and commit to an availability and/or delivery inside the sold-out zone. However, there are no free lunches here, and sales must be asked, and must answer to, which currently booked customer order or orders scheduled for time period 2 are to be shipped later. The answer to this question establishes customer order priorities and tells the master planner and/or master scheduler how to reschedule availability and delivery dates.

At this point the master planner and/or master scheduler knows that the expected demand for the option in question is the sum of the top three lines in the MPS matrix—the item forecast (independent demand), the option forecast (dependent demand), and actual demand (customer orders). Thus, in time period 2, the total demand is for 12 red options, since there is *no* service demand, *no* option forecast, and *only* 12 committed to customers.

The Partially-Sold-Out Zone (Periods 4 Through 7 in Example) and the No Orders Zone (Period 8 in Example and Beyond in the Real World)

In the *partially-sold-out zone*, total expected demand is not so easily identified. Here, some firm customer orders are in hand and others are anticipated by the forecast. The item forecast line states that *no* service demand is expected, while the actual demand is for seven red options in time period 4 and five red options in time period 6 (obtained through a customer service or order-entry process). The remaining question is: How many additional red options should be forecasted to satisfy anticipated demand in time period 4 and time period 6? Here the master planner and/or master scheduler is faced with a range of alternatives. Period 4 is analyzed first:

1. *No conference center chairs requiring the red option.* Even though red is a 50 percent option, the four chairs remaining to be sold in time period 4 may *not* be red. Perhaps red has simply gone out of fashion. Or a sales representative has just landed an order for four black chairs and committed them to a period 4 availability and future delivery. The right answer in this case is zero.

2. *One conference center chair requiring the red option.* Sales of 40 conference center chairs are anticipated for each month (time periods 1 through 4 and time periods 5 through 8) with 20 being red (using the 50 percent probability factor). Actual demand for red chairs during the first month (time periods 1 through 4) indicates that 19 red chairs have been sold to date and scheduled for delivery (12 to be available for chair configuration in time periods 2 and 7 to be available for configuration in time period 4).

   Therefore, current sales information combined with historical knowledge make it plausible that only one additional red chair will be sold and scheduled to be available during the month. This logic assumes that the events that have already occurred in the month will have an impact on events yet to occur. In other words, over a month, the predicted sale of conference center chairs will equal the probability (initially) chosen, that of 50 percent.

3. *Two conference center chairs requiring the red option.* A case can also be made that two of the four conference center chairs (50 percent probability) still left to promise in period 4 will be for the red option. The available-to-promise in time period 4 at the conference center chair level is four chairs. The important point here is that the master planner and/or master scheduler has four sets of common items available-to-promise in that time period. To build a conference center chair, the company needs a set of common items as well as the black or red option items. Therefore, the company in this example expects a demand for only four more chairs in time period 4.

   If the red option has a 50 percent probability, the option forecast for that red option in time period 4 is two additional chairs. This case proceeds from the notion that the future probability for conference center chair sale options is *independent* from the actual sales history in periods 1, 2, and 3—just as the probability of a coin's turning up as heads is 50 percent, even though previous coin flips may have all been heads or all tails.

4. *Three conference center chairs requiring the red option.* According to the established demand and production rate for the conference center chair family, 20 chairs are anticipated to be promised to be available to go into the configuration process in time period 4. Since the red option is a 50 percent option, we might have expected that 10 of the promised chairs (50 percent of the aggregate 20) for the time period would require the red option. A review of the actual demand in time period 4 for the red option shows that seven chairs have already been committed, leaving three out of the next four conference center chair customer orders to require this option. This

logic assumes that the previous events in the customer order booking cycle affect future events.

5. *Four conference center chairs requiring the red option.* Even though red is a 50 percent option, the four chairs remaining to be sold in time period 4 may be all red. Perhaps red is a *new hot color.* Or a sales representative just landed an order for four red chairs and committed them to a time period 4 availability to be sent to the configuration process. The right answer in this case is four.

Master planning and scheduling (MPS) systems generally support one, two, or three of the types of logic just represented—specifically, option forecasts in examples 2, 3, and 4. In example 2, the master planning and scheduling system takes the aggregate production rate for a make-to-order product for a group of time periods and explodes it through the planning bill; it then subtracts the actual demand for those time periods to determine the option forecast. In example 3, the master planning and scheduling system takes the available-to-promise value and explodes it through the planning bill, multiplying ATP by the probability associated with the option in question. In example 4, the master planning and scheduling system takes the planned production (MTO) or demand (MTS) rate for the time period and explodes it through the planning bill; it then subtracts the actual demand for that time period to determine the option forecast.

The ATP-driven explosion through the planning bill approach is probably the most commonly used, and for that reason is the basis for the remaining examples used in this book. Applying this logic, the forecast in time period 4 for the red option is identified as two conference center chairs. With this information, the master planner and/or master scheduler knows that nine is the total expected demand for the red option in time period 4—two to support the option forecast, and seven to support actual demand.

Continuing the use of the ATP explosion logic, look at time period 6, where 12 more conference center chairs are available-to-promise. If that ATP is exploded through the planning bill, a demand for six red options are identified in time period 6. The same logic can be applied in time period 8 (the no orders zone), where 20 conference center chairs are available-to-promise. Exploding that quantity through the planning bill results in a red option forecast of 10 conference center chairs.

Regardless of the method chosen, the reader should check the company's demand management, supply chain management, and master planning and scheduling software to determine alternatives. The total demand for each of the master planned and/or master scheduled options must be determined before the master plan and/or master schedule that satisfies the anticipated demand and stays within the approved supply plan constraints can be created.

Creating the Master Plan and/or Master Schedule for Products Using a Make-to-Order Manufacturing Strategy

A make-to-order product is one made *after* receipt of a customer order. Frequently, long-lead-time components are planned prior to receipt of an order as a means of reducing customer delivery time. In cases in which options or other intermediates are stocked prior to customer order receipt, the terms *assemble-to-order*, *finish-to-order*, *kit-to-order*, or *package-to-order* are commonly used.

The master planner and/or master scheduler working with products in the make-to-order environment needs to understand the shape of the company's backlog curve and which time periods are *sold out*, *partially sold out*, or *void of booked orders*. The following sections analyze each of these *zones* in terms of the conference center chair example used in this chapter.

The Sold-Out Zone

The first demand appears in time period 2—when 12 red options are expected to be available and delivered to the finishing (configuration) process (refer to Figure 9.4 on page 283). Here the question becomes, How many red options should be currently scheduled to be available in period 2? This question suggests three others:

1. What is the very *least* that should be scheduled?

2. What is the very *most* that should be scheduled?

3. What number will *most likely* satisfy demand?

The answer to the first question (the least) for time period 2 is 12 because 12 conference center chairs are already booked and promised. If less than 12 are planned and scheduled, a risk of missing a customer promise in time period 2 is not only possible, but probable.

The answer to the next question—the *most* that should be scheduled—is, again, 12. This is the sold-out zone, and there are *no* more common items to promise. The reason the ATP at the conference center chair product family level is zero is that all 20 sets of common items are committed—12 required for red chairs and the other 8 required for black chairs. *Theoretically, this is fine!*

However, a master planner or master scheduler might argue, "But if sales has an oppor-tunity to sell an additional conference center chair and commit it to be available to enter the configuration process in time period 2, can I really tell them *not* to take the order? After all, we're not in the business of turning away orders." No one wants to lose orders but consider the risk of committing that additional unit (that is not available) to be sent to configuration and/or finishing in time period 2. The old saying, *you can't build something out of nothing,* might apply here.

Based on the integrated business planning (IBP) or sales and operations planning (S&OP) process, executive management has agreed that 20 conference center chairs should be promised to be available for delivery to the configuration and/or finishing process in time period 2. This decision has been made in consideration of capacities, materials, capital, marketplace presence, quality, and competition. Therefore, the master planner and/or master scheduler has planned to have 20 sets of common items. Since every conference center chair needs a set of common items, selling more conference center chairs than there are common items is making a *bad* promise.

The sales force could, however, book and commit an additional customer order in the sold-out zone and shift a set of common items from, say, a customer who ordered a black conference center chair to a customer who ordered a red one. Or sales could request the shifting of the common items from one customer order to another customer order, both for the same-colored option. In either case, the items in the unique options must be available before the shift can take place. But the fact that such a manipulation is possible is no basis for planning and scheduling more than the anticipated volume of conference center chairs.

Now consider the converse situation—sales books only 18 conference center chairs, two *less* than the expected demand. Since a complete conference center chair cannot be made from the two sets of uncommitted common items, the master planner or master scheduler must either reschedule them out into the future, move something up to build earlier, produce something to stock, or place the individual completed common items into inventory.

Finally, the third question—the number *most likely* to satisfy demand. Answer: The aggregate of the three demands. Figure 9.4 on page 283 indicates an item forecast of zero, an option forecast of zero, and an actual demand of 12; the most likely demand is 12, and we should expect that 12 options sets would be scheduled for receipt in time period 2.

Thus, an important rule for products in the make-to-order environment: *For a **pseudo item,** the master plan or master schedule should equal the actual demand for all time peri-ods in the sold-out zone. This rule makes master planning and scheduling in the sold-out zone relatively easy compared to the partially sold-out zone,* the next subject for discussion.

The Partially-Sold-Out Zone

In the conference center chair example, the partially sold-out zone lies somewhere between time periods 3 and 7 (refer to Figure 9.4 on page 283). Here, four conference center chairs remain in time period 4's available-to-promise, the first time period in the partially sold-out zone. As a first step in determining how many to master plan and/or master schedule, again ask the three questions: What is the *least* that should be scheduled? What is the *most* that should be scheduled? What number will *most likely* satisfy demand in the time period? The actual demand line for time period 4 indicates that seven red options are committed to customer orders, so the *very least* that should be scheduled is seven—enough to satisfy firm customer demand.

That covers the red conference center chairs already sold, but how many more conference center chairs requiring the red option could possibly be promised in this time period? The answer is four because even though *only half* of the remaining four required conference center chairs are predicted to be red, it is possible that *all four* could be sold as red conference room chairs. Therefore, the *most* that should be master planned and/or master scheduled in time period 4 is 11—the seven *already promised* to customer orders and the four that *could be so promised*.

Finally, what is the *most likely* number of red options that could be scheduled to satisfy expected demand in time period 4? Answer: nine. This is determined as follows:

1. There is zero service demand (the red option is an artificial collection of items and therefore it is classified as a *pseudo* and cannot be built or sold by itself).

2. Four more sets of common items are available-to-promise; half of these are expected to go with the red option. Therefore two of the four expected demand should be red.

3. Seven demands for red chairs are already in hand and require the red option.

4. The most likely total demand is nine, which is calculated (0 + 2 + 7) using the conclusions stated in 1 through 3.

Moving on to time period 6, ask the three questions again. The answers received: The *least* that should be planned and scheduled would be 5—the actual demand; the *most* that should be scheduled is the 5 that are committed plus the conference center chair ATP of 12, or 17; and the *most likely* number to satisfy demand is the sum of the three demand lines, or 11, which is calculated (0 + 6 + 5) using the numbers highlighted in this sentence.

So, the expected demand range for time period 6 is between 5 and 17, with 11 being the most likely expected demand (refer to Figure 9.4 on page 283).

The No-Orders Zone

The *no-orders,* or *forecast, zone* is by definition one in which (theoretically) no product configurations have been ordered and committed. With no orders in hand, and with the forecast as a sole guide, the master planner and/or master scheduler must nevertheless plan and schedule material and capacity; again, the three questions offer guidance. The time period in question is period 8.

The *least* that could be scheduled is zero since no actual demand exists. The *most* that should be scheduled is 20, calculated by taking the zero actual demand and adding it to the 20 available-to-promise from the product family. Here, the assumption is that every one of the conference center chair sales forecasted and supply planned to be available to enter the configuration phase in time period 8 would require the red option.

What about the *most likely* scenario for the red option? Here again, the answer is the sum of the three demand streams: the service demand of zero, the actual demand of zero, and the option forecast of 10. Thus, 10 is the *most likely* value. This scenario assumes that 50 percent of the conference center chairs sold requiring a time period 8 availability to enter configuration and/or finishing will have the red option.

So, what should the master plan and/or master schedule for the red option be for time periods 2, 4, 6, and 8?

- **Time Period 2:** It should have 12 red options scheduled for receipt—no more, no less. For a pseudo item like the red option, the master plan and/or master schedule should equal the actual demand in the sold-out zone.

- **Time Period 4:** We have already determined that in time period 4 the *least* is 7, the *most* is 11, and the *most likely* is 9. We know the master plan and/or master schedule in time period 4 should be somewhere between 7 and 11. Hold that thought for now, as the next section on option overplanning will shed more light on what should be scheduled in this time period.

- **Time Period 6:** This is similar to time period 4 in that it is in the partially sold-out zone. For now, let's say the master plan and/or master schedule has 11 red options in time period 6—the most likely expected demand.

- **Time Period 8:** The master planner and/or master scheduler should adopt the *most likely* expected demand and schedule 10 red options in this time period.

Option Overplanning

As has been stressed so far, the more difficult issue is not coming up with a forecast for common items, but with the forecast for the right mix of unique option-related items. The question always remains, *What are the chances that the actual sales will match the fore-casted demand exactly or even within a given tolerance?* Since the answer is invariably *not* very likely, it may be necessary to protect the company and its ability to satisfy customer demand from possible forecast error.

One way to protect against forecast error is to provide safety stock for the items required to build a conference center chair. *This could be expensive, and if the safety stock carried is forecasted wrong, the company may pay for the error at least four times:*

1. In stocking items not required by actual booked customer orders.

2. In lost sales because the wrong items are stocked, and the company lacked the complete sets of items to build entire products for shipment.

3. In stocked items being broken, lost, stolen, or otherwise unavailable (i.e., shelf life expires) when needed.

4. In overstocking items that are common to each product sold and thereby not needing forecast error protection.

Alternately, a company could safety stock finished products to cover their bases. But that would be both impractical and expensive in terms of inventory, space, production, obsolescence risk, and so on.[1]

A much better approach to protecting the plan and schedule from forecast error is option overplanning, a technique that entails increasing the master plan and/or master schedule (depending on if and where planning bills are used to aid mix demand planning or forecasting) for unique options in the partially sold-out zone to provide protection against demand variation.

To understand option overplanning, ask this question: "When a customer places an order, when does he or she usually want delivery?" In most cases, the answer is yesterday, as soon as possible, or right now!

---

[1] One wonders how often manufacturers have disassembled or torn down finished stock to retrieve common items needed for the product configurations the customers actually wanted.

Look again at the backlog curve for Soft Seat shown in Figure 9.3 on page 280. If a new customer order appears now, the earliest that delivery to the configuration and/or finishing production line can possibly be promised (if other orders and the master plan and/or master schedule are not manipulated) is the first time period of the partially sold-out zone, only if available-to-promise shows the necessary unique options and common items along with the required configuration/finishing capacity. This makes sense, since all production capacity and material in the sold-out zone are already committed to customer orders.

In the Soft Seat example, the first unsold time period is period 4, and that is where protection should be applied (refer to Figure 9.4 on page 283). But what should be protected? Earlier discussion suggests that no protection for common items is needed, since a one-for-one relationship exists between the product family plan and the required common items; the referenced product family is probably the best set of numbers available since product family planning is done at the aggregate, not detailed, level.

If four conference center chairs remain available-to-promise, then four sets of common items should be available since the master plan and/or master schedule for common items is generally set up to match expected demand. (Note: In more complex environments, there are cases when multiple common item groupings are used, one set of common items for the entire product family and others for groupings of similar products within a product family.) Again, the problem of forecasting demand and satisfying customer requirements surfaces with respect to the unique items, the color options in our example.

From earlier discussion we know that the least number of red chairs that should be scheduled for time period 4 is 7, the most is 11, and the most likely is 9. To provide 100 percent forecast-error protection to the first unsold time period (period 4 in the example), we would set the schedule to match the most demand that could be received. In the case of the red option, that is 11 red option sets.

Thus, there would be adequate supply of red options to cover demand even if the forecast were 100 percent wrong. Consider this: Even if the demand forecast of colored options is completely wrong in the first unsold time period, the company and supply function is still able to meet customer demand, and it does this without filling the company's warehouse with unnecessary common parts or finished good inventory.

Option overplanning is an excellent forecast protection vehicle, especially for products that are part of a make-to-order manufacturing strategy. Let's take a look at exactly what option overplanning buys a company.

- Option overplanning provides protection against demand variation in the first unsold time period for the product in question. It is in this period that the customer usually wants delivery.

- Option overplanning drives the material requirements planning (time-phased material planning) system. Material requirements planning, in turn, tells planners and schedulers what must be done to satisfy the master plan and/or master schedule in *matched* sets of parts or items, ensuring that master planned and/or master scheduled items can be produced as promised.

- Option overplanning creates inventory *only* for material with a lead time greater than the backlog horizon. The benefit, of course, is the reduction of unneeded inventory (a company does not need safety inventory across the *sold-out zone*—the customer has told the supplying company what they want).

Although option overplanning is a powerful technique, it potentially creates inventory and must be used with caution; it must be managed in terms of quantities and dates. Option overplanning also tends to move around, as we will observe in the next chapter. It must be managed and scheduled properly, usually in the first unsold time period of the *partially sold-out zone*. However, option overplanning is not necessarily confined to this first unsold time period—there are reasons to spread out the option overplanning, which will be addressed later in this chapter.

Let's say it again: *There is no reason to have any material protection or option overplanning in the sold-out zone* (the company is sold out, since all sets of common items are committed to already booked customer orders). Likewise, it probably is *not* a good use of funds to provide material protection in the no-orders zone. A well-informed master planner and/or master scheduler also knows that they have the option overplanning throughout the partially sold-out zone.

Calculating Projected Available Balance for Pseudo Items

Once the master plan and/or master schedule is created, the master planning and scheduling computer software will calculate the projected available balance (PAB). As shown in Figure 9.4 on page 283, there is a starting PAB of zero—not surprising, since the red option is a pseudo item and, thus, cannot be built (pseudo items are artificial items and only used for planning purposes). Nor should it be surprising to see that PAB remains zero through time period 3 since this is a pseudo item and the master plan and/or master schedule is set equal to the actual demand. As a reminder, in creating the master plan and/or master schedule for the *sold-out time periods*, it was said that the master plan and/ or master schedule line must balance with the actual demand line. This done, the PAB will be zero.

In time period 1 there is no activity, and in time period 2 there are 12 red option sets master planned and/or master scheduled against an equal total demand. Time period 3 is zero because there is no additional activity. Calculating time period 4, zero red option sets are projected to be available at the end of time period 3; these are added to the 11 red option sets that are master planned and/or master scheduled (expected receipts), resulting in a total supply of 11 red option sets against a total anticipated (or most likely) demand of 9 red option sets. The difference of two red option sets represent the option overplanned quantity. In other words, for a pseudo item, the projected available balance line on the master plan and/or master schedule reflects the time-phased option overplanning for the option sets in question.

Moving forward in the discussion, the projected available balance remains at two red option sets in time period 5, since there is no activity. In time period 6, there are the two red option sets from time period 5's PAB plus the 11 red option sets from the MPS line, minus total demand of 11 red option sets, which again leaves two red option sets. The same logic applies to time periods 7 and 8.[2]

Calculating Available-to-Promise

In calculating the available-to-promise (ATP) quantity for the red option sets, the calculation works backward from time period 8 (right to left instead of the popular left to right in the English language). The first step is to take what is master planned and/or master scheduled and subtract the commitments (customer orders booked but not yet shipped).

The idea of ATP is to inform the sales organization, customer service, and/or customer order entry what can be promised (product, option configurations, order quantities, lead times, delivery date) and then protecting all promises the company makes to its customers.

---

[2] Note: Option overplanning is generally done in the first unsold time period, although for various reasons (e.g., budget) the master planner and/or master scheduler may wish to spread the overplanning over the first few time periods in the partially sold-out zone for forecast-inaccuracy protection. For example, since time period 6 is still in the partially sold-out zone, the master planner and/or master scheduler could overplan and schedule up to a total of 17 units, the most red options that could be required to service customer needs in that time period.

A sales forecast is *not* a commitment, but rather a prediction or request for product; thus, sales forecasts are *generally* (most of the time—a discussion of exceptions is in Chapter 17, on demand management for two-demand streams) ignored in the ATP calculation.

Working right to left starting in time period 8, 10 red option sets are master planned and/or master scheduled, and zero red option sets are committed (see actual demand line, time period 8), so the ATP is 10 red option sets from time period 8—a noncumulative value. The master planning and scheduling computer software has more calculations to perform before it can display the total red option sets available-to-promise in time period 8.

For period 6, 11 red option sets are master planned and/or master scheduled, and the actual demand is 5 red option sets, leaving 6 red option sets available-to-promise in that period (noncumulative) to any incoming new orders. In time period 4, the 11 red option sets that are master planned and/or master scheduled have commitments totaling 7 against them, resulting in 4 red option sets being available-to-promise. For time period 2, 12 red option sets are master planned and/or master scheduled and 12 are committed, leaving an ATP of zero.

These ATP values are noncumulative. To calculate a cumulative value or carry over the values, simply add the ATP from each time period working left to right. Why is this important? What if a customer calls and asks, "How many red conference center chairs can you give us by time period 8?" The answer is 20, assuming the 20 sets of common items needed are also available (see ATP, time period 8, cumulative value, Figure 9.4 on page 283).

At this point, a complete master plan and/or master schedule is available, not only for red option sets, but for the common items as well as the other product family colors offered (see Figure 9.5 on pages 298–299); for simplicity the only other option color in the discussion is black. The next step in understanding the process is to actually commit an order using the ATP information.

As stated earlier, a pseudo item cannot be built, but it can be master planned and/or master scheduled. And if a pseudo item can be planned and/or scheduled, it is possible that a projected available balance could be calculated to be a positive number. If this is so, as Figure 9.4 time period 4 indicates, the system is telling us how much overplanning the master planner and/or master scheduler is doing. In this instance there are two (2) extra sets of the components that make up the red option pseudo item.

Using Available-to-Promise to Commit Customer Orders

In the next example, the customer has requested 10 conference center chairs to be delivered in time period 6: Of the 10 conference center chairs ordered, 9 are to be red and 1 is to be black. Can this order be accepted? Use Figure 9.5 on the following pages to answer this question. The common items' ATP line in time period 6 indicates that 12 sets of common items are available-to-promise in that time period. In fact, a total of 16 sets of common items are available-to-promise, as shown on the cumulative ATP line.

The cumulative ATP in time period 6 on the red option set schedule indicates that 10 sets of red option items are available-to-sell and commit. Continuing the analysis, 10 sets of black option items are available through time period 6, as the master plan and/or master schedule for that option makes clear. Thus, demand management, customer service, customer order entry, and the master planner and/or master scheduler now know that the order can be taken.

However, committing to customer orders always requires that *two questions be asked and answered.* The first is: *Can the order be taken?* An accurate ATP provides the answer to this question. The second question is: *Does the business want to take the customer order and commit to its delivery requirements?* In other words, in this example is the company willing to sell 10 conference center chairs here and have only 6 conference center chairs left to sell for the next six time periods of which only one conference center chair can be red? This second question requires a management decision. If both questions are answered in the affirmative, the next step is to book the customer order.

First, look at time period 6, the actual demand line, in the conference center chair product family plan and/or schedule (top of Figure 9.5 on page 298). Currently, it shows that 8 red option sets are committed to customers, but with the new customer order of 10 conference center chairs, it will become 18 conference center chairs committed to customers (see Figure 9.6 on pages 300–301). The ATP of 12 conference center chairs will be reduced by 10, leaving an ATP of 2 conference center chairs for the same time time period and 6 cumulative.

The same process is true for the common items since the product family and the common items pseudo bill have a one-for-one relationship. Now, dropping down into the red option master plan and/or master schedule for the time period under discussion, the actual demand of 5 red conference center chairs in time period 6 will increase by 9, to a total of 14 red conference center chairs. The black option's actual demand in time period 6 will increase by 1 conference center chair, to 4 black conference center chairs.

Conference Center Chair Product Family

MPS MATRIX	Past Due	1	2	3	4	5	6	7	8	Total
Item Forecast			0		4		12		20	36
Option Forecast			0		0		0		0	0
Actual Demand			20		16		8		0	44
Total Demand			20		20		20		20	80
Projected Available Balance	0	0	0	0	0	0	0	0	0	0
Available-to-Promise			0		4		12		20	36
		0	0	0	4	4	16	16	36	
Master Schedule			20		20		20		20	80

Common Items (100 Percent Probability)

MPS MATRIX	Past Due	1	2	3	4	5	6	7	8	Total
Item Forecast			0		0		0		0	0
Option Forecast			0		4		12		20	36
Actual Demand			20		16		8		0	44
Total Demand			20		20		20		20	80
Projected Available Balance	0	0	0	0	0	0	0	0	0	0
Available-to-Promise			0		4		12		20	36
		0	0	0	4	4	16	16	36	
Master Schedule			20		20		20		20	80

Figure 9.5   Complete Master Plan and/or Master Schedule for Conference Center Chair Product Family, Common Items, and Options

Red Option (50 Percent Probability)

MPS MATRIX	Past Due	1	2	3	4	5	6	7	8	Total
Item Forecast			0		0		0		0	0
Option Forecast			0		2		6		10	18
Actual Demand			12		7		5		0	24
Total Demand			12		9		11		10	42
Projected Available Balance	0	0	0	0	2	2	2	2	2	2
Available-to-Promise			0		4		6		10	20
		0	0	0	4	4	10	10	20	
Master Schedule			12		11		11		10	44

Black Option (50 Percent Probability)

MPS MATRIX	Past Due	1	2	3	4	5	6	7	8	Total
Item Forecast			0		0		0		0	0
Option Forecast			0		2		6		10	18
Actual Demand			8		9		3		0	20
Total Demand			8		11		9		10	38
Projected Available Balance	0	0	0	0	1	1	2	2	2	2
Available-to-Promise			0		3		7		10	20
		0	0	0	3	3	10	10	20	
Master Schedule			8		12		10		10	40

Figure 9.5 *Continued*

Conference Center Chair Product Family

MPS MATRIX	Past Due	1	2	3	4	5	6	7	8	Total
Item Forecast			0		4		2		20	36
Option Forecast			0		0		0		0	0
Actual Demand			20		16		18		0	54
Total Demand			20		20		20		20	80
Projected Available Balance	0	0	0	0	0	0	0	0	0	0
Available-to-Promise			0		4		2		20	26
		0	0	0	4	4	6	6	26	
Master Schedule			20		20		20		20	80

Common Items (100 Percent Probability)

MPS MATRIX	Past Due	1	2	3	4	5	6	7	8	Total
Item Forecast			0		0		0		0	0
Option Forecast			0		4		2		20	36
Actual Demand			20		16		18		0	54
Total Demand			20		20		20		20	80
Projected Available Balance	0	0	0	0	0	0	0	0	0	0
Available-to-Promise			0		4		2		20	26
		0	0	0	4	4	6	6	26	
Master Schedule			20		20		20		20	80

Figure 9.6 Complete Master Plan and/or Master Schedule for Conference Center Chair Product Family, Common Items, and Options After Booking Order for 10 Chairs (9 Red and 1 Black)

Red Option (50 Percent Probability)

MPS MATRIX	Past Due	1	2	3	4	5	6	7	8	Total
Item Forecast			0		0		0		0	0
Option Forecast			0		2		1		10	13
Actual Demand			12		7		14		0	33
Total Demand			12		9		15		10	46
Projected Available Balance	0	0	0	0	2	2	−2	−2	−2	−2
Available-to-Promise		0	0	0	1 / 1	1	0 / 1	1	10 / 11	11
Master Schedule			12		11		11		10	44

Black Option (50 Percent Probability)

MPS MATRIX	Past Due	1	2	3	4	5	6	7	8	Total
Item Forecast			0		0		0		0	0
Option Forecast			0		2		1		10	13
Actual Demand			8		9		4		0	21
Total Demand			8		11		5		10	34
Projected Available Balance	0	0	0	0	1	1	6	6	6	6
Available-to-Promise		0	0	0	3 / 3	3	6 / 9	9	10 / 19	19
Master Schedule			8		12		10		10	40

Figure 9.6 *Continued*

The master planning and scheduling system then recalculates the option forecast; it takes the ATP for the conference center chair product family, two chairs in this case, and explodes it through the planning bill, applying the probability of 50 percent, leaving an option forecast of one chair each for both red and black options. What we have just seen is the enterprise resource planning (ERP) system automatically consuming the forecast at the option level.

It's important to note that not only does the master planning and scheduling module of the ERP system **consume the forecast for products and options sold,** *but it also* **consumes (reduces) the forecast for products and options not being sold.** This is the only consumption logic known to the authors that does this—forecast consumption logic generally only consumes (reduces) what's sold, *not* what's *not* sold. (The reader is cautioned here that *not* all ERP and MPS software on today's market has this vital feature; the key here is to have ERP and MPS system capability to explode the ATP from the parent level into the option demand/forecast at the child level or master schedule level.)

Total demand for the red conference center chair option increases to 15 in time period 6, which is the total of zero service forecast (it's a pseudo item and thereby cannot be built or sold), an option forecast of 1, and 14 actual demand. The black option's total demand in time period 6 is 5 conference center chairs. To recalculate the red option ATP, we note that 9 additional red conference center chairs have been booked, resulting in a total committed demand of 14 red conference center chairs for that time period (5 + 9). Since 11 red conference center chairs are master planned and/or master scheduled in time period 6 and 14 have been committed, the resulting ATP is –3. Since an ATP of –3 does not make much sense for the red conference center chair option, the ATP in time period 6 will become zero; the total master plan and/or master schedule in time period 6 is consumed.

To protect the entire commitment of the 9 additional red conference center chairs, the master planner and/or master scheduler (really the master planning and scheduling software) must cover a demand of 3 more red conference center chairs (the –3 discussed above). The MPS line shows an MPS lot of 10 red conference center chairs in time period 8, but these red option sets will be too late to commit to a time period 6 demand. Working back in time, the master planner and/or master scheduler finds four red conference center chair option sets available-to-promise in time period 4. By using three of these red conference center chair option sets for time period 6 coverage and taking them out of the ATP in time period 4, one red conference center chair option set would remain available-to-promise in time period 4.

By working back in time, from time period 6 to period 4, a master planner and/or master scheduler can use ATP to protect customer promises without committing current inventory any earlier than necessary. To complete the example for the red conference center chair option, the cumulative ATP would then drop to 1 up through time period 7, while time period 8 would drop to 11. Remember, we started with a total ATP of 20 red conference center chair option sets and sold 9 red conference center chairs, leaving the 11 displayed in the cumulative available-to-promise line.

The same process is followed to complete the black conference center chair option. The good news here is that most master planning and scheduling software does these mechanics for the user, allowing the master planner and/or master scheduler time to manage the information and required business decisions.

Changes in Projected Available Balance

The projected available balance is also affected by the booking process. Continuing the booked customer order discussed in the previous section, time periods 1 through 5 remain the same, since no product or option requirement occurred to change the total demand in those time periods; the booking was for product to be available to enter the configuration and/or finishing process in time period 6. Two red conference center chair option sets were originally projected to be available at the end of time period 5, due in part to red conference center chair option overplanning.

If these two red conference center chair option sets are added to the master plan and/or master schedule of 11 red conference center chair option sets in time period 6, the result would be a projected available balance of 13 red conference center chair option sets, which is calculated by taking the 11 in the time period and adding them to the 2 projected to be available going into the time period (11 + 2). The new red conference center chair option total demand is 15, which is calculated by adding the 1 on the option forecast line to the 14 on the actual demand line (1 + 14), leaving a potential deficit of 2 red conference center chair option sets. Time periods 7 and 8 also have a cumulative potential deficit of 2 red option sets, since the master plan and/or master schedule in time period 8 equals the total demand.

Returning to time periods 4 and 6, two additional red conference center chair option sets over the current actual demand are expected to be required in time period 4 and one additional red conference center chair option set in time period 6 (option forecast line), yielding a total red conference center chair option forecast of three red conference center chair option sets through time period 6. Look at the master plan and/or master schedule line in time period 4.

Remember (from Figure 9.5 on pages 298 and 299, prior to taking the sales order) that the master planner and/or master scheduler overplanned the red conference center chair option sets by 2 red conference center chair option sets (a master plan and/or master schedule of 11 against a total demand of 9). If that had not been done, then the ATP in Figure 9.5, time period 4 would have been 2 red option sets instead of 4 red option sets, which means that the business would not have been able to satisfy the customer's request for all the conference center chairs—only 8 red conference center chairs could have been promised and committed. However, since the red conference center chair option sets were overplanned, the company could commit to fulfilling the entire customer order request for 9 red conference center chairs and 1 black conference center chair.

Time period 4 was overplanned by 2 red conference center chair option sets. At this point, 1 of the overplanned red conference center chair option sets has been given up by taking the order for 9 red conference chairs (remember, only 8 red conference chairs could have been promised without the option overplanning). In time period 6, there is a projected deficit of 2 red conference center chair option sets. Remember the option forecast above for 3 red conference center chair option sets. If that 3 do not come in, then the projected available balance for red conference center chair option sets will be *plus one (1)*. That plus one (1) is the remaining overplanned red conference center chair option sets. So, sales and/or customer service can take only 1 more red chair customer order through period 6, *not* 3, unless an adjustment is made to the master plan and/or master schedule.

There's another interesting point that can be highlighted here. Prior to the booking of the customer order for 10 conference center chairs, the company had option over-planned the red conference center chair option by 2 red sets in time period 6 (see projected available balance in Figure 9.5). After the customer order was booked (9 of the chairs being red), the red conference center chair option overplanning in time period 6 for the red conference center chair option sets is –2 (projected available balance). That is a shift of 4 units (+2 to –2). The only place these 4 units could have gone is to the black option.

Prior to the customer order booking, the option overplanning for the black conference center chair option sets in time period 6 was 2 units (projected available balance in Figure 9.5); after the customer order booking occurred, it is 6 units (projected available balance in Figure 9.6 on pages 300 and 301), which includes the 4 red option sets that shifted to the black option sets.

Option Overplanning for Products in the Make-to-Stock Environment

Working with products in a make-to-stock environment (the strategy is to ship directly off the shelf) most likely forces the manufacturing company to build to a demand forecast or planned inventory level so that product is available when the customer requests it. We have spent enough time discussing the fact that forecasts usually contain some degree of error. So, look at this situation. Let's say the company's integrated business planning (IBP) or sales and operations planning (S&OP) output calls for the company to build and deliver 100 Type AB products (AB product family) to the marketplace during a particular month.

For discussion purposes, this product family has two items (A and B) in it. Therefore, it is sales and marketing's responsibility to forecast the expected demand for each product, since product A and product B are advertised as being ready for shipment upon receiving the customer's order. For this example's purpose, let's say that sales and marketing forecast that 60 units will be for product A and 40 units will be for product B. Since the 60/40 split between products A and B is a mix forecast, what are the chances of the sales force bringing in customer orders that will perfectly match this expected demand? We should not be surprised if the answer is not very good!

If this expectation is true, then the *chance of the company meeting its overall volume target is nil*. If the company sells 61 units of A and 39 units of B, the total product that can be delivered on time is 99, assuming manufacturing built 60 product A items and 40 product B items (and the company is carrying no safety stock). So, to protect itself from this losing condition, many (if not most) manufacturing companies do decide to carry some amount of safety stock on the finished product A and product B units (say they hold 10 extra product A and 8 extra product B or some defined extra quantity of stock on individual, lower-level items).

While this approach may work sometimes, it can be expensive as well as hard to forecast. Is there another way? Sometimes a company may be able to provide forecast-error protection for products in the MTS environment by overplanning some of the unique items that make up the finished product.

Figure 9.7 on page 306 is an example of a make-to-stock strategy being employed on product A and product B. As the figure illustrates, product A is made from unique lower-level components W and X and 25 common components that are also used to make product B. Product B is made from unique lower-level components Y and Z and the same

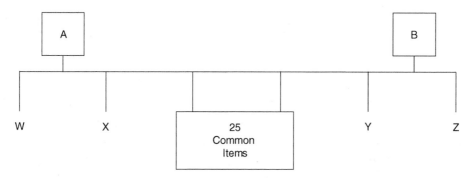

Figure 9.7   Make-to-Stock Product Structures for Stocked Finished Items A and B

25 common components that are used to make product A. In this example it is assumed that there's a short finishing cycle, there's a variable demand pattern, and that the unique lower-level components W, X, Y, and Z are used in other places. The master planner and/ or master scheduler has decided to do some dependent overplanning and use the time-phased, material requirements planning system to overplan the unique lower-level components in matched sets of components.

To do this, two planning bills are created—one for product A's unique lower-level components and one for product B's unique lower-level components. Figure 9.8 shows these simple planning bills with their unique lower-level components, identified as A-OP and B-OP. Since the common components are needed to build either product A or product B, both A-OP and B-OP are classified and treated as pseudo items with planning bills (for planning purposes) attached.

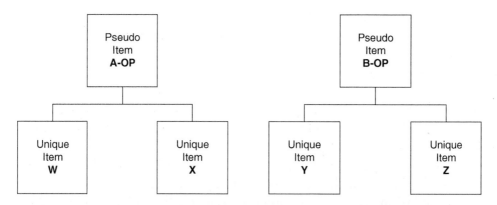

Figure 9.8   Planning Bills for Unique Components in Product Structures A and B (A-OP is Product A Option Bill and B-OP is Product B Option Bill)

The next step is to create a master plan and/or master schedule for the product A option and product B option equal to the overplanning desired. Since period 1 may be inside the finishing lead time, the overplanning in the example has been done in periods 2 and 3. The master planner and/or master scheduler has placed firm planned orders (planned scheduled receipts) for the product A option in period 2 for 20 sets and in period 3 for 10 sets. The product B option has been scheduled for 15 planned scheduled receipts in period 2 and 5 planned scheduled receipts in period 3. The total overplanning for A-OP and B-OP is 50 unique component sets for both products in both time periods. (Remember: This overplanning is only being applied to the unique lower-level components, W, X, Y, and Z.)

By creating the unique lower-level component planning bills and by master planning and scheduling the product A option and product B option (pseudo items can't be built, but they can be planned and scheduled), the master planner and/or master scheduler has provided unique component protection for expected forecast error in *matched sets of unique components*. This is done by driving the material requirements planning system with the master plan and/or master schedule for the product A option and product B option (refer to Figure 9.9 on page 308 to see how it actually works).

Products A and B are forecasted at the 60/40 split. Using these probabilities, 60 product A units are scheduled to be produced in time periods 1, 2, and 3. At the same time, 40 product B units are also scheduled to be produced in each of those time periods. Using the A-OP plan and/or schedule, 20 sets of unique components W and X are planned to be available in time period 2, while an additional 10 sets are planned to be available in time period 3. Using the B-OP plan and/or schedule, we expect 15 sets of unique components Y and Z to be available in time period 2, and 5 more Y and Z sets to be available in time period 3.

So, what has this bought the master planner and/or master scheduler? To answer this question, let's ask the following questions: What is the maximum number of A products that could be committed in time period 2? What is the maximum number of B products that could be committed in time period 2? What is the maximum number of A products that could be committed in time period 3? What is the maximum number of B products that could be committed in time period 3?

Using Figure 9.9 on page 308 to answer each question, the reader can see the benefit(s) of this overplanning technique. The maximum number of A products that can be committed in time period 2 is 80—the 60 A products scheduled and using the 20 A-OP overplanning of W and X to produce an additional 20 A products. It should also be remembered that the company in this example has a short manufacturing cycle. However, if 80 A products are committed in time period 2, then only 20 B products can be committed in time

100 Units/Period

A & B Family	1	2	3
A	60	60	60
B	40	40	40
Total	100	100	100
A-OP	0	20	10
B-OP	0	15	5
Total	0	35	15
A	60	(45) (80)	(55) (70)
B	40	(20) (55)	(30) (45)
Total	100	135	115

Figure 9.9 Master Plan and Schedule for Products A and B as well as Pseudo Items A-OP and B-OP

period 2; again, remember that only a combined total of 100 A and B products can be made due to only having 100 sets of common components.

The maximum number of B products that can be committed in time period 2 is 55—the 40 B products B and using the 15 B-OP overplanning of Y and Z to produce an additional 15 B products; again, remember that the company in this example has a short manufacturing cycle. However, if 55 B products are committed in time period 2, only 45 A products can be committed (a combined total of 100 A and B products). One more time, this is true because we *only* have 100 sets of common components—*no* overplanning has been done for those 25 common components.

What does this really mean? Imagine going to sales and telling them that they had to create the *perfect forecast* or the company would not be able to achieve its overall shipping plan. Or telling finance that a *safety stock* for all stocked items must be carried or the company would not be able to achieve its shipping plan. Finance might ask if inventory *goals and targets are more important to the business than safely making money and a profit*.

By employing the technique illustrated in the example, the master planner and/or master scheduler can respond in a different way. If the sales organization books and commits delivery for A products in time period 2 somewhere between 45 and 80, and for B products somewhere between 20 and 55, the company will be able to reach their goals. But remember, only 100 total units (A and B together) can be sold and committed in any time period because of the common items' constraint.

Looking at time period 3, if customer orders for the A product are somewhere between 55 and 70, and orders for the B product are somewhere between 30 and 45, the plan can be achieved. By using this *overplanning* technique, a wide range of possibilities will now satisfy the business's leadership and management's desired shipping plans. And it didn't cost the master planner and/or master scheduler or the company a great amount of time or money.

Master Planning and Scheduling Products in Make-to-Stock and Make-to-Order Environments: A Comparison

Make-to-stock (MTS) products are generally master planned and/or master scheduled at the end item level. By contrast, products in the make-to-order (MTO) environment call for master planning and scheduling below the end item level, often working with pseudo bills-of-material to manage hundreds of options.

Another difference is that make-to-stock transactions are often simpler—the customer wants a standard electric switch box, and the manufacturer simply pulls one out of finished-goods inventory. Transactions in the make-to-order environment, though, are more complex in that several actions must take place.

First, the customer must indicate product specifications and a desired delivery date. Second, the manufacturer must match the desired specifications and delivery date with the requisite common and unique items. Third, the customer order must be booked identifying the required date for all the unique components plus the common components to be delivered to the configuration/finishing production line(s). Finally, the timing of production and meeting promised customer deliveries must be coordinated through customer service, master planning and scheduling, logistics planning and execution, inventory management, finishing functions, and quality control.

To ensure customer satisfaction for products in the MTS environment (where immediate or near immediate delivery is required), conventional statistical techniques are often used to analyze desired customer service levels and compute how much safety stock should be carried for each end item being master planned and scheduled. But for products in a make-to-order environment, it doesn't make sense to stock completed items, since the final configurations required by customers will be unknown until the customer order appears.

Trying to safety stock individual components and/or raw materials is also impractical. How do you decide which items need safety stock, in what quantities, and so on, when literally thousands of unique products are made by a single company? Therefore, techniques such as option overplanning in the first unsold time period should be used.

Yet another difference centers around finishing schedules (discussed in depth in Chapter 12). For products living in the MTS world, finished products are usually built to a demand forecast using available, planned, and/or demonstrated capacity. For products living in an MTO environment, the customer order must precede the finishing or final assembly process. Moreover, information in the customer order must be communicated to the manufacturing facility; all the required items listed on the pseudo bills-of-material must be sent to the right operation on the finishing line at the right time.

In addition, process instructions detailing the configured customer order must be developed. In short, master planning and scheduling products in the MTO world is generally somewhat tougher than simply planning to build a red conference center chair and placing it on the shelf.

Regarding the bills-of-material (BOMs) being used, companies that have products that are make-to-stock use standard BOMs for the entire planning, scheduling, and building phases. Planning products in a make-to-order environment, though, do not universally use standard BOMs, at least at the upper levels. Instead, multilevel planning and pseudo bills are common. Many times, in an MTO environment, a conventional bill is restructured into a planning bill, possibly several levels down, based on the competition's lead time, the company's cumulative lead time, the company's willingness to invest in inventory, and the capacity needed to finish the order to a customer specification.

This restructuring is done for three reasons: first, to allow a company to master plan and schedule the fewest number of items; second, to give marketing and sales a better chance at creating an accurate forecast (the accuracy of the forecast will always be better at the aggregate level than at the detail level); and third, by separating the common components from the unique components, option overplanning can be applied to just the unique components, thus reducing the inventory carried as protection against demand variability.

Most of the discussion in this chapter concerned itself with the mechanics of two-level (or multilevel) master planning and scheduling and how planning bills are used to assist the master planner and/or master scheduler in determining the demand and/or requirements at the MPS second level. It also has dealt with the logic used to create the master plan and/or master schedule, and how, when, and where to use option overplanning. With the knowledge of two-level (or multilevel) master planning and scheduling, we are now ready to return to the job of the master planner and master scheduler and the process of master planning and scheduling products using a make-to-order manufacturing strategy.

If the reader is in the busines of making heavily optioned, complex products, he or she should not shy away from two-level or multilevel master planning and scheduling because it appears to be hard to do. Unfortunately, there is no shortcut answer to doing the work the best way possible and beating the competition every time! Yes, master planning and scheduling products in a make-to-order and/or design/engineer-to-order environment is more difficult than master planning and scheduling products in the make-to-stock world. However, MTO and DTO/ETO might be the best manufacturing strategy for the reader's company to follow.

The next chapter follows the same format as Chapter 5, which presented situations for the master planner and/or master scheduler to use when analyzing information and data presented via real-time computer screens. By using what some call a Class A master planning and scheduling process supported by an ERP computer system, the master planner and/or master scheduler can draw conclusions quickly during the decision-making process. The goal of Chapter 10 is not to provide a set of *right* answers, but rather an understanding of how to do master planning and scheduling when it comes to meeting the customer with a product that is somewhere between the completed product design and a completed finished product on the shelf.

10

Using Master Planning and Scheduling Output for Make-to-Order Products

In the absence of facts, arguments will persist.

This chapter considers how the master planner and/or master scheduler working with products in a make-to-order (MTO) environment uses the information presented by the master planning and scheduling (MPS) system. Special attention is given to the following:

- Differences in the information used for make-to-stock (MTS) and make-to-order (MTO) products;

- Using the planning bill to generate demand forecasts for master planned and/or master scheduled items;

- Balancing the master plan and/or master schedule to actual and anticipated demand for pseudo items;

- How available-to-promise (ATP) information and forecast consumption data are handled;

- Overplanning MTO products at the option level in the partially sold-out zone;

- Action messages supplied by the enterprise resource planning (ERP) and master planning and scheduling (MPS) computer system and how the master planner and/or master scheduler may respond to those action messages.

To maintain continuity, this chapter uses the winch example introduced in Chapter 5. Figure 10.1 on page 314 describes the three winch models, WA01, WA04, and WA06,

		WA01	WA04	WA06	Characteristic
A100	Carriage Assembly	1	1	1	Common
C100	2000# Cable Assembly	1			Unique
C101	4000# Cable Assembly		1		Unique
C102	6000# Cable Assembly			1	Unique
D100	Drum – 50', 1/4" Cable, 1"	1			Unique
D102	Drum – 50', 3/8" Cable, 1.5"		1		Unique
D103	Drum – 50', 1/2" Cable, 1.5"			1	Unique
G102	Gearbox 4 FPM, 1" Shaft	1	1	1	Common
M100	5 HP Motor	1			Unique
M103	8 HP Motor		1		Unique
M105	10 HP Motor			1	Unique
P100	Pendant Assembly	1	1	1	Common
S100	Shaft, 1" x 24"	1			Unique
S101	Shaft, 1.5" x 24"		1	1	Unique
	Lift Speed (Feet Per Minute)	4	4	4	
	Capacity (In Thousand Pounds)	1	4	6	

Figure 10.1   Winch Product Comparison

listing all major components. The matrix used here is a helpful way of identifying what is common and what is unique within the product structure of the winch product family. Notice that the A100 carriage assembly, G102 gearbox 4 fpm, 1-inch shaft, and P100 pendant assembly are common to all three winches.

All these winches have the same lift speed—4 feet per minute (fpm)—but vary as to lift capacity (1,000, 4,000, and 6,000 pounds). *The G102 gearbox is a common item as long as the lift speeds remain at 4 fpm.* However, this has changed, as described in the next paragraph.

Using Planning Bills to Simplify Option Scheduling

Assume for a moment that management of the company producing the identified winches wants to expand its offerings. Instead of offering just three winches with the same lift speed, the company will offer winches that operate and lift at speeds of 4, 6, and 10 feet per minute. In addition, winches with 2,000-, 3,000-, and 5,000-pound lift capacity will be added to the product line offering. Thus, the company will make available winches with three different lift speeds and six different capacities—18 different configurations instead of the previous 3 offered configurations.[1]

The company's decision to expand its winch product family means that MPS at the end-item level will be significantly expanded and made more complex. To simplify matters, the company has decided to create a planning bill for winch family (WXYY) that contains both a common components (5500) bill—common components now consist of the carriage assembly (A100) and pendant assembly (P100)—along with the various option bills for the different capacities and lift speeds (1,000#, 2,000#, 3,000#, 4,000#, 5,000#, 6,000#, 4 fpm, 6 fpm, and 10 fpm). With the planning bill structure in place, marketing and sales provided the probability of sales that will include the various options. The winch product family planning bill with the best estimate for each of the various options is shown in Figure 10.2 on page 316.

The planning bill shown in the figure thus reflects all option component sets as well as the common components. This planning bill structure makes it possible to cut out nearly 50 percent of the otherwise master planned and/or master scheduled items, reducing their numbers from 18 to 10. The 10 remaining MPS items are the common group (1), capacity options (6), and various gearboxes (3).

The previous chapters covering planning bills as well as master planning and scheduling products using an MTO manufacturing strategy show that MPS is done at the option

---

[1] Here we make the assumption that all of the gearboxes work with any of the capacity options.

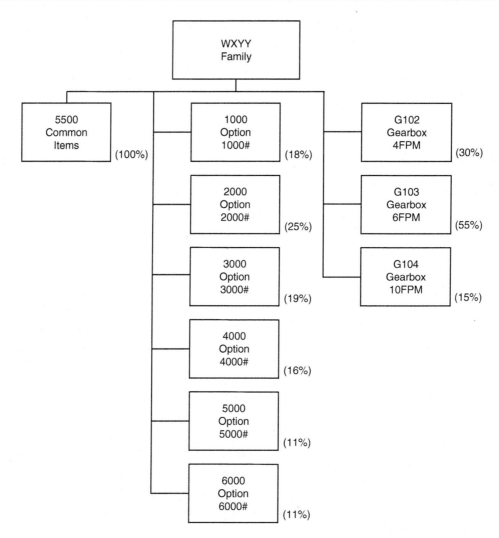

Figure 10.2   Winch Product Family Planning Bill

or feature level, and not at the level of the end item. Applying this logic, the master planner and/or master scheduler for the winch product family does the same, dropping down one level to gain better control, ease the job of forecasting, add flexibility in manufacturing, and better serve the customer.

The Scheduling Process

In the example, the winch product family's common components and various lift capacity options are all defined as *pseudo planning bills*—that is, artificial groupings of items that can be scheduled but not built. The gearboxes are purchased items and therefore *not defined as pseudo items*.

Since the gearboxes are purchased complete, the common components bill contains only common components from the lift capacity options (no common items between the various gearboxes are included). If the gearboxes were manufactured in-house, an opportunity to add the common components in the gearboxes to the common components bill would exist, and any company building a product similar to the winch product family should seize this opportunity if it presents itself.

Time-Phased Bills-of-Material

Once structured, the planning bill for the common components as well as each of the lift capacity options can be time phased. Time-phasing the master planned and master scheduled items simply means that each parent item is exploded through its bill-of-material into its underlying sublevel items (i.e., assemblies, subassemblies, components, raw materials, and packaging materials); additionally, the total length of time required for material and capacity planning, material procurement, capacity adjustment, manufacturing operations, assembly, quality testing, packaging, and shipping is shown using the extended horizontal lines against the time scale above (weeks in this example). Time-phased bills-of-material (BOMs) for the common components and for one of the lift (capacity) options (3,000#) are shown in Figures 10.3 and 10.4, respectively on page 318. (Refer to Chapter 5 for details on creating time-phased bills.)

The figures indicate a cumulative lead time for the common components and option components of 16 weeks, with the greatest lead time component being the housing casting (1200C) in the common components and the drum casting (D101C) in the 3000# option bill. Figure 10.3 indicates that two major assemblies make up the common components: the A100 carriage assembly and the P100 pendant assembly. The A100 is itself made from item 1000 (an axle), item 1100 (a 6-inch wheel), and item 1200 (a housing). Figure 10.4 shows that the lifting capacity option is also made up of two major assemblies, a 7-horsepower motor (M102) and a winding assembly (3001).

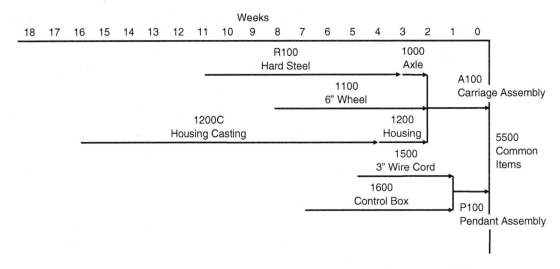

Figure 10.3 Time-Phased Common Items Planning Bill

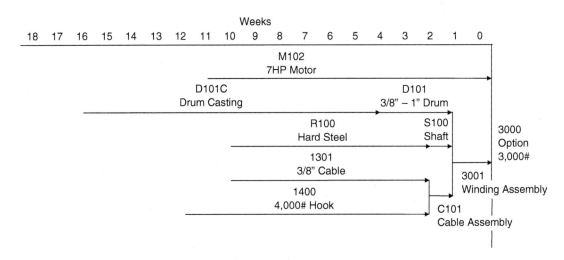

Figure 10.4 Time-Phased 3,000# Option Planning Bill

For purposes of illustration, assume that manufacturing has added the winding assembly (3001) to increase efficiency in production. This winding assembly includes a 3/8–1-inch drum, a shaft, and a cable assembly. Grouping and assembling materials into intermediates is often done for purposes of efficiency, control, and manufacturing flexibility. These intermediates can either be built and placed in stock or remain on the manufacturing floor for immediate consumption by a parent item. In the latter case, the intermediate item is commonly referred to as a phantom item—that is, an item that is real but not planned to be stocked.

In the example, the 3001 winding assembly is actually a produced item. This not only creates greater efficiencies in manufacturing but allows for the creation of a modular subassembly. The same logic can be used in the other lift capacity option bills. Such time-phased bills can help the master planner and/or master scheduler determine which items will be affected by a process change.

For example, if a change were to be made nine weeks prior to shipment, the time-phased planning bill would make it possible for the master planner and/or master scheduler to quickly identify the several affected items. Thus, among the common components in Figure 10.3, the hard steel and housing casting would be affected. In the 3,000# option in Figure 10.4 the motor, drum casting, hard steel, cable, and hook are affected.

Item Numbering System

To continue with the example, assume that a significant item numbering system is being used at the end-item level.[2] Now consider the WXYY product family in terms of its significant item number system, as described in Figure 10.5.

The first character defines the product family (W = winches), the second character defines the lift speed, and the last two define capacity. With 18 possible configurations to deal with, this significant item number approach is useful in sales planning and for

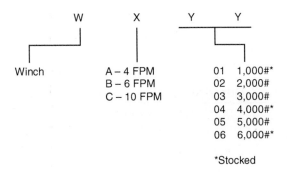

Figure 10.5   Significant Item Numbering System (WXYY)

---

[2] This is *not* a recommendation; it is simply used here for illustration purposes. Some companies use product configurations driven by a significant item-numbering scheme for entering customer order requirements.

customer order entry purposes. In such a case, the sale of a WC05 would mean a winch that operates at 10 fpm and lifts up to 5,000 pounds.

When customer orders are received for products in a make-to-order environment, the customer generally defines the configuration required, the number of units needed, and the product requested delivery date. For example, the customer order entry screen reproduced in Figure 10.6 indicates that the customer has ordered two winches, each lifting at 6 fpm and a 3,000-pound lift capacity and requested delivery on October 14.

To satisfy this particular customer order, the master planner and/or master scheduler needs the following:

- Two sets of common components

- Two sets of 3,000# option components

- Two 6 fpm gearboxes

With this background for the winch example, attention can be turned to using the MPS information to make decisions in the make-to-order, assemble-to-order, finish-to-order, kit-to-order, and package-to-order manufacturing environments, starting with the common components. From this point forward in this chapter, our discussion will center around **master scheduling** products where the company is using a **make-to-order manufacturing strategy**.

Order #	Customer Name	Credit
C3456	Liftum-High Machine Tool	S

Line	Item	Description	Qty Req'd	Date Req'd
1	WB03	3,000#, 6 FPM Winch	2	10/14
2	5500	Common Items	2	10/14
3	3000	3,000# Option	2	10/14
4	G103	6 FPM Gearbox	2	10/7

Figure 10.6   Customer Order Entry Screen

If the reader's company has need for both a master plan and master schedule, the formats used in this chapter to support our master scheduling discussion would be very similar if not the same (the contents would be different, but the matrix format would be the same).

Master Scheduling Common Components

Figure 10.7 on pages 322–323 is a representation of a software screen used for master scheduling the common components (5500) used in the winch. The screen format is divided into several major sections: item information, planning horizon summaries of demand and supply, and detail data sections containing information on requirements and replenishment order status, exception-driven action messages, and various reference data.

The master schedule screen summarizes critical details used by the master scheduler in managing, aligning, and synchronizing demand and supply. These screen formats are the same as those used in Chapter 5. Here it would be useful to highlight some of the data elements that makes this particular screen unique to a make-to-order (MTO) environment.

Item Information Section

This section of the master schedule screen contains background information about the item being scheduled: item number, item description, product family, and the like. It also contains information specific to the item that helps the master scheduler to properly manage the item's progress through production: lot size, order quantity, lead time, the position of time fences (planning time fence and demand time fence), and so forth.

In Chapter 5, the *item status* on the winches was *STK* (stock). In this case the common components bill is a pseudo; thus, its item status is *PSDO*. Under *demand manager* and *forecast consumption*, the screen notes *PLANBL* for planning bill. This means that, in this case, the demand manager identified by name in Chapter 5 (Ferguson) is actually a planning bill, and the items in the planning bill are forecasted automatically.

Note that even though the demand is calculated and disaggregated automatically through the planning bill percentages, it remains the responsibility of the demand/commercial organization to assess and update the planning bill percentages on a regular basis. Also, the demand forecast is automatically consumed using the planning bill. The technique used to consume the demand forecast is to explode the available-to-promise (ATP)

Item Number	Primary Description		Item Status	Product Family		Master Scheduler	Demand Manager
5500	COMMON ITEMS		PSDO	WXYY		PROUD	PLANBL

Balance on Hand	Lot Size		Safety Stock		Time Fence					Lead Time	Cuml. Lead Time	Stnd. Cost
	Rule	Factor	Policy	Factor	PTF	DTF	MTF	CTF	RTF			
0	LFL	1	NO	0	13			12		1	16	$565

Period	Past Due	10/13	10/20	10/27	11/03	11/10	11/17
Item Forecast							
Option Forecast		10	0	265	370	400	400
Actual Demand		385	405	135	30		
Total Demand		395	405	400	400	400	400
Projected Available Balance	0	5	0	0	0	0	0
Available-to-Promise		10	0	265	370	400	400
Master Schedule		400	400	400	400	400	400

Period	1/12	1/19	1/26	2/02	2/09	2/16	2/23
Item Forecast							
Option Forecast	440	440	440	440	440	440	440
Actual Demand							
Total Demand	440	440	440	440	440	440	440
Projected Available Balance	0	0	0	0	0	0	0
Available-to-Promise		440	440	440	440	440	440
Master Schedule		440	440	440	440	440	440

Master Schedule Detail						
Required Date	Order Number	Lot Number	Order			Recommended Action
			Quantity	Type	Status	
10/13	5500	413	400	MPS	FIRM	
10/20	5500	414	400	MPS	FIRM	
10/27	5500	415	400	MPS	FIRM	
11/03	5500	416	400	MPS	FIRM	
11/10	5500	417	400	MPS	FIRM	
11/17	5500	418	400	MPS	FIRM	
11/24	5500	419	400	MPS	FIRM	
12/01	5500	420	400	MPS	FIRM	
12/08	5500	421	420	MPS	FIRM	
12/15	5500	422	420	MPS	FIRM	
12/22	5500	423	420	MPS	FIRM	
1/05	5500	434	430	MPS	FIRM	
1/12	5500	425	430	MPS	FIRM	
1/19	5500		440			PLAN

Figure 10.7 Master Schedule Screen, Common Components

Forecast Consumption	Resource Profile	Critical Resources					
		Resource	Resource	Resource	Resource	Resource	Resource
PLANBL	WXYY	MCH	SUB	ASSM	KIT	–	–
Selling Price	Special Instructions			Date Run		Actions Recommended	
$1,010	SAFETY-HOUSING CAST			XX-XX-XX		PLN	

11/24	12/01	12/08	12/15	12/22	1/05	Period
						Item Forecast
400	400	400	400	400	400	Option Forecast
					80	Actual Demand
400	400	400	400	400	480	Total Demand
		20	40	60	10	Projected Available Balance
400	400	420	420	420	350	Available-to-Promise
400	400	420	420	420	430	Master Schedule

3/02	3/09	3/16	3/23	3/30	4/06	Period
						Item Forecast
440	440	440	440	440	440	Option Forecast
						Actual Demand
440	440	440	440	440	440	Total Demand
0	0	0	0	0	0	Projected Available Balance
440	440	440	440	440	440	Available-to-Promise
440	440	440	440	440	440	Master Schedule

Actual Demand Detail													
Required Date	Order Quantity	Reference Number	Order Number	T	S	C	Required Date	Order Quantity	Reference Number	Order Number	T	S	C
10/13	35	Main Mfg	C1759	A	R		10/20	30	Everglass	C1819	A	F	
10/13	60	WA01	M0814	F	R		10/20	15	Phillips	C1825	A	F	
10/13	45	WA04	M0815	F	R		10/20	5	Pacific Inc	C1831	A	F	
10/13	25	WA06	M0816	F	R		10/20	10	Moore Mfg	C1832	A	F	
10/13	15	Allen Mfg	C1802	A	R		10/20	50	Eagle Betts	C1829	A	F	
10/13	40	WC02	M0817	F	R		10/20	35	Riverbend	C1830	A	F	
10/13	14	Capt Mtrs	C1746	A	R		10/20	100	West Coast	C1849	A	F	
10/13	70	Desert Co	C1811	A	R		10/27	60	WA01	M0820	F	F	
10/13	20	Deer Crs	C1814	A	R		10/27	40	Excor	C1835	A	F	
10/13	36	G Gregory	C1815	A	R		10/27	10	Smith Co	C1837	A	F	
10/20	25	Intl Energy	C1821	A	R		10/27	25	Ames Mfg	C1841	A	F	
10/20	40	Chuck Mfg	C1823	A	R		11/03	30	MPRS	C1856	A	F	
10/20	50	WC04	M0818	F	R		1/05	80	Daly & Son	C1801	A	F	A
10/20	10	Roadman	C1824	A	F								
10/20	60	M0819	M0819	F	F								

Figure 10.7 *Continued*

(Note: This figure will be referred to several times in the coming text. The reader may wish to bookmark this page for easy reference.)

quantities through the percentages that reside in the planning bill, as explained in the previous chapter.

On the next information line, the *balance on hand* is zero, which is not surprising since a pseudo cannot be built or stocked. As for *lot size,* discrete lot sizing rules are generally applied to pseudo items; therefore, lot-for-lot (LFL) is used in the example. Also, since a pseudo item cannot be stocked, it should have no *safety stock* indicated.

The *lead time* one level down is set to 1 week in the example, while the *cumulative lead time* is set to 16 weeks (the time required to pull together all the common components from scratch). To shorten that lead time, the master scheduler has chosen to safety stock the housing casting, which in the time-phased bill-of-material was shown to be the long-lead-time component. The master scheduler is reminded of this decision by the text under *special instructions.* By safety stocking the housing casting, its contribution to the cumulative lead time is effectively reduced and the manufacturer is able to deliver the common components four time periods sooner.

This explains why the *planning time fence* (PTF) may be set at 13 time periods, which is inside the cumulative lead time of 16 time periods but outside the cumulative material ordering time of 12 time periods (16 – 4 = 12). Of course, there is no reason why the master scheduler could not set the planning time fence at 12 time periods. It also could be set at 14 time periods. The setting of the PTF does not need to line up exactly with the cumulative lead time or any other lead time.

Planning Horizons Section

This section of the master schedule screen contains the demand and supply information needed to manage the master schedule. This screen summarizes booked orders on the actual demand line by time period. In addition to showing actual demand, the master schedule screen provides the available-to-promise (ATP) quantity described in Chapter 9. Thus, for time period 10/13, there are booked orders needing 385 sets of the winch common components.

The master scheduler has placed two time fences in this example: a capacity fence (CTF) set at the end of week 1/05, and a planning time fence (PTF) at the end of the following time period. The capacity time fence is a memo-type time fence indicating that it is difficult to make capacity adjustments within this capacity time fence. The planning time fence is used to control computer software behavior; all master (supply) scheduled orders within the PTF are controlled by the master scheduler respectively, while those outside the planning time fence are generally controlled by the master planning and scheduling computer software.

Detail Data Section

The bottom portion of this master schedule screen contains two separate categories of information, both generated by the MPS software system using data from various order files—that is, manufacturing and supplier orders on the supply side, and customer and stocked orders on the demand side.

The first category of information is master schedule detail, which identifies the supply released orders as well as the firm planned orders (FPOs) already placed, along with their respective identification numbers (lot) and required dates. The master schedule detail section also includes a recommended action column. In the case of the last supply order (required date 1/19), the recommended action is *PLAN*, or *it is time to convert the computer planned order (CPO) in question into a firm planned order (FPO)*.

The section labeled *Actual Demand Detail* indicates the source of demand on the line of that name in the planning horizon summaries. This section calls out the required date, quantity ordered, order reference number, and order number.

Analyzing the Detail Data

With the general sections of the master schedule screen understood, we consider the finer details. Begin with the planning horizon in the 10/13 column. On the master schedule line of that time period, the master schedule shows an FPO for 400 sets of common components ready to be applied to customer orders. That was the plan, but a review of the plan for this time period indicates that actual demand is for only 385 sets of common components.

Eleven separate customer orders, each listed individually in the actual demand detail section of the screen, are the source of this demand. For example, on 10/13 there is an order for 35 units for Main Manufacturing (customer order C1759). The "A" in the *T* column indicates that the unit is using an assemble-to-order (ATO) manufacturing strategy. The order beneath this indicates a quantity of 60 units required on 10/13. This requirement has a reference number—WA01—which is not the name of a customer but one of the company's own product numbers. In this case the master scheduler has committed 60 sets of common components to a finished goods order. (In addition to building and configuring to customer orders, the master scheduler may at times choose to build popular configurations to stock as noted by the asterisks in Figure 10.5 on page 319.)

Order M0814 indicates that this order is a manufacturing order rather than a customer order. The "F" next to it indicates that the product is being built for finished goods. Thus, the master scheduler is building to customer order as well as to company stock.

Determining Available-to-Promise (ATP). Since the 11 lines of detail demand summarize to the 385 units shown in the 10/13 time period's actual demand, the ATP quantity for this time period can be calculated by subtracting actual demand for the time period from the 400 sets of common components scheduled to be due in 10/13, yielding an ATP of 15 units.

Oddly, the master schedule screen shows an ATP in time period 10/13 of only 10 units, which is explained as follows. Looking ahead to time period 10/20, the reader can see that the master scheduler has planned for another 400 sets of common components to be available. Since the actual demand for that time period is 405 units (5 over the amount master scheduled), the need for common components in that time period is overbooked by 5 units.

To ensure the company's ability to satisfy each customer promise, the master scheduler plans to use 5 sets of the 10/13 time period's common components' surplus to cover the 10/20 overbooking. As a result, the ATP in 10/13 is reduced by 5 units, resulting in the indicated ATP of 10 units.

Available-to-Promise (ATP) and the Sold-Out Zone. Time periods 10/13 and 10/20 are in the *sold-out zone*, meaning that no more customer orders are expected. This zone is sold out even though 10 units are still available-to-promise.

To understand this, the master scheduler needs to ask the question "Will sales be bringing in a last-minute order?" If the answer is yes, it's time for sales to define the configuration needed. Remember, we're talking about the current time period. If sales doesn't have a customer order in hand that requests the remaining 10 units in the sold-out zone, the master scheduler must take other action.

What is to be done with the 10 sets of common components that are available-to-promise in time period 10/13? If no action is taken by the master scheduler, and if no customer orders appear at the beginning of the time period, then there will be 10 sets of common components for which there is *no* home.

Balancing the Sold-Out Zone for Common Components

As time period 10/13 begins, the master scheduler must ask, "What are the chances of a customer order coming in the door with a delivery (to configuration and/or finishing process) time of one period or less?" To make good on such an order, the customer order must appear right away, and the winch configuration must be known. If a customer order for 10 winches magically appeared, the problem of excess common components would go away, as the customer order would consume the option forecast and planned production (ATP would become zero).

More likely than not, a customer order will not appear just in time to solve the master scheduler's common components problem, and the company will face two undesirable realities: (1) having the capacity to assemble 10 winches that will remain idle, and (2) carrying inventory of all the material identified in the common components planning bill. Neither of these choices is satisfactory from the company's point of view, but what other alternatives are available?

The master scheduler has several alternatives (four of which will be discussed here) for meeting the challenge presented in the example's sold-out zone. The first alternative is to look into the future and see if any customer order can be moved up.

For instance, the actual demand detail section in Figure 10.7 (see pp. 322–323) indicates a customer order of exactly 10 units (Moore Manufacturing, order number C1832) required for delivery in time period 10/20. Perhaps this customer would be agreeable to taking early delivery, making it possible to pull that 10-unit order into time period 10/13. But first, the master scheduler must determine which capacity options and gearboxes that the customer has requested and examine the various option screens to make sure that those options are also available in 10/13.

This alternative would solve only the current time period issue, *not* the sold-out zone problem. The capacity consumed in time period 10/13 by moving the order for 10 units in from 10/20 would increase available capacity in time period 10/20. So, the master scheduler should look beyond the sold-out zone for other possible orders to move up. In this case, the entry for Smith Company in time period 10/27 is a possible candidate.

The Smith Company order of 10 units is scheduled for the first time period of the partially sold-out zone. If this order can be pulled into either the 10/13 or 10/20 time period (the sold-out zone), the problem of losing the capacity in that zone can be solved. But first, the master scheduler must look up Smith Company customer order (C1837) and find out which capacity options and gearboxes go with it, then check the master schedule for those options to be sure that the needed materials are or will be available.

The second alternative is to split a customer order into multiple deliveries. There are some large orders in time period 10/27 and further out that might be split up—some to be produced with the capacity available in the sold-out zone and the remainder to be produced in the originally scheduled time period. The customer order of 40 units for Excor, for example, might be broken into 10 units and 30 units, with 10 units moved into time period 10/13 and the remaining 30 units staying where they are currently scheduled. It might be better from a business standpoint to produce the 10 units early and hold them as inventory than to lose the capacity. Of course, the customer should be given the opportunity to accept an earlier delivery; the earlier delivery would be the best of both worlds for the company, allowing it to build earlier yet not carry the inventory.

Instead of getting the demand to match the master schedule, a third alternative is to decrease the master schedule so that it equals the actual demand. In this example, the total of the master schedule for the sold-out zone must be 790 units—385 units for the demand in time period 10/13 and 405 units for the demand in time period 10/20. The perfectly balanced master schedule would require reducing the lot of 400 units in time period 10/13 to 385 units and increasing the master schedule in time period 10/20 to 405 units. This would mean that 5 sets of common components would be rescheduled into time period 10/20 and 10 sets would be rescheduled into some time period beyond 10/20.

The fourth alternative is to build a popular configuration to stock. As already discussed, the winch company seems to do this as a regular practice. Look at the actual demand detail: You see WA01, WA04, and WA06 winches being built on manufacturing orders for finished goods. The master scheduler should analyze the options to determine what material is available. That information, in addition to consultation with sales, marketing, demand management, manufacturing, and finance, should lead to a decision and possibly production authorization with respect to the inventoried configuration.

Handling Abnormal Demand

With the immediate problem of cleaning up the sold-out zone (reducing the ATP to zero) taken care of, the master scheduler must look further into the future to determine what else needs to be done. For the company represented in the Figure 10.7 (pages 322–323) master schedule screen, the future planning zone for common components 5500 begins in time period 11/10 and continues to the end of the planning horizon. Normally, this planning zone contains no orders. But in this case a customer order for 80 sets of common components exists in time period 1/05 of the planning horizon.

This customer order is from a customer with whom the company normally doesn't do business, which means that it represents abnormal demand. Abnormal demands are composed of customer orders not anticipated or called out in the regular sales forecast. In this case, sales and/or customer service has indicated that the customer order for 80 units represents abnormal demand (code A) in the detail section.

Time period 1/05 contains an option forecast of 400 units and actual demand (known to be abnormal) of 80 units. Notice that the total demand calculated for time period 1/05 is 480, indicating that the abnormal demand did not consume the forecast but was considered additive. Since we know that abnormal demand is not part of the forecast, some adjustment to the master schedule must be made to ensure that an extra 80 sets of common components are available to satisfy that abnormal demand. The master scheduler has, in this example, already made that adjustment.

The Figure 10.7 master schedule screen indicates that by time period 1/05, 90 more units are scheduled than are forecasted. This was done by increasing the master schedule by 20 units in time periods 12/08, 12/15, and 12/22 and again by 30 units in time period 1/05. The master scheduler has decided to get the common components ready early, thus ensuring that sufficient common components are available to handle the abnormal demand order.

But the abnormal demand customer order is for only 80 units; why the 10 extra units? The answer is that the demand forecast for time period 1/12 jumps abruptly from the typical 400 units to 440 units. By increasing the master schedule in time period 1/05 to 430 units and holding it through time period 1/12 (stabilizing the master schedule and using small, incremental adjustments), the expected demand orders can be satisfied.

The buildup thus helps solve the abnormal demand issue and in addition helps to solve the expected increased demand in the forecast. In planning the buildup over the six time periods in question, the master scheduler would have returned to the time-phased bill-of-material for the common components (Figure 10.3, p. 318) to make sure of the availability of materials.

So, starting with time period 12/08, when the master schedule amount increases to 420 units, the master scheduler would have to check the R100 hard steel and the 1200C housing casting. The beauty of the time-phased bill-of-material is that the master scheduler can instantly determine the items that are impacted by a change in the master plan and/or master schedule.

To review how the MPS system handles abnormal demand, look at time period 12/22, where there is a projected available balance (PAB) of 60 units. The master scheduler has arranged for an additional 430 sets of common components to be available in time period 1/05, making a total of 490 sets of common components available (60 units plus 430 units master scheduled equals a total of 490 units). With a forecasted demand of 400 in that time period, 90 units will be left over. Since the 80 units is a result of the abnormal demand customer order—and not considered part of the forecast—it is also subtracted from the remaining 90 units, leaving a PAB of 10 units.

Action Messages

As the master scheduler looks further out on the planning horizon, he or she observes in time period 1/19 a computer planned order (CPO) of 440 units and in the master schedule detail section a recommendation to convert that CPO to a firm planned order (FPO). The reason for the recommendation stems from the fact that time period 1/19 is the first time period outside the planning time fence (PTF). Therefore, the master scheduler should convert this CPO to an FPO, so that the 440 units show up inside the PTF the next time the MPS system is run.

At the end of the current time period, 10/13, we would expect the 385 units to be shipped and all subsequent time periods to shift to the left. But at this point, the 440 units are still a CPO, and the master scheduler needs to convert it to an FPO. If no action is taken, the PTF would move to the end of time period 1/19, and the 440 units in that time period would be moved with it to the right—outside the planning time fence, since CPOs cannot exist inside the PTF. In that case, the master scheduled lot of 440 units in time period 1/26 (the new first time period outside the PTF after the system shifts all time periods to the left) would be doubled, from the 440 units to 880 units. An accompanying message would also inform the master scheduler of a negative available balance inside the PTF. The ATP would drop to zero in time period 1/19 because the master (supply) scheduled quantity was moved out of the time period.

Working the Pseudo Options

With the current situation for the common components in the continuing example now understood, and some actions in future time periods taken, the next step is to analyze the remainder of the options to determine what further actions might be necessary to ensure a complete and valid master schedule. Here, the option issues are illustrated through analysis of the 1,000# and 3,000# lift capacity options and the G102 gearbox.

The 1,000# Option

Item Information Section. The data contained in this section of the screen (Figure 10.8 on pp. 332–333) for the 1,000# option is basically the same as the item information in the common components screen; however, there are a few differences. Under *special instructions,* for example, this option is listed as being part of the winch product family, 18 percent of whose sales are expected to require this option configuration (note that the 18 percent is taken directly from the planning bill).

Master Schedule Detail Section. This section shows a series of action messages for the master scheduled item. Here, the master planning and scheduling software logic recommends a number of reschedule-ins and the conversion of a CPO to an FPO. The master scheduler would quickly see that 12 of the 13 master schedule lots are currently scheduled incorrectly, as evidenced by the R/I-01 (reschedule-in—one-period) messages. At first blush there appears to be a serious timing problem. But a complete analysis should take place before any knee-jerk action is taken.

Planning Horizons Section. The first step toward determining the source of the potential problem is to examine the *sold-out zone,* time periods 10/13 and 10/20. Time period 10/13 has 72 sets of the 1,000# option planned and/or scheduled to be received. In-house customer orders, however, total 74 units for this time period, and there are still 2 more units forecasted. Therefore, the total demand shown is 76 units (74 units + 2 units). Since only 72 units are scheduled to be available, the projected demand exceeds supply by four option sets.

Now review the next time period, 10/20. Again, 72 sets of the 1,000# option are planned and/or scheduled against a total projected demand (all in-hand customer orders) of 75 units, resulting in demand exceeding supply by 3 option sets. The PAB in that time period has gone from –4 units to –7 units, because of the 3 overbooked options. The difference between the –7 PAB, which is a cumulative number, and the cumulative ATP for the two time periods –5 is the option forecast for time period 10/13 (remember, ATP does *not* take forecast into account, whereas PAB accounts for *all* demand).

At this point, the master scheduler must ask: "Is current scheduling in the sold-out zone a problem?" Here it must be remembered that in the current time period of the sold-out zone, the chance of bringing in a customer order to use the common components is/was slim. So, when analyzing the common components earlier in this chapter, the master scheduler decided to either pull in a demand order that had been scheduled already and possibly ship it early, split a customer order and move some forward, decrease the master schedule to equal the actual demand, or build a popular configuration to stock.

Item Number	Primary Description		Item Status	Product Family				Master Scheduler		Demand Manager
1000	1000# OPTION		PSDO	WXYY				PROUD		PLANBL

Balance on Hand	Lot Size		Safety Stock		Time Fence					Lead Time	Cuml. Lead Time	Stnd. Cost
	Rule	Factor	Policy	Factor	PTF	DTF	MTF	CTF	RTF			
0	LFL	1	NO	0	13		12			1	16	$1,305

Period	Past Due	10/13	10/20	10/27	11/03	11/10	11/17
Item Forecast							
Option Forecast		2	0	48	67	72	72
Actual Demand		74	75	60			
Total Demand		76	75	108	67	72	72
Projected Available Balance	0	−4	−7	−30	−25	−25	−25
Available-to-Promise		−2	−3	20	72	72	72
Master Schedule		72	72	85	72	72	72

Period	1/12	1/19	1/26	2/02	2/09	2/16	2/23
Item Forecast							
Option Forecast	80	79	79	79	79	80	79
Actual Demand							
Total Demand	80	79	79	79	79	80	79
Projected Available Balance	−25	0	0	0	0	0	0
Available-to-Promise	80	105	79	79	79	80	79
Master Schedule	80	105	79	79	79	80	79

Master Schedule Detail						
Required Date	Order Number	Lot Number	Order			Recommended Action
			Quantity	Type	Status	
10/13	1000	226	72	MPS	FIRM	
10/20	1000	227	72	MPS	FIRM	R/I - 01
10/27	1000	228	85	MPS	FIRM	R/I - 01
11/03	1000	229	72	MPS	FIRM	R/I - 01
11/10	1000	230	72	MPS	FIRM	R/I - 01
11/17	1000	231	72	MPS	FIRM	R/I - 01
11/24	1000	232	72	MPS	FIRM	R/I - 01
12/01	1000	233	72	MPS	FIRM	R/I - 01
12/08	1000	234	72	MPS	FIRM	R/I - 01
12/15	1000	235	72	MPS	FIRM	R/I - 01
12/22	1000	236	72	MPS	FIRM	R/I - 01
1/05	1000	237	72	MPS	FIRM	R/I - 01
1/12	1000	238	80	MPS	FIRM	R/I - 01
1/19	1000		105			PLAN

Figure 10.8   Master Schedule Screen, 1,000# Option

Forecast Consumption	Resource Profile	Critical Resources					
		Resource	Resource	Resource	Resource	Resource	Resource
PLANBL	WXYY	MCH	SUB	ASSM	KIT	–	–

Selling Price	Special Instructions	Date Run	Actions Recommended		
$1,650	WXYY-18% OPTION	XX-XX-XX	NEG	R/I	PLN

11/24	12/01	12/08	12/15	12/22	1/05	Period
						Item Forecast
72	72	75	75	75	63	Option Forecast
						Actual Demand
72	72	75	75	75	63	Total Demand
−25	−25	−28	−31	−34	−25	Projected Available Balance
72	72	72	72	72	72	Available-to-Promise
72	72	72	72	72	72	Master Schedule

3/02	3/09	3/16	3/23	3/30	4/06	Period
						Item Forecast
79	79	79	80	79	79	Option Forecast
						Actual Demand
						Total Demand
0	0	0	0	0	0	Projected Available Balance
79	79	79	80	79	79	Available-to-Promise
79	79	79	80	79	79	Master Schedule

Actual Demand Detail												
Required Date	Order Quantity	Reference Number	Order Number	T	S	C	Required Date	Order Quantity	Reference Number	Order Number	T	S	C
10/13	60	WA01	M0814	F	R							
10/13	14	Capt Mtrs	C1746	A	R							
10/20	40	Chuck Mfg	C1823	A	R							
10/20	35	Riverbend	C1830	A	F							
10/27	60	WA01	M0820	F	F							

Figure 10.8 *Continued*

(Note: This figure will be referred to several times in the coming text. The reader may wish to bookmark this page for easy reference.)

In each case, the ATP at the common components and product family levels would go to zero. Remember, that is a responsibility of the master scheduler to make the master schedule line equal to the actual demand line in the *sold-out zone* for all *pseudo* items. If the ATP of 10 goes to zero at the product family level, that zero will be exploded through the planning bill (which obviously yields zero) to generate a forecast for all options and common components. When this is done, the option forecast for the 1,000# option will become zero in time period 10/13. The additional option forecast of two 1,000# options then vanishes into thin air. If the option forecast of two in time period 10/13 disappears, the PAB increases –4 units to –2 units. In time period 10/20, the PAB increases from –7 units to –5 units.

Solving the Problem. The solution to bringing the master schedule into balance begins by examining the actual demand detail section of Figure 10.8 on pages 332–333. In time periods 10/13 and 10/20, 74 units and 75 units of actual demand appear, respectively. The actual demand detail section indicates the sources of those numbers.

With respect to the 74 units of demand, the detail section indicates two sources. The first is an order for 60 sets for WA01, under manufacturing order M0814. The second is for 14 units for Captain Motors, customer order C1746. The customer order for Captain Motors is a regular assemble-to-order product; we know this because of the code "A" in order type. But the manufacturing order for 60 option sets is being built for stock on a manufacturing order ticket; again, the code "F" (for finished goods) makes this clear.

In other words, 60 option sets of those 74 option sets are for the company's own stock inventory! In attempting to bring actual demand and the master scheduled quantities into balance, which of these two demand sources might be easier to manipulate? The Captain Motors customer order may be untouchable for customer service purposes, but perhaps the manufacturing order to add to the company's inventory could be reduced from 60 option sets to 58 option sets or even something less. If that is possible, the problem in time period 10/13 will be solved.

Time period 10/20 is also oversold, as evidenced by the negative ATP, this time by 3 units. Again, the solution begins with determining the source(s) of actual demand. Here, there are two orders, one of 40 units for Chuck Manufacturing and one of 35 units for Riverbend. These are real customer orders for which promises have been made. The question that now must be asked is: "Can the master scheduler reduce the finished-goods order in the first time period from 60 option sets to 55 option sets or less?" If we can, the problem is solved. This would, in fact, result in 3 units being on hand as time period 10/13 ends, enough to cover the deficit in time period 10/20, and provide a perfect balance through the sold-out zone.

Thus, what appears to be a complicated and messy situation can be resolved simply by the demand and supply sides of the house reducing one stock order. *So, what is the moral of this example? Simply, to know the customers, including the needs of both external and internal customers; don't panic and jump to immediate conclusions; analyze the planning horizon as a whole; and use people's product and process knowledge to do what's best for the customer as well as the supplying company.*

When examining master schedule screens, it is easy to believe that the numbers represented in them are scientifically derived and absolutely valid. This is rarely the case in today's master planning and scheduling world (although some believe that it is improving at the speed of light); since the authors expect the master planning and scheduling process to be driven more and more by computer technology over the next decade, it can be said that MPS and the people working in this environment are on the path to truly knowing that the numbers represented in the MPS are scientifically (algorithmically) derived and absolutely valid (provided the inputs and master data are accurate).

However, the authors and readers are in today's environment and people are still involved in the equation. So, let's look at ways to rebalance the schedule; it is legitimate to continually challenge the numbers.

- Are items being made for inventory really critical?

- Is the lot size or supply order quantity optimal, or has it been arbitrarily set?

- Is there a bias in the demand forecast to ensure abundant supply?

- Is the ship date for a big order being dictated by the customer's needs, or by a salesperson's commission calendar?

- Has the lead time requested been padded by safety time, just in case?

These are all legitimate questions (it's called open and honest communications) for a master planner and/or master scheduler to ask as he or she attempts to balance supply and demand within a time frame that meets market needs. Again, let's all remember that the two bookend business objectives are to satisfy customers (and sales) while safely making money and a profit (for the business).

Returning to time period 10/13 for the 1,000# option (Figure 10.8 on pp. 332–333), we see that by dropping the WA01 demand order to 55 option sets (this should only be done by the person or function creating the demand, *not* the master scheduler), the first two reschedule-in messages would vanish—there would be no need to reschedule the master schedule lot in time period 10/20 into time period 10/13, or the 85 units in time period

10/27 into time period 10/20, as the PAB at the end of time period 10/20 would be zero, not a negative number.

In time period 10/27, another demand order for 60 option sets is on tap. Above that is demand for 48 additional sets of the 1,000# option, which is/was generated by the WXYY product family (Figure 10.2 on page 316) exploding its ATP through the planning bill (18 percent probability). To see how that happens, return to the common components (Figure 10.7 on pp. 322–323). There, the ATP in time period 10/27 is 265 units for the common components set. Due to the 100 percent or 1:1 ratio of the common components to the WXYY family in the planning BOM, the common-components ATP is the same as the WXYY product family ATP, therefore the common-components ATP can be used as a proxy for WXYY family ATP for demonstration purposes.

By exploding 265 units through the planning bill at the designated 18 percent probability for the 1,000# option, the result is 48 units, which appear in the option forecast line of that option's master schedule screen. Adding the 48 option sets forecasted to the 60 option sets already booked yields a total demand of 108 units against a master schedule of 85 option sets. Therefore, since the 60 option sets booked are for inventory (as indicated in the actual demand detail), the source of the problem is once again internal demand.

Demand is managed by sales and marketing; supply is managed by supply chain management or manufacturing. The problem revealed in our example is that the company has overbooked the master schedule—in this case with demand from a finished-goods item.

Another of the master scheduler's challenges is to understand what constitutes *real* demand and how to satisfy it. As the example implies, *not all demand is real and necessary.* The master scheduler works closely with the demand manager and with sales and marketing when determining who gets what and which orders receive priority.

The last item for discussion on the 1,000# option is the ATP in time period 10/27. Here the reader sees that 85 option sets are scheduled for receipt.[3] Actual demand is 60 option sets, which is subtracted from the MPS receipt of 85 option sets, leaving 25 option sets, *not 20.* The ATP of 20 option sets is a result of the system's using 5 available options to cover the oversold 5 option sets in time periods 10/13 and 10/20. In other words, the master scheduler should not commit more than 20 of the 1,000# options through time period 10/27.

Handling the Action Messages. Getting the 60-unit inventory order reduced makes all the reschedule action messages in this example disappear. The last task of the 1,000# option master scheduler is to convert the CPO for 105 units in time period 1/19 (just beyond the planning time fence) into an FPO. As time passes and time period 10/13 disappears, all remaining time periods shift to the left, but *no* CPOs on the master schedule

---

[3] This is a good example of overplanning, since the other master planning and schedule receipts are for 72; this 85 is also scheduled in the first unsold time period.

line can shift inside the PTF without their conversion to FPOs by the master scheduler. Failure to do so would result in the CPO being moved out into time period 1/26. The master scheduler should follow the system's recommendation and convert the CPO into an FPO, with the quantity being dependent upon the action taken when balancing the demand and supply in the sold-out zone.

The 3,000# Option

The 3,000# option is another pseudo-option, just like the 1,000# option. The difference is simply the lift capacity. The item information indicates nothing unusual (refer to Figure 10.9 on pp. 338–339). The PTF is the same for both options, as are the lot sizes. One difference is that the 3,000# option is planned as a 19 percent option instead of an 18 percent option.

Next, the master scheduler should look at the planning horizons data. In time period 10/13, notice the option forecast of 2 units. This will automatically vanish when the common components and winch product family's sold-out zone is cleaned up. Also, in time period 10/13, there is an actual demand of 71 option sets, and a master schedule lot of 76 option sets. The PAB in that time period will now be 5 option sets (adding 2 option sets to the PAB of 3 option sets to take into account the option forecast dropping to zero), indicating that 5 more sets of the 3,000# option are scheduled than exist as in-house manufacturing orders. Since the chances of bringing in a customer order of 5 option sets for this time period are slim, the master scheduler needs to clean up the sold-out zone for the 3,000# option.

Cleanup first requires a look ahead to time period 10/20, where the actual demand is for 75 option sets and the option forecast is zero—the company is not expecting to sell any more winches during the first two time periods. In the example, the master scheduler needs to cover the actual demand of 146 option sets (71 + 75) for the sold-out zone, for which 166 option sets of the 3,000# option sets are scheduled, leaving a surplus of 20 option sets of the 3,000# option.

Also notice in time period 10/20 that the PAB is 18 option sets and the ATP is 15 option sets. This PAB will increase to 20 option sets once the option forecast in time period 10/13 is reduced to zero. A majority of this surplus is caused by the master schedule receipt of 90 option sets. A significant portion (14) of this master schedule lot probably represents option overplanning done to compensate for expected forecast error. Here, the overplanning has moved into the sold-out zone.

Since no additional winch orders are planned to be received for immediate delivery in the sold-out zone, it makes no sense to schedule more 3,000# options than are required

Item Number	Primary Description		Item Status	Product Family					Master Scheduler	Demand Manager	
3000	3000# OPTION		PSDO	WXYY					PROUD	PLANBL	
Balance on Hand	Lot Size		Safety Stock		Time Fence					Lead Time	Cuml. Lead Time	Stnd. Cost
	Rule	Factor	Policy	Factor	PTF	DTF	MTF	CTF	RTF			
0	LFL	1	NO	0	13		12			1	16	$1,540

Period	Past Due	10/13	10/20	10/27	11/03	11/10	11/17
Item Forecast							
Option Forecast		2	0	50	70	76	76
Actual Demand		71	75	25			
Total Demand		73	75	75	70	76	76
Projected Available Balance	0	3	18	19	25	25	25
Available-to-Promise		5	15	51	76	76	76
Master Schedule		76	90	76	76	76	76

Period	1/12	1/19	1/26	2/02	2/09	2/16	2/23
Item Forecast							
Option Forecast	84	83	84	84	83	84	83
Actual Demand							
Total Demand	84	83	84	84	83	84	83
Projected Available Balance	23	0	0	0	0	0	0
Available-to-Promise	84	60	84	84	83	84	83
Master Schedule	84	60	84	84	83	84	83

Master Schedule Detail					
Required Date	Order Number	Lot Number	Order		Recommended Action
			Quantity	Type	Status	
10/13	3000	216	76	MPS	FIRM	
10/20	3000	217	90	MPS	FIRM	
10/27	3000	218	76	MPS	FIRM	
11/03	3000	219	76	MPS	FIRM	
11/10	3000	220	76	MPS	FIRM	
11/17	3000	221	76	MPS	FIRM	
11/24	3000	222	76	MPS	FIRM	
12/01	3000	223	76	MPS	FIRM	
12/08	3000	224	76	MPS	FIRM	
12/15	3000	225	76	MPS	FIRM	
12/22	3000	226	76	MPS	FIRM	
1/05	3000	227	76	MPS	FIRM	
1/12	3000	228	84	MPS	FIRM	
1/19	3000		60			PLAN

Figure 10.9   Master Schedule Screen, 3,000# Option

Forecast Consumption	Resource Profile	Critical Resources					
		Resource	Resource	Resource	Resource	Resource	Resource
PLANBL	WXYY	MCH	SUB	ASSM	KIT	–	–

Selling Price	Special Instructions	Date Run	Actions Recommended	
$1,980	WXYY-19% OPTION	XX-XX-XX	PLN	

11/24	12/01	12/08	12/15	12/22	1/05	Period
						Item Forecast
76	76	80	80	79	67	Option Forecast
						Actual Demand
76	76	80	80	79	67	Total Demand
25	25	21	17	14	23	Projected Available Balance
76	76	76	76	76	76	Available-to-Promise
76	76	76	76	76	76	Master Schedule

3/02	3/09	3/16	3/23	3/30	4/06	Period
						Item Forecast
84	84	83	84	83	84	Option Forecast
						Actual Demand
84	84	83	84	83	84	Total Demand
0	0	0	0	0	0	Projected Available Balance
84	84	83	84	83	84	Available-to-Promise
84	84	83	84	83	84	Master Schedule

Actual Demand Detail												
Required Date	Order Quantity	Reference Number	Order Number	T	S	C	Required Date	Order Quantity	Reference Number	Order Number	T	S	C
10/13	35	Main Mfg	C1759	A	R							
10/13	36	G Gregory	C1815	A	R							
10/20	15	Phillips	C1825	A	F							
10/20	10	Moore Mfg	C1832	A	F							
10/20	50	Eagle Betts	C1829	A	F							
10/27	25	Ames Mfg	C1841	A	F							

Figure 10.9 *Continued*

(Note: This figure will be referred to several times in the coming text. The reader may wish to bookmark this page for easy reference.)

by customer orders. Therefore, the master scheduler should reschedule the overplanning (established at 14 option sets in the example) to the first unsold time period in the partially sold-out zone, which is time period 10/27, or prepare to use them. Master planning and scheduling software systems may not make this suggestion; thus, the master scheduler may have to personally and carefully manage the overplanning dates and quantities.

Here the same alternatives confront the master scheduler as those presented earlier with respect to common components. The availability of the 3,000# option suggests that the pulling up of a customer order might be a good decision. Looking at the actual demand detail, we see that the company has a customer order for Ames Manufacturing (C1841) requiring 25 units of the 3,000# option winches in time period 10/27. This being the case, the master scheduler could elect to build some of these configurations ahead of time and either ship early (with customer approval) or store the completed products for a time period or two.

The master scheduler could also choose to build a *popular* configuration early, using the common components available and overplanned gearboxes, whatever they may be. (An examination of the gearbox master planning and schedule's ATP would determine the feasibility of this alternative.) The point here is that demand, as well as supply, can be managed in an effort to balance the master schedule in the sold-out zone.

If demand cannot be altered, then the supply must be changed. If the master scheduler decides to reduce supply, the approach would entail moving the 14 overplanned options to time period 10/27 from time period 10/20. The master scheduler would again lower the 76 option sets in time period 10/13 to 71 option sets, and in time period 10/20 the master schedule would read 75 option sets.

The master scheduler should also pay attention to the fact that the PABs in the future are too high, indicating an inventory buildup. The overplanning quantity is set at 14 option sets. Is this too much? Since the PAB continues to be positive, overplanning may need to be reduced.

Consider the master schedule detail in Figure 10.9 (page 338) for time period 1/19. The MPS system is recommending the conversion of the CPO for 60 option sets to an FPO for 60 option sets. The planning horizon data for this same time period indicates that it is time to make this conversion. But why the quantity of 60? The lot size for a pseudo is generally lot-for-lot (LFL). Using this logic, the computer software asks what should be released to put demand and supply in balance.

In time period 1/12 shown in Figure 10.9, the PAB is 23 option sets, indicating that there is expected to be 23 option sets available at the end of this time period. Since demand for the 3,000# option in time period 1/19 is 83 option sets, and 23 option sets are projected to be available at the end of the prior time period, a CPO for 60 option sets is created.

As the example highlights, the master planning and scheduling software adjusts the supply to equal the demand in the first time period outside the PTF, the first time period when and where CPOs can be placed.

Master Scheduling Purchased Items in the Planning Bill

Now we turn to the master schedule screen for the 4 fpm gearbox, a purchased item (Figure 10.10 on pp. 342–343). Master scheduling a purchased item in the make-to-order (MTO) environment is a combination of the logic discussed in Chapter 5 (on using the master scheduling approach in a make-to-stock [MTS] environment) and this chapter's logic on using master scheduling techniques supported by planning bills in a make-to-order (MTO) environment.

Item Information Section. The item information section contains the item number (G102) and other key information used by the master scheduler:

- On-hand balance equals 320 units (this is a *real* item).

- Lot sizes are fixed at 500 units per order (minimum order quantity).

- The company intends to maintain a safety stock of 100 units.

- The gearbox is a stocked (STK) item, *not* a pseudo item.

- The lead time is 12 time periods—it takes 12 time periods to receive a gearbox from the supplier after a supply order is placed. The planning time fence (PTF) is set at 12 time periods from the current time period.

- Thirty percent (30%) of winch family sales are forecasted to include this 4 fpm gearbox feature.

- Reschedule-in action is recommended.

Planning Horizons Section. Beginning in time period 10/13, there is an item forecast demand of 8 units, indicating that not only is the gearbox part of the winch's final assembly (noted in the option forecast), but it is sold as a spare or service item and is forecasted as

Item Number	Primary Description		Item Status	Product Family		Master Scheduler	Demand Manager
G102	4FPM GEARBOX		STK	WXYY		PROUD	PLANBL

Balance On Hand	Lot Size		Safety Stock		Time Fence					Lead Time	Cuml. Lead Time	Stnd. Cost
	Rule	Factor	Policy	Factor	PTF	DTF	MTF	CTF	RTF			
320	FIXD	500	QTY	100	12					12	12	$300

Period	Past Due	10/13	10/20	10/27	11/03	11/10	11/17
Item Forecast		8			20		
Option Forecast		3	0	80	111	120	120
Actual Demand		120	110	77			
Total Demand		131	110	157	131	120	120
Projected Available Balance	320	189	79	422	291	171	51
Available-to-Promise				423			
Master Schedule				500			

Period	1/12	1/19	1/26	2/02	2/09	2/16	2/23
Item Forecast				20			
Option Forecast	129	132	132	132	132	132	132
Actual Demand							
Total Demand	129	132	132	152	132	132	132
Projected Available Balance	159	527	395	243	111	479	347
Available-to-Promise		500				500	
Master Schedule		500				500	

Master Schedule Detail						
Required Date	Order Number	Lot Number	Order			Recommended Action
			Quantity	Type	Status	
10/27	G102	005	500	PUR	RLSD	R/I-01
11/24	G102	006	500	PUR	RLSD	R/I-01
12/15	G102	007	600	PUR	RLSD	

Figure 10.10 Master Schedule Screen, 4 fpm Gearbox

Forecast Consumption	Resource Profile	Critical Resources					
		Resource	Resource	Resource	Resource	Resource	Resource
PLANBL	NONE	–	–	–	–	–	–
Selling Price	Special Instructions		Date Run		Actions Recommended		
$440	WXYY-30% OPTION		XX-XX-XX		R/I		

11/24	12/01	12/08	12/15	12/22	1/05	Period
	20				20	Item Forecast
120	120	126	126	126	105	Option Forecast
20					80	Actual Demand
140	140	126	126	126	205	Total Demand
411	271	145	619	493	288	Projected Available Balance
480			520			Available-to-Promise
500			600			Master Schedule

3/02	3/09	3/16	3/23	3/30	4/06	Period
20					20	Item Forecast
132	132	132	132	132	132	Option Forecast
						Actual Demand
152	132	132	132	132	152	Total Demand
195	563	431	299	167	515	Projected Available Balance
	500				500	Available-to-Promise
	500				500	Master Schedule

Actual Demand Detail												
Required Date	Order Quantity	Reference Number	Order Number	T	S	C	Required Date	Order Quantity	Reference Number	Order Number	T	S	C
10/13	60	WA01	M0814	F	R							
10/13	45	WA04	M0815	F	R							
10/13	15	Allen Mfg	C1802	A	R							
10/20	60	WA06	M0819	F	F							
10/20	30	Everglass	C1819	A	F							
10/20	15	Phillips	C1825	A	F							
10/20	5	Pacific Inc	C1831	A	F							
10/27	60	WA01	M0820	F	F							
10/27	10	Smith Co	C1837	A	F							
10/31	7	Liftem Hi	C1834	S	S							
11/28	20	SGA	C1813	S	F	A						
1/05	80	Daly & Son	C1801	A	F	A						

Figure 10.10 *Continued*

(Note: This figure will be referred to several times in the coming text. The reader may wish to bookmark this page for easy reference.)

independent demand. This means that the gearbox option has a dual demand stream. A forecast of 20 units for expected service demand is found in the first time period of each month, rather than being spread evenly at 5 per time period.

Returning to time period 10/13, where the remaining service forecast is 8 units, one might speculate that the initial quantity for the month of October was 20 units. In this case the 8 units tells us that customer orders have been taken for 12 gearboxes, leaving the 8 gearboxes of the initial 20 gearboxes unconsumed. How have those 12 units been consumed? The actual demand detail section for time period 10/31 provides part of the answer: A customer order for 7 of the 4 fpm gearboxes has been promised to customer Liftem-Hi (C1834), with a promised delivery of 10/31. This customer order has consumed the demand forecast that precedes it by date.

In time period 10/27, there is actual demand of 77 gearboxes and 7 of those are the service order (S) from Liftem-Hi. Since no more service orders are listed in the demand detail section, the master scheduler (or reader) would have to assume that the missing 5 service orders have already been shipped or the initial forecast for October was 15 gearboxes, not 20.

The option forecast line for the 4 fpm gearbox is simply derived by exploding the ATP of the WXYY product family (see the ATP line of the common components, Figure 10.7 on page 322–323, as a proxy) through the 30 percent in the planning bill. Thus, if 400 winches (of all descriptions) were forecasted for time period 11/10, then 120 winches of the 4 fpm gearboxes would be forecasted (400 × 30% = 120).

This gearbox option forecast is automatically consumed every time an order (customer or manufacturing for stock) for a winch is booked (this is so because the gearbox is part of the winch's planning bill). In this gearbox's master schedule screen (Figure 10.10, pages 342–343), forecast consumption is taking place two different ways: one by the planning bill (affects the option forecast) and one by the forecasting logic in the master planning and scheduling system itself (item or service forecast).

Troubleshooting the Planning Horizon. The fact that the example company has a safety stock policy of maintaining a 100-unit inventory of gearbox G102 should send a signal to the master scheduler to scan the planning horizon for any violation of that requirement. The PAB line tells the tale. There are two violations—in time period 10/20, 79 gearboxes are projected to be available while in time period 11/17, 51 gearboxes are projected to be available.

These safety stock policy violations are the source of the action messages in the master plan and schedule detail section and the reason for the recommendations to move 500 gearboxes into time periods 10/20 and 11/17, respectively. If left to its own devices, the master planning and scheduling software system would follow these recommendations. However, before the master scheduler does any rescheduling, he or she should give some thought to the company's unwritten policy of stable master plans and/or master schedules, avoiding mountains of stock, and having enough inventory to satisfy customer demand. Before moving in an order of 500 gearboxes to satisfy a 21-unit safety stock problem (100 – 79 = 21), the master scheduler should make an attempt to finesse the situation.

The search for a solution to this problem begins at the sources of demand for the 4 fpm gearboxes: the various finished-goods winch configurations for which this gearbox is a bill-of-material item, service or spares demand, and safety stock.

We have already seen how the master scheduler got demand reduced for the 1,000# option. One part of that reduction was the product family's available-to-promise (ATP) of 10 option sets being reduced to zero. That reduction would also explode down to the 4 fpm gearbox in question, reducing demand for it by 3 units. Suppose, as discussed earlier in this chapter, that the master scheduler got the finished-goods order for the WA01 (1,000# options, 4 fpm gearboxes) reduced from 60 units to 55 units in time period 10/13, and from 60 units to 30 units in time period 10/27.

These reductions of 35 units would flow down to the 4 fpm gearbox level, reducing demand for it—more than enough to eliminate the first reschedule-in recommendation. Of course, the reason for this reduction is that the stocking orders in question use the 4 fpm gearbox.

Another point to consider before blindly following the computer software's rescheduling recommendations is the safety stock policy itself. Safety stock is *not* sacred; it is there to be used when it suits the best interests of the company and its customers—when unexpected customer orders (or manufacturing orders for stock) need to be satisfied, when production shortfalls occur, and to save the company from ordering 500 gearboxes (possibly the supplier's required order quantity) when only a handful are needed!

Time period 11/17 shows a projected available balance (PAB) of 5 units—49 units fewer than the 100 units required by the safety stock policy. The demand reductions for WA01 winches just mentioned would reduce that shortfall, leaving what many experienced master planners and/or master schedulers would view as a somewhat comfortable level of safety stock.

A novice might jump in and act quickly on the second reschedule-in message (which is why some master planners and/or master schedulers are nicknamed *Pogo—move the order in, move the order out, increase the volume, decrease the volume, etc.*) without understanding the impact on the supply chain, while the veteran master planner and/or master scheduler may ignore it and move on (maybe the veteran should have the nickname *Firm, not Frozen*).

Abnormal Demand. Finally, looking at time period 1/05, the 80 units in the actual demand line of Figure 10.10 (page 343) represent abnormal demand (the customer order for Daly & Sons we saw listed on the common components screen). In time period 11/28 there is another abnormal demand—20 units for SGA (see actual demand detail). Since this SGA order is a service requirement (indicated with an *S*) and is abnormal (indicated with an *A*), the booking of these 20 units did not consume the spares forecast. Remember, abnormal demand is incremental demand, and a system with an automated forecast consumption mechanism should *not* consume the forecast with any demand indicated as abnormal (the reader is advised to review his or her MPS software to understand how the system handles abnormal demand; many MPS software systems are *not* configured to handle abnormal demand correctly [authors' experience]). The handling of the 80 units of abnormal demand in time period 1/05 has already been discussed under common components.

The difference between master scheduling this gearbox and the pseudo common components above basically centers around the fact that real (buildable or purchased) gearboxes can be inventoried, while pseudo items (artificial collection of items, not buildable or purchased by itself) cannot.

Linking the Master Plan to the Master Schedule to the Material Plan

To understand the connection between the master planning and scheduling (MPS) and material requirements planning (MRP) for pseudo items, refer back to the 3,000# option (see Figure 10.9 on pp. 338–339). Recall that a winding assembly (item 3001) had been structured in as part of this option, and therefore demand for the 3,000# option triggers a one-for-one demand for the winding assembly through the MRP system. The MRP screen for the 3001 winding assembly is seen in Figure 10.11 on pages 348–349.

The MRP screen format is the same as the one introduced in Chapter 5 and similar to the MRP screens worked through earlier in this book. However, there are a few differences. Generally, the MRP system is driven by the master schedule line within the MPS system. Thus, if the master schedule for the 3,000# option calls for 90 units in time period 10/20, that triggers a projected gross requirement of 90 winding assemblies in time period 10/13—one lead-time period earlier. However, the 3,000# option is a pseudo item and requires a slight modification to that logic.

The MRP System

The *past due* time period in Figure 10.11 (page 348) indicates projected gross requirements of 41 units of part 3001 and a scheduled receipt of 8 units. Therefore, the starting projected available balance (PAB) can be calculated as follows:

Requirements Detail Section. The requirements detail in Figure 10.11 is analogous to the actual demand detail of the master schedule screen and explains the origins of demand for the item being analyzed. In this case, notice the first two lines of the requirements detail. The first line is for 36 units for customer G. Gregory; the second is for 5 3,000# option sets. The 36 units for G. Gregory are a customer requirement. The second is to fill an expected requirement for the 3,000# option.

Looking back to the actual demand detail in the master schedule screen for the 3,000# option (Figure 10.9 on pp. 338–339), that requirement—36 units for customer G. Gregory—is for time period 10/13. That is the required date to the finishing or final assembly line. But to meet this date, the one-period lead time for option 3,000# requires work to start on the item in time period 10/07. This can be observed both in the planning horizon for that date and in the requirements detail section.

The 5 units from the second line of the actual demand detail (Figure 10.11, page 349) represent the winding assemblies expected to be required by the 3,000# option in time period 10/13 and are a direct result of the ATP quantity at the master schedule option level, the quantity still not committed. Therefore, what is passed to material requirements planning from master scheduling for a pseudo item is a combination of the actual demand and the available-to-promise (ATP).

Now look at the 3,000# option in time period 10/13 of Figure 10.9 (pages 338–339), where the actual demand is 71 units. Two orders are found in the details section of that screen: one for 35 units and one for 36 units for Main Mfg and G Gregory respectively.

    249 Units on-hand balance at the beginning of the current time period

−   41 Units (number needed to satisfy the past-due requirement; the master scheduler should challenge why these items have not been issued if they are on hand)

+   8 Units past due supply, but expected to be received instantly (software coding) since they have not been rescheduled
_____

    216 Starting balance for next time period

Item Number	Primary Description	Item Status	U/M	Item Type	Comm. Code	MRP Planner	Value Class
3001	WINDING ASSEMBLY	STK	EA	SUB	NONE	MCGUIRE	A

| Balance on Hand | Safety Stock | | Scrap Factor | Annual Gross Requirements | Total Released Requirements |
	Policy	Factor			
249	NO	0	0%	4,180	136

Period	Past Due	10/13	10/20	10/27	11/03	11/10	11/17
Service Requirements							
Production Requirements	41	90	76	76	76	76	76
Scheduled Receipts	8						
Projected Available Balance	216	126	50	−26	−102	−178	−254
Planned Order Release			178			228	

Period	1/12	1/19	1/26	2/02	2/09	2/16	2/23
Service Requirements							
Production Requirements	69	84	84	83	84	83	84
Scheduled Receipts							
Projected Available Balance	−779	−863	−947	−1,030	−1,114	−1,197	−1,281
Planned Order Release		251			251		

| Master Schedule Detail | | | | | | | | |
Required Date	Promised Date	Order Number	Lot No.	Rem. Qty	Received	Type	Status	Recomm. Action
10/06	10/06	3001	86	8	220	MFG	RLSD	R/O-03
10/27	10/27	3001	87	178				Order

Figure 10.11   Material Requirements Planning Screen, 3001 Winding Assembly

Lead Time	Cumulative Lead Time	Order		Minimum Order Qty	Maximum Order Qty	Multiple Release Requirements
		Policy	Qty/Time			
1	16	POQ	3	100	NONE	NONE

Total Scheduled Receipts	Special Instructions	Date Run	Actions Recommended		
8	NONE	XX-XX-XX	R/O	ORDER	

11/24	12/01	12/08	12/15	12/22	1/05	Period
						Service Requirements
76	76	76	76	76	76	Production Requirements
						Scheduled Receipts
−330	−406	−482	−558	−634	−710	Projected Available Balance
	228			237		Planned Order Release

3/02	3/09	3/16	3/23	3/30	4/06	Period
						Service Requirements
84	83	84	83	84	83	Production Requirements
						Scheduled Receipts
−1,365	−1,448	−1,532	−1,615	−1,699	−1,782	Projected Available Balance
250			84			Planned Order Release

Actual Demand Detail												
Req'd Date	Req'd Qty.	Reference Number	Order No.	Lot	T	S	Req'd Date	Req'd Qty.	Reference Number	Order No.	Lot	T	S
10/07	36	G Gregory	C1815		A		12/15	76	3000		226	P	F
10/07	5	3000		216	P		12/22	76	3000		227	P	F
10/13	15	3000		217	P		1/05	84	3000		228	P	F
10/13	15	Phillips	C1825		A		1/12	69	3000			P	P
10/13	10	Moore Mfg	C1832		A		1/19	84	3000			P	P
10/13	50	Eagle Betts	C1829		A		1/26	84	3000			P	P
10/20	25	Ames Mfg	C1841		A		2/02	83	3000			P	P
10/20	51	3000		218	P		2/09	84	3000			P	P
10/27	76	3000		219	P		2/16	83	3000			P	P
11/03	76	3000		220	P		2/23	84	3000			P	P
11/10	76	3000		221	P		3/02	84	3000			P	P
11/17	76	3000		222	P		3/09	83	3000			P	P
11/24	76	3000		223	P		3/16	84	3000			P	P
12/01	76	3000		224	P		3/23	83	3000			P	P
12/08	76	3000		225	P		3/30	84	3000			P	P

Figure 10.11 *Continued*

Since only the order for 36 units appears in the material requirements planning screen (Figure 10.11, pages 348–349), the master scheduler knows that the requirements for 35 units of the 3001 winding assembly have already been satisfied. The remainder of this material requirements planning screen example is provided as reference material for the reader who wants to dig a little deeper into the MPS and MRP integration program.

In working through the several make-to-order (MTO) examples in this chapter, the reader should get a sense of the difficulty of master planning and scheduling in the MTO environment—the use of pseudo planning bills having contributed an added level of complexity. Difficult though it may be, it is a job that must be done if companies hope to be successful in satisfying customer orders within the lead time demanded by the marketplace.

Manufacturing Strategies—Products in the Make-to-Order Environment

Determining where the company wants to meet the customer (what state the company wants its product in when the customer order is received) is probably the *most important* decision the company will make regarding master planning and scheduling. There are several factors that need to be taken into account as the company decides the stage of product completeness for each product family, product subfamily, product groupings, and/or finished product.

We have discussed products in the make-to-stock environment in some length. We also have discussed products that the supplying company does not desire to hold finished goods in stock due to loss of flexibility and high cost of inventorying many variations of finished products offered by the company.

Where to meet the customer is determined for each product and/or product grouping. Some of the factors that a company reviews during the *where to meet the customer* discussion are as follows:

- Company's cumulative lead time required to build a product from scratch;

- Marketplace lead-time demands (windows of opportunity);

- Customer required lead times (all customers are equal; it's just that some are more equal than others);

- Competition's quoted delivery lead times (the company must win in either delivery, price, or quality);

- Cost of carrying inventory (warehousing, equipment, insurance, people, technology);

- Capacity reserved for finishing the product build in advance of customer order being received;

- Complexity of environment using pseudo bills, including probability percentages;

- Technology available to master plan and schedule the three backlog curve zones;

- Planner's and scheduler's skill in working in the product make-to-order world;

- Understanding of how to effectively apply option overplanning to master planning and scheduling.

Figure 10.12 outlines the various manufacturing strategy choices a company has in front of it. It is recommended that a time-phased bill-of-material be created for each major product grouping. Once this is done, the master planning and scheduling team (working with demand management) draw a line down at the lead time where the company must or desires to meet the customer.

For instance, maybe the company's cumulative lead time is 18 weeks, but the marketplace, potential customers, and competition dictate that the company be able to put a customer-configured product on the street in 12 weeks. This means that the company (if it desires to remain competitive in delivery times) must cut 6 weeks of lead time.

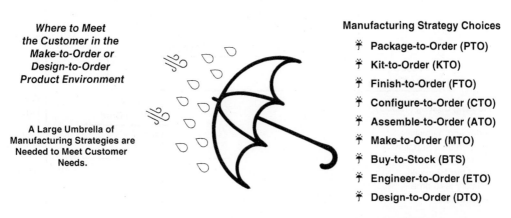

Where to Meet the Customer in the Make-to-Order or Design-to-Order Product Environment

A Large Umbrella of Manufacturing Strategies are Needed to Meet Customer Needs.

Manufacturing Strategy Choices

- Package-to-Order (PTO)
- Kit-to-Order (KTO)
- Finish-to-Order (FTO)
- Configure-to-Order (CTO)
- Assemble-to-Order (ATO)
- Make-to-Order (MTO)
- Buy-to-Stock (BTS)
- Engineer-to-Order (ETO)
- Design-to-Order (DTO)

Figure 10.12   Manufacturing Strategies Under Make-to-Order Umbrella

Cutting lead times can be done by applying various lean manufacturing techniques, simplifying or eliminating various non-value-adding operations, improving methods and processes related to value-adding activities, and so forth. However, these activities may not be enough to cut the required 6 weeks of lead time in this simple discussion.

Therefore, again, if the company still desires to remain competitive regarding lead-time delivery, the product must be stocked at the point where the 12-week line is drawn on the time-phased bill-of-material (refer to Figures 10.13 and 10.14 for an example of a time-phased bill-of-material being used to determine what needs to be stocked or on order for the company to meet the customer delivery requirements of 12 weeks).

What this says is that the company will purchase materials (in our example, the housing casting highlighted in Figure 10.13 and drum casting highlighted in Figure 10.14 on page 353) and (if necessary) build its product to an intermediate point but will *not* finish the manufacturing process until the customer order and customer specifications are received from the customer. It also means that the company will have the capacity in place to take the incomplete product to a complete product within the allotted lead time, 12 weeks in our example.

The most desired position is to meet the customer with a minimal amount of purchased material and no manufacturing done or completed (meeting the customer with a product that is truly make-to-order). However, the marketplace, customer, and competition may

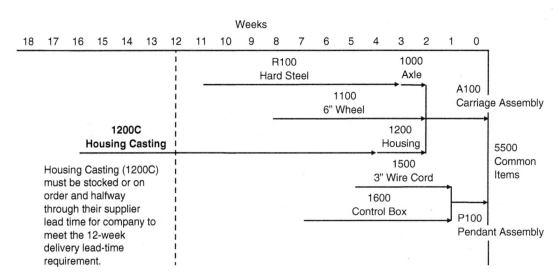

Figure 10.13   Time-Phased Common Components Planning Bill Linked to Lead-Time Reduction Strategy

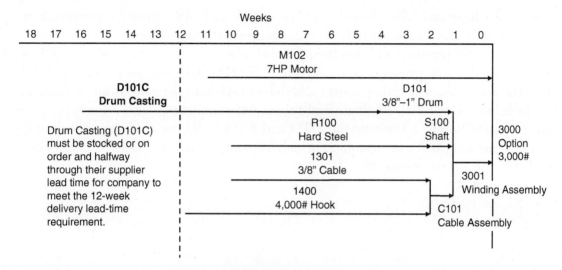

Figure 10.14 Time-Phased 3000# Option Planning Bill Linked to Lead-Time Reduction Strategy

again dictate that the company does some manufacturing prior to receiving the customer order in order to reduce delivery lead time once the customer order is received (meeting the customer with a product that is assemble-to-order, configure-to-order, finish-to-order). Maybe, just maybe, the delivery lead time is still too long for the company to be competitive, and more lead time must be trimmed.

As customer and marketplace delivery demand lead-time requirements to become shorter and shorter, the supplying company may be pushed into using a kit-to-order and/or package-to-order manufacturing strategy. For example, a company that supports surgeons during surgical procedures with instruments may build all the individual instruments to stock and prepare kits of instruments when the surgeon and surgical procedure is known.

Another example is that the company may build the finished goods items to stock and package them upon receipt of the customer order for different country deliveries (packaging requirements may well be different for various countries as well as labels printed in various languages).

Working with products in the make-to-order world is by far the most difficult environment that a master planner and/or master scheduler might work. However, manufacturing professionals, including master planners and master schedulers, know how to do it and do it right. It may be harder to work in this pseudo infected environment, but for many companies it is the most effective and efficient way to run the business. The alternative choices of make-to-stock or design-to-order just won't get the job done.

Since we have now discussed the make-to-stock and make-to-order manufacturing strategies, let's take a look at the final manufacturing strategy a company can choose to use in its master planning and scheduling world. The next chapter considers that other environment: custom products and design-to-order (DTO) or engineer-to-order (ETO). Here the master planner and/or master scheduler must make decisions in an environment in which bills-of-material, routings, lead times, and completion dates are *not* predetermined. In addition to addressing the DTO and ETO world, we shall take a look at the make-to-contract (MTC) environment, which has some similarities to the MTO as well as the DTO or ETO environments.

11

Master Planning and Scheduling in Custom-Product Environments

Failure to plan on your part does not constitute an emergency on my part.

Back in Chapter 6, several manufacturing strategies—make-to-stock, package-to-order, kit-to-order, finish-to-order, assemble-to-order, make-to-order, engineer-to-order, and design-to-order—were introduced and discussed. Each strategy was partially dictated by the competitive environment faced by the company and the need to meet the customer at some point in time earlier or later in the production process. In this chapter our focus will be on the design-to-order (DTO) and engineer-to-order (ETO) strategies, and on the particulars of master planning and scheduling in these environments. The process of developing and introducing a new product for which no actual demand yet exists, whether it be for a make-to-stock or make-to-order product, is a unique application of the design-to-order or engineer-to-order strategy.

As a brief review, recall that companies utilizing a DTO or ETO supply chain strategy generally do not begin the design and/or manufacturing process until a customer order, contract, or letter of intent is actually in hand. Specialized industrial equipment, large passenger aircraft, high-tech military equipment, commuter subway cars, and shopping malls are typical of DTO and ETO products. Because these products are expensive and suited for a limited number of customers and applications, their manufacturers cannot afford to design, build, and hold them in inventory in the expectation of future orders. Unlike companies that make products to stock so they can meet their customers at or near the time of delivery, companies using the DTO and ETO manufacturing strategy design and engineer their products to order; their customers are willing to wait months and even years before completion and delivery of the final product.

This is not to say that companies that design product to order and engineer product to order do not, or need not, forecast future business activity or practice the disciplines of integrated business planning or sales and operations planning, product portfolio management, demand management, supply management, logistics management, and financial management. The mere fact that these companies have designers, engineers, supply chain professionals, and manufacturing personnel on the payroll is clear evidence that future designing, engineering, supply chain planning, and manufacturing activities are anticipated and that some future planning (e.g., demand forecasting) is, in fact, required and taking place. The only real differences among all the various supply chain or manufacturing strategies are the planning time horizon and where master planning and scheduling is done.

The Unique Challenges of the DTO and ETO Environments

To appreciate the challenges facing master planners and master schedulers in companies that design products to order and/or engineer products to order products, consider Figure 11.1, which roughly describes the value-/cost-adding activities that must go on within the company between its customer contract or promise and actual delivery of the finished product. For perspective, companies that make products to stock and make products to order are added to the figure.

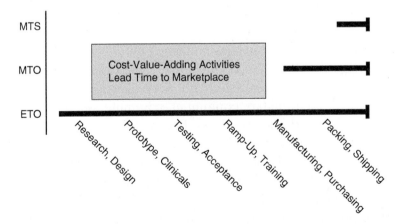

Figure 11.1 Tasks of Manufacturing Strategies Compared

The bottom axis of Figure 11.1 on the prior page is a timeline along which these activities are listed. As the figure makes clear, the company that designs to order and/or engineers to order all or some of their products faces the product management, demand management, supply management, logistics management, and financial management chores that other companies face, but these challenges are just the tip of the iceberg, so to speak—other major planning and scheduling tasks lie beneath the surface:

- Product specifications must be worked out, usually in collaboration with the customer;

- A prototype or sample must be produced and tested;

- Feedback from prototype testing must be reflected in design and engineering changes;

- Marketing and promotional activities usually commence before a product exist;

- New structures and processes must be integrated with current structures and processes;

- Bills-of-material, formulas, or recipes, as well as process routings, must be created;

- Master planning and scheduling uses a combination of standard and pseudo product structures;

- Those with a need to know must be educated and trained on the new products, structures, and processes;

- Thought must be given to the products, structures, and processes that will be eliminated or modified;

- Ramp-up to final demand and supply planning as well as manufacturing levels must begin.

Many of these activities precede the traditional master planning and scheduling (MPS) and material requirements planning (MRP) activities so far discussed. This does not mean, however, that the master planner and/or master scheduler and the tools for balancing demand and supply cannot be useful in these earlier activities. Quite the contrary; the master planner and/or master scheduler, being one of the individuals responsible for getting the final product to the customer, is a logical candidate for coordinating the DTO and ETO activities; it needs to be noted here that the MPS techniques are eminently suited to DTO and ETO product environments from design/engineering through supply chain planning through master planning and scheduling through material purchasing through manufacturing operations through packaging and shipping.

The main difference between master planning and scheduling manufacturing activities and engineering activities is that instead of bringing materials and manufacturing capabilities together within certain build times, the DTO and ETO master planner and/or master scheduler must provide for human resources and elapsed times for products thought of in a much broader sense: research specifications, product designs, engineering drawings, tooling configurations, planning that which is unknown, people and machine requirements for that which is known as well as unknown, testing and learning activities, marketplace acceptance, packaging/labeling, and so forth.

The Case of New Product Introduction

Design-to-order and engineer-to-order master planning and scheduling issues are equally relevant to companies that make products to stock and/or make products to order when they plan and introduce new products. In these instances, a product is being designed to order or engineered to order at the behest of executive management and the marketing function, who have determined the feasibility and sales potential of the item. New products for these companies must pass through the same research and development activities—research, design, prototype, clinical trials, testing, acceptance, ramp-up, training, full purchasing and manufacturing phases—as do DTO and ETO products.

The same challenges apply to both environments. Demand must be forecasted; product specifications or formulations must be developed; design changes based on prototype or clinical testing must be made; agency approvals need to be granted (not in all cases); and processes for manufacturing, packaging/labeling, and shipping the final new product must be arranged. In fact, new products create two extra levels of planning and scheduling difficulties regardless of the supply chain or manufacturing strategy chosen: (1) timing the introduction, and (2) planning for the impact of the new product on current lines of business. Generally, these two difficulties are not unrelated.

Timing New-Product Introductions

New-product introductions are always risky. Product development requires high expenses for research and development, design, engineering, and the tooling to bring the product to market. These costs are incurred before even one dollar of revenue is generated and must be paid, regardless of whether the product is a success or failure. *And there is no assurance that the new product will succeed.* No matter how much thought goes into market research, no matter how much money is spent on promotion designed to introduce the new product to the marketplace, high failure rates for new products are the rule in many industries.

Minimizing the risks associated with new-product introductions requires careful planning—that is, forecasting and coordination of procurement/purchasing/operations/ manufacturing with sales and marketing. From the master planner's and/or master scheduler's perspective, this means working closely with marketing and new product technology to hit roll-out dates planned in the company's promotional strategy.

The confusion and damage caused by poor coordination between production and promotion can be great and are well illustrated in these five cases:

1. In the late 1980s, Lotus Development Corporation spent months and millions preparing its large base of Lotus 1-2-3 users to switch over to a forthcoming upgrade of its popular spreadsheet program. The customers were ready, but the product was not. Month after month of production delays caused confusion and frustration for both the company and the marketplace.

2. In late 1991, Apple Computer Company introduced its low-priced Classic model of the Macintosh. The product rolled out of Apple's new, state-of-the-art plant built especially for this machine; Apple was right on time for the Christmas buying season. The Classic was an immediate success in all but one respect: Demand was more than twice what had been forecast. The result: angry dealers who were allocated a few machines at a time, demoralized salespeople, and many customers who simply gave up waiting for their promised Classics and bought competing machines to put under the Christmas tree.

3. In late 2000, one of this book's authors (John) read an article in *Road and Track* magazine about the BMW M5 (named R&T sedan of the year) coming to the United States. Being a car enthusiast and having picked up his first BMW in Germany in 1985, John immediately set his sights on acquiring one of these vehicles in 2000. When John showed up at his local BMW dealer, he was told that they would put

him on the waiting list (number 28); John was also told that the dealership was allocated only two M5s in 2000 while future allocations were still up in the air! (Story's Conclusion > John got lucky!)

One of John's golfing friends was driving by a BMW dealer in the greater Los Angeles area and saw its sign that read, *M5s available*. John's friend called John (the friend knew John was looking to secure an M5) to let him know about his discovery (that was on a Sunday). On Monday morning John set out to visit that dealer (he was on his way to commencing a somewhat local consulting assignment starting Tuesday) to see what was truly available. Well, John selected one of the three M5s available (the West Coast dealer had acquired three M5 vehicles from an East Coast dealer) and closed the deal. So, this became a win/lose and lose situation: John got his M5 by paying over manufacturer's suggested price while John's local dealer lost a high-end sale. By the way, John still owns and drives that M5!

4. In 2016, Samsung introduced the Galaxy Note S7. Samsung had been steadily gaining market share against its rival Apple and had surpassed the Apple iPhone sales in several markets. The pressure was on to maintain momentum. Two months after launch, reports began circulating that the Galaxy Note S7 had a minor problem: It tended to burst into flames due to short-circuit flaws with the battery. The phone was banned on airline flights and 2.5 million units were recalled by Samsung. Samsung identified the issue and ramped up production at a second battery manufacturer, only to have the same problem occur again! The result was $3 billion in losses due to damage control, a drop in market capitalization of over $14 billion due to frightened investors selling shares in the company, and a severely bruised reputation that set back prior gains in market share. In short, the pressure to compete and maintain launch schedules can lead to costly quality errors in design, planning, scheduling, manufacturing, and execution.

5. In late 2020 Apple announced its iPhone 12. The question at the time was, How is Apple going to handle its expected demand this time around (remembering what happened 30 years ago—see #2)? Well, if a consumer wants a new iPhone 12 in November, that consumer needs to preorder the phone (and probably pay for it in advance). By taking this action, Apple created a situation that was a win/win for the customer and supplier; the customer got one of the first new phones available on the market (promised delivery date was placed out into the future, probably taking lead time and the entire supply chain into account) and the supplier, Apple, got the best demand forecast possible, that of customer orders.

These are only five stories (one per decade) that have happened in the past 50 years. Of course, there are tens, hundreds, and probably thousands more that master planners and schedulers are aware of (there may be several within the reader's own company walls). The place to start the required communication among product management, demand management, supply management, logistics management, and financial management is the monthly integrated business planning (IBP) process. As a reminder, the IBP monthly process consists of the product portfolio review, demand review, supply review, integrated reconciliation review, and management business review supported by financial appraisals along the way. Besides planning the new product launch dates into the marketplace, the participants in the IBP process need to establish business expectations regarding products that are already in the marketplace (especially the products that generate significant revenues for the company).

Planning for the Impact on Existing Products

The introduction of a new product generally has some impact on a company's existing products. In some cases, the new product is an intended replacement of a current product and, except for service or spare parts, supply planning and manufacturing of the existing product is discontinued; the annual model changes of automobiles are a good example. In other cases, it is assumed that the new product will cannibalize some sales from the company's existing products; one might assume Apple's introduction of the PowerBook and MacBook surely had that effect on its other basic, monochrome screen models. How about the over-the-counter drug manufacturers who promote a new, improved aspirin on television, causing significant impact on demand. In some cases, as with the introduction of new products in separate product markets, no impact on existing products would be expected; Samsung's introduction of a new television model, for example, would have no measurable impact on sales of its popular cell phone.

Consider a company preparing for the introduction of a new product that it hopes to eventually replace demand for an existing product. In planning its initial periods of supply, the company needs to do several things: It must continue satisfying demand for the old product until the new product catches on in the marketplace, it must plan on the elimination of inventory for the old product, and it must phase in operations and manufacturing of the new product as demand and production for the old one taper off (Figure 11.2, page 362).

In this case, the company planned the new-product introduction for time period 3 and planned for the gradual displacement of the old product by the new product over time periods 3 through 6. This is a simple case, without lead time or inventory complications. Nor does it recognize the possibility that the production line may have to be shut down for

	1	2	3	4	5	6
Old Product	20	20	15	10	5	0
New Product	0	0	5	10	15	20
Total Production	20	20	20	20	20	20

Figure 11.2   Introduction of a New Product (in Time Period 3)

production training and product changeover. But this case should make the point about the issues the master planner as well as the master scheduler must consider in planning new-product introductions. Let's take a look at the process for getting a new product to the marketplace.

Launching a New Product

The job of putting a new product into the marketplace in a respectable time frame has proven to be a frustrating experience for many organizations. To improve the process, a number of companies have adopted a four-step approach to new-product introductions.[1]

1. Use a task force to plan and create data structures and process routings as well as to maintain control of these structures and routings. The task force usually consists of four to seven people representing research, design, marketing, process engineering, master planning and scheduling, material and capacity planning, operations and manufacturing, procurement and purchasing, possibly regulations and trials, packaging and labeling, and shipping and tracking.

2. Make all new products and their market introductions part of the integrated business planning or sales and operations planning process. Each new product is added to the monthly agenda, with discussions revolving around design

---

[1] For a complete discussion of new product launches, see Jerry Clement, Andy Coldrick, and John Sari, *Manufacturing Data Structures* (New York: John Wiley & Sons, 1992).

documentation, material availability, manufacturing capabilities, marketing promotion, introductory pricing, and strategy issues.

3. Create a bill-of-activities (sometimes referred to as a bill-of-events) that includes all the activities and events that must take place between product idea approval and actual product launch. Couple this bill-of-activities or bill-of-events with resource templates to generate priorities and resource requirements. Eventually, these bills-of-activities or bills-of-events will be replaced with actual bills-of-material, recipes, formulations, and process routings.

4. Use best-practice planning and control concepts of master planning and scheduling (MPS) and enterprise resource planning (ERP) to execute materials and activities requirements. This makes it possible for the company to plan, schedule, execute, control and report progress, and to know at all times what needs to be done, the nature of resource requirements, and when each activity is to be completed.

Master Planning and Scheduling—Activities and Events

Virtually any set of items, activities, or events can be master planned and scheduled. In the traditional sense, master planning and scheduling typically means ensuring that operations and/or manufacturing has the materials and capacity required when it commences the product's production steps, such as putting together the items or ingredients to produce a ballpoint pen, a bottle of shampoo, an automobile, a can of paint, and so forth.

In the design-to-order (DTO) and engineer-to-order (ETO) and new-product environment as seen in Figure 11.3 on page 364, many of those activities and events take place at computer design screens, in testing laboratories, in sales brochures, around conference tables, on conference calls, and in web-based meetings. These activities and events can and should be master planned and scheduled.

This goes back to the earlier questions of what and where do we master plan and schedule? Some of the candidates for the answer to these questions are packaged products, end items, option sets, material groupings, raw materials, and so on. Here (for products in the DTO and ETO environment), we plan and schedule activities and events, and instead of master planning and scheduling from recipes or bills-of-materials, bills-of-activities or bills-of-events are among the tools of the master planner's and/or master scheduler's trade.

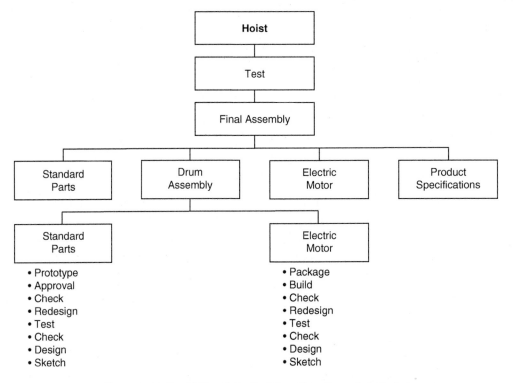

Figure 11.3   Bill-of-Activities for Special Hoist

Consider Levitation Lift Corporation (LLC), which is in the heavy-duty hoist and crane business. Working with executive management and marketing, LLC's research and development center has proven a new hoist technology that it is ready to give to supply chain planning and manufacturing. A small-scale model based on off-the-shelf materials has been tested in the laboratory and in the field, and it is time to bring it up to full scale through design and engineering and ready it for operations and/or manufacturing.

No design specifications and no bills-of-material currently exist for this new product, but the master planner and/or master scheduler can still apply his or her art and tools to this project following these steps:

1. *Classify the scope of the change.* Is the hoist a major or minor product change, or does it represent a new-product concept? Does it fit into any existing product family? This information imparts a feel for the complexity and difficulty associated with the upcoming change.

2. *Create a dummy item number for the finished hoist.* Ask design engineering (or research and development) to release a number that will be used for planning purposes. At some future point the new product will either carry this number or be assigned a new one.

3. *Identify significant activities.* Here the master planner and/or master scheduler or master planning and scheduling task force would list the set of important tasks necessary for designing/engineering and producing the hoist—ideally, in the sequence in which they must take place. In this case, design, detail engineering, perhaps a customer approval of the detailed design, drafting, checking the drawings, creating of a prototype, and so forth, all the way through the assembly, testing, and shipping activities, might make up this list. Even significant sales and marketing activities should be identified.

   Naturally, the master planner and/or master scheduler cannot know in detail all significant activities and events associated with the creation of this hoist: They do not yet exist. But knowledge of the products of his or her business and close consultation with relevant parties within the company make a close approximation possible. And at this stage, a close approximation is all that is required.

4. *Create a bill-of-activities or bill-of-events.* At this point a bill-of-activities or bill-of-events like the one in Figure 11.3 (page 364) can be constructed. The product will be built from the bottom up, but anyone looking at the bill will know that to get the special hoist onto the shipping dock, a test will have to be made.

   Four significant events must take place before that test can be made: Product specifications must be developed and produced; an off-the-shelf motor must be obtained; a drum assembly must be designed and built; and some standard parts must be procured as their significance to the hoist is spelled out. Each of these four significant events has its own bill-of-activities, bill-of-events, or defined bill-of-materials. As unknown events are entered into the bills-of-activities or bill-of-events, use dummy numbers.

5. *Estimate total resources and lead time for each activity or event.* In the example, we would consider the resources required to complete each of the four significant activities (and their subactivities) and the test involved in making the special hoist (Figure 11.4 on page 366). The lead times for performing each of these activities and/or events can be estimated from past projects and programs as well as conversations

Activity	Elapsed Time (Weeks)	Hours Required	Competition/ End of Week #
Sketch	3	120	3
Design	4	165	7
Check	1	15	8
Test	1	10	9
Redesign	2	80	11
Check	1	15	12
Build	3	120	15
Package	1	20	16
Total	16	545	16

Figure 11.4   Loading and Scheduling the Activities

with the relevant company functions, and these can be used to create the planning lead times and a cumulative time frame for the entire DTO and ETO project or program.

Taking just one activity as an example, LLC might schedule the *tooling for the drums* as follows: *Combine the master plan and schedule for the drum tooling with similar master plan schedule for each of the other significant activities to construct an overall project lead-time schedule.* This is then available for the next step.

6. *Rough cutting the project or program lead-time schedule.* The methodology for rough cut capacity planning (Chapter 15) is here brought to bear on the hoist's schedule of the project to determine if the plan is feasible, given the company's resources and other commitments.

7. *Replace dummy item numbers with real numbers.* As the bill-of-activities or bill-of-events becomes more fully articulated with design specifications and actual materials or ingredients required, obtain real numbers from design and engineering for those items and substitute them for the *dummy numbers* in the original plan.

8. *Validate/adjust lead times and resources as required.* Over time, as more information becomes available, the original estimates for lead times and resource requirements will need to be validated and, where appropriate, adjusted. The ERP software system using the MPS module logic (maybe in conjunction with a project management system) can then be used to recalibrate the entire project or program.

9. *Reprioritize all materials and activities.* This is where a master planning and scheduling and network system can be of the greatest use. If all marketing, design, engineering, material planning, capacity planning, manufacturing, product testing, logistics planning, and shipping activities are driven by a common master plan and/or master schedule, each event will be in line with the others to ensure continuity with the entire master plan and/or master schedule.

Prices and Promises to Keep

The schedule developed through the steps just listed has three uses in design-to-order, engineer-to-order, and new-product introduction situations:

1. *To determine a delivery date for the marketplace, sales force, and customer.* In new-product introductions, as in the Apple anecdote cited earlier in this chapter, it was important to be able to tell dealers, sales representatives, and end users when the product would be available. They need this information for their planning purposes, and woe unto the manufacturer that fails to deliver on its promises. Delivery dates are also critical to the negotiating process between company and customer on design-to-order and engineer-to-order products.

2. *To determine required activities and events that must be done in order to bring the new product into the marketplace.* In cases for which a delivery date requirement has already been determined, the bill-of-activities product schedule allows the company to *backward schedule* from the product's due date to obtain all the event start and required completion dates that will make the delivery date feasible. These become the *start and due dates* for all individual tasks.

3. *To create a structure for benefit and cost analysis.* In the absence of bills-of-material, formulations, or recipes, the master plan and/or master schedule and bills-of-activities (remember, bills-of-activities are also called bills-of-events) just described form a basis upon which the company can estimate its costs in time and materials on the DTO and/or ETO product including the new-product introduction. These costs are an important element in pricing the forthcoming product, which is generally required in competitive bidding situations for DTO and ETO products.[2]

What Can Go Wrong

The new-product master plan and/or master schedule for design-to-order and/or engineer-to-order products can be upset by a number of unforeseen problems. In fact, the longer the planning horizon, the greater the potential for these problems to manifest themselves. Among the sources of master planning and scheduling problems are the following:

- *New or unknown processes and technologies.* Since the company is dealing with a new product, it is possible that the processes necessary to produce it may also be new. Of course, the same can be said for the technology needed to bring the product to the marketplace.

- *Lack of product specifications, at least initially.* It is not unusual in this environment for design and/or engineering to release to supply chain planning and manufacturing an incomplete set of specifications.

- *Frequent design and engineering changes.* For example, in master planning and scheduling the introduction of a complex new product, a period of many months may elapse between the point at which certain materials are specified within the design along with the engineering and the date at which materials are actually scheduled

---

[2] American and European firms have tended to determine product price on the basis of their manufacturing and development costs. Japanese firms generally have adopted a "target price" approach, first determining a price that will allow their new products to penetrate or create a market, and then working back through manufacturing and materials to design and engineer the product with a cost structure that allows them to meet that price objective profitably.

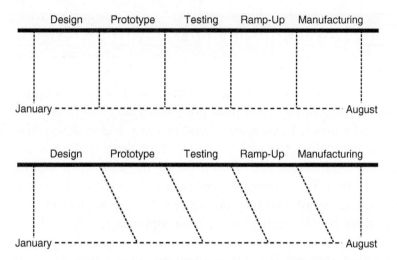

Figure 11.5   Effects of Scheduling Delays

for purchase. During this time, and unknown to the manufacturer, the supplier of that material may have gone out of business or switched to a different material, which may not be compatible with the design and/or engineering. This adversely affects the schedule.[3] This would not happen if the supplier was part of the team.

What typically happens in many development projects is seen in Figure 11.5. This shows planned activities and their schedule along a timeline from project inception in January to manufacturing and shipping in late August.

The first part of the figure is what was planned; the second part shows what can happen! Here design and engineering has consumed more time than planned, and since the activities are sequential, all the remaining activities must be squeezed into a shortened time frame if commitments to the marketplace and customers are to be met. *It should not be surprising if product quality suffers and people frustrations mount as a result.*

---

[3] For a very complete description of the problems of product development management, with emphasis on the worldwide auto industry, see Kim B. Clark and Takahiro Fujimoto, *Product Development Performance* (Boston, MA: Harvard Business School Press, 1991). Other research performed by the Ford Motor Company in 1986 indicated that the typical U.S. automaker accelerated the frequency of its engineering changes up to the time of the first production run, and even continued those engineering changes at a high pace several months into the production phase of the new-model introduction. The result was surely much confusion, delays, and poor-quality automobiles until such time as the level of changes stabilized. The same Ford study indicated that engineering changes for Japanese auto firms peaked out 16 to 20 months before the first production run; very few changes were made in the months just prior to initial production, and virtually no changes once production was in full swing.

Integrating Design and Operation Activities

Design, engineering, and manufacturing schedules must be integrated so that all energy in the company is focused on a common goal—satisfying customer needs while safely making money and a profit. In companies that produce highly designed and engineered products, and in companies for which new-product development is a major strategic thrust, design and engineering and related functions make up a significant portion of schedule time and costs. These design and engineering activities precede supply planning and manufacturing activities, and they do not stop with new-product design and release but continue in the form of ongoing engineering support.

Even though it is easy to see why design and engineering and manufacturing activities should be integrated, they are not always integrated in practice. This is because design, engineering, and product development schedules typically are not derived from manufacturing and procurement schedules that trace their origins back through the master plan and/or master schedule to sales plans and customer commitments.

Figure 11.6 on page 371 illustrates the relationship between design/engineering and manufacturing/production activities in moving from the early stages of a project to a delivered product. This relationship goes beyond product engineering to tooling and process flow design.

Many companies fail to integrate design and engineering activities with manufacturing and production activities or drive them with a common master plan and/or master schedule. This is a typical source of trouble. It does very little good to be ready to perform a manufacturing operation on time when the product design and/or engineering is not yet complete; nor does it help company efficiency and effectiveness when different design and/or engineering projects converge on a design or engineer resource bottleneck at the same time.

The solution to the problem of engineering-manufacturing integration is to drive all requirements—whether design, engineering, sales, marketing, supply chain planning, manufacturing, product testing, quality, or finance—with a common master plan and/or master schedule (Figure 11.7 on page 372).

A common master plan and/or master schedule ensures that a company's total resource requirements are aligned with the goal of satisfying customer needs while safely making money and a profit. It is tied directly to the output of the integrated business planning or sales and operations planning process.

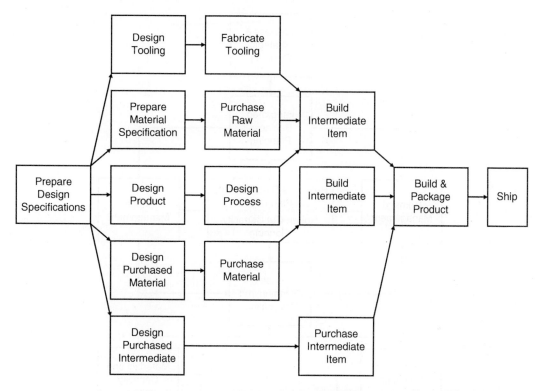

Figure 11.6 Engineering and Manufacturing Dependent Relationship

By generating need dates through enterprise resource planning and master planning and scheduling, design and engineering personnel are informed of required dates for its *products* (drawings, specifications, process instructions, etc.). These required dates can be passed upstream until all activities and priorities are scheduled.

For years, manufacturing companies have used a combination of the master plan and/or master schedule, process routings, and work center resource data to plan and control capacities. To do the same for design and engineering resources, process templates that define tasks for each designing and engineering job need to be created. These templates identify the sequence of tasks, where work will be done (e.g., in the laboratory), and the time estimated to complete each task.

With the templates in hand, a resource capacity plan can be generated for design, engineering, supply chain planning, manufacturing, product testing, and logistics work. Tasks that require common resources (e.g., drawing, checking) are highlighted as potential impediments to the scheduled completion of design and/or engineering requirements.

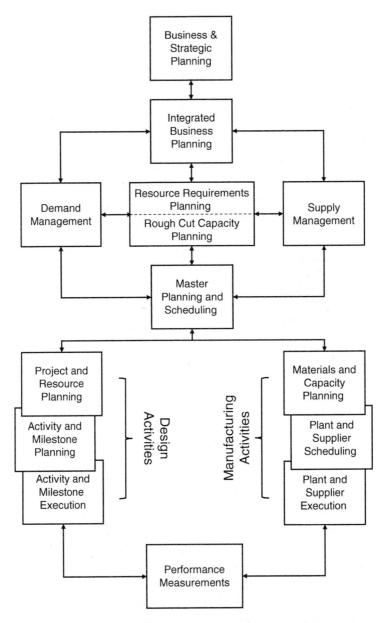

Figure 11.7   Design and Manufacturing Activities Planning Using a Common Master Plan and/or Master Schedule

This process is known as design or engineering resource planning. It is a methodology that integrates design, engineering, and manufacturing requirements by means of a common master plan and/or master schedule. Basically, design or engineering resource planning is a time-phased planning process similar to enterprise resource planning.

Instead of just planning materials and capacity to support the manufacturing build process, design or engineering resource planning plans design and engineering capacity requirements, production capacity requirements, required materials to support operations and manufacturing (and can also plan materials to support design and engineering), and unknown processes/capacities early in the game (uses the best data and information available at the time). And it's *all integrated* and driven by the master of all plans and schedules, the master plan and/or master schedule.

Plan Down, Replan Up

Design engineering has products just like manufacturing. Some of these products consist of drawings, bills-of-material, routings, recipes, formulations, process sheets, and specifications. In order to produce these products, a series of activities or events like designing, engineering, drafting, checking, and documenting must take place.

Therefore, if a company can tie together these design and engineering activities, identify the amount of expected or anticipated lead time necessary to complete each activity, and determine the due date for the product or project, a detailed activity plan can be created. Figure 11.8 on page 374 is an example of a customized product that requires standard manufactured items and operations plus yet-to-be-designed and/or engineered materials and tooling.

In a demand-driven business, the initial plan is created by starting with the demand due date (and quantity) and planning down through all of the activities needed to satisfy this demand due date (and quantity). The due date for the product in this example is workday 145 (the start of planning shown on the left side of the boxes in the figure). The final configuration of the product is estimated to take five days of work once the two standard items and the one new item are available.

Taking this into account, the start date for the final configuration process is workday 140. This start date creates the due dates for the new and standard items. Although the remainder of discussion will concentrate on start and due dates (this is done to simplify a complex discussion as well as a complex figure), item quantities are generally planned at the same time.

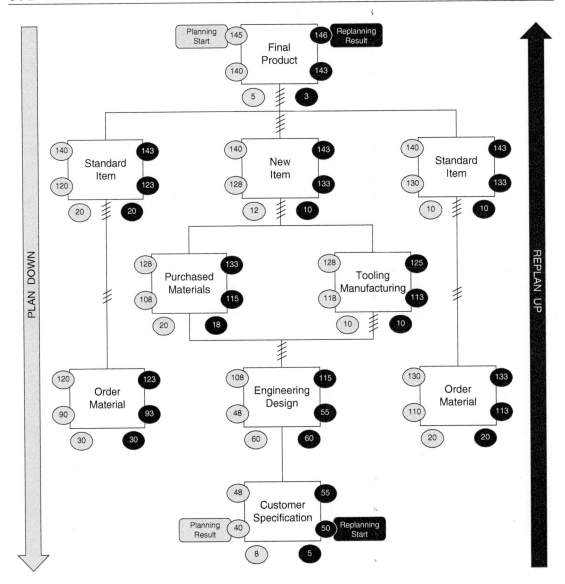

Figure 11.8 Plan and Replan Example

All initial planning numbers are shown on the left side of each activity box while the replanning numbers are shown on the right side of the activity box. The start dates are shown at the bottom of the activity boxes while the due dates appear at the top of the boxes. The logic used here is standard master planning and scheduling and event requirements planning for the standard items. The process continues as shown in Figure 11.8 on the prior page. However, there is more to this product build than just the standard item. What about the new item?

The due date of the new item is workday 140. Once the new materials and tooling are available, it is estimated that it will take 12 days to assemble/manufacture this new item. Therefore, the planned start date for the new item is workday 128. This means that the materials and tooling must be available on workday 128. The lead time for the purchased materials is 20 days, creating a start date or purchase date of workday 108. The tooling, which will be built in parallel to the purchase material, has a start date of workday 118 due to its 10 days of lead time.

The example indicates an engineering design group that is responsible for both the material and tooling designs. With this in mind, the earliest start date (workday 108 for the purchasing of the new materials and workday 118 for the tooling manufacturing) is used as a due date for the completed designs (workday 108). The designs are anticipated to take 60 more days, and therefore must be started on workday 48. This means that the customer's completed order and company's (i.e., engineering's) understanding of the design specification must be available on workday 48. The company in this example has planned 8 workdays to study and analyze the customer's specification. This means the customer must deliver its order specification on or before workday 40. What the company has now is a detailed activity plan. Once this plan is done, it is time for execution.

For discussion purposes, let's say the customer in this example missed the order specification delivery date by 10 days, delivering the specification on workday 50. Since the plan was for the company to have this specification on workday 40, a potential problem exists in meeting the final product delivery date. The good news is that this potential problem has surfaced on workday 50, not workday 145, the product delivery date. The process now moves from a downward planning effort to an upward replanning effort.

Going back to Figure 11.8 on page 374 and starting at the bottom (replanning start), the company determines if the specification can be studied and understood in less than 8 days, perhaps even 5. If this can be done, the specifications will be available in engineering design on workday 55. The next question is if engineering design can cut their lead time to delivery.

In the example, let's say the answer is no. Therefore, the materials and tooling design will be available on workday 115. This tooling design delivery date does not present any problems to tool manufacturing since the initial plan calls for a delivery of the tooling on workday 128. (Tooling will be ready on workday 125, assuming a 10-day lead time.) The problem is the purchased material.

Can the supplier shorten its lead time of 20 days? Let's assume the answer in the example is a little—maybe 2 days. With the design arriving in purchasing on workday 115 and a purchasing lead time of 18 days, the materials can be expected on workday 133. This means that the manufacturing of the new item can start on workday 133.

Can the expected or anticipated 12-day manufacturing lead time be compressed? Let's assume yes, by another 2 days. Adding the 10-day manufacturing lead time to the start date of 133 gives us an expected completion date of 143. This means that the final configuration process can start on workday 143.

The final product configuration is planned to take 5 days, but let's assume that this also can be reduced, say to 3 days. (Final assembly has committed to doing this because of

CAPACITY-DRIVEN ENVIRONMENTS

Just a few weeks on the job were enough to convince Bill Childs that he was dealing with a different set of master planning and scheduling challenges. As a master planner and/or master scheduler with 10 years of experience in the automotive-parts industry, Childs was used to situations in which master planning and scheduling the flow and assembly of materials and parts was the foremost concern. Indeed, ensuring the smooth movement of materials into the finishing stage of production for alternators, starter motors, and other auto parts had defined his previous work. But at Testing Systems, Inc., his new company, Childs was up against something quite different.

Testing Systems was a high-technology company that engineered hardware and software for diagnostic testing of both electromechanical and microprocessor-based equipment. This was an environment in which engineers and software programmers were many and assemblers were few, where output was measured more in circuitry designs and lines of programming code than in products shipped, and it required a different approach to master planning and scheduling.

Childs found that he needed to change his thinking about many of the basics of master planning and scheduling that had served him well in the auto-parts industry. Instead of working back from end product demand through traditional bills-of-material, this environment required a focus on getting the most out of the company's cadre of highly paid, highly educated *knowledge workers*. It was, after all, their capacity to design and program exotic electronic equipment that was Testing System's *product*; manufacturing and assembly were not where value was added and were, in fact, generally subcontracted to other firms.

the notification time it received. Remember, this replanning effort is taking place around workday 50 and we're discussing schedule changes for workday 143.) By reducing the lead time of the final configuration process, the new due date for the final product is projected to be workday 146, one day late. Chances are the company can find another day to pull out of the schedule somewhere if the replanning is continued.

The message here is that bad news early is better than bad news late. The earlier the problem is identified, the better chance a company has to positively respond. This example shows real customer service. The customer shows up 10 days late with the specification and the example company expects to deliver on time or, at worse, one day later than the original due date.

Bill Childs's situation is no longer unique in modern industry and actually represents a growing segment of a master planning and scheduling craft. The real growth industries of the past quarter century—software, electronics, microprocessors, medical technology, biotechnology, and aerospace—present situations in which traditional manufacturing and assembly are often the tail of the value-adding and cost process, and science, design, engineering, and development are the dog that wags that tail.

Thus, master planners and master schedulers have had to learn to measure and manage capacities similar to those presented above, and this learning will undoubtedly continue into the near-term future. These are capacity-driven environments, and they represent a departure from the material-driven environment typical of those represented elsewhere in this book.

To understand the difference between the material-driven and the capacity-driven environments, consider Figure 11.9, in which the unique concerns of the two are contrasted. This figure makes it clear that the focus of the master planner's and/or master scheduler's attention in the capacity-driven environment is on the key resources of the company, and every opportunity is sought for getting the most from those resources.

Material-Driven	**Capacity-Driven**
• Schedule to meet demand	• Schedule to utilize resources
• Schedule fewest number of items	• Schedule bottlenecks
• Back schedule from end item or option	• Forward schedule after bottleneck; back schedule before bottleneck
• Schedule materials, then balance capacity	• Schedule capacity, then balance materials
• Customer demand is the controlling variable	• Capacity resources are the controlling variable

Figure 11.9   Two Different Scheduling Environments

In a job shop, the internal resources might be metal machining equipment; in a law firm, they might be billable hours; in a software development company, they might be the capacity to create lines of programming code; in a plate-glass-making facility that utilizes multimillion-dollar continuous-process equipment, they might be machine hours.

Where and What to Master Plan and Schedule

Unlike material-driven companies, such as a computer producer, capacity-driven companies focus their master planning and scheduling not on the final product but the capacity that produces it. When the question, "Where and what should a company center its master planning and scheduling efforts?" is asked, the computer company invariably answers, "Finished computers or major options that can be configured into a workable computer in a short lead time." The capacity-driven company, such as a machine-tooling company, might focus on machine-hour capacity.

Consider just such a machine-tooling company and the situation described in Figure 11.10. This company has three items on its schedule, Items 121, 122, and 123. The master planner and/or master scheduler has learned through experience the amount of drilling-machine time required for each of these items. By multiplying the machine hours per hundred items by the quantity of expected demand (in hundreds), the total capacity requirements for each item can be determined.

Like all demand, machine time has both a quantity and time dimension (i.e., the customer wants an item in a certain quantity and by, or at, a certain time). Figure 11.11 on page 379 is the master planning and scheduling matrix that matches demand and supply

Item	Machine Hours Required per 100
121	1.00
122	1.25
123	1.40

Figure 11.10   Capacity Matrix

	1	2	3	4	5	6
Actual Demand	240	254	182	140	70	0
Available-to-Promise	0	−14	58	140	210	280
MPS (Capacity)	240	240	240	280	280	280

Figure 11.11   Master Schedule Matrix for Drilling

for the drilling operation. Here the master plan and/or master schedule lists demand not in terms of the number of items to be built or number of items sold, but by the machine hours required for the build and/or sold items. Available-to-promise (ATP) and the master plan and/or master schedule lines are likewise expressed in machine-hour terms.

Reviewing the MPS matrix for the drilling operation, the master planner and/or master scheduler sees that he or she is sold out through time period 2. In fact, time period 2 shows that the company is oversold by 14 hours. As with master planning and scheduling in other environments, the shortfall could be eliminated through the simple expedients of either 14 hours of overtime, off-loading some of the demand to another drilling work center, or subcontracting the work to an outside source.

As in the materials-driven environment, the ATP line is a handy guide to determining whether new demand can be accepted and when. Beginning with time period 3, for example, the master planner and/or master scheduler notices a positive ATP, signifying that drilling capacity is available to commit and sell.

The MPS matrix can help a capacity-driven company commit to customer deliveries without overselling its capacity. Figure 11.12 on page 380 shows four customer orders in which the required capacity has been calculated. If these customer orders are to be sequenced in the order shown, when can the master planner and/or master scheduler commit each without further planning overtime, and so forth?

This example assumes that the master planner and/or master scheduler has decided to work overtime to satisfy the 14 hours oversold in time period 2. However, no more overtime will be planned. The first order for item 121 requires 50 hours; it can be committed for a time period 3 delivery, which leaves 8 hours in time period 3's ATP (58–50). The next order (122) will use the remaining 8 hours of ATP in time period 3 plus 4.5 hours of time period 4's ATP, leaving 135.5 hours available-to-promise in time period 4.

Item	Machine Hours Required per 100	Order Quantity (100s)	Total Required Machine Hours
121	1.00	50	50.0
122	1.25	10	12.5
123	1.40	12	16.8
121	1.00	120	120.0

Figure 11.12   Matrix Showing Required Capacities

The next order, for item 123, requires 16.8 hours. It, too, can be promised in time period 4, leaving an ATP of 118.7 hours of capacity. The last order in the example is again for item 121, which requires 1.00 hour of capacity per 100 units. The request is for 12,000 units, which will require 120 hours of capacity. The numbers tell us that time period 5 should be the promise date (only 118.7 hours of capacity in time period 4 being available-to-promise), but the experienced master planner and/or master scheduler, hoping to satisfy the customer and use company resources most effectively, may commit a time period 4 delivery.

Even though the rules are *not* to plan any extra capacity, the person working with capacity numbers must remember that capacity is aggregated planning and not an *exact science*. Of course, the specified work may also take longer than estimated! Knowing what to do in this instance is part of the *art* of *master planning and scheduling*.

Capacity Master Schedules

In the capacity-driven environment, the focus tends to be on bottlenecks or constraints in the operation. Like the hourglass-shaped situations faced by many assemble-to-order manufacturers of option-laden products, many capacity-driven companies have pinch points in their operations, and these are the critical scheduling points.

By developing routings or bills-of-events, such as those shown in this chapter, master planners and/or master schedulers can work backward to determine the latest possible start date required for each operation that precedes the bottleneck or constraining operation. Likewise, they can determine the earliest expected finish date by doing the same for all events and processes that occur beyond the bottleneck or constraining operation.

Make-to-Contract Environments

In the custom-products environments, many companies do little or nothing until they have a customer contract in hand for a particular product program or project. At that point, development work begins, as do the other tasks that lead toward the completed work.

This was not the case at Hyster Company when the late Larry Wilson, a former Oliver Wight Principal and long-time friend, was the master scheduler. Hyster had an engineer-to-order product that was master scheduled using pseudo planning bills that contained total hours required on their major shops, an estimate of capacity for key suppliers and typical people-weeks required in engineering, and so forth. The pseudo planning bill was used to master plan and schedule 18 months into the future and was replaced with the actual bill-of-material upon receiving a customer's letter of intent. The process was then managed as described in this chapter.

The make-to-contract (MTC) world is very similar to the engineer-to-order world; however, in the make-to-contract environment, the company may very well have completed the design work, and there may already be a working prototype. This is very much the situation in the aerospace industry, in which an aircraft producer may have to approach the U.S. Department of Defense with an operating prototype of the new fighter plane it hopes to sell.

At this point, the company has no orders, but it has already invested millions, or even billions, in design, new-materials development, tooling, and flight testing. This is often the price of admission to the formal competition for the megabillion-dollar-contract award for the next generation of fighter aircraft.

In other cases, the producer may already have an established product that it is selling to a new customer. In winning a customer contract, it is only building the same product (perhaps with some minor design changes) for the specified quantity and to the time specification of that customer.

Make-to-contract jobs, especially with the government, very often have strong inducements for on-time delivery—namely, late penalties. Thus, the master planner and/or master scheduler has a critical role to play not only in the successful planning and control of the program or project but in its profitability to the company. These contracts sometimes feature partial-completion payouts to the contractor, in which the company is paid for materials and other expenses as incurred; this is quite different than being paid for the work on delivery dates and has an effect on the master planning and scheduling policy of the producer.

The Need for Standards—A Long Time Ago

"The aerospace/defense industry is characterized by change in high volume often at rates that seem beyond human responsiveness," according to the late Paul Hemmen, a former Oliver Wight Principal and long-time friend.[4]

The application of computer technology to the manufacturing environment, in which precise processes are used to produce exacting engineered designs subject to change, offer a solution for maintaining control and responsiveness to change. Using today's computer software technology to crunch the numbers (as often as necessary to keep essential data current) is also required.

Enterprise resource planning (ERP) system components—the computer hardware, planning software, and knowledgeable people—have provided the so often sought-after control potential for the commercial industry for several decades. ERP systems are ideally suited for the aerospace/defense industry as well. In fact, the basic logic of ERP (with its predecessor, MRPII) was born in the industry some 50 years ago on the U.S. government submarine programs.

So much progress has been made since then, especially adapted by commercial users, that it may seem as though the A&D industry stood still in updating their information technology and management systems. It might not be too far a stretch to say that A&D systems have become nearly as sophisticated as the weapons systems being produced (of course, this comment depends on what information technology and management systems are being discussed).

Commercial users, having found the secret to planning and control in manufacturing several years ago, have on the other hand simplified their systems by applying lean manufacturing concepts in their plants/mills that are driven by excellent planning and control processes, such as master planning and scheduling. Hence the need for standards that provide a coherent, simple means for applying the ERP concepts and using ERP systems in the A&D industry.

The Standards

Early in 1987, the fate of MRP systems for the A&D industry was essentially on hold awaiting application criteria and guidance. Government and industry worked as a team

[4] Paul G. Hemmen, "The Standard for Master Production Schedules," *APICS A&D SIG Digest*, Edition II, April 1991.

and reached agreement, which provided the 10 key elements subsequently promulgated as standards in application DFAR sections Subpart 242.72. The ad hoc committee selected the widely known and proven quality standards for successful use of enterprise resource planning (ERP) and manufacturing resource planning (MRPII) systems as they would be applied for materials management and accounting systems.

Standard Number 2 states in part: "Assure that costs of purchased and fabricated material charged or allocated to a contract are based on valid time-phased requirements as impacted by minimum/economic order quantity restrictions. A 98 percent bill of material accuracy and 95 percent master (production) schedule accuracy are desirable as a goal in order to assure that requirements are both valid and appropriately time phased." The MPS definition in this book (and the authors' choice) is master planning and scheduling, *not* master production scheduling. MPS is a lot more than just *production scheduling*.

When these accuracy levels are not evident, the contractor is burdened with proving the relevant cost significance to the government. Of the standards, this one is the meat-and-potatoes issue!

Some divergence of views and debate remains, however, about this key element, as to whether it means 95 percent accuracy or performance. ERP users have established by overwhelming precedent of proof testing and pain in the manufacturing environment the realities and benefits of this goal.

As early users discovered, MRPII and ERP without an initial master planning and scheduling (MPS) step in the process produced no more than computerized order launching. The essence of the MPS is to inject a clearly distinguishable management step in the process to achieve balance, stability, and validity for requirements and schedules.

The master schedule is management's *anticipated build schedule* and as such must pass the test of doable regarding capacity resources and materials availability on a continuing basis. It is not a static parameter containing a snapshot of the contract requirements. Rather, the master plan and schedule is dynamic data representing forward-looking supply planning, product configuration and flow, and performance feedback, within the constraints of reasonable capability and expectation for the company.

The master plan and/or master schedule is management's steering control over all planned activity as it portrays supply versus demand. Continuous feedback (closed loop in the ERP process) and performance reporting are essential to progress toward the goal of 95 to 99.5 percent performance to the master plan and/or master schedule. What makes master planning and scheduling (MPS) and bills-of-material (BOM) the meat and potatoes of supply chain management is that they answer three of the four fundamental questions in the manufacturing equation:

1. What is the company going to make? The answer is on the master plan and/or master schedule!

2. What does it take to make it? The answer is on the bill-of-material!

3. What does the company need (and when) to make or buy what's needed? The answer is noted on the material requirements plan coupled with system-generated, exception-driven, action messages output!

4. What does the company already have? The answer is in the highly accurate inventory records! Note: This assumption is based on standard number 5, which sets the quality level for inventory record accuracy (IRA) at 95 percent.

The essence of the master plan and/or master schedule is to inject a clearly distinguishable management step in the process to achieve balance, stability, and validity for requirements and schedules. This is an everyday occurrence in Class A companies.

Satisfying the Customer and the Standard

Figure 11.13 is the master plan and schedule for an aerospace company that holds a contract to make and deliver air-to-ground missiles. *The contract is the demand* in this make-to-contract (MTC) situation, and here the actual demand line indicates the contract delivery dates (20 missiles in time period 4 followed by 20 missiles in time period 8). *The master plan and/or schedule line is the anticipated supply*. Late penalties are part of this particular contract.

	Past Due	1	2	3	4	5	6	7	8
Actual Demand					20				20
Projected Available Balance	0	5	10	15	0	5	10	15	0
Master Schedule		5	5	5	5	5	5	5	5

Figure 11.13   MTC Master Plan and/or Master Schedule, Missiles, Level-Loaded

	Past Due	1	2	3	4	5	6	7	8
Actual Demand					20				20
Projected Available Balance	0	6	12	18	2	7	12	17	0
Master Schedule		6	6	6	4	5	5	5	3

Figure 11.14 MTC Master Plan and/or Master Schedule, Missiles, Build Ahead

The level-loaded master plan and/or master schedule in Figure 11.13 on the prior page works out just fine in terms of the dates and quantities required by the customer contract, but in its fear of encountering an unanticipated delay that might cause it to miss the delivery dates—and thus incur a financial penalty—the missile producer may sometimes decide to build ahead of the customer contract (take a risk), as shown in Figure 11.14. Here the producer is leaving some slack in certain periods—slack that could be used to catch up if any delays occur.

In building slack or buffer into the master plan and/or master schedule, the missile producer knows that if there is a delay in time periods 1 through 3 or time periods 5 through 7, time could be used to make up for any delay in time periods 4 and 8. If that time is not needed, the production lines might be scheduled for some other work, maintenance, or training (e.g., worker safety training).

Building unnecessary inventory is generally avoided by companies that use an MTC manufacturing strategy, but here the extra inventory might be viewed as a prudent safety stock against a possible financial penalty, and it may be that the government is paying the missile company for materials and other expenses as work is completed, not on delivery, in which case inventory has minimal carrying cost to the company. However, someone pays for early inventory; *it's not free!*

This same missile producer may have a design change to phase in or have another customer contract for a different missile design that requires that work begin in time period 9. In this situation, the company determines that it must close down its line for all of time period 8 to make the changeover to begin building the new missile. Since the customer contract terms for the first missile remain unchanged, the company would have to schedule time periods 1 through 7 differently. Figure 11.15 on page 386 shows just one of the many possibilities.

Variations of these master planning and scheduling approaches are applicable to accommodate short weeks due to holidays, slow ramp-up to full production of a new product,

	Past Due	1	2	3	4	5	6	7	8
Actual Demand					20				20
Projected Available Balance	0	6	12	18	4	10	16	20	0
Master Schedule		6	6	6	6	6	6	4	0

Figure 11.15 MTC Master Plan and/or Master Schedule, Missiles, Line Closing (Time Period 8)

slow ramp-down to phase out one product and introduce another, and so forth. The possibilities are many. The only constant is that the customer contract defines the obligation to deliver in terms of product, specifications, quantities, and dates. As a reminder, the supply schedule need not be the same as the customer contract delivery.

When Supply Can't Satisfy Demand

Despite what many defense contractors believe, *that the customer won't let us change the master plan and/or master schedule*, the company can and should do what it believes is valid and necessary with the master plan and/or master schedule as long as customer specifications, quality, costs, delivery dates, and quantities are satisfied. The misguided notion that the customer contract controls the supply schedule (we're not talking about the delivery schedule) leads to all manner of dysfunctional behavior among companies.

It is not atypical, for example, for a defense contractor to fall behind schedule, to the point that delivery dates cannot *possibly* be met, and yet refuse to do the rescheduling of material and capacity that will bring the process back under rational control. The excuse for not rescheduling is that *the customer won't let us change the master plan and/or master schedule*. Perhaps the customer will not let the company change the committed *delivery date* but changing the supply schedule generally is under the supply company's control.

Producers must control the master plan and/or master schedule, and when the facts dictate that delivery dates cannot be met, the master plan and/or master schedule must be adjusted to the new reality. A *past-due* master plan and/or master schedule *cannot* be made as scheduled no matter how hard the company may try.

If today is February 15, the unfinished product scheduled for completion on February 1 will not be completed on time or as currently scheduled. Leaving the master plan and/or master schedule completion date February 1 sends invalid information throughout the system. *So why not work to valid schedules, ones that can be made for which people can be held accountable?*

Up to this point, we have concentrated our efforts on master planning and scheduling and the planning of materials and capacities to build products and satisfy customer needs. The next challenge is to schedule production by communicating these real customer needs to manufacturing. The formal communication lines are supported by various techniques, some of which the next chapter on finishing addresses.

12

Finishing or Final Assembly Scheduling

Rolling delivery promises gather no reorders.

Up to this point, the focus has been on bringing together the material and the capacity to build products that customers will eventually order. At some point the manufacturing floor must be told what to produce, in what quantities, and in what configurations. This communication is accomplished through the finishing (or final assembly) process. The finishing process converts the master plan and/or master schedule from a plan into manufacturing action.

The finishing schedule establishes work authorization—that is, approval to perform work on defined products, using specified capacity and materials—according to a schedule that identifies the sequence in which the work is to be performed. The finishing schedule sets priorities for finishing, assembly, filling, testing, kitting, packaging, and so forth. This communication has a variety of labels: work orders, production orders, shop orders, factory orders, job orders, campaigns, batches, detailed production or line schedules, scheduling boards, run rates, and kanbans.

Manufacturing Strategy Tied to Finishing/Final Assembly Schedules

The manufacturing strategy of the company has an impact on how and when work authorization should be released to the finishing and/or final assembly process. Is the company

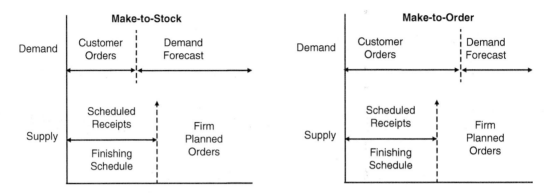

Figure 12.1   Finishing or Final Assembly Schedules for Products Made Using a Make-to-Stock or Make-to-Order Manufacturing Strategy

pursuing a make-to-stock, finish-to-order, make-to-order, engineer-to-order, or design-to-order manufacturing strategy on the various products the company produces? Or is it something in between, like package-to-order or buy-to-stock?

To understand why manufacturing strategy matters, look at Figure 12.1. On the left, the company using a make-to-stock strategy for its products has a typically short backlog of customer orders because the product is delivered off the finished goods shelf. Over the time periods prior to receipt of the customer order, the company must plan demand using a forecast or anticipated customer order receipt.

For products in a make-to-order environment—on the right side of the figure—the backlog is much longer, and the company does not need to plan demand using a forecast to nearly the same extent. This is because in the make-to-order environment, the customer places the order and typically expects to wait a reasonable amount of time for delivery.

The important point here is that the time allotted to the finishing process may be less than the sum of the customer backlog. In a company that makes its products using a make-to-stock manufacturing strategy, the time allotted to finish the product is often greater than the sum of the customer backlog.

Satisfying these two different demand patterns requires different scheduling patterns. For products in a make-to-stock environment, the product must be on the finished goods shelf prior to receipt of the customer order. Therefore, released production and/or buy schedules must be created prior to receiving the customer orders, and the master planner and/or master scheduler must key the finishing or final assembly schedule to the demand forecast.

In contrast, products in the make-to-order environment are ones in which the final product is not built until the customer order is in hand, with all option requirements specified.

Here, the customer expects to wait some amount of time while the supplying company's manufacturing unit releases and executes the finishing or final assembly schedule.

Although the company's selected manufacturing strategy impacts how and when to release work authorization into the finishing or final assembly process, other variables also need to be addressed. These questions should be asked:

- Is manufacturing set up with a job shop orientation, or does it operate in a continuous-flow-type environment?

- What is the volume of product or products moving down the production line?

- How about the product mix? Are there many choices or just a few? Is mix and match popular?

- Is the manufacturing lead time short or long? What about the material procurement cycle?

- Are the logistics plans, i.e., transportation, planned or already in place?

The answers to these questions can affect how best to schedule, sequence, and communicate what needs to be done.[1] For instance, a continuous-flow production line that builds a few types of products with a short manufacturing lead time may choose to use the production schedule to authorize work; no work order may be necessary.

As it has long been said regarding master planning and scheduling, it's all about understanding the choices available and then selecting the choice that will be most effective in realizing the company key objectives—satisfying customers while safely making money and a profit!

Manufacturing Strategy Approaches

Having a manufacturing strategy is just part of what a company needs; beneath the level of manufacturing strategy must be some chosen tactic or approach to fulfilling the manufacturing strategy. For most companies, the approach will be either job/intermittent or flow/process manufacturing. Both are represented graphically in Figure 12.2 on page 392.

---

[1] See John Dougherty and John Proud, "From Master Schedules to Finishing Schedules in the 1990s" (*APICS 33rd International Conference Proceedings*, 1990).

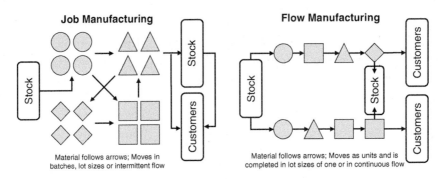

Figure 12.2 Job and Flow Manufacturing

Job or Intermittent Production Environments

The left side of Figure 12.2 represents a job or intermittent production–type environment. In the job shop (intermittent production), work centers and resources are grouped by like functions (saws together, presses together, etc.), so work flows to the various work centers in the sequence of steps needed to be performed. Here, the manufacturing process begins with material in a stock location. Material leaves this location to enter a queue at the first work center, where it awaits processing. When that job becomes the priority, work commences.

From the first work center, the partially processed product is moved to either an intermediate stock location or into the queue at the second work center in the identified production sequence. And, so it goes, until each step of the manufacturing process has been completed, and the transformed material/product enters the finished-goods inventory or is shipped to a customer. Assembled products built in various lot sizes, design-to-order and engineer-to-order products, low-volume make-to-order products, and others characterized by high product variation are generally manufactured in this way.

Continuous Flow or Process Production Type Manufacturing Environments

The right side of Figure 12.2 represents the continuous flow or process type environment. In the continuous flow environment, work centers or cells and resources are grouped in the normal sequence that work is performed. Here, material starts at the beginning of the production line and is subject to processing operations and/or added materials as it literally flows down the line. Other materials flow into the line as required.

A good example of a continuous flow or process production environment is found in plate-glass manufacturing, a continuous process in which raw materials are added to one end of a furnace tank and molten glass pours out of the other, forming a continuous ribbon of glass. This glass ribbon is subjected to continuous forming, annealing, and cutting operations at various points on the production line. Make-to-stock, quick-speed, and high-volume make-to-order products with minimal product variation—particularly nonassembled products like glass, nylon, chemicals, engineered lumber, and so forth—are most frequently manufactured using this approach.

Mixed Approaches

Job/intermittent and continuous flow manufacturing approaches to production are not mutually exclusive. It is quite common to have a job shop feeding a flow line, a flow line feeding a job shop, a flow line feeding another flow line, or one job shop feeding another job shop. The combination of approaches used, and their order, is determined by the requirements of the business and by the state of its process technology.[2]

Other Manufacturing Issues

Finishing and/or final assembly schedules need to consider issues other than the manner in which manufacturing will take place. These are volume, the level of product variability in the product mix, and required completion lead times.

Volume

The finishing and/or final assembly schedule for inexpensive ballpoint pens, a high-volume operation with quick speeds, is much different than that of a commercial aircraft manufacturer or other producers of high-cost, low-volume products with slow speeds. In the high-volume, quick-speed operation, completed products may come off the production line at hundreds per minute—for example, 50,000 pens per shift.

To ask manufacturing to report unit completions to a work order would be overwhelming and counterproductive. In the low-volume environment, however, using a work order to collect data and information about each operation is not overwhelming.

---

[2] These issues are addressed in James M. Utterback, *Mastering the Dynamics of Innovation* (Boston: Harvard Business School Press, 1994). Utterback points out how the interaction of product and process innovation has often transformed traditional job shop operations, first into traditional job shop routines interspersed by *islands of automation*, and eventually into continuous-flow manufacturing.

Variability in the Product Mix

The amount of variability in the product mix not only influences the choice of job shop versus continuous flow manufacturing, but it also impacts the finishing and/or final assembly schedule. High product variability often causes a company to utilize the planning bill concept and plan and schedule pseudo items, which need to be pulled together in the finishing and/or final assembly process to correctly communicate what the customer has ordered.

Take, for example, a company that manufactures cosmetics. A continuous-flow production line may be used to produce bulk or semi-finished product. Once the customer order is received, the bulk may be used in a filling and/or packaging operation.

Completion Lead Time

Does it take a long time to actually produce the product, or is the manufacturing cycle short? The answer to this question may impact how the finishing and/or final assembly schedule is communicated to manufacturing. If a long completion lead time is required, the master planner and/or master scheduler might lean toward the use of a work order.

But if the company's business is producing sewing needles by the hundreds of thousands, or if its product takes just a few seconds to manufacture, then a work order may not make as much sense, and some form of line schedule may be appropriate. A line schedule (sometimes supported by a manual or electronic schedule board) announces what is to be run: by type, quantity, item number, batch, sequence, and so forth.

Manufacturing and Operational Sequencing

During the creation of the master plan and/or master schedule, individual manufacturing sequences of products are generally not considered in many environments, specifically job shop or intermittent production facilities. What mattered then was what needed to be produced in what period (days or weeks or months) to satisfy anticipated or firm demand. Specific sequencing takes on critical importance in the finishing and/or final assembly process, and for several different reasons.

A printer, for example, may need to run the light colors first, then run the sheets again, this time with the darker colors (assuming a single-color machine). A textile producer of athletic socks may choose to run the socks requiring light dyes before the dark dyes are used. An engineered lumber producer may want to run the narrow widths before the wider widths due to machine adjustments, and to gradually run wider and wider widths to minimize setup and changeover times.

However, there are manufacturing environments where the sequencing and grouping of batches may take place earlier in the process—that is, during the master plan and/or master schedule preparation. This may be desired due to the use of common materials (once the bag of powder is open, we want to use it all) and processes (set up adjustment on a constant, rate-based production line). Chemical, food, and cosmetic producers are examples of companies that might plan sequencing early in the game.

Traditional Means of Communicating the Master Plan and/or Master Schedule

One traditional way master planners, master schedulers, and production schedulers communicate to the manufacturing floor is by means of the detail production order (also commonly called a job order, shop order, or work order). Generally, enterprise resource planning (ERP) computer software systems support this form of schedule communications fairly well.

A production order is a document or group of documents (both manual and electronic documents are used in today's manufacturing environments), conveying authority for the manufacture of specified items or products in specified quantities by a defined due date. It generally includes a bill-of-material for manufacturing the product, a list of operations or steps required by work center, and various other documents specifying tooling, equipment settings, required inspections, and testing requirements. It may include documents to be used as turnaround forms to report material consumption, manufacturing activity, or completion of particular steps in the process.

Data contained on separate bills-of-material and routing documents can be combined into a single document with additional information. To do this, each component within the bill-of-material must be identified to the operation or manufacturing step where it is needed. Additionally, the manufacturing location where material is to be delivered must be identified. With this information, a finishing or final assembly document can be created.

Another way to communicate finishing and/or final assembly schedules is by means of work location or work center schedules. Many job shops and intermittent production facilities use these schedules as final authorizations and to set work location or work center priorities.

Do All Companies Really Need These Computers to Do Detailed Production Scheduling?

One of the most interesting scheduling boards seen by one of the authors was located in the plant of a Japanese rubber belt manufacturer (Figure 12.3). It was not merely a scheduling board, but an inventory-control system as well. Each item was represented by a vertical tube into which wooden blocks of varying thickness (lot size) could be placed, representing the current inventory level (height of the blocks in each tube) and the required level for the current time frame (pieces of string attached by pins across each tube that could be moved up and down as demand for the item changed).

As work was completed, the block of wood representing the inventory was placed in the tube and the physical material was placed in an outbound stocking location. The operator would then move the next-in-line block of wood from the "out" tube. This block was his or her authorization to begin work on the next item (identified by the block of wood). This simple board served as inventory control, demand driver, work authorization, and priority system. It was simple, and seemed to work without benefit of electricity, computer chips, or mega-yen software.

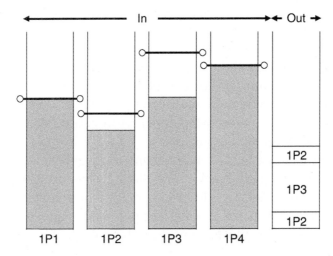

Figure 12.3   Manual Scheduling Board

Yet another means of finishing and/or final assembly schedule communication is by means of a production line schedule, which is most applicable in a continuous flow environment. When it comes to process, repetitive, or lean manufacturing environments, companies may find it beneficial to simply use line or batch schedules without work orders.

A line or batch schedule can be a very simple directive, as in *run four lines and two shifts to make this product*. Or it can be more definitive, as in *run product 123 on line 1 at 2,000 units per shift* or *run product 345 on line 2 at 6,000 units per day for three days*.

Line schedules can be displayed on manually maintained schedule boards or electronic computer scoreboards (today, the authors still see manually maintained schedule boards as well as electronic computer schedule boards in small to large companies—sometimes, simplicity is the ultimate sophistication). These boards (manually maintained or electronic computer-based) notify personnel which job to run next, along with date and quantity specification requirements.

The Role of People and Computers in Finishing and Final Assembly Scheduling—Past, Present, and Future

You can't control what you haven't planned! Said another way, if you don't know where you are going, any road will get you there! Supply chain professionals have known for a long time that planning, both aggregate and detailed, must be done if a company is to satisfy the two bookend objectives of a service and/or manufacturing business or company, that of satisfying customers while safely making money and a profit.

Well, going back some 75 years, these all-important planning activities were done entirely by people using pencils, paper, chalkboards, adding machines, typewriters, and so forth. Computers? Automation? What are you talking about?

Not until Alan Turing (father of computers [authors' opinion]) was able to put his vision and creativity into practical and understandable reality (inventing a machine eventually called a computer) did machines have anything to do with planning; people did it all! And by the way, the planning was more successful than unsuccessful in companies that did it right.

As time passed, computers became more and more important in business management. It all started in manufacturing businesses when computers were used in finance to do payroll tasks. Again, as time passed, the use of computers in production and inventory management found their way into the demand and supply sides of the business with processes such as focus forecasting, customer order entry, material reorder point inventory control, material requirements planning, shop dispatching, and so forth. So, some 50 years ago, people and computers jointly did the required planning for a manufacturing operation. And by the way, the planning was more successful than unsuccessful in companies that did it the right way.

Time continued to pass, and the turn of the century (some 20-plus years ago) saw more advancements in computers and machines performing tasks that people previously did. Supply chain management professionals were using computer technology and supporting systems such as master production scheduling, manufacturing resource planning, enterprise resource planning, and so forth.

During this time, people in planning had the tasks of creating and inputting the planning data (beginning of the planning process) as well as analyzing the output and system recommendations and making executable decisions based on this output data and information (ending of the planning process). The computer and its associated software did a large amount of the number crunching between the beginning of the planning cycle (entering of the planning data) and the ending of the planning cycle (taking action on the output recommendations generated by the computer software).

Fast forward to the 202X decade! Computer and machine technology continued its advancement at lightning speed during the years 2000 to 2020. So, what's happening now? Well, every day during the beginning of this decade, computers and machines are performing more and more tasks that people do in the supply chain management arena.

In fact, today there are many advocates of turning *all* supply chain planning over to the computer and its associated software. And by the way, the planning may be more successful than not in companies that do it the right way (Oliver Wight calls the right way, Class A). *Refer to Chapters 18–20 in this book to secure an understanding of how to do it right when it comes to master planning and scheduling.*

The basic issue today (of turning *all* planning activities over to the computer and its associated software) is that *judgment and creativity are things people do fairly well*, and *computers do not do that well—at least at this time.* So, if there is a significant amount of *judgment and/or creativity in a situation, people still are needed in the equation.* And let's not forget about accountability; people know how to hold people accountable to do what those people said they were going to do, but people and/or machines do *not* know how to hold machines (i.e., computers) accountable—at least at this time.

However, the landscape is changing, and computers and machines are becoming more effective and humanized as they learn at "lights out" speed. The authors share a more detailed discussion regarding people in master planning and scheduling, use of computers in master planning and scheduling, supply planning professionals, including those in master planning and scheduling, and each's role in the overall activity known as value chain management or supply chain management during this 2020's decade in this book's closing comments, entitled Final Thoughts, pages 783–808.

The Kanban System

Kanban, the Japanese term for *signal,* is another popular method of communicating to manufacturing. The signal itself can be a card attached to a bin, a square painted on the floor, or simply a container holding assembled components or raw materials. Japanese manufacturers originally created *kanbans* as a means for indicating when some action was to take place.

The entire kanban process is set in motion by a demand-pull originating with a customer or stocked order. A demand order creates requirements for products, which in turn pull materials through the entire system of production and suppliers. In the ideal kanban system, nothing moves until a customer (or stock) order is taken, but when that customer (or stock) order does appear, every level of the production system becomes the customer of the next-lower level of production or supply.

As manufacturing depletes materials from a kanban container, the empty container becomes an order to refill—a source of demand pulling more of the same materials through the production and supplier process. When the container is full, that sector of the production and supplier system comes to a halt and stops.

The kanban system was designed as a simple but elegant way to tightly link production and suppliers with the company's demand, thereby eliminating the need for costly inventory and finished goods for which there might be no demand.[3] Raw materials and components are delivered by suppliers only as they are needed—that is, just-in-time—and are brought to manufacturing only as needed. The manufacturing floor builds products only to fill orders. When demand is slack, workers perform machine maintenance, discuss improvements, do housekeeping, and so forth.

---

[3] The kanban method is based upon the waste-reduction methodology that motivated Japan's postwar industrialists. Devastated by the war, and short on capital and materials, they viewed American production methods of the 1950s and 1960s (it continued through the remainder of the century and some think it still continues [author's note]) as creating profligate levels of inventory for which orders might or might not appear. Far better, they thought, to only order materials and build things for which there were orders.

This system, which operates on the basis more of actual demand than on forecasted demand, has many obvious merits but also some serious weaknesses, especially insofar as products with long lead times and fluctuating demand are concerned. In a sense, companies that use kanbans have adopted a make-to-order manufacturing strategy in competitive environments where others would use the make-to-stock manufacturing strategy. At the same time, they have corrected some of the lead-time problems normally associated with this strategy by pioneering new methods of rapid line changeover, shorter cycle times, lean manufacturing, and just-in-time delivery of materials from suppliers.

Product-Dependent Kanbans

There are two types of demand-pull systems: product-dependent and product-independent. With product-dependent kanbans, the kanban itself is identified to a material. The product-dependent kanban is labeled with the item number, description, and kanban quantity. These kanbans are the visible records needed to set the system in motion. Think of the manufacturing floor and refer to Figure 12.4 on page 401. Imagine that each work cell has at least one outbound stocking location. This (or these) outbound stocking location(s) are identified to a product. In the example, work cell B has three locations for 1S1, two locations for 1S2, and one location for 1S3.

For work cell A, there are five outbound stocking locations. The inbound stocking location for work cell A might be the warehouse. The way product-dependent kanban works is as follows: *If the kanban is empty, fill it. If the kanban is full, stop work and/or production. If all kanbans are full, the line is shut down.*

Now let's assume that all kanbans are full, the production line is full, and a customer needs a 1S1. That customer can be a customer from outside the plant or the next operation (each work cell has customers and suppliers). Referring to Figure 12.5 on page 402, we see that satisfying this demand leaves an empty kanban square formerly occupied by 1S1—which authorizes work cell B to produce a 1S1.

Assume that it takes a 1P1 and 1P3 to manufacture the 1S1. Work cell B would get or request a 1P1 and 1P3 from work cell A's outbound stocking location, move those two items to work cell B, and commence the operations necessary to produce the 1S1. What this action does is free up two more kanbans—the 1P1 and 1P3. That now authorizes work cell A to fill those two kanbans.

Assume that it takes a 1R5 to make a 1P1. Work cell A would get or request a 1R5 from the warehouse and commence working on the 1P1. When finished, work cell A would place the 1P1 in its outbound stocking location designated for 1P and would still know that it has a 1P3 to build, which takes a 1R3. Work cell A would get or request a 1R3 from the warehouse, build the 1P3, and place it in the outbound stocking location labeled 1P3. This

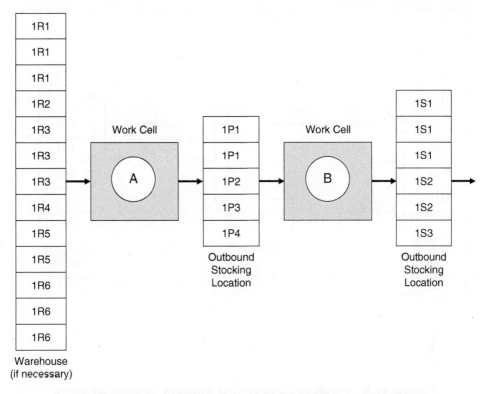

Figure 12.4 Product-Dependent Kanban Example

action would free up the warehouse space for 1R5 followed by 1R3, which are replenished in the same manner as the work cell's outbound stocking locations.

Product-Independent Kanbans

This system uses unlabeled outbound stocking locations (refer to Figure 12.6 on page 402). Assume that the production line is full. A demand pull for the 1S1 sets the line in motion. The outbound stocking location for work cell B is now empty, which authorizes work cell B to produce another product.

The work cell B operator looks back and pulls the 1S2 forward into his or her workspace (the worker may use additional materials from other feeder lines) and commences work cell B's operations by taking the 1S2 (semi-completed item) and doing what is necessary to complete the product. When finished, work cell B would move the 1S2 to its outbound stocking location. The initial pull action also puts work cell A into action since its outbound stocking location has been freed up.

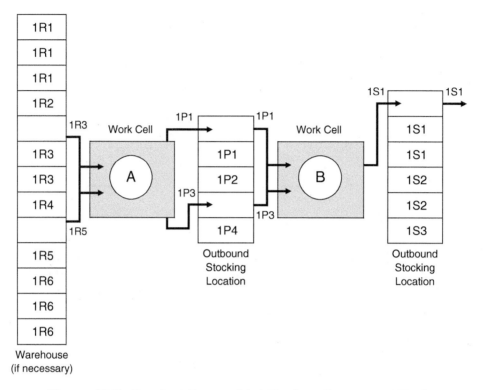

Figure 12.5 Product-Dependent Kanban System at Work

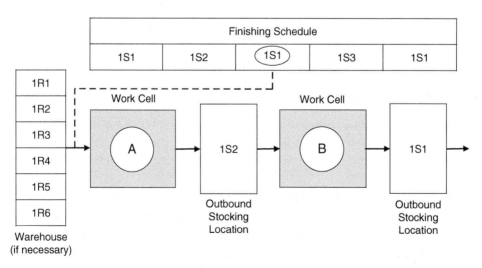

Figure 12.6 Product-Independent Kanban System Example

The next question is, What does work cell A start to work on? The decision is made by using a master plan, master schedule, finishing schedule, final assembly schedule, or detailed production schedule (company policy dictates which schedule is to be used when product-independent kanbans are being used).

In the example let's say that the chosen line priority driver is the finishing or final assembly schedule, which states (for the example) that a 1S1 is the next desired item. Therefore, the gateway operation will commence building a 1S1, which is then passed down the production line as kanbans are freed up by satisfying customers.

Tying It All Together (Aggregate Integrated Business Planning Through Master Planning and Scheduling Through Detailed Production Scheduling)

The Soft Seat example used in Chapters 8 and 9 dealt with a conference center chair product family. In Chapter 8 we discussed the process of restructuring the conference center chair's bill-of-material into a series of pseudo or planning bills. This was done to facilitate forecasting, bill-of-material database maintenance, master planning and scheduling, and option overplanning. Let's return to the Soft Seat chair example and see how these pseudo bills and the overall planning bill concept is used during the finishing or final assembly process.

When the conference center chair planning bill was structured (refer to Figures 8.6 and 8.7, pp. 266 and 267, for a review), five options were identified: seat assembly, chair back splat assembly (albeit a purchased assembly in the example), left leg assembly, hardware kit, and right leg assembly. The seat and back splat assemblies were color sensitive, so we took the seat and back splat assemblies and put them into a color-sensitive option bill. This meant that a selection of the red option required the red seat assembly and the red back splat assembly. The other three items (right leg assembly, left leg assembly, and hardware kit) were common to all conference center chairs.

Therefore, these items were structured into a common-items bill. This structuring was done assuming that the marketplace was permitting a two-period (e.g., two-day or two-week) delivery time. The use of the time-phased bill-of-material and knowledge of where the company desires or needs to meet the customer are very important when determining the best way to structure the planning bills.

How would the following scenarios impact the planning bill structure? What if, by compressing the manufacturing and procurement lead times, the company being discussed could remain competitive and not stock completed colored chair seat assemblies? Alternatively, what if the competition began quoting longer lead times so that the company being discussed didn't have to stock completed colored chair seat assemblies? If the company being discussed didn't have to stock completed chair seat assemblies, then the color-sensitive items would become the colored all-weather cloth and the colored chair back splat assembly—the seat inners and the label contained in the chair seat assembly become common parts (see Figures 12.7 on this page and 12.8 on page 405).

The new or restructured planning bill looks like Figure 12.8 on page 405. As you can see, the common items bill now contains the label, seat inners, hardware kit, right leg assembly, and left leg assembly. The red option bill contains the red all-weather cloth and the red back splat assembly.

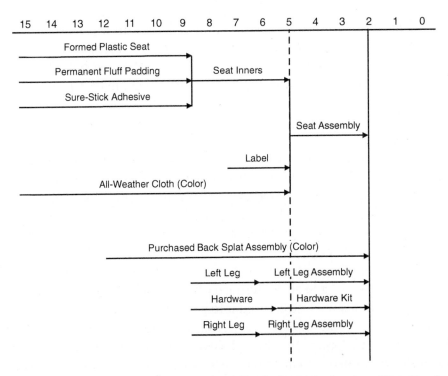

Figure 12.7   Planning Bills When Colored Chair Seats Are Not Stocked

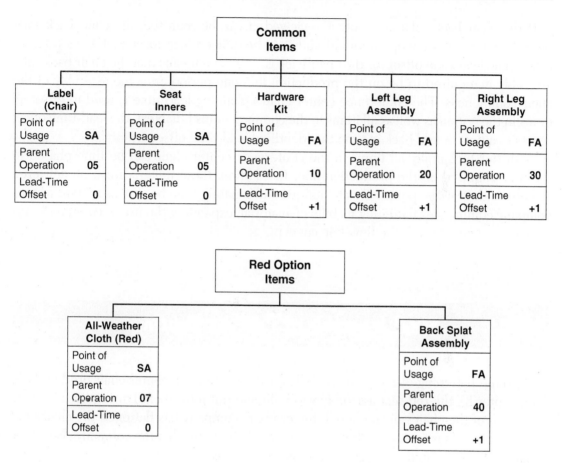

Figure 12.8   New or Restructured Planning Bill

Besides the planning bill structure, the master planner and/or master scheduler may desire to put other useful and meaningful data on each item in the pseudo bill. This data may include delivery point of usage, parent operation number, and lead-time offset.

Review the red option pseudo bill at the bottom of Figure 12.8. The all-weather seat cloth and chair back splat assembly are the items in this bill. Notice that the cloth is required for operation 07, which is done in work center SA. This tells the master planner and/or master scheduler that the all-weather seat cloth will need to be delivered to location SA when operation 07 is started. The all-weather seat cloth item (as Figure 12.8 states) has a lead-time offset equal to zero. In other words, the cloth is needed when the manufacturing work for the conference center chair commences.

If the chair back splat assembly is reviewed, it can be seen that the chair back splat assembly is needed for operation 40 and is to be delivered to location FA, its point of usage. The lead-time offset for the chair back is +1, which means that the chair back splat assembly is required to be on the production line one period after the assembly of the chair commences. The conference center chair's planning lead time is used to offset all items in the option as well as all items in the common items bill. Next, the lead-time offset serves to adjust or add back in time the identified lead-time offset.

With this technique, all items in the conference center chair can be time phased to the time required on the production line. In addition, these materials can be delivered directly to their usage points. This technique and capability can be very important when a company commences flattening its bills-of-material, expanding the use of common-items bills, and moving toward the flow-line concept.

Final Assembly or Process Routings

Prior to the flattening of the planning bills for the conference center chair product family (Chapter 8), the red seat assembly was built and put into stock. During this chapter's discussion of the chair's planning bill, the example company has flattened the chair's bill and no longer plans to stock red seat assemblies. This means that the company also needs to flatten the associated routings or process instructions.

A routing is defined as the sequence of activities or events necessary to build or produce a product. Figure 12.9 on page 407 identifies two routings: one for the final assembly of the conference center chair (the top half of the figure) and one for the subassembly of the seat assembly (the bottom half of the figure).

However, the company being discussed no longer plans to build and stock the seat assembly—it has been removed from the planning bill structure (see Figure 12.8 on page 405). But the company's master planner and/or master scheduler knows the manufacturer still needs to build the chair seat if the company is to produce a conference center chair. The red chair seat is composed of seat inners, a label, and red all-weather cloth (see Figures 12.7 on page 404 and 12.9's on page 407 subassembly routing section).

Since the company no longer has a seat assembly in the planning bill to attach the required operations documentation, the master planner and/or master scheduler has resequenced the operations of the subassembly work (operation 10, which states to attach the

Operation	Final Assembly Routing	Point of Usage
10	Lay out hardware kit per instructions	FA
20	Assemble left leg assembly to seat assembly using provided hardware	FA
30	Assemble right leg assembly to seat assembly using provided hardware	FA
40	Attach back splat assembly	FA
Subassembly Routing		
10 → 05	Attach label to seat inners	SA
20 → 07	Attach all-weather cloth to seat inners	SA

Figure 12.9   Final Assembly and Subassembly Routings

label to the seat inners, has become operation 05, and operation 20, which states to attach the colored all-weather cloth, has become operation 07). These two operations are now the first two operations in the conference center chair's build sequence.

The six-step process (two for the seat work and four for the final chair work) is now one complete routing for the final chair assembly (Figure 12.10 on page 408). This complete routing is attached to the common items' parent, as it (the common item's parent) *will be required for all conference center chairs* that need to be built, the same requirement that is placed on the common items.

The routing for the conference center chair has also taken on the characteristics of a generic or common chair. Look at operation 07 in Figure 12.10. It states that the all-weather cloth will be the color stated on the customer order. The same is true for operation 40. With the addition of these instructions, this assembly routing can be used to communicate to the manufacturing floor the activities and/or events that must take place in order to produce a customer's desired colored chair, be it red or black.

Operation	Final Assembly Routing	Point of Usage
05	Attach label to seat inners	SA
07	Attach all-weather cloth to seat inners (color per customer order)	SA
10	Lay out hardware kit per instructions	FA
20	Assemble left leg assembly using provided hardware	FA
30	Assemble right leg assembly using provided hardware	FA
40	Attach back splat assembly (color per customer order)	FA

Figure 12.10   Generic Conference Center Chair Routing Attached to Common Items

Continuing to look at Figure 12.10, we see the operation number and point of usage that were attached to the planning bill. Look at operation 05 again. It states that the label needs to be attached to the seat inners. This tells the master planner and/or master scheduler that the label and seat inners are needed to support operation 05. Since operation 05 is done in location SA, that's where the label and seat inners need to be delivered (the point of usage).

If we look at operation 10, we see that the hardware kit is required in location FA. The routing states that operations 05 and 07 will be started in location SA one period prior to operations 10 through 40, which are done in location FA. This is the reason behind the lead-time offset of +1 for all items required in work center FA versus work center SA.

Configuring and Building to a Customer Order

We now have in place the database necessary to respond to a customer request and order. If the demand management, supply management, master planning and scheduling, material management, and manufacturing processes work, the materials required to support a customer request for delivery in two to five time periods (which equates in the example being discussed to where the company has decided to meet the customer) and the resources necessary to produce the final configuration should be in place. The next step is to book a customer order, commit to a delivery date (assuming the materials and capacity are or will be available), and produce the desired product.

Figure 12.11 identifies what's needed to produce a red conference center chair. This figure shows that in order to produce a red chair, one set of common items (a label, seat inners assembly, hardware kit, left leg assembly, right leg assembly) and one set of red option items (the red cloth and the red back splat) are needed. From this data, a material list for the real material items such as the label, left leg assembly, right leg assembly, back splat, and so forth can be generated. So, if a customer should order a red conference center chair, we can use the planning bills and specific configuration desired to identify all the engineered items required (see Figure 12.12 on page 410).

Reviewing the figure, the reader can see the item, description, quantity needed (dependent on the customer order—the example shows that five red conference center chairs have been ordered), point of usage (location to deliver the items), and date required. The date required for each component is calculated by the master planning and scheduling system using the customer's due date and conference center chair's planned lead time plus each item's lead-time offset.

Say the chair has a planned lead time of two periods and the left leg assembly has a lead time offset of +1. The left leg assembly would be required on the production line in location FA one time period after the build start date of the conference center chair; the

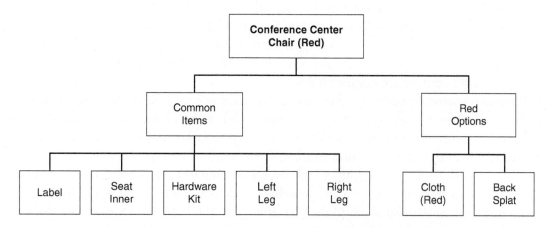

Figure 12.11   Red Conference Center Chair Planning Bill-of-Material

Materials List	Finish Order F1234			
Item	Description	Qty	Point of Usage	Date
125	Chair Label	5	SA	6/9/XX
420	Seat Inners	5	SA	6/9/XX
780	All-Weather Cloth	5	SA	6/9/XX
861	Hardware Kit	5	FA	6/16/XX
122	Left Leg Assembly	5	FA	6/16/XX
128	Right Leg Assembly	5	FA	6/16/XX
880	Back Splat Assembly	5	FA	6/16/XX

Figure 12.12   Finishing or Final Assembly Materials for Conference Center Chair

example being discussed needs the left leg assembly on June 16 versus a build start of June 9. Using the lead-time offset capability means that material can be scheduled to arrive on the production line the day it is actually needed. Lead time is offset by day.

Along with the material list shown in Figure 12.12, a set of process instructions (Figure 12.13 on page 411) can also be generated by the master planning and scheduling system. Remember, a generic routing was attached to the common items, which is also needed to build conference center chairs.

When the customer order is taken and a due date is committed, this generic routing can be used to determine when each operation needs to be done. This is done either by backward scheduling from the due date to identify the latest possible start date, forward scheduling from the first operation to identify the earliest expected completion date, or mid-point (bottleneck) scheduling, which uses a combination of backward (starting with the bottleneck's start date, backward schedule to determine the first operation's anticipated start date) and forward scheduling (starting with the bottleneck's start date, forward schedule to determine the last operation's expected completion date). In most cases the choice should be to backward schedule from the customer's need and promise date.

Operations List Finish Order F1234

Sequence	Description	Work Center	Date
05	Attach label to seat inners	SA	10 Jun
07	Attach all-weather cloth to seat inners (color per customer order)	SA	16 Jun
10	Lay out hardware kit per instructions	FA	17 Jun
20	Assemble left leg assembly using provided hardware	FA	19 Jun
30	Assemble right leg assembly using provided hardware	FA	21 Jun
40	Attach back splat assembly (color per customer order)	FA	23 Jun

Figure 12.13   Finishing or Final Assembly Routing for Conference Center Chair

Finishing or Final Assembly Combined Materials and Operations List

At this point we have successfully used the planning bill and the generic routing to create a materials list and to identify all the operations that must be performed in order to produce the customer's requested product—five red conference center chairs. Since we know the operation and when the material is needed, a combined materials and operations list can be created on one screen, as shown in Figure 12.14 on page 412.

This screen shows that the first activity or event is operation 05. In this operation the manufacturing floor is being instructed to attach the label to the seat inners. In order to do this, labels and seat inners are needed on June 9 in location SA. The attaching of the labels to the seat inners will be done five times, and all the work is to be completed by June 10.

Operation	Material	Description	Qty.	Wrk. Ctr.	Date
05		Attach label to seat inners	5	SA	10 Jun
	125	Chair Label	5		9 Jun
	420	Seat Inners	5		9 Jun
07		Attach all-weather cloth to seat inners (color per customer order)	5	SA	16 Jun
	780	All-Weather Cloth	5		9 Jun
10		Lay out hardware kit per instructions	5	FA	17 Jun
	861	Hardware Kit	5		16 Jun
20		Assemble left leg assembly using provided hardware	5	FA	19 Jun
	122	Left Leg Assembly	5		16 Jun
30		Assemble right leg assembly using provided hardware	5	FA	21 Jun
	128	Right Leg Assembly	5		16 Jun
40		Attach back splat assembly (color per customer order)	5	FA	23 Jun
	880	Back Splat Assembly	5		16 Jun

Figure 12.14   Final Assembly (and Subassembly) Combined Materials and Operations List

The next activity or event in the sequence is operation 07, where the all-weather seat cloth (color per customer order) is attached to the seat inner assembly. In order to complete this operation, five pieces of cloth (color identified by customer order) must be delivered to SA by June 9. When this work is completed, we will have an all-weather colored seat. This seat then flows to location FA, where the next operation (which is 10) will be worked.

During operation 10, the hardware kit is made ready for use in final assembly. This means that the hardware kit is needed to be delivered to FA by June 16. Operation 10 is scheduled to be completed by June 17, which was determined by backward scheduling from the customer order commit date.

This process continues until all the operations have been completed and the total customer order is finished. During the process, the manufacturing floor can report progress by each operation, defined milestones, checkpoint operations, or completed chair or groups of chairs. This choice is dependent upon the environment, manufacturing strategy chosen, product lead time, product volume, desired or needed information, and the company's computer software capability.

Choosing the Most Effective Approach

There is no one right approach to communicating the schedule to manufacturing. The key to making the best choice is keeping the ultimate purpose of the finishing or final assembly schedule in mind: the simple and clear communication of work authorization, specifications, and priority.

The best choice is also a function of previously discussed environmental issues. While no ironclad rules are possible, some approaches to finishing and final assembly schedules are used more often in certain environments. In a business with a job shop organization, low volumes, high potential product mix, long lead times, and high need for proper sequencing, it is normal to see individual work orders and bills-of-material traveling with the work to communicate work authorization and specifications.

Conversely, in environments with a flow-line organization, high volumes, few product variations, and short lead times, manual or electronic-generated line schedules such as schedule boards communicate end-product priorities. Kanbans may be used to trigger work authorization and signal priorities for all feeder lines and departments that supply the production line.

Most manufacturing environments are somewhere between these two ends of the spectrum. The influence of continuous-improvement programs is pushing more job type environments toward the flow-line scenario. It is also pushing high-volume flow lines toward shorter, quicker runs that can be better supported by the vigorous use of kanbans in all upstream-process steps. Thus, there is something of a convergence of the two extreme models of manufacturing.

Master Plans versus Master Schedules versus Finishing Schedules

Master planning and scheduling is a process to schedule and prioritize material and capacity in anticipation of delivering final products to customers. It is typically organized into weekly and sometimes daily time periods. In the finishing or final assembly process, however, the manufacturing schedule may be stated in days or hours or even minutes (one Motorola plant that one of the authors worked with several years ago scheduled to the minute). This difference in the required precision of planning periods is not the only difference between finishing, final assembly scheduling, and master planning and scheduling.

The master plan as well as the master schedule is driven by the integrated business planning or sales and operations planning process through the product management (new product launches), demand management (sales and marketing), and supply (manufacturing, procurement, purchasing) plans, while the finishing or final assembly process is driven by the master schedule, stock replenishments, customer orders, and process requirements (i.e., process industry plants). This naturally results in quite different time horizons—the cumulative lead time being the minimum planning horizon for the master plan and master schedule, and the finishing or final assembly lead time for the finishing and/or final assembly schedule.

When the master plan and/or master schedule is put together, the actual build sequence is generally not considered in many if not most environments; only the date when the product is expected to be needed is identified. This is not true when looking at the finishing or final assembly schedule. It is very important to analyze the situation and define the best sequence to produce the various products scheduled.

Take the athletic sock manufacturer—it would not be smart to dye the blue socks before the yellow socks. If this is done, a complete clean-out or wash-down would be needed before the lighter dye could be used. Additionally, the changeover and setup times required to modify the production line for the next product need to be minimized.

The master plan's and/or master schedule's function is to ensure that the material and capacity will be available when it is needed to produce the product. The finishing or final assembly schedule's function is to drive the finishing and final assembly process using the materials and capacity the master planner and/or master scheduler has preplanned. In other words, the finishing or final assembly schedule relieves the master plan and/or master schedule.

Once the finishing or final assembly process commences, the job of the master planning and scheduling function may come to an end and the completion process might be managed under the eyes of the finishing or final assembly process leads (this depends on the company environment).

Master planning and scheduling and finishing and final assembly scheduling are keys to a successful enterprise resource planning (ERP) implementation. If a company's master planning and scheduling effort fails, it is going to be very difficult for that company to reach Class A standards. The same can be said for the finishing or final assembly process.

Master Scheduling Logistics (Sharing In/Out Information)

Information is power! This is so true today and will be even more true tomorrow. However, for information to be power, it must be communicated to those with a need to know or, said differently, to those who would like to know. This chapter and the chapters that preceded it have discussed planning and control from a master plan to a master schedule to a finishing or final assembly schedule. That information is used to plan materials and capacity so that the manufacturing operation will be in a state to produce product when it is needed and/or ordered by a customer.

The supply chain management organization uses the master planning and scheduling (MPS) system to assist the master planners and master schedulers to determine what materials as well as what capacity will be needed in future time periods. Using this time-phased planning, procurement and purchasing professionals place material orders with suppliers to meet the anticipated, time-phased need for those materials. Additionally, operations and manufacturing professionals secure machines and tooling along with hiring people to build product to meet the anticipated, time-phased product demand.

Think about it; that's a lot of data and information that other functions within the company can use (assuming the data and information are reliable and up to Class A standards). One of those functions that really can use this type of information is logistics (receiving, receiving inspection, inventory control, stockroom, order picking, packaging, labeling, and shipping).

Master planning and scheduling coupled with finishing and final assembly scheduling can and should provide to the logistics function when it expects materials to be received and finished products to be shipped as well as logistics needs between receiving and shipping. The information is there, and it needs to be shared! However, let's say again that this valuable information must be accurate, trustworthy, and timely if it is to be of use in logistics planning.

To ensure an orderly and smooth master planning and scheduling along with a finishing and final assembly scheduling implementation, a defined process has been developed. This defined process and the various elements necessary to effectively implement master planning and scheduling into a company is the subject of the next eight chapters, which cover data integrity (Chapter 13), supporting integration (Chapters 14–17), and implementation (Chapters 18–20).

13

Data Integrity Requirements to Support Master Planning and Scheduling

If you don't have integrity, nothing else matters.
If you have integrity, nothing else matters.

The past 12 chapters contain many examples of simulated computer grids and otherwise calculated master planning and scheduling outputs (e.g., projected available balance, available-to-promise) based on actual and forecasted demand data, computer planned orders, firm planned orders, scheduled (supply) receipts, bills-of-material structures, safety stock settings, planning time fence parameters, and the like. Future chapters will more deeply explore aggregate planning, resource planning, and demand/supply planning parameters, including inputs and outputs as well as other data elements.

At the risk of stating the obvious, none of these system calculations, algorithms, recommendations, and reports work without clean data. The somewhat tired adage "garbage in, garbage out" remains as relevant today as when it was first printed in 1957 and attributed to Army Specialist William D. Mellin.[1]

---

[1] The phrase "garbage in/garbage out," or GIGO, was first widely seen in print by the *Times Daily,* Hammond, Indiana, November 10, 1957, paraphrasing Mellin on his work with Army data scientists and early computers. Mellin himself does not take credit for the invention of the phrase, so the true source is still up for debate. Similar phrases have been attributed to the reporter Raymond J. Crowley and computer pioneer Charles Babbage.

In this chapter, we explain what data integrity is, why it is important, and define the four pillars of data integrity that drive greater understanding, accountability, responsibility, control, accuracy, and consistency of data needed for effective master planning and scheduling processes.

What Is Data Integrity and Why Is It Important?

What Is Data Integrity?

Planners, schedulers, woodworkers, airplane mechanics, artists, and nearly anyone involved in creating and maintaining high-quality work know the difference between working in a clean, organized environment and a dirty, disorganized environment. Sifting through stacks of papers and e-mails, piles of crusty paintbrushes, drawers of jumbled wrenches, and wondering where the tape measure went is frustrating and unproductive. In addition to being clean and organized, a *craftsperson*, no matter what their trade, relies on the fitness and accuracy of the tools that they use.

Airplane mechanics (and everyone who is going to fly on the airplane that they are maintaining) depend on the accuracy of their torque wrenches when gauging the amount of pressure to apply to tightening a bolt, nut, or screw. If a mechanic doesn't routinely calibrate their torque wrench, the bolts, nuts, and screws they are installing get overtightened or undertightened, things break or come loose, and then bad things can happen.

Planning software systems, their functionality, and the data supporting that functionality are the planner's and scheduler's workspace and tools, *their workshop and torque wrench*, so to speak. To operate effectively and efficiently, a planner and/or scheduler needs to know where the tools are and that the tools are accurate and fit for use. Otherwise, again, bad things can happen!

Planning software functionality is highly dependent on the *integrity of the data* that supports it. Integrity goes beyond simply being accurate. Data integrity is defined as the accuracy and consistency of stored data, supported by standard rules and procedures that ensure that data has not been changed accidentally or deliberately without authority, and that the data is accurate, complete, and on time. In short, integrity means that the data is correct, worthy of trust, and there are processes in place to keep it that way so that when one needs to use it, the data is fit for its purpose.

Master Data (Static)	Supporting Data (Dynamic)
Item/Material Master	Approved Supply Plan (including Actions)
Planning Bills of Material	Demand Plan (including Sales Orders)
Resource/Load Profiles	MPS Process/Production/Work Orders
Work Locations/Centers	MPS Rough-Cut Capacity Plan
Bills-of-Material	MPS Procurement/Purchase Orders
Logistics Master	MPS Item Inventory Records
Customer Master	MPS Item Quality Status

Figure 13.1   Examples of Data Required to Support Master Planning and Scheduling

Data integrity can be broken down into two parts: (1) master data integrity (MDI), or integrity as it applies to *static* system data (e.g., nontransactional, relatively unchanging) and (2) supporting data integrity (SDI), or integrity as it applies to *dynamic* (e.g., frequently changing) system *data structures* (e.g., orders, plans, transactional records). Enterprise resource planning (ERP) systems in their entirety have thousands upon thousands of data elements and records supporting customer service, demand management, sales, marketing, product development, quality, supply management, manufacturing, procurement, finance, and other functions required to run a business.

The fundamental processes for achieving and maintaining a high level of data integrity apply to all types of datasets within the system, regardless of the business area. This chapter focuses on the general processes and principles required to achieve data integrity and specifically on data that is required to support master planning and scheduling, examples of which can be seen in Figure 13.1.

Why Is Data Integrity Important?

Despite the critical importance of data integrity to the effectiveness of enterprise resource planning systems (or any software systems, for that matter), data integrity rarely makes it onto the meeting agenda of C-suites or boardrooms. Perhaps this is due to the lack of awareness of the critical nature of data integrity or perhaps the topic of data integrity lacks the strategic allure possessed by other competing priorities. Ironically, something that frequently makes the leadership team's agenda is the implementation of new software systems!

With the advent of "big data" and the technology used to take advantage of that data (e.g., machine learning, artificial intelligence, data analytics), the need for clean and accessible data is becoming increasingly important. Leadership teams that are developing *digital strategies* must include *data integrity* as an important component of that strategy for it to be effective.

The business impact of poor data integrity is troubling, to say the least. Everything built upon a poor and crumbling *data foundation* is at risk (see Figure 13.2, left side). In a *poor data integrity environment*, the planning software functionality and its supporting data are *poorly understood, inaccurate,* and are *not creating value*. There are *no* formal and routine processes in place, beyond perhaps what regulatory bodies and safety would require, to assess the quality of the data, much less improve and maintain it. As a result, the planning system is producing plans and recommendations that are, at best, in need of a deep scrub before being communicated and executed.

Master planners and master schedulers frequently resort to using offline systems (e.g., spreadsheets, hotlists, and homegrown databases) to develop a *better plan* than the expensive, often state-of-the-art planning software in which the company heavily invested. Ironically, offline systems require data as well, so while plans may be more easily manipulated and force-fit to the planner's and scheduler's liking, the validity of the plans and schedules continues to be suspect. Finally, *offline systems are far less integrated and frequently less visible* to all that need to see them, so e-mails, texts, and phone traffic increase just to relay information.

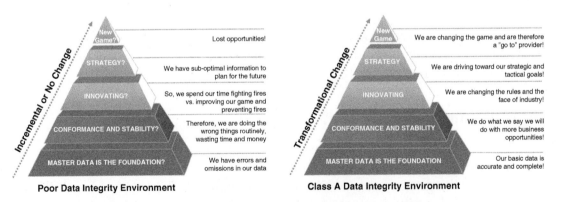

Figure 13.2   The Business Impact of Poor versus Class A Data Integrity Environments

With a poor data foundation resulting in poor plans, execution suffers! The people working for the company find themselves spending a lot of time chasing orders (sometimes called *Pur-Chasing*), putting out fires (also participating in dragon slaying), and apologizing (instead of selling or servicing) to customers and their bosses. After a day spent with one's hair on fire, there is little energy left for actually improving processes and the cycle continues. To compound the problem, *poor plans and data not only affect execution*, but they also *make it very difficult to effectively develop and execute tactical and strategic plans*. Of course, this is no way to *compete* and be a *game-changing* company.

Contrast the environment that was just described with that of a Class A data integrity environment (see Figure 13.2 on page 420, right side). In this environment, from the leadership team to front-line execution, the importance of data has been internalized and processes supporting data integrity are an integral part of daily operations. With a solid data foundation, plans within the planning system are more accurately produced, reflect reality, and are visible to all who need to use them. There are fewer surprises as a result, and the company gains a reputation for reliability, both internally and externally. The company and the people in it *do what they say they will do,* and the data and performance prove it. For more information regarding Class A structure and its structured approach, refer to Chapters 18–20 and Appendix A).

When routine things are more routinely executed to plan, most of the time that was spent firefighting and dragon slaying can be invested on innovative, rule-changing new ways of working. When seasoned practitioners and experts within a company are able to focus more of their energy on developing more productive ways of doing what they do, the company is increasingly capable of outcompeting other companies in their industry. A virtuous cycle is created. This ability to innovate, execute, and outcompete at the tactical level enables the executive team to spend far less time worrying about the near term and far more time on executing strategic plans for the future (to be explained further in Chapter 14, on integrated business planning). In short, rule-changing tactical processes allow for a game-changing strategy that has a much higher chance of being executed. This is how companies can disrupt the status quo and change the game.

Just as a strong foundation is needed for a safe and sturdy home, a strong foundation rooted in clean and accurate data is needed for the effective use of master planning and scheduling (MPS) software in developing reliable and effective master (supply) plans and master (supply) schedules. Now, let's explore how the data and value chain management (sometimes referred to as supply chain management) processes link together to enable planning and control of the business.

Gaining Control and Integration Points

From the time that trading goods and services became a way of life for human beings, tradespeople who were trading in physical goods have had to figure out what their customers want, what they have on hand to sell them, what they need to make (or grow, harvest, etc.), what it was going to take to make the product (time/capacity/capability), and what materials they needed to get or do to support the above. The same was true for service-based organizations, with some modification of what one considers *on hand to sell*, raw materials required, and so on. Not much has changed in those fundamental equations or objectives from early trading civilizations to today.

However, planning and scheduling processes, techniques and tools, and planning and scheduling software systems in support of these simple business objectives or equations have evolved and improved over time. The two models in Figure 13.3 are visual depictions of the processes required to run an entire company (the integrated business model on the top) and to run a *supply point* (the integrated planning and control model on the bottom). For the purposes of discussion, we will assume a supply point to be a manufacturing plant or production factory; however, a supply point can also be a distribution center or another node within an integrated value or supply chain.

The integrated business model on the top of Figure 13.3 on page 423 depicts an entire business (or a division within a business) and the processes and elements required to run it well. The following description of the model is intended to be a brief overview. The processes and standards of excellence are described in more detail in *The Oliver Wight Class A Standard for Business Excellence*, seventh edition, as well as other Oliver Wight publications (from John Wiley & Sons and Ross Publishing). At the top and bottom of the integrated business model, we have performance improvement processes (e.g., measures, continuous improvement mindset, accountability) and people, values, and knowledge management processes (e.g., education, training, communication, lived mission and vision statements) required for all functions of a business.

For purposes of understanding, the interior of the model can be divided north and south into two hemispheres (the authors included a dashed line for clarity). *Above-the-line* (northern hemisphere) elements of the model show what is required to develop and deliver the company's strategic objectives, enabled through effective integrated business planning (IBP), described in Chapter 14, and strategic planning/management. *Above-the-line* processes are performed by middle and upper management, with a frequency of monthly in the case of IBP, or in the case of strategy development and strategy refresh processes, on a quarterly, semi-annual, or annual basis.

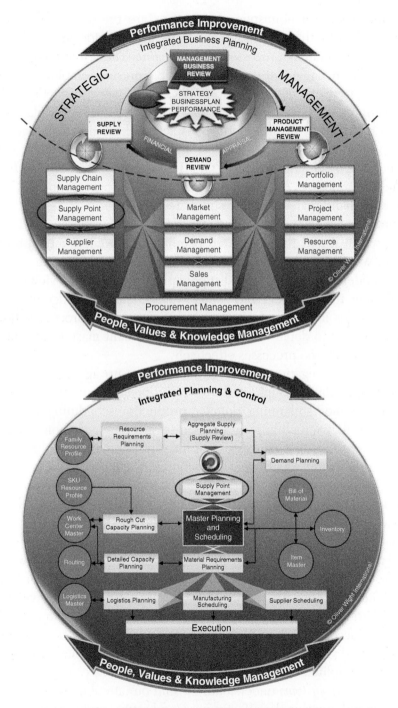

**Figure 13.3   The Integrated Business Planning and
Integrated Planning and Control Models**

Below-the-line (southern hemisphere) processes are the detailed planning, control, and execution processes that take direction from, and provide feedback to, the afore-mentioned aggregate planning processes *above-the-line*. The *below-the-line* processes are executed by middle management, supervisors, and front-line employees. From right to left *below-the-line*, portfolio management processes (e.g., new product introduction, renovations, discontinuations), sales and marketing processes, and supply planning processes are depicted. Procurement management spans across these detailed processes because sourcing and procurement activities support all three categories. Finally, note the integration between the *below-the-line* processes (horizontally) and between *below-the-line* and *above-the-line* processes (vertically) through their connection to IBP by way of the product review, demand review, and the supply review.

Supply point management is circled in the integrated business model to emphasize the linkage between it and the integrated planning and control model on the bottom of Figure 13.3, where supply point management is also circled. Note some additional overlap in the models where aggregated supply planning (supply review) is depicted, as well as performance improvement and people, values, and knowledge management processes. The rectangles in the model represent key supportive processes, flowing top to bottom from aggregate to detail, while the circles represent master data and supporting data required to execute the processes effectively.

The top-down disaggregation/planning (and bottom-up aggregation/replanning) of the aggregate supply plan through master (supply) planning, master (supply) scheduling, material requirements planning, detailed production scheduling, logistics planning and execution, supplier scheduling, and execution are touched upon in other chapters in this book. Done well, these processes are linked to one another through enterprise resource planning software, using clean and accurate master data (the circles), to ensure that the moving parts are meshed together and effectively operating as a single machine.

One can think of an enterprise resource planning (ERP) system as a data repository coupled with an integrated calculator (we will discuss how this is changing in a moment). Human beings enter data, or data is received from linked systems using an electronic data interface, and the ERP system stores that data and uses it to calculate new stored data.

For example, sales order quantities and dates are used, along with demand forecasts/plans, to calculate total customer requirements. This is the input by which supportive supply plans, schedules, capacity plans, and goods receipts are developed and executed. Accounts payable, accounts receivable, and other finance processes keep track of all of the money associated with those processes and transactions through a single integrated system. Using this simplified view, several *laws of ERP systems* can be described:

With the *laws of ERP systems* understood, we shift our attention to how companies can abide by the laws and improve the effectiveness (and return on investment) of their ERP

1st Law:	ERP systems never question the integrity of the data they process.
2nd Law:	ERP system recommendations are dependent upon the integrity of the data they process.
3rd Law:	Corrupt data results in poor recommendations, disappointing results, planner mistrust, and ERP implementation failure.
4th Law:	Root cause analysis is required on the 3rd Law. The question "Why is there corrupt data in the ERP system?" must be asked five times—*why, why, why, why, and why*. The most likely answer (perhaps at several "levels of why") will be *people* not knowing what or how to do the required input or maintenance tasks correctly, not caring or paying attention to doing the required tasks, not having the necessary time to do the required tasks correctly, and so forth.
5th Law:	Corrective action must be designed and implemented to address the answers to the five whys. The most effective designs will involve replacing people-dependent tasks with technology-dependent tasks (it's called "fail-safing" the data integrity process).
6th Law:	Highly accurate and trustworthy data result in good recommendations, rewarding results, planner/scheduler trust, and system implementation success. Most ERP systems will achieve desired results.

systems through four pillars of data integrity. In fact, the authors have experienced that companies can sometimes (perhaps often) avoid costly upgrades and implementations of new ERP software by addressing the underlying problem—that is, repairing the existing processes (and data) and *reimplementing* their existing systems to a Class A level of performance.

The Four Pillars of Data Integrity

Achieving data integrity relies on a set of processes that are executed by educated and trained people, with clear roles and responsibilities, measured for performance, and governed by policy. Like any successful endeavor that requires change in behavior, implementing a data integrity program and supporting processes requires change management

Figure 13.4   The Four Pillars of Data Integrity

and discipline to the point that it becomes a new *habit* in the organization. The real goal is *not just* to singularly *achieve* data integrity; the real goal is to *become the kind of company in which data integrity is regarded as a fundamental part of successful operations and a respect for data integrity is a condition for employment.*

There are four pillars or key principles for establishing an effective data integrity program in support of Class A master planning and scheduling (see Figure 13.4). We will start with an overview and then get more specific regarding choices and options to be considered, depending on the data and the business environment.

Education and Training

Education and training are often treated as the same in casual conversation, but they have clearly different roles. Education is commonly defined as the transfer of *theoretical* knowledge (the *why* and the *what*) while training is regarded as the transfer of specific skills (the *how* and *when*). Both are critical to the successful implementation of any new process, starting with education squarely up front to set the stage and gain excitement for, and commitment to, change. After processes have been designed and are ready for implementation, training can commence.

From an education perspective, all of the process elements and linkages within the two models in Figure 13.3 on page 423 would come into play depending upon the audience and focus of the data integrity program (data integrity can be applied to most, if not all, aspects of a business). Education is focused on the fundamentals of time-phased planning supported by an ERP system and is generally *not* focused on the ERP brand or software provider (*training* is more brand-specific). Education would include top-down and bottom-up planning from aggregate planning to detailed execution, inventory planning and control concepts, the theory and practicality behind safety stocks, where and when to use time fences (i.e., planning time fence), how process routings work and the typical data used within them, levels of capacity planning and roles and responsibilities, to name but a few.

Training, in the context of a data integrity program, is more specific to the individual process execution steps and where to find and adjust settings and parameters within the company's specific ERP system and other planning systems of record. One can think of training as *button pushing* exercises to learn how to operate within the system, but it also includes training on communication protocols, process flows, and the like.

For example, once the master planner and/or master scheduler has been educated on the concept of using planning time fences (see Chapter 3), made responsible for their upkeep, and it has been determined through a set of rules (i.e., policy and procedure) that the planning time fence for a specific part number should be set to 30 days, the master planner and/or master scheduler has to know where that setting exists within the master data tables in the ERP system.

Furthermore, the master planner and/or master scheduler needs to understand how the planning time fence setting interacts with other settings in the system, such as the parameters that dictate what happens when a computer-planned order hits the planning time fence. These data elements need to be synchronized in order for the system to behave as designed and provide the correct recommendations.

When the stakeholders and users of an ERP system have been *educated and trained*, then and only then has the company made them *aware of their role(s)* and are they truly *able to execute their responsibilities along with being held accountable for so doing*. Awareness and ability are the foundations upon which ownership and accountability can firmly rest. It is plainly unethical to hold someone accountable for a policy or procedure for which they were unaware through no fault of their own or for which they haven't been provided the proper tools and training to execute.

Ownership

Much like the terms *education* and *training*, the terms *accountability* and *responsibility* are often inaccurately applied. The accountable role is the person (singular) who is ultimately *answerable* for the performance their department or span of control (the buck stops here). The responsible party(s) is the person(s) who *does the work* to achieve the expected performance of that department. If a person or team isn't performing, the senior-most leaders should be looking to the accountable party for answers.

The accountable party needs to assess the awareness and ability of those responsible for doing the job. If they are aware and able and still *not* performing, they may be unwilling (unlikely, but it does happen), and we all know that situation doesn't typically end well for the responsible party.

Accountability for data integrity, within the specific scope of master planning and scheduling, resides with the person in charge of that functional area of the business, such as a vice-president or director of supply chain or the senior-most role in the planning organization. Accountability for overall data integrity for the entire company must reside with a member of the executive team (an executive champion), such as the chief operating officer or the president/chief executive officer.

While not a showstopper per se, it is the authors' opinion that the executive champion for data integrity function should *not* reside with a chief information officer or other information technology or information systems leadership. This is *not* to diminish the importance of these absolutely critical functions in running a business! Placing accountability with the vice president of supply (VPS), chief operating officer (COO), or president (CEO) reinforces the concept that data integrity is *not a software or technical function* owned by an IT/IS group; *it's a business objective in which everyone plays a part.*

Responsibility for data integrity, again within the context of master planning and scheduling, resides with the master planners and master schedulers (no surprise!). They do the work to audit and maintain target levels of data integrity, among other responsibilities. There are other roles within a complete data integrity program, of course. Examples of the various roles and responsibilities are highlighted in Figures 13.5 and 13.6 on pages 429 and 430 respectively.

A RACI (responsible, accountable, consulted, informed) matrix or one of its permutations (examples provided further on in the application sections) is typically used to define and communicate responsible and accountable roles. For the sake of brevity, the consulted and informed roles will not be detailed in this chapter's example, Figure 13.6. Consulted parties are typically subject matter experts whose opinions are needed for policy and process development or execution of a task. Informed parties are just that, informed of progress or completion of tasks and/or improvement plans.

Once a company has educated and trained the appropriate people and accountability and responsibilities have been assigned, all parties must act in concert with one another to maintain control of the data within the ERP system. It is near impossible to measure data integrity and perform meaningful root cause analysis and corrective action on processes that are out of control. The next section highlights key principles for controlling changes to the data in an ERP environment.

Role	Responsibilities
Executive Champion (Accountable) (Informed)	• Ensures that data integrity is continuously promoted (and funded) and a priority • Liaison to the executive team for data-related issues • Embodies the level of commitment of the organization to MDI
Functional Leaders (Accountable) (Informed)	• Ensure that policy is established and communicated • Ensure that policy is enforced and being followed • Routinely review data integrity metrics • Contribute to data-related strategic initiatives and risk management • Ensure that a continuous education/training curriculum exists and is being used
Users (Responsible)	• Responsible for the integrity of their assigned critical fields • Take part in establishment/modification of data auditing rules • Take part in auditing critical fields • Perform root cause analysis and develop corrective action
Super Users (Responsible) (Consulted)	• First line of support for users • Representative for the department/process team on data projects • Functional experts for training • Testing experts for system architecture changes • Outstanding system training • Able to document processes, functional specification, etc.
Data Steward (Responsible) (Consulted)	• Ensures that data elements are clearly defined • Eliminates data conflicts/duplicates • Removes unused data elements • Ensures that data is being used consistently in various systems • Ensures that data is fit for purpose—Coordinates the auditing and accuracy reporting process. • Ensures that the auditing process is effective and efficient (e.g., rules-based automation) • Ensures adequate documentation on appropriate usage and rules for data exists • Documents the origin and sources of authority on each data element (ownership) • Ensures that data is protected against unauthorized access or change

Figure 13.5   Examples of Roles and Responsibilities within a Data Integrity Program

Data Fields	Accounting Manager	Global Master Data Manager	Global Procurement Manager	Local Master Data Manager	Quality Manager	Distribution Manager	Supply Chain Manager	Warehouse Manager	Buyer	Cost Analyst	Global Master Data Team	Inventory Control	Logistics Specialist	Master Data Specialist	Quality Specialist	Distribution Specialist	Master Scheduler	Warehouse Specialist
	Accountable Roles								**Responsible Roles**									
Account Assignment Group	A									R								
Base Unit of Measure		A												R				
Batch Management			A												R			
Storage Capacity Usage								A										R
Certificate Type					A										R			
Costing Lot Size	A									R								
Distribution Channel						A										R		
Documentation Required					A										R			
EAN Category		A														R		
EAN/UPC Code		A														R		
In-House Production							A										R	
Lot size key							A										R	
Material		A										R						
Material description		A												R				
Material Type		A										R						
Minimum lot size							A										R	
Minimum Safety Stock							A										R	
Planned delivery time							A										R	
Purchasing group			A											R				
Storage Location				A										R				
Material group			A						R									

Figure 13.6 Supply Chain Master Data Integrity (Static) Ownership RACI Example

Change Control

Change control policies and procedures define who is authorized to change a data element and how the change is managed through a defined workflow. There is a balance to be struck here, as shown in Figure 13.7 on page 431, that seeks to manage both control and agility. The more centralized (globally controlled) the process is, the more control there is, but it comes with a tradeoff in agility. The opposite is true with the decentralized model.

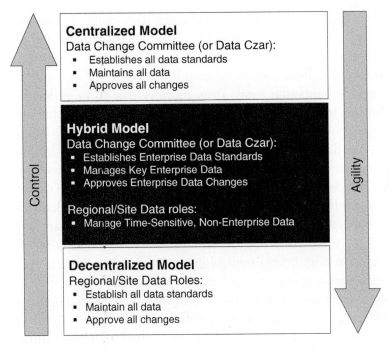

Figure 13.7   Change Control Models

In a centralized change control model, fewer expert-level users are authorized to make changes, and therefore control over change is very high. This is a reasonable and effective approach for globally relevant data that could have an enterprise-wide impact if errors occur (think financial data structures, tax codes, item numbers and descriptions, etc.). In this model, it can take days, weeks, or sometimes months for a change to be made in the system, depending on the approval workflow and regulatory environment. This length of elapsed time is often unacceptable for many data changes, including most planning parameters.

The decentralized model allows more changes to be made by a broader base of users. When educated and trained users spot errors or data elements out of tolerance, they can quickly address them and update their plans accordingly. This provides autonomy, agility, and empowerment to the users. However, in a decentralized change control environment with users who *haven't* been properly educated or trained, the data environment can be pure chaos. In a chaotic data environment, it is not uncommon to see one user changing a data field just to have another user change the same data field right back! Furthermore, *mass update aficionados* can unwittingly destroy swaths of previously acceptable data at the push of a button. A decentralized approach and the benefits of its agility have to be *earned* through education and training.

The best option is a hybrid model in which each data element is assessed and assigned for central control or local control based on business structures, the impact of potential errors, regulatory restrictions, and the like. An objective should be, within reason, to empower users at the local (decentralized) level to control as much of their own data as practical. Data elements may move from more central to more local control and vice versa, depending on the environment and education and training initiatives. The hybrid approach strikes a prescriptive balance between control and agility.

After making the determinations regarding centralized and decentralized control, the process must be documented (flow charts, policies, procedures, work instructions, metrics), and roles and responsibilities assigned (RACI diagrams, job or role descriptions). For data over which there is decentralized control, the user can change the data as they see fit so long as it is within their role and responsibility and they are following the rules for the appropriate values that can be entered or changed. This is typically managed through role-based system access control governed by data integrity policy, transaction procedures, work/desk instructions, and accuracy metrics.

Change control processes that are more centralized are often supported by dedicated workflow software or workflow modules within an ERP system (see Figure 13.8 on page 433). A change request is initiated by a user, which then goes through some gating process to categorize and accept or reject the request. Following the gating procedure, the appropriate individuals are notified (in parallel and/or sequentially) to execute their part in the change process, typically through e-mail, texts, or system notification. When the process is complete, the initiator and appropriate parties are notified of the request close-out. Decentralized sounds easier, doesn't it? There are many benefits to education and training, and enabling the decentralization of change control is clearly one of them!

With users and leadership educated and trained, roles and responsibilities assigned, and the change control process in place, a company will have established sufficient overall control of data integrity processes to implement effective auditing supported by root cause analysis and corrective action. Of course, prior to this work, baseline audits can be taken to gain a general understanding of the integrity of the data within the ERP system in order to influence and promote action.

Audits

Lord Kelvin, the nineteenth-century mathematical physicist, once said, "When you can measure what you are speaking about, and express it in numbers, you know something about it; when you cannot express it in numbers, your knowledge is of a meager and

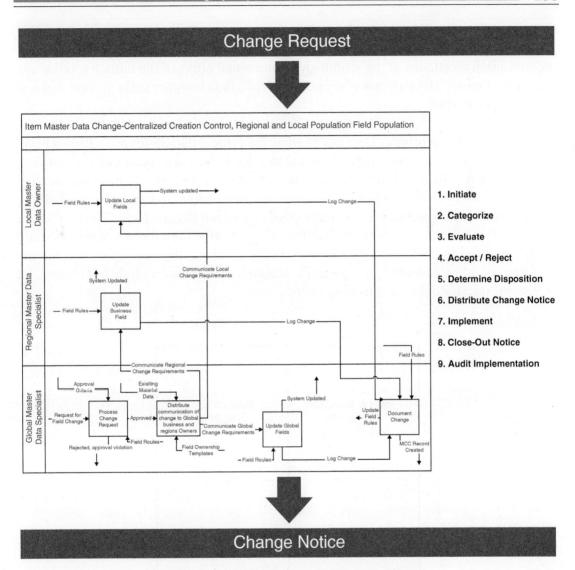

Figure 13.8   Change Control Process

unsatisfactory kind." It is often the case in companies, when asked, "How accurate are your lead times?" that the answer that is returned is, "Pretty good . . . I think." In order for master planning and scheduling systems to function effectively, practitioners have to advance beyond "I think" to a confident "I know!"

Auditing data for accuracy can be a daunting prospect. Enterprise resource planning (ERP) systems are packed with data across many modules and business functions. Practitioners, often crestfallen at the seemingly monumental effort of the initiative, often ask, "Where do I start?" Here are some key principals of a data integrity audit process that one can use to get started:

1. *Don't audit everything.* Determine what the critical data fields are within a functional scope (e.g., those data elements that have the most impact on the outputs, calculations, or recommendations related to the processes they support) and then rank those critical data fields (static) or data structures (dynamic) for probability of error and impact of error using a *quad chart* (see Figure 13.9). Those fields or structures that have a high probability of error and a high impact of error should be audited in each audit cycle (i.e., weekly or, at a minimum, monthly) for the item numbers selected for the audit. Examples here may include lead times, lot sizes, safety stocks, or purchase orders.

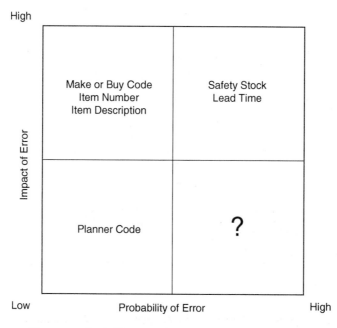

Figure 13.9 Probability and Impact Quad Chart Example

Conversely, for those fields that ranked low/low or even low impact/high probability, one may choose to audit those fields once per quarter or even once per year. An example here may include the code that designates which items belong to which planners and/or schedulers. The likely chance of error is moderate to low and it wouldn't be a disaster if there were an error, but a company should clean up the list and review master planner, master scheduler, material planner, capacity planner, and production scheduler designations at least once per year.

2. *Clearly define what "accurate" means for each field or data construct.* Before data can be deemed accurate, the rules—data sets, comparators/benchmarks, analysis, tolerances—must be defined. Once one knows the rules, a hit/miss analysis can be done on the data across the selected pool and a percentage accuracy metric can be calculated. Let's take procurement lead time as an example.

A company may define procurement lead time as the elapsed time, in whole days, from the moment a purchase requisition (if used) is created until the material is received on the company's dock. This is the standard (based on reality) that is maintained in the procurement lead time filed in the ERP system. This definition includes the conversion of a purchase requisition to a purchase order (if used), the communication of that purchase order (if used and not using a supplier scheduling program) to the supplier, the supplier producing the product, the transit time from the supplier to the company, and the time it takes to receive the product.

Distinctly missing from this definition is quality inspection time and put-away time in the warehouse. Perhaps the quality inspection and put-away times are encompassed in a different field within the ERP system. At any rate, it is important to understand what the procurement lead time does in the ERP system and what it includes (see education and training) in order to develop the rules.

From there, continuing with the procurement lead time example, one can measure from the point of purchase requisition (if used) creation to goods receipt across several past deliveries and compare the actuals to the procurement lead time field in the ERP database. Here again, rules are required. Should the accuracy of the field be based on the average of the past three actual procurement lead times? Should one compare against the longest lead time of the past three actuals? The shortest? The median? There is no right answer per se.

The average of the actual lead times may not give you a very reliable predictive lead time if there is high variability in the actual data. Using the longest actual lead time as the basis for accuracy would drive a planner to make some conservative purchasing decisions, lowering risk but also increasing inventory by ordering too early more often than not.

Perhaps a variability metric (e.g., coefficient of variation or CV—the ratio of standard deviation over the mean) could be added to the rule set. For example, if the CV of the data set is high (>1), then take the longest actual lead time as the comparator to the master data. This is the most risk-averse planning stance in a highly variable environment. If the CV is low (<1), then the average of the data set is used as a comparator.

Finally, understanding variability (standard deviation) may enable the use of a tolerance such as +/– 5 percent; that is, if the comparator is within 5% of the field data, the planner and/or scheduler will consider the field data to be accurate.

The rules around data accuracy can be very simple or very complex, depending on the data field and its variability. What is important is that the subject matter experts are engaged in setting the rules, with the ultimate goal being increasingly accurate master planning and scheduling recommendations from the system.

3. *Where possible, develop a systematic/algorithmic approach to assessing accuracy.* The more thought and precision that go into developing the rules, the easier it is to automate the auditing process. A person with reasonable spreadsheet skills could automate the analysis described in #2. If auditing a particular field can be automated, more attention can be dedicated to root cause analysis and corrective action on the failures. Furthermore, larger data sets (or the entire data set) can be routinely audited when automation is achieved.

4. *Design the audit scope, or item selection criteria to produce the most benefit.* For items that can be audited systematically (i.e., automated), the scope is limitless. A computer can audit all of the data available at the push of a button. A company may choose to run the algorithm quarterly or annually to keep certain fields clean and weekly or monthly for others (see #1). For fields that are more difficult to automate or for companies that have yet to achieve the system capability to do so, a more manual method of audit is necessary (i.e., a person must compare each field against the accuracy rules and make a determination) and

therefore a more limited scope of audit is necessary to complete the audit in a reasonable time frame.

One method for determining audit scope is to determine a statistically significant sample size based on the number of item numbers, purchase orders, process orders, and so on in the population and the confidence level and confidence interval one wishes to achieve. Once the sample size is determined, a random selection equal to that sample size can be culled from the total pool of item numbers and those items can be audited. There are many calculators available, through a simple Internet search, for taking statistical samples. While this method can give confidence as a whole, it runs the risk of selecting items that haven't been used in quite some time or may not be used in quite some time.

Another method for determining audit scope is to audit the pool of items that is likely to be transacted upon in the near future, preferably before reaching their respective cumulative lead times (see Chapter 3 for further explanation of cumulative lead times). This method will ensure that audit time is focused on those items that the company is about to produce and/or procure before decisions are made and money is spent. In this methodology, some concessions may have to be made for high turning items so as not to overaudit a single item number.

5. *Incorporate the auditing responsibilities into a planner's or scheduler's job description and workload.* For any of these to work, time and focus are needed. The responsibility for data integrity and the time and resources needed to fulfill that responsibility must be clearly stated in the responsible party's job or role description and calculated into the person's workload (e.g., the number/complexity of items for which the planner and/or scheduler is responsible). Data integrity simply has to be viewed as part of the job, not a project or event.

A final note on audits. A primary goal of auditing is to find errors. *If the audit process is not finding errors, it may be time to tighten the tolerances and/or readdress the rules.* Finding errors in a single item presents the opportunity to perform root cause analysis and corrective action that may uncover systemic issues that impact many other items. In this way, the master planning and scheduling system becomes increasingly refined and increasingly able to make good recommendations, allowing for planners and schedulers to spend more time with their colleagues on improving overall processes in the company and changing the game!

Applying the Four Pillars of Data Integrity in Support of Master Planning and Scheduling

In the world of competitive barbequing (including serious backyard aficionados), many factors determine whether the chef serves up the meal of a lifetime or a product destined for the dog's bowl. The chef has to know *what* they are cooking (Beef brisket? Pork ribs? Tofu? Seitan?) and *how* they are going to cook it (Slow smoked over indirect heat? Grilled directly over the flames? Buried in a pit wrapped in banana leaves?). They must select the appropriate ingredients for the seasonings.

They must select the appropriate equipment. The source of heat and/or smoke must be determined. One could use charcoal briquets, lump hardwood charcoal, wood, or gas. Smoke can be produced using a variety of woods—cherry, apple, mesquite, oak, hickory— all having different flavor profiles. All of these choices are analogous to *static master data*. These are the *inputs* into the barbeque process, all having choices and tradeoffs, but ultimately must be best suited for the job at hand.

Any competent barbeque chef who wants to make an award-winning meal knows that one cannot just prepare the ingredients, start the fire, and let everything else take care of itself. The cooking process is dynamic, and it needs monitoring, tending, and adjusting along the way. The chef must ensure that the cooking temperature and environment is being maintained, monitor the state of the food being cooked, baste, season, taste (there *are* advantages to being the chef), and make other additions and adjustments to the process along the way. In other words, the chef must manage the *outputs* of the barbeque process as well. This is analogous to managing *dynamic supporting data*.

The four pillars of data integrity described in the previous section (refer back to Figure 13.4 on page 426) apply to master data integrity (static) and supporting data integrity (dynamic) alike. Users responsible for both data sets must be educated and trained, ownership and responsibility must be assigned, control over changes to the data must be established, and audits must be conducted to measure and ensure integrity. However, there are nuances in the *application* of the four pillars to static and dynamic data that are described as we move through this chapter. This is particularly true for change control and audits.

Education and Training for Master Planning and Scheduling Data Integrity Processes

Master plans and schedules, as their names imply, are the masters of all plans and schedules within the supply chain execution environment (e.g., production volumes, material plans, capacity plans, production schedules). As such, education in master planning and scheduling (MPS) must cover the practices involved in MPS but also include the integrated processes that feed into the MPS process (e.g., demand management) and then take direction from MPS (e.g., material requirements planning).

An example of an education syllabus and participants is displayed in Figure 13.10. Education must be delivered by a professional (e.g., subject matter expert) who has experience

Master Planning and Scheduling Education	
Target Audience	• Senior Supply Chain Leadership (Directors, VPs) – Minimum attendance indicated by asterisk (*) below • Supply Chain Managers • Master Planners and/or Schedulers • Demand Managers • Material Planners • Those with "skin in the game" related to data integrity (IT and supporting functions)
Duration	• Typically 2–3 Days
Syllabus (subject to modification based on environment, but generally the contents of this book!)	• Kickoff and Objectives of the Course* • Overview of Class A Principles and Integration (People, Processes, Tools)* • Overview of the Integrated Business Model and Integrated Planning and Control (Figure 13.3)* • General Mechanics of Time-Phased Planning in an ERP Environment with Emphasis on MPS* • Master Planning Processes, Key Data Elements, Measures (including Resource Requirements Planning) • Master Scheduling Processes, Key Data Elements, Measures (including Rough Cut Capacity Planning) • Integration Points with MPS (Demand Management, Distribution Requirements Planning, Material Requirements Planning) • Data Change Control Strategies for MPS Data • Data Audit Strategies for MPS Data • Root Cause Analysis and Corrective Action Techniques • Data Integrity Program Implementation* • Wrapup*

Figure 13.10 Education for a Data Integrity Program in Support of Master Planning and Scheduling

in the processes in question. Often this means that companies outsource their education until such time as enough internal expertise is built up to perform education on their own. In Class A companies, ongoing education is a critical part of the Own Phase in the Oliver Wight Proven Path for Business Excellence (see Chapters 18–20).

Training is delivered to focused groups of users and is more *transactional* in nature, meaning that real button pushing in the master planning and/or master scheduling system(s) takes place. In addition to training on system functionality, users must be trained on company policies, procedures, process flows, work instructions, and planning and scheduling techniques that support the process for which they are responsible and the data integrity program in general (see Figure 13.11 on page 441). Training is typically delivered by planning system experts (e.g., key users) and relevant subject matter experts.

Prior to detailed education and training on master planning and scheduling processes and the data integrity program to support it, there are a number of activities that must be undertaken to bring the organization to this point. The Oliver Wight Proven Path for Business Excellence provides a roadmap of these activities and is explained in detail in Chapters 18 through 20.

Ownership for Master Planning and Scheduling Data Integrity Processes

As previously stated, accountability for data integrity in support of master planning and scheduling lies squarely with supply chain management leadership. The senior supply chain planning leader (e.g., supply manager and/or master supply planner) at a supply point or node in the supply chain, such as a plant or distribution center, would be the obvious choice for ultimate accountability for data integrity supporting master planning and scheduling at that supply point.

A director of supply chain or similar role with accountability for multiple nodes within the supply chain would be the accountable party for master plans and/or master schedules (*requests for production*) from IBP-approved supply plans to the supplying sites. The master planner and/or master scheduler role would be responsible for ensuring that those plans and/or schedules are valid and that the data is accurate. Additional layers of accountability at the executive level are expected across value or supply chains and for the company as a whole.

While there must be only one name/role in the accountability box, that person/role can also be *responsible* for activities related to data integrity. For example, in smaller organizations/sites, the site planning manager may be accountable for data integrity supporting MPS at that site, but also is responsible for conducting periodic *bench audits* of

Master Planning and Scheduling Training	
Target Audience	• Senior Supply Chain Leadership (Directors, VPs) – Minimum attendance indicated by asterisk (*) below • Supply Chain Managers/Supervisors • Master Planners and/or Schedulers • Those with "skin in the game" related to data integrity (IT and supporting functions)
Duration	• ~1–2 Weeks for MPS (can be intermittent, often in sandbox environment)

Training Content	• Kickoff and Objectives of the Training*
	• Review of Class A Principles and Integration (People, Processes, Tools)
	• Review of the Integrated Business Model and Integrated Planning and Control (Figure 13.3)
	• Master Planning and Scheduling (MPS) Process
	  ◦ MPS policies, flow diagrams, procedures, and work instructions
	  ◦ System transactions and timing (monthly/weekly/daily)
	  ◦ The purpose and function of key data elements and structures
	• Specific data management procedures and work instructions for MPS
	  ◦ Education/training in MPS system tools used in supporting and master data maintenance
	  ◦ MPS data change control policies, flow diagrams, procedures, and work instructions
	  ◦ MPS data auditing policies, flow diagrams, procedures, and work instructions (including root cause, corrective action)
	  ◦ MPS control reports for monitoring MPS health
	• Implementation Plan
	• Wrapup*

Figure 13.11 Training for a Data Integrity Program in Support of Master Planning and Scheduling

dynamic data like MPS production orders or MPS plans within the planning time fence (see this chapter's audits section for more detail). In larger organizations, he or she may delegate that responsibility to a more front-line role such as a planning supervisor or operations lead.

Responsibility assignments will depend in part on the change control required for the data. For master planning and scheduling parameters, responsibility should reside with the master planner and/or the master scheduler (remember, education and training open the door to well-managed decentralized control).

When tight central control is necessary (e.g., global finance hierarchies), a corporate steward may be assigned to be responsible for the data. Both the accountable and responsible parties need to be assigned (see the example in Figure 13.12 on page 443) by *each critical master data element (static) and supporting data structure (dynamic)* determined in the data integrity program design.

In the end, when it comes to ownership, documentation is necessary but insufficient. Offices are often replete with three-ring binders full of organizational charts and RACI-type matrices that are collecting dust. What is most important is that the planning team can look each other in the eye during the process design and accept responsibility for their part in the data integrity program, full stop.

Data integrity is a non-negotiable *part of the job* of a master planner and/or master scheduler and must be included in the formal job description. Those accountable must look the team in the eye and assure them that the master planners and/or master schedulers *will have the resources (skills, time, tools) to execute their responsibilities*. It is these *commitments* that are the most important outcome of the ownership design exercise.

Change Control for Master Planning and Scheduling Data Integrity Processes

With the need for a corporate change control policy, procedures, and workflow established in the prior section, let's talk in practical terms how this is applied to master planning and scheduling. Change is a weekly, daily, hourly, by-the-minute part of a master planner's and/or master scheduler's job. New product introductions represent changes to the portfolio for which a planner and/or scheduler is responsible. Changes to the demand and supply balance require analysis and potential adjustments to master plans and/or master schedules.

Waning performance, changes to policy, or change notifications from suppliers may precipitate changes to master data settings to enable the master planning and scheduling system to make the best recommendations in the future. It is critical that master planners and/or master schedulers play an active role in all of these changes.

Data	Type	Supply Chain Director (Corp)	Master Planner (Corp)	Planning Manager (Site)	Master Scheduler (Site)
Order Quantity	Static			A	R
Make or Buy Indicators	Static			A	R
Min/Max Lot Sizes	Static			A	R
Rounding Value	Static			A	R
Safety Stock	Static			A	R
Planner Code	Static			A	R
Lead Time	Static			A	R
Planning Time Fence	Static			A	R
Yield/Scrap Factors	Static			A	R
IBP Supply Planning Parameters	Static	A	R		
Resource Profiles (Resource Requirements Planning)	Static	A	R		
Resource Profiles (Rough Cut Capacity Planning)	Static			A	R
Planning BOM (Request for Supply)	Static	A	R		
Planning BOM (Multi-Level Master Scheduling)	Static			A	R
IBP Product Family Hierarchy	Static	A	R		
IBP Supply Plans	Dynamic	A	R		
MPS Process/Production/ Work Orders	Dynamic			A	R
Rough Cut Capacity Plans	Dynamic			A	R
Resource Requirements Plans	Dynamic	A	R		
MPS Purchase Orders	Dynamic			A	R

Figure 13.12   MPS Specific Data Integrity Ownership RACI Example

PORTFOLIO DATA CHANGE CONTROL In a properly controlled environment, master data population for new product introductions goes through a workflow with each respective subject matter expert populating the data required to build out a complete system record for that item (e.g., customer service parameters, data needed for logistics planning and execution, storage information needed for inventory management, planning parameters needed for material planning and production). *Note: This workflow also applies, often in a more truncated form, to master data changes for existing product renovations where changes have been made to a product's production process and/or required materials.*

A mistake that companies often make is assigning the responsibility for these portfolio-related data changes to a *data steward* who lacks the knowledge of the product to make informed decisions about the master data. By default, the steward will often copy and paste data from an item that they deem to be similar to the item they are working on, hoping that any inaccuracies will get caught by the right person down the road. Sometimes this is done purely for expediency and (false) efficiency.

Hope is not a strategy, and unfairly expecting a steward who is not an expert in the fields of master planning and scheduling to properly set the planning parameters is a recipe for disaster that simply causes more inefficiencies later. For this reason, it is imperative that master planners and schedulers be a part of the portfolio change workflow. This is a simple thing to do once ownership over the data has been established.

It is the (R)esponsible party on the RACI matrix that would be inserted into the workflow for adding or updating the critical fields assigned to them. They would use the data auditing *rules* and other pertinent information from manufacturing and/or suppliers to make a qualified judgment about the data and enter it accordingly. In this way, master planners and/or master schedulers take responsibility for their data from cradle to grave.

MASTER (STATIC) DATA CHANGE CONTROL In the simplest terms, the master data elements for which master planners and/or master schedulers have been made responsible (RACI) can be changed by them at any time they see fit, so long as the changes are made within the rules and boundaries covered by policy and procedure for that field. The data auditing process provides feedback on the performance of the process. The audit is a measure of the users' capability to make changes effectively and in a timely manner. This kind of agile and empowering environment is enabled through education and training.

SUPPORTING (DYNAMIC) DATA CHANGE CONTROL Changes to supporting data structures such as MPS process orders, MPS purchase orders, site-level master plans (i.e., *requests for production*) emanating from IBP-approved supply plans, and so forth are also subject to policy and procedure guidelines. Again, it is the master planner's and/or master scheduler's role as a (R)esponsible party to make these changes within the approved company rules. The use of defined time zones, the six (sometimes seven) key questions to answer before changing the master plan(s) and/or master schedule(s), and other master planning and scheduling management techniques were discussed in Chapter 4 and must be applied to change control in the context of supporting data.

Audits for Master Planning and Scheduling Data Integrity Processes

With the proper controls in place, audits of process effectiveness (i.e., accurate, timely data) can begin. This does not, and should not, preclude a company from performing a preliminary audit of data against some reasonable set of rules to get a rough estimate of the current state of data integrity. This is especially important if one is trying to get the program on the radar screen of executives and secure funding for a data integrity initiative.

ROOT CAUSE ANALYSIS AND CORRECTIVE ACTION PROCESSES   Before taking any routine measurements beyond a baseline assessment, it is vitally important to design and gain consensus on how root cause analysis and corrective action will be performed and reported. Far too many organizations either don't undertake any analysis of any kind when performance isn't where it should be (metrics that are always red and/or glossed over in reporting) or, more often, they only make it *one-why deep* in the *five whys* root cause analysis methodology.[2]

There is seemingly no end to the list of problem-solving and root cause analysis techniques from which to choose. Let's review a few common ones. These approaches should be used within an overall continuous improvement framework and requires education, design, and training in its own right. If your company has a strong lean/Six Sigma[3] organization, they would likely be a good source for information as well.

- **Pareto Analysis:** Often referred to as the *80/20* rule, wherein 80 percent of the problems can be attributed to 20 percent of the causes, Pareto analysis is a method of categorizing causal occurrences and ranking them in order to address the causes with the most occurrences, thereby providing the most leverage in identifying

---

[2] The five whys technique was developed by Sakichi Toyoda of the Toyota Motor Corporation. The tool is commonly used for root cause analysis in lean manufacturing and Six Sigma practices.

[3] Six Sigma is a set of process improvement tools, developed at Motorola in the late 1980s, that are used to measure, reduce, and eliminate causes of defects and variability within a process.

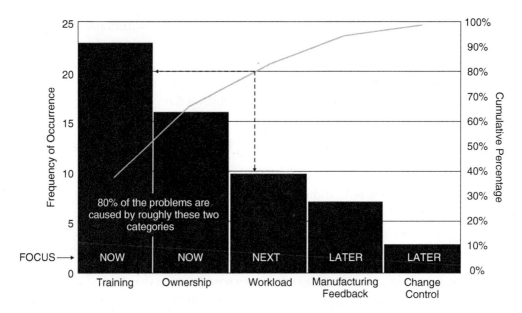

Figure 13.13 Pareto Chart

and fixing the problem. Simply put, Pareto analysis narrows the focus of teams to address the critical few causes among the many that are typically competing for attention.

In the context of data integrity, general error categories can be established and data errors that are detected can be assigned to those categories. The categories that account for ~80 percent of the errors should be prioritized and addressed. (See Figure 13.13.)

Example categories for data integrity may include

Education/training (I didn't know what to do).

Ownership (I didn't know I was supposed to do it).

Time management (I have too many e-mails, phone calls, texts, and distractions in my day).

Workload (I'm effective with my time, but still couldn't get to data maintenance— something had to give).

Change control process breakdown (I wasn't informed of that change to the supplier).

Unauthorized change (someone screwed up my data).

Manufacturing feedback process breakdown (I wasn't informed that the machine was running faster).

Error in BOM creation/maintenance (I put the wrong quantity in the BOM for that part).

Error in new product introduction data maintenance (the wrong lead time was entered during launch).

- **Five Whys:** A process in which the interrogator(s) repeatedly asks "why" a problem has occurred, peeling back layers by asking the next "why" question in reference to the answer from the previous "why" in an effort to get to the root cause. Often, this will lead to *multiple branches of causes* that can be managed using an *Ishikawa fishbone diagram or recorded in a tabular format.*

  Why did our lead time accuracy fall below 95 percent? Entry errors during our vendor consolidation initiative.

  Why were there entry errors? The deadline was approaching, folks were overwhelmed, entry got sloppy.

  Why were folks overwhelmed? Workload; we had to do our regular job in addition to the initiative.

  Why did we underestimate the workload? Because we don't do capacity planning for planner workload.

  Why don't we do capacity planning? Because we haven't taken the time to do it properly.

  Corrective Action: *Develop a rough cut capacity planning process for planner workload.*

- **A3 Problem Solving:** A structured approach to problem solving developed by Toyota Motor Corporation and popular with lean practitioners, the process uses a prescribed form (which fits on an ISO A3 paper size, hence the name) to guide teams through problem solving and continuous improvement (see Figure 13.14 on page 448).

Header Information	Body Information
A3 Number and Name	1. Clarify the Problem (Is, Is Not, Problem Statement)
Team Leader and Contact Info	2. Break Down the Problem
Team Members (Name and Role)	3. Set the Target
Stakeholders (Name and Role)	4. Analyze the Root Cause (Five Whys, Pareto)
Department	5. Develop Countermeasures (including impact on Target)
Organization Objective	6. Implement Countermeasures
Start Date	7. Monitor Results and Process
Planned Duration	8. Standardize and Share Success

Figure 13.14   A3 Form Components

MASTER (STATIC) DATA AUDITS Master data audits are performed much like inventory cycle counts in a warehouse. In cycle counting, inventory is ranked in importance based on movement velocity and/or value and is counted (audited) accordingly. Generally, slow-moving and/or low-cost items are counted less frequently than fast-moving, expensive items.

Master data elements can also be ranked in order of *importance* by determining probability of error and impact of error, and those with high probability and/or impact of error are audited more frequently than those with low probability and/or impact of error. Some judgments must be made in certain situations on the high-impact/low-probability or low-impact/high-probability data elements, but it's a reasonable framework to start (see Figure 13.15 on page 449).

The basic audit process is highlighted as we conclude our discussion on data integrity requirements to support a best-practice master planning and scheduling process. It is useful to have the IT/IS or data governance organization help coordinate these efforts by automating the selection of items codes and facilitating/consolidating the feedback reporting among the various teams. A data steward or coordinator would be perfect for this coordinating task. It bears repeating that, if the auditing of the key field can be automated through a rules-based algorithm, the (R)esponsible party need

Data	Type	Supply Chain Director (Corp)	Master Planner (Corp)	Planning Manager (Site)	Master Scheduler (Site)	Probability	Impact	Frequency
Order Quantity	Static			A	R	L	H	Q
Make or Buy Indicators	Static			A	R	L	H	Q
Min/Max Lot Sizes	Static			A	R	L	H	Q
Rounding Value	Static			A	R	L	H	Q
Safety Stock	Static			A	R	H	H	M
Planner Code	Static			A	R	L	L	A
Lead Time	Static			A	R	H	H	M
Planning Time Fence	Static			A	R	L	H	M
Yield/Scrap Factors	Static			A	R	L	H	M
IBP Supply Planning Parameters	Static	A	R			L	L	M
Resource Profiles (Resource Requirements Planning)	Static	A	R			L	H	Q
Resource Profiles (Rough Cut Capacity Planning)	Static			A	R	L	H	M
Planning BOM (Request for Supply)	Static	A	R			L	H	Q
Planning BOM (Multilevel Master Scheduling)	Static			A	R	L	H	Q
IBP Product Family Hierarchy	Static	A	R			L	L	A

A = Annually
Q = Quarterly
M = Monthly

Figure 13.15   RACI Diagram with Audit Frequency

not *perform the audit* but must be *appraised of the results* to *perform root cause and corrective action*.

1. Select the item codes to be audited for the month (see Figure 13.9 on page 434 and following paragraphs).

2. Audit the key fields (i.e., the data—static examples in Figure 13.15) against the defined rules. Audit key fields designated as *monthly* frequency each monthly cycle, audit the *quarterly* designations in the first month of each quarter, and *annual* designations once per year. Automated audits can be run monthly.

3. Report percent accuracy, by key field, for the group of item codes audited.

    Accuracy per Key Field =
    Accurate Key Field Data / Total Items Audited × 100

4. Perform root cause analysis and corrective action on key fields falling below acceptable standards, report and rectify.

The requirement minimums for a Class A (Capable) Milestone[*] and to support an effective master planning and scheduling process are set at 95+ percent.

---

[*] See Chapters 18 through 20 and Appendix A for a discussion and definition regarding Class A requirements.

Note that bills-of-material receive extra scrutiny at 98+ percent accuracy, as an incorrect BOM can cause havoc across multiple avenues in master planning and scheduling, material planning, capacity planning, and cost accounting.

Item Master Records (support MPS process itself)	95%+
Inventory Records (support MPS process itself)	95%+
Planning Bills (if used, to support MPS)	98%+
Resource Profiles (support RCCP and MPS)	95%+
Bills-of-Material (support detailed material planning)	98%+
Process Routings (support detailed capacity planning)	95%+
Work Location Master Records (support RCCP/CRP/DPS)	95%+
Valid Price and Cost Data (support costed MPS)	95%+
Logistics Master Records (support logistics planning)	95%+

SUPPORTING (DYNAMIC) DATA AUDITS Auditing supporting data structures, such as master plans, master schedules, and/or rough cut capacity plans, takes on a slightly different flavor than auditing static master data. Putting together a valid master plan and/or master schedule (i.e., the product/service is needed and the schedule can be achieved in terms of material and capacity) often requires tradeoffs and decision making that is not so easily assessed through *mechanical* means.

As a result, the audit is typically performed by a planning manager or supervisor, sitting with a master planner and/or master scheduler, and reviewing a set of master plans and/or master schedules to test for validity and, in doing so, better understand the master planner's and/or master scheduler's critical decision-making skills.

In selecting the product families, product subfamilies, master planned, or master scheduled items to audit, one must remember that the *purpose of an audit is to expose problems in an efficient and effective way*. When a single problem is revealed, it may shed light on similar problems across many product families or items, and therefore the solution will also touch many product families and/or items.

Therefore, it is helpful to select product families and items that are *active*; that is, there is reasonable volume velocity and demand/supply/inventory/capacity balancing activities in play. An audit of an item with no demand forecast, no corresponding master plan and/or master schedule, and a pile of inventory sitting on the shelf may be interesting to an inventory management team and may require a post-mortem examination, but it would not shed much light on the forward-looking planning process or the capabilities of the master planner and/or master scheduler.

Once the items or product families have been selected for that audit time period (*minimum monthly*), the planning manager or supervisor schedules time with the master planner and/or master scheduler and reviews the master plan(s) and/or master schedule(s) for those product families or items. A series of questions should be asked for both master plan(s) and/or master schedule(s) (see Figure 13.16). Let's take a look, shall we?

Supporting Data Audit Questions	
Master Plans	Master Schedules
Is the request for supply directed to the correct plants and/or suppliers?	Are there any past dues?
Are demand and supply balanced appropriately?	Are demand and supply balanced appropriately?
Are inventory or backlog projections within acceptable range?	Are inventory or backlog projections within acceptable range?
Are resources requirement plans valid?	Are rough cut capacity plans valid?
Are the assumptions supporting the plan clearly captured?	Have exception messages been reviewed and acted upon?
Are issues, risks, and opportunities being addressed?	Are issues, risks, and opportunities being addressed?
Is the master plan tied to the approved supply plan?	Have MPS process/production orders been released correctly?
Is accountability for MPS due-date adherence clearly understood?	Have MPS purchase orders been released correctly?

Figure 13.16 Supporting Data Audit Questions

Finally, a series of control reports can be run on a routine basis that will also shed light on the health of the master plan(s) and/or master schedule(s). The data reported can include the examples that follow and are often dynamic, depending on when the snapshot is taken.

For example, the numbers tend to increase after a master planning and scheduling system regeneration runs and decrease as master planners and/or master schedulers work their exception-driven action messages. Early on in the process improvement journey, one may find that there are hundreds, if not thousands, of orders that are past due or that haven't been transacted in a timely manner. With the truth on the table and assuming best-practice processes have been established and implemented, the planning supervisors or operational leads can use control reports to help monitor the health of the plans in the master planning and scheduling system.

Examples of Data Reported on Control Reports

- Number of planned orders past start date and not yet released
- Number of planned orders past finish date and not yet released
- Number of process orders past due (finish date in the past)
- Number of purchase orders past due (finish date in the past)
- Number of exception messages by type and planner

Summary

As stated previously in this chapter, data integrity is a topic for which it is difficult to muster widespread enthusiasm or passion, but it is essential to running a business effectively. Estimations of the risks and productivity losses associated with bad data often help in gaining the attention of leadership. That said, there is often at least one person or a group of people within a company who has a natural interest and passion for systems and data and one can start there in building support.

Companies don't have to wait for perfect functional processes to be in place to establish a data integrity program based on the four pillars described here. As the functional processes mature, the inputs to the data integrity program will improve—education and training will improve, understanding of accountabilities and responsibilities will improve, key data elements will be more widely used and adopted, and the data rules will improve. The message here is to *start now*!

Keep data integrity principles in mind as we explore the master planning and scheduling (MPS) supporting integrated business planning (IBP) process in the next chapter. One of the reasons companies fail to make timely decisions in MPS and/or IBP is a mistrust of the data available and underlying assumptions made. *Confidence in the data (even roughly right) goes a long way in enabling confidence in decisions.*

14

Integrated Business Planning

Strategy without tactics is the slowest route to victory.
Tactics without strategy is the noise before defeat.

In business, as in war, failures often stem from lack of *horizontal* coordination between essential functions and lack of *vertical* integration with the strategic objectives of the business. On the battlefield, armies that fail to coordinate the movement of infantry with support from artillery, air, and armor typically are defeated by opponents whose main force and support functions operate as one. Furthermore, if the army is fighting the wrong battle, regardless of victory or defeat, it has done little or nothing to advance the strategic objective of winning the war. On the contrary, it has likely squandered valuable time, materials, money, and lives.

In business, the company whose sales force is out booking orders and promising delivery dates without the concurrence of finance, engineering, and manufacturing are likewise imperiled. If the company is developing, launching, selling, and manufacturing goods or providing services without a connection to a clear strategy on *how the company will win*, the company can be very good at all of the aforementioned functions and still go out of business.

While *horizontal and vertical integration and coordination* among business functions is obviously essential, it does not just happen; it needs a formal mechanism to ensure that it occurs. That mechanism is *integrated business planning (IBP)*. Integrated business planning represents the further evolution of sales and operations planning (S&OP) from its production planning roots, through foundational demand/supply/inventory/backlog balancing, into a fully integrated business management process. Oliver Wight defines integrated business planning as follows:

Integrated Business Planning is a process led by senior management that evaluates and revises time-phased projections for demand, supply, portfolio, strategic projects and the resulting financial plans. This is done on a monthly basis and planned on a minimum 24-month rolling horizon.

It is a decision-making process that realigns the tactical plans for all business functions in all geographies to support the company's business goals, strategies and targets.

A primary objective of the process is to reach consensus on a single operating plan, to which executives of the management team hold themselves accountable and allocates the critical resources of people, equipment, inventory, materials, time and money to most effectively satisfy customers in a profitable way.

The key functions of the organization are engaged in the monthly IBP process and ensure that individual plans are synchronized with each other and aligned with the business strategy. The Oliver Wight standard five-step IBP process is depicted in Figure 14.1.

Integrated business planning covers a rolling planning horizon of at least two years but often extends to three years and beyond to account for product development pipelines or resource plans that require longer visibility to manage change. Integrated business planning

Figure 14.1   The Integrated Business Planning Model

(IBP) deals with demand and supply volumes at a product family level (e.g., groups and subgroups of similar products or services) and speaks in the language of sales and manufacturing (markets, regions, forecasts, shipments, bookings, production, units, hours, etc. as well as in financial terms). In addition to serving as a means of generating other plans, IBP is the process for developing a *volume budget* for individual manufacturing sites (e.g., plants, mills, factories) and the master plan and/or master schedule.

Each step review, described in the next section, is owned by the executive that is accountable for that business function. The executive step owner chairs their respective review, provides leadership direction, makes timely decisions when needed, officially approves the plan, and is accountable for the overall effectiveness of the IBP process.

Each step owner is supported by a step leader. The step leader, typically a manager or director-level position, is accountable for delivering the information *packet* that effectively communicates past performance, forward-looking plans and assumptions, and actions or decisions required to close gaps to business objectives and achieve strategic goals. The step leader marshals the step review participants and other resources to assist him or her in preparing this packet for distribution to the review's participants 24 to 48 hours prior to the formal session.

Integrated Business Planning Process Elements in Brief

The following sections will introduce the fundamental elements of the integrated business planning process. The renowned statistician George Box once said, "All models are wrong, some are useful." The IBP process should be tailored to the needs of the business—small versus complex, local versus global, one division versus multiple divisions, and so on—while keeping these best-practice elements embedded.

Strategy and Business Plan Performance

Strategy and business plan performance lies in the center of the model in Figure 14.1 on prior page for a reason. The integrated business planning (IBP) process is an excellent mechanism to ensure that all of the forward-looking plans are concurrent with strategy. Resources must be adequately applied to the strategic objectives and decisions must be made to align to the objectives. Often this means deciding *what the business isn't going to do* in favor of a *what the business is going to do* strategy.

For example, if part of the business strategy is to grow through new product innovation, one would expect new product vitality (the percent of revenue from new products) to be assessed monthly in the product management review (PMR). The PMR team must ensure that resources are being deployed to achieve vitality results, which may mean a shift of resources from existing product renovations.

Likewise, if another strategic objective is to expand the business into emerging markets, one would expect resources to be applied, measures developed, and progress toward this goal to be reported in the demand review. Finally, if cost-out initiatives, supply chain segmentation, or footprint expansions were part of the strategy, progress should be reported in the supply review.

Figure 14.2 depicts how a company's vision is supported by goals that are broken down into strategies, tactics, and actions that should be monitored and measured for progress. (Figure 14.2 shows one such goal being cascaded for simplicity, but a similar cascade should be in place for the other goals depicted.)

It is surprisingly easy to stray away from the three- to five-year strategic plan when under pressure to deliver financials every quarter! IBP ensures that the business functions and leadership looks beyond the quarter and remembers what they signed up for when they developed the strategy.

Product Management Review—Step 1 in the IBP Process

The primary objective of the product management review (also referred to as the portfolio management review) is to raise the visibility of the product and/or service portfolio

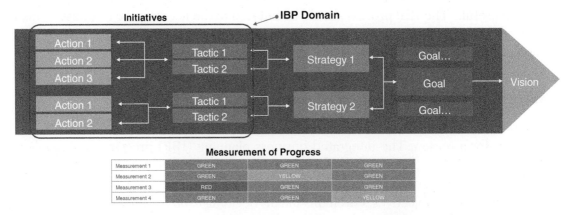

Figure 14.2   Strategy Deployment and Alignment

agenda across the business and approve a valid and achievable portfolio plan that supports the business strategy. To do this, the PMR team must monitor and manage the health and sufficiency of the project funnel to ensure that, when everything is summed up, the pipeline of new product innovations, existing product renovations, value (profit) research/engineering, and stock-keeping unit (SKU) rationalization projects will achieve the business objectives. Changes or risks to the current and projected portfolio must be identified and evaluated for impact, and the PMR team must reach consensus on the aggregate summary of projects and ensure that the portfolio is adequately resourced and aligned to the business strategy.

The master planner (sometimes the supply manager) and master scheduler would likely play a role on individual project teams as new products and/or changes to existing products are being planned and scheduled through the facility (pilot runs and production). The impact of PMR projects on available capacity and materials must be understood in order to communicate an effective supply chain response.

Figure 14.3 is a visual representation of a company's portfolio plan. The portfolio includes all of the products currently for sale. The projected portfolio also includes products entering the portfolio and products leaving the portfolio over time. A healthy business requires a range of new product introductions or, at a minimum, significant renovations to existing products to remain competitive in the face of changing technologies and customer demographics.

Reducing product costs and making "new and improved" modifications to existing products may extend the life of a product or brand but may not grow the business. The key to growth and profitability is to include in the portfolio a mix of product improvements

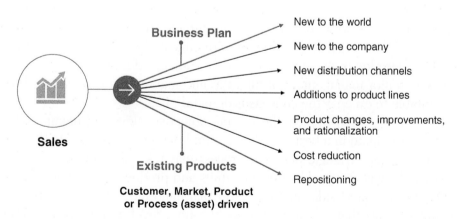

Figure 14.3   Product Portfolio Planning

and the products that are new to the company and, occasionally, new to the world to grow the business.

The emphasis in companies tends to be on what is entering the portfolio. It is also important to plan the effect that new products will have on existing products. The plan must also include information on products that ought to leave the portfolio (the end-of-life and rationalization of products), which companies are often reluctant to eliminate.

The expectation is that a process exists that compares the existing product's sales plan to the business plan goals and plans/replans on how to achieve the goals and strategic plan. The product management review provides visibility of changes in the product portfolio goals, objectives, and strategies and how those changes will affect the demand, supply, logistics, and financials of the business.

Demand Review—Step 2 in the IBP Process

The primary objective of the demand review is to reach consensus on a single demand plan and the activities and investments that are required to execute the plan. A *single demand plan* includes not only the latest best estimate of anticipated demand, but also the high-side and low-side scenarios to communicate the impact of opportunities and risks on the plan. The goal is to reach consensus on an *unconstrained, unbiased, time-phased demand plan and the resulting financials* (volume, revenue, and margin). *Unconstrained* here means that the demand team does not (at least initially) constrain the plans based on the supply chain's ability to supply; however, the demand organization might constrain the demand related to strategic direction, sales and marketing budgets, and the like.

The business must also seek to understand and agree on underlying assumptions (the story) supporting the plan so that it can be effectively communicated beyond just quoting a number. When gaps to strategy or annual sales targets are uncovered, the team sets priorities and action plans to close gaps to commitments and performance measure targets, mitigate risks and exploit opportunities, and make trade-off decisions with clear alignment to strategy. The senior management of the sales and marketing organizations hold themselves accountable to execute the consensus demand plan.

Figure 14.4 on page 461 depicts the varying objectives, levels of detail, and business functions that participate in a best-practice demand planning process. On the right-hand side, the visioning and strategic planning process may take place on an annual or semi-annual basis, looking at demand by business units and product families over an extended horizon. On the left-hand side, in short-term planning and execution, a team is managing the mix of sales that are coming in at the item level and adjusting to abnormal demand and/or unexpected supply constraints as needed. Integrated business planning

Demand Review	Short-Term Planning and Execution	Integrated Business Planning Process Focus	Visioning Strategic Planning
	Horizons		
	0–13 weeks	4–24 months	3–5 years
Objective	Meet Customer Requirements; manage critical supply issues	Ensure business plan is met, close gaps to plan(s), deliver against the strategy and goals while realizing the vision.	Set long-term direction for the business. product/service, customer, infrastructure plan.
Functions that influence	• Supply Chain • Orders • Distribution	• Sales and Marketing Strategies • Leadership Objectives • Demand Plan • Finance	• Leadership Objective • Vision Statement
Detail needed	Item/Location	Product Family/Subfamily	Business Unit/Product Family

Figure 14.4 Demand Planning Horizons and Objectives

lies between these zones to ensure that execution activities are connected to, and guided by, the business strategy and vision.

The master planner and/or master scheduler play a key role in evaluating the demand-related risks, opportunities, and alternate scenarios, working closely with the demand manager to develop the best course of action in order to exploit opportunities and minimize the impact of risks to the business. The demand plan is considered a request for product from demand to the supply organization, so the master planner and/or master scheduler must understand the demand plan deeply enough to develop an effective response to that request.

Supply Review—Step 3 in the IBP Process

The primary objective of the supply review is to answer the demand organization's request for product by aligning the needed supply with demand, considering cross-business implications and developing alternatives when demand and supply cannot be easily aligned. Furthermore, the supply team must ensure that critical resources are available to support the supply plan using resource requirements planning techniques (sometimes referred to as rough cut capacity planning at the aggregate level).

When identified, the supply team works together to develop gap-closing plans for gaps to performance metrics or strategic plans. When agreed-upon inventory, lead time, and backlog tolerances will be exceeded in order to align demand and supply plans, the impact of the deviations will be summarized and positioned for approval. Strategic initiatives such as cost reduction programs, footprint expansions, and so forth will be reviewed for progress.

The master planner and/or master scheduler play a key role in evaluating the incoming product and demand plans, alternate scenarios, opportunities, and risks to develop a supply chain management (SCM) response and communicate back to the overall organization, not just the demand organization.

Figure 14.5 shows that the scope of the supply review extends beyond individual manufacturing sites to include the extended supply chain. Opportunities, risks, costs, and performance related to the supply plan reside in each node of a supply chain and need to be considered when developing the plan and alternate scenarios. Master planners and/or master schedulers at each node in the supply chain (e.g., planners at a company's suppliers and customers) may take part in the supply planning processes, especially in scenario planning.

After evaluating, a product on the demand plan may become constrained by supply, but it is the supply organization's objective to say yes to demand and work the options ("yes, if . . ." and "yes, but . . ." and "yes, and this is what it will take").

Financial Appraisal—Step 4a in the IBP Process and Integral Part of Each Step

A financial appraisal takes place at each process step review and a summary is prepared at the business level for the integrated reconciliation review. A representative from the finance organization attends each review and ensures both that the financial plans are being derived from the operational numbers (i.e., no separate financial forecasting) and that the financial outcomes are right, valid, and realistic. *Right* means that the calculations to convert operational numbers into financials are done correctly.

For example, a weighted average selling price is used to convert family-level unit volumes into dollars, and it is the financial representative's job to make sure that is done correctly. *Valid* means that the planned financial results meet the needs of the business. *Realistic* means that the plans are achievable; the finance organization often plays the part

Figure 14.5 Scope of Supply Management in the Supply Review

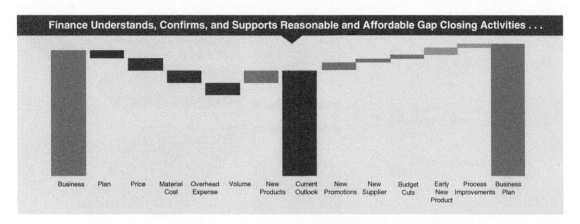

Figure 14.6 Finance's Role in Integrated Business Planning

of a third-party observer, appropriately questioning the plans when assumptions, opportunities, and risks are not clear.

Figure 14.6 depicts a waterfall chart (sometimes referred to as a bridge chart) that graphically shows the building blocks and assumptions related to the current outlook; that is, the plan put forward in the current IBP cycle and the opportunities and risks that must be managed to get back on track to the business plan if need be. A sign of successful financial integration into a company's IBP process is when the finance team walks shoulder-to-shoulder with the other functions of the business (product, demand, supply) and stands behind the plan as *our plan and the truth as we know it today*, as opposed to separate operational and financial projections.

The master planner and/or master scheduler work closely with finance when developing their plans and alternate scenarios to ensure that the impacts (e.g., inventory, customer backlogs, logistics cost, absorption variances, etc.) are appropriately communicated for decision making.

Integrated Reconciliation Review—Step 4b in the IBP Process

Integrated reconciliation is a *process* that takes place during the IBP cycle and is a formal *review* prior to the management business review. Both the process and the integrated reconciliation review are primarily executed through the team of IBP step leaders. The objective of the process is to find and manage any gaps or misalignment early in the process and at the lowest practical level. Figure 14.7 (on page 464) shows that the company's bottom-up planning processes (i.e., continuous replanning through IBP) and top-down

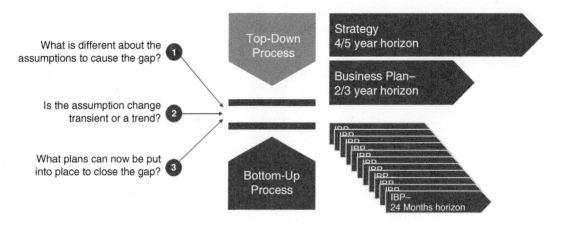

Figure 14.7 Gap Management Approach

planning processes (the strategy cascade described in Figure 14.2 on page 458) must be reconciled on a monthly basis to stay in alignment.

The team of IBP step leaders should take every opportunity to resolve issues between steps before escalating them to the integrated reconciliation review (IRR) and potentially the management business review (MBR). Should issues require escalation to the IRR, the IBP step ladders will use the IRR to prepare recommendations on decisions required in the MBR based on well-defined, quantified scenarios.

The IRR team also ensures that plans are aligned and optimized across the process and that performance measures and improvement plans are appropriately assessed and communicated. Finally, the team sets the formal agenda for the management business review, publishes the MBR information deck, and ensures readiness for decision making.

The supply manager, master planner, and/or master scheduler may play a role in developing scenarios and recommending decisions. For sure, if the supply manager, master planner, or master scheduler is the supply review leader, they will take part in the IRR every month.

Management Business Review—Step 5 in the IBP Process

The primary objective of the management business review (MBR) is to approve the updated plans coming from the product management review, demand review, supply review, and the various financial appraisals. The IBP step owners and the extended executive team participate in the review, assess gaps in the latest plans versus strategic and business goals and measures, and they ensure actions are taken to close the gaps. They are also tasked with making decisions and resources available to execute the approved plans. They hold each other accountable for success in execution.

The executive team must hold themselves accountable to ensure that the fundamental questions in Figure 14.8 are asked and answered each month. The executive team should *expect to hear the truth* and the IBP participants should be prepared to *deliver the truth as they know it at that time!*

Upon completion of the management business review, the approved product (launches, discontinuations), demand (sales, marketing), supply (manufacturing, procurement, purchasing, logistics), and financial (revenue, margin, cost) plans are distributed along with the review's minutes and open action items to all relevant managers. Of course, this is to include the supply director, supply manager, and master planner and/or master scheduler.

How are we performing compared to our strategic initiatives?	How are the individual product families performing (actual and projected)?	Senior leaders of the business are responsible for ensuring that these questions are asked and answered every month.
Are we on plan financially?		
How are we performing operationally?	Are we comfortable with the projections between months 4 and 24?	
Has there been significant learning since last month (actual vs. projected)?	Do we have any reason to revisit our company goals, strategies, strategic initiatives, or business vision?	
What new or different risks must we understand or consider?	How good is our reliability at developing a plan and performing to the plan?	
What decisions must we make today? Within the next few months?		

Figure 14.8   Some Fundamental Questions Answered Through Integrated Business Planning

Workable, Adjustable Plans

One of the *principal benefits* of the IBP process is its focus on *workable plans*. Natural optimism and business units planning in isolation are factors that can lead to plans that cannot be fulfilled within reasonable costs or cannot be fulfilled at all. Workable plans can be created only by processes that have built-in reality checks.

The IBP process offers those checks by starting at the top and providing verification at lower levels. The participation of all major functions is mandated by the process, and the feasibility of each function's plans is assessed by the others through the natural *pitch and catch* of an integrated information flow. Feedback loops ensure that plans that are beyond the current capabilities of related functions are assessed, and alternatives are jointly developed in an attempt to alleviate the constraints.

Thus, an increase in the sales plan put forth by marketing and sales is critiqued by supply chain planning and manufacturing, which may not have nearly the resource capacity or required materials to deliver product at the requested level, assuming planned sales volume is reached. Manufacturing may respond with *what if* alternatives, trade-offs, and costs to meet demand and, in the process, ensure that the organization is truly committed to execution.

Figure 14.9 on page 467 indicates where IBP fits into the scheme of other company activities and the points where feedback can and should take place. Integrated business planning ties the company's high-level business and strategic plans to the operations of each department. The feedback loops in Figure 14.9 indicate how each department participates in the process. All major functions of the company are involved, ensuring that plans are attainable from top to bottom, bottom to top, and side to side. The absence of these linkages creates the potential for loss of control and for significant miscommunication within the organization. For example, production operations might be working from one set of numbers while sales or product development is planning on something quite different. The potential for confusion and failure in such a case is obviously great, and IBP can eliminate its occurrence.

Customers cancel firm orders; unexpected new orders miraculously appear; manufacturing capacity slips as unanticipated breakdowns occur. Several years back, British Prime Minister Benjamin Disraeli said that "what we anticipate seldom occurs, what we least expect generally happens." This statement applies equally to politics, war, and business. The events we plan often unfold in ways we do not expect. Even well-coordinated plans can lead us into failure if they are carved in stone.

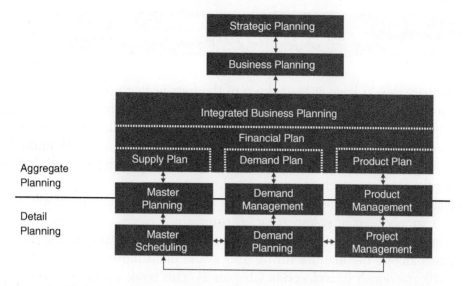

Note: Master planning is referred to as supply management in some companies; master planning is (occasionally) referred to as master scheduling in some companies (for clarity, see this book's Glossary).

Figure 14.9 Integrated Business Planning and Other Company Functions

To be successful, we need plans that are sufficiently *flexible,* or *robust,* to accommodate the contingencies that naturally occur. Fortunately, the IBP process, with its regular monitoring and inputs from many sources, provides an opportunity for planning adjustments as needed.

As a result, IBP (along with master planning and scheduling) is an exceptional process for managing change. All the information needed to make adjustments ends up on the table, and each of the parties whose agreement to those adjustments is critical has a seat at the table.

Moreover, because IBP links high-level plans together while the supply chain management (SCM) and master planning and scheduling (MPS) using the enterprise resource planning (ERP) system links high-level and low-level plans, changes made at the IBP level are formally communicated down into the detailed plans required for action and execution. This channel of information enables different functions in the company to seize opportunities and avoid potential disasters.

Integrated business planning also allows companies to better manage finished-goods inventory, customer backlog, and demand as well as supply lead times. The right people come together to make decisions in a structured planning (and control) process that reflects top management's expectations. And finally, IBP provides a basis for measuring accuracy and performance, which is critical to any organization that is serious about continuous improvement.

Master Supply Planning

Every company should have at least three of the four near- to mid-term planning levels depicted in Figure 14.10 on page 469. Those three levels are integrated business planning at the corporate or divisional level, master (supply) scheduling at the plant level, and detailed production scheduling (also at the plant level). Companies with multiple manufacturing sites (especially those that can produce the same product at multiple sites) need to consider the master (supply) planning level.

As described earlier in this chapter, one of the outputs of the IBP supply review is a family-level supply plan in volume (e.g., cartons, tons, pieces). The role of the master (supply) planner (supply manager in larger supply organizations) is to divide the aggregate volume plans among the manufacturing sites as the plans move closer to execution (see Figure 14.10, previously introduced in Chapter 2). This is *not* simple mathematics.

The inputs that the master (supply) planner may use in making decisions as to where to direct volume include resource requirements plans from the supply review process, plant quality levels, plant costs and absorption, proximity to key accounts that will be buying the volume, and so forth. The decisions must align with the strategies and tactics reviewed and approved in the supply review. In this way, the mix across the plants (especially where there is conflict) is guided and directed by senior leadership to achieve the optimal outcome for the business, not a single plant.

The master (supply) planning function can clearly reside at the corporate level, directing volume to the sites. However, it is not simply a matter of creating a more detailed breakdown of the aggregate plans and using bill-of-material and material requirements planning (MRP) functionality to drive requirements through the extended site footprint from a lofty control tower. Theoretically, the control tower model seems attractive, and perhaps with advancing technologies will become increasingly realistic (see the Epilogue and Final Thoughts following Chapter 20 in this book).

However, experience still dictates *today* that there may be too many variables within many manufacturing sites (if not most) to accurately plan from a remote distance. People *call in sick*, equipment starts *acting up*, suppliers get *stuck in traffic*, and events get *planned that aren't communicated* in the ERP system. Any number of variables can affect the ability of a plant to execute and, therefore, *today* in many manufacturing companies (if not most) it is necessary to have a master scheduling role at the plant that has a better understanding of these variables and can make more realistic and reliable plans using these inputs (see Figure 14.11 on page 469).

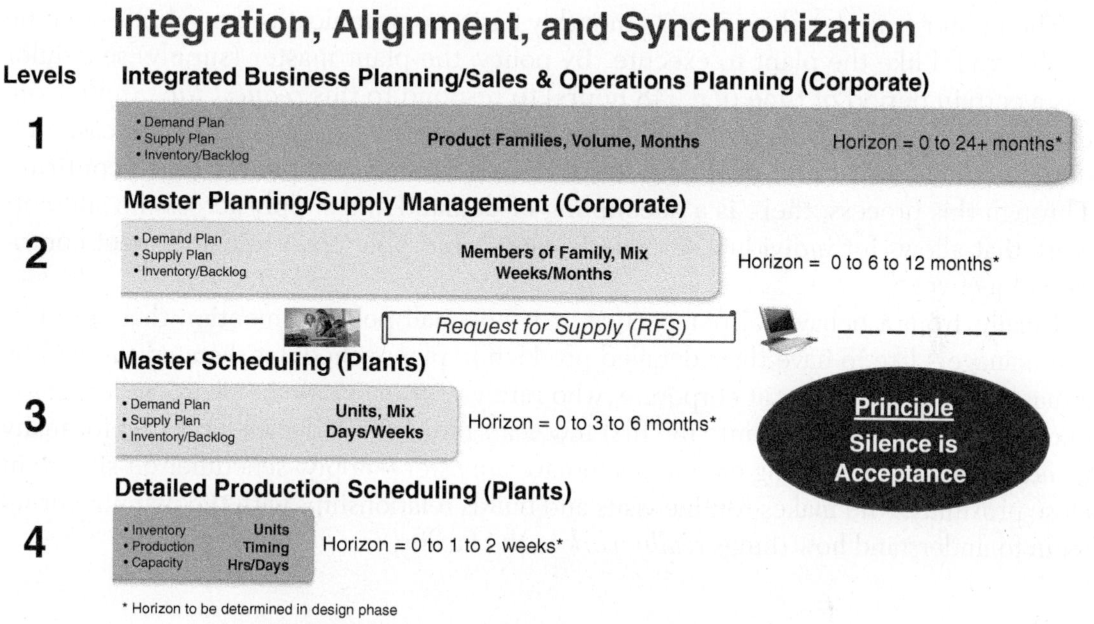

Integration, Alignment, and Synchronization
Levels
Integrated Business Planning/Sales & Operations Planning (Corporate)
1
• Demand Plan
• Supply Plan
• Inventory/Backlog
Product Families, Volume, Months
Horizon = 0 to 24+ months*
Master Planning/Supply Management (Corporate)
2
• Demand Plan
• Supply Plan
• Inventory/Backlog
Members of Family, Mix
Weeks/Months
Horizon = 0 to 6 to 12 months*
Request for Supply (RFS)
Master Scheduling (Plants)
3
• Demand Plan
• Supply Plan
• Inventory/Backlog
Units, Mix
Days/Weeks
Horizon = 0 to 3 to 6 months*
Principle
Silence is Acceptance
Detailed Production Scheduling (Plants)
4
• Inventory
• Production
• Capacity
Units
Timing
Hrs/Days
Horizon = 0 to 1 to 2 weeks*
* Horizon to be determined in design phase

Figure 14.10 Four Levels of Planning

Works
MPS
MRP
MPS
MRP
MPS
MRP
Customers
Customers
Customers
Finished Product Plant
Finished Product Plant
Finished Product Plant
Component Plant
Component Plant
Sub-Component Plant
Sub-Component Plant
Doesn't Work
MPS
MRP
MRP
MRP
MRP
MRP

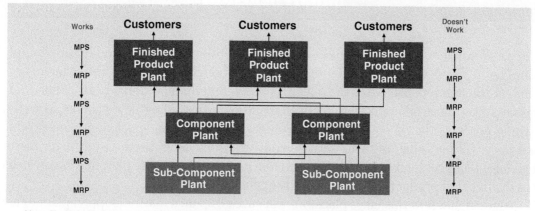

Note: Today's Environment. In the decade ahead the need for an onsite master scheduler will most likely be history (tasks required to be done by a person today will most likely be done by a computer or robot [authors' opinion]).

Figure 14.11 Master Planning and Scheduling at Each Level

The master (supply) planner, on a monthly basis, communicates the volumes that he or she would like the plant to execute. By policy, the plant master (supply) scheduler has a certain period of time (e.g., 48 hours) to respond to this *request for supply* from the master (supply) planner with a *yes* or *no* answer (or a *yes, if* . . . in the case of a decision that needs to be made before or during the next supply review to confirm). Through this process, there is a decoupling of demand and supply across the site network that allows for individual sites to develop achievable plans and still meet corporate objectives.

Finally, from a behavioral perspective, it is no small point to mention that very few site managers like to have their detailed production plans/schedules dictated to them by a master (supply) planner at corporate, who rarely (if ever) visits the plant! So let's say it one more time, as we move into the first few years of the 202X decade, it is best for many (if not most) manufacturing operations to have a master (supply) scheduler on-site, or in close proximity, who makes routine visits and builds relationships with the manufacturing team to understand how things *really work* in the facility.

Integrated Business Planning and the Master Supply Schedule

The past few pages painted a picture of integrated business planning and master (supply) planning in very broad strokes, demonstrating the benefits of each to the company as a whole. From the prospective of the master (supply) scheduler, more detail is needed. The business plan must be converted into a demand plan (including new product as well as existing product) that is converted into a master (supply) plan specifying plant production rates (volume) that, in turn, must be converted to a detail product-mix plan (master schedule) that eventually is converted into a material and capacity plan that is converted into the detailed production schedule and supplier schedule.

To understand how this takes place, we will eavesdrop on a master (supply) planner and a master (supply) scheduler preparing for a supply review as part of the company's IBP process. The example is purposefully simplified and manual in nature in order to explain the concepts.

These days, advancements in technology and SCM software and analytics support the process greatly, but one must still understand the business and the story behind the numbers. Picking up the phone and meeting with your partners in the IBP process now and again doesn't hurt, either!

The executive summary (page 472) highlights the major changes from last cycle, the issues to be discussed and decisions required, and allows for Jim to set the tone of the review and focus participants' attention. Following the pre-read and minor changes, if necessary, Diana committed to publishing and forwarding the information deck to the participants at least 24 hours (48 hours prior to the supply review is the goal) in advance of the review to allow the team to digest the information and come prepared to support the decision-making process.

Of course, the timing discussed in the AutoTek story is not really realistic for most manufacturing companies using the integrated business planning (IBP) process discussed earlier in this chapter. AutoTek's planning horizon is far too short. And making decisions at the IBP level for the near-term time periods is *not* best-practice IBP; making those near-term decisions is more of a master planning and scheduling effort (master planning and scheduling generally works in the near-term to mid-term periods of the planning horizon).

To review, integrated business planning is a process that has a planning horizon of 24 months or greater, and generally planning and/or replanning is done for months 4 through 24 (or more if the IBP planning horizon stretches out beyond 24 months).

From the master (supply) planner and the master (supply) scheduler's prospective, this supply review has provided the numerical ingredients of new product, demand, supply, inventory, backlog, and shipments that will guide Diana's and Bill's activities between this point and the end of the next scheduled IBP cycle. They know that the numbers will not hold up in the absolute sense, but they have the benefit of reflecting the best judgment of a roomful of people who have intimate knowledge of the company's operations.

Further, the approved supply plan Diana will work with has been subject to a reality check called *resource requirements planning* or *rough cut capacity planning*, which compares the supply plan to the internal as well as external capabilities of the company. Just how that reality check is accomplished is the subject of the next chapter.

Before proceeding to the discussion on rough cut capacity planning, let's take a look at the next enhancement to the integrated business planning information AutoTek may choose to use in the future. Numbers are the facts that tell the story (of course, accurate numbers make for an accurate story). However, before leadership or top management dives into the detailed numbers, they may want to look at a few charts (graphs) to get an overall picture.

THE CASE OF INTEGRATED BUSINESS PLANNING AT AUTOTEK

AutoTek Corporation, a manufacturer of automotive parts and a subsidiary of the industrial giant Execor Industries, had just completed their monthly demand review in their IBP process. Diana, a senior master supply planner and the supply review leader, attended the demand review to better understand the updated demand plan and supporting assumptions.

"It looks like we'll see a significant upturn in sales," she thought to herself, studying the information in their IBP planning tool. "The new sales promotion has really grabbed the marketplace. The commercial organization plans to grow the business by 15 percent over the next six months . . . maybe by 20 percent if the most optimistic projections come true. I've got to get down to work and figure out how we're going to support demand if they really do hit those targets."

Diana reviewed the company's aggregate performance in comparison to the business plan. She looked at how they had performed with respect to demand, supply, and inventory projections across the manufacturing sites. She also examined the backlog and shipment projections. Next, she reviewed the assumptions for the coming time period, which included the hiring and training of 10 new people in the next 60 days at their primary production facility. These added personnel were expected to help AutoTek increase production rates if necessary.

In addition, the company directors speculated about their major competitors during the demand review. Jelco was facing a general strike, and JDR Enterprises was threatened by acquisition by Murco & Watts. She could see that there was both opportunity and risk/danger for AutoTek in these developments.

Diana started with the make-to-stock muffler family, reviewing the 90 days of history beginning in February (see Figure 14.12 on page 473). Sales had planned to sell 32,000 units per month, but they actually booked 36,000 units in February, 34,000 in March, and 37,000 in April. The third line on the chart shows the monthly differences between planned demand and actual demand; the fourth line shows cumulative differences by month, which increased to 11,000 units in April.

She remembers the conversation in the demand review. "On the whole, we're pretty pleased with our performance," said Sally Lattimer, vice president of sales. "Not only are we selling over the plan, we're within 10 percent of what we said we would do." She also remembers thinking to herself, "If we keep overselling the plan, we might end up in a heap of trouble. *It's a good problem to have, but it's still a problem!*" Next, she focused on the supply plan.

Stocked Muffler Family		History			IBP Plan	Future Plan				
Demand Plan		FEB	MAR	APR		MAY	JUN	JUL	AUG	SEP...
Planned		32,000	32,000	32,000	Last Cycle	32,000	32,000	32,000	32,000	32,000
Actual	109% Performance	36,000	34,000	37,000	Current Cycle	36,000	36,000	36,000	36,000	36,000
Monthly Variance		+4,000	+2,000	+5,000						
Cumulative Difference	Start 0	+4,000	+6,000	+11,000						
Supply Plan		FEB	MAR	APR		MAY	JUN	JUL	AUG	SEP...
Planned		35,000	35,000	35,000	Last Cycle	35,000	30,000	30,000	25,000	25,000
Actual	95% Performance	34,000	33,000	33,000	Current Cycle	35,000	35,000	37,000	37,000	37,000
Monthly Variance		−1,000	−2,000	−2,000						
Cumulative Difference	Start 0	−1,000	−3,000	−5,000						
Finished Goods Inventory		FEB	MAR	APR		MAY	JUN	JUL	AUG	SEP...
Planned		23,000	26,000	29,000	Last Cycle	32,000	30,000	28,000	21,000	14,000
Actual	Start 20,000	18,000	17,000	13,000	Current Cycle	12,000	11,000	12,000	13,000	14,000
Monthly Variance	45% of Plan	−5,000	−9,000	−16,000						

Figure 14.12 Demand and Supply Plans, Stocked Muffler Family

Manufacturing had a planned supply rate of 35,000 mufflers for February, March, and April, but they fell short by 1,000 in February, 2,000 in March, and another 2,000 in April, making them short by 5,000 units overall. She thought, "Still, the performance over these 90 days was 95 percent of plan . . . not bad over the aggregate period, but also *not* good! *Overselling and underproducing is not a good formula for success.*"

She moved on to the inventory position on mufflers. Sure enough, she could see from the data that they entered February with a starting balance of 20,000 units and planned to boost that level to 29,000 units by the end of April to meet the expected growth in our business. But the higher-than-expected sales and lower-than-planned production have resulted in a net depletion of muffler inventory—just the opposite of the plan.

Diana studied the information, noting how every month's pattern of higher-than-planned demand and lower-than-planned supply had progressively reduced inventory. That was good in the sense that AutoTek had less inventory to finance during those three months, but it was abundantly clear that unless this pattern was reversed, demand would very quickly outpace the company's supply (from production and from inventory), resulting in angry customers, missed sales, and opportunities for competitors to expand market share at AutoTek's expense.

She wondered how management planned to deal with this problem, knowing that the decision would affect her directly. She wanted to know how supply (production) rates would be adjusted; these, she knew, would be driven by whatever demand projections the sales and marketing people assumed for the coming periods.

She recalled Lattimer's comments: "The plan that we all agreed to last month called for demand of 32,000 units each month. We've been doing some analysis since the last meeting, and we are prepared to boost the forecast by 4,000 units per month through September. We believe the demand is very real, and that our overselling the plan in each of the past three months is not a fluke."

From the master planner's prospective, this was a critical point in the process. She needed to know the projected supply rate—something that could not be determined without considering future sales.

She got to work on developing a plan. First, she looked back at the previous month's inventory projection, noting its shortfalls. To satisfy the expected demand and to provide some demand protection for variation to plan, Jim Saunders, the vice president of supply chain management, had authorized raising inventory levels to a maximum of 32,000 units in May, then gradually reducing it to 14,000 units in September. The current inventory position was planned to be at 29,000 units; however, due to the situation described earlier, muffler inventory had fallen to 13,000 units. "How are we ever going to get back on plan?" she asked herself.

The new demand projections and shortfall in inventory demanded a workable response from manufacturing. Diana picked up the phone and called Bill Weston, the plant master scheduler. He offered this prospective: "It sounds like we need to ramp up production to meet the increased demand plan. But we can't do it instantly. We will need to hire and train a few more people and likely bring in some new equipment, and that will take time."

"How much time?" Diana asked.

"Let me check with Javier and get back to you with an estimate," Bill responded. Bill walked down the hall to discuss the scenario with the plant manager, Javier Carbajal. They did some back-of-the-envelope calculations and Bill returned to his desk to call Diana.

"Probably 40 days or so," Weston told Diana. "We're confident that we will be able to sustain a run rate of 35,000 for the next two months while we are getting prepared for the increased supply rate. We have had problems coming up to 35,000 units in the past, but I think those problems are now behind us. The way I figure it, our inventory position will be at 11,000 units in 40 days if we produce at a rate of 35,000 per month and sell at a rate of 36,000 per month. In principle, we believe that we can meet the higher-demand projection, but I want to figure out a way to meet it and still run the plant at a reasonable and level rate of production."

Weston wanted to keep the supply plan level because shifts in production rates were expensive due to changeovers, adding and laying off personnel, and so forth. Therefore, Diana computed a level supply plan as follows:

- Sum the forecast or demand plan, then add or subtract the expected or desired change in the inventory levels.

- Divide the result by the number of months in the planning period.

For July, August, and September, Diana began with total demand of 108,000 units (36,000 per month). To compute the desired change in inventory levels stipulated by Saunders, she looked at the target for the last period, September, which was 14,000, then subtracted the expected beginning inventory for July of 11,000 units (June month-end). Thus, ending inventory needed to increase by 3,000 units. It made sense to just add this requirement to projected customer demand of 108,000 to get a total demand for July through September of 111,000 units, or a supply (production) rate of 37,000 per month (111,000 divided by three months).

Would this approach satisfy the plan? To find out, the new demand and supply figures were entered into the system and a new inventory projection was calculated (Figure 14.13, page 476). In July, August, and September, the company would produce 1,000 more units than it planned to sell and ship. That surplus production would increase AutoTek's inventory. The ending September inventory figure would be 14,000 units—just what Saunders had asked for.

However, before pronouncing the new plan as workable, Bill needed to check plant capacity as well as AutoTek's key or critical suppliers. (Assume for now that the plan has been checked for realism by Bill, and Diana is ready to move on with its analysis of the customized muffler product family.) A detailed discussion of how to "sanity check" the proposed supply (production) plan against capacity and key resources follows in Chapter 15, on rough cut capacity planning.

Even though Diana had determined that the plan was realistic, questions remained. "What's the high watermark?" she asked herself. "How high could sales really go?"

Diana reviewed the opportunities and risks ledger in the demand review information deck and called Todd, the demand manager, to confirm. "We could possibly hit 38,000 from May through September," Todd confirmed.

"And if you bomb out?" asked Diana. "Worst-case scenario, 30,000," he shot back. "We've already studied that possibility in the demand consensus part of the review."

With the best- and worst-case scenarios numerically defined, Diana was then able to project inventory levels for either case (Figure 14.13). If sales succeeded on the high side, inventory would drop to a low of 4,000 units in September; if sales were poor, AutoTek would find itself with 44,000 units on the shelf at the end of that month.

Stocked Muffler Family		History			IBP Plan	Future Plan				
Demand Plan		FEB	MAR	APR		MAY	JUN	JUL	AUG	SEP...
Planned		32,000	32,000	32,000	Last Cycle	32,000	32,000	32,000	32,000	32,000
Actual	109% Performance	36,000	34,000	37,000	Current Cycle	36,000	36,000	36,000	36,000	36,000
Monthly Variance		+4,000	+2,000	+5,000	High	38,000	38,000	38,000	38,000	38,000
Cumulative Difference	Start 0	+4,000	+6,000	+11,000	Low	30,000	30,000	30,000	30,000	30,000
Supply Plan		FEB	MAR	APR		MAY	JUN	JUL	AUG	SEP...
Planned		35,000	35,000	35,000	Last Cycle	35,000	30,000	30,000	25,000	25,000
Actual	95% Performance	34,000	33,000	33,000	Current Cycle	35,000	35,000	37,000	37,000	37,000
Monthly Variance		−1,000	−2,000	−2,000						
Cumulative Difference	Start 0	−1,000	−3,000	−5,000						
Finished Goods Inventory		FEB	MAR	APR		MAY	JUN	JUL	AUG	SEP...
Planned		23,000	26,000	29,000	Last Cycle	32,000	30,000	28,000	21,000	14,000
Actual	Start 20,000	18,000	17,000	13,000	Current Cycle	12,000	11,000	12,000	13,000	14,000
Monthly Variance	45% of Plan	−5,000	−9,000	−16,000	High	10,000	7,000	6,000	5,000	4,000
Approval Decision Required This Cycle		Jim Saunders			Low	18,000	23,000	30,000	37,000	44,000

Figure 14.13 Recalculation of Demand, Supply, and Inventory

Now that she knew what the opportunities and risks were, she documented the upside, downside, and most likely scenarios for the upcoming supply review to drive consensus on the path forward. Then, she moved on to the manifold product family.

The new supply plan is the budget that will be used by Bill Watson, AutoTek's master scheduler, when he constructs the master schedule for the product family individual members. It's not enough for Watson to just create the master schedule; he must also ensure that when aggregated by product family, it equals the supply plan by volume.

Diana went through the same routine with manifolds, adjusting and testing the plan in terms of demand, supply, and inventory, carrying out a validity check at each step. When she finished with all make-to-stock families, she took a break before switching over to make-to-order products, which included customized mufflers and spoilers. The make-to-order items represented a smaller, but higher-margin, part of the business.

Diana reviewed the data for the customized muffler family (Figure 14.14, page 477). The format was basically the same as the one used for the make-to-stock products, with

Customized Muffler Family	History			IBP Plan	Future Plan				
Demand Plan	FEB	MAR	APR		MAY	JUN	JUL	AUG	SEP...
Planned	800	800	800	Last Cycle	800	800	800	800	800
Actual _(108% Performance)_	840	860	880	Current Cycle	850	850	900	900	1,000
Monthly Variance	+40	+60	+80						
Cumulative Difference _Start 0_	+40	+100	+180						
Supply Plan	FEB	MAR	APR		MAY	JUN	JUL	AUG	SEP...
Planned	850	850	850	Last Cycle	850	800	800	800	800
Actual _(97% Performance)_	820	830	820	Current Cycle	850	850	1,050	1,050	1,050
Monthly Variance	−30	−20	−30						
Cumulative Difference _Start 0_	−30	−50	−80						
Backlog	FEB	MAR	APR		MAY	JUN	JUL	AUG	SEP...
Planned	970	920	870	Last Cycle	820	820	820	820	820
Actual _Start 1,020_	1,040	1,070	1,130	Current Cycle	1,130	1,130	980	830	780
Monthly Variance _130% of Plan_	+70	+150	+260						

Figure 14.14 Demand and Supply Plans, Customized Muffler Family

the demand plan on top, followed by the supply plan. The make-to-stock planning screens displayed finished-goods inventory, the make-to-order plan focused on *backlog* (*customer orders booked but not yet shipped*)—*not to be confused with back orders*, which are *past-due customer orders*.

Generally, backlog refers to orders promised to customers for a future delivery, and these booked orders have not been shipped to the customer (and possibly not even built). In the make-to-order business, customer orders are accepted and delivery is committed respective of a defined customer lead time (give us the order and we will then make it). Some time ago, a company in Portland, Oregon, appropriately labeled these customer orders "future history."

Diana began with the demand plan, seeing the actual demand versus planned demand lines, and understanding the difference (180 over plan for the last three months). She noted that performance to the sales (demand) plan was right at 108 percent. Once again, over-selling the demand plan. As with the make-to-stock muffler example, Lattimer proposed that the company would experience an increase in sales, from 800 to 850 in May and June, from 800 to 900 in July and August, and from 900 to 1,000 in September.

Diana moved on to the company's backlog position, shown on the bottom of the matrix. She thought, "90 days ago we had 1,020 units in the backlog. We wanted to take that 1,020 and work it down to 820 by the end of September. The 820 units represented approximately one month's production. What has happened is that as we look back over the last three months, the actual backlog went from 1,020 to 1,130. That means that we're looking at about five to six weeks of backlog, based on the original plans. This is not the direction in which we want the backlog to go."

Diana called Bill Weston again. "We came in a tad low," he confessed, "but we're nevertheless 97 percent performance to plan. The problem is that the backlog simply isn't decreasing because sales is booking at a higher rate than plan and we are producing slightly below the plan. If we are sitting on five to six weeks of backlog, we should be quoting lead times of five to six weeks—assuming, of course, that the customers requested delivery as early as possible [the shape of this backlog curve is important to know since it affects the lead times used to quote and promise customer deliveries]. We need to change something if we are to achieve the backlog desired position. If quoted lead times are to be reduced to one month or less, we'll have to create a supply (production) plan that works off part of the backlog over the next few months."

"As we evaluate the plan, let's bear in mind that ramping up supply (production) in May and June will be difficult," Weston cautioned. "But with the training discussed earlier today, Javier and I believe we'll achieve our planned supply of 850 units in May and June. In July, we can increase production to satisfy the increase in demand and begin to work down that backlog."

Weston agreed that at the end of June, Diana could increase supply/production to 1,043 units for the months of July, August, and September, and a level supply plan was computed by taking the projected beginning backlog (1,130 in June) and subtracting the desired ending backlog (800 units, which equals the originally planned production for July through September). That left a desired change of 330 units. Adding that to the 2,800 expected bookings in the demand plan for the planning period July through September (900 + 900 + 1,000) yielded 3,130 units that needed to be shipped if the company was to hit its goal by the end of September. The 3,130 units divided by three months gave a level production rate of 1,043 units per month.

If both Carbajal and Lattimer achieved their respective plans, the target of a one-month backlog would be realized. However, if Carbajal could raise production to 1,050, the goal of less than one month quoted lead time could be achieved by September (see Figure 14.14 on page 477, a projected backlog of 780). The next step was to do a sanity check of the proposed supply plan by running it through rough cut capacity planning (see Chapter 15).

Once Diana felt that these two plans were reasonable and realistic, the next step was to combine the make-to-stock and make-to-order muffler families on the same IBP matrix (see

Figure 14.15). This required computing an aggregate demand plan, supply plan, inventory projection, backlog projection, and shipment projection derived by summing the make-to-stock (MTS) and make-to-order (MTO) product family data.

In May, for example, the new MTS demand plan called for 36,000 units (Figure 14.13 on page 476), while the new MTO demand plan called for 850 units (Figure 14.14 on page 477), summing to 36,850 units (Figure 14.15). The process of aggregating the demand plans was continued for each month through completion. The same logic was used to aggregate the supply plan, using the MTS supply plan and the MTO supply plan figures.

The next step was to look at the inventory, backlog, and shipment projections. The muffler family inventory was a result of make-to-stock planning, whereas the backlog position was the result of make-to-order planning. Therefore, the projected muffler family inventory at the end of May (Figure 14.15) was equal to the MTS muffler inventory at the end of May (Figure 14.13, page 476). The projected muffler family backlog at the end of May

Combined Muffler Family		History			IBP Plan	Future Plan				
Demand Plan		FEB	MAR	APR		MAY	JUN	JUL	AUG	SEP...
Planned		32,800	32,800	32,800	Last Cycle	32,800	32,800	32,800	32,800	32,800
Actual	111% Performance	36,840	34,860	37,880	Current Cycle	36,850	36,850	36,900	36,900	37,000
Monthly Variance		+4,040	+2,060	+5,080						
Cumulative Difference	Start 0	+4,040	+6,100	+11,180						
Supply Plan		FEB	MAR	APR		MAY	JUN	JUL	AUG	SEP...
Planned		35,850	35,850	35,850	Last Cycle	35,850	30,800	30,800	25,800	25,800
Actual	95% Performance	820	830	820	Current Cycle	35,850	35,850	38,050	38,050	38,050
Monthly Variance		−1,030	−2,020	−2,030						
Cumulative Difference	Start 0	−1,030	−3,050	−5,080						
Inventory/Backlog		FEB	MAR	APR		MAY	JUN	JUL	AUG	SEP...
Inventory	Start 20,000	18,000	17,000	13,000	Current Cycle	12,000	11,000	12,000	13,000	14,000
Backlog	Start 1,020	1,040	1,070	1,130	Current Cycle	1,130	1,130	980	830	780
Shipment Projections		36,820	34,830	37,820	Current Cycle	36,850	36,850	37,050	37,050	37,050

Figure 14.15   Demand and Supply Plans, Including Inventory, Backlog, and Shipment Projections

(Figure 14.15, page 479) was equal to the MTO muffler backlog at the end of May (Figure 14.14, page 477). This process was continued for the remaining months (June through September).

The last thing that needed to be determined are the projected shipments. Here the group took the demand plan (bookings and expected shipments) from the muffler make-to-stock family (in companies with MTS products, products are generally shipped from finished goods inventory as customer orders are received and booked) and added these totals to the muffler make-to-order supply plan (in companies with MTO products, products are shipped as they are built; they do not go into inventory). The result was an aggregate shipping projection for the muffler product family. If we again look at May, Figure 14.13 on page 476 shows expected shipments of 36,000 units (demand plan) for the stocked muffler family. Figure 14.14 on page 477 shows expected shipments of 850 units (supply plan) for the customized muffler family. Therefore, the total expected shipments are 36,850 units (Figure 14.15, page 479). This process was continued for the remaining months (June through September).

Once she had computed the basic numbers, Diana generated a rough cut capacity plan for the entire muffler family to ensure that the resources and capacity were, or would be, available when needed. This was yet another check, determining whether the business plan could be fulfilled if everyone accomplished their stated plans with respect to demand, supply, inventory, backlog, shipments, and finances.

With the product family business settled, Diana reviewed the product management review information deck to understand the new products and their possible impact on future business. This was an important area of concern to both Diana and AutoTek's master scheduler, Bill Watson, since both needed to understand data relevant to each new-product introduction. Diana and Bill both understood the fact that new products were becoming more and more important to the business. Once this part of the agenda was complete, Diana reviewed the status updates, provided by the supply review team, covering the major projects the company was currently working on. This review included an update on the new production line being installed.

With the core of the supply review developed, Diana reviewed the updates to the action items taken at the prior review and prepared the draft deck for a *pre-read* with Jim Saunders, the supply review owner. Diana and Jim would meet prior to the supply review to review the highlights of the deck and allow for Jim to prepare to make decisions and ask questions of Diana. Also, during this pre-read, Jim and Diana would jointly craft the executive summary used to kick off the review.

Synchronizing and Assessing Demand and Supply

Integrated business planning is an integrated demand-driven supply planning process. Once the demand is known or anticipated (including new products), a supply plan is put together. To get started, several supply plans may be created. The primary supply plan (or *base scenario*) may be aligned with demand while achieving inventory and backlog objectives. However, in doing this, resource requirements planning may highlight potential resource problems over the planning horizon that need to be addressed.

Secondary supply plans may use selected opportunity and risk information flowing from the IBP process to develop scenarios and contingency planning. By adjusting plans at the aggregate product family level, the supply planner can model the potential supply chain response to an increase in demand (i.e., key market opportunities exploited), a decrease in demand (i.e., key market risks coming true), and potential supply-side constraints related to capacity and materials.

Similar modeling may be done using potential supply chain risks and opportunities. Depending on the timing and likelihood of the demand and supply opportunities and risks, the final supply plan may be a compromise between the scenarios that were developed and would become the recommended supply plan for approval and execution. To highlight for leadership and the supply manager possible issues and concerns, a synchronization chart showing demand, supply, and inventory may be helpful (Figure 14.16, page 482).

Reviewing the chart, the AutoTek's IBP participants see bars, lines, and background highlights. The bars in the example synchronization chart represent demand over a two-year time period (24 months) for a seasonal *product line or family* (brackets). The bars in the first three periods (–3, –2, –1) show historical data regarding actual demand (shipments). As the AutoTek participant looks at future time periods 1–3, the lightly shaded part of the bars represents firm customer orders (not yet delivered) while the darkly shaded part of the bars represent the demand plan (anticipated orders). The dotted line labeled *backlog* shows the order book, with a starting backlog in period –1 of 600,000 units (the sum of future orders in time periods 1 through 3), depleting over time until it reaches zero in time period 3, when the last of the current firm orders are planned to ship.

Using this information, it is easy to see *what time periods demand and supply (the dark line labeled supply plan) are not equal. If the demand and supply are not equal (decoupled), the result is an increase or decrease in inventory.*

The background in Figure 14.16 shows the inventory position by time period. As one can see, in time periods 1 through 6, the supply volume is generally greater than demand

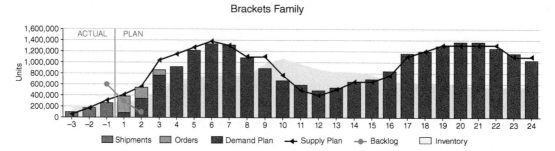

Figure 14.16 Synchronization of Demand, Supply, and Inventory

with the exception of time periods 3 and 5. As a result, the inventory is expected to rise in advance of the peak sales season.

Beginning in time period 7, supply volumes dip below the demand volumes and inventory begins to decrease as the business moves into the slow season. In the supply review, there would likely be questions regarding the supply plan, for example "Why does production dip in time periods 3 and 5?" The supply review leader is expected to document and publish the assumptions supporting this supply plan in order for leadership to understand the chosen demand/supply balance and inventory projections in an attempt to *answer questions before they are asked.*

Someone once said a picture is worth a thousand words (or, in this example, a thousand numbers). The synchronization of demand, supply, inventory, and/or backlog is fundamentally important in integrated business planning. By using this type of information chart, time-phased demand is brought together with time-phased supply and the resulting time-phased inventory and backlog projections.

Once the demand and supply plans are synchronized for all product families, management takes a look at the inventory levels (dollars, days of inventory, and/or units) to ensure that the resulting inventory projections are in line with the business objectives. Figures 14.17 and 14.18 on page 483 display inventory by days of inventory and dollars for the brackets product family. Similar projections should be aggregated for the entire business.

The examples in Figures 14.17 and 14.18 show 3 months of history plus 24 months of future projections. The shaded background is the inventory projection related to the synchronization chart shown in Figure 14.16 but translated from units into days of inventory and dollars. The projections also include the target inventory (the business objective) and some guardrails (minimum and maximum inventory). The guardrails are important to allow for some flexibility in planning and reduce overly reactive responses when inventory isn't exactly on target.

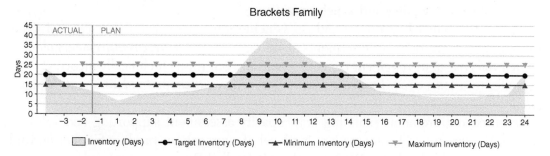

Figure 14.17   Inventory Projection in Days of Inventory

The minimum inventory may represent an inventory level, below which significant customer service issues begin to appear. The maximum inventory may represent an inventory level at which significant cash, warehouse space, or other implications begin to appear.

The end result shows that the master (supply) planner and/or master (supply) scheduler developed a plan that is within the inventory guardrails established as a business. Furthermore, as we can see in Figure 14.17, the chart shows graphically why the master (supply) planner and/or master (supply) scheduler may have chosen to reduce supply volumes in time periods 3 and 5 in order to keep inventory within the guardrails.

That, of course, is *not* the only choice at the master (supply) planner's and/or master (supply) scheduler's disposal. It may be a legitimate option to keep the supply plans in time periods 3 and 5 at higher volumes consistent with surrounding months and exceed maximum inventory for a time period or two to protect customer service in the busy season and better optimize production scheduling. If this were the case, the master (supply) planner and/or master (supply) scheduler would need to document this recommendation (with alternatives and implications) and ask for approval in the supply review.

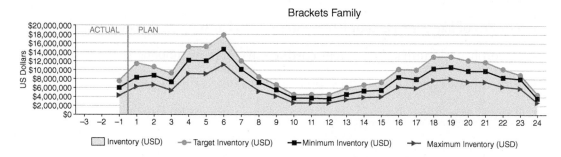

Figure 14.18   Inventory Projection in Dollars

In addition to aligning and synchronizing aggregate demand, supply, inventory, and backlog projections, a key process and assessment required for approving valid and achievable IBP plans is resource requirements planning (RRP). *Resource requirements planning is often referred to as rough cut capacity planning*, but this is technically incorrect (some also refer to *resource requirements planning* as *rough cut capacity planning at the aggregate level*).

Resource requirements planning is a capacity assessment supporting and validating plans at the integrated business planning level of aggregation (product families and subfamilies in monthly buckets). RRP is applicable to all IBP process steps and includes only the *critical few resources* (or groups of resources) needed to validate and support the IBP plans and business objectives.

Rough cut capacity planning (RCCP), on the other hand, is applied at the master (supply) planning and/or master scheduling level of aggregation (subfamilies, SKUs, or groups of SKUs in weekly buckets) and typically assesses more resources than RRP (but not *all* resources). More detail on the mechanics of both RRP and RCCP processes can be found in Chapter 15. With a little ingenuity, resource requirements planning can be performed on any resource/resource grouping deemed *critical* to the success of the IBP plans or business objectives. Some examples include:

- Project or product management resources needed to support new product introductions or product renovations;

- Material sourcing personnel needed to support the new product pipeline;

- Research and development personnel needed to support innovation plans;

- Sales or marketing resources needed to execute promotional activities;

- Warehouse space needed to store projected inventory;

- Engineers needed to support manufacturing plans;

- Groups of like assets and/or labor pools needed to support the supply plan;

- Severely underutilized resources costing the company money;

- Critical raw materials used to support the projected supply plans;

- Project resources needed to execute strategic projects for the business.

Here again, a resource requirements planning chart can be used to quickly highlight issues, concerns, problems, and balance. Figures 14.19 and 14.20 are examples of resource requirements plans for a defined resource. The charts use bars to represent the required capacity to meet the supply plan (shades representing the families that load the resource).

The examples also show three lines (demonstrated capacity and planned capacity are overlapping over two-thirds of the horizon). The two lower lines represent the demonstrated and planned capacity out over time. The top line is the maximum capacity (see Chapter 15, on rough cut capacity planning, for the definitions of these capacity lines that also apply to resource requirements planning).

Using this information, one can see in the model that time periods 1–4 are slightly under demonstrated capacity and planned capacity, indicating that they may encounter a utilization or absorption problem in the near term related to that asset. If the model were based on labor, the production manager may choose to deploy those resources to other activities (maintenance, clean outs, etc.) or reduce shifts.

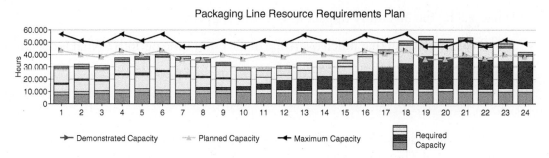

Figure 14.19 Resource Requirements Plan

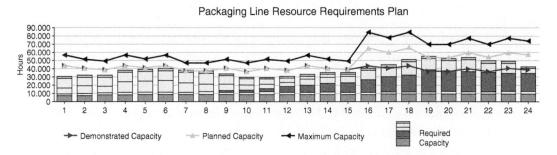

Figure 14.20 Resource Requirements Plan/Rough Cut Capacity Plan

Time periods 5–8 show required capacity fairly well balanced to demonstrated and planned capacity. In time periods 9–15, the underloaded projection returns, which may need some decisions to be made again to resolve. Time periods 17–18 show that required capacity exceeds the demonstrated and planned capacity but is within the maximum capacity. In time periods 19–22, the required capacity exceeds the maximum capacity and then drops back down.

Therefore, if this supply plan is approved as currently written, the company must be able to sustain some form of overtime or flex above the demonstrated and planned capacity time periods 17–24 and must recognize the upcoming problem in time periods 19–22 (remember that these time periods are 16–24 months out from the current planning time period).

So, what does top management and the supply manager do with this information? First of all, the company probably doesn't want to approve this plan without some action plan in place (securing answers to the listed questions):

- Do we move supply plans to fill in the underloaded time periods?

- What will be the inventory impact if we move supply?

- Can the company run that much overtime in the outer time periods? What is the cost?

- What will it take to raise to maximum capacity in time periods 18–22?

- When does top management need to make these decisions?

These charts don't solve the problems; they highlight the problems. People in today's world (refer to Final Thoughts, pages 783–808, for a discussion on technology advancements and the use of computers/robots in the problem-solving arena) solve the problems (machines continue to be used in making routine decisions and solving minor to intermediate problems). Perhaps a resolution may be to add another shift starting in time period 16.

Figure 14.20 on page 485 shows this addition by the deviation of the planned capacity line from the demonstrated capacity line. The maximum capacity increases accordingly. However, as one can see, this solves for the required capacity peak but leaves some stranded capacity in months where required capacity does not meet planned capacity. This potential resolution may need to be massaged as time moves closer to the hiring lead time (the potential problem is recognized 16 months in advance instead of 16 days or 16 hours or 16 minutes in advance as it is in many companies).

Measuring Accuracy and Performance

As was stated earlier, the numbers supported by graphics tell a story. When the story is told, it's up to the supply manager and/or master (supply) planner along with executive leadership or top management to change the story if they do not like what they are reading. This is what integrated business planning (IBP) is all about—creating and changing the supply chain's or company's story. Fundamentally, all participants in the IBP process have to trust in the story and the underlying plans. Nothing builds trust like proven, measured accuracy and performance.

In addition to building trust, a primary function of accuracy and performance measurements is to help a company or function improve. As such, accuracy and performance measures must be designed to send signals that can (and should) be acted upon through root cause analysis and corrective action processes. Tolerances are often established for the measure so that action is only taken when the measurement results stray far enough from perfect to have a significant negative impact to the business. Tolerances vary depending on the measure and business impact (see Figure 14.21, page 488).

For example, when measuring production quantity variances, there may be a broader tolerance for inexpensive components than for an expensive end item. In short, tolerances establish the boundaries for when the company or function starts feeling pain. Once performance is consistently proven within established tolerances, it is incumbent upon the responsible owner of the measure to tighten tolerances to further improve performance. This is how one beats the competition—not by being good enough, but by being the best!

While there are many key accuracy and performance indicators that can be employed to measure supply chain accuracy and performance (and several are defined throughout this book), in this section we will cover a few fundamental measures used in the supply review as part of the integrated business planning process:

- Customer service performance

- Aggregate supply plan performance

- Master plan and/or master schedule performance

- Inventory and/or backlog plan performance

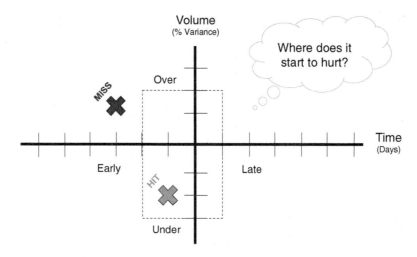

Figure 14.21   Measurement Tolerances

Customer Service Performance

Good (and poor) customer service is the outcome of an integrated system of planning, control, and execution. Sales, order entry, master planning and scheduling, material planning and control, capacity planning and control, production scheduling and execution, procurement and purchasing, warehousing and distribution management, logistics management, and finance/accounting are several of the functions that affect the customer's delivery experience. As such, customer service performance is truly a shared metric! That said, it often lands in the demand review and/or supply review for monitoring and improvement. We will focus on two practical levels of customer service that can be measured (order on-time-in-full and order line-on-time-in-full) as well as two dates by which a company can measure performance (promise date and request date).

Finally, we will look at perfect order performance, which is the pinnacle of customer service measures, but is often difficult to measure due to the complexity of gathering the data. There is a proxy for perfect order called rolled throughput yield or perfect order index that we will provide that is much easier to calculate and has the benefit of highlighting where in the order execution process to focus for improvement.

When placing an order, a customer typically communicates a requested date upon which they would like to receive the order (request date). In response, the customer service representative (or automated system) will communicate a promised date back to the customer. This is accomplished through the available-to-promise process (described in more detail in Chapters 9 and 17), supported by software. If the customer's

Measure	Definition	Calculation	Class A Milestone Target
Orders On Time In Full to Request Date	Complete orders shipped on time, in full, to the customer's request date within established tolerances.	$$\frac{\text{Number of Orders Shipped On Time In Full}}{\text{Number of Orders Due}} \times 100$$	95%
Orders On Time In Full to Promise Date	Complete orders shipped on time, in full, to the promise date communicated to the customer within established tolerances.	$$\frac{\text{Number of Orders Shipped On Time In Full}}{\text{Number of Orders Due}} \times 100$$	95%
Order Lines On Time In Full to Request Date	Complete order lines shipped on time, in full, to the customer's request date within established tolerances.	$$\frac{\text{Number of Order Lines Shipped On Time In Full}}{\text{Number of Order Lines Due}} \times 100$$	95%
Order Lines On Time In Full to Promise Date	Complete order lines shipped on time, in full, to the promise date communicated to the customer within established tolerances.	$$\frac{\text{Number of Order Lines Shipped On Time In Full}}{\text{Number of Order Lines Due}} \times 100$$	95%*

*Order Lines On Time In Full to Promise Date is the only mandatory measure in this list for Class A accreditation. The others are recommended measures.

Figure 14.22   Customer Service Performance Measures

requested date and the company's promise date are the same, no further discussion is necessary, and it is up to the company to execute. If the requested date and the promise date are different, a negotiation may ensue to gain agreement on a date.

A company can measure itself (many times these measurements are done by the company's customer) both against the requested date and the promise date of an order and against the full order and the individual lines on the order. Performance against the requested date is a measure of *responsiveness* to the marketplace. Performance against the promise date is a measure of the company's *reliability*. Performance against the entire order represents more complete customer satisfaction. Performance against individual order lines represents only a part of customer satisfaction related to an order.

In Figure 14.22 on page 489, the standard measures are listed along with their calculations and the minimum level of performance required to achieve a Class A milestone accreditation (more on Class A milestone accreditation and Class A certification in Chapters 18 through 20 as well as in Appendix A).

Perfect order performance is a measure of flawless order execution. For an order to be *perfect*, there can be no errors in order entry, manufacturing, quality, shipment, customer receipt, or documentation (e.g., invoicing). It is literally the perfect customer experience. While theoretically possible to record and report each stage of a customer order, one can imagine how cumbersome that might be across hundreds or thousands of orders being transacted (again, in today's world as we enter the 202X decade).

As stated previously, rolled throughput yield or perfect order index is a way to measure the *probability* of a customer receiving a perfect order from the company without having to track each individual order. The calculation consists of multiplying the performance scores (on time, in full, no errors) of each stage in the order fulfillment process together to determine the probability of a perfect outcome.

Figure 14.23 on page 490 shows that, even with relatively high performance at each stage in the fulfillment process, the probability of a perfect experience is surprisingly low. That said, it is easy to see the areas of opportunity to improve the probability of a perfect experience (in this case, manufacturing on-time-in-full would be a good place to start).

Perfect Order Index						
Order Entry	Manufacturing	Quality	Shipping	Receipt	Invoicing	Result
98%	95%	97%	99%	99%	99%	88%

Figure 14.23 Perfect Order Index

Aggregate Supply Plan Performance

Supply plan volumes are approved, by product family, in the supply review each month. The supply plan volumes consist of manufactured items, purchased items or services to be rendered that are grouped into product families for the purposes of mid- to long-term planning. Since the supply plan is a fundamental input in calculating inventory and capacity projections over the integrated business planning horizon, the capability of the supply chain to execute on that supply plan is of critical importance.

For the purposes of integrated business planning, the aggregate product family-level volumes are measured (See Figure 14.24 on page 492). In the near term, as the supply plan is executed, variability in the mix (i.e., individual items or subfamilies within each product family) is expected to exist and may be masked by the aggregate volume performance. This is an acceptable trade-off to simplify the process of developing a *roughly right* plan over the 24+-month IBP planning horizon. If variability in the mix is significantly off-plan in the details, one would see the variances manifest themselves in other measures such as master plan performance, master schedule performance, cost of goods sold, and customer service.

To measure aggregate supply plan performance, a snapshot is taken of the current month's plans and, when the month is complete, the actual results are compared against those plans. If a change to the plan is authorized, then the measure is against the newly authorized plan.

For products in a make-to-order environment, when the level of demand is more or less than the plan, then the measurement is against the received demand volumes. At an aggregate level, the expectations of achieving the total volume are pretty high (+/– 2 percent). Furthermore, one can look across the mix of families and report how many families are achieving this +/–2 percent performance level. The minimum standard for a Class A milestone is that 75 percent of the product families achieve a +/–2 percent aggregate supply plan performance.

Some companies choose to weight their product families by *importance* when applying their aggregate supply plan performance measurements. For example, the average cost of the products in the family may be a weighting factor or the strategic significance of *getting it right* in the family may be another (e.g., a new product that is going to thwart the competition only if the company is first to market).

For example, say that there were 10 product families being measured and 9 out of 10 were within +/–2 percent aggregate supply plan performance. That would be a Class A result by the book. However, if that 10th family that was out of tolerance happened to be the family that contained $100 million rocket engines, the business results of being out of tolerance in that family may *not* feel like Class A.

Measure	Definition	Calculation	Class A Milestone Target
Aggregate Supply Plan Performance	A measure of the actual volume against the approved supply plan volume, by month. If a change to the plan is authorized, then the measure is against the newly authorized plan. In a make-to-order environment, when the level of demand is more or less than the plan, then the measurement is against the received demand volumes.	$\dfrac{\text{Actual volume by family}}{\text{Planned volume by family}} \times 100$	Within +/−2% 75% of families achieve this goal.

Figure 14.24   Aggregate Supply Plan Performance

Alternatively, the business may be performing well against all of the major "important" families, but a few supporting families that are out of tolerance may drive the score below a Class A level, which wouldn't be how the business results *really feel* through excellent performance, where it really counts. Whatever the method of reporting aggregate supply plan performance, it is important to document the rationale and the calculation so that everyone has the same understanding of what is being measured and, more importantly, *why* it is being measured.

Master Plan and/or Master Schedule

As early as the business improvement evaluation and overall planning is being done, an initial *skunkworks team* develops a set of ideas about the kinds of goals that the new people behaviors, business processes, and computer hardware/software system should have in order for the company to become a best-practice business within its industry. This is an important activity as the company's leadership and management determine their next process improvement initiatives.

However, goals by themselves are *not* helpful unless they can be rendered into *specific measurements*, *root cause* analysis, *corrective action* plans and *implementations*, *fail-safe* the process, and executive *reporting*. No one can tell how they are doing—and certainly cannot measure progress—unless accuracy and performance can be measured.

During the *Proven Path* Lead Phase (see Chapter 18 for a detailed explanation of the Lead Phase), an initiative core group considers what *accuracy and performance goals* would be appropriate for the company if *a fully integrated business planning (IBP) and master planning and scheduling (MPS) implementation* were to take place. Oliver Wight's operational and business excellence standards along with defined milestones have several accuracy and performance goals along with defined Class A measurement requirements (and acceptable tolerances) that are linked directly (or indirectly) to MPS and IBP.

For instance, master planning performance (intermediate-level product subfamilies or groupings), master schedule performance (intermediate-level groupings or stock-keeping unit/mix), and detailed manufacturing schedule performance (stock-keeping unit/work authorization, i.e., work order) need to be 95 percent or better according to the Class A Planning and Control Milestone criteria as defined in *The Oliver Wight Class A Standard for Business Excellence,* seventh edition. It should also be noted that *full* Class A certification in managing internal supply and master planning and scheduling requires the company to have schedule performance in the company's industry top quartile or at a minimum of 99.5 percent (within defined tolerances).

Database accuracy across MPS-related elements (e.g., lead times, lot sizes, etc.) need to be maintained at a minimum level of 95 percent (again, within defined tolerances). Accuracy also applies directly to the master plan as well as the master schedule. The master plan along with the master schedule must be free of past-due work and be realistic and doable (refer to upcoming discussions on rough cut capacity planning in Chapter 15 as well as prior discussions on material planning as part of Chapters 3, 5, and 10).

Accuracy and performance to the master plan and/or master schedule notifies leadership and management just how well the overall business is performing and where corrective interventions may be required. Accuracy and performance measures become matters of ongoing importance to the operation and continuous improvement of the MPS process. Therefore, it is recommended that master plan performance, master schedule performance, master plan accuracy, and master schedule accuracy be reported monthly as part of the supply review (SR) and management business review (MBR).

Inventory and/or Backlog Plan Performance

Similar to customer service performance, inventory and/or backlog plan performance is an output of an equation that includes inputs from both the demand and supply organizations and is truly a shared metric. From the finished goods point of view, inventory is product on the shelf waiting to be shipped, typically employed in a make-to-stock supply strategy. Backlog represents an order book out over the horizon (i.e., customer orders taken but not yet shipped). Backlog is not to be confused with back orders, the latter being orders that are past due. Back orders must be rescheduled out into a future period where they are anticipated to be shipped.

Therefore, there may be *back orders* in the company's *backlog*, but other orders in the backlog can be on schedule to promise but just not yet shipped. In simple terms, if the commercial team sells products that supply didn't make, it generally results in lower-than-expected inventory, higher-than-expected backlog, stock-outs, and poor customer service over time. If the supply organization makes products that the commercial team doesn't sell, it generally results in higher-than-expected inventory, lower-than-expected backlog, cash flow problems, and a warehouse that is bursting at the seams.

In the worst cases, inventory and backlog are treated as *inputs* to an equation and drastic actions are taken to right-size inventory and backlog without addressing the root causes (i.e., *real* inputs) of the problem. For example, some companies dramatically cut manufacturing or procurement to achieve a year-end inventory target, causing supply chain and customer service to suffer, only to ramp up production (usually with expensive overtime) early in the next fiscal year to re-establish order from the self-inflicted chaos.

In addition, year-end price incentives are often used to entice customers to buy ahead of their normal procurement cycle, further eroding margins. This vicious cycle is a terrible waste of money, time, and resources. On the bright side, it can be permanently fixed through proper new product, demand, supply, and logistics planning (resulting in inventory and backlog projections) using a well-running integrated business planning process.

To build trust in the forward-looking inventory and backlog projections, one must provide sound assumptions upon which the projections are based (e.g., supporting documentation regarding related product portfolio, demand, supply, logistics, and finances) and also measure how well the resulting inventory and/or backlog is ultimately predicted. The measure is similar to that of aggregate supply plan performance and is defined in Figure 14.25 on page 495.

The Evolution of Integrated Business Planning

Integrated business planning (IBP) evolved over time from its production planning roots to foundational sales and operations planning to the strategy deployment process it is today. The examples that were shown in the case of IBP at AutoTek and in the synchronizing demand and supply sections display the basic demand, supply, inventory, backlog, and capacity balancing core at the heart of a foundational IBP process. These are typically the areas where a master (supply) planner and/or master (supply) scheduler would be most active in the process.

Doing this well can bring huge benefits to a company. These basic processes were the essence of what was called sales and operations planning in the 1980s. Many companies get *stuck* at the 1980s-level of maturity and fail to progress to the integrated business planning level of maturity in today's world. Exponential improvement in results can be achieved through the transition to IBP, with the integration of new product introductions and portfolio planning, financial planning, and the use of the IBP process as the primary vehicle through which strategy is deployed (see Figure 14.26, page 496).

Measure	Definition	Calculation	Class A Mile-stone Target
Inventory or Backlog Plan Performance	A measure of the actual inventory/ backlog against the approved inventory/ backlog plan by month. If a change to the plan is authorized, then the measure is against the newly authorized plan.	$\dfrac{\text{Actual inventory / Backlog by family}}{\text{Planned inventory / Backlog by family}} \times 100$	Recommended, but not a Class A requirement

Figure 14.25   Inventory Plan Performance

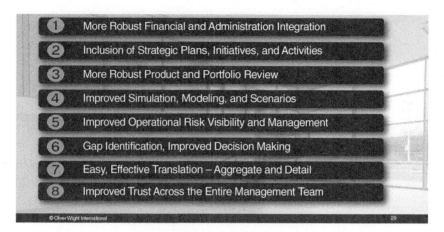

1. More Robust Financial and Administration Integration
2. Inclusion of Strategic Plans, Initiatives, and Activities
3. More Robust Product and Portfolio Review
4. Improved Simulation, Modeling, and Scenarios
5. Improved Operational Risk Visibility and Management
6. Gap Identification, Improved Decision Making
7. Easy, Effective Translation – Aggregate and Detail
8. Improved Trust Across the Entire Management Team

© Oliver Wight International

Figure 14.26   Sales and Operations Planning (S&OP) versus Integrated Business Planning (IBP)

The IBP process continues to evolve. With the support of increasingly advanced technology (e.g., data analytics, artificial intelligence), the process promises to drive increasingly integrated and effective decision making. End-to-end supply chain integration (e.g., linkage of systems and data, including with customers and suppliers) coupled with improved data visibility (e.g., heat maps, dashboards) will help executive teams to identify and prevent a broader array of problems, further out on the horizon, before they happen. Oliver Wight continues to be on the leading edge of IBP development. Stay tuned!

You can learn more about integrated business planning by reading *Enterprise Sales and Operations Planning*[1] and its companion book, *The Transition from Sales and Operations Planning to Integrated Business Planning*,[2] both written by George Palmatier and Colleen Crum, former Oliver Wight principals. Additionally, John Wiley & Sons has published *The Oliver Wight Class A Standard for Business Excellence*[3] while Oliver Wight Publications has published *The Oliver Wight Class A Integrated Business Planning Milestone Workbook*.[4]

---

[1] George Palmatier and Colleen Crum, *Enterprise Sales and Operations Planning* (Boca Raton, FL: J. Ross Publishing, 2003).

[2] George Palmatier and Colleen Crum, *The Transition from Sales and Operations Planning to Integrated Business Planning* (New London, NH: Oliver Wight International, 2013).

[3] *The Oliver Wight Class A Standard for Business Excellence*, seventh edition (Hoboken, NJ: John Wiley & Sons, 2017).

[4] *The Class A Integrated Business Planning Milestone Workbook* is offered to Oliver Wight clients as an addendum to *The Class A Standard for Business Excellence* (Hoboken, NJ: John Wiley & Sons, 2017). At the time of this writing, the Workbook is not offered as a standalone product for sale.

Finally, the Oliver Wight website contains several white (as in Oliver Wight) papers and case studies on the topic. Now that the reader has a general understanding of integrated business planning (IBP) along with master planning and scheduling (MPS) and the information available by using these processes, let's turn our attention to a detailed discussion of resource requirements planning (RRP) and rough cut capacity planning (RCCP).

15

Resource Requirements Planning and Rough Cut Capacity Planning

It is forgivable to be defeated, but never to be surprised.

Imagine that your job is hauling stacks of crates from Los Angeles, California (USA), to San Diego, California (USA), on a flatbed truck. You have decided to take Interstate 5 (I-5), a highway that you know travels beneath several underpasses. Along the way you discover that your cargo is loaded 15 feet high, but the underpasses have only 14 feet of clearance. How can you continue your journey? Here are some possibilities:

- Crash on through, knowing that your top crates will wind up as two-dimensional displays on the pavement.

- Unload enough crates to allow the truck to pass under each overpass, then reload the truck on the other side.

- Let some air out of the tires to lower the truck's height, then fill the tires with air on the other side and continue your journey.

- Take an exit and take a detour to bypass each underpass by going around them.

- Reconstruct the underpasses.

None of these options is either practical or acceptable. You should have planned ahead, loading the truck with respect to the height of the underpasses. This could mean stacking the boxes to a compatible height or picking a route that allows for safe passage of your cargo. Perhaps other constraints force you to stack the boxes to a certain height, making clearance under two of the underpasses impossible. In that case, you might still take I-5 but seek other roads as you approach the two low underpasses. Either way, as the old saying goes, the best time to make an escape plan is before you need one.

Know Before You Go

The overloaded truck has a direct analogy in manufacturing. Managers cannot just take a supply (manufacturing) plan and a master plan and/or master schedule and toss them onto the production floor and hope for the best. Chances are that this approach will bump into some low underpasses: a work center with too few people to assemble the product as called for in the approved supply plan, master plan, or master schedule; too little lead time in another work center; a production line overloaded due to equipment constraints; insufficient space on the manufacturing floor that month or week or day; a lack of design engineers available to start the process; the inability of the sole supplier of a critical material to deliver on time.

To avoid being caught by such unpleasant surprises, team leaders, master planners, and master schedulers need a couple manufacturing road maps called *resource requirements planning* (RRP) used as part of the integrated business planning process (see Chapter 14) and *rough cut capacity planning* (RCCP) used as part of the master planning and scheduling process. Both resource requirements planning and rough cut capacity planning basically ask and answer *one question: Does the business have a chance of meeting the supply (production) plan, master plan, and/or master schedule as currently written?*

If the answer to this one question is yes, the supply manager, master planner, and/or master scheduler is directed (in a sense) to *get more detail* in the form of detailed capacity requirements planning (CRP) and/or material requirements planning (MRP). *If the answer to this one question is no*, then *there isn't any reason* for the supply manager, master planner, and/or master scheduler *to get more detail*; if a company doesn't have enough capacity for the supply manager, master planner, and/or master scheduler to feel somewhat comfortable about successfully producing what's on the aggregate supply plan (remember that this aggregate supply plan is at the volume level, not the mix level), no more detail is going to change that comfort level!

Resource requirements planning and rough cut capacity planning each help to identify the material and personnel shortages, the lead-time constraints, and the capacity issues that make it possible to create a supply (production) plan, master plan, and/or master schedule that can be executed with every expectation of success. It also suggests possible options for navigating around process and material constraints. In short, both RRP and RCCP make it possible (1) to test the validity of a supply (production) plan, master plan, and/or master schedule before doing any detailed material/capacity planning, and (2) to initiate action for making mid- to long-range capacity adjustments.

One way or another, everyone does some form of RRP and RCCP. It might be as simple as saying, "My plan calls for shipping 3 million dollars' worth of product this month, and we've always been able to ship 4 million dollars' worth of product per month. Therefore, we have the proven capacity to meet the plan."

Alternately, one might say, "Management wants to ship 7 million dollars' worth of product a month during the summer season. We have no precedent for being able to do that. Therefore, management's new plan appears to be unrealistic at this time." At the other extreme, a formal resource requirements plan and/or rough cut capacity plan might be carried out that evaluates all key resources and determines the feasibility of fulfilling the approved integrated business planning (IBP) or sales and operations planning (S&OP) output plans.

This chapter focuses on the formal master planning and scheduling approach and covers all of the essential elements and techniques needed to make RCCP understandable and workable. Some reference will be made to RRP in this chapter, but the focus will be on RCCP in support of master planning and scheduling (suffice it to say that the mechanics of RRP and RCCP are identical but applied at different levels of aggregation).

Resource requirements planning (RRP) and rough cut capacity planning (RCCP) are used to test validity and initiate action for making capacity and/or supply plan, master plan, and/or master schedule adjustments. The difference between a supply plan and production plan is that a supply plan can include purchased product whereas a production plan is strictly for production.

Another difference between the supply plan, master plan, and master schedule is the detail regarding discussion level (volume vs. mix vs. schedule), group identification (product family vs. product subfamily vs. item grouping vs. stock-keeping unit), length of time periods (months vs. weeks vs. days), and time horizon (24 months vs. 18 months vs. 12 months vs. 6 months vs. 3 months).

The remainder of this chapter uses the master plan and/or master schedule as the principle driver to the RCCP process. Let's take a look.

Rough Cut Revealed

Simply put, RRP and RCCP attempts to identify 80 to 90 percent of the issues or potential problems that may occur on the manufacturing floor before detailed production schedules and capacity plans are either developed or contemplated. The other 10 to 20 percent typically surface in the course of material and capacity requirements planning. These problems might be related to space or machinery, or the ever-present bottlenecks that ultimately limit output. Similarly, a gateway work center where the entire production process begins may be a potential problem. Perhaps limited storage tank space will cause a problem. Because every manufacturing process has potential limitations to output, the list could go on for pages and would be unique to each company.

With RRP and RCCP, supply managers, master planners, master schedulers, and team leaders can quickly identify obstacles to the plan or schedule (either the aggregate supply plan, master plan, or master schedule) that they are creating/reviewing without wading through all the detail. These supply managers, master planners, master schedulers, and team leaders do this by focusing on the critical or key resources within the company. These critical or key resources may be identified as critical or key due to required labor, equipment, materials, floor space, suppliers' capabilities, and, in some cases, money.

The Rough Cut Process[*]

To carry out rough cut capacity planning (RCCP) in a company with simple products and bills-of-material, recipes, or formulas, an old technology cell phone or even just a clipboard, a pencil, and a simple hand-held calculator may suffice. If a company has products of average complexity and more extensive bills-of-material, recipes, or formulas, a smartphone or computer with a spreadsheet program or master planning and scheduling software is very helpful. For very complex planning operations, enterprise resource planning (ERP) software that includes a master planning and scheduling

---

[*] Logic for resource requirements planning (RRP) is the same as that of rough cut capacity planning (RCCP). The only difference is the driver (aggregate supply plan for RRP and master plan and master schedule for RCCP).

(MPS) coupled with a rough cut capacity planning (RCCP) module as well as a finite capacity loader may be necessary. Whatever the situation, RCCP tools must be interactive with the user.

As a starting point, we need to understand a few key terms:

- **Required capacity:** The capacity needed to meet the approved supply plan, master plan, and/or master schedule. This is derived by taking the supply plan, master plan, and/or master schedule and extending it by the setup time and run time necessary to produce or purchase the product.

- **Available capacity:** The capacity that a work location (production line, work center, work cell) would have if it operated at a one hundred percent productivity level (based on present staffing, equipment, and number of shifts worked).

- **Demonstrated capacity:** The proven or historical capacity of a critical resource, key resource, work location, work center, work cell, group of resources (e.g., labor pools, machines), or production line calculated on the basis of actual output performance.

- **Planned capacity:** Demonstrated capacity plus or minus anticipated adjustments to that capacity in the future. Adjustments might include the addition of equipment or people, or reductions in machines or staff.

- **Maximum capacity:** The highest level of capacity at which a manufacturing and/or production system is able to operate without additional capital expenditures.

With these basic definitions understood, we can consider rough cut capacity planning (as well as the resource requirements planning) process itself, which, simply put, entails three basic steps:

1. Calculate the capacity required to meet the proposed supply plan, master plan, and/or master schedule.

2. Compare the required capacity to the planned capacity.

3. If necessary, adjust the planned and/or required capacity so that the two are in balance.

As Figure 15.1 on page 504 indicates, the validation process begins when data from the supply plan, master plan, and/or master schedule is entered into the RRP and/or RCCP system module (e.g., ERP capacity planning module, capacity planning spreadsheet, etc.). Data from two other sources is then drawn upon: the resource or load profile database, which contains information about the company's use of critical or key resources to build or purchase products, and the production and supplier database, which has information

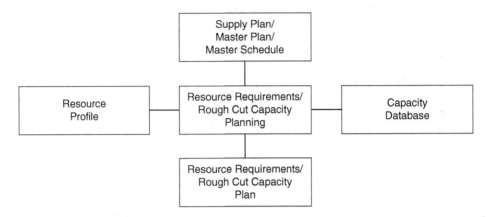

Figure 15.1   Resource Requirements and/or Rough Cut Capacity Planning Process

about the available as well as the demonstrated and planned capacity of each critical or key resource used to manufacture or procure the products in question.

Combining information from the various supply plans and the resource profiles, the resource requirements planning (RRP) and/or rough cut capacity planning (RCCP) software module determines the *required capacity* necessary to meet the supply plan, master plan, and/or master schedule. This required capacity is then compared to the production's and supplier's *planned capacity* and *capabilities* to determine whether adequate capacity exists or will exist.

If the critical or key resource's planned capacity for the aggregate supply plan is adequate, the supply plan is deemed realistic and it is used to create the master plan and/or master schedule as well as detailed material and capacity plans (indirectly), if and as necessary. If RRP determines that the critical or key resource's planned capacity cannot support the aggregate supply plan, that information is given to management and the supply manager, master (supply) planner, and/or master planner supported by the master scheduler(s), who then must either alter the aggregate supply plan or increase the resource's capacity.

Essentially, management must balance the aggregate supply plan's required capacity against a critical or key resource's planned capacity by asking these questions:

- What is the required capacity by time period?

- What is the planned capacity by time period?

- Do the required and planned capacities balance by time period?

- What is the difference between the two?

These questions make it possible to identify potential problem areas and to make adjustments before moving on to any required detailed material and capacity requirements planning.

The next two sections explain the creation of resource profiles and work location, work center, or production line capacity data. Be aware that this activity involves both art and science, resulting in a refined guess, albeit one with high predictive value.

Creating the Resource Profile

A resource profile is a statement of the critical or key resources needed to build the product being evaluated by resource requirements planning (RRP) and/or rough cut capacity planning (RCCP). It is created through the following process: Identify the key suppliers, work centers, production lines, and critical/key resources needed to support the various, higher-level supply plans (aggregate supply plan itself, master (supply) plan, and master (supply) schedule). This is done by a quaint but effective method: asking people in manufacturing, in purchasing, in design, and in engineering. Those who deal with the engineering, production, and buying processes every day know what the critical and/or key resources, process constraints, bottlenecks, and supplier-furnished materials are for any particular product normally run through the plant. Typical responses will be influenced, but not limited, by the following elements:

- Constraining or bottlenecked work centers or cells;

- One-of-a-kind or special tooling needed in a particular work area;

- Processes that are difficult to subcontract because they require special skills or equipment;

- High *mix sensitivity* where large numbers of options exist;

- Purchased materials from identified constraining suppliers;

- Suppliers supplying special materials having *out-of-normal* requirements, such as long lead times, tight tolerances, shelf-life considerations, and so forth;

- Physical properties of the product that make it easy for the production process to get out of control, causing yields to vary;

- Unwillingness to offload work because of technology issues.

To be systematic in identifying all the critical and/or key resources, the person charged with identifying the critical or key resources and creating the resource profiles may find it helpful to use a matrix like the one in Figure 15.2 on page 507. On the left side, the critical or key resources required to support the aggregate supply plan, master plan, and/or master schedule are listed. Across the top, the reasons these resources may pose obstacles to achieving the plan and/or plans are listed.

For example, assembly, drilling, mixing, blending, and fabricating, among other resources, could be listed in the left column. Across the top, such obstacles as bottlenecks, difficulty of offloading, special skills requirements, reluctance to share technology, or single-source suppliers may be listed.

Once the matrix is complete, determine whether any of the resources identified can be combined. For example, three drill presses might be grouped into "drilling department"; a drilling and milling machine might be grouped into "fabrication"; mixing, filling, and packing operations might be grouped into a "production line." Keep the resource profile as simple as possible and with as few entries as absolutely necessary, remembering that the purpose of RRP and RCCP is to *only answer the one question*: *Do we have a chance of meeting this aggregate supply plan, master plan, and/or master schedule as currently written?*

Next, determine the times and standards associated with each of the critical or key resources. *Times* and *standards* refer to setup time and run time (operational or processing time required), as opposed to queue time, wait time, and move time (interoperational times). In traditional manufacturing, setup and run times impact the workload on a resource because they actually tie up that resource. In contrast, the queue, wait, and move times impact the time it takes to move work through the facility, but these interoperational times do not affect the load at any particular resource, which is the real consideration when it comes to testing the validity of the aggregate supply plan, master (supply) plan, and/or master (supply) schedule.

Critical or Key Resources	Reasons							
	Bottleneck or Process Constraint	Not Easy to Off-Load	Mix Sensitivity	Physical Properties	Can't Change Over Quickly	Costly to Underutilize	Special Skills Required	Travel Distance
Tooling (Dies)	✓	✓				✓		
Packing Operations	✓	✓			✓			
Semifinished Operations			✓	✓				
Assembly/Test						✓	✓	
Design Engineering		✓				✓	✓	
Plating				✓				✓
Press 1	✓	✓						
Press 2	✓				✓	✓		
Random, Inc. (Special Material)		✓		✓				✓
Fabrication		✓	✓			✓	✓	

Figure 15.2   Critical or Key Resources Worksheet

Here is a four-step method for deriving the resource profile's operational or processing time:

1. Select the product family, product subfamily, item grouping, and/or stock-keeping unit for which the resource profile is being created.

2. Explode the product family, product subfamily, item grouping, and/or stock-keeping unit using the entire bill-of-material, recipe, formulation, or pseudo bill.

3. Search each of the associated detail routings to determine whether a previously identified critical or key resource is involved in the procurement and/or manufacture of the product family, product subfamily, item grouping, and or stock-keeping unit.

4. Determine the resource profile times for each time element required by each identified critical or key resource. This can be time consuming, but is readily done using one of the following methods:

   - *Choose a typical or representative item or group of items,* one that most ideally represents the entire product line—perhaps one or more from a similar product family or product subfamily—and use it as a proxy for the planned item.

   - *Compute an arithmetic average for the resource.* Add up the time spent on all items within the product family, product subfamily, item grouping, and/or stock-keeping unit that pass through the critical or key resource and divide that time by the number of items or group of items processed.

   - *Compute a weighted average.* This requires that a weight, which correlates to the anticipated product mix, is applied to the group of items or individual item's time. The weighted times are then summed to create a weighted average for the resource.

   - *Estimate the time it takes for the planned product to be secured from a critical or key supplier or pass through a critical or key work center or down a critical or key production line.* Ask people on the manufacturing floor or in the plant or mill how long it takes for an average lot size or batch to go through the critical or key resources and extrapolate the time for the planned product from this input.

These methods will yield estimated times that are useful for developing predictive resource profiles. If detailed routings and process sheets are available with engineering standards, the resource profile times created using one of the above methods can be quite accurate.

Once they are estimated, enter the operational/processing and interoperational times for each resource in a matrix that breaks out each key resource by product family, product subfamily, group of items, stock-keeping unit (SKU), as shown in Figure 15.3 on page 509. The matrix in Figure 15.3 constitutes a *resource profile by product family*.

Key Resources	Unit of Measure	IBP/S&OP Family A	IBP/S&OP Family B	IBP/S&OP Family C	IBP/S&OP Family D	IBP/S&OP Family E
Filling Lines 1 & 2	Machine Hours	1.1	1.1		0.8	1.5
Filling Line 3	Machine Hours	0.8	2.0		2.2	2.25
Filling Line 4	Machine Hours	1.0		4.0		
Finishing Line	Labor Hours	15.0	28.0	48.0	24.0	26.0
In-Process Storage	Lbs.	15,000				
Processing Department	Equipment Hours	265.0		22.0	33.0	20.0
Incoming Test	Labor Hours	13.0		8.0	26.0	6.0
Supplier 100	Lbs.	450		215	335	
Supplier 200	Cases	250		1,000		

Figure 15.3   Resource Profile by Product Family (per 1,000 Units)

We also need to determine what is called *lead-time offset*. The lead-time offset is the time between the *need* for the resource and the date that the product has been *promised*. The application of lead-time offset is necessary if a product has longer lead times—generally more than a month or two when doing resource requirements planning in the integrated business planning (IBP) or sales and operations planning (S&OP) processes. In that case, you may have to use the offset so that the need for the resource can be identified in the proper time period in the resource requirements plan (generated by RRP) and/or rough cut capacity plan (generated by RCCP).

Figure 15.4 on page 511 shows a simple two-level bill-of-material for a customized pen, detailed routings for the pen and body assembly, and a timeline for the pen product. A review of the bill-of-material (Figure 15.4, Section A) indicates that the pen is composed of one body assembly and one cap. The body assembly in turn is made up of one barrel, one ink filler, and one filler cap. The expected ship date or promised date for delivery of the product is identified with the completed pen. But body assemblies must be manufactured or assembled (in this example) before pens can be produced.

For purposes of discussion, assume that we have identified two critical or key resources, work centers 250 and 900. The detail routing (Figure 15.4, Section B) for the body assembly reveals four operations. As we look at the routing, we notice that the first critical or key resource encountered in the body assembly is operation 20, which takes place at work center 250. On the timeline shown at the bottom (Figure 15.4, Section C), operation 20 in work center 250 for body assemblies is required 35 days prior to the due date assigned for the pen product. Therefore, this resource has a lead-time offset of 35 days.

The next critical or key resource encountered is operation 40 for the body assembly, which is to be performed in work center 900. In this case, the resource is required 16 days prior to the completion of the pen and is assigned a lead-time offset of 16 days. The customized pen's routing is shown at the top of Figure 15.4, Section B, and also contains the two critical or key resources, a pass through work center 250, and a pass through work center 900. As the timeline shows, the lead-time offsets assigned are 12 days, 8 days, and 2 days, respectively, from the pen's planned completion date.

By definition, *every* critical or key resource has a lead-time offset. But in practice, if the offset is less than 30 days (when at the IBP or S&OP level), it does not need to be entered into your calculations when you are evaluating the validity of the aggregate supply plan (rough cutting the master supply plan and master supply schedule may require more precision). This is because IBP or S&OP supply planning is generally done on a monthly basis. In fact, some companies even represent lead-time offset in months when planning at this aggregate level.

Every resource required within 30 days falls within the month that the supply of product is due. Offsets between 30 and 60 days fall in the month immediately preceding the month the product is due, and so forth. The choice is arbitrary and one that a company must make prior to implementing resource requirements planning (RRP) and/or rough cut capacity planning (RCCP).

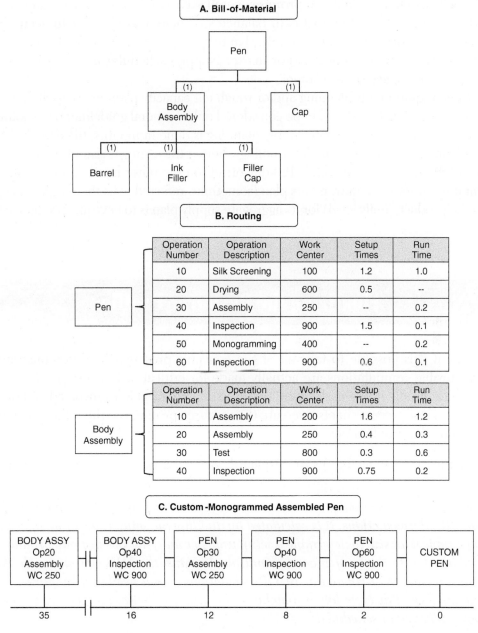

A. Bill-of-Material

B. Routing

Pen

Operation Number	Operation Description	Work Center	Setup Times	Run Time
10	Silk Screening	100	1.2	1.0
20	Drying	600	0.5	--
30	Assembly	250	--	0.2
40	Inspection	900	1.5	0.1
50	Monogramming	400	--	0.2
60	Inspection	900	0.6	0.1

Body Assembly

Operation Number	Operation Description	Work Center	Setup Times	Run Time
10	Assembly	200	1.6	1.2
20	Assembly	250	0.4	0.3
30	Test	800	0.3	0.6
40	Inspection	900	0.75	0.2

C. Custom-Monogrammed Assembled Pen

Figure 15.4   Two-Level Bill-of-Material and Timeline Illustrations: Lead-Time Offsets, Pen Product

This arbitrary choice might compromise overall accuracy. But it doesn't really matter—with RRP and/or RCCP, the goal is to balance simplicity and speed with accuracy and feasibility, and to determine if the supply plan in question is valid and realistic. The team leader, master (supply) planner, and/or master (supply) scheduler is not trying to match the precision of a space shuttle launch.

Resource requirements planning and/or rough cut capacity planning is applied common sense, not hard science, and should be considered only a general guideline. If a resource has an offset of 35 days and aggregate supply planning is done in months, the extra 5 days will not make much of a difference in determining whether the aggregate supply plan is realistic. The lead time of a resource with a 120-day offset, on the other hand, must be taken into account if the resource requirements plan (sometimes referred to as the rough cut capacity plan at the product family level) for its aggregate supply plan is to have any predictive value.

Finalizing the Resource Profile

At this point it is possible to take all of the concepts presented and demonstrate how resource profile computations are actually made for critical or key resources. The computations are simple if you understand the fundamental principles involved. When using detail routings or process sheets to create the resource profile, use the following equation to determine the profile times:

$$\left(\text{Run time} + \text{Setup factor}^{*}\right) \times \text{BOM quantity} = \text{Total time required per unit produced}$$

> ** Setup time is essentially turned into a setup factor or setup rate to simplify the RRP and RCCP calculations. It is calculated by dividing the setup time for an operation by a typical lot size to determine a setup time per unit, not per discrete production batch or lot. In this way, it can be multiplied against the MPS volume much like a run rate, and the RRP and/or RCCP calculations do not need to take into account the number of discrete lots or batches to be produced within a given time period being planned or scheduled.*

This yields the total *time required per unit* of produced product for the resource in question. Using that total *time per unit*, one can simply multiply against the volume in the master (supply) plan and/or master (supply) schedule to determine the total resource time required for the resource in a given time period (refer to Figure 15.4 on page 511).

For pens, there are two critical or key resources: an assembly operation (in work center 250) and several inspection operations (in work center 900). Note, there is an assembly operation (work center 200) that is *not* considered a key resource, and therefore not included in the analysis. Each operation has a setup and run time that can be used in the profile time equation. Let's take a look at the assembly work center (WC 250) and inspection work center (900) calculations.

Assembly Work Center 250   **Total**

Body Assembly (or BA, Op 20): [0.3hrs run time per BA + (0.4hrs setup time per 10* BAs)] x 1** = 0.34hrs

Pen (Op 30):   [0.2hrs per Pen + (0.0hrs Setup per 10* Pens)] x 1** = 0.2hrs
                                                                                                                ———————
                                                                                                                0.54hrs

*Typical batch size. The setup factor or rate is calculated by dividing the setup time by the typical batch size. The setup factor is then added to the run rate to determine the total hours needed for each pen on the MPS.

**The Quantity Per on the BOM must also be factored in. In this case, there is only one (1) Body Assembly and of course only one (1) Pen per final pen product. If there were three (3) Body Assemblies per final pen product, then the time required by Body Assemblies on each resource would have to increase by a factor of three (3)

Inspection Work Center 900   **Total**

Body Assembly (or BA, Op 40): [0.2hrs run time per BA + (0.75hrs setup time per 10* BAs)] x 1** = 0.275hrs

Pen (Op 40):   [0.1hrs run time per Pen + (1.5hrs setup time per 10* Pens)] x 1** = 0.25hrs

Pen (Op 60):   [0.1hrs run time per Pen + (0.6hrs setup time per 10* Pens)] x 1** = 0.16hrs
                                                                                                                ———————
                                                                                                                0.685hrs

*Typical batch size. The setup factor or rate is calculated by dividing the setup time by the typical batch size. The setup factor is then added to the run rate to determine the total hours needed for each pen on the MPS.

**The Quantity Per on the BOM must also be factored in. In this case, there is only one (1) Body Assembly and of course only one (1) Pen per final pen product. If there were three (3) Body Assemblies per final pen product, then the time required by Body Assemblies on each resource would have to increase by a factor of three (3)

The calculations given show that every pen product master (supply) planned, or master (supply) scheduled will require a total time of 0.54 hours *per complete pen planned/ scheduled* on the assembly work center. Likewise, every complete pen will require 0.685 hours *per complete pen planned/scheduled* on the inspection work center. Note that the rough math shown is not taking into account any lead time offsets.

The first assembly operation performed on the body assembly (Op 20) takes place 35 days prior to the completion of the final pen. It may be okay to not use a lead time offset for that operation for the purposes of integrated business planning or sales and operations planning in monthly buckets.

However, when master scheduling in weekly buckets, a master scheduler may wish to apply a 35-day (~7 workweek) lead time offset to the time required for body assembly operation 20 in the assembly work center 250 and plan for the time 35 days or 7 weeks earlier. Similarly, the master scheduler may choose to offset the time required for body assembly operation 40 in the inspection work center 900 by 16 days or 3 workweeks.

At this point, the resource profile is complete and the master planner and/or master scheduler can move on to the other input for the resource requirements planning (RRP) and/or rough cut capacity planning (RCCP) process, that of planned capacity, which is to be compared to the required capacity.

Capacity Inputs

The integrated business planning (IBP) or sales and operations planning (S&OP) process yields an aggregate supply (eventually an approved aggregate supply plan) plan, establishing supply volumes by product family. An example of such an aggregate supply plan is shown in Figure 15.5 on page 515.

This particular supply plan covers five product families with three future months' worth of data. Here we will see what happens when the aggregate supply plan is exploded through the resource profile.

The aggregate supply plan calls for 30,000 units of product family A in July. Referring back to the resource profile for product family A (see Figure 15.3 on p. 509), the required time for the first critical or key resource, filling lines 1 and 2, is 1.1 hours per 1,000 units. That means that 30,000 units will require 33 hours on production filling line

Month		Family A	Family B	Family C	Family D	Family E
July		30,000	10,000	4,000	3,000	3,000
August		25,000	5,000	4,000	3,000	3,000
September		25,000	5,000	5,000	4,000	3,000
Total		80,000	20,000	13,000	10,000	9,000

Figure 15.5 Aggregate Supply Plan

either 1 or 2—30,000 units divided by 1,000 and multiplied by 1.1 equals 33 hours of required capacity.

For product family B, the resource profile indicates that 1.8 hours per 1,000 units are required on production filling line either 1 or 2. Since the aggregate supply plan for product family B calls for 10,000 units in July, the required capacity will be 18 hours—10,000 units divided by 1,000 and multiplied by 1.8 equaling 18 hours of required capacity.

Continuing this simple calculation for each product family in the aggregate supply plan, the required capacity for the entire aggregate supply plan can be determined. Figure 15.6 on page 516 shows this required capacity for the aggregate supply plan shown in Figure 15.5 using the resource profile developed in Figure 15.3 on page 509.

Once the aggregate supply plan's required capacity has been calculated by using the resource requirements or rough cut technique or method discussed, the next step is to compare that required capacity to the actual capacity at the supply manager's, master planner's, and/or master scheduler's disposal. This comparison determines whether adjustments need to be made to available resources or the aggregate supply plan. A company's capacity really consists of several types of capacities, two of which (demonstrated and planned) are described in further detail in the following sections.

Demonstrated Capacity. This was earlier shown to be the proven or historical capacity of a critical or key resource or work center. To illustrate demonstrated capacity, consider a racing car.

Imagine that you've been working for the past five years to design a very fast vehicle. During the design process, you have determined that the car should be able to achieve a speed of 200 miles per hour (mph). Actual time trials, however, reveal that the car never exceeds 180 mph. No matter what your engineers and mechanics do, the car never exceeds

Key Resource	Unit of Measure	Month	Family A	Family B	Family C	Family D	Family E	Required Capacity
Filling Lines 1&2	Machine Hours	July	33.0	18.0		2.4	4.5	58
		August	27.5	9.0		2.4	4.5	43
		September	27.5	9.0		3.2	4.5	44
		TOTAL	88.0	36.0		8.0	13.5	145
Filling Line 3	Machine Hours	July	24.0	20.0		6.6	6.75	57
		August	20.0	10.0		6.6	6.75	43
		September	20.0	10.0		8.8	6.75	46
		TOTAL	64.0	40.0		22.0	20.25	146
Filling Line 4	Machine Hours	July	30.0		16.0			46
		August	35.0		16.0			51
		September	25.0		20.0			45
		TOTAL	80.0		52.0			132
Finishing Line	Labor Hours	July	450.0	280.0	192.0	72.0	78.0	1,072
		August	375.0	140.0	192.0	72.0	78.0	857
		September	375.0	140.0	240.0	96.0	78.0	929
		TOTAL	1,200	560.0	624.0	240.0	234.0	2,858
In-Process Storage	Lbs.	July	450,000					450,000
		August	375,000					375,000
		September	375,000					375,000
		TOTAL	1,200,000					1,200,000
Processing Department	Equipment Hours	July	7,950		88.0	99.0	60.0	8,197
		August	6,625		99.0	99.0	60.0	6,872
		September	6,625		110.0	132.0	60.0	6,972
		TOTAL	21,200		268.0	330.0	180.0	21,996
Incoming Test	Labor Hours	July	390.0		32.0	78.0	18.0	518.0
		August	325.0		32.0	78.0	18.0	453.0
		September	325.0		40.0	104.0	18.0	487.0
		TOTAL	1,040		104.0	260.0	54.0	1,458
Supplier 100	Lbs.	July	13,500		860.0	1,005		15,365
		August	11,250		860.0	1,005		13,115
		September	11,250		1,075	1,340		13,665
		TOTAL	36,000		2,795	3,350		42,145
Supplier 200	Cases	July	7,500		4,000			11,500
		August	6,250		4,000			10.250
		September	6,250		5,000			11,250
		TOTAL	20,000		13,000			33,000

Figure 15.6   Resource Requirements or Rough Cut Required Capacity

180 mph. So, what is the demonstrated speed of the vehicle? Obviously, it is 180 mph or less, and it would be foolish to enter the vehicle in a race that requires 200 mph.

The same mechanism applies in manufacturing. It is foolish to adopt a plan that loads a factory, plant, mill, production line, or a critical/key resource with 200 units of work per month when past experience indicates that 180 units of work per month is the best that has been (or most likely will be) achieved. More than a few manufacturing companies do just that! While this can-do attitude may appear admirable, attempts to exceed demonstrated capacity are invariably doomed to failure and should *not* receive support.

Adequate demonstrated capacity in itself, however, is *not* sufficient to make the decision to adopt the aggregate supply plan—demonstrated capacity could potentially change if resources are added or if operations are altered. Planned adjustments to capacity must be considered before making an evaluation of the aggregate supply plan.

Planned Capacity. This is demonstrated capacity plus or minus anticipated changes or adjustments to the production process (e.g., improved/reduced productivity) or resources (e.g., added/reduced equipment). To understand this better, let us return to the racing car analogy for a moment.

Perhaps later tests determine that by installing an exotic, special-purpose air blower, your car can achieve 200 mph. The air blower manufacturer indicated that it could deliver the new part at the end of five weeks. This means the car can be expected to clock at 180 mph for the next five weeks and at 200 mph in the sixth week. Now you have a decision to make:

Should you adjust your racing strategy today, increasing the car's expected clocking to be 200 mph come the sixth week? Here you need to analyze the possibility of really being able to compete at 200 mph in the future. If you are confident that the design is good, that production will deliver as promised, and that you will be able to achieve 200 mph six weeks out, then it seems reasonable to adjust your planned racing speed for the car.

Likewise, if a manufacturing unit has regularly demonstrated its ability to produce 180 units per month, an upward adjustment to 200 units per month beginning sometime in the future might be reasonable if operators are scheduled for special training or additional equipment is expected to be available.

With this sort of knowledge in hand, the supply management team, master planner, and/or master scheduler can begin to make valid comparisons of the required capacity and the planned capacity (Figure 15.7 on page 518).

In some cases, there are underloads (*less* capacity is required than is planned to be available), while in other cases there may be overloads (*more* capacity is required than is planned to be available). For example, in the finishing operation shown in Figure 15.7 (fourth row), a total of 857 hours is required in August, yet current plans have only 600

Key Resource	Unit of Measure	Month	Required Capacity	Net Difference	Planned Capacity	Maximum Capacity
Filling Lines 1 & 2	Machine Hours	July	58	56	114	152
		August	43	17	60	80
		September	44	100	144	192
		TOTAL	145	173	318	424
Filling Line 3	Machine Hours	July	57	76	133	171
		August	43	27	70	90
		September	46	122	168	216
		TOTAL	146	225	371	477
Filling Line 4	Machine Hours	July	46	49	95	114
		August	51	−1	50	60
		September	45	75	120	144
		TOTAL	132	123	265	318
Finishing Line	Labor Hours	July	1,072	68	1,140	1,596
		August	857	−257	600	840
		September	929	511	1,440	2,016
		TOTAL	2,858	322	3,180	4,452
In-Process Storage	Lbs.	July	450,000	690,000	1,140,000	1,140,000
		August	375,000	225,000	600,000	600,000
		September	375,000	1,065,000	1,440,000	1,440,000
		TOTAL	1,200,000	1,980,000	3,180,000	3,180,000
Processing Department	Equipment Hours	July	8,197	2,253	10,450	12,350
		August	6,872	−1,372	5,500	6,500
		September	6,972	6,273	13,200	15,600
		TOTAL	21,996	7,154	29,150	34,450
Incoming Test	Labor Hours	July	518.0	14	532	551
		August	453.0	−173	280	320
		September	487.0	185	672	768
		TOTAL	1,458	26	1,484	1,639
Supplier 100	Lbs.	July	15,365	29,635	45,000	45,000
		August	13,115	31,885	45,000	45,000
		September	13,665	31,335	45,000	45,000
		TOTAL	42,145	92,885	135,000	135,000
Supplier 200	Cases	July	11,500	7,500	19,000	23,000
		August	10.250	−250	10,000	12,000
		September	11,250	12,750	24,000	29,000
		TOTAL	33,000	20,000	53,000	64,000

Figure 15.7 Required Capacity versus Planned Capacity

hours available. Do such potential overloads truly indicate that the aggregate supply plan cannot be met? Not necessarily. Management might be able to increase the capacity at selected critical or key resources. This prompts our next subject: maximum capacity.

Maximum Capacity. By definition, this is the heaviest load a resource can handle under any reasonable set of circumstances and without capital expenditures. It can be achieved through a number of means. In the case of personnel, the use of overtime, including added shifts and weekends, or outright staff additions can increase the resource. In the case of a critical supplier, some work might be offloaded to another supplier, the company could agree to pay extra for supply priority, or premium freight methods could be used to expedite material delivery. In the case of machine time, an extra shift might be added.

Attempts to operate a production system beyond its maximum capacity generally lead to confusion in manufacturing, and almost always lead to a failure to achieve planned supply (production) quantities. Remember, no amount of work or maneuvering in the details can make up for a mistake (e.g., overloading) in aggregate plans.

Evaluating the Plan

Clearly, flexing capacity up or down or using any other approaches to boost or lower capacity may have a cost impact and must therefore be carefully evaluated by management. Resource requirements planning and rough cut capacity planning answers questions about critical capacity and material requirements in terms of numbers. Each point out at its respective planning level where potential problems are likely to occur and reveals what happens when alternatives (e.g., maximum capacity) are applied.

The resource requirements plan and rough cut capacity plan provides an opportunity for people to exercise skill, knowledge, and creativity in balancing demand for product with the supply of resources. It makes it possible to *manage by the numbers* and to evaluate whether a supply plan, master plan, and/or master schedule is achievable or merely an unrealistic gleam in someone's eyes.

Resource requirements planning and rough cut capacity planning can also determine where the energies of management should be focused. If product family A is an elephant (refer to Figure 15.6 on p. 516) compared to the other product families—that is, if it has by far the largest need for capacity and creates the biggest problems—management can focus its efforts on that product family.

Overloading Demonstrated and/or Planned Capacity

Panware has a work center that makes saucepans and matching covers. Assume that it takes the same amount of time to make the saucepan as it takes to make the cover. The resource in question has a demonstrated capacity of 5,000 total unit pieces (assuming planned capacity is equal to demonstrated capacity and no adjustments are made to that planned capacity) per time period. Therefore, manufacturing can build 2,500 complete packages during any given time period (2,500 saucepans and 2,500 matching covers).

Management wants 2,750 packages per time period. The master (supply) planner and/or master (supply) scheduler appropriately responds, "Yes, we can do that, but we will need a new piece of equipment." To this, management counters, "No, we are not going to buy any new equipment."

"Okay, we'll need to work an extra shift." "No, we're not going to work another shift."

"Okay, we will work a few weekends of overtime." "No, we are not going to work any overtime."

"Okay, how about offloading some work to a subcontractor?" "No, we will not offload any work."

At some point, the master (supply) planner and/or master (supply) scheduler needs to respond with a firm *"no"* to the requested 2,750 packages per period. Even though the supply manager, master (supply) planner, and/or master (supply) scheduler know that his or her job is to say *"yes" to demand and "this is what it will take,"* when all suggested roads lead to a dead end, the driver (the company's supply manager, master planner, and/or master scheduler) does not want to risk a crash by making a bad promise to the customer as well as the demand organization.

After a few minutes of thought, management goes through this logic: "If we ask for 2,500 packages, the most we will get is 2,500 packages. However, if we ask for 2,750 packages, we may not get 2,750 packages, but we may get 2,650 packages. This is closer to the 2,750 that is desired than the 2,500 packages, and we didn't authorize any additional spending. So, let's schedule more than we can do, just in case we may get more" (see Figure 15.8 on page 521).

As directed, the master planner and/or master scheduler has scheduled 2,750 packages per time period over the next four time periods. Work authorization for the four lots of 2,750 packages has been given. Manufacturing commences work on the 2,750 saucepans due in time period one. Once this work is done, a changeover is made to the pan covers.

Time Periods	Package Schedule	Saucepan Builds	Pan Cover Builds	Package Shipments	Saucepan Inventory	Pan Cover Inventory
1	2,750	2,750	2,250	2,250	500	0
2	2,750	1,750	3,250	2,250	0	1,000
3	2,750	3,750	1,250	2,250	1,500	0
4	2,750	750	4,250	2,250	0	2,000

Figure 15.8   Overloading the Master Plan and Schedule

The master (supply) planner and/or master (supply) scheduler has released an authorization for 2,750 covers. However, only 2,250 covers can be completed during time period one due to capacity constraints (2,750 saucepans plus 2,250 saucepan covers equals 5,000 total units). Therefore, only 2,250 completed packages can be shipped at the end of time period one.

As time period two commences, manufacturing will complete the open order for 2,750 saucepan covers (500 remain to be completed). Now, since the resource is already set up for pan covers, the decision is made to continue working on the 2,750 covers scheduled for completion in time period two.

When this work is completed, a total of 3,250 units of capacity have been spent. The production line is changed over to saucepans, and 1,750 of the 2,750 pans scheduled are completed. Manufacturing takes these 1,750 saucepans plus the 500 in inventory, adds the 2,250 saucepan covers, and ships 2,250 packages. And so it goes. . . .

Managing to demonstrated and/or realistic planned capacity is critically important in effectively running a manufacturing operation. *More isn't always better*. As Figure 15.8 suggests, the total number of packages shipped per time period continues to be 2,250 units over the four-time-period horizon. The most packages that can be shipped in the example is 2,500—the demonstrated and planned capacity. *Scheduling more has proven disastrous*.

Rough Cut Capacity Planning at the Master Planning and Master Scheduling Levels

Figure 15.9 on page 523 recaps the relationship between integrated business planning (IBP) or sales and operations planning (S&OP), resource requirements planning (RRP), master supply planning, master supply scheduling, and rough cut capacity planning (RCCP). Here, the aggregate production/supply plan is developed in the IBP or S&OP process. Next, the aggregate production/supply plan is sanity checked for validity and reasonability through the RRP (sometimes referred to as RCCP at the IBP level) process and adjusted as necessary.

Once the executive team determines that a realistic plan exists, the approved supply plan becomes the driver and constraint in the master planning and scheduling process, which translates the approved, aggregate supply plan into discrete item groupings or item numbers, quantities, and due dates. This accomplished, the master (supply) plan and/or master (supply) schedule drives the material and capacity planning processes.

Important Note: Material and capacity are planned to support the master (supply) plan and/or master (supply) schedule, not the demand plan or sales forecast. Material and capacity are needed to support what the company plans to build, not what it plans to sell! Yes, demand and supply could be the same, but quite often they are different.

While all companies need to do RRP or RCCP at the aggregate supply planning level, many manufacturing environments require a second or even a third pass through the rough cut analysis, this time at the master plan and/or master schedule level. Companies with highly varied mixes of product are among these. This remainder of this section covers techniques for carrying out rough cut capacity planning (RCCP) for complex product mixes.

Rough cut capacity planning at the master planning and master scheduling levels uses the same principles as resource requirements planning or rough cut capacity planning at the aggregate supply plan level but extends the calculations down one or two additional levels. This is done by exploding the master (supply) plan and/or master (supply) schedule, instead of the aggregate supply plan, through an MPS item's resource profile to generate the required capacity to meet the master (supply) plan and/or master (supply) schedule.

As Figure 15.10 on page 524 indicates, each IBP or S&OP product family may be divided into constituent items. Product family A, for example, consists of items A1, A2, A3, and A4.

The critical or key resources are listed on the left side of the resource profile, along with the associated times and standards. In addition, the resource profile contains the

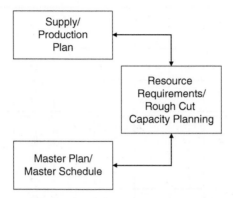

Figure 15.9   Resource Requirements and Rough Cut Capacity Planning and Operational Relationships

predicted mix probability for each item or group of items. In the case of product family A, for example, each product is indicated as having a 25 percent probability of sale selection; that is, there is a 25 percent probability that demand of product family A will be for an A1, or an A2, or an A3, and an A4.[1]

This product mix percentage is very important at the master plan and/or master schedule level, because it yields a much more detailed estimate of how the various critical or key resources will be deployed for each item within the product family. Consider product family D, which has just two items, the first of which (D1) constitutes 33 percent of the mix. That means that when a customer orders a product D, one-third of the time we would expect the customer to order a D1 and two-thirds of the time we expect the customer to order a D2.

Jump back to the B product family. This is different. Three of the items (B1, B2, and B3) are very much alike and use the same key resources. The same is true for items B11, B12, and B13. Therefore, two groups were formed, and respective resource profiles were created to cover the two groupings. As shown in Figure 15.10 on page 524, when an item in the B product family is needed, 60 percent of the time we expect it to be a B1, B2, or B3. The remaining 40 percent of the time we expect to need a B11, B12, or B13.

In addition to this breakout by individual items within a product family, the master (supply) plan's and/or master (supply) schedule's rough cut capacity planning resource profile also shows the average resource times developed for the aggregate product family (see Figure 15.10, average columns). Now take a close look at filling lines 1 and 2 for the IBP or S&OP product family A.

---

[1] These probabilities are established by management as part of the IBP or S&OP process.

Key Resource	Unit of Measure	A: A1	A2	A3	A4	Average	B: B1 B2 B3	B11 B12 B13	Average	C: C1	C2	Average	D: D1	D2	Average	E: E1	E2	Average
Typical Mix %		25%	25%	25%	25%	100%	60%	40%	100%	50%	50%	100%	33%	67%	100%	50%	50%	100%
Lines 1 & 2	Hours	2.0	2.4			1.1	3.0		1.8				2.4		0.8	3.0		1.5
Line 3	Hours			3.1		0.8		5.0	2.0	3.0	5.0	4.0		3.3	2.2		4.5	2.25
Line 4	Hours				4.0	1.0												
Finishing Department	Hours	12.0	12.5	16.7	20.0	15.0	18	45	28	36	60	48	19	26	24	24	27	26
In-Process Storage	Lbs.	10,000	10,000	20,000	20,000	15,000												
Processing Department	Hours	160.0	260.0	320.0	320.0	265.0				15.0	29.0	22.0	24.0	45.0	38.0	13.0	27.0	20.0
Incoming Test	Hours	8.0	12.0	16.0	16.0	13.0				7.0	9.0	8.0	18.0	30.0	26.0	5.0	7.0	6.0
Supplier 100	Lbs.		1,800			450				150	280	215	225	390	335			
Supplier 200	Cases				1,000	250				1,000	1,000	1,000						

Figure 15.10   Resource Profile by MPS Item (Per 1,000 Units)

In the resource profile for product family A, we learned that production lines 1 and 2 required 1.1 hours per 1,000 units. Using the master (supply) plan and/or master (supply) schedule resource (load) profile by item, we review the computation of this weighted average for lines 1 and 2.

Item A1 requires 2.0 hours per 1,000 units.

Item A2 requires 2.4 hours per 1,000 units.

Items A3 and A4 do not use lines 1 and 2.

Since all items are predicted to be 25 percent of the total mix, the times for each unit would be:

A1 = 2.0 × 25% = 0.5 hour

A2 = 2.4 × 25% = 0.5 hour

A3 = 0.0 × 25% = 0.0 hours

A4 = 0.0 × 25% = 0.0 hours

Weighted average = $1.1 \text{ hours} (0.5 + 0.6 + 0.0 + 0.0)$

The same calculation is performed for each critical or key resource in the resource profile for each product family. Once average hours (times) or standards have been computed for each critical or key resource, rough cut capacity planning (RCCP) can be used to evaluate the capacity for each resource on a month-by-month basis using the aggregate supply and/or master plan and on a week-by-week basis using the master (supply) plan and/or master (supply) schedule (each company decides whether the master plan is in months or weeks). This process has already been examined at the aggregate supply plan level. Now we examine the process at the master (supply) plan and master (supply) schedule level.

The example shown in Figure 15.11 provides the quantities scheduled for each master (supply) plan and/or master (supply) schedule item. Note that the totals for these master (supply) plan and/or master (supply) schedule items are identical to those stipulated in the aggregate supply plan (see Figure 15.5 on page 515). What's different is that the item quantities have been broken out as components of the aggregate supply plan totals.

These item quantities are the result of the master (supply) planner's and/or master (supply) scheduler's taking the aggregate supply plan and translating it into discrete items, quantities, and weekly due dates based on the predicted mix and inventories available.

Family	A	B	C	D	E	Total
July Week 1		B1 4,000 B2 4,000 B3 2,000				10,000
Week 2	A1 6,000		C1 1,000	D1 2,000 D2 1,000	E1 3,000	13,000
Week 3	A3 2,000 A4 10,000		C2 1,000			13,000
Week 4	A4 12,000		C2 2,000			14,000
Total	30,000	10,000	4,000	3,000	3,000	50,000

Figure 15.11   Master Schedule for July

In other words, firm planned orders have been created by the master (supply) planner and/or master (supply) scheduler for the items, as shown in the figure.

During the RCCP process, the quantities for each master (supply) planned and/or master (supply) scheduled item are multiplied by the time requirements in the resource profile. This results in a week-by-week summary of total required capacity. The total required capacity is then compared to the planned and maximum capacities for each master (supply) plan and/or master (supply) schedule item (see Figure 15.12 on the following page).

Again, note that the aggregate supply plan quantities by product family (Figures 15.5 on page 515 and 15.11 above) equal the totals of the master (supply) plan and/or master (supply) schedule quantities within each product family. But the master (supply) plan and/or master (supply) schedule rough cut capacity plan clearly yields more detailed information, since it is at an item group level or item level.

This additional detailed information allows us to assess whether the master plan and/or master schedule is valid and realistic given the planned and maximum capacity. As we begin looking at specific master (supply) plan and/or master (supply) schedule line items, a couple of guidelines (which the authors have used for years) may be useful.

Family		A	B	C	D	E	Required Capacity	Net Difference	Planned Capacity	Maximum Capacity
Lines 1 & 2	Week 1		30				30	−6	24	32
	Week 2	12			5	9	26	4	30	40
	Week 3						0	30	30	40
	Week 4						0	30	30	40
	Total	12	30	0	5	9	56	58	114	152
Line 3	Week 1						0	28	28	36
	Week 2				3		3	32	35	45
	Week 3	6					6	29	35	45
	Week 4						0	35	35	45
	Total	6	0	0	3	0	9	124	133	171
Line 4	Week 1						0	20	20	24
	Week 2			3			3	22	25	30
	Week 3	40		5			45	−20	25	30
	Week 4	48		10			58	−33	25	30
	Total	88	0	18	0	0	106	−11	95	114

Figure 15.12   Rough Cut Capacity Plan by MPS Item

If the required capacity is:

- No more than 10 percent greater than the planned capacity, the master (supply) plan and/or master (supply) schedule seems to be realistic, and more detail should be pursued (detailed material/capacity requirements planning plus plant scheduling).

- More than 20 percent greater than the planned capacity, the master (supply) plan and/or master (supply) schedule seems to be unrealistic, and a corrective action plan should be derived before proceeding.

- Between 10 and 20 percent greater than the planned capacity, the master (supply) plan and/or master (supply) schedule is in the gray area, and prior resource behavior (what we know about the resource in question) must determine what is to be done.

For example, if Mary runs the resource in question and it seems that Mary can always get a little bit more out of the resource when push comes to shove, we might go forward with a predicted overload of 20 percent or so. However, if Ernie runs the resource in question and Ernie is known to be very close to the vest on his capacity availability, in other words, if Ernie says he can get you 100 units in a certain period of time, he may be able to get you 101 or 102 and sometimes only 98 or 99, but chances are not good for 103 or more, or it would be a big surprise if only 97 or less were made available.

At this point we can apply the general guidelines to an analysis of the weekly rough cut capacity requirements in July for production lines 1 through 4 (Figure 15.12, page 527). Whereas the aggregate supply plan revealed an underload for lines 1 and 2, at the master (supply) planning and/or master (supply) scheduling level, we observe an expected overload in the first week of July (required capacity versus planned capacity) and underloads in the third and fourth weeks.

Is the overload a reason for changing the master (supply) plan and/or master (supply) schedule? Maybe not, because it is within the 20 percent guideline. Besides, the maximum capacity is 32 hours. Remember, you only want to know if we have a chance to achieve the master (supply) plan and/or master (supply) schedule, not if we will be able to accomplish it in every detail. Of course, in selected environments, such as the process industry, these guidelines most likely need tighter tolerances, say, 5 to 10 percent, or even 2 to 5 percent.

For production line 3, significant underloads are indicated in each week, and for production line 4, an underloaded condition appears in weeks 1 and 2, and overloads in excess of 20 percent in weeks 3 and 4. In fact, required capacity in weeks 3 and 4 greatly exceeds maximum capacity.

Handling Under- and Overloads

Several options exist for dealing with under- and overloads. First, for production lines 1 and 2, it might be possible to move some of the workload from week 1 of July into June or into weeks 3 and 4 of July, where underloads are projected. By looking back at the master plan and/or master schedule (Figure 15.11, p. 526), items B1, B2, and B3 are the candidates for load shifting since they are the only units planned to run during the first week in July. Each 1,000-unit run requires three hours.

Therefore, if we want to balance required and planned capacity, we must either shift 2,000 units of B1, B2, or B3 into another time period or increase the planned capacity or a combination of the two choices. Of course, any discussion of moving out a master (supply) planned and/or master (supply) scheduled item requires consideration of the impact of that move on the ability to meet the customer promise dates.

Analysis of weeks 3 and 4 in July for production line 4 indicates a significant potential overload. What is causing this potential problem, and what can be done about it? To determine the cause of the overload, look back at Figure 15.11 to see which master planned and/or master scheduled items are planned or scheduled to run in weeks 3 and 4.

There we note that items A3, A4, and C2 are scheduled for production. Items A3 and C2, however, do not use production line 4 (Figure 15.11).

Therefore, we need to concern ourselves only with the 10,000 units of A4 scheduled in week 3 and the 12,000 units of A4 scheduled in week 4. What started out to be a potential problem that we may not have even recognized has been reduced to a single master (supply) planned and/or master (supply) scheduled item over a two-week period, further illustrating another payback of the rough cut capacity planning (RCCP) process. Now, the master (supply) planner and/or master (supply) scheduler must determine if load shifting from weeks 3 and 4 to weeks 1 and 2 can be accomplished within the framework of the master (supply) plan and/or master (supply) schedule.

When dealing with the underloaded condition in weeks 3 and 4 in July for production lines 1 and 2, the master (supply) planner and/or master (supply) scheduler may decide to allow the equipment on these production lines to sit idle in weeks 3 and 4 and do productive or preventive maintenance. Another possibility is to plan to move people from one work area to another.

The people who work on production lines 1 through 4 may be people with the same skills, or they could all be people who work on various filling lines and therefore possess similar skills. Perhaps these workers could be moved to production line 4 in weeks 3 and 4, along with a group of operators from line 3, who will be virtually without activities for the entire month.

By using rough cut capacity planning (RCCP) to validate the master plan and/or master schedule, it is possible to validate whether the aggregate supply plan derived during the IBP or S&OP process can be met at the product mix level. This validity check brings us full circle in the RRP and RCCP processes.

Resource Requirements and Rough Cut Capacity Planning Graphs

A picture is worth a thousand words, as the old saying goes! Well, when it comes to resource requirements planning (RRP) in support of integrated business planning (IBP) and rough cut capacity planning (RCCP) in support of master (supply) planning (MSP) and master (supply) scheduling (MSS), this old saying certainly applies. In today's world, leaders, managers, planners, and schedulers want to get and digest information quickly and pictures and graphs relating to a supply chain situation can and does assist them in doing just that, getting and digesting information about the situation quickly.

As an example, a common response from master planning and scheduling professionals regarding a potential delivery issue such as "Demand just doubled their monthly expected sales for our most important customer—What should we now do?" is, "Show me the picture (graph) and I will then decide whether or not I need to look at the numbers in detail."

Technology advancements since the third edition of this book are somewhat *mind-boggling*. And it's *not* the end of those technology advancements; in fact, it's just the beginning! Yes, technology and machines are doing tasks such as creating graphs (and sometimes making decisions based on those graphs) that people in supply chain management have done for years (see Final Thoughts in this book for further discussion regarding the master planning and scheduling profession and where it is going during this decade).

Let's review the discussion that we had in the previous chapter regarding resource requirements planning and rough cut capacity planning. It was stated in that chapter that data and information required for supply management and/or master (supply) planning and/or master (supply) scheduling is either resource requirements planned or rough cut capacity planned using available system technology.

It was also stated that a chart or graph can be used to quickly highlight issues, concerns, problems, and balance. Figures 15.13 and 15.14 are examples of resource requirements plans (sometimes referred to a rough cut capacity plans) for a defined resource (charts and discussion with additional comments that follow the charts is repeated from Chapter 14 for the reader's convenience).

These charts use bars to represent the required capacity to meet the supply plan (shades representing the families that load the resource). The figures also show three lines (demonstrated capacity and planned capacity are overlapping over the entire horizon in Figure 15.13 below and over two-thirds of the horizon in 15.14 on page 531). The two lower lines represent the demonstrated and planned capacity out over time while the top line is the maximum.

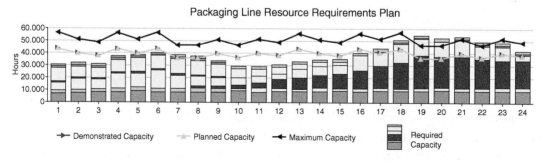

Figure 15.13   Resource Requirements Plan in Support of Integrated Business Planning

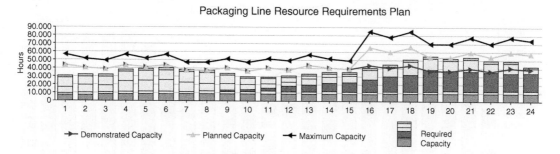

Figure 15.14 Resource Requirements Plan / Rough Cut Capacity Plan at IBP Level

Using this information, one can see in the model in Figure 15.13 that time periods 1–4 are slightly under demonstrated and planned capacity, indicating that they may encounter a utilization or absorption problem in the near term related to that asset. If the model were solely based on labor, the supply or production manager may choose to deploy those resources to other activities (maintenance, clean outs, etc.) or reduce shifts. Time periods 5–8 show required capacity fairly well balanced to demonstrated and planned capacity.

In time periods 9–15, the underloaded projection returns and some decisions may need to be made again to resolve. Time periods 17–18 show that required capacity exceeds the demonstrated and planned capacity but is within the maximum capacity. In time periods 19–22, the required capacity exceeds the maximum capacity and then drops back down. Therefore, if this supply plan is approved as currently written, the company must be able to sustain some form of overtime or flextime above the demonstrated and planned capacity periods 17–24 and must recognize the upcoming problem in time periods 19–22 (remember that these time periods are 16–24 months out from the current planning time period).

So, what does top management and the supply manager do with this information? First of all, the company probably doesn't want to approve this plan without some action plan in place (securing answers to the listed questions):

- Do we move supply plans to fill in the underloaded periods?

- What will be the inventory impact if we move supply?

- Can the company run that much overtime in the outer time periods? What is the cost?

- What will it take to raise to maximum capacity in time periods 18–22?

- When does top management need to make these decisions?

Again, these charts don't solve the problem(s); they just highlight the problem(s). People in today's world (refer to Final Thoughts, pages 783–808, for a discussion on technology

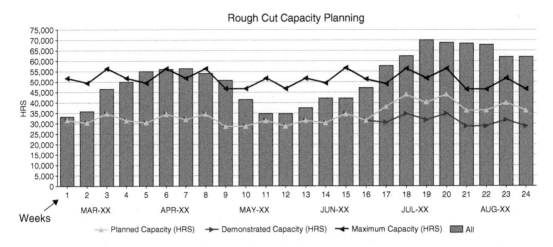

Figure 15.15   Rough Cut Capacity Plan at Master Planning and Scheduling (MPS) Level

advancements and the use of computers/machines/robots in the problem-solving arena) use these types of charts and graphs to solve an identified problem or identified multiple problems.

However, computers/machines/robots continue to be used in making routine decisions and solving minor to intermediate problems. Perhaps a resolution may be to add another shift, starting in time period 16. Figure 15.14 (page 531) shows this addition by the deviation of the planned capacity line from the demonstrated capacity line. The maximum capacity increases accordingly.

However, as one can see, this solves for the required capacity peak but leaves some stranded capacity in months where required capacity does not meet planned capacity. This potential resolution may need to be massaged as time moves closer to the hiring lead time (the potential problem is recognized 16 months in advance instead of 16 days or 16 hours or 16 minutes in advance, as it is in many companies).

Rough cut capacity planning charts and graphs used in supply chain management and master planning and scheduling this decade look very much the same as the charts and graphs used in resource requirements planning. Figure 15.15 is an example of a rough cut capacity plan (graphic format) supporting a master (supply) planning and/or a master (supply) scheduling function or what jointly is referred to as a company's master planning and scheduling (MPS) process.

The differences between the resource requirements planning (RRP) chart in support of integrated business planning (IBP) shown in Figure 15.14 and rough cut capacity planning (RCCP) chart in support of MPS shown in Figure 15.15 are as follows:

- The planning horizon is shorter in rough cut capacity planning than in resource requirements planning.

- In RCCP, time periods are in weeks (possibly days at the beginning of the planning horizon) rather than in months.

- Identified capacity hours are less in RCCP than in RRP due to shorter time periods.

- Required reaction time for changes needed as a result of RCCP is most likely less than the required reaction time for changes needed as a result of RRP.

A best-practice master planning and scheduling process requires that a best-practice rough cut capacity planning process be part of it! And while we're discussing it, charts and graphs displaying capacity data and information is how that data and information must be available (today) for a company's master (supply) planner and/or master (supply) scheduler to do their job effectively. So, what does it mean for a master (supply) planner and/or master (supply) scheduler to do their job effectively? Let's take a look!

Using and Working the Rough Cut Capacity Plan

Now that the method and use of resource requirements planning (RRP) and rough cut capacity planning (RCCP) at the aggregate supply plan, master plan, and master schedule levels has been explained, it is time to look more deeply into the evaluation process. Let's continue our discussion using the RRP and/or RCCP example already developed in this chapter (refer to Figure 15.7 on p. 518).

Going back to the example in Figure 15.7 on page 518, a review of the necessary capacity shows that for production lines 1 and 2, the potential problem is a projected *underload* in July (58 hours required capacity versus 114 planned capacity), August (44 hours required capacity versus 60 planned capacity), and September (44 hours required capacity versus 144 planned capacity). This indicates that the plan is realistic in terms of having *sufficient* resources to satisfy *required supply capacity*, at least at the aggregate level.

The same appears to be true for production lines 3. Line 4 is overloaded by one hour (51 required hours versus a planned capacity of 50 hours) in August. The overload on line 4 is small and well within the maximum capacity of 60 hours, so we will make the assumption that it can be covered by a focused use of limited overtime.

So far, so good! Now consider the next key resource, finishing. Here the situation is tight—1,072 required hours versus 1,140 planned hours in the month of July. If everything goes smoothly, the plan should work. But if anything goes astray or unexpected customer orders roll in the door, the situation could quickly shift from an acceptable condition to an *overload* situation.

There is definite trouble in August—an *overload* of 257 hours above planned capacity, which represents a potential *overload* of approximately 30 percent, and 17 hours above the maximum capacity of 840 hours. In September the finishing work center appears to have sufficient capacity.

Up to this point, only one of four critical or key resources has a potential significant problem—finishing, in August. As the reader can see, this analysis has narrowed down the critical or key resources that are potential obstacles to meeting the aggregate supply plan.

Move down the list of critical or key resources in Figure 15.7 and compare required and planned capacities. Here the capacity planner finds that in-process storage contains no problem for any of the three months. The processing department, however, contains a potential *overload*, again in August; but the adequate capacity in July and September for this resource suggests that some load shift may alleviate the problem.

For the incoming test resource, capacity is marginally adequate for July, but August is *overloaded* by 50 percent. September appears to be in good shape. Material from supplier 100 is more than adequate in all three months, and for supplier 200, material is sufficient for July and September, but marginal for August.

In effect, this exercise has reduced the potential obstacles to meeting the aggregate supply plan from nine critical or key resource areas to four critical or key resource areas. Within those four problematic resources, only three—finishing, processing, and incoming test—represent significant issues, and then only in the month of August. Knowing the locations and depth of these problems makes the search for solutions possible. The example also points out the importance of evaluating resources on at least a monthly basis.

Look at the three-month totals. From a quarterly, aggregate perspective, sufficient resources are available for all critical or key resources. However, the month of August is clearly problematic now, since three resources and one critical or key supplier will be overloaded during that month.

The process thus entails moving from the aggregate to the pegged-detail level as the supply manager, master planner, and/or master scheduler determine that more information is necessary to answer the question, "Do we have a chance of meeting the aggregate supply plan, master (supply) plan, and/or master (supply) schedule as currently written?"

Taking Action as a Result of Resource Requirements Planning and/or Rough Cut Capacity Planning

Once the problem resources have been identified and analyzed as much as possible, the next step is to evaluate potential solutions. First, determine whether action really needs to be taken in August for each of the critical or key resources identified. Recall the general action guidelines stated earlier—the challenge is to have the required capacity equal the planned capacity *within the tolerances* established by such guidelines.

In an out-of-balance situation, there are only three choices of action: (1) modify the supply plan so that required capacity equals planned capacity; (2) adjust the planned capacity to equal required capacity in support of the current supply plan; and (3) do a combination of the two actions just noted. The second option is generally preferable if at all possible. Let's see how this might be achieved to resolve the problems anticipated for August.

Working Capacity Overloaded Situations

Several actions may be taken in order to adjust the planned capacity for each overloaded resource:

- Work overtime or extra shifts.
- Transfer people from underloaded work areas to boost the resources in the overloaded work areas.
- Reroute some of the work to an alternate work center, work cell, or production line if one is available.
- Subcontract all or a portion of the work.
- Hire temporary workers.
- Install more equipment.
- Build a new facility.

Working Capacity Underloaded Situations

As the example in Figure 15.7 on page 518 demonstrates, a number of *underload* situations exist (production lines 1 through 3). These may be undesirable situations, but they also present opportunities to:

- Deploy workers on other lines;

- Conduct education and training sessions;

- Do productive or preventive maintenance on idle equipment and/or housekeeping in idle work areas;

- Reduce shifts and/or overtime;

- Assign production line workers to other functions like design or engineering. The workers can then learn what these functions have in mind as they develop a product. The production line workers can then give engineers ideas and possible solutions to manufacturing-related problems that appear in the company's manufacturing operation (plant, factory, mill, shop);

- Run a promotion to increase demand, thereby increasing required capacity;

- Establish an improvement task force to reduce setup and changeover times.

And the list goes on. Clearly, dealing with underloads, like overloads, requires good communication among marketing, sales, finance, engineering, manufacturing, purchasing, and human resources. Each option must be examined in light of the capacity needed as well as the planned and maximum capacity anticipated to be available.

In the case of the finishing resource, for example, we see that the most capacity that can be expected is 840 hours (maximum capacity). But the required capacity is 857 hours. Therefore, even bringing the finishing resource up to its maximum capacity of 840 hours by moving people from production line 3 would not alleviate an overloaded condition. Moreover, the movement of workers from one work center to another might create negative impacts elsewhere. There generally is *no free lunch*. A key question that always needs to be answered is whether the action to be taken alleviates the original problem and/or creates a new one.

Finessing the Situation with Customers

In addition to looking for possible move-ins and move-outs in the plant, factory, mill, or shop, sales and marketing may find customers willing to receive their orders early or late. A financial incentive may be cost-effective in getting them to accept rescheduled deliveries.

For example, MultiTech, Inc., may be happy to take delivery of a commercial vehicle a month sooner if it is offered an added option or engine upgrade at no additional cost.

Turbo Brothers might be willing to take early delivery of a vehicle from the manufacturer's current inventory without all the features it originally ordered if a special warrantee package is offered. In cases like these, the aggregate supply plan, master supply plan, and/or master supply schedule can be modified by moving some orders forward in the plan and/or schedule and others back.

Lot Splitting

Another alternative is to do a *lot split*. For example, an August run of 10,000 might be split into a run of 5,000 in July and 5,000 in August, thus alleviating a predicted capacity shortage. The master (supply) planner and/or master (supply) scheduler could also plan to ship the product early (if the company's demand organization and the company's customer agree) or hold the early build and then ship the entire lot as planned so the company continues to honor any and all promises made to the customer. Of course, in some industries, the splitting of lots or batches is controlled by product specifications, recipes, and formulations.

When Capacity Cannot Be Adjusted

If the planned capacity for the finishing line cannot be adjusted in August, it may become necessary to modify the aggregate supply plan, master plan, and/or master schedule. This requires asking what the plan and/or schedule hoped to achieve in the first place.

If the plan and/or schedule was trying to build product to satisfy firm customer orders, sales and marketing must decide which customer orders, if any, can get moved out of the problem period. If the plan and/or schedule was devised to satisfy a combination of customer orders and replenish some warehouse stock, sales and marketing must again decide whether the customer or the warehouses take priority.

Perhaps one of the demands in question includes a very large order from a new customer. This customer order may well be a candidate for splitting or moving some of that new customer's requirements into an earlier time period, into a later time period, or a combination of some of the requirements being moved into an earlier time period while the remaining requirement stays in the promised time period or is moved out into a future time period. As was stated, master planning and scheduling is part science and part art. Working the master (supply) plan and/or master (supply) schedule is the *art* piece of the MPS process!

Simulations—Rough Cut Capacity Planning

Sales and marketing have just notified the master (supply) planner and/or master (supply) scheduler that because of an unexpected strike at a competitor's plant, several key changes will take place in the approved supply plan for product family C (Figure 15.16). For product family C, the anticipated demand in July and August will increase from 4,000 to 6,000 units per month. In September, the old, approved supply plan called for 5,000 units, while the new, approved supply plan calls for 10,000.

What will be the impact on the identified critical and/or key resources over and beyond the problems the company is already facing? It should be noted that (assuming the supply organization can favorably respond), the increase in demand has been approved by the company's leadership team!

The new capacity requirements are shown in Figure 15.17 on page 539. As can be seen, the same four critical and/or key resources that were identified earlier as potential problems are affected by this change, but the predicted capacity overloads in August are more severe. Production line 4, which only had a small overload of one hour in August, is now approaching its maximum capacity. In addition, the underloads for finishing and incoming tests in July have now vanished, and an overloaded condition is predicted.

Rough cut capacity planning makes it possible for management to see the impact of the proposed changes very clearly. Additionally, the *"What If"* capability built into RCCP

Month	Family A	Family B	Family C	Family D	Family E
July	30,000	10,000	6,000	3,000	3,000
August	25,000	5,000	6,000	3,000	3,000
September	25,000	5,000	10,000	4,000	3,000
Total	80,000	20,000	22,000	10,000	9,000

Figure 15.16   Modified Supply Plan, Product Family C

Key Resource	Unit of Measure	Month	Family C	Required Capacity	Net Difference	Planned Capacity	Maximum Capacity
Filling Lines 1 & 2	Machine Hours	July		58	56	114	152
		August		44	16	60	80
		September		44	100	144	192
		TOTAL		146	172	318	424
Filling Line 3	Machine Hours	July		57	76	133	171
		August		43	27	70	90
		September		46	122	168	216
		TOTAL		146	225	371	477
Filling Line 4	Machine Hours	July	24	54	41	95	114
		August	24	59	−9	50	60
		September	40	65	55	120	144
		TOTAL	88	168	97	265	318
Finishing Line	Labor Hours	July	288	1,164	−24	1,140	1,596
		August	288	953	−353	600	840
		September	480	1,169	271	1,440	2,016
		TOTAL	1,056	3,286	−106	3,180	4,452
In-Process Storage	Lbs.	July		450,000	690,000	1,140,000	1,140,000
		August		375,000	225,000	600,000	600,000
		September		375,000	1,065,000	1,440,000	1,440,000
		TOTAL		1,200,000	1,980,000	3,180,000	3,180,000
Processing Department	Equipment Hours	July	132	8,241	2,209	10,450	12,350
		August	132	6,916	−1,416	5,500	6,500
		September	220	7,037	6,163	13,200	15,600
		TOTAL	484	22,194	6,956	29,150	34,450
Incoming Test	Labor Hours	July	48	534	−2	532	551
		August	48	469	−189	280	320
		September	80	527	145	672	768
		TOTAL	176	1,530	−46	1,484	1,639
Supplier 100	Lbs.	July	1,290	15,795	29,205	45,000	45,000
		August	1,290	13,545	31,455	45,000	45,000
		September	2,150	14,740	30,260	45,000	45,000
		TOTAL	4,730	44,080	90,920	135,000	135,000
Supplier 200	Cases	July	6,000	13,500	5,500	19,000	23,000
		August	6,000	12,250	−2,250	10,000	12,000
		September	10,000	16,250	7,750	24,000	29,000
		TOTAL	22,000	42,000	11,000	53,000	64,000

Figure 15.17   Revised Rough Cut Capacity Plan

software makes it possible for management to juggle the numbers—shifting workers, rescheduling-in as well as rescheduling-out, splitting lots, and so forth—until the aggregate supply plan becomes realistic, achievable, and the new approved supply plan.

Screen and Report Formats

There are several screen and report formats among current off-the-shelf planning systems. The choice is a matter of preference. A few of the more commonly used formats are discussed here.

Information Displayed Horizontally

In this screen format, the units of time are displayed across the top (e.g., July, August, and September). The left side displays the maximum, planned, and required capacities, followed by the period and cumulative variances (see Figure 15.18). In some software, this arrangement is reversed to display units of time vertically.

Key Resource: Finishing (Hours)

	July	August	September	Total
Maximum Capacity	1,596	840	2,016	4,452
Planned Capacity	1,140	600	1,440	3,180
Required Capacity	1,164	953	1,169	3,286
Difference	−24	−353	271	−106
Cumulative Difference	−24	−377	−106	−106

Figure 15.18 Horizonal Format, Rough Cut Capacity Plan Screen

Key Resource: Finishing (Hours)

	Required Capacity	Planned Capacity	Period Difference	Cumulative Difference	Maximum Capacity
July	1,164	1,140	−24	−24	1,596
August	953	600	−353	−377	840
September	1,169	1,440	271	−106	2,016
Total	−24	−353	−106	−106	4,452

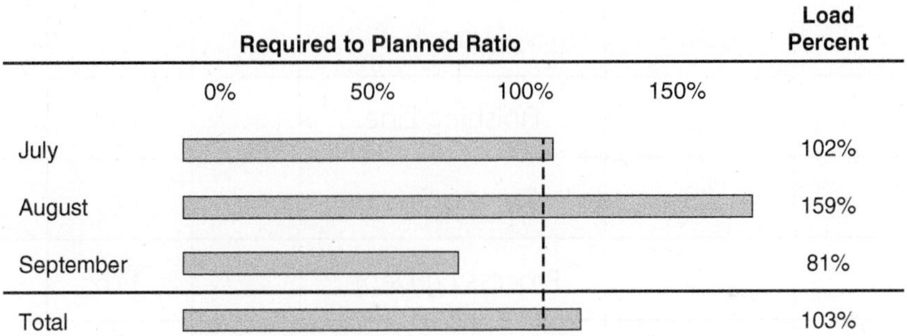

	Required to Planned Ratio				Load Percent
	0%	50%	100%	150%	
July					102%
August					159%
September					81%
Total					103%

Figure 15.19 Combined Tabular and Graphic Screen

Combined Tabular/Graphic Report

A variant of the horizontal and vertical screens includes a graphic representation of the capacity situation. In the sample screen shown in Figure 15.19, an additional column has been included. This provides a graphic view of the required capacity versus the planned capacity for a critical and/or key resource.

Exception Screen

The exception screen shows only the problematic work locations, work centers, or production lines (see Figure 15.20 on page 542). It is useful for highlighting underloads and overloads. The middle of the screen lists the critical and/or key resources that have an exception to parameters entered by the user. This means that the user defines an underload or overload condition in its own terms. This is done by setting target levels for underloads (e.g., less than 60 percent loaded) and overloads (e.g., greater than 120 percent loaded).

Underload Indicators Percent: 60			Key Resource	Overload Indicators Percent: 120		
July	August	September		July	August	September
51		31	Lines 1 & 2			
43		27	Line 3			
57		54	Line 4			
			Finishing Line		159	
39		26	In-Process Storage			
		53	Processing Dept.		126	
			Incoming Test		168	
35	30	33	Supplier 100			
			Supplier 200		123	

Figure 15.20   Rough Cut Capacity Plan Exception Screen

The left side of the screen shows the potential underloads, represented by periods of time (weeks, months, quarters, etc.). When a load ratio is shown in any column, it indicates that the required capacity is less than 60 percent of the planned capacity (the target level of the minimum capacity chosen for this example). Again, the target percentages are determined by the company's master planning and scheduling system user.

Overloads are represented on the right side of the screen. When a load ratio is shown in any column, the critical and/or key resource is projected to require capacity in excess of 120 percent of the planned capacity and therefore is considered in an overloaded condition. (Again, 120 percent was arbitrarily chosen for this example.)

Rough Cut Capacity Planning at a Process Company (Industry Example)

Rough cut capacity planning is a process used by all Class A companies to test the validity and feasibility of their master (supply) plan as well as their master (supply) schedule. Additionally, resource requirements planning system logic (again, sometimes referred to as rough cut capacity planning at the integrated business planning level) is used to test the validity and feasibility of the aggregate supply plan before releasing an approved supply plan to the master (supply) planning and/or master (supply) scheduling organization for further detail and refinement (volume to mix, months to weeks, longer-planning horizon to shorter-planning horizon).

Only Organic Options, known as O-Cubed in the food industry, is working on bringing its current integrated business planning, master (supply) planning, and master (supply) scheduling processes up to Class A standards. Currently, O-Cubed has a Class A demand and supply process but falls short in their product management (new products), integrated reconciliation, and management business review process in order to be certified Class A in integrated business planning.

However, O-Cubed uses rough cut capacity planning extremely well during their demand and supply balancing process. Let's take a look at their story in the past, currently in the present, and planned for the future.

O-CUBED GETS IT DONE AND GETS IT DONE FAST; THE FOOD INDUSTRY REQUIRES FRESHNESS IN DELIVERY AND QUALITY

Prior to partnering with Oliver Wight, we thought we were cross-functional and had integrated processes, but in reality, we all stood behind our departmental walls and rarely looked outside to others for input. In fact, each department had their own interpretation of how the weekly *demand forecast* was going to be consumed. We used the term *demand forecast*, as opposed to *demand plan*, given that there wasn't much *demand planning* used to generate the *demand forecast*. Some groups considered the prior rolling 6 weeks as the new trend; some groups used the prior 13 weeks.

We just didn't have a standard or universal approach. We lacked one source of truth, one clear signal from the demand side of the house to the supply side as to what was needed for execution. We actually had a process where we constrained or locked next week's forecast each Thursday and then when demand materialized differently than expected, we were often not prepared to cover customer orders, or were late to cover those customer orders. This led to customer order shortages that resulted in artificial demand being added to the demand forecast, knowing that it would never materialize, which finally ended without any control of disposals . . . the perfect storm!

One area we did excel at was our ability to firefight today's and tomorrow's issues, as this was all we knew (which seems logical, given our lack of forward planning), but it was exhausting. A lot of finger pointing and fighting between departments, providing little to no value, little to no corrective action or root cause analysis, resulting in processes being developed that didn't address the real problem or correct the problem.

The processes we created were often *Band-Aids* to larger issues, thus referred to as *workarounds*. Enter the Oliver Wight team to assess our planning/execution/performance, after which we received a Class D mark . . . humbling to say the least, but at least we knew where we needed to focus and had a road map of how to achieve business excellence.

We then created (after the initial proven path lead phase work) a high-level design of the work needing to be done to correct our sins and rebuild our foundation; the leadership team excitedly approved the request . . . time to go to work! We developed demand, supply, and master scheduling teams and began our journey.

Within a few months we worked through the task lists, creating a sustainable planning process that generated conversation and began to shift the focus to the future as opposed to the historical. Historical performance is important, but it can only be an input to generating the future plan. Now, we're ready to kick off our first attempt at real demand and supply reviews. It was a lot of work, but the teams were engaged and mostly had a vested interest in a change for the better. . . . I say mostly because change is difficult, and it took a while to break the old mantra of "we've always done it that way!"

We now have Class A functioning demand and supply reviews that are assumption- and scenario-driven to ensure we're communicating the best possible, single set of numbers to our business partners. Assumptions and scenarios are vetted by cross-functional groups to ensure they qualify as such (not all assumptions can be the basis for a good plan) and while we're always looking to improve in these reviews, our primary focus has shifted to developing product management reviews and improving our integrated reconciliation and management business reviews.

To anyone considering this journey, I would suggest developing all five of the reviews at the same time, as piecing them together can be quite frustrating. Think of a baseball team that requires nine players to be on the field at the same time and how ineffective it would be to take the field with six players, or how frustrating it would be to have all nine players on the field at the same time, each with a different strategy or set of rules.

In the six-player example, those who are playing must carry the load of the missing three players in order to compete, and in the latter example, a team cannot be successful if they're not all playing the same game. It is to be noted that Oliver Wight suggested that our company implement a complete sales and operations process including all five reviews at the same time; unfortunately, functional management running the new product and finance departments at the time decided to go down a slightly different path (which might be one reason we are now working on bringing those functions into the integrated business planning process).

Focusing more specifically on supply planning and rough cut capacity planning, we historically only looked at equipment capacity at the weekly level, for peak or holiday rush periods, during our annual budgeting process. Picture a massive Excel spreadsheet, broken down into stock-keeping units/resource level, each combination with varying throughputs, all to see how taxed the manufacturing facilities were a few weeks of the year. While the spreadsheet tool was powerful, it was cumbersome to first jump straight to the production floor, without first doing any aggregate-based analysis.

I'll never forget a comment made to me by the Oliver Wight team early on, stating, "no amount of detailed planning can correct an error/problem at the aggregate level." Conversely, we can't only stay at the aggregate level, either; it's simply the best place to start. But then we continue to get more granular, confirming that we can meet our supply plan until we reach our lowest level of planning (hours/day).

But what about our other resources, specifically our most sought-after commodities? With commodities, we historically looked no further out than four months, with a deep focus on the next three weeks. It was then that we recognized an opportunity to start looking at our business through a different lens.

In a highly perishable, fresh food industry, a 24-month forward-looking plan at first seemed out of touch . . . almost absurd. But quickly, we discovered that there is a place for the 24-month horizon and that place is the monthly supply review. This is where we'll evaluate an individual facility's total equipment capacity used/available to then make decisions on capital expenditures for facility expansion, adding on incremental production lines, moving volume either in or out of network (co-pack), or maybe, worst case, delaying or moving demand. This analysis is conducted at the product family level as our critical resources are directly tied to banks of like equipment—bagger bank A is tied to product family 1, bagger bank B is tied to product family 2, and so on (see Figure 15.21 on page 546).

In the example shown in Figure 15.21, we're looking at the rough cut capacity plan for product family A packaging lines. We've identified the assumptions behind our demonstrated, planned, and maximum capacity (spikes tied to our financial calendar).

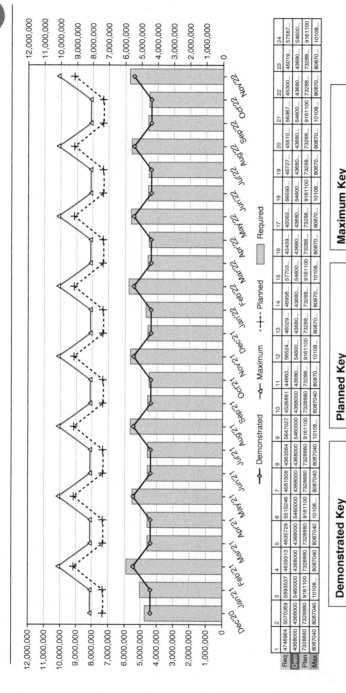

Figure 15.21 Processed Foods Resource Requirements Plan (sometimes referred to as Rough Cut Capacity Plan)

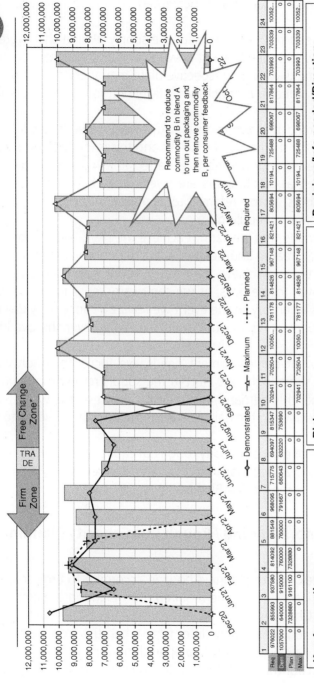

Commodity 'B' Scenario: Do we consider a BOM change to Blend 'A'?

Recommend to reduce commodity B in blend A to run out packaging and then remove commodity B, per consumer feedback

	1	2	3	4	5	6	7	8	9	10	11	12	13	14	15	16	17	18	19	20	21	22	23	24
Req	976022	855993	937580	814092	881549	968095	715775	694097	815347	702941	702504	10050...	781178	814826	967148	821421	805694	10194...	725488	698067	817864	703993	703339	10052...
Dem	1057000	640000	915000	760000	760000	791667	680643	632220	753690															
Plan	0	7328880	9161100	7328880	7328880	0	0	0	0	702941	732504	10050...	781177	814826	967148	821421	805694	10194...	725488	698067	817864	703993	703339	10052...
Max						0	0	0	0	0	0	0	0	0	0	0	0	0	0	0	0	0	0	0

◇ Demonstrated —△— Maximum —+— Planned ▓ Required

Key Assumptions:
- Demonstrated is contracted lbs w/o PPV.
- Planned includes open market purchases...no PPV projected.
- Max identifies periods without contracted volumes.
- Historically, June – August require open market purchases resulting in PPV due to transition between growing areas and insect pressures.
- Projecting shortages April '21 – August '21.
- Consumers have advised that reduced amounts of commodity D could be an improvement to the item.
- This commodity is most costly item in this blend.
- 3% margin improvement by reducing/removing commodity B.

Risks:
- Shortages to Blend 'A' resulting in lost sales and/or lost customers.
  - Apr 21: 122k lbs
  - May 21: 176k lbs
  - June 21: 56k lbs
  - July 21: 62k lbs
  - Aug 21: 62k lbs
- PPV to cover above shortages could exceed $1mm of unplanned expense
- If we eliminate commodity B in blend A we will have to change packaging...currently have packaging inventory through Aug '21 (we can however reduce amount and use current packaging)

Decisions/Info needed/Direction:
- Do we have budgeted contigency to cover unplanned expense of $1mm to cover shortages?
- What is the probability that historical events reducing available supply will occur again this year?
- Should we consider reducing amount of commodity B in blend A to eliminate risk of lost sales/customers through contracted periods and then reduce future contract volumes to eliminate future risk and cost to blend B?

Figure 15.22 Scenario Planning Including Recommendations

We, however, refer to our *planned capacity* as a percentage of our overall capacity as opposed to *flex capacity*.

Once we've reviewed and agreed that we can meet the supply plan at the aggregate/monthly level in the supply review, we then break it down a level and evaluate the weekly needs in our tactical weekly meetings with the respective plant managers, focusing on the next 26–52 weeks. This review is still at a product family level (authors' note—referred to as master supply planning).

Once we've reviewed and agreed that we can meet the weekly needs, we'll break it down and review the daily needs for the next three weeks and this is the first review at the stock-keeping-unit and bagger levels (authors' note—referred to as master supply scheduling). Lastly, we look to ensure that our baggers are level-loaded based on number of hours they can run per day (authors' note—referred to as master supply scheduling and the beginning of detailed production scheduling).

If during the analysis we determine that we cannot achieve the plan, we'll make adjustments, then verify that we haven't created another problem at a prior level (we plan down, replan up until we've confirmed we can achieve the plan). Given the perishable nature of our business, we have to get down to the days, as we can't carry more than one to one and a half days of finished goods inventory. In the event we realize a capacity by day issue, we lean on another manufacturing facility in our network to help cover the overloaded condition.

Once we complete the review of our equipment needs, we focus on rough cutting our raw commodities, using the same logic. We start in the supply review evaluating the aggregate needs to meet the monthly demand and then go down to the week level in weekly tactical meetings, finally reviewing the daily needs for the next three weeks to meet the required supply levels.

Let's look at an example of one of our commodity rough cut capacity plans (Figure 15.22 on page 547). Here, we are looking at a scenario to cover an extended supply shortage in one of our most popular blends . . . we'll call it Blend A.

Using Resource Requirements Planning / Rough Cut Capacity Planning Data and Information

First, a little background. We break up our planning horizon according to firm, trade, and free zones. The firm zone identifies the lead time required from planting the crop until it arrives at the processing facility. Changes inside this firm zone can be the most risky and costly to the business should the required supply differ from when the crop was planted. The trade zone adds on the time needed for ground preparation to the growing time, and changes here can typically be accounted for with little to no cost or risk. Finally, there is the free (change) zone where changes can occur without concern to the business, so long as they are within our business strategy (strategy is determined in monthly management business review).

Then we have our demonstrated, planned, and maximum capacity. In our world, *demonstrated capacity* refers to the amount of product we contracted for prior to being in the respective firm zone. Demonstrated capacity above or below the required supply can be caused by a myriad of events including, but not limited to, weather events, crop disease, insect pressures, or changes to required supply triggered by a demand change.

Then, we use planned capacity to identify changes to our available supply that can include the aforementioned events, as well as increased supply due to open market/field purchases. Finally, we use maximum capacity to identify time periods we haven't yet contracted for, and these time periods are set to equal the required supply each month until the contracts are written.

Next, we have the key assumptions, risks, opportunities, and decisions/information needed/direction boxes (information and data included on supply charts). These information and data boxes are the foundation of our chart visuals (we use them on nearly every chart visual). They paint the picture and drive the conversation.

For example, in the scenario shown in the chart (Figure 15.22 on page 547), we've recognized a shortage of supply without a current plan to correct the situation. However, after participating in the rest of the monthly reviews, I learned a little more about a few key pieces of information that I'm now using to support our recommendation.

First, in the product management review, I learned that consumers actually would prefer that Blend A had less of commodity B. I then learned in the demand review that Blend B's sales aren't growing at their previous rates, and sales has concerns that this could result in a gap in our demand plan should this slowdown continue at its current rate.

In preparation for the supply review, we recognized the shortfall so, working with the procurement and finance teams, we determined that we could probably buy raw materials on the open market to cover the shortage, but it would be costly, as this commodity is the most expensive component in Blend A. All signs were pointing to a bill-of-material (BOM) change to reduce or eliminate commodity B, but I had to make sure that we weren't at risk of incurring a packaging write-off by changing the BOM, as completely eliminating the item from the blend would violate marketing/nutrition callouts on the bag.

Sure enough, we have packaging inventory to cover us into August (remember, Blend A sales are softening) but we can still alter the BOM and be compliant with packaging regulations. *Perfect!*

We'll propose to alter the BOM, avoid a packaging write-off, avoid lost sales/customers because we'll now have the supply to cover the shortages, avoid the unplanned cost of buying commodity B to fill the gap, and be more profitable on the item because we'll no longer require as much supply.

Authors' note: O-Cubed's integrated business planning process, including each monthly review, contributed to the director of planning's recommendation, which it looks like will yield several benefits, the subject of the next section in this chapter.

Rough cut scenario planning is one of the most rewarding aspects of supply planning. It brings out the creativity of the team and can be highly effective, so long as there is enough due diligence behind the recommendation. Invest the time in monthly reviews and offline meetings, gathering the information and data, and be sure to ask questions and get input from others along the way so that when you come to the table with a recommendation, you already have the backing from your coworkers (reader suggestion from O-Cubed team). It's a process and takes time to polish, but the payoff is worth it.

So, what's next for O-Cubed? Earlier in the story, I mentioned that we started the integrated business planning (sometimes referred to as the sales and operations planning process), focusing on only two of the five monthly reviews. Seeing the benefits, we (as a company) have realized in the demand and supply reviews that the business is eager to realize the full potential of the remainder of the integrated business planning process; so, we're now focusing on developing and strengthening our product management, integrated reconciliation, and management business reviews. This doesn't mean that we can't improve on demand and supply reviews; it means that there's only so far we can go in those reviews without having the rest of the process fully functioning.

Then, there's tool enhancement/implementation, as we're largely dependent on Excel, which, while powerful, has limitations when it comes to full integration and expedient decision-making. It is, however, a challenge to identify what tools you need when you don't fully grasp all the needs or requirements of the business when we haven't developed the business processes to support a best-in-class tool. If there's one thing I've learned along this journey, it's that patience is vital and being too quick to make a strategic decision can often lead to large/significant mistakes!

Using best-practice rough cut capacity planning processes and techniques requires education, awareness, dedication, integrity, commitment, and training to do it right the first time! O-Cubed now recognizes this and is well on our way to being certified as a Class A company in integrated business planning as well as in master planning and scheduling. The leadership and management team at Only Organic Options hopes that the reader enjoyed reading how its company uses rough cut capacity planning along with scenario planning and change recommendations on a regular basis (monthly in our integrated business planning process, weekly in our tactical master planning and scheduling process, and daily in our operational production scheduling process).

As stated in the story, O-Cubed also does detailed capacity requirements planning once the company's corporate master (supply) plan and its plants' master (supply) schedules have been released. For a more detailed discussion on capacity requirements planning (CRP), refer to the Oliver Wight Series book entitled *Gaining Control: Capacity Management and Scheduling.*[2]

Note: The O-Cubed story is a real story told and written for the authors by Only Organic Options' (company name has been changed) director of planning and contract manufacturing with an objective of serving as an example of how one company effectively uses rough cut capacity planning and master planning and scheduling.

The Benefits and Limitations of Rough Cut Capacity Planning

Like all tools, rough cut capacity planning (RCCP) provides benefits to the user in particular situations. But again like all tools, its very design limits those situations for which it is appropriate. Let's take a look at some of those benefits followed by some limitations of the process being discussed, that of rough cut capacity planning.

Benefits

One of the major benefits of resource requirements planning (RRP) and rough cut capacity planning (RCCP) is that master (supply) planners and/or master (supply) schedulers do not need a detail routing for every item in the plan and/or schedule. This is what makes RRP and RCCP simple and quick tools to use.

In contrast, detail capacity requirements planning (CRP) requires master planning and scheduling (MPS), material requirements planning (MRP), inventory record control (IRC), bills-of-material (BOM), detail process routings (DPR), and detailed production scheduling (DPS). In addition, CRP requires a high degree of accuracy in bills-of-material, detail routings, and inventory records. Only then can accurate, detail capacity planning be done.

On the average, RRP and RCCP can be productively used in as few as 15 to 30 days after implementing an integrated business planning and master planning and scheduling system respectively. In the standard implementation scheme, CRP is not generally effective until 12 to 15 months after the manufacturing resource planning (the supply part of enterprise resource planning) implementation is commenced.

---

[2] For a detailed discussion on CRP, see James G. Correll and Kevin Herbert, *Gaining Control: Capacity Management and Scheduling* (Hoboken, NJ: John Wiley & Sons, 2006).

A related benefit is that RRP and RCCP can be run as often as needed prior to execution of the aggregate supply plan, master (supply) plan, and/or master (supply) schedule. Because it requires minimal computer time (relative to CRP), it is a better simulation tool than capacity requirements planning (CRP), although its output is more of a shadow of reality owing to its use of only critical or key (as technology continues to improve and computer speeds continue to increase, this is less of a benefit than it was a decade or two ago).

Simulations possible with resource requirements planning cover scenarios such as the effect of changing aggregate demand plans to meet financial objectives or changing aggregate supply plans to meet intermediate- to long-term inventory projections. Simulations with rough cut capacity planning cover scenarios such as the effect of changing the mix of expected demand, the booking of a large order, or the shifting of replenishment orders either in or out on the planning horizon.

Since RRP and RCCP are simple simulation tools, you can use them to test the impact of proposed actions before putting those actions into practice. Rough cut capacity planning also allows the master planner and/or master scheduler to test the proposed master (supply) plan and/or master (supply) schedule, if necessary, before obtaining more detail via detailed material requirements planning (MRP) and capacity requirements planning (CRP). Figure 15.23 illustrates the differences between RRP, RCCP, and CRP.

Limitations

It is important to bear in mind that resource profiles are based on representative products for an entire family. Incoming orders, however, may not exactly fit the predicted mix, causing discrepancies between aggregate and detail planning. Also, the manner in which setup time is handled may affect load predictions in various ways.

For instance, suppose that a particular machine requires eight hours for setup, and the rough cut resource profile assumes runs of 10,000 pieces. If it turns out that only 100 units of one product line are actually run, the rough cut assessment may be invalid. The reason for this is that the setup time (say, 8 hours) either is assumed to be required for any run quantity or it has been divided by the expected run quantity to establish the setup time per unit. Thus, suppose you plan to run 100 units. What's the setup time required? Is it 4.8 minutes (8 hours multiplied by 60 minutes multiplied by 100 units divided by the 10,000-unit lot size), or is it 8 hours (the setup time per lot)? Someone must make a decision.

Another limitation of rough cut capacity planning is that it ignores work-in-process and work completed. This negates its value as a short-term planning tool—where these balances matter—and limits it to an intermediate- and long-range planning tool. To understand this fully, let us review the logic of RCCP.

	RRP	RCCP	CRP
What	Projected Gross Capacity Requirements for Key Resource Groups	Projected Gross Capacity Requirements for Key Resources	Projected Net Capacity Requirements for Each Work Center
How	Explode IBP Supply Plan Through Resource Profiles	Explode Master Plan or Master Schedule Through Resource Profiles	Explode MPS and MRP Planned Orders Through Detailed Routings: Combine with Current WIP Status from Shop Floor Control
When	As Required for Simulation	As Required for Simulation	Annual & Quarterly Budget Development; Weekly, Monthly
Why	1. Pre-MPS Evaluation of Supply Plan 2. Intermediate to Long-Range Planning	1. Pre-MRP Evaluation of Master Plan and/ or Master Schedule 2. Short to Intermediate-Range Planning	1. Post-MRP Detailed Analysis 2. Periodic Check of All Work Centers
Precision	Aggregate or Gross — Key Resources Only	Aggregate or Gross — Key Resources Only	Detailed — Considers Inventory, Lot Sizing, WIP Completions, Work Center Lead Times — Voluminous Data
Complexity	Less Than RCCP	Much Less Than CRP	Usually Exceeds MRP
Planning Horizon	Integrated Business Planning Limits	Master Plan and/or Master Schedule Limits	MRP Horizon Less Lead-Time Offsetting
Implementation	Short (Manual or Spreadsheet at First)	Short (Manual or Spreadsheet at First)	Requires Work Centers, Routing, MPS, MRP, and WIP Status from SFC

Figure 15.23 Differences Between Resource Requirements Planning, Rough Cut Capacity Planning, and Capacity Requirements Planning

The logic starts by exploding the aggregate supply plan, master (supply) plan, or master (supply) schedule through the resource profile to determine the required capacity. The results of this explosion are compared to the planned capacity, and from this comparison an action plan to move forward is created. At no time during this process does RCCP look at the work-in-process or at what work is or was completed. This work-in-process netting does not take place until material requirements planning, capacity requirements planning, and detailed production scheduling or shop floor control systems are run (refer to Chapter 2's discussion of closed-loop enterprise resource planning). Thus, rough cut capacity planning (RCCP) data is often invalid in the short term. It is not useful in planning for this week's production; its eyes are on the future.

Finally, RCCP is limited by the fact that it considers only critical or key resources. Actual building of a product, however, requires the resources in all work centers. It is in this sense that RCCP is limited to answering the following questions:

1. Do we have a chance to meet the aggregate supply plan as currently written?

2. Do we have a chance to meet the master supply plan as currently written?

3. Do we have a chance to meet the master supply schedule as currently written?

Thus, execution of an approved supply plan, master (supply) plan, and master (supply) schedule are always vulnerable to contingencies not highlighted during the rough-cut process. Rough cut capacity planning is targeted at being simple and getting information to the user (supply owner, supply leader, master planner, master scheduler) quickly!

Implementing the Rough Cut Capacity Planning Process

Unlike most other manufacturing processes, techniques, and systems, rough cut capacity planning (RCCP) does *not* generally require a lengthy cost justification, a large budget, a full project team, or a major educational and training effort. As mentioned earlier, for products with simple bills-of-materials and steady mixes, a laptop computer using a spreadsheet, a smartphone with spreadsheet capability, or even a number 2 pencil with a piece of paper, and the steps outlined in this chapter are enough to do the rough cut capacity planning job. Those steps can be summarized as follows:

1. Identify the key resources using the resource matrix.

2. Develop resource profiles for the critical or key resources using the best times and standards available.

3. Get supply plan numbers from the integrated business planning (IBP) or sales and operations planning (S&OP) process, master (supply) plan from the master (supply) planner, and the master (supply) schedule from the master (supply) scheduler.

4. Calculate the required capacity by exploding the aggregate supply (production) plan, master (supply) plan, and/or the master (supply) schedule through the appropriate product resource profiles.

5. Compare required capacity and planned capacity.

6. Identify the potential over- and underloads by time period.

7. If necessary, identify alternatives that balance the required capacity and the planned capacity.

8. Determine the best course of action and implement solutions by either increasing/decreasing the planned capacity or increasing/decreasing the supply (production) plan, master (supply) plan, and/or master (supply) schedule.

The payback from following these steps can be immense in terms of better supply plans and schedules and a more refined supply planning process. The reader would be hard pressed to find many, if any, Class A companies that do not use some form of detail in their rough cut capacity planning efforts. However, this detail is then presented to the supply chain user in graphic formats—a picture is worth a thousand words is the old saying!

Closing Comments Regarding Resource Requirements Planning and Rough Cut Capacity Planning

Remember the time-honored expression KISS (Keep It Simple, Stupid!). This should be the supply's vice president, supply director's, supply manager's, master (supply) planner's, and master (supply) scheduler's motto when designing a rough cut capacity planning

(RCCP) system and deciding what to rough cut capacity plan. Every company needs to do some form of rough cut capacity planning at the aggregate supply plan level before converting that aggregate supply plan into a master (supply) plan and/or master (supply) schedule.

But is this enough to proceed with detail material and capacity planning? The answer is simple: If you do not require RCCP beyond the aggregate supply (production) plan level, *don't* do it. There is no reason to rough cut capacity plan at a detail level just to put numbers on a screen or a piece of paper. A general guideline when using RCCP is expressed with one word: *simplify*! Remember, the idea is to look only for information necessary for making quick, informed decisions.

The Pareto Principle tells us that 80 percent of our results typically come from just 20 percent of our efforts. This is a rule of thumb that has proven its value in many fields. With respect to detailed capacity requirements planning, the Pareto Principle explains why a small number of critical or key resources can be used to predict large-scale outcomes, and it is used to reduce the number of constraints in a supply chain management system to just a small number of problems.

If a critical or key work location, work center, or production line represents a problem, the supply owner, supply leader, master planner, and/or master scheduler need to take another step—identify what makes it a problem. Perhaps there are several reasons for a particular work location, work center, or production line being a constraint or bottleneck—the equipment, the suppliers, the operators, and so forth.

Now ask which of these several reasons would yield the highest benefit if it were eliminated. Equipment overheating might represent 80 percent of the problem in this particular work location, work center, or production line; eliminating overheating as a problem through productive or preventive maintenance would represent the most efficient course of action to take. Using the Pareto technique in this way helps managers, master (supply) planners, and master (supply) schedulers to refine their analysis of critical and/or key resources and to improve the predictive value of the rough cut capacity planning system.

Since enterprise resource planning (ERP) requires a realistic aggregate supply plan as a starting point, Class A ERP companies use RCCP simulation tools to assist in creating valid and realistic supply (production) plans. Since the manufacturing part of ERP begins with the aggregate supply plan, that plan must be valid and realistic. Rough cut capacity planning allows companies to sanity check their aggregate supply plans and master (supply) plans as well as their master (supply) schedules and, consequently, get the very most out of their ERP system.

Aggregate supply plans, master (supply) plans, master (supply) schedules, and detailed manufacturing (production) schedules are only half of the equation—the supply half. In order for ERP and MPS to work well in a company, the other side of the equation—demand—must also be addressed. Chapters 16 and 17 address these important integrated processes. While these next two chapters concentrate on supply and demand management, the reader is reminded that new product and product management also play key roles in a company's strategic and tactical planning process (review Chapters 11 and 14 for a brief discussion regarding new product and product management).

The next chapter will give the reader a flavor of aggregate supply planning and management as viewed through the perspective of master planning and scheduling (MPS). Since ERP is an integrated demand-driven (supply) planning process, the MPS process is very dependent upon the demand and supply management activities. The better these demand and supply activities are done, the better the master planning and scheduling process will be done and there's a better chance that the company is or will be operating in or at a Class A level.

16

Supply Management and Aggregate Master Planning

Don't change the plan and/or schedule faster than the real world can respond.

Imagine a company that manufactures two families of computer equipment, Quantum and Phaser. Lightning Computer Company has hundreds of suppliers and thousands of customers in different parts of the world. Its six assembly plants are located on three continents.

While corporate has a couple of master (supply) planners requesting production volumes (approved through the integrated business planning [IBP] or sales and operations planning [S&OP] process) from each of its six plants, each of the plants has a master (supply) scheduler whose responsibilities include balancing the planned supply of material and capacity with anticipated customer and stock orders expected to come into the plant. If Lightning Computer is well managed, it is because someone above the plant level has taken responsibility for understanding overall demand for the company's different computers and has optimized the way in which that demand will be satisfied.

Lightning Computer Company has two Asian assembly plants, one in Malaysia and another in Taiwan. These plants are near some important component suppliers but are far away from others. The Asian plants are the company's newest and most productive, but the fact that most of their finished goods must be shipped to North America and Europe offsets part of their cost-effectiveness.

Of the company's other four assembly plants, two are in the United States (specifically, California and Colorado), one is in Canada, and the other is in Spain; these are much closer to the majority of customers but are less cost-efficient assemblers. Despite these drawbacks, the non-Asian plants score slightly better on quality ratings and are better suited to building most members of the Quantum and Phaser product families. The Malaysian plant is new and qualified to build only one of the Quantum and one of the Phaser computers, products that can be built in other plants as well; the Taiwan plant can build only one Quantum and one Phaser computer and is the *only* plant capable of doing so.

Since this company normally builds and ships several thousand computers each month, optimizing its production through the six different plants really pays off at the bottom line. As a result, someone must be proactive in making a number of difficult decisions about how work will be assigned.

Previous chapters of this book have presented the subject of master planning and scheduling through the eyes of the corporate-level supply planner/scheduler as well as the plant-level supply planner/scheduler. These individuals most likely must support manufacturing of several products utilizing the capacity of one or more production lines. So, let's raise our sights a notch from the plant level to the regional or corporate level.

Here, we find that some individual (or individuals) must take responsibility for balancing demand and supply at a more aggregate level than the plant level master (supply) scheduler, but with more detail than the supply executive works with at the IBP or S&OP level. We will call this individual the supply manager or the master (supply) planner.[1] Generally, in today's world, the supply manager or master (supply) planner does not schedule any of the various plants; instead, he or she *requests* certain types and quantities of products to be built in order to meet anticipated demand.

The master planning and scheduling process that relies on site master (supply) planners/schedulers is changing (during the writing of this book revision) in larger manufacturing operations. The master planning and scheduling process that will be used more and more this decade is sometimes referred to as end-to-end (E2E) planning (see this book's Final Thoughts for a discussion regarding end-to-end planning and the future of the master planning and scheduling process as well as that of the master planning and scheduling profession as we move through the third decade of the twenty-first century).

To appreciate the role of the supply manager and/or master (supply) planner, let's revisit the top portion of the enterprise resource planning chart (Figure 16.1 on page 561), introduced earlier in the book as Figure 2.7 (page 41). The relationships between corporate-wide IBP or S&OP, demand management, supply management, and master planning and scheduling are shown to be highly integrated. Resource requirements planning and rough cut capacity planning are also important processes used in support of these functions.

---

[1] The size of the company, the number of businesses, the number of plants, plant locations, the number of products, and the like are variables that need to be considered when creating the supply management and/or master (supply) planning function. This function consists of one or more individuals.

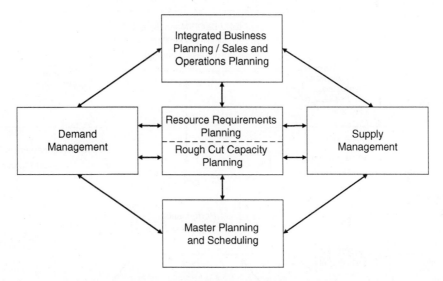

Figure 16.1   Enterprise Resource Planning Coupling Supply Management with Master Planning

The ball begins rolling during the corporate IBP or S&OP process.[2] Anticipated demand (usually referred to as the sales forecast) over a horizon of 24 (plus) months, along with plans and actions to achieve that demand, is reviewed and approved by corporate leaders and managers. This anticipated demand is described in aggregate terms—that is, volume of expected sales bookings and/or shipments per month by product family. However, when it comes to multiple business units and multiple plants, the IBP or S&OP process takes on a different posture (Figure 16.2 on page 562).

The goal of IBP or S&OP in a multi-business/multi-plant environment is to balance corporate-wide demand—which may originate on several continents as well as from new products or new product variations—with the production capability and capacity of the enterprise and to assign manufacturing responsibility to the various plants within the enterprise. A product plan for new product launches, existing product renovations and product discontinuations for each month of the planning horizon is created, and the vice president of marketing (the product management review owner, accountable for the overall product portfolio plans) is assigned accountability for developing and communicating the portfolio plans, including assumptions and information required to develop corresponding demand and supply plans.

---

[2] The reader may wish to review integrated business planning (IBP), which was covered in Chapter 14.

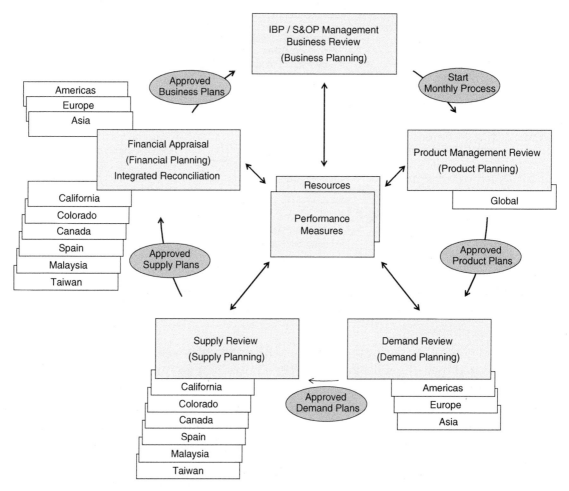

Figure 16.2   Integrated Business Planning—Lightning Computer Company

A sales plan for each product family for each month of the planning horizon is created, and the vice president of sales (demand review owner, accountable for the overall demand plans) is assigned accountability for selling that number of units. Likewise, a supply plan for each product family is created covering the same planning horizon, and the vice president of manufacturing (supply review owner, accountable for the overall supply plans) takes accountability for producing or purchasing that number of units.

The job and responsibility of the supply manager and/or master planner is to make sure that the approved demand plan is satisfied with product and the approved supply plan is optimally assigned to the different manufacturing facilities. Additionally, the supply manager and/or master (supply) planner monitors projected inventory and backlogs to ensure that neither gets out of IBP or S&OP approved tolerances. Thus, the supply manager or master (supply) planner acts as a corporate-level balancer of product, demand, and supply using many of the same techniques used by the plant-level master (supply) schedulers (key difference is that supply managers generally work at an aggregate level, master (supply) planners work at both an aggregate as well as a detailed level, and master (supply) schedulers work at a somewhat detailed level).

A properly educated and trained supply manager and/or master (supply) planner is practically indispensable in a multi-business/multi-plant company. This person (or people) must understand the importance of customer service, the productive capacities of the company's different plants, their relative production efficiencies and effectiveness, output quality to the customer, lead times to get things done, and the ability of individual plants to deliver on their promises. Given this knowledge, a competent supply manager and/or master (supply) planner (assisted by the demand organization's demand manager and/or demand planner) can do the following things:

- Create sufficient supply (production as well as purchased) volume to meet corporate-wide demand;

- Optimize product manufacturing across all plants;

- Ensure that product build requests only go to plants that have the capability and capacity to build those products;

- Plan inventory stocking levels while taking logistics issues into account;

- Reduce backlogs and thereby reduce delivery lead times to the customer;

- Reschedule production among the plants as problems occur;

- Consult with the demand manager on customer priorities and allocation issues.

In the absence of centralized supply management, a multi-plant company runs these risks:

- Some plants being idle while others are buried under backlogs (some backlog being back orders) and running three shifts per day;

- Being out of stock on some items and overstocked on others;

- Requesting work from different plants without regard to relative cost and quality factors;

- Carrying excess inventories at one plant and minimal or zero inventories at others;

- Building products without regard to logistic and storage considerations;
- Putting customers on back order out of one plant when another plant could solve the problem.

Our computer company is a good example of how a multi-business/multi-plant company can effectively deal with supply questions. Lightning Computer Company has three business units; these handle sales in North America (from Los Angeles), Europe (from Barcelona), and Asia (from Hong Kong). Of its six manufacturing plants, three are in North America, one is in Europe, and two are in Asia. The company conducts its business, including the monthly IBP or S&OP process, from its headquarters in Los Angeles, California. (Note: Lightning Computer is in the middle of upgrading their S&OP process to an IBP process.)

The monthly corporate IBP or S&OP management business review is preceded by substantial preparation. Each business unit must add a new month's demand forecast to a rolling 24-month demand plan, dropping the current month at the same time.

For example, as July 202X approaches its conclusion, the demand forecast for July 202Y is added to the rolling 24-month plan, and July 202X falls into history. The three business unit plans are then rolled into the Lightning Computer Company aggregate demand plan. The corporate demand manager (who could be a business unit demand manager) analyzes and adjusts the aggregate and unit demand plans as needed to satisfy the company's all-important customers while staying within defined constraints.

When this task is completed and consensus is received from the demand review participants, the demand plan(s) is/are forwarded to the supply manager or master (supply) planner. Using the various demand plans, the supply manager and/or master (supply) planner creates supply plans for both the individual plants and the company as a whole. This exercise aims to optimize the capabilities and capacities of the company's six plants.

Financial assessment and monetization of the volumetric plans (e.g., revenue, margin, costs) happens throughout the cycle in the appropriate review steps. Once the demand plans and supply plans are in balance, the financial manager evaluates and finalizes anticipated revenues, overhead expenses, manufacturing costs, and so on, and summarizes them into financial plans for each of the business units, the manufacturing plants, and the entire company. These plans are then compared with Lightning's overall business plan to ensure alignment.

After making any necessary adjustments, the financial manager pulls these diverse plans together into a single set of numbers, which is distributed to all direct participants (and needing and authorized indirect participants) of the IBP or S&OP management business review (MBR) 24 to 48 hours prior to the actual MBR taking place. The approved demand and supply plans that emerge from the IBP or S&OP MBR are distributed to Lightning's demand and supply managers, business unit owners, and manufacturing plant management.

As noted earlier, this book and chapter concentrates on demand and supply balancing; this does not mean that new product and product management as well as financial management are not as important to the company as demand management and supply management. The reason for limiting most of our discussion to demand and supply is because this book is about master (supply) planning and master (supply) scheduling which by definition is supply management at different levels with different levels of aggregation and detail.

So, the reader may ask, why is demand included? Well, a company's supply chain management process, including master planning and scheduling, is a demand-driven process during planning; during execution, supply can be either demand-driven (fruit generally doesn't get any better sitting in an inventory for long periods of time) or supply-driven (if the vegetables don't come out of the ground, it doesn't really matter what the demand is for vegetables!).

Also, as the reader will recall, one of a company's bookend objectives is to satisfy customer demand and the sales organization's promises and commitments made to those customers. As a review, the other bookend is for the company to safely make money and a profit!

Supply Management and Master Planning in Action

We can use Lightning Computer Company to illustrate how a supply manager and/or master (supply) planner might request work for various products from multiple plants. To make our discussion more manageable, Figure 16.3 on page 566 maps out the details for the Quantum product family. Here we consider company products employing a make-to-stock manufacturing strategy. The Phaser computer product family will be used later to demonstrate the same issues for products using a make-to-order manufacturing strategy.

The Quantum is a specialized and powerful computer that can be configured in four different ways to meet customer needs: products Q99A1, Q99A2, Q99A3, and Q99A4. Experience indicates that 40 percent of Quantum customer orders will be for the Q99A1 configuration, 30 percent will specify the Q99A2 configuration, 20 percent will specify the Q99A3 configuration, and the remaining 10 percent will request the Q99A4 configuration, as shown in the figure. Assuming that a particular month's approved demand for

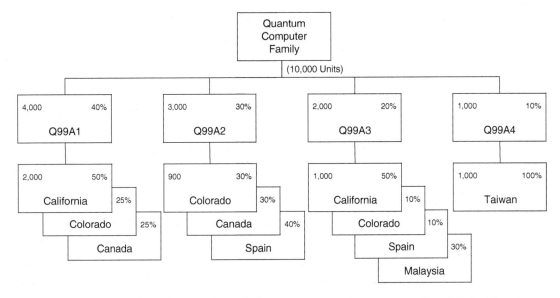

Figure 16.3 Planning Network for Quantum Computers (Multiple Plant Environment—Make-to-Stock Products)

Quantum product family computers is 10,000 units, the company translates this product family rate into the demand for specific computers in each of the four configurations:[3]

- 4,000 Q99A1 (10,000 multiplied by .40)

- 3,000 Q99A2 (10,000 multiplied by .30)

- 2,000 Q99A3 (10,000 multiplied by .20)

- 1,000 Q99A4 (10,000 multiplied by .10)

[3] Experienced demand and supply managers know that actual orders rarely match the forecasted demand for the different product family member products. Safety stocking, as well as option overplanning, are two ways a company protects itself from demand variation.

At this point, the supply manager or master (supply) planner must ask, "Given what I know about the current and future workloads of our six plants, their capabilities and capacities, cost efficiencies, and distances from customers and suppliers, what is the optimal approach to requesting work for this particular month's Quantum product family supply (production or purchased)?"

Some master (supply) planners and/or master (supply) schedulers use computerized algorithms to answer this question, while others simply use the computers between their ears and draw on their years of experience. Still others use a combination of computer models and experience. To get us started, the planning bill in Figure 16.3 (page 566) displays the percentages used to plan the Quantum computer product family mix demand.

When requesting the total number of computers during the period in question from the six manufacturing plants, the supply manager and/or master (supply) planner must also recognize that (1) the company will have some level of finished-goods inventory (the example in the figure is for stocked products) for each computer configuration at the beginning of the supply/production period, and (2) the company will desire some level of inventory at the end of the supply/production period. Remember, the customer expects products built using a make-to-stock strategy to be in inventory when they place the order; in other words, there is a short wait time until the customer order is satisfied and the product is delivered.

The Impact of New Product in Supply Management and Master Planning

As the reader may have noted in the integrated business planning discussion in Chapter 14, the sequence of reviews is something like this: (1) product management review planning new product and the company's product portfolio; (2) demand review planning new product as well as current saleable products; (3) supply review planning how the supply organization is to respond to the demand organization's request for product; (4a) financial appraisal—sometimes a formal review meeting, other times a formal *process*, or both—regarding the monetization of proposed product, demand, and supply plans and (4b) integrated reconciliation review, working out issues between proposed product, demand, and supply plans; and (5) management business review reviewing, making decisions, ensuring resources are available, and approving the newly updated product, demand, supply, and financial plans.

The company's *product pipeline* or *funnel* (i.e., new or renovated products, strategically, that are expected to be available for the marketplace) and master product launch (and discontinuation) plan (i.e., when new or renovated product is expected to be available and ordered by the customer and when discontinued product will no longer be available for sale) have a direct impact on the supply organization capability, capacity, inventory, and suppliers. Master (supply) planners as well as master (supply) schedulers need to understand these plans along with their accuracy and reliability. Let's spend a little time looking at an example of a master product launch plan followed by short discussions regarding both the new product funnel and the sales funnel (both funnels impact master planning and scheduling).

A company's master product launch plan is most likely tied to the sales pipeline. Using the master product launch plan, the master (supply) planner and/or master (supply) scheduler can make plans for product development's material needs, tooling requirements, use of various product line capabilities for testing, inspection requirement capacities, and so forth. The master product launch plan also alerts supply chain management when materials from suppliers will be needed as well as when production capacity needs to be available for building of the product. Figure 16.4a on page 569 is an example of what a master launch plan for new products (including major renovations to existing products) may look like. Figure 16.4b shows the relationship between the Product Management Review in the IBP cycle discussed in Chapter 14 as well as the Portfolio, Project, and Resource Management activities supporting the Product Management Review.

Reviewing the figures, the reader can see products under development, type of product, whether a product is forecasted (i.e., in the demand approved plan), anticipated launch date, and reschedules made to the last master product launch plan. Additionally, issues regarding product launches are called out along with a summary of delays, accelerations, and projects moved in or out. All of this information is valuable to the company's supply chain management team.

Next, displayed in Figure 16.5 on page 570 is an example of a product development pipeline coupled with financials. Reviewing this figure, the reader can see the various stages of the product development cycle. The figure displays an area to note ideas followed by the company's stages and gates followed by product going to market.

Additionally, the new product funnel lists gross and net anticipated portfolio financial contributions (i.e., net after considering risk adjustments, typically using product drop-out rate based on type of project and location within the funnel) and net anticipated financials that are *included in the approved demand plan*, typically after a specific milestone or gate (Stage 4 in the example) has been passed within the portfolio management process. The entire pipeline is pointed toward delivery of strategic objectives noted in financial or other identified terms. Again, this valuable information is very important to include in the company's master (supply) plan and master (supply) schedule.

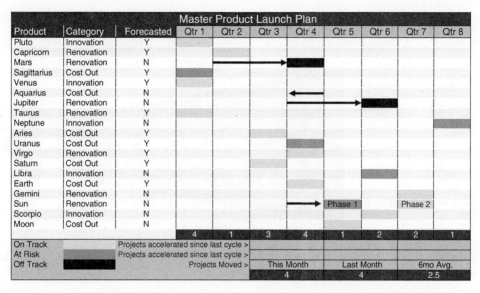

			Master Product Launch Plan							
Product	Category	Forecasted	Qtr 1	Qtr 2	Qtr 3	Qtr 4	Qtr 5	Qtr 6	Qtr 7	Qtr 8
Pluto	Innovation	Y								
Capricorn	Renovation	Y								
Mars	Renovation	N								
Sagittarius	Cost Out	Y								
Venus	Innovation	Y								
Aquarius	Cost Out	N								
Jupiter	Renovation	N								
Taurus	Renovation	Y								
Neptune	Innovation	N								
Aries	Cost Out	Y								
Uranus	Cost Out	Y								
Virgo	Renovation	Y								
Saturn	Cost Out	Y								
Libra	Innovation	N								
Earth	Cost Out	Y								
Gemini	Renovation	N								
Sun	Renovation	N						Phase 1		Phase 2	
Scorpio	Innovation	N								
Moon	Cost Out	N								
			4	1	3	4	1	2	2	1

On Track		Projects accelerated since last cycle >				
At Risk		Projects accelerated since last cycle >				
Off Track		Projects Moved >	This Month		Last Month	6mo Avg.
			4		4	2.5

Figure 16.4a   Master Product Launch Plan for New Products

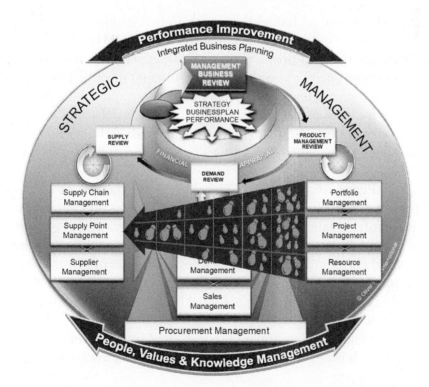

**Figure 16.4b   Integrated Business Model with Emphasis on
Product Launch**

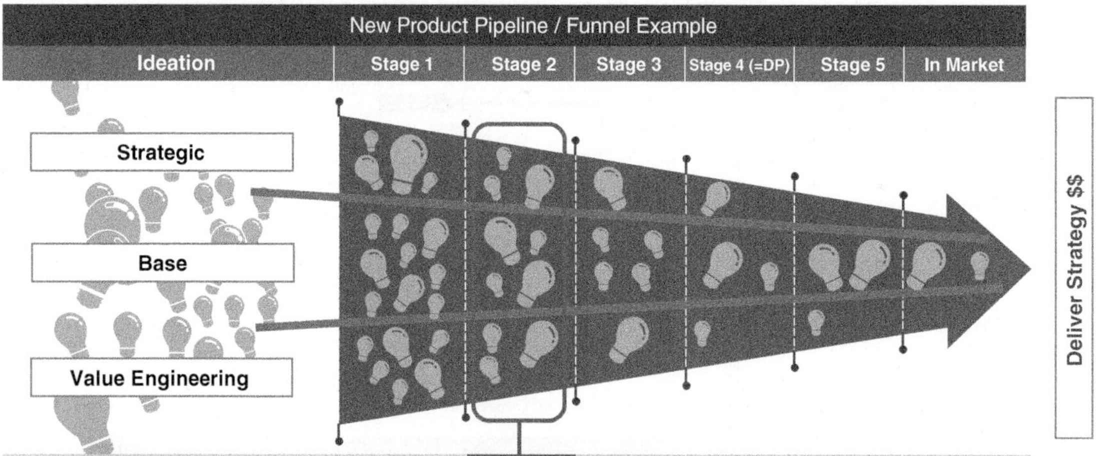

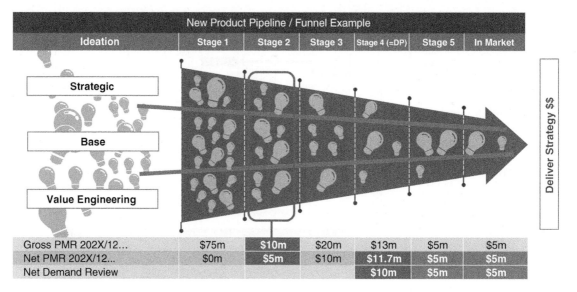

	Stage 1	Stage 2	Stage 3	Stage 4 (=DP)	Stage 5	In Market
Gross PMR 202X/12...	$75m	$10m	$20m	$13m	$5m	$5m
Net PMR 202X/12...	$0m	$5m	$10m	$11.7m	$5m	$5m
Net Demand Review				$10m	$5m	$5m

Figure 16.5 New Product Pipeline with Financials

There's another pipeline or funnel that needs to be included in the master planning and scheduling process. Since supply chain management (SCM) and master planning and scheduling (MPS) are demand-driven processes during planning, the demand (including potential business from current as well as new customers) must be known by the master (supply) planner and/or master (supply) scheduler. The sooner this information can be made available to the master planning and scheduling team, the better. In most companies, making arrangements to secure the required materials and capacity takes money and time (as time passes, more money for various reasons is required to secure the needed material and capacity).

Take a look at Figure 16.6 on page 571, which is an example of a company's sales pipeline funnel. As we review the information displayed in the figure, the reader can see a column identifying sales suspects that have been categorized as growth, sustaining, and strategic potential customer sales. Following the suspect column, we have the sales activity phases and check milestones for the sales cycle, that of prospecting, qualifying, meeting (relationship building), proposing, contracting, and closing. These stages or milestones lead to prospects becoming potential business to becoming active customers within the business.

Additionally, the sales pipeline funnel lists potential future revenues for growth, sustaining, and strategic business. The entire pipeline is pointed toward a delivered revenue

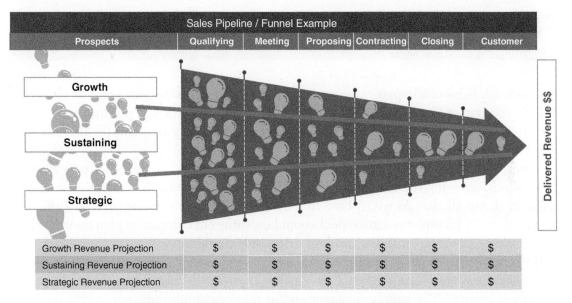

Sales Pipeline / Funnel Example						
Prospects	Qualifying	Meeting	Proposing	Contracting	Closing	Customer

	Qualifying	Meeting	Proposing	Contracting	Closing	Customer
Growth Revenue Projection	$	$	$	$	$	$
Sustaining Revenue Projection	$	$	$	$	$	$
Strategic Revenue Projection	$	$	$	$	$	$

Figure 16.6   Potential Customer Pipeline

financial objective. Let's say it one more time: This known, discussed, and reviewed (within the demand organization) information is very important to include in the company's master (supply) plan and master (supply) schedule. It's there for the taking and should *not* be ignored.

As has been noted earlier, today's master planning and scheduling is more art than science (yes, that's all changing in this and future decades). So, until master planning and scheduling truly becomes more science than art within a company, a process should be in place to ensure that those in master planning and scheduling are given the data and information that they need to know. *As the old saying goes, if you don't know where you are going, any road will get you there!*

The art and science of master planning and scheduling begin with the art and science of integrated business planning, including product planning, demand planning, supply planning, and financial planning. Well, there are numerous environments and situations that require supply planning—product-driven aggregate inventory planning, product-driven aggregate backlog planning, product-driven disaggregated inventory planning, and product-driven disaggregated backlog planning, to name a few. The following sections discuss these environments, along with some of the planning elements that master (supply) planners and/or master (supply) schedulers must take into account during their planning activities.

Inventory Projection and Planning

We normally think of computer companies like Lightning as *product-* or *material-driven*—that is, companies that orient their production around the particular product orders they anticipate or actually receive from their customers. Satisfying demand for these orders drives everything else.

Later in this chapter, we'll see that some companies are what we call *production-* or *capacity-driven*—for them the need to maintain costly production facilities near full capacity drives all else. As we will see in the following sections, being product-driven or production-driven explains a great deal about how different companies plan their production capacity. Let's start with the product-driven environment.

To simplify the situation example a bit, we will assume for now that Lightning Computer has one central warehouse in Los Angeles where the different manufacturing plants ship their output.[4] The supply manager and/or master (supply) planner in this scenario is merely concerned with inventory *in the aggregate*—*where* the finished computers are located does not really matter. Later, we will consider what happens when the six production plants maintain finished-goods inventory on site.

For Quantum computers, the projected beginning inventory and desired level of ending inventory for each specific configuration at the central warehouse for the time period in question are given in the following table:

Thus, if demand for the Q99A1 product during the period is 4,000 units (see Figure 16.3 on page 566), the desired ending inventory is 800 units, and the beginning inventory is 1,600 units, the required supply (production) for the period will be 3,200 units, as shown

Inventory	Q99A1	Q99A2	Q99A3	Q99A4
Beginning	1,600	0	600	800
Ending	800	600	400	200
Change	−800	+600	−200	−600

---

[4] Having a centralized warehouse for this global company is, of course, unrealistic; we use this contrivance for purposes of demonstration only. If the company had all of its plants clustered in one geographic region, the example would be feasible.

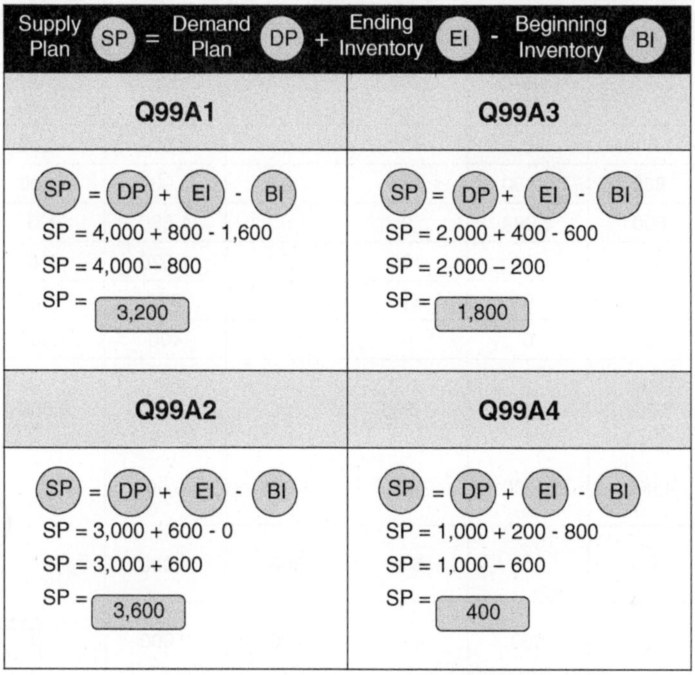

**Figure 16.7   Quantum Computers Supply Plan Calculations
(Aggregated Inventory Planning)**

in Figure 16.7. Using the same basic logic, some companies use a desired inventory days of supply or days forward coverage (DFC) to calculate the aggregate supply plan. This is the total Q99A1 production that the supply manager and/or master (supply) planner will need to request from the three plants that build this computer.

So, to calculate the total required production for any member of a product family in a product-driven, aggregated inventory-planning environment, the supply manager and/or master (supply) planner adds the desired change in inventory to the anticipated demand. Using this logic, Figure 16.7 indicates the production required for each member of the Quantum computer family.

Once the aggregate production by computer configuration is known, the supply manager and/or master (supply) planner must decide *which* plants should build these products, and in what quantities. For instance, the supply manager and/or master (supply) planner may decide that half of the 3,200 Q99A1 computers (1,600 units) should be built in California, with the rest divided equally between the Colorado (800 units) and Canadian (800 units) plants. This division of total required production is a *request for supply* from each plant and/or supplier.

	PRODUCT						
PLANT	Q99A1	Q99A2	Q99A3	Q99A4	Required Capacity (Units)	Planned Capacity (Units)	Maximum Capacity (Units)
California	1,600	0	900	0	2,500	1,800	2,200
Colorado	800	1,080	180	0	2,060	1,800	2,200
Canada	800	1,080	0	0	1,880	900	1,100
Spain	0	1,440	180	0	1,620	900	1,100
Malaysia	0	0	540	0	540	1,800	2,200
Taiwan	0	0	0	400	400	1,800	2,200
Supply Plan	3,200	3,600	1,800	400	9,000	9,000	11,000
Demand Plan	4,000	3,000	2,000	1,000	10,000		
Beginning Inventory	1,600	0	600	800	3,000		
Desired Ending Inventory	800	600	400	200	2,000		
Projected Ending Inventory	800	600	400	200	2,000		

Figure 16.8 Quantum Computers Supply Plan (Product-Driven, Aggregated Inventory Planning)

The top half of Figure 16.8 shows the result by plant of the *request for supply* calculation for each specific computer configuration. The bottom of the figure shows the totals by planning period for each configuration. In this case,

- Supply equals total production from all plants; or

- Demand equals total demand by product configuration; or

- Beginning inventory equals the projected starting on-hand balances by product configuration; or

- Desired ending inventory equals what the company would like to have on hand; or

- Ending inventory is the quantity projected to be in inventory.

Will the Plan Work?

The supply manager and/or master (supply) planner must then ask, "How realistic is this plan? Will each of the plants be able to comply with these production requests during the time period in question?" The supply manager and/or master (supply) planner could answer these questions by calling, texting, or e-mailing the master schedulers at each of the six plants. A more fruitful first step, however, would be to rough cut or sanity check the plan in Figure 16.5 (page 570) against planned plant capacities; doing so would indicate whether the plan has a chance of succeeding.

As Figure 16.8 (page 574) indicates, overloaded conditions exist in California (140 percent), Colorado (115 percent), Canada (200 percent), and Spain (180 percent). The two Asian plants are severely underloaded: Malaysia by 70 percent and Taiwan by almost 80 percent.[5] In this particular case, we will assume that none of the six plants can materially alter its maximum capacity, at least in the short to intermediate time frame. Therefore, the supply manager and/or master (supply) planner must make some adjustments to the supply plan and/or master (supply) plan before releasing it to the plants.

As the supply manager and/or master (supply) planner begin(s) looking for adjustment opportunities, the Taiwanese plant will surely catch his or her attention. As shown in Figure 16.8, this plant has a planned capacity of 1,800 units per period, and that number could be expanded to 2,200 in a crunch (through subcontracting, overtime, added shifts, and so on).

Since this plant is only being asked to build 400 Q99A4 units, it has plenty of excess capacity. But remember, this plant can *only* build Q99A4 Quantum computers! As a result, that idle capacity cannot help the supply manager or master (supply) planner) alleviate overloading elsewhere in the system. Taiwan is locked in![6]

The situation in Malaysia appears more promising. The initial supply plan is only requesting 540 Q99A3 units against this plant's 1,800-unit capacity (which is entirely devoted to Q99A3 units). Given the overload situations in California, Colorado, and Spain, the supply manager and/or master (supply) planner would be tempted to shift *all* Q99A3 production to this location. Doing so would bring the Malaysian plant up to capacity; it would also solve *all* overloading problems in California and some—but not all—elsewhere.

---

[5] The over- and underload percentages are calculated by dividing the required production by the planned productions (rounded for simplicity).

[6] If serious underloading at the Taiwan plant was chronic, occurring in many periods, senior management would have to consider either upgrading the plant to handle other product configurations or reducing its capacity. Alternatively, marketing schemes to increase the demand for Q99A4 computers could be used to more closely match demand and this plant's capacity.

Further adjustments, such as moving some planned Q99A1 production from Colorado and Canada to California, would solve the Colorado plant's overload problem, but Canada and Spain would continue to be overloaded. For example, Spain would be asked to build 1,440 Q99A2 units and nothing else, but this single request would be in excess of its *maximum* production capacity.

Of course, getting these under- and overloading conditions worked out involves more than simply matching demand with the capabilities and capacities of various plants. A number of other issues must also be considered:

- Differences in shipping costs;

- Customer bundling requirements;

- Plant-specific manufacturing costs;

- Inventory storage areas;

- Product build sequences;

- Availability of components;

- Distances from suppliers and customers;

- Quality differences between plants.

These issues must enter into the supply manager's and/or master (supply) planner's final analysis and decision making. In this case the supply manager and/or master (supply) scheduler may have little choice but to request that capacity be increased to near maximum in California, Colorado, Canada, and Spain while decreasing the capacity in Taiwan. In a product-driven environment like this one, failing to meet demand *on time* can drive customers into the arms of competitors, perhaps permanently!

The complexity of optimizing product demand, plant capacities, and the many other factors mentioned here is usually beyond the processing ability of the human mind, which explains why so many companies are beginning or continuing to use computerized finite-capacity scheduling algorithms to plan and schedule production. The next step is to move these advanced production planning and scheduling systems into the hands of the supply manager, master (supply) planner, and/or master (supply) scheduler.

What we've described so far seems simple enough, but what happens when we make the situation more realistic and consider the fact that each of the plants has and maintains inventory? The supply manager and/or master (supply) planner must then plan supply (produced or purchased) by taking plant inventory and customer location into account.

Product-Driven, Disaggregated Inventory Planning

The previous section made the assumption that *where* finished computers were inventoried did not affect supply planning. This assumption simplified our explanation of Lightning Computer's supply planning. A company with plants clustered in one region (e.g., the northeastern United States), and possibly operating out of a single centralized warehouse in that region, could plan supply (production) using this convenient assumption.

Companies operating in different regions or countries, however, cannot; they generally must plan to hold finished-goods inventories at multiple locations—for example, in the finished-goods warehouses of their far-flung manufacturing facilities or strategically located distribution centers. We'll now assume that Lightning Computer is one of these companies.

Figure 16.9 on the following page shows Lightning's projected inventory, by plant, at the beginning of the planning period. Figure 16.10 indicates the leadership team's desired inventory at the end of the period. We can see that the aggregate beginning inventory for Q99A1 is 1,600 units; 1,000 of these are inventoried at the California plant with the balance at the Colorado plant. By the end of the period, Lightning Computer would like to have a total of 800 Quantum computers on hand: 400 in California, 200 in Colorado, and 200 in Canada.

The desired ending inventory by plant creates another factor for the supply manager and/or master planner to consider when allocating production requests to the six plants slated to build Quantum computers. For example, the California and Colorado plants might be the optimal source of Q99A1 production during this particular time period, and they might have the capacity to handle the *entire* 3,200 units needed.

However, since the inventory plan calls for an ending balance of 200 units at the Canadian facility, the fact that Canada has zero inventory as a projected starting balance might

PLANT	PRODUCT				
	Q99A1	Q99A2	Q99A3	Q99A4	Totals
California	1,000	0	150	0	1,150
Colorado	600	0	150	0	750
Canada	0	0	0	0	0
Spain	0	0	150	0	150
Malaysia	0	0	150	0	150
Taiwan	0	0	0	800	800
Totals	1,600	0	600	800	3,000

Figure 16.9   Beginning Inventories for Quantum Computers

PLANT	PRODUCT				
	Q99A1	Q99A2	Q99A3	Q99A4	Totals
California	400	0	200	0	600
Colorado	200	180	40	0	420
Canada	200	180	0	0	380
Spain	0	240	40	0	280
Malaysia	0	0	120	0	120
Taiwan	0	0	0	200	200
Totals	800	600	400	200	2,000

Figure 16.10   Desired Ending Inventories for Quantum Computers

induce the supply manager and/or master (supply) planner to allocate *at least* 200 units of production to it. The alternative would be to build in California and/or Colorado and ship to Canada—possibly a bad idea when transportation costs are considered.

Considering all factors, the supply manager and/or master (supply) planner in this example is using the same logic explained in the product-driven, aggregated inventory planning section. The only difference is the fact that inventory needs to be planned by plant. Refer to Figure 16.11 on page 580 for all the calculations.

With the results of these calculations taken into account, the production required for each computer by plant is shown in the top half of Figure 16.12 on page 581; the bottom half shows total demand, supply, and inventory by computer model.[7] Reviewing production by plant, the reader will again observe overloaded conditions in California, Canada, and Spain, while Malaysia and Taiwan remain underloaded. Colorado, fortunately, is near full capacity.

Thus, before releasing this supply plan, the supply manager and/or master (supply) planner must think about *re*balancing the supply plan while keeping all planning parameters in mind. He or she will seek ways to offload some work from California and Spain to Malaysia, as discussed in the previous section. This is the type of complex situation in which the computing power of finite planning and scheduling software is extremely helpful.

It should be clear that the job of requesting supply (produced or purchased) from multiple plants or suppliers requires the supply manager and/or master (supply) planner to take into account many different policies and constraints. The next section adds still another variable: backlog.

Backlog and lead time to the customer must be considered for products using a make-to-order manufacturing strategy. As a refresher on the term *backlog*, the reader will remember that backlog (we're not talking about back orders) is defined as *customer orders booked but not shipped*.

Product-Driven, Aggregated Backlog Planning

We have now covered various situations the supply manager and/or master (supply) planner must contend with in a product-driven, inventory-based environment. This type of

---

[7] The format of this figure is the same as Figure 16.5, which was explained earlier in the chapter. The numbers differ here because we have considered *disaggregated* inventory.

Supply Plan SP	=	Demand Plan DP	+	Ending Inventory EI	−	Beginning Inventory BI

Plant	**Q99A1** (SP) 3,200	Plant	**Q99A3** (SP) 1,800
California	SP = 2,000 + 400 - 1,000 SP = 2,000 – 600 SP = 1,400	California	SP = 1,000 + 200 - 150 SP = 1,000 – 50 SP = 1,050
Colorado	SP = 1,000 + 200 - 600 SP = 1,000 – 400 SP = 600	Colorado	SP = 200 + 40 - 150 SP = 200 – 110 SP = 90
Canada	SP = 1,000 + 200 - 0 SP = 1,000 + 200 SP = 1,200	Spain	SP = 200 + 40 - 150 SP = 200 – 110 SP = 90
Plant	**Q99A2** (SP) 3,600	Malaysia	SP = 600 + 120 - 150 SP = 600 – 30 SP = 570
California	SP = 900 + 180 - 0 SP = 900 + 180 SP = 1,080	Plant	**Q99A4** (SP) 400
Colorado	SP = 900 + 180 - 0 SP = 900 + 180 SP = 1,080	Taiwan	SP = 1,000 + 200 - 800 SP = 1,000 – 600 SP = 400
Canada	SP = 1,200 + 240 - 0 SP = 1,200 + 240 SP = 1,440		

Figure 16.11   Quantum Computers Supply Plan (Disaggregated Inventory Planning)

environment generally looks very much like a company using a make-to-stock manufacturing strategy.

But what about the company that uses a make-to-order manufacturing strategy? The job of supply management is similar to that used for products built using the make-to-stock manufacturing strategy except that the company deals with changing backlogs instead of changing inventories.

Again, backlog is defined as customer orders that have been booked but not shipped. For products using the make-to-order manufacturing strategy, a salesperson takes the customer order and commits to a delivery date. When the customer's order is taken, it is

PLANT	PRODUCT						
	Q99A1	Q99A2	Q99A3	Q99A4	Required Capacity (Units)	Planned Capacity (Units)	Maximum Capacity (Units)
California	1,400	0	1,050	0	2,450	1,800	2,200
Colorado	600	1,080	90	0	1,770	1,800	2,200
Canada	1,200	1,080	0	0	2,280	900	1,100
Spain	0	1,440	90	0	1,530	900	1,100
Malaysia	0	0	570	0	570	1,800	2,200
Taiwan	0	0	0	400	400	1,800	2,200
Supply Plan	3,200	3,600	1,800	400	9,000	9,000	11,000
Demand Plan	4,000	3,000	2,000	1,000	10,000		
Beginning Inventory	1,600	0	600	800	3,000		
Desired Ending Inventory	800	600	400	200	2,000		
Projected Ending Inventory	800	600	400	200	2,000		

Figure 16.12   Quantum Computers Supply Plan
(Disaggregated Inventory Planning)

placed in the company's backlog. When the product is built and shipped, the customer order is removed from the company's backlog.

Let's return to the Lightning Computer Company to consider how demand, supply, and backlogs can be handled in the supply planning process, using the company's other product family, the Phaser computer, as an example. In this section, we'll deal with the simpler case: backlogs in aggregate. Here, as in the Quantum aggregated inventory planning example, we'll assume that the company has a centralized order-entry and customer service function; customer orders are treated in aggregate to simplify our initial Phaser computer example; we'll drop this assumption in the next section.

There are four members of the Phaser product family: P99B1, P99B2, P99B3, and P99B4. Again, the company has estimated the percentage of total demand that each

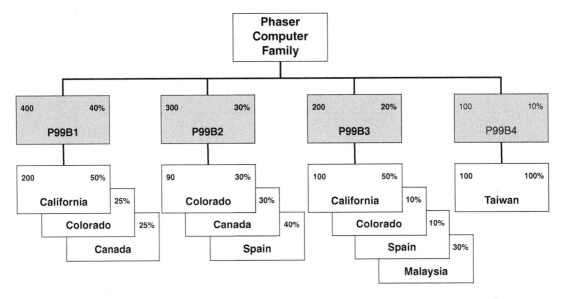

Figure 16.13 Phaser Computers (Multiple Plant Environment—Make-to-Order)

of these configurations is likely to represent. These estimates are represented in Figure 16.13, which also indicates the company's expectation of which of its six plants will build those computers, again in terms of percentages.

For example, it expects 40 percent of total Phaser demand during the planning period to be for the popular P99B1 model; the California plant is expected to build half of these units, with the balance shared equally by the plants in Colorado and Canada.[8]

Since Phaser computers are planned to be made to order, most (if not all) individual configurations offered have customer orders on the books. Looking at the projected demand for the Phaser computer family in the planning period in question, the supply manager and/or master (supply) planner can quickly translate this volume (1,000 computers) into the anticipated mix demand using the percentage figures contained in the Phaser planning bill (Figure 16.13). (The reader will note that this procedure is the same procedure used in the inventory situation described earlier.)

For our Phaser computers, the projected beginning and desired level of ending backlogs for the time period in question are given in the following table:

---

[8] The authors chose to use the same numbers as in the Quantum example so that the reader can more easily recognize the differences between products using a make-to-order versus a make-to-stock manufacturing strategy. The demand for the Phaser product line is 10 percent of the demand for the Quantum product line of computers.

Backlog	P99B1	P99B2	P99B3	P99B4
Beginning	160	0	60	80
Ending	80	60	40	20
Change	−80	+60	−20	−60

From these numbers, coupled with the anticipated product demand, a total supply plan is generated (Figure 16.14)—again, without respect to *where* backlogs exist. The result is very reminiscent of the supply plan developed for the Quantum family. As the reader can see, the supply manager and/or master (supply) planner anticipates needing 480 units of P99B1, 240 units of P99B2, 220 units of P99B3, and 160 units of P99B4.

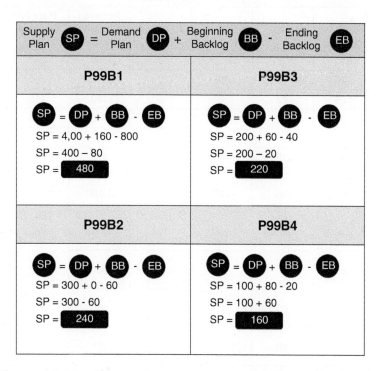

Figure 16.14   Phaser Computers Supply Plan Calculations

The supply manager and/or master (supply) planner must then determine from which plants to *request this production*. Using the planning bill in Figure 16.13 on page 582 for P99B1, the initial plan would request 240 units from the California plant and 120 units each from Colorado and Canada. This follows precisely the percentages dictated by Figure 16.13.

The process continues until the entire initial supply plan is created (Figure 16.15). But is this initial plan workable? Unfortunately, a quick scan of the required capacity (in units) and the planned capacity (in units) indicates some under- and overloaded conditions. California and Canada are severely overloaded, while Malaysia and Taiwan are severely underloaded. Some adjustment—moving some work from here to there—will have to be made prior to requesting production from these plants.

This section has been a condensed version of the multi-business/multi-plant supply planning process found in companies using a make-to-order manufacturing strategy for

PLANT	PRODUCT						
	P99B1	P99B2	P99B3	P99B4	Required Capacity (Units)	Planned Capacity (Units)	Maximum Capacity (Units)
California	240	0	110	0	350	220	300
Colorado	120	72	22	0	214	220	300
Canada	120	72	0	0	192	110	150
Spain	0	96	22	0	118	110	150
Malaysia	0	0	66	0	66	220	300
Taiwan	0	0	0	160	160	220	300
Supply Plan	480	240	220	160	1,100	1,100	1,500
Demand Plan	400	300	200	100	1,000		
Beginning Backlog	160	0	60	80	300		
Desired Ending Backlog	80	60	40	20	200		
Projected Ending Backlog	80	60	40	20	200		

Figure 16.15   Phaser Computers Supply Plan (Aggregated Backlog Planning)

selected product families. As the reader can see, the supply planning process is similar for backlog and inventory planning. For this reason, we will not go into every detail.[9] Continuing with this condensed approach, let's turn our attention to product-driven, disaggregated backlog planning.

Product-Driven, Disaggregated Backlog Planning

In the previous section, Lightning Computer Company treated its backlog as a total, paying no attention to which plant would satisfy that backlog. What if this was *not* the case? What if customer orders were received by the individual plants and satisfied by them directly? This would create a different situation for the supply manager and/or master (supply) planner. Two figures provide the details for our computer company using this disaggregated scenario. Figure 16.16 on page 586 shows the beginning backlog for the Phaser computer line, while Figure 16.17 displays management's desired level of backlog at the end of the planning period in question.

To determine a supply plan for each manufacturing plant in this scenario, the supply manager and/or master (supply) planner will follow the same steps outlined in the section "Product-Driven, Disaggregated Inventory Planning." Again, the difference is a changing backlog instead of changing inventory levels. Figure 16.18 on page 587 shows the calculations for each Phaser computer by plant.

The anticipated demand for each product and plant is derived using the planning bill shown earlier in Figure 16.13 (page 582). That demand is added to the desired change in backlog by plant. The initial supply plan (results of the calculation in Figure 16.18) is shown in Figure 16.19 on page 588.

As the supply manager and/or master (supply) planner reviews this initial plan, he or she once again observes that the required capacity in units exceeds the planned capacity in units in four of the six manufacturing plants; again, the two Asian plants show underloads. The supply manager and/or master (supply) planner notices overloads in Canada, Colorado, Spain, and California.

---

[9] For more detail on supply and backlog planning, the reader should review Chapter 14 as well as the previous two sections of this chapter.

PLANT	PRODUCT				
	P99B1	P99B2	P99B3	P99B4	Totals
California	100	0	15	0	115
Colorado	60	0	15	0	75
Canada	0	0	0	0	0
Spain	0	0	15	0	15
Malaysia	0	0	15	0	15
Taiwan	0	0	0	80	80
Totals	160	0	60	80	300

Figure 16.16   Beginning Backlog for Phaser Computers

PLANT	PRODUCT				
	P99B1	P99B2	P99B3	P99B4	Totals
California	40	0	20	0	60
Colorado	20	18	4	0	42
Canada	20	18	0	0	38
Spain	0	24	4	0	28
Malaysia	0	0	12	0	12
Taiwan	0	0	0	20	20
Totals	80	60	40	20	200

Figure 16.17   Desired Ending Backlog for Phaser Computers

Supply Plan (SP) = Demand Plan (DP) + Beginning Backlog (BB) - Ending Backlog (EB)				
Plant	**P99B1** (SP) 480		Plant	**P99B3** (SP) 220
California	SP = 200 + 100 - 40 SP = 200 + 60 SP = **260**		California	SP = 100 + 15 - 20 SP = 100 – 5 SP = **95**
Colorado	SP = 100 + 60 - 20 SP = 100 + 40 SP = **140**		Colorado	SP = 20 + 15 - 4 SP = 20 + 11 SP = **31**
Canada	SP = 100 + 0 - 20 SP = 100 + 40 SP = **80**		Spain	SP = 20 + 15 - 4 SP = 20 + 11 SP = **31**
Plant	**P99B2** (SP) 240		Malaysia	SP = 60 + 15 - 12 SP = 60 + 3 SP = **63**
California	SP = 90 + 0 - 18 SP = 90 - 18 SP = **72**		Plant	**P99B4** (SP) 160
Colorado	SP = 90 + 0 - 18 SP = 90 - 18 SP = **72**		Taiwan	SP = 1,00 + 80 - 20 SP = 100 + 60 SP = **160**
Canada	SP = 120 + 0 - 24 SP = 120 - 24 SP = **96**			

Figure 16.18   Phaser Computers Supply Plan Calculations

The first three of these overloads could be solved by increasing capacity. California represents a more difficult case. Maximizing output there would solve some of the overload problem, but *not* all of the problems identified. At maximum capacity, it would remain overloaded by 55 units. However, these could be offloaded to Colorado if it raises its capacity to maximum. Alternatively, some production could be offloaded to Spain if planned production were raised at that location.

Of course, the Asian plant underload condition cannot be solved by raising the capacity of the other plants. As we observed earlier, Taiwan is the *only* plant capable of building P99B4 computers; in fact, it can build nothing else in the Phaser line. Therefore, *not* much can be done to immediately relieve its 25 percent undercapacity problem. Malaysia is another matter. Since it builds P99B3 computers, all requests for production of that particular model now directed to California, Colorado, and Spain could be shifted to that location.

PLANT	PRODUCT						
	P99B1	P99B2	P99B3	P99B4	Required Capacity (Units)	Planned Capacity (Units)	Maximum Capacity (Units)
California	260	0	95	0	350	220	300
Colorado	140	72	31	0	243	220	300
Canada	80	72	0	0	152	110	150
Spain	0	96	31	0	127	110	150
Malaysia	0	0	63	0	63	220	300
Taiwan	0	0	0	160	160	220	300
Supply Plan	480	240	220	160	1,100	1,100	1,500
Demand Plan	400	300	200	100	1,000		
Beginning Backlog	160	0	60	80	300		
Desired Ending Backlog	80	60	40	20	200		
Projected Ending Backlog	80	60	40	20	200		

Figure 16.19   Product-Driven, Disaggregated Backlog Planning

But there's another problem: Building computers in Malaysia and shipping them halfway around the world to customers in Europe and North America may not be cost effective. And so it goes.

This condensed example points out the need for computer software support. A supply manager and/or master (supply) planner who deals with the balancing and optimizing of multi-product/multi-plant production should seriously consider implementing an advanced finite-capacity planning and scheduling software package. There are so many parameters that our between-the-ears computers are incapable of storing and processing them all in a timely way.

Without some electronic computer assistance, the task is often reduced to an ineffective sequence of trial and error. This is particularly true in a production-driven environment, which is the subject of the next section.

Production-Driven Environments

Supply planning does not have to begin with the product and work down to plant assignments, as shown in the previous sections. Instead, the supply manager and/or master (supply) planner may begin at the plant level, determining what percentage of the anticipated gross demand should be handled by each, and only then determine which product family members should be built in each plant.

This approach may be preferred when keeping production facilities fully utilized is the overwhelming concern—more important than the mix of products built. For example, a company with highly capitalized new plants and customers who will buy just about all of their production may choose this approach. In this environment, the supply manager's and/or master (supply) planner's mission is clear: Keep those plants rolling!

Let's suppose that Lightning Computer Company found itself in this type of production-driven (or capacity-driven) environment: Its computers are in such demand that management's policy is to run all plants at full capacity.[10] Figure 16.20 on page 590 indicates the supply manager's and/or master (supply) planner's supply (production and/or purchased) plan by plant for each of the company's Quantum configurations.

Note that the requested capacity for each plant matches planned capacity in equivalent units. This supply plan meets customer demand and satisfies the desire of management to keep its plants fully loaded. However, management cannot have its cake and eat it too: Satisfying this policy has created a problem of mix inventory.

The company is projected to be overstocked in some product configurations and understocked in others. Perhaps the company's marketers can solve the overstock problem through a special promotion of Q99A4s, of which there are projected to be 1,400 more than desired. The understocked condition of Q99A1 and Q99A2 is very serious for Lightning Computer. Management desires an ending inventory for both of these configurations at the end of this planning period. But the initial supply plan projects zero ending inventory for both. This both fails to satisfy management's requirement and creates a dangerous situation for the company.

Therefore, the company's leadership team may want to turn its attention to the plant in Taiwan, which is seriously underloaded because of its ability to produce only one

---

[10] This may be unrealistic for a computer company, but it is certainly likely for a company in food processing, chemicals, or other highly capitalized manufacturing businesses.

PLANT	\multicolumn{7}{c}{PRODUCT}
	Q99A1	Q99A2	Q99A3	Q99A4	Required Capacity (Units)	Planned Capacity (Units)	Maximum Capacity (Units)
California	1,800	0	0	0	1,800	1,800	1,800
Colorado	600	1,200	0	0	1,800	1,800	1,800
Canada	0	900	0	0	900	900	900
Spain	0	900	0	0	900	900	900
Malaysia	0	0	1,800	0	1,800	1,800	1,800
Taiwan	0	0	0	1,800	1,800	1,800	1,800
Supply Plan	2,400	3,000	1,800	1,800	9,000	9,000	11,000
Demand Plan	4,000	3,000	2,000	1,000	10,000		
Beginning Inventory	1,600	0	600	800	3,000		
Desired Ending Inventory	800	600	400	200	2,000		
Projected Ending Inventory	0	0	400	1,600	2,000		

Figure 16.20   Quantum Computer's Supply Plan (Inventory Planning)

Quantum model. If this plant were equipped, staffed, and qualified to produce Q99A1s and Q99A2s, the company's inventory shortcomings for those products could disappear; the overstock of Q99A4 models at that location would also be reduced.

Most examples are not this simple, and the use of finite-capacity planning and scheduling software is practically a must in creating a viable supply plan. Unfortunately, explaining all of the optimizing features in these systems is beyond the scope of this book.[11] Once the supply plan is created, it must be approved by the executive team in order to move forward in the company's master planning and scheduling function. The reader may be asking, *What does this all mean?*

[11] Readers who desire more information about advanced planning (production) scheduling software should see the many articles published on the subject. Other sources include software suppliers and consultants specializing in production- and capacity-driven environments.

Reviewing and Approving the Aggregate Supply Plan

Master planning and scheduling is the function and process a best-practice company uses to tie the aggregate supply plan to lower-level detailed supply plans. Additionally, master planning and scheduling is also used to translate the approved supply plan into detailed terms that are understood by personnel in middle management as well as those personnel charged with executing the detail (plan) that makes up the aggregate (plan).

Figure 16.21 shows the integration of integrated business planning with the monthly supply review process with the supply management function with the master planning and scheduling function and process. This all-important planning process that ties these functions and processes together starting at the top (planning level) and tying it to the bottom (planning level) as well as tying the bottom (planning level) to top (planning level).

Additionally, let's *not* forget that these functions and processes also need to be tied side to side, meaning that the supply review must be integrated with the demand review as well as the logistics review and supply management must be integrated with demand management and logistics management. The approved supply plan(s) is/are then the input to a company's master planning and scheduling function (refer to the figure for a visual of this integrated environment).

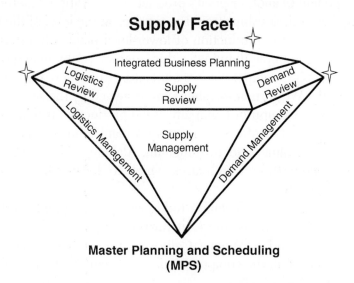

Figure 16.21   Tying the Approved Supply Plan to Integrated Business Planning and Master Planning and Scheduling

Key to best-practice and Class A master planning and scheduling is a combination of knowledgeable people behaving in a Class A manner, integrated Class A best practices throughout the supply chain management function, up-to-date Class A technology and systems, and Class A data integrity in all supporting records (i.e., inventory record accuracy and accurate bills-of-material coupled with accurate process routings). Another key to a company's demonstrating Class A best-practice behaviors is that of linking, not only its departments and functions together, but also its sales offices, inventory warehouses, transportation entities, and each manufacturing facility. Although this integration may *not* be easy (see the next section for tough environments), it's just what Class A companies routinely do!

Interplant Product Integration

The problem of multi-plant planning and scheduling along with supply management becomes even more difficult when executed within a *multiple-tiered* corporate system of component, intermediate, and finishing plants. In this environment, the finished output of one plant is a component of another plant's product. The traditional method of scheduling and rescheduling these relationships from the top (i.e., at the level of the finishing plants) and *automatically* driving the production of lower-level plants often has adverse consequences. The following example illuminates this common problem and offers a solution.

Minuteman Electronics Company is a manufacturer of a new line of laptop computers sold throughout the Western hemisphere and is owned by the same holding company that owns the Lightning Computer Company. Final production is done at three facilities in the United States: Boston, Massachusetts (in a plant adjoining corporate headquarters); Raleigh, North Carolina; and Birmingham, Alabama. These finishing plants ship completed goods to one of three warehouses, which are located in Boston (at the plant), Chicago, and San Francisco.

Minuteman's finishing plants are supported by component plants located in Durham, North Carolina, and Waco, Texas; these in turn are supported by two subcomponent plants located in Durham and in Pomona, California. Both subcomponent plants produce printed circuit boards used in the component plants' circuit board assemblies.

In the world of modern manufacturing, in which vertically integrated companies may have several finishing plants (in different countries) for different product lines and several component and subcomponent plants serving these and outside customers, the level of complexity increases dramatically for the supply manager, master (supply) planner, and master (supply) scheduler.

Figure 16.22 describes just such a situation. Here the company operates three levels of production facilities: finishing plants, component plants, and subcomponent plants. Customers and company-owned distribution centers provide demand to the finishing plants, and the finishing plants in turn create demand for components and subcomponents plants. This demand is placed on the various plants through a series of iterations using the master planning and scheduling and material requirements planning systems.

Where should the master planning and scheduling function be located in this interplant system? In a centralized planning and scheduling approach, master planning and scheduling is located at the finishing plant level. Demand comes down from customers,

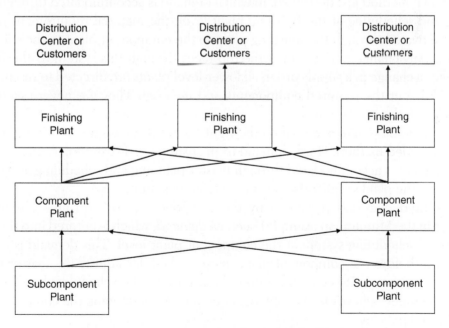

Figure 16.22   Interplant Demand and Supply

distribution centers, or centralized supply management; the production to satisfy that demand is master planned and scheduled at the finishing plant; and the material requirements planning system reaches back through the underlying layers of component and subcomponent facilities to plan and schedule and order all necessary materials and capacity for the facilities. This approach is the norm in many companies, but it has severe negative side effects, as any plant manager at a lower-tier plant will confirm.

What happens in this automated, fully integrated arrangement is that demand changes at the top (at the finishing plant level) cascade downward through the time-phased material planning or material requirement planning system, creating a whipsaw effect at lower levels. Component and subcomponent plants, which must respond mindlessly to customer order changes from above, are burdened with constant production and material schedule adjustments. They cannot decouple themselves from demand at the finishing plant level, nor can they refuse an order that is beyond their capacities. *They cannot, in a sense, control their own destinies*. The result is often chaos for all facilities involved.

Figure 16.23 on page 595 diagrams this situation. On the left-hand side of the figure is the traditional method just described, in which demand is accommodated through master planning and scheduling at the finishing plant level; the material requirement planning system is activated through the finishing plant to the component plant to the subcomponent plant. Any change in demand at the top races through this system. If the finishing plant makes a change in a supply order, all lower-level plants are directed to reschedule-in or reschedule-out the required components and material. They are never asked if they can accomplish the reschedule.

A better way to operate is shown on the right-hand side of Figure 16.23. Today, this is the recommended method. Here, demand from customers, distribution centers, and supply management is accommodated through master planning and scheduling at the finishing plant and the plant's enterprise resource planning system.

The required materials produced by the component plant's (printed circuit board assemblies in the Minuteman example) become *demand*, which is entered into the master planning and scheduling system at the component plant level. This demand is reviewed and analyzed before the component plant master scheduler adjusts the master (supply) schedule to support it. It is only put into the master (supply) schedule when the master (supply) scheduler believes that demand can be met while keeping the component plant within defined policies.

This leads to a very important principle: *People should be held accountable only for those things they can control*. When finishing plants change their production schedules,

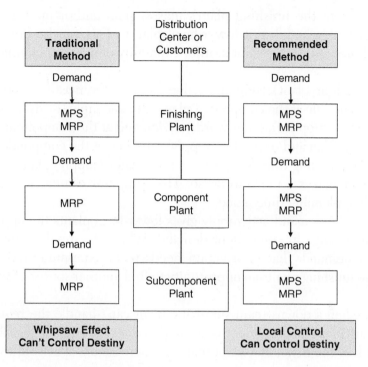

Figure 16.23 Interplant Master Schedule and Material Requirements Planning

and supporting plants are directed to fall in step—without regard to their capabilities and/or capacities—supporting plants are almost automatically set up for failure. In many instances, these supporting plants miss schedules or build and carry unnecessary levels of inventory.

However, this is the way of the future for manufacturing throughout the world. But first, the problem of accountability must be solved. Management knows how to hold people accountable for their actions; how do you hold computer hardware and software accountable for its actions? We don't know how to do this today, but the authors feel we will figure it out in the not-too-distant future (see Final Thoughts on page 783–808 in this book for a discussion on master planning and scheduling in the next couple of decades).

Component and subcomponent plants are in business to support upstream plants. These component and subcomponent plants want to satisfy their customers (upstream plants), but they need a chance to do it right. What is needed is a way to prevent wholesale changes in the finishing plant's master plan and/or master schedule from causing *automatic* reschedules at lower-level plants. This can be done by using the planning time fence and firm planned order capability of master planning and scheduling software.[12]

Driving the finishing plant's component demand into the master (supply) plan and/or master (supply) schedule at the component plants can decouple (by using a planning time fence) demand from supply. In other words, as demand at the component plant changes, the master (supply) plan and/or master (supply) schedule at the component plant will *not* change inside the planning time fence unless the master (supply) planner and/or master (supply) scheduler makes a move to do so. The computer cannot make any *automatic* changes inside the planning time fence.

The decoupling of demand and supply gives lower-level plants the opportunity to say *yes* or *no* to any change in component demand. When the supply plant cannot satisfy that component demand, that information needs to be communicated up the supply chain, giving the finishing plants an opportunity to find another source of supply or replan appropriately.

Additionally, when a downstream supplying plant can't handle the *request for supply* from an upstream plant, management is notified of the situation and possibly can make a decision that solves the issue, like authorizing an increase of capacity at the desired supplying plant.

This same process is continued from the component plants down to the subcomponent plants. In this case, the component's master (supply) plan and/or master (supply) schedule drives lower-level requirements through the enterprise resource planning system, generating demand for circuit boards. This demand enters the master (supply plan) and/or master (supply) schedule of the subcomponent plant. The process just described at the component plant is the same at the subcomponent plant.

The benefit of this recommended method is that it gives greater control to management at each level—the people with the greatest knowledge of local capabilities and constraints. If a subcomponent production line is experiencing a breakdown or scheduled maintenance, or if problems with a supplier have constrained the availability of materials, these plant personnel will know about it. Under the traditional method, master (supply) planners and/or master (supply) schedulers who instigate change at high levels may be oblivious to these lower-level problems.

---

[12] For a review of planning time fences and firm planned order capability, see Chapters 3 through 5.

Key Performance Metrics—Calculations, Colors, Standards

One way to improve record accuracy and supply chain performance is to *measure it, analyze it, and correct it!* Just paying attention to record accuracy and/or performance will generate improvement; "now, that's not so hard to do" might be a general reaction. No, it's not! But you have to do it. And when you do it, you might as well take a look at the measurement results and do something with those results.

There are three defined accuracy (bills-of-material, routings, inventory records) and three or four defined performance (approved aggregate supply plan, master (supply) plan and/or master (supply) schedule, detailed manufacturing or production schedule) criteria that must be met for a company to achieve Class A. Best practice as well as Class A for each of these criteria is defined as 95 percent or better for achieving the *integrated planning and control milestone* and 99.5 percent or the upper quartile of a company's business industry for *true best-practice and/or Class A in managing internal supply!* There is one exception to the Class A milestone 95 percent criteria just stated: bills-of-material accuracy must be 98 percent or above.

Many companies, especially Class A companies, like to color code (red, yellow, green, and sometimes blue) their monthly accuracy and performance results. These color codes quickly display a picture of how the company is doing, what the company does well, what the company does not do so well, and what needs the company's attention. As most supply chain professionals know, green means good, yellow means caution, red means bad, and blue might mean outstanding and better than good.

Once the color coding is done, the action taken from this point forward is what might make or break the use of an accuracy or performance measurement system. Some companies just post the number and color on a chart and hang that chart in the lobby, hallway, cafeteria, and so on.

By doing so, chances are good that accuracy and performance will probably improve, but will it improve to what's actually possible? The answer to this question is, probably not! More can be done by implementing a key performance indicator (KPI) program that uses a defined measurement process, color coding, measurement posting, Pareto analysis, corrective action identification, corrective action approval, corrective action implementation, result posting and reporting, and improvement follow-up!

A simple flow diagram showing the different activities and actions that might be taken once an accuracy or performance result has been identified is a useful tool in managing performance. The measurement passes through a series of yes-or-no questions and, depending on the answers to those questions, follow-on activities are identified. An example of this flow diagram is shown in Chapter 20, Figure 20.2 on page 757.

For example, if the master (supply) plan and/or master (supply) schedule is measured and reported to be 97 percent in a particular month, it might be coded *green* in regard to the MPS Class A milestone. The next question regarding this input is to determine if this result has been attained for three consecutive months.

If the answer to this question is *yes*, a reward of some kind might be given to those that made this happen. If the answer to this last question is *no*, a discussion on how to sustain this lofty performance is conducted. And so, the process continues for all the accuracy and performance results gathered each month.

Again, just paying attention to KPIs can generate improvement, but doing the identified analysis and taking corrective action can move accuracy and performance toward those best-practice goals rather quickly. Today, companies rely on people to do this analysis, identify problem areas, develop suitable solutions, secure approvals required, and do or support the implementation of the noted corrective action.

In other words, people play an integral part when it comes to an accuracy and performance measurement program. The next section discusses some additional (over and beyond ensuring company-defined accuracy and performance compliance) responsibilities assigned a supply manager or master (supply) planner.

Should Companies Have Supply Managers and/or Master Planners?

This chapter has spelled out the many tasks of the supply manager and/or master (supply) planner. In a simpler world, when companies operated out of single manufacturing facilities, the idea of having a corporate-level associate assigned to these tasks would not have been particularly compelling. The manufacturing manager and plant master (supply) scheduler would have handled those tasks.

But that simpler world has largely disappeared for a number of major companies, and someone (or more than one) must take responsibility for their greater supply planning and supply coordination needs. That someone is the corporate supply manager and/or master (supply) planner. Although many of these large manufacturers do not staff such a position, most should.

The cost of salary and benefits for a good supply manager and/or master (supply) planner is minuscule when compared to the losses incurred through unnecessary overstocks, unfilled customer orders, over- and underloaded plants, and production snafus in general.

But what are the specific responsibilities of a supply manager and/or master (supply) planner?

1. Working closely with demand management to establish a supply plan consistent with company policies.

2. Optimizing the performance of manufacturing plants while satisfying firm and anticipated demand.

3. Evaluating current supply capabilities relative to the company supply plan and recommend production changes as required.

4. Coordinating the aggregation of current and planned plant production information and incorporating that information into the company supply plan.

5. Coordinating raw material supply with purchasing and plant production to ensure their availability with respect to the company supply plan, company master (supply) plan, and plant master (supply) schedules.

6. Ensuring that the supply manager's and/or master (supply) planner's monthly *requests for production* are reflected in actual plant output.

7. Advising the demand manager and/or demand planner regarding changes in plant capabilities, particularly as they may affect the ability to satisfy customers.

8. Communicating regularly with plant-level master (supply) schedulers to determine demonstrated plant capacities and the impact of production changes on the company supply plan, company master (supply) plan, and on individual master (supply) schedules.

9. Ensuring that inventory levels fall within approved ranges.

10. Ensuring that backlogs are managed to competitive and approved levels.

To fulfill these responsibilities, the supply manager and/or master (supply) planner must bring certain knowledge, experience, and personal abilities to the job. He or she must have a solid understanding of the company's plant production processes, production and inventory control system, order management routines, and shipping/transportation scheduling procedures.

Knowledge of raw materials, plant resources, and an understanding of the company's sales structure, product lines, and customer base are also very important; so too is a thorough understanding of the master planning and scheduling process, policies, procedures, work instructions, planning and control techniques, current state technology, and tools (i.e., Microsoft office products, process flow diagrams, etc.).

A good supply manager and/or master (supply) planner also has a number of skills and personal qualities:

- Analytical, mathematical, and problem-solving skills;

- The ability to communicate effectively, verbally as well as through written texts, e-mails, and reports;

- An ability to work with personnel in many functional areas;

- Good planning, execution, and time management skills.

The overarching responsibilities of a supply manager and/or master (supply) planner are represented in Figure 16.24 on page 601. There we can see that the supply manager and/or master (supply) planner interfaces with each of the key planning functions in manufacturing: aggregate supply planning, resource requirements planning at the product family level, master (supply) planning, master (supply) scheduling, rough cut capacity planning at the group or finished goods level, materials planning, capacity planning, plant scheduling, supplier scheduling, and logistics planning.

The supply manager and/or master (supply) planner stands, in effect, between these planning functions and the demand side of the business, which forms the left-hand side of the figure. This central position is shared with the supply manager's counterpart, the demand manager and/or the master supply planner's counterpart, the demand planner; together they represent the yin and yang of effective and orderly manufacturing in a complex world. The demand and supply managers share common performance goals and performance measures. Thus, they must work closely together to get the job done.

The tasks of demand management parallel those of supply management and these demand management tasks are the subject of our next chapter. Until the past couple decades or so, few individuals were uniquely assigned responsibility for either set of tasks. Instead, their functions were parceled out to different managers or worse, were the responsibility of no one in particular.

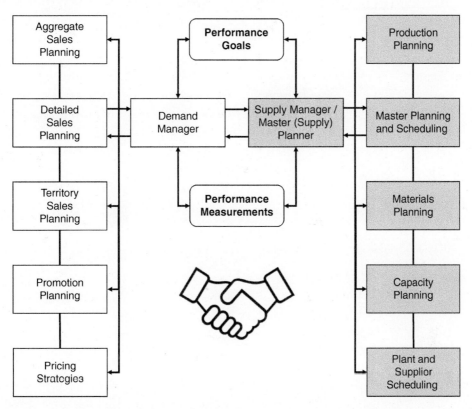

Figure 16.24 **The Role of the Supply Manager and/or Master (Supply) Planner**

Fortunately, a growing number of companies have recognized the importance of demand and supply management, and many are creating management (in some cases, director) positions with those titles. Doing so is one of the most important steps that a multi-business/multi-plant company can take to ensure that demand and supply is balanced in the most cost-efficient and customer-satisfying way.

17

Demand Management and Aggregate Master Planning

Customers can order anything they want as long as it agrees with the forecast.

In the final analysis, virtually all of us show up at work on Monday morning for one reason: to either create or satisfy demand for our company's products or services. Customer demand is the spark that ignites our entire economic system, and it serves as the controlling factor in all productive activities. While product supply can sometimes get out of balance and the imbalance appears as unsold inventory or poor customer service, the clear signal of customer demand eventually brings production back into equilibrium.

The master (supply) planner's and/or master (supply) scheduler's role in this dynamic process has already been discussed: to harmonize the *when* and *how much* of supply (produced or purchased) with actual and forecasted customer demand. If forecasted demand was always reliable, this would be a simpler job. But as we will see shortly, nothing is simple in predicting the future of customer orders.

What Is Demand Management?

The idea of supply management is easy enough to understand: It implies controlling the production and procurement processes to specified levels of output. Since manufacturing facilities and labor are under the control of the company's management, these ideas seem straightforward.

The concept of demand management requires more explanation. Demand generally comes from outside the company and is thus beyond the full control of the company's leadership and management teams, prompting many to ask, "What's to manage? Bring it on!" To a sales representative living and working a thousand miles away from the company's production facility or facilities, the idea of managing demand seems unimportant. All he or she may be interested in is managing the order book—getting as many orders booked as quickly as possible. More orders mean more commissions, and more compliments from management. If February's customer orders are twice those of January's, that is an unqualified achievement. If everyone doubled his or her customer orders, however, manufacturing could be thrown into chaos, and possibly only about half of those customer orders would be filled on time and as promised.

Because demand is largely external to the company, it would be convenient to proceed with the notion that demand should be left to rise and fall of its own accord, with all of management's attention directed toward supply. However, this notion fails on several counts:

- Few manufacturing facilities are so flexible with respect to volume that they can operate efficiently with low output in one period and high output in the next. This violates the basic principle of load leveling.

- Not all demand is external to the company—at least in the larger sense. Much of modern production simply creates intermediates or components for use in final products manufactured by the same company or its subsidiaries. At the end of the twentieth century, for example, General Motors Corporation *in*sourced 70 percent of its components and subassemblies. Thus, even though the final customer decision is external, demand is not entirely created from outside the company.

- Demand can be created, or its timing shifted, through marketing. Thus, the idea of managing demand is reasonable and necessary if customer demand and the company's supply capabilities are to be kept in balance.[1]

---

[1] For a complete treatment of demand management and forecasting, see Colleen Crum and George E. Palmatier, *Demand Management Best Practices: Process, Principles and Collaboration* (Boca Raton, FL: J. Ross Publishing, 2003).

Demand management has four fundamental requirements:

1. *Prediction*—Maintaining a balance of demand and supply requires some ability to know the level of incoming orders *in advance*, especially for products the company is using a make-to-stock manufacturing strategy for and/or for products the company is using a package-to-order, kit-to-order, finish-to-order, assembly-to-order, or make-to-order manufacturing strategy for coupled with supply lead times that are shorter than competitive demand lead times.

2. *Communication*—Infantry units have traditionally established listening posts to detect and give early warning of approaching enemy forces. Successful companies know that they will have a chance of preparing for incoming demand if they maintain their own listening posts near the customers. Typically, this is done through the field sales force, which visits customer facilities, talks with procurement and purchasing managers, and otherwise tries to gauge the level and timing of future orders.

3. *Influence*—Communication leads to knowledge, and knowledge leads to influence. As described earlier, manufacturing works to level the load on the production facility; it abhors a situation where it works at 100 percent of capacity in odd-numbered months and at 50 percent during even-numbered months. Ideally, the plant manager would like work scheduled at 75, 85, or 95 (sometimes 100) percent of capacity *every* month.

   The master planner and/or master scheduler uses his or her influence with sales and marketing to negotiate, where necessary, the shifting of customer demand to produce a better situation on the manufacturing floor—one that makes better use of fixed assets and human resources. This might take the form of a phone call, e-mail, or text message to marketing or to the sales representative to ask, "Do you really need this big order in October? Would it be helpful to you if we shipped a third of it in September and two-thirds of it in October? Or would it be a problem for you if we shipped half of it in October and the other half in November?"

   Marketing can also influence demand, both its quantity and timing, through the use of advertising, pricing, and incentives to dealers, sales representatives, and customers.

4. *Prioritization and Allocation*—The idea behind demand management and master planning and scheduling is to satisfy all customer demand while safely making money and a profit for the company. However, if a situation presents itself in which less product exists than requested, or the materials and resources needed to produce

the required product are not available, then a decision must be made as to which customers get their orders filled as requested and which ones need to wait (another way to say this is which customers have the highest priority). This decision is the responsibility of sales and marketing.

Allocation is the process used when the company cannot produce enough product to cover the demand, whereas prioritization is the process used to determine which customer's order is filled first. If a company cannot produce enough product, then some business may have to be turned away. In this case, the available product needs to be allocated so that the company does not oversell and overcommit its ability to produce.

Thus, the idea of planning and managing demand is reasonable and has plenty of precedents. Let's take a look at a sample company that uses forecasting techniques to attempt to understand its customer's ordering pattern(s).

THE ROLE OF FORECASTING IN A COMPANY: THE CASE OF HASTINGS & BROWN

Richard Phillips sat in front of his computer, checking all the numbers he had just entered into an elaborate spreadsheet. The first column listed each of the company's 50 key products, which collectively accounted for almost 95 percent of company revenues. Arrayed across the top were the company's 42 sales territories. The number he entered into each cell represented a sales forecast by product as determined by a field representative, based upon contacts with customers who were just then beginning the lengthy process of making purchase decisions.

Phillips was assistant sales director for Hastings & Brown (H&B), a U.S. publisher of college textbooks with annual revenues of $38 million. H&B's customers were college professors scattered across North America who determined which textbooks their students would be required to use during the next fall semester. Their purchase decisions were generally made between April 15 and June 15.

Each April, Phillips had to prepare a sales forecast for July through September, the period during which fall semester books would be ordered. Although this was his third experience of handling the fall forecast, this year would be more difficult than ever. Many new editions of H&B texts were just now being published, and their acceptance by the marketplace would be one large question mark until actual customer orders came in from the field. The competition had been active in both new publications and promotions. Forecasting fall sales this year would clearly be more difficult than in any of the past few years.

In H&B's industry, every new book was an experiment. Many, in fact, joked that "the first printing is our market research." Some of the books published in the spring would catch on and be ordered in large numbers for the fall and for subsequent semesters; most, however, would be used by just a few schools and would disappear from the marketplace in a year or two. Determining the winners and losers at this point was the tough part.

Many in H&B management needed the forecast and would rely on it for a variety of purposes. Phillips's boss needed it for his report to the president. He would also comb through it for evidence of big winners to be touted to the sales force to spur them on to even larger sales.

The production manager would use the forecast to plan reprints. Since the first printing of a new title was indeed a form of market research, initial printings were deliberately kept small. Once the winners were identified by the field sales force, plans for second printings had to be made; the same had to be done for other, older publications.

The company's financial manager also had a keen interest in the forecast, as he would have to finance production and budget further expenses. Finally, H&B's president would be making his quarterly trek to New York, where he was expected to report to the parent company's board of directors on the plans and progress of the subsidiary company he managed. The fall sales forecast would be his primary resource in preparing for that important meeting.

All forecasted sales figures were submitted directly by the field sales representatives, who were (or were supposed to be) in regular contact with their customers. As a former field representative who knew most of the field staff, Phillips was suspicious of many of their forecasts. He remembered the Nashville representative, Rhett Farnsworthy, as a self-styled big shot. Farnsworthy's forecasts were always higher than just about everyone else's, yet his optimism was never supported by actual sales. Joan Sommerville of Seattle, on the other hand, was a high-performing sales representative who invariably turned in a low forecast.

Phillips liked to think that the overly optimistic and overly pessimistic figures submitted by individual field representatives would naturally cancel each other out when the figures were aggregated by dollars into a final forecast. But he had neither the time nor a method to empirically evaluate that theory.

He suspected some field representatives of simply pulling numbers out of a hat. Because the forecast played no part in establishing sales quotas for their territories, and since no rewards or penalties were ever assessed for accurate or inaccurate forecasts, the largely unsupervised field representatives had no particular incentive to take the forecasting job seriously. To many, it was an annual chore that took away from their selling time. H&B management had never emphasized the importance of good sales forecasting to the overall workings of the company, nor had it provided them with a methodology for doing the job systematically.

One who did take the forecasting job seriously was Arthur Petersen, of the Wisconsin territory. Petersen had a reputation for being diligent in developing his territory forecast for each major project. He kept careful records of past order quantities, called his customers frequently about their plans, and used early customer order patterns to project future orders. This attention to detail paid off in booking customer orders and in more accurate forecasts for the Wisconsin territory. But Petersen was an exception to the rule.

Phillips continued the tedious business of compiling the forecast figures, and as he did so he determined that he would ask Petersen to develop a short training program on sales forecasting for the other sales representatives. But not until next year.

This story of sales forecasting at Hastings & Brown is not meant to be typical, but to illustrate good and bad forecasting methods and show how forecasts are used by different parties in a company.

Master planning and scheduling is one of those parties or functions that relies heavily on an accurate forecast or, better said, a forecast created by demand professionals who (to the best of their ability) highlight potential future business (as they know it) at the time the forecast is created. It is a known fact that most forecasts are *wrong*, or, again better said, are somewhat *inaccurate*.

Regardless of inaccuracies contained in a company's forecast, it is (and should be) used during the planning phase of demand management. Another key takeaway from this story is that the demand organization needs to be responsible and accountable for informing the supply organization of anticipated and booked demand by product (new offerings as well as current offerings), quantity (volumes as well as mix), and due date (one-time as well as recurring).

The Impact of New Product in Demand Management

This book has emphasized over and over again that supply chain management (sometimes referred to as value chain management) is a demand-driven process during planning and is either a demand-driven or supply-driven process during execution. As stated earlier in this chapter, demand generally comes from outside the company and is thus beyond the full control of the company's leadership and management teams, prompting many to ask, "What's to manage?" This question was addressed earlier in the opening section of this chapter on demand management and aggregate master planning (and master scheduling).

Anticipated demand comes in a couple different flavors, those of current market offerings and new market offerings. New market offerings are generally referred to as new product and planned by when these product ideas enter the new product development pipeline funnel as well as the new product master launch plan. The good news is that portfolio management plans the company's new product ideas through to launching defined new products into the marketplace.

However, many companies do *not* include this data and information in their demand plan, much less in either the company's master (supply) plan or the master (supply) schedule. Why, oh why, is this so true, so often? Unfortunately, the authors do *not* have an answer for the reader on this one.

Ignoring this data and information doesn't make any sense. In order for a company to have a complete, valid, realistic, and informative demand plan, all anticipated demands as known at the time of creating the demand plan must be included on the demand plan!

Don't bother worrying whether it's about Class A through Class D, it just is *common sense*, or what Oliver Wight principals refer to as *organized common sense*. The next section is a modified description of what was discussed in the previous chapter on supply management and aggregate master planning—including the new product launch plan and new product pipeline funnel in the demand management process.

Master Launch Plan and Pipeline Funnel Examples for New Products

As a review of the integrated business planning (IBP) discussion in Chapters 14 through 16, the reader should have noted and digested the sequence of IBP reviews: (1) close the books for the prior month, (2) portfolio and/or product (management) review, planning new products and the company's product portfolio, (3) demand (management) review planning new products as well as current saleable products, (4) supply (management) review planning how the supply organization is to respond to the demand organization's request for product, (5) integrated reconciliation review working out issues between the proposed demand plan and the proposed supply plan, (6) financial (management) appraisal regarding proposed demand and supply plans, and (7) management business review planning/reviewing/replanning/approving moving forward with newly updated product, demand, supply, and financial plans. Closely following the closing of the prior month's books (sometimes even before the book closing is completed), the company's new products' launch and pipeline plans are reviewed and replanned as necessary.

The company's launch (when a new product is expected to enter development as well as when the new product is anticipated to be available for the marketplace) and demand pipelines (when the new product is expected to be available for the sales organization to sell to customers) have a direct impact on the demand organization's sales targets, expected revenues, commission structures, market shares, company growth, and so forth. Demand managers and demand planners need to understand these new product plans along with their accuracy and reliability.

Now, let's spend a little time looking at an example of a master launch plan followed by short discussions regarding both the new product funnel as well as the sales funnel; both funnels impact demand management in addition to master planning and scheduling.

A company's master launch plan is most likely tied to the sales pipeline. Using the master (new product) launch plan, the demand manager and/or demand planner can make plans for product development's new product entering the marketplace, product growth in marketplace, new product marketplace promotions, and so forth. The master product launch plan also alerts demand management when account management and account managers will be needed as well as when after-market service needs to be available for supporting product implementations.

For review (the master launch plan was introduced in Chapter 16), Figure 17.1a on page 611 is an example of what a master launch plan for new product may look like. The reader will see similarities to Chapter 16 examples or, in some cases, repeats of Chapter 16 examples for continuity and understanding.

Reviewing the figure, the reader can see products under development, type of product, whether the product is forecasted, anticipated launch date, and reschedules made to the last master launch plan. Additionally, issues regarding product launches are called out along with a summary of delays, accelerations, and projects moved in or out. All of this information is valuable to the company's demand management team.

Next, displayed in Figure 17.2 on page 612 is the example of the product development pipeline coupled with financials. Again, reviewing this figure, the reader can see the various stages of the product development cycle. The figure displays an area to note ideas followed by the company's stages and gates followed by product going to market.

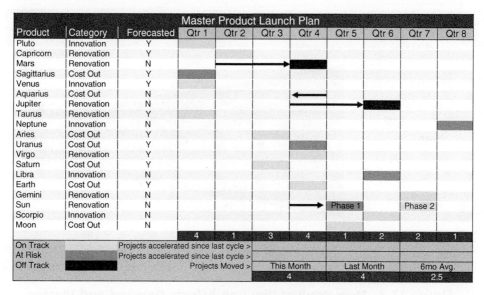

Product	Category	Forecasted	Qtr 1	Qtr 2	Qtr 3	Qtr 4	Qtr 5	Qtr 6	Qtr 7	Qtr 8
			Master Product Launch Plan							
Pluto	Innovation	Y								
Capricorn	Renovation	Y								
Mars	Renovation	N		→		■				
Sagittarius	Cost Out	Y								
Venus	Innovation	Y								
Aquarius	Cost Out	N				←				
Jupiter	Renovation	N				→		■		
Taurus	Renovation	Y								
Neptune	Innovation	N								
Aries	Cost Out	Y								
Uranus	Cost Out	Y								
Virgo	Renovation	Y								
Saturn	Cost Out	Y								
Libra	Innovation	N								
Earth	Cost Out	Y								
Gemini	Renovation	N								
Sun	Renovation	N				→	Phase 1		Phase 2	
Scorpio	Innovation	N								
Moon	Cost Out	N								
			4	1	3	4	1	2	2	1

On Track	Projects accelerated since last cycle >	
At Risk	Projects accelerated since last cycle >	
Off Track	Projects Moved >	This Month / Last Month / 6mo Avg.
		4 / 4 / 2.5

Figure 17.1a Product Launch Plans Affect Demand and Master (Supply) Planning

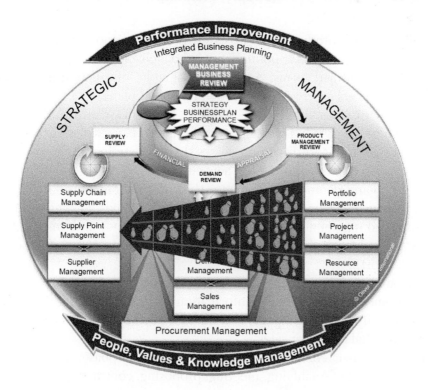

Figure 17.1b Integrated Business Model with Emphasis on Product Launch

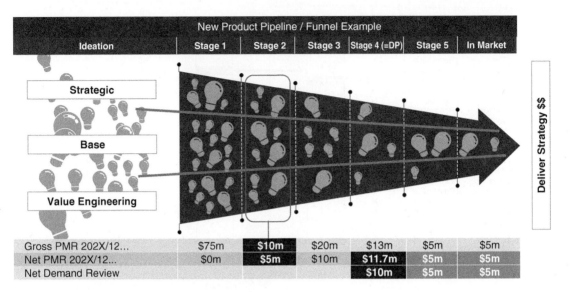

New Product Pipeline / Funnel Example						
Ideation	Stage 1	Stage 2	Stage 3	Stage 4 (=DP)	Stage 5	In Market

Strategic

Base

Value Engineering

Deliver Strategy $$

	Stage 1	Stage 2	Stage 3	Stage 4 (=DP)	Stage 5	In Market
Gross PMR 202X/12...	$75m	$10m	$20m	$13m	$5m	$5m
Net PMR 202X/12...	$0m	$5m	$10m	$11.7m	$5m	$5m
Net Demand Review				$10m	$5m	$5m

Figure 17.2   New Product Pipeline Affects Demand and Master (Supply) Planning

Additionally, the new product funnel lists gross demand and net anticipated demand financials. The entire pipeline is pointed toward a delivery strategy objective noted in financial or other identified terms. Again, this valuable information is so important to include in the company's aggregate and detailed demand plans.

There's another pipeline funnel that needs to be included in the demand management process. Since the demand management (DM) and master planning and scheduling (MPS) processes are demand-driven processes during planning, the demand (including potential business from current as well as new customers) must be known by the demand managers and demand planners. The sooner this information can be made available to the demand management team, the better. In most companies, making arrangements to secure the required market and customer support takes money and time (as time passes, more money for various reasons is required to secure the needed customer service and after-market support).

Take a look at Figure 17.3 on the following page, which is an example of a company's sales pipeline funnel. As we review the information displayed in the figure, the reader can see a column identifying sales suspects that have been categorized as growth, sustaining, and strategic potential customer sales.

Following the prospect column, we have the sales activity phases and check milestones for the sales cycle, that of qualifying, meeting, proposing, contracting, and closing. These

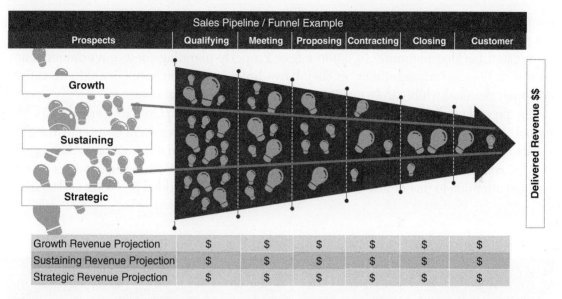

Sales Pipeline / Funnel Example						
Prospects	Qualifying	Meeting	Proposing	Contracting	Closing	Customer

Growth Revenue Projection	$	$	$	$	$	$
Sustaining Revenue Projection	$	$	$	$	$	$
Strategic Revenue Projection	$	$	$	$	$	$

Figure 17.3   Customer Pipeline Affects Demand and Master (Supply) Planning

phases and milestones lead to prospects becoming potential business to becoming active customers within the business.

Additionally, the sales pipeline funnel lists potential future revenues for growth, sustaining, and strategic business. The entire pipeline is pointed toward a delivered revenue financial objective. Let's say it one more time: This known, discussed, and reviewed (within the demand organization) information is very important to include in the company's demand plan(s). It's there for the taking and should *not* be ignored.

As has been noted earlier, today's demand management and master planning and scheduling is more art than science (yes, that's all changing in this and future decades). So, until demand management and master planning and scheduling truly become more science than art within a company (see this book's Final Thoughts on pages 783–808), a process should be in place to ensure that those in demand management as well as supply management are given the data and information that they need to know. *As the old saying goes, if you don't know where you are going, any road will get you there!*

The art and science of demand management, supply management, and master planning and scheduling begin with the art and science of integrated business planning, including portfolio and/or product planning, demand planning, supply planning, and financial planning. Well, there are numerous environments and situations that require demand planning—product-driven aggregate inventory planning, product-driven aggregate back-log planning, product-driven disaggregated inventory planning, and product-driven dis-aggregated backlog planning, to name a few. Properly planning these environments are a must in demand management, as they have direct impact on supply's ability to satisfy customer demand while safely making money and profit for the company.

The preceding discussion regarding the new product launch plan, new product pipeline funnel, and sales pipeline funnel is repeated from the supply management chapter to assist the reader in understanding the importance of including this data and information in their aggregate, as well as detailed, demand and supply planning processes. With that all said, it's time to turn our attention to that demand forecast coupled with its embedded problems and issues.

Problems with the Demand Forecast

Virtually every industry employs one or more individuals to forecast future levels of business activity; in the H&B case, this task was done by unsupervised field sales representatives. Other companies use more formal processes. The many sectors of the energy industry, for example, attempt to predict demand for coal, natural gas, and petroleum so that production, distribution, and financing can be arranged in an orderly fashion. Large individual companies like money center banks, auto producers, and chemical giants have traditionally employed individuals with specialized training to develop proprietary forecasts of future business activity.

Whichever way demand forecasting is conducted, one thing can be said with some certainty: The forecast is never 100 percent accurate. (One of the authors had the privilege of working with one Class A company that did have 100 percent forecast accuracy. That company built only one product, had only one customer, and a customer backlog that stretched out for around eight years—forecasting was not their problem.)

Economist John Kenneth Galbraith once remarked, "We have two classes of forecasters: those who don't know, and those who don't know they don't know." Predicting the behavior of thousands, if not millions, of individual decision makers is by nature a questionable business, no matter how scientifically done.

The result is that forecasts are invariably inaccurate to some degree. Economic and stock market forecasters are often held up for special ridicule; indeed, many joke that economic seers exist solely for the purpose of making astrologers look good.

The Impact of Demand Bias on Supply Chain Management

Demand and supply management along with master planning and scheduling are once again driven by anticipated customer demand, certainly during the planning process. Best practice dictates that this anticipated demand be the best forecast of future needs as known at the time of creating the demand plan. To say this in a few different words, the master planning and scheduling function, as part of the supply management function and in support of the demand management function, must receive notification of what the demand organization really thinks it can sell and/or what the marketplace will buy in future time periods.

This statement of anticipated demand must *not* be influenced by the supply organization's current capability to deliver the requested product. Again, in other words, the anticipated demand is *not* supply constrained. Although the anticipated demand is *not* supply constrained, it is constrained by the company's strategy; that is, company's strategy might be to focus on big box stores, not small, single-site operations.

With this said, most, if not all, demand organizations seem to want to take the supply organization's capability and capacity into account during the demand planning phase (the authors' experience through all these years). Unfortunately, by doing so, potential business and sales may be left on the table (given enough time and money, supply can do a lot in satisfying true, unconstrained demand).

Even though the demand organization may understand the concept of demand that is unconstrained by supply (remember, demand is constrained by business strategy), it is possible that bias will be built into the anticipated demand plan. This bias can also present problems for master planning and scheduling and the supply chain management function.

Figure 17.4 on page 616 displays a couple of charts showing negative and positive biases. A *negative bias* is one where the demand plan is continually *under* the actual demand received from the marketplace. A *positive bias* is one where the demand plan is continually *over* the actual demand received from the marketplace.

If the noted biases are unknown, both situations create an unhealthy master planning and scheduling environment. Whether the demand plan submitted to the supply organization contains negative or positive bias, the people using a demand plan known to contain some level of bias may have reservations about and be resistant to creating supply plans that commit the company to purchasing materials and/or producing products in order to satisfy the received demand plan.

Identifying and Recognizing the Impact of Bias

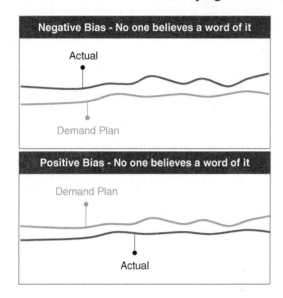

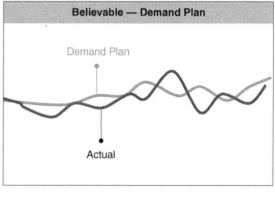

Figure 17.4 Demand Bias Affects Master Planning and Scheduling

What tends to happen is known in industry as *second guessing*! Said another way, the supply organization just won't believe the demand plan and will create their own anticipated demand plan. How's that for having people that far away from the marketplace and customer base thinking they know what those customers are going to buy? This is known in industry as a *lose-lose* situation. ***Accountability is all but lost!***

What's needed is a demand plan that is free from demand biases and supply constraints. Of course, this is the ideal situation, but it is hard to realize this happening in many companies, certainly at the beginning of a company's journey to best practices and the achievement of something referred to as Class A by Oliver Wight Principals. As an interim step to truly practicing Class A principles in demand management, it is suggested that known demand plan biases be shared and documented for those with a need to know (i.e., supply chain management professionals).

Is this book biased in securing valid and useable demand data and information for master planners and schedulers?) Yes, it is! There, it's on the table.

The right side of Figure 17.4 shows a chart where sometimes actual demand exceeds the demand plan and sometimes the demand plan exceeds actual demand. Chances are good that this demand pattern is what most master planners and/or master schedulers will be faced with if all (or most) of demand bias is removed from the demand plan. Demand planning is somewhat like capacity planning—both are a form of aggregate planning.

One final note regarding the *lose-lose* situation highlighted a couple paragraphs ago. Although a *lose-lose* situation is not a *win-win* situation, there is some good news (along with more bad news) in it. The reader needs to understand that those who are second guessing are really trying to do the right thing, that of keeping the company out of trouble due to an invalid and unrealistic demand plan. That's the good news; the bad news is that those people generally don't communicate their second-guessing thoughts.

And when this second guessing happens, the second guessers really hope the demand creators are wrong, because if the demand creators are right, the company has a few more problems to deal with, like promises made to customers and suppliers that won't be kept, inventory that doesn't get better with age, increased backlogs that cause longer delivery lead times, lost business due to lack of product availability, red-faced demand and supply personnel, and so forth. It's just not a good situation!

Putting aside demand planning constraining anticipated demand by current supply capability and capacity along with introducing both negative and positive biases into the demand plan, there are other elements that need to be taken into account when creating the all-important demand plan. It is not an easy job to visualize entirely what the marketplace and customers will be buying next week, next month, next quarter, and even next year!

Forecasting, like master planning and scheduling, is a combination of art and science. The question is, "Is the forecast more art than science or is it more science than art?" Regardless of the answer, chances are good that the forecast does contain errors and is not one hundred percent accurate. So, what does a company do about using this inaccurate forecast to drive the internal (and, sometimes, external) supply or value chain management?

Coping with Forecast Inaccuracies

Even though demand forecasts are imperfect, they are necessary, and companies have developed a number of ways to make the most of the situation. Over the years, the authors have observed how different companies cope with the inherent inaccuracies of demand

Accountability	Lead-Time Reduction
Communication	Manufacturing Flexibility
Customer/Supplier Linking	Performance Measurement
Demand Management	Reserve Capacity
Forecasting Systems	IBP, S&OP, and MPS Policies
Frequent Reviews	Safety Stocks and Option Overplanning

forecasting. Here are the 12 most popular techniques used in today's environment, listed alphabetically.

The reader may be asking, "What is the number-one way companies cope with the inaccurate forecast?" Well, the authors for years collected this information and even though it might not be the best solution for coping with the inaccurate forecast, the answer is, by far, **safety stocking**! The others that make the top five responses are **communications, manufacturing flexibility, reserve capacity,** and **demand management** (the subject of this chapter).

Accountability, frequent reviews, performance measurements, and **lead time reduction** all are in the top 12 responses, but they are further down on the list (*Are you surprised?*). *These last-mentioned four ways to cope with forecast inaccuracies are among the best solutions!* Just *paying attention to the numbers* and *measuring the accuracy of these numbers* generally increase the accuracy of the forecast. And, for sure, *reducing the lead time* (overall planning, material ordering, queue staging, product building, etc.) is one of the very best ways to cope with the inaccuracies of the demand forecast (the further out on the planning horizon that sales and marketing has to predict demand, the less accurate that prediction will be! Last, but not least, is the all-important *accountability*; identifying who is accountable and holding that person truly accountable can work miracles.

The two previous paragraphs covered 9 of the 12 ways to cope with forecast inaccuracies; what was left out? There's *customer/supplier linking, forecast systems,* and *IBP/S&OP/MPS policies*. While these three solutions do address the issue of an inaccurate forecast, they probably should and do find their place on the bottom of the list (this is not to say they are poor choices, but rather to say that the other choices might be better and more effective). Certainly, linking and sharing information with a company's customer and/or supplier is a big plus; however, sometimes the company's customers and suppliers are dealing with the same or similar issues and problems that the company doing the forecasting is also experiencing.

Additionally, creating, documenting, training, and implementing policies (the rules to be followed) do *not* guarantee that all the issues and problems with the forecast will disappear. Of course, if the creators and users of the demand forecast don't know the rules and/or they don't follow them, it becomes a *so-what* scenario. Now, truly implementing an integrated business planning or sales and operations planning and master planning and scheduling process at a Class A level requires a company to shore up the driver of this overall planning process (again, bookend company objectives are to satisfy customers and sales while safely making money and a profit).

Finally, technology advancements in today's world are mandatory in product and/or portfolio management, demand management, supply management, logistics management, and financial management. Using an up-to-date forecasting system is a big plus in the efforts to create what some might call a realistic and usable demand forecast.

Reviewing and Approving the Aggregate Demand Plan

Master planning and scheduling is the function and process a best-practice company uses to tie the aggregate demand plan to lower-level detailed demand plans. Additionally, master planning and scheduling is also used to translate the approved demand plan into detailed terms that are understood by personnel in middle management as well as those personnel charged with executing the detail (plan) that makes up the aggregate (plan).

Figure 17.5 on page 620 shows the integration of integrated business planning with the monthly demand review process and its demand management function with master planning and scheduling function and its supply management function. These all-important planning processes tie the demand and supply functions and their processes together, starting at the top (planning level) and moving to the bottom (planning level) along with tying the bottom (planning level) to the top (planning level).

Additionally, let's *not* forget that these functions and processes also need to be tied side-to-side, meaning that the demand review must be integrated with the product and portfolio

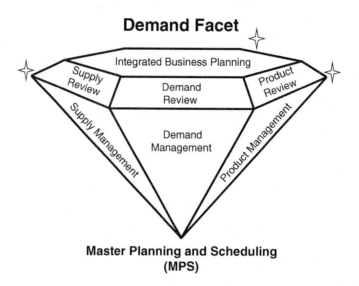

Figure 17.5 Tying the Approved Demand Plan to Integrated Business Planning and Master Planning and Scheduling

review as well as integrated with the supply review and that demand management must be integrated with product and portfolio management as well as supply management. This is not to say that demand management isn't integrated with the other functions of the company; in fact, Class A companies are integrated and linked throughout the company!

The approved demand plan(s) is/are then the input to the company's master planning and scheduling function (refer to Figure 17.6 for a visual of this integrated environment).

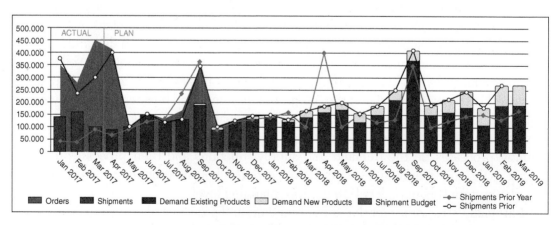

Figure 17.6 Demand Management Includes a Formal Demand Plan

As illustrated in the figure (as an example), the beginning time periods display past demand orders received and shipped (Shipments). Moving out throughout the demand planning horizon, booked customer orders along with anticipated customer orders are shown by demands for existing products and demands for new products. Completing the chart are references to actual shipments by month for the same period in the prior year (Shipments Prior Year) as well as the approved demand plan from the prior IBP/S&OP cycle (Shipments Prior) as compared to the anticipated shipments in the next two years.

Key to best practice and Class A demand management and supply management including master planning and scheduling is a combination of knowledgeable people behaving in a Class A manner, integrated Class A best practices throughout the demand and supply management functions, up-to-date Class A technology and support systems, and Class A data integrity in all supporting records (i.e., customer record accuracy and accurate forecasts coupled with accurate sales order processing, accurate inventory records, and so forth).

Another key to a company demonstrating Class A best-practice behaviors is that of linking, not only its sales and marketing functions together, but also its sales offices, distribution warehouses, transportation entities, and all of the supplying facilities. Again, although this integration may *not* be easy, it's just what Class A companies routinely do!

It's About Quantities

To be useful to the master planner and/or master scheduler, forecasts must be expressed as items or groups of items (or product subfamilies), quantities, and dates. A forecast of $10 million in sales revenue is of little value to the multiproduct company when it needs to schedule its production. A forecast of 1,000 red golf shirts, 2,000 blue golf shirts, and 1,500 blue sport shirts with red trim is more useful. Getting from a useless to a useful demand forecast is a challenging activity in which marketing, sales, manufacturing, and logistics can participate for mutual benefit.

Breaking Down the Forecast

For the company with multiple product lines, the forecast may be developed in the aggregate but must then be broken down into manufacturable segments. Consider an office furniture manufacturer with a very simple offering of two products whose forecast for a time period looks like Figure 17.7.

If these products were made in one style and color, this forecast would be directly usable by the master planner and/or master scheduler. There would be two discrete products to be built in specified quantities, and each of these would have a specific bill-of-materials. But business is rarely that simple, and each of these chairs is actually a product family that comes in three colors: black, gray, and burgundy.

For products using a make-to-order manufacturing strategy in which the color variety can be made as part of the finishing process, master planning and scheduling can be done to the point where the color items are added. But assuming that this is not the way the chairs are built, or if the finishing stage is to be master planned and/or master scheduled, then marketing with assistance from sales needs to break down its forecast into color-specific categories for each period, as in Figure 17.8.

Product Line	Forecast (in units)
Deskmate Secretarial Chairs	5,000
Executive Chairs	1,000

Figure 17.7   Demand Forecast for the Two-Product Company

Color	Secretarial		Executive	
	Percentage	Forecast	Percentage	Forecast
Black	20	1,000	70	700
Gray	50	2,500	20	200
Burgundy	30	1,500	10	100
Total	100	5,000	100	1,000

Figure 17.8   Deskmate Secretarial Chair Product Family

This is a product mix forecast for the company's two product families, in one time period. Here, the marketing and sales department estimated how, as percentages, customer orders would be distributed among the product options within the product family. In most cases, breaking down an aggregate sales forecast is not this simple as there are usually many more product items, colors, and options.

It's About Time

Knowing the *what* of the demand or sales forecast is just half of what is needed by the master planner and/or master scheduler. The other half is *when* those items are needed.

Booking Date and Product Demand Date

In demand planning (also known as demand forecasting), there are two (sometimes more) important dates that resonate within a company. For the commercial organization, sales in particular, the forecasted date is typically expressed by *booking date*—that is, when the customer order is to be received. This is the red-letter day for sales and marketing, as getting customer orders is the reason for its existence. In fact, it is only fair to measure forecast accuracy using bookings versus the plan—that is, did sales get the order when they said they would?

For master planners and schedulers, one of their primary roles is to satisfy those customer orders (bookings) with completed products while balancing the requirements for capacity and materials. Therefore, the master planner and/or master scheduler needs to know the *real demand date*, which, most often, is the company's *desired shipping date*, although sometimes it's the customer's desired delivery date (or other times it can be dates in between, such as milestones along a build plan for design/engineer-to-order products).

Other functions need to know these dates as well, including logistics and finance (ship dates are typically when revenue is realized, for example). Suffice it to say, the master planner and/or scheduler needs to line their plans up to the *appropriate demand date* to ensure that the master planned and/or master scheduled item(s) is available in the right configuration to ship, package, kit, finish, or assemble.

The degree to which customer order bookings and demand dates differ depends on the nature of the business and its product manufacturing strategy. For products in the make-to-stock part of the business, for example, the two dates may be separated by just a few hours or a day—just long enough to pull, pack, label, ship, and invoice the items from finished goods inventory. For products in the make-to-order or design/engineer-to-order part of the business, a greater time gap between the customer order booking date and the pull, pack, label, ship, and invoice date typically exists because the items are in some incomplete stage of production (perhaps not even designed) when the customer orders are booked. Here, a lead time is added to the booking date to get the true expected delivery (or ship) demand date (or milestone dates).

For simplicity, let's stick to make-to-stock (MTS) and make-to-order (MTO) manufacturing strategies. Figure 17.9 illustrates the difference between the two. For general learning purposes, a make-to-order situation in which a single blanket order with multiple shipments is also shown.

Period	1	2	3	4	5
MTS (0 Periods Lead Time)					
Bookings	100	150	125	150	
Demand	100	150	125	150	

MTO (1 Period Lead Time)					
Bookings	100	150	125	150	
Shipment		100	150	125	150

MTO — Scheduled Shipments, Blanket Order (1 Period Lead Time)					
Bookings	1,000				
Shipment		250	250	250	250

Figure 17.9 Demand Bookings versus Shipment Demand

In the MTS grid, the booking and demand dates align, as there is very little time between order booking and the demand (ship) date. In the first MTO grid, the booking date and the demand (ship) date are offset by the lead time (one time period) to make/assemble/finish the product. In the second MTO grid, the demand (ship) dates are broken up into four shipments corresponding to the booked sale of 1,000 units. This could be by customer request and/or negotiated due to capacity constraints or manufacturing capability.

The master planner's and/or master scheduler's focus on the demand date pays off particularly well when the customer is focused on the same date(s). Consider a candy company whose big seasons are Easter and Halloween. The candy company may give their supplier's sales representative an order for chocolate Easter eggs in January, but they have a definite delivery date (demand date) in mind—not January (the booking date), but sometime just before Easter, which in the United States is in March or April.

Again, while booking dates are important in demand management and to the commercial organization in particular, what's key in supply management is for the supplying company's master planner and/or master scheduler to understand when the ordered *product needs to be completed or shipped or delivered to satisfy the customer by the promise date* committed by the sales and/or customer service organization.

The integrated business planning (IBP) process described in Chapter 14 is performed at a company's product family level. In other words, the IBP participants are working with aggregate, volume plans for product, demand, supply, and financial management purposes. While working at an aggregate level is good and where executive leadership should be working, it (aggregate volume planning) is *not* good enough for middle management using a master planning and scheduling (MPS) process. Here, middle management must deal with product mix issues and therefore must understand potential demand at that mix level.

This is one of the more complex areas that a master planner and/or master scheduler must plan and schedule. The main issues that need to be dealt with are forecasting or predicting what products or product configurations the customer is going to order while product build time is quickly slipping away (especially for MTO products).

As the make-to-order manufacturing strategy suggests, once the customer places the order, there is still some remaining manufacturing or assembling or kitting or packaging to be done. In order for the supplying company to do this remaining product processing, material must be on hand or on order, capacity must be available, and the finishing operations scheduled. Of course, this is called *planning and scheduling and execution*!

This entire book has stressed the notion that master planning and scheduling is a demand-driven process through the planning phases and demand-driven and/or supply-driven through the execution phases. This section of the demand management chapter centers its discussion on planning level 2 (aggregate/detailed master planning) as well as planning level 3 (groupings/detailed master scheduling). Both the master planning and master scheduling processes use basically the same logic that is about to be discussed regarding disaggregating volume level planning into mix level planning (see Figure 17.10).

The basic disaggregation logic is to take either the approved, aggregate demand plan or approved, aggregate supply plan, *explode* it through the planning bill's defined percentages (referred to as the disaggregation translator in Figure 17.10), *back off* the necessary lead time required to complete the product's build cycle, and *populate* the appropriate demand cells in the MPS time-phased matrix.

That logic is pretty straightforward; what's not so straightforward is choosing the driver, either the demand plan or supply plan. Again, Figure 17.9 (page 624) showed the timing differences between the booking of customer orders and demand for the ordered product to be shipped. Discussion of those differences is key to selecting the driver for this disaggregation process.

Let's start with the make-to-order product. Again, as the strategy suggests, once the customer order is received, there's still some work to be done; *it's make-to-order (customer places the order and the supplying company works to make it)*!

Therefore, a positive lead time offset must occur from the booking date to the expected product completion date, taking into account the time required to finish the product build

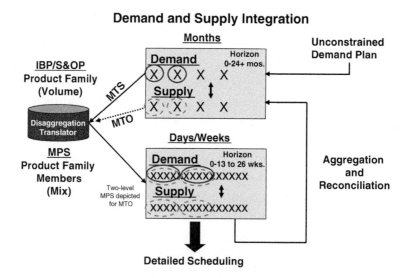

Figure 17.10   Using a Planning Bill to Disaggregate Volume Plan(s) into Mix Plan(s)

cycle to the defined customer specifications. Once this positive lead time offset has been applied to the booking date so as to identify the expected completion and promised ship date, the supply (production or purchase) due date is matched to that promised ship date. This is the product, quantity, and due date that needs to drive the disaggregation process for all MTO products, since the company does not plan to carry finished goods inventory for MTO products (once the product build is complete, ship it).

Now let's turn our attention to the make-to-stock manufacturing strategy. Although the use of planning bills for make-to-stock products is somewhat limited from a supply perspective, there are companies that choose to use the planning bill capability as an aid to disaggregate the approved, volume demand plan into a product mix demand plan. In fact, it is standard disaggregation logic in demand management software. Yes, the authors are implying that the approved, aggregate demand plan be used as the driver during the disaggregation process for products using a make-to-stock manufacturing strategy. The reader may be asking, why is this the case?

When a company chooses a make-to-stock manufacturing strategy for a group of products, it is making a decision that it will carry inventory to shorten its customer delivery lead time or enhance its ability to be more efficient and effective on the manufacturing floor. Therefore, when a customer order is booked, it is assumed that the product is in inventory and can immediately be shipped. In other words, the booking date is the same as the expected shipping date (refer to Figure 17.10 on previous page for a visual presentation).

Producing or procuring the product that is assumed to be in finished goods inventory when the customer order is received was done prior to the date the customer order was received or booked! After disaggregating the demand plan and using standard planning logic to develop the master plan and/or schedule, the MPS must be reaggregated and checked against the approved IBP/S&OP supply plan to ensure that the mix-level MPS is in line with approved supply plans after having made adjustments in the mix-level detail.

The disaggregation process using a planning bill is not only very useful for all products considered under the design/make-to-order umbrella but might be considered mandatory. In Chapter 8 the reasoning behind using a planning bill when many possible configurations are possible was coupled with how to structure these planning bills along with establishing the probability percentages.

Figure 17.11 on the following page gives the reader another reason (identifying where the company plans to meet its customer or what state the product is in when the customer order is received) for using the planning bill capability. This reason quite possibly might be the most important reason for using the planning bill technique in master planning and scheduling. Master planners and/or master schedulers need to know how much lead time they have to complete, package, and ship the product after the customer order is received.

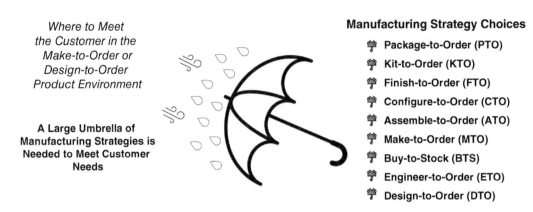

Where to Meet the Customer in the Make-to-Order or Design-to-Order Product Environment

A Large Umbrella of Manufacturing Strategies is Needed to Meet Customer Needs

Manufacturing Strategy Choices

- Package-to-Order (PTO)
- Kit-to-Order (KTO)
- Finish-to-Order (FTO)
- Configure-to-Order (CTO)
- Assemble-to-Order (ATO)
- Make-to-Order (MTO)
- Buy-to-Stock (BTS)
- Engineer-to-Order (ETO)
- Design-to-Order (DTO)

Figure 17.11   Various Planning Strategies Used in MPS

Where the supplying company plans to *meet its customer with product* using a combination of MTO and/or DTO manufacturing strategy implies how much effort has already been put into planning and building the product being ordered. For example, all the required raw materials to satisfy a customer order may already be in stock, but *no* manufacturing has taken place. Or all the required manufacturing has been done, but the subassembly and final assembly work still needs to happen before the product is ready to ship. Or nothing has been done in terms of materials, but design and engineering capacity (people) are in place. Figure 17.11 lists some of the manufacturing strategies available to the manufacturing company—package-to-order, kit-to-order, finish-to-order, configure-to-order, assemble-to-order, true make-to-order, and design/engineer-to-order.

The process described in this section is used to populate the option forecast (sometimes called the production forecast line) on the MPS matrix. What master planners and/or master schedulers have here is MPS system logic that takes an approved demand or supply plan (plan with accountability) and then converts it into a forecast (prediction with less accountability using percentages, but at a more detailed level).

Even though some may be skeptical of introducing prediction back into the equation, this logic has proved over time to yield better predictions at the mix level than any other disaggregation logic, and it does it with less people time. However, the reader is still cautioned that, unfortunately, potential forecast accuracy issues are being introduced into the MPS system; it just happens to be the best practice for working with products using a make-to-order manufacturing strategy that master planners and master schedulers are aware of today.

Spreading the Demand Forecast by Time Period

Sales (demand) forecasts are typically made for large blocks of time: The current year's sales forecast is 3.2 million units. That may be helpful information to the board of directors, but down in the trenches the figure is not that useful. Since master planning and scheduling needs information to establish ship and delivery dates, a phone call, e-mail, and/or text message goes over to marketing and sales.

"Can you give me some shipping or delivery dates for next month?" the master (supply) planner and/or master (supply) scheduler asks. The sales director checks his computer. "No dates, but we've forecasted 12,000 units of product number 7352. Does that help you?" "Yes," the master (supply) planner and/or master (supply) scheduler says with suppressed sarcasm, "that information is of tremendous help."

If sales and marketing do not know when forecasted customer orders will need to be shipped or delivered during November, it is certain that the master planner and/or master scheduler does not know either. One approach to master planning and scheduling 12,000 units would be to look at the record of actual shipments of product number 7352 during November of the previous two or three years. Is there a pattern? In a seasonal business, like those of chocolate Easter eggs or ski apparel, a strong pattern may exist.[2]

If no strong pattern exists, the company may simply spread the 12,000 forecasted units evenly over the days or weeks in the month. With this many units forecasted the law of large numbers favors this even distribution. The law of large numbers holds that, barring some internal bias, outcomes will be evenly distributed around the mean (average). Thus, the shipping dates for the 12,000 units should be scattered evenly through November, and the master planner and/or master scheduler can earmark them for production in this fashion.

If the company's products are something like furniture, in which just 100 to 150 units were forecasted for November, no such assumption of even distribution can be made; half of them might be part of a single large order, due for shipping on one particular date. Sales should be asked directly if these units are expected to come in many small customer orders or from one or two large customers.

A monthly sales forecast can be broken down, based upon the number of working days in a given week, taking into account holidays and plant maintenance shutdowns. This could also take into account the fact that the month in question may begin and end in the middle of a week. Here sales forecasts from different months need to be blended within weekly time periods. For example, Monday and Tuesday might be part of October and Wednesday through Sunday part of November.

---

[2] *Warning:* If the pattern shows past November orders skewed toward the end of the month, do not automatically assume that this is when the customers wanted the product. It may merely indicate the company's tendency to experience the end-of-the-month nightmare described in Chapter 1.

The World of Small Numbers in Master Planning and Scheduling

While the Law of Large Numbers is a useful tool in a number of statistical applications, small numbers frequently confront the unwary master planner and/or master scheduler. Let's take a look at a situation where a company is dealing with ones and tens instead of hundreds and thousands.

Consider a situation in which the product mix demand is being determined. The marketing and sales department states that one particular option of a product family will account for 6 percent of its total demand, which is figured as follows using enterprise resource planning software:

Period	1	2	3	4	5	6	Totals
Forecast	10	10	10	10	10	10	60
6% Option	0.6	0.6	0.6	0.6	0.6	0.6	
Anticipate Demand*	1	1	1	1	1	1	6

*Rounded Up

Because some software rounds less than whole numbers, demand for this option is not 6 percent of the product family, but 10 percent (6 divided by 60).

Virtually all enterprise resource planning software includes this troublesome feature. One way the problem can be eliminated is by entering fractional reminders as artificial inventory that is carried over from period to period. When this artificial inventory reaches a value equal to or greater than the demand, it is accommodated in the demand line. (The answer is rounded down and the fraction is reduced by the amount needed.)

This is a way of keeping the fractional values in the system and making the mathematics work correctly. To see how this works, consider the same example, but with fractional remainders carried forward:

Period	1	2	3	4	5	6	Totals
Forecast	10	10	10	10	10	10	60
6% Option	0.6	0.6	0.6	0.6	0.6	0.6	
Anticipated Demand*	1	1	0	1	0	1	4
Cumulative Reminder	0.4	0.8	0.2	0.6	0	0.4	

*Rounded Up and Down

In this situation, demand has totaled to four units, which is 6 percent of the total forecast for the six periods (4 divided by 60).

Demand and Forecast Adjustment

In addition to discussing how the sales forecast is developed, it is also necessary to understand how to use it in the master planning and scheduling (MPS) process. Consider Figure 17.12, which contains a one-month sales (demand) forecast of 400 units.

This demand came from the integrated business planning process described in Chapter 14; the breakdown of this aggregate figure of 400 into weekly time periods was accomplished through collaboration between supply chain management, sales, and marketing. Thus, weeks (time periods) 1 through 4 are each forecasted at 100 units, which both parties deemed reasonable in terms of past order patterns and future expectations. The figure also contains lines for normal actual demand, abnormal actual demand, and total demand, all of which will be addressed soon.

Actual Demand

The second line of the example in Figures 17.12 and 17.13 on the following page represents normal actual demand, that is, the quantity of product for which the company has firm customer commitments against what was forecasted. In the figures, each week has less actual demand than what had been forecasted. The actual demand line is updated as confirmed orders are received.[3] These quantities remain in this line, however, until those items are produced and shipped.

	1	2	3	4
Product Forecast	100	100	100	100
Actual Demand	85	0	90	50
Abnormal Demand				
Total Demand				

Figure 17.12   Aggregate Demand Forecast of 400 Spread Over Time

---

[3] Updating of normal actual demand may be accomplished automatically through the company's order entry system.

	1	2	3	4
Unconsumed Forecast	15	100	10	50
Actual Demand	85	0	90	50
Abnormal Demand				
Total Demand	100	100	100	100

Figure 17.13   Consumption of the Demand Forecast

Forecast Consumption

As normal actual demand appears and is entered into the matrix, that demand consumes part of the forecast. Thus, in Figure 17.13, the 85 units of normal actual demand in time period 1 consume that same amount of the forecast, leaving 15 units of forecast remaining. The 90 units of normal actual demand in time period 3 consume all but 10 units of that time period's forecast, and half of the original forecast of 100 in time period 4 is consumed by normal actual demand in that period.

Notice, however, that *total demand* remains the same as the original forecast of 100 per week. Here an assumption has been made that the normal actual demand represents demand already anticipated during the development of the forecast.

Timing versus Demand Problems

Time passes, and as the end of week 1 is reached, the forecasting system automatically drops that column and shifts the remaining three weeks to the left. But if no new orders came in to consume the remaining 15 units of the original sales forecast in week 1, what would we do with those 15 units?

This question highlights a perennial problem for demand and supply managers: determining whether the forecast was inaccurate in quantity—in which case those orders will never appear—or whether the forecasted orders are simply delayed. Here, two options are available: (1) Assume that customer orders for the 15 units will never come in and drop them entirely, or (2) Assume that the orders for the 15 units are merely delayed and carry them over as part of the unconsumed forecast.

The first option involves a change in the forecast volume—from 400 units to 385 units—which may require consultation with other parties in the company (marketing, sales, and finance, in particular). Many enterprise resource planning software systems will automatically drop the 15 unsold units as they update the records with the passage of time. This may not be prudent, however, and the demand manager/demand planner and/or master planner/master scheduler would be advised to check with sales and marketing about any variance between actual demand and the sales (demand) forecast before the time period is closed out.

If the second option is chosen—that is, the missing orders that total 15 units are merely delayed—no change to the overall volume forecast of 400 units for the month is made, and the unsold 15 units are rolled forward. But how? There are many possible approaches to this situation, and Figure 17.14 shows just a few choices.

The first option is to roll all 15 units forward and front-load the unconsumed forecast into the very next time period; another option is to roll all 15 units forward and back-load the unconsumed forecast into the last time period of the month. Subsequent options may roll the unconsumed forecast forward but spread the 15 evenly across all remaining time periods in the month or spread the 15 based on sales' input.

	Past Due	1	2	3
Original Forecast	100	100	100	100
Unconsumed Forecast	15	100	100	100
New Forecast (Option 1)		115	100	100
New Forecast (Option 2)		110	105	100
New Forecast (Option 3)		105	105	105
New Forecast (Option 4)		100	100	115
Etc.			Etc.	

Figure 17.14 Rolling the Demand Forecast

Demand managers and/or demand planners as well as master planners and/or master schedulers should know that there is no best way of rolling the unconsumed forecast forward that fits all companies and all situations. Ultimately, the company's business and demand planning team must exercise judgment based upon demand patterns experienced by their own company and the input of knowledgeable and affected parties.

One general decision rule that bears following, however, is that customer orders that fail to materialize in an aggregate forecasting time period should not be automatically rolled into the next forecasting period (someone in the demand organization needs to review unconsumed forecast when it is not totally consumed in the month). For example, the situation in Figure 17.14 (page 633) represents an aggregate forecasting period of one month, let's say four weeks; 400 units of demand are anticipated during that time period. The 15 units that failed to materialize in the past-due week might be rolled forward into new weeks 1, 2, and 3 by any means viewed as reasonable.

However, a new aggregate forecasting time period would take effect in weeks 5 through 8, and it should not be burdened by any inaccuracies that manifested themselves in the previous forecasting time period. Prudence dictates that—barring reliable information to the contrary—demand that fails to materialize in weeks 1 through 4 or month 1 could be assumed to be lost, and therefore need not be rolled forward into weeks 5 through 8. Instead, it could be dropped. If that demand were still lurking in the market, one would expect that the new forecast would have picked it up.

The best way to handle this situation is to have someone in marketing, sales, and demand management review the prior period's forecast and make a determination as to whether the unconsumed forecast should be rolled forward or dropped. Doing this prevents loss of accountability for forecast accuracy.

Tracking Cumulative Demand

In the case described in Figure 17.14 on page 633, a shortage of normal actual demand in the first time period would most likely be rolled over into one or more time periods in the current month. Demand managers and/or demand planners as well as master planners and/or master schedulers would not be losing any sleep at this point, knowing that the forecast is most likely inaccurate to some degree and that the division of the 400 units into four discrete demand time periods was, after all, based more on intuition than on science. Besides, there are three more weeks available in the month's forecast planning horizon.

As the days and weeks slip by, however, variances between normal actual demand and the forecast have fewer and fewer opportunities to come into balance. How can we deal with variances as time passes?

Technology as in Computer Alert
Still a Problem After All These Years

One trait of almost all master planning and scheduling software is the fact that it looks at the demand forecast and the actual demand for each time period and takes the greater of the two as total demand. On the surface this seems to make sense; if actual demand outstrips the demand forecast, the master planner and/or master scheduler needs to build to that demand level. If the demand forecast exceeds actual demand, it might be assumed that the customer orders are just late.

Look at the situation below. Marketing and sales forecast the need for 400 units over four time periods. But the system software logic has automatically taken the greater of the demand forecast and actual demand, thus increasing the demand forecast by 20 units, to 420 units.

	1	2	3	4	Total
Product Forecast	(100)	(100)	100	100	400
Actual Demand	(100)	80	(110)	(110)	400
Abnormal Demand					
Total Demand*	100	100	110	110	420

Now consider what happens when a customer calls to request a rescheduling-out of an order so that 40 units of actual demand are shifted from time period 2 to time period 3 (80 – 40 = 40 and 110 + 40 = 150). Remember, this is not an increase in demand, just a reschedule-out. As shown below, the system software logic does its thing, taking the greater of demand forecast and actual demand in determining total demand, and in so doing increases total demand by 40 units (from 420 to 460) out of thin air (so to speak)!

	1	2	3	4	Total
Product Forecast	(100)	(100)	100	100	400
Actual Demand	(100)	40	(150)	(110)	400
Abnormal Demand					
Total Demand*	100	100	150	110	460

*Greater of forecast and actual demand lines.

One useful approach to dealing with deviations from the sales (demand) forecast over periods of time is through the tracking of demand on a cumulative basis—that is, by comparing the *total* of normal actual demand over a period of time to the *total* forecasted for that same elapsed period. This technique filters out the effects of timing problems from inaccuracies in the forecast quantity. Figure 17.15 applies this technique to the example we have been following.

Here a range using high and low indicators is established to accommodate the inevitable inaccuracy of the forecast. This range is the sum for both the expected timing errors and the expected forecast errors. Any values that fall outside these high and low boundaries are signals to demand and supply management to investigate.

Another line is added to indicate the deviation of normal actual demand from forecasted demand, expressed as a percentage of forecasted demand. Over time, this deviation should decrease and approach the acceptable forecast error for the month.

Since the first period is less likely (percentage wise) to correspond to the forecast than would the four weeks taken as a whole, the anticipated spread between the high and low boundaries is assumed to be its greatest. But this spread should narrow progressively over time. Why? Simply because the passing of time allows the timing problems to work themselves out, leaving only the inaccuracies of the sales forecast quantity as the source of deviation. The result, in a normal situation, should look something like Figure 17.16 on the following page.

How does demand management use these tracking signals? If the normal actual demand in time period 1 of the example is fewer than 40 units (low), a signal is sent (the yellow flag is up) to watch this product through the coming weeks because the forecast could be biased high. If the actual demand at the end of time period 1 is greater than 160 units

	1	2	3	4
Low	40	100	200	320
Forecast	100	200	300	400
High	160	300	400	480
Deviation from Forecast	60%	50%	33%	20%

Figure 17.15   Tracking Cumulative Demand

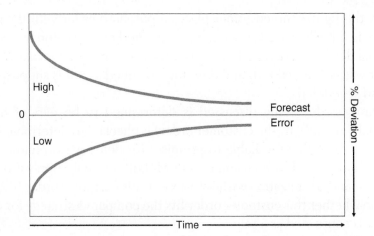

Figure 17.16   Converging Deviation from Demand Forecast Over Time

(high), a signal is sent (the red flag is up) to demand management that the forecast may be biased low or some unexpected demand may have appeared.

This situation could result in the forecast being understated. Incremental demand not anticipated is known as abnormal demand and must be recognized if demand planning and master planning and scheduling (MPS) are to work effectively.

Customer Order Processing with Process Flow Diagram Example

Demand planning and control within a demand management process is vital to the success of a company's efficient and effective, best-practice master planning (as well as a best-practice master scheduling) implementation and operating environment. One element of a demand management as well as master planning and scheduling process is that of taking and processing customer orders. As customer orders are processed, attention must be paid to whether the noted customer order is part of forecasted or anticipated demand and whether the noted customer order can be supported by supply regarding the promise that the demand organization is making or about to make to the customer. Figure 17.17 on page 639 displays a process flow for taking, reviewing, accepting or not accepting, and confirming or not confirming a customer request for product.

As shown in the figure, the customer places a purchase order with the supplier. This purchase order is initially reviewed to determine whether it was forecasted as expected demand (normal demand is demand that was forecasted versus abnormal demand, which is demand that was *not* forecasted) and therefore assumed that it is supply planned (master planned and scheduled).

If the customer order being discussed is determined to be part of the forecasted demand (normal demand), it (the customer order) is checked to determine if the product whether or will be available (available-to-promise) for delivery as requested by the customer (quantity and date). If this customer order is both normal, supply is or will be available, and the demand organization wishes to accept this customer order (the check might be to determine whether this customer order fits the company's strategy for business), the customer order is confirmed as a sale.

However, if either of these three checks show possible issues (the customer order is classified as abnormal demand and/or the requested customer order cannot be supported with product availability and/or the customer order is from a small company that is in conflict with the sales strategy of wanting to deal only with box stores), additional analysis should (actually must) be done before accepting and making a promise to the customer. Figure 17.17 shows a process flow for the company deciding the fate of the entered customer order.

Major elements of this process flow are increasing/decreasing/changing the approved demand plan, increasing/decreasing/changing the approved supply plan, shifting other customer orders to other time periods, moving planned and/or scheduled supply to other time periods, and declining or not accepting the customer order (partial or complete customer order). Regardless of the company decision, the customer needs to be informed of the decision and the reason for the course of action (taken or to be taken).

The described process flow is included in this demand management section as an example of how demand managers and demand planners use process flows and sales/marketing guidelines to ensure that valid and realistic promises are made to the customer. The figure also includes a review of the six or seven questions (the morale effect on the supply organization is sometimes noted as a seventh question that must be answered before the master plan and/or master schedule is changed) that need to be asked if the customer booking requires a change to the existing master plan and/or master schedule. When a customer order is booked, the company is making a promise to the customer that the product ordered, quantity ordered, and due date agreed to will be honored. *Remember, a promise made is a debt unpaid!*

The following sections discuss possible problems with accepting abnormal demand and evaluating the acceptance of customer orders using the available-to-promise capability of

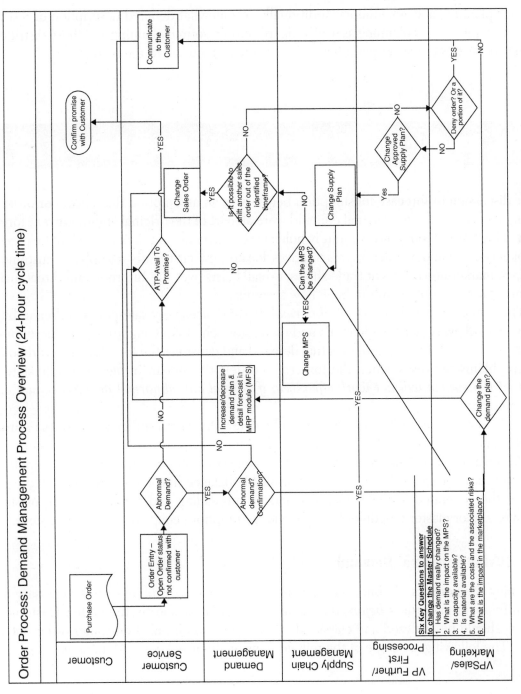

Figure 17.17 Customer Order Processing Flow

master planning and scheduling. Additionally, a somewhat detailed description of distribution requirements planning as well as distribution resource planning and these distribution process ties to master planning and scheduling is offered to the reader.

Possible Problems Caused by Abnormal Demand

Our discussion of forecast consumption began with an assumption that customer orders being entered as (normal) actual demand were all part of the original and/or current forecast. This assumption, however, rarely holds up in a dynamic marketplace. Unanticipated bookings are made as sales representatives locate new customers and obtain customer orders; marketing's efforts at trade shows, e-mail blasts over the Internet, and direct mail campaigns sometimes result in huge new accounts.

These unanticipated orders, or *abnormal demand*, are every salesperson's dream, but they can be every master planner's and/or master scheduler's nightmare. If these customer orders enter the system as actual demand and consume the forecast, big overbooking problems can result when the forecasted orders do appear. In fact, it can be stated that a *MPS system will not work effectively if normal and abnormal demand cannot be differentiated*.

Without this ability, total demand cannot be determined with sufficient accuracy to produce a reliable projected available balance line on the MPS matrix. And it is from this projected available balance line that the MPS system generates the all-important exception-driven action messages. If the projected available balance line cannot be calculated correctly, the generated action messages could be misleading and could cause the master planner and/or master scheduler to make poor assumptions coupled with bad decisions.

Identifying Abnormal Demand

To enjoy the benefits of abnormal demand and to avoid its problems, it is necessary to identify abnormal orders *before* they enter the system or shortly thereafter. Customer orders should be analyzed and classified as normal or abnormal at customer order entry time. The following are some of the telltale signs of abnormal demand, to name a few:

- A new customer account;

- The wrong seasonal pattern;

- A one-time sales order;

- A larger-than-normal customer order;

- A sales order that comes through a nontraditional distribution channel.

Marketing and sales personnel should be encouraged to help in this process, and demand managers and/or demand planners as well as master planners and/or master schedulers should communicate with these individuals when in doubt about any suspicious demand orders (sometimes it's better to be cautious than surprised). This is not to say that getting a chance to book abnormal demand is a bad thing; no, selling and receiving demand (regardless of whether it is forecasted or not forecasted) is a good thing (most of the time). It's just that when a company and its master planning and scheduling function must deal with abnormal demand, caution needs to be taken to ensure that the customer is given a commitment that can be met (*our company and its associates and/or employees do what we say we are going to do*).

Accommodating Abnormal Demand

Once abnormal demand is properly identified, working it into the demand forecast and master plan and schedule is straightforward. Figure 17.18 on the following page demonstrates a situation in which a one-time customer order is submitted in time period 3 as a result of attendance by marketing at an industry trade show. The customer is a foreign company that wants to buy 150 units on an experimental basis. Only time will tell if this company becomes a regular customer.

Notice here that these 150 units, categorized as abnormal demand by sales and marketing, are added to the unconsumed forecast of 10 and the (normal) actual demand of 90, to obtain a total anticipated demand of 250 units. The original/current forecast is unchanged, as is the unconsumed forecast. What's changed is the total anticipated demand, which shows an incremental total demand increase equal to the abnormal demand.

	1	2	3	4
Unconsumed Forecast	15	100	10	50
Actual Demand	85	0	90	50
Abnormal Demand			150	
Total Demand	100	100	250	100

Figure 17.18   Treatment of Abnormal Demand

Customer Linking

The difficulty of determining customer demand has already been explained. Difficult and imprecise as it is, sales forecasting is nevertheless a requirement of modern business. But what if we could get the customers to do this forecasting? Who, after all, could possibly know their needs with greater certainty? A number of companies do, in fact, have such a forecasting system, which is generally known as *customer collaboration* or *linking*.[4] They are most prevalent and applicable when the customer is an upstream producer, distributor, or retailer for whom the company acts as a supplier.

Customer collaboration and linking uses the logic of enterprise resource planning (ERP) and distribution resource planning (DRP) to create demand plans at the manufacturing plant and master planning and schedule level (see Figure 17.19, page 643). These planning systems take the customer's product forecast, booked demand, inventories, open purchase orders, open manufacturing orders, and bills-of-distribution to create planned receipts of products needed in order to prevent stock-out conditions.

Once a customer determines replenishment requirements for its various products, these demands are communicated to the supplier. This has long been done using traditional purchase orders. But why use the purchase order? Why not send the supplier the

---

[4] For a very complete treatment of distribution resource planning and customer connectivity, see André J. Martin, *Distribution Resource Planning* (New York: John Wiley & Sons, 1990).

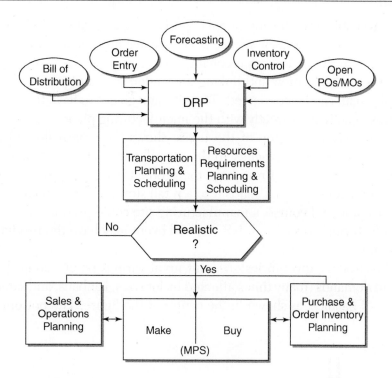

Source: Reprinted from *Distribution Resource Planning* by André J. Martin (New York: John Wiley & Sons, Inc., 1990), with permission of the publisher.

Figure 17.19   Distribution Resource Planning

expected demand directly in the form of a shipment schedule? This can be done by having the customer's ERP or DRP system determine the plant's required shipping date by offsetting the transportation time necessary to move the product from the supplier to the customer's delivery point.

This demand along with other customer demands is aggregated and used in the integrated business planning or sales and operations planning process to plan *make* items; it is used by procurement to plan *buy* items; and it is used by master planning scheduling to plan both *make* and *buy* items. This same customer demand data is also used in logistics planning, capacity requirements planning, and detailed production scheduling.

While customer collaboration and linking solve many of the issues associated with demand, the master planner and/or master scheduler must still analyze the expected supply to see whether the demand can be satisfied. If it cannot be satisfied, it is the responsibility of the master planner and/or master scheduler to ensure that the customer is informed of the problem, either directly or through sales and marketing. If sufficient supply will be available, then no additional communication is generally necessary and the principle of *silence is approval* or *silence is acceptance* applies, and the product can be expected to arrive on the customer's receiving dock as requested.

Once customer collaboration and linking are understood and put in place, the entire demand/supply chain can be connected. The ultimate goal is to have the customer linked through a series of activities directly with the manufacturing plant.

Look at Figure 17.20. The top of the figure shows the typical flow of product as it moves from the manufacturing facility to the manufacturer's distribution center or to its customer's manufacturing site. From here the product continues its journey, possibly to a retail distribution center, which sends it to a retail store, which ultimately puts it in the hands of the customer. Of course, a manufacturing site could produce its product, send it to other manufacturing sites or warehouses, and eventually have the product wind up at the customer site.

Through this process, inventories are built up at various points along the way. These inventories and demands (many times affected by lot sizes, kanbans, and safety stocks) are quite often out of balance, as shown in the center of the figure. The bottom of the figure

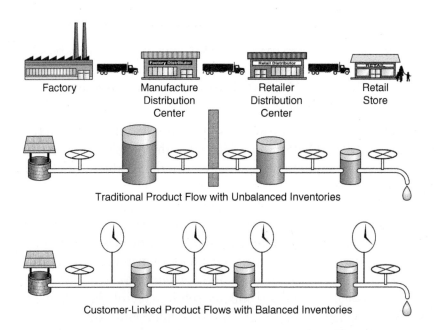

Source: Reprinted from *Distribution Resource Planning* by André J. Martin (New York: John Wiley & Sons, Inc., 1990), with permission of the publisher.

Figure 17.20 Typical and Improved Pipelines

is where most companies would like to be, a smooth flow with pockets of reduced inventories that are balanced with the feeding operations (suppliers) and the needing operations (customers). The challenge is to link all these operations together and balance the flow.

Getting Sales Pipeline Control

Customer and supplier linking offers many opportunities for the manufacturing company using a well-defined master planning and scheduling (MPS) process. We have already discussed how forecasting can be improved by connecting up to the customer's requirements. We have also discussed the opportunity to eliminate the use of purchase orders by using the customer's supplier schedules. In fact, several companies, such as Xerox Corporation, have been using electronic data interchange as a means to communicate with one another for a very long time.

When companies get their sales pipeline under control, the next logical step is to remove *all* waste that may be resident in the flow. This waste may exist in the form of multiple stocking locations, transportation, obsolete materials, damaged goods, unnecessary paperwork, and unnecessary communications. Figure 17.21 shows the typical communication links between the traditional customer and supplier.

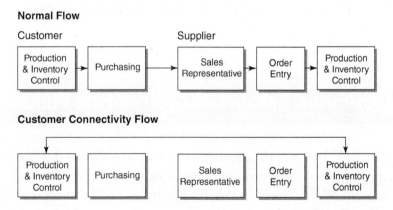

Source: Reprinted from *Distribution Resource Planning* by André J. Martin (New York: John Wiley & Sons, Inc., 1990), with permission of the publisher.

Figure 17.21 Customer and Supplier Information Flow (in Today's World, Production and Inventory Control Is Referred to as Supply Chain Management)

The traditional flow shows a material planner at the customer site, reviewing material requirements (requisitions) with their procurement and/or purchasing department. The material planner typically uses some form of material requirements planning or distribution requirements planning to determine what needs to be ordered and when it needs to be ordered.

Procurement and/or purchasing then communicates with the supplier's sales department, who places the order (demand or request for product) into their order entry system. This demand is communicated to the scheduling department of the supplier, which further communicates it to the manufacturing function. Looks like a lot of touches and possibly stress-filled wasted motions.

What if the company could get its procurement and/or purchasing function to work out a volume agreement with the supplier's sales function that covers a defined planning horizon? If this could be arranged and an agreement drawn up, then why not have the customer's supply chain planning or supply chain management (production and inventory control) function talk and/or text and make releases directly to the supplier's supply chain planning or supply chain management (production and inventory control) function?

These people speak the same language. Think of all the communication and miscommunication problems that could be avoided. And what about the time factor? Talk about eliminating waste! Customer collaboration and connectivity is a win-win situation.

By doing this (which resembles the supplier-linking process, but from the other side), the sales force is focused on what it's good at—selling. It removes huge amounts of administrative time requirements that are generally needed to place multiple orders and releases. And most companies that implement customer and supplier linking are finding that they do less expediting. That alone makes it worth looking into the concept.

Distribution Resource/Requirements Planning

In military operations, logistics personnel attempt to site all foreseeable people power, equipment, supply, and material requirements as close to battlefield operations as practical. This is its method for ensuring the availability of critical resources. In Operation Desert Storm, for example, a six-month supply of equipment and materials was shipped to Saudi Arabia before any major engagements were undertaken. In times of conflict, of course, the military does not have shareholders screaming about excess inventories!

Many manufacturers follow a similar model—though tempered by concerns for inventory cost—shipping finished goods out to regional distribution points where they are more readily available to the customer. This strategy has three purposes:

1. ***To reduce lead time***—If shipping from a manufacturing plant in North Carolina to a customer in Utah normally requires four days by overland truck, at least three of those days can be eliminated by siting inventory in Utah itself. This reduction in lead time may be an important element of customer service (for both products and spares) and increase the company's competitive position.

2. ***Reduce transportation cost***—Distributed inventories are sometimes motivated by greater transportation cost efficiencies. For example, in the case just given, shipping individual orders on demand by truck from North Carolina to customers in Utah would be much more costly than would sending planned, full truckload shipments to a Utah distribution center. This latter approach might also eliminate the need for periodic air-freight shipments to satisfy special customer needs.

3. ***Control the market channel***—For many common consumer and industrial goods, a true market presence can sometimes be established only when a local inventory and distribution system is in place. Control of shelf space in the supermarkets of Salt Lake City, Utah, for example, could not be established or maintained by a potato chip maker in Pennsylvania unless it had a distribution center in that metropolitan area. Effective shelf stocking at supermarkets and convenience stores could not possibly be accomplished from Pennsylvania in a cost-effective way.

Of course, distributed inventory is not a panacea for solving every business problem. Distribution centers are cost centers and must ultimately be judged in terms of the value their costs add to the company and its customers. It should also be noted that there are third-party companies that provide warehousing and distribution services; sometimes, it might be a good business decision to use this type of service rather than operating company owned distribution centers.

The Mechanics of Distribution Requirements Planning

Minuteman Electronics Company (MEC), the laptop computer manufacturer, was introduced earlier in this book. As shown in Figure 17.22 on page 648, Minuteman produces its finished computers in Boston. This manufacturing plant ships finished products to

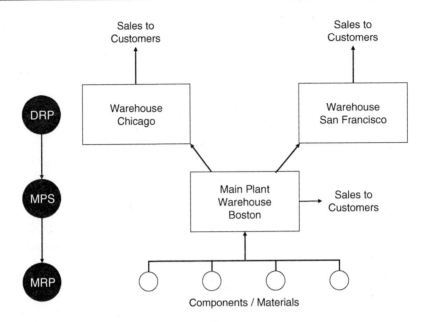

Figure 17.22 Distribution Scheme and Planning Tools, MEC

distribution centers located in Boston, Chicago, and San Francisco. Figure 17.22 illustrates the Minuteman distribution scheme and—on the left side of the figure—the planning tools used to build and move products through it.

From the master planner's and/or master scheduler's perspective, Minuteman products are built according to the master plan and/or master schedule supported by a master planning and scheduling (MPS) system at the company's main plant, a system that reaches down to material and capacity levels using material and capacity planning (finite or infinite) logic. This same MPS system is driven by demand from three sources: direct sales to customers out of Boston, orders placed by the warehouse located in Chicago, and orders placed by the warehouse located in San Francisco—each of which is viewed as a customer.

For direct customer sales—those filled from the plant warehouse—demand is forecasted by Minuteman's local sales and marketing team. Sales to Midwestern and West Coast customers, however, are forecasted by the sales and marketing organizations based in Chicago and San Francisco, respectively.

Figure 17.23 on page 649 provides a more detailed look at the linkage between the manufacturing plant and the two MEC distribution centers with respect to just one product: item 247. As the figure makes clear, each of the distribution centers has an on-hand

Chicago DC

O/H: 500 O/Q: 400 L/T: 1 WK S/S: 1 WK		Period (Weeks)							
		1	2	3	4	5	6	7	8
Sales Forecast		200	200	200	200	200	200	200	200
In Transit									
Projected Available Balance	500	300	500	300	500	300	500	300	500
Planned Order Release		400		400		400		400	

San Francisco DC

O/H: 350 O/Q: 300 L/T: 2 WK S/S: 300		Period (Weeks)							
		1	2	3	4	5	6	7	8
Sales Forecast		150	150	150	150	150	150	150	150
In Transit		300							
Projected Available Balance	350	500	350	500	350	500	350	500	350
Planned Order Release		300		300		300		300	

Boston Plant/Warehouse

O/H: 350 O/Q: 300 L/T: 2 WK S/S: 300		Period (Weeks)							
		1	2	3	4	5	6	7	8
Sales (BOS) Forecast		100	100	100	100	100	100	100	100
Warehouse (CHI) Requirements		400		400		400		400	
Warehouse (SF) Requirements		300		300		300		300	
Total Demand		800	100	800	100	800	100	800	100
Projected Available Balance	1,300	500	1,400	600	500	700	600	800	700
Master Schedule			1,000			1,000		1,000	

Figure 17.23   Distribution Resource Planning Linkages, Item 247

(O/H) balance, specific order quantity (O/Q), transit lead time (L/T), and safety stock (S/S) defined for the item. The Chicago facility, for example, begins the current period with an on-hand balance of 500 units, has an order quantity of 400 units, a safety stock of 200 units (one week's worth of demand), and a lead-time requirement of one week.

How activities at the distribution centers signal activities at the manufacturing plant becomes clear as we examine several periods in Figure 17.23. Here, the Chicago distribution center's first-time-period forecast of 200 is expected to use all but 300 units of the on-hand balance of item 247—leaving 300 units as a projected available balance at the end of time period 1. The second week's demand is also 200 units, which will leave 100 units (300 – 200) projected available balance at the end of time period 2.

Since that number is below the safety stock requirement, a planned order release is made for 400 units—the specified minimum order quantity. That order is required to be received in time period 2 but must be shipped from the Boston manufacturing plant in week 1 (transportation lead time is one time period). When the plant acknowledges or ships the order, the planned order release will be changed into a scheduled receipt and show up on the "in transit" line by its due date, which is week 2. This process would continue through the Chicago distribution center's horizon. As the reader can see, a series of planned orders is being created for the Chicago distribution center, which will translate into request for product from the Boston plant.

A similar set of events is going on at the San Francisco distribution center, though an "in transit" shipment is expected to arrive during week 1, obviously due to a planned order released earlier (two weeks earlier, given the expected in-transit lead time to move the product to that facility). Again, a series of request-for-product notifications is being placed on the Boston manufacturing plant from the San Francisco distribution center.

The Impact of Distribution Center Orders on the Plant

The manufacturing facility that receives distribution center orders views them as another source of demand. In the current example, the MPS system at the Boston plant indicates three sources of demand: its own sales forecast of regional sales (100 units per week), Chicago's warehouse requirements of 400 every other week, and San Francisco's warehouse requirements of 300 units every other week. In week 1 of the example, these warehouse requirements total 800 units: 100 from Boston, 400 units Chicago, and 300 from San Francisco. Together, the warehouse requirements from each location and for each week in the planning horizon constitute total demand to which the master planner and/or master scheduler needs to respond.

In addition to understanding the total demand, the master (supply) planner and/or master (supply) scheduler must also know which distribution center is placing the demand. This requirement is supported by the pegging capability in the master planning and scheduling (MPS) system. Pegging informs the master (supply) planner and/or master (supply) scheduler which warehouse caused the demand. The reader should understand some of the reasons for this requirement: assigning priorities, if necessary, and effective shipping, to name just two.

Distribution Requirements Planning versus Distribution Resource Planning

The information system that makes distribution *requirements* planning possible also makes distribution *resource* planning feasible. This extends a company's ability from simply building and shipping items to the ability to maximize the total resources of the company. As an example, Minuteman's information system enables the master (supply) planner and/or master (supply) scheduler to intelligently manage demand and supply throughout the company and its distribution system; in addition, this same information system very likely has enough stored data to develop a shipping routine that minimizes costs and balances transportation loads.

In Figure 17.24, item 247 is shown to be just one of four for which quantity, space, and weight have been calculated to facilitate balanced shipping in weeks 1 and 2.

Based on this information, the master (supply) planner and/or master (supply) scheduler or the logistics and/or transportation planner can reserve an appropriate level of transportation capabilities to move combined orders at the most effective cost from the Boston plant to the Chicago distribution center.

Item No.	Week 1				Week 2			
	Qty (ea)	Space (ft2)	Weight (lbs.)	Notes (*)	Qty (ea)	Space (ft2)	Weight (lbs.)	Notes (*)
141	250	27	1,250		250	27	1,250	
223	100	16	824					
247	400	36	2,000					
288	200	20	1,700		200	20	1,700	
Etc.	. . . . .	. . . . .	. . . . .		. . . . .	. . . . .	. . . . .	
Total	2,900	312	16,974		1,370	135	6,650	

Figure 17.24   Transportation Plan, Chicago Distribution Center

The next question must be this: If we can get the distribution centers to communicate their planned requirements, why can't we get the customers to communicate their planned requirements? It's the next logical step and is similar to the interplant environment, described earlier for Minuteman Electronics Company.[5] And it impacts a subject of fundamental importance to the manufacturer—load leveling.

Expected Results

Companies that use distribution resource planning (DRP) and/or supply chain management (SCM) processes and systems continue to experience improved customer service with reduced inventories. This is being done with less reliance on sales forecasting and improved sales productivity by keeping the sales representatives doing what they are paid to do, which is to sell. Periodic demand monitoring and transportation planning, coupled with the other DRP and SCM processes, can lead to increased product pipeline velocity and reduced lead times from supplier to customer. And let's not forget the reduction of distribution and manufacturing costs associated with the benefits already stated.

Overall, the customer-linking process can give a company the opportunity to eliminate all unnecessary activities. This is a continuous-improvement program expanding to include the distribution and logistics network.

The notion of DRP and linking with the outside or within the company is not without issues and risks, but also opportunities, as the following scenario makes clear.

MULTIPLANT COMMUNICATIONS

Larger companies generally support production through a number of production plants. The automobile industry, whose finished products contain upward of 4,500 parts, is a case in point. Final assembly and finishing are supported by separate production facilities for engines, interiors, metal stamping, and so forth.

---

[5] Both the manufacturer and its customers should be Class A companies for this to be feasible.

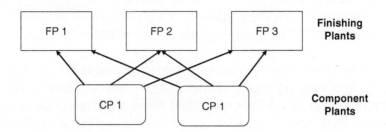

Consider a simpler example: a company with three finishing plants and two component plants.

The component plants may be total captives of the finishing plants, serving their needs exclusively. They may, on the other hand, have some outside customers to whom they sell part of their output. In either case, good communication among plants is an important element in successful manufacturing. The finishing plants establish demand for the component plants, which, in turn, attempt to produce an adequate supply. When finishing and component plants fail to communicate and fail to work together, manufacturing productivity and output generally suffer.

Scheduling practitioners recognize one problem of multiplant communications that stands out above all others: Lower-level plants have trouble controlling their own schedules and are often whipsawed by the changing demand situation at the upper-level plants they serve. Unlike the independent company, which has a *right of refusal* with respect to customer demand, the lower-level plant as part of the larger corporate machinery typically cannot just say no to demand from a finishing plant or corporate office. Nor does it have much latitude in shifting or splitting orders, or in outsourcing the work. Overloading of the master plan and/or master schedule at lower-level plants is the typical result.

Management Issues

When a finishing plant passes down an order to a component plant, its knowledge of the scheduling and manufacturing situation at the component plant is often imperfect (it certainly is better in the third decade than it was in the first and second decades of the twenty-first century). Lack of communications and general lack of insight into current production issues and problems at the lower-level plant provoke a number of management concerns, one going directly to the heart of how people should be managed.

Most management practitioners acknowledge that an individual should never be held responsible or accountable for the results of operations over which he or she lacks control.

Yet this hallowed principle is routinely violated by a great number of manufacturers whose corporate schedulers control the master plans and/or master schedules of their component plants.

General managers of component plants are held accountable for stabilizing production, controlling costs, and meeting supply demands from finishing plants, even though the strings that control schedules on their own plant floors are often pulled by someone else, perhaps by a lower-level staffer located in corporate offices thousands of miles away. "We could be having equipment problems, materials shortages, whatever, and this would not be reflected in the schedule we're expected to follow" is a common complaint. "Just tell us what you want, and when, and let us figure out the best way to schedule the work at our facility."

Managers of lower-level plants, in the authors' experience, would generally prefer a multiplant system in which they have greater autonomy in meeting the requirements of higher-level plants—their *best customers*. That greater autonomy would give them control of their own master (supply) plans and/or master (supply) schedules, the ability to negotiate movement and splitting of orders, the right to *refuse an order*—in effect, the same autonomy enjoyed by independent companies that must adhere to the sharp discipline of the marketplace if they hope to survive and prosper.

Corporate staffers are often uncomfortable with this notion of component plant independence and their own loss of control. In cases observed by the authors, that discomfort stems from a lack of confidence in the planning and scheduling capabilities of lower-level supply managers and schedulers.

But experience indicates that good things usually happen when decision-making responsibility is pushed down to the lowest possible level. This has been one of the important lessons of the quality movement and the practice of continuous improvement in manufacturing. Here, control is maintained through accountability for performance and through incentives that naturally align the interest of the component plant manager with those of the corporation.

Multiplant planning and scheduling problems affect just about everyone, so solving them is in everyone's interests. Sales and marketing have a problem when customer orders are not shipped on time because the component plant fails to deliver due to overloading and overscheduling the manufacturing facility.

Manufacturing managers and production supervisors at component plants often see some of their own problems as the result of scheduling failures higher up ("they just dump all of their scheduling and forecasting mistakes onto us"). Finance wonders where all the profits are going—reschedules, expediting, overtime, and the like cost money. In the long run, accountability is lost and overall performance suffers.

Tells Us What You Want and We'll Do the Rest, Sir!

One of the lessons (learned some 50-plus years ago) from America's military experience in Vietnam was that command and control cannot be exercised effectively from afar (50-plus years ago [Authors' Note: This has and continues to change]). To the great frustration of U.S. field commanders, much of the war (officially a conflict) was run directly from the Pentagon. Analysts and staffers working and living in the comfortable environments of Washington, D.C., plotted campaigns for corps commanders and selected targets for bomber pilots stationed half a world away.

Lacking a feel for local resources and circumstances, many of their directives were either ineffective or outright damaging to U.S. war efforts. While overall strategy was logically the domain of the White House, high-echelon military officers, and their staffs, believed that the business of effecting that strategy should have been left to the discretion of local commanders who had a better grasp of conditions on the ground.

This important lesson from Vietnam was not lost on the captains and majors who, 20 years later, filled the general officer ranks of the U.S. armed forces during the Gulf War. As the new generation of U.S. commanders, they defined the broader strategy of driving Iraqi forces from Kuwait, but they gave local commanders broad discretion in implementing the strategy. And it worked exceedingly well.

Available-to-Promise

A promise made is a debt unpaid! This little sentence by Robert Service ought to be posted prominently wherever demand management, customer service, supply management, and master planning and scheduling (MPS) personnel work, as it articulates one of the primary responsibilities of their functions.

When a customer requests a product, the sales representative(s), account manager, demand manager, demand planner, customer service representative, order entry personnel, supply manager, master planner, or master scheduler must respond to that request and commit to a date for shipment. This constitutes an explicit promise to the customer, and the available-to-promise (ATP) information of the master plan and/or master schedule is an important tool in making good on promises. In this sense it is an important element of demand management.

The ATP line of the master plan and/or master schedule matrix indicates the portion of scheduled production that is unconsumed after all other commitments are covered and tells demand management, customer service, order entry, field sales, supply management, master planning, and master scheduling what is available to fill new requests. While the mechanics of ATP were briefly touched on in Chapters 3 and 9, a little refresher is appropriate here.

Consider the following example of a ballpoint pen manufacturer (Figure 17.25). This producer, who begins the current period with an on-hand balance of 150 cases of pens, has

	Past Due	1	2	3	4	5	6	7	8
Product Forecast		100	100	100	100	100	100	100	100
Option Forecast									
Actual Demand									
Total Demand		100	100	100	100	100	100	100	100
Projected Available Balance	150	50	250	150	50	250	150	50	250
Available-to-Promise									
Master Schedule		300			300				300

Figure 17.25   Projected Available Balance and Available-to-Promise, Pen Manufacturer

a demand forecast of 100 cases per week over an eight-week horizon. Given that demand forecast, the master planner and/or master scheduler has placed three firm planned orders of 300 cases each in time periods 2, 5, and 8.

Given the on-hand balance, total demand, and existing master planned and/or master scheduled supply orders, the master planning and scheduling (MPS) system can calculate the projected available balance for all future periods as shown in the figure. The reader should notice that Figure 17.25 defines the last line in its matrix as the master (supply) schedule; this type of matrix is also used for master (supply) planning.

In determining the quantities available to promise to a customer, the master (supply) planner's and/or master (supply) scheduler's first concern is in protecting commitments already made—namely, protecting the actual demand indicated in the MPS matrix.

The master (supply) planner's and/or master (supply) scheduler's second concern is in protecting those commitments in the most efficient manner; here, this means protecting demand with the closest master (supply) planned and/or master (supply) scheduled lot that immediately precedes it. Thus, if an actual customer order for a time period 8 delivery is received and accepted, it would be more efficient to protect that commitment from supply expected to be available as near to, but preceding, time period 8 as possible.

In the situation given here, for example, an experienced demand manager, master (supply) planner, or master (supply) scheduler would never protect a time period 8 demand with on-hand inventory when a source of supply is anticipated in time period 8. *Note: Does the reader think that maybe, just maybe, the authors saw such behaviors a few times during their supply chain management and master planning and scheduling professional careers?*

To deal with these two concerns, the MPS system calculates ATP from right to left—here moving from time period 8 to time period 1. An ATP is calculated for all MPS supply orders, the ones scheduled in time periods 8, 5, and 2, plus time period 1, since there are pens on hand and they are available to sell or promise.

Since ATP is the master (supply) planned and/or master (supply) scheduled quantity less actual demand, the ATP for time period 8 is 300 cases (300 − 0, as shown in Figure 17.26 on the following page). There are at least 300 cases of pens available-to-promise to any customer that needs delivery in that time period. However, this calculation is only for the eighth time period and does not take into account previous time periods' available-to-promise (ATP).

Moving to time period 5 (Figure 17.26), the next time period in which supply is scheduled, the calculation is again straightforward: 300 cases firm planned orders − 60 actual demand = 240 ATP. Time period 2 is a little more complicated. A demand of 100 cases of pens is committed in this time period, but there is also demand in time periods 3 and 4. With no other supply anticipated to intervene until time period 5, all of the demand in

	Past Due	1	2	3	4	5	6	7	8
Product Forecast		100	100	100	100	100	100	100	100
Option Forecast									
Actual Demand		90	100	60	50	60			
Total Demand		100	100	100	100	100	100	100	100
Projected Available Balance	150	50	250	150	50	250	150	50	250
Available-to-Promise		60	90			240			300
		60	150	150	150	390	390	390	390
Master Schedule			300			300			300

Figure 17.26   Available-to-Promise, Period-by-Period, and Cumulative-by-Period

time periods 2, 3, and 4 must be protected by the firm planned order of 300 cases scheduled for completion in time period 2. Thus, the ATP for time period 2 is 300 cases (time period 2's FPO) – (100 actual demand in time period 2 + 60 actual demand in time period 3 + 50 actual demand in time period 4) or ATP = 300 – 210, which equals 90 units.

Time period 1 has 90 cases of actual demand, and that is covered by the 150 cases on hand. The ATP for time period one then is 150 cases – 90 cases = 60 cases. Once the ATP by time period is known, the MPS system can calculate the cumulative ATP (the bottom row of numbers on the available-to-promise line in the matrix), as shown in Figure 17.26.

This cumulative result is calculated by adding each time period's ATP on the planning horizon to the prior time period's cumulative ATP value. Available-to-promise logic is generally used to support products that are planning to use a make-to-order manufacturing strategy more than products planned to use a make-to-stock manufacturing strategy since customer-committed backlog reaches further into the future for make-to-order products than it does for make-to-stock products.

ATP with Two Demand Streams

So far, we have looked at the classical available-to-promise (ATP) calculation and its use. This classical approach is valid and works for most companies as they commit product for customer delivery. However, as in most manufacturing situations, there are incidents or events that cause the standard logic to falter. This is the case when a company has multiple demand streams, such as one source of demand being to support customer orders for the company's finished and completed product while another source of demand might be to support customer orders for service or spare parts used to repair or maintain one of the company's products. Refer to Figure 17.27 on the following page during the discussion of this expanded ATP logic.

The ATP (normal) has been calculated as described earlier for time periods 1, 4, and 8 (noncumulative values). As you can see, the ATP in period 1 is 11. Let's say that production calls the person committing inventory and requests that all the items available be sent to the floor no later than time period 3.

To satisfy this request and to ensure that other promises are protected, the person doing the committing reviews the ATP in time period 1, sees that 11 units are available to promise according to the ATP, and makes the commitment to production to send them 11 units right away. Everything looks good!

The next event that occurs is a phone call from the service parts organization requesting the two items that they forecasted a need for in time period 1. What does the person tell them? "Oops! Don't have them!" What about time period 2? "Oops! Don't have them!" What about time period 3? "Oops! Don't have them!" Okay, three strikes and you're out! The next time the service parts organization forecasts its anticipated orders, it will likely forecast hundreds, thousands, millions, and so on.

	Past Due	1	2	3	4	5	6	7	8
Service Forecast		2	2	2	2	2	2	2	2
Production Forecast				4	4	4	4	4	4
Actual Demand		5	4						
Total Demand		7	6	6	6	6	6	6	6
Projected Available Balance	20	13	7	1	20	14	8	2	21
Available-to-Promise (Normal)		11			25				25
Available-to-Promise (Service)		7			9				9
Available-to-Promise (Production)		5			17				17
Master Schedule					25				25

Figure 17.27   Available-to-Promise with Two Demand Streams

Here is a case where the forecaster tried to do what's right: tell the master (supply) planner and/or master (supply) scheduler what he or she really thinks will be needed. However, it didn't work, so it's back to the old way of doing business (request more than might be needed and hope for the best).

If a company has the two-demand-stream situation, the logic of calculating ATP may need to be changed in order to protect the *forecast*. In the case being addressed in Figure 17.27, three ATP lines are shown: one for the aggregate ATP (normal), one for production, and one for service.

One way to calculate the ATP for production is for the MPS system to use the standard logic (on hand, which equals 20 units, plus the master supply plan and/or master supply schedule of zero, minus the actual demand of 9 units), resulting in 11 units of ATP. Taking this result, the MPS system can now subtract the service forecast of 6 units (2 units each in time periods 1, 2, and 3), leaving an ATP for production equal to 5 units (20 + 0 – 9 – 6). This approach in essence is reserving or allocating 6 units for the service part of the business.

Turning our attention to the service ATP, the system takes the on-hand balance of 20 units, plus the master supply plan and/or master supply schedule of zero, minus the actual demand of 9 units minus the remaining production forecast of 4 units, leaving 7 units ATP for service (20 + 0 – 9 – 4). Again, by subtracting the production forecast of 4 units from the ATP for service, you essentially reserve or allocate those units for production.

These calculations create an interesting situation. Look at the ATP results in time period 1 for service and production. It is easy to see that the summation of 5 units ATP for production and 7 units ATP for service does *not* equal the 11 units total ATP (there are only 11 units actually available-to-promise). There is one (1) unit up for grabs. First come, first served! When the first request for the extra unit is satisfied, the ATP will be recalculated and adjusted to take this into account (Figure 17.28, page 662).

Let's go back to production's phone call—production needs as many as there are available by time period 3. The answer to that question is now 5 units, not 11 units, based on the protection of the service forecast (see Figure 17.27 on page 660). So, let's take the customer order of 5 units and commit to delivery in time period 3. When this is done, the production forecast in time period 3 is consumed and reduced to zero. In the example, the forecast in time period 4 has been reduced to 3 units. This forecast consumption technique is one of many choices and is called *forward consumption*.

The new ATP for production is the on-hand inventory of 20 units, plus the master (supply) plan and/or master (supply) schedule of zero, minus the actual demand of 14 units (5 + 4 + 5) minus the service parts forecast of 6 units, equaling zero units (20 – 14 – 6). The new ATP for service is the on-hand inventory of 20 units, plus the master (supply) plan and/or master (supply) schedule of zero, minus the actual demand of 14 units minus the production forecast of zero units equaling 6 units (20 – 14 – 0). As you can see, the extra unit has been committed, the production commitments have been acknowledged and protected, and the service forecast has likewise been protected.

	Past Due	1	2	3	4	5	6	7	8
Service Forecast		2	2	2	2	2	2	2	2
Production Forecast					3	4	4	4	4
Actual Demand		5	4	5					
Total Demand		7	6	7	5	6	6	6	6
Projected Available Balance	20	13	7	0	20	14	8	2	21
Available-to-Promise (Normal)		6			25				25
Available-to-Promise (Service)		6			9				9
Available-to-Promise (Production)		0			17				17
Master Schedule					25				25

Figure 17.28 Available-to-Promise with Two Demand Streams After Accepting Production Order for Five Units in Time Period 3

Another method used by companies facing the two or multiple demand stream issue is to allocate the on-hand inventory balance and master (supply) plan and/or master (supply) schedule by percentage. Let's say the company decides that 30 percent of the manufactured or purchased items will be for spares, while the remaining 70 percent will be for production of the company's finished product (Figure 17.29, page 664). If the company has an on-hand balance of 20 units, 6 units would be allocated for spares while 14 units would be held for production's use. The same logic can be applied to the master (supply) plan and/or master (supply) schedule lots. In this case, 30 percent of 25 units is 8 units (rounded up), while 70 percent of 25 units is 17 units (rounded down).

Reviewing the first three time periods' ATP, we see a spares customer order for 2 units in time period 1 and another for 1 unit in time period 2. There are 20 units in inventory. Using our percentage allocation, 30 percent of the 20 units is 6 units, which are reserved for spares. Therefore, subtracting the 3 units committed, the ATP for spares in time period one has been reduced to 3 units.

In production's case 14 units were originally allocated, establishing an opening ATP of 14 units. However, a total of 14 units have been committed to production (5 units in time period 1, 4 units in time period 2, 5 units in time period 3), thus reducing the ATP in time period 1 for production to zero units. (Production is sold out unless spares releases some of their allocation; this is a management decision.)

These examples have shown the need to modify the standard ATP logic in order to deal with the more complex multiple-demand-stream environment. The reader should not expect that standard MPS software logic will support these types of calculations; most of the time the MPS software system must be modified in order to protect forecast as well as actual demand. What's important is that the logic of the MPS system be such that it supports the people making the decisions. In order to do this, the information presented must be accurate, timely, and factual.

Should Companies Have Demand Managers?

Hopefully, this chapter has made clear the importance of good demand management to the supply chain management, including master planning and scheduling. Without it, supply chain management and master planning and scheduling is at the mercy of external forces over which it has little or no control.

	Past Due	1	2	3	4	5	6	7	8
Service Forecast			1	2	2	2	2	2	2
Production Forecast					3	4	4	4	4
Actual Demand (Spares)		2	1						
Actual Demand (Production)		5	4	5					
Total Demand		7	6	7	5	6	6	6	6
Projected Available Balance	20	13	7	0	20	14	8	2	21
Available-to-Promise (Normal)		3			25				25
Available-to-Promise (Service)		3			8				8
Available-to-Promise (Production)		0			17				17
Master Schedule					25				25

Figure 17.29   Available-to-Promise Using MPS Allocation by Percentage

Over the years, manufacturing companies have seen the wisdom of having an individual (or more than one individual) dedicated to the job of supply management or the managing of its manufacturing schedules; this is done by a supply manager, master (supply) planner, and/or a master (supply) scheduler. Class A companies give the same attention to demand management. In many ways, these are parallel functions. A demand manager and/or demand planner position (usually reporting to a marketing function) is not universally present in many manufacturing companies, but it is highly recommended.

Figure 17.30 presents a process diagram of how a demand manager and/or demand planner interacts with the demand side of the business and how that same function is linked with the supply management function, which benefits directly from more accurate and robust information about demand.

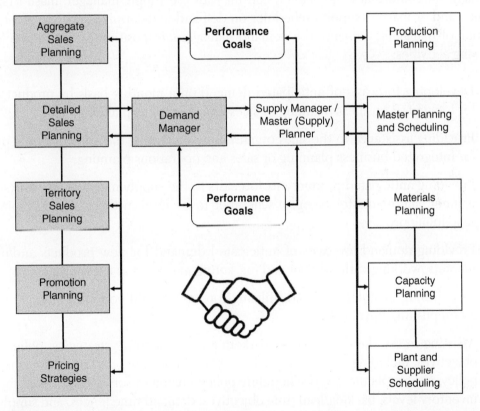

Note: Depending on the size and complexity of the organization, some companies use a demand planner in place of a demand manager and master (supply) planner (possibly a master scheduler wearing multiple hats) in place of a supply manager.

Figure 17.30   The Role of the Demand Manager or Demand Planner

Sales and marketing play important roles in demand management, and their active involvement leads to improved supply planning and master planning and scheduling. These organizations are responsible for developing and maintaining sales plans, both at the aggregate level and disaggregated or detailed level. Sales and marketing must take responsibility for predicting the product mix, customer order promising, and identification of abnormal demands.

Additionally, as members of management, sales and marketing must have a role in formulating company policies with respect to lead-time definitions, rescheduling time zones, safety stocks, overplanning, inventory levels, and customer service levels. As participants in the integrated business planning or sales and operations planning process, sales and marketing also should have inputs to development of the aggregate supply plan.

Finally, sales and marketing should consult with the supply manager, master (supply) planner, and/or master (supply) scheduler on demand-and-supply issues. To assist in the function of managing demand, the demand management position is responsible for the following activities:

1. Developing forecasts of anticipated demand on a monthly basis by product family for integrated business planning or sales and operations planning;

2. Providing assistance to the sales organization facilitating the sales planning process for integrated business planning or sales and operations planning;

3. Providing anticipated product mix forecasts to the supply manager, master (supply) planner, and/or master (supply) scheduler to be used in the master planning and scheduling process;

4. Providing demand forecasts of anticipated demand for new products and/or new markets, working with product and marketing managers as appropriate;

5. Establishing, maintaining, and utilizing forecasting and communications tools for accomplishing the above;

6. Assisting in the development of marketing/manufacturing strategies, policies, and objectives, including integrated business planning or sales and operations planning policy, master planning and scheduling policy, customer service objectives, targeted inventory levels, backlog/lead time objectives, demand time fences, and supply time fences (planning time fence);

7. Assisting with planning bills (especially product mix factors) and product structures;

8. Monitoring the company's performance to approved plans while providing detailed input to sales and marketing management for use at the integrated business planning or sales and operations planning reviews;

9. Developing and documenting the factors and assumptions supporting the company sales plan;[6]

10. Advising the supply manager, master (supply) planner, and/or master (supply) scheduler on allocation and prioritization issues.

Overall, the demand manager or demand planner is to sales and marketing what the supply manager, master (supply) planner, or master (supply) scheduler is to manufacturing and production operations. The primary qualifications for the demand management (planning) position include:

- Experience in sales, marketing, and customer service;

- Knowledge of the company's products and services;

- Knowledge of enterprise resource planning, including integrated business planning and/or sales and operations planning, demand management, supply management, and master planning and scheduling;

- Excellent communication skills;

- Credibility throughout the company, with top management, sales, marketing, manufacturing, supply chain management, research and development, engineering, finance, and other support organizations;

- Knowledge of the company's manufacturing processes; and

- Current technology and computer skills.

The last 17 chapters have discussed the *why(s)*, *what(s)*, and *how(s)* of master planning and scheduling (MPS). Much of this discussion has been in the format of what the demand manager, demand planner, supply manager, master (supply) planner, and/or master (supply) scheduler must do in order to become effective in demand and supply management as well as master planning and scheduling.

---

[6] George E. Palmatier and Joseph S. Shull, *The Marketing Edge* (New York: John Wiley & Sons, 1989).

The last four chapters on integrated business planning, rough cut capacity planning, supply management and aggregate master planning, and demand management and aggregate master planning have addressed many MPS integration points.

The next three chapters (before looking into the future of master planning and scheduling) are designed to provide the reader with a proven methodology to educate the people with a need to know on MPS concepts, implement an effective master planning and scheduling (MPS) process, design and/or implement the required supporting tools and technology, ensure that the company's data integrity will support a well-run MPS system, and achieve those lofty Class A operating results.

18

The Proven Path to a Successful Master Planning and Scheduling Implementation (Phase 1)

Executives Lead MPS Behavior and Process Evaluation and Planning

If you always do what you've always done, you will always get what you've always gotten.

From the Original Implementation Plan to the Current Proven Path

Over the past 75 years, thousands of companies have taken steps in the direction of greater effectiveness, quality, and customer service. Perhaps at no time since the early years of the Industrial Revolution has the impulse toward self-improvement been so widespread. In North America and Europe, the motive for that impulse is not difficult to understand: Intense competition from foreign competitors—primarily Asian corporations—threatens both the profitability and the survival of companies in a wide range of industries.

An important set of tools used by companies in their drive toward improvement in manufacturing has been manufacturing resource planning (MRPII), enterprise resource planning (ERP), and integrated, time-phased, demand-driven supply chain management (SCM). Thousands of companies in a variety of industries have turned to these highly effective processes and increasingly advanced software tools as a means of improving customer service, shortening delivery times, increasing productivity, and reducing inventory costs. Of these companies, hundreds (possibly greater than a thousand) have reached the coveted status of Class A in Operational and/or Business Excellence.

In 1976 the late Oliver Wight, who did so much to develop and popularize these powerful processes and tools, asked his colleague Darryl Landvater to investigate and document the critical activities and steps taken by companies that had been successful in adopting manufacturing resource planning and making it their operating philosophy. The purpose of this investigation was to provide implementation guidelines that others might follow—what the Oliver Wight Companies would call *The Proven Path*. Not surprisingly, Landvater found that successful implementation of manufacturing resource planning does not happen by chance, luck, or sorcery, but through thoughtful planning, teamwork, and execution.

The original, or what might be called the first version of *The Proven Path* (although not referred to as such at that time) was/is documented as *The Implementation Plan* in a few books: (1) *MRPII: Unlocking America's Productivity Potential*; (2) *Manufacturing Resource Planning (MRPII): Unlocking America's Productivity Potential*, revised edition, and (3) *The Executive Guide to Successful MRPII*, all written by the late Oliver Wight.[1]

The first time a graphic version of The Implementation Plan and the term *The Proven Path* was referenced in print was Tom F. Wallace's *MRPII: Making It Happen* in 1985, followed by Wallace's second edition of the book in 1990.[2] All of these volumes fully spell out in detail the steps and activities needed to successfully implement manufacturing resource planning.

In 1989 a somewhat significant update was made to the now-called *Proven Path* (second edition) and it was/is documented in a couple of standalone books titled *The Proven Path: A Roadmap to Class A—The Integrated Approach to MRPII, JIT/TQC, and DRP* published by Oliver Wight Limited Publications, Inc. in 1989 (revised edition, January 1990). That *Proven Path* version was used in the original release of this book in 1994, while succeeding

---

[1] Oliver W. Wight, *MRPII: Unlocking America's Productivity Potential* (Oliver Wight Limited Publications, Inc., 1981); Oliver W. Wight, *Manufacturing Resource Planning: MRPII, Unlocking America's Productivity Potential*, rev. ed. (Oliver Wight Limited Publications, Inc., 1981); Oliver W. Wight, *The Executive Guide to Successful MRPII* (Oliver Wight Limited Publications, Inc., 1982); and Oliver W. Wight, *The Executive Guide to Successful MRPII*, 2nd ed. (Oliver Wight Publications, Inc., 1983).

[2] Thomas F. Wallace, *MRPII: Making It Happen*, 2nd ed. (New York: John Wiley & Sons, 1990).

versions of *Master Scheduling: A Practical Guide to Competitive Manufacturing* by John F. Proud continued to refer to it and use it (targeted at master scheduling implementation) as a tool and guide when pursuing a master scheduling and rough cut capacity planning implementation (it's just worked for so many years). *The Proven Path* is also discussed in various Wight Papers (also referred to as White Papers) written by Oliver Wight Principals.

Well, time marched on and in 2005 *The Proven Path* received another makeover coinciding with the release of Oliver Wight's *Class A Checklist for Business Excellence*, 6th edition.[3] So, in the 28+-year tradition of this book, the authors decided to briefly describe that latest *Proven Path* along with overlaying it with the MPS activities necessary (described in the text within each section) in a master planning and scheduling implementation. However, before we do that, let's go back and review how *The Proven Path* works (and we do mean **works**) in a company's supply chain management improvement initiative involving master planning and scheduling.

Master planning and scheduling is a subsystem of manufacturing resource planning (MRPII), enterprise resource planning (ERP), supply chain management (SCM), operational excellence, and business excellence. Because of this, the process of implementing master planning and scheduling has many parallels to the implementation of these processes. For that reason, it is worth taking just a few moments to review some of those processes.

The Proven Path to Successful Operational Excellence

Research by the Oliver Wight Companies has found that those who pursue a course of implementing *operational excellence* spend between 12 and 24 months (longer for *business excellence*, which includes nine enabling disciplines of which master planning and scheduling is but a part of the managing internal supply discipline) in a series of activities that involve the participation of managers and technical workers from the top to the lower levels of the organization. Typically, these activities are similar to those represented in Figure 18.1.

To get us started, let's briefly review the 2nd version of *The Proven Path* (documented by Oliver Wight International in the noted *Proven Path* books) for movement to operational

---

[3] Oliver Wight International, Inc., *The Oliver Wight Class A Checklist for Business Excellence*, 6th ed. (Hoboken, NJ: John Wiley & Sons, 2005).

The (Past) Proven Path, Version 2

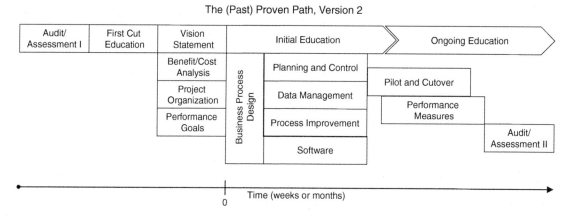

Figure 18.1   The Oliver Wight Operational Excellence Proven Path

excellence as well as *The Proven Path* for the master planning and scheduling (see Figure 18.3). Once that is done, discussion of the 3rd version of *The Proven Path* will take place for those who are pursuing or wish to pursue a course of implementing business excellence, including master planning and scheduling (see Figure 18.5 on page 684).

This documented discussion is the main focus of Chapters 18 through 20. Chapter 18 focuses on *evaluation and planning* for a supply chain management and/or enterprise resource planning implementation (let's say it one more time—master planning and scheduling is part of a supply chain management and/or enterprise resource planning implementation), while Chapter 19 focuses on the *design and structure* activities required for a successful SCM and/or ERP implementation, and Chapter 20's discussion focuses on an effective *launch and cutover* (including *success measurements*) of the designed or redesigned processes, software support enhancements, and new people behaviors. Of course, data integrity to best-practice standards is a must! For a moment or two, let's go back and visit history.

The Proven Path (2nd version) process began with an *audit/assessment* of the company's current situation—its operations, problems, strategies, and opportunities—and its readiness to adopt operational excellence. This exercise not only forced managers to take a hard look at existing practices but formed a valuable baseline against which future programs would eventually be measured.

The next step was *first-cut education,* in which both the executive team and operating team learned about operational excellence: what it is, how it operates, and what it takes to implement it properly. This group also had to determine whether *operational excellence* made sense for their particular business.

Assuming that this step had a positive outcome, the same set of team leaders then developed a *vision statement,* a written document that described the company and its competitive capabilities once *operational excellence* was adopted and integrated company-wide. Taking place concurrently with the beginning of the vision statement process were three critically important activities, which were performed in parallel: *benefit/cost analysis, project (initiative) organization,* and the development of *performance goals.*

Benefit/cost analysis results, again, in a formal written document that articulates all the anticipated benefits and costs that were expected to accrue to the company if and when *operational excellence* was adopted and implemented. Project organization and performance goals were developed in parallel to the benefit/cost analysis. In effect, they consider two issues: If *operational excellence* were to be adopted, how would the implementation be organized within the company? And what levels of accuracy and performance would be expected in areas touched by the *operational excellence* implementation?

The Decision Point

At this point, the company and its management were in a position to make an informed decision to either continue business as usual or adopt the *operational excellence* approach. If their decision was to go with operational excellence, they would face a one- to two-year period of implementation activities, some of which were sequential while others were approached in parallel.

When the authors discuss *The Proven Path* for Business Excellence (remember, there are nine enabling disciplines required for Oliver Wight Class A Certification in Business Excellence), the implementing company can be looking at three to five (maybe even 10) years of implementation and improvement activities (it's a journey, not a destination). The speed at which a company can implement these improvements depends on its beginning state, its willingness to focus on the improvement initiative, and resources available.

Therefore, some companies may progress faster than others. In short, speed of results can vary, but skipping steps in *The Proven Path* to increase speed (or for any other reason) only serves to increase the risk to achieving success. As an intermediate step on this somewhat long journey to Class A in Business Excellence, several companies over the years chose (or now choose) to take on a few milestones (as defined in Oliver Wight's Class A Standard as chapters) at a time, such as Integrated Business Planning, Managing Market Demand,

and Managing Internal Supply (which is where the master planning and scheduling process is designed/redesigned, documented/approved, and implemented/reimplemented).

However, for now let's continue our brief discussion regarding *The Proven Path* (2nd version) to achieve operational excellence (again, master planning and scheduling is a significant part of an operational excellence implementation). The first set of these activities was the preparation for converting the company's entire process over to the operational excellence approach. This crossover could include the implementation of a new ERP/SCM software system(s) or a reimplementation of the system(s) already installed.

Prior to the full cutover, a series of pilot operations were performed to minimize the risk of failure and to increase the overall chances of achieving Class A results (several hundreds of companies achieved operational excellence by following *The Proven Path* methodology being described). The preparation activities just mentioned included the following:

- Creation of a detailed implementation plan (a sample is in this book's Appendix B);

- Education and training of key and affected company associates;

- Design of the business processes as they would look once operational excellence was implemented;

- Writing and implementing company policies and procedures with respect to tactical planning, execution, and control (policy, flow diagram, and procedure listings are included in Appendix C);

- Development of an accurate database for inventory records, product definitions, process routings, production lines, manufacturing cells or centers, and variable parameters (see Chapter 13);

- Aggregate forecast/customer order and production/procurement/purchasing planning (today's terms are aggregate demand planning and aggregate supply planning) implemented early;

- Computer, conference room, and live pilot operations completed successfully (go/no go decisions);

- Necessary levels of data integrity in place for all items (see Chapter 13 for MPS support requirements);

- Feedback links in place for plant production and procurement and purchasing;

- Identification and implementation of process acceleration and improvements that would make the entire supply chain system work more effectively and efficiently;

- Acquisition, installation, and maintenance of the software needed to support operational excellence (and business excellence) as well as related activities;

- Identification of accuracy and performance measurements and methods of tracking them.

Going on the Air

Once these activities were successfully completed (recognizing that education and training are *never* really completed), the company was ready to "go on the air," to use an Oliver Wight term. There, the policies, procedures, guidelines, workflows, work instructions, accuracy and performance metrics, and computer systems developed earlier around conference room tables were tested in a series of measured experiments. This was done with a small set of products, so that if the new process or system failed or contained system bugs, operations within the company would not be jeopardized. Pilot operations also provided opportunities for personnel to learn to operate the process and system in measured steps.

Satisfactory pilot operations then led to a full cutover to the newly designed, time-phased, integrated, demand-driven ERP (now referred to as SCM) process and system(s)—again, in measured steps. At this point, data on accuracy and performance was collected for comparison to the accuracy and performance goals set earlier in the design stage. The personnel involved with and using the newly implemented business process(es), along with the newly implemented software and/or software enhancements, worked hard for a few months getting used to the system's input requirements as well as with using the system's output information then available.

The last step on the company's journey to Class A using *The Proven Path* (2nd version) was the *audit/assessment II*, or the *call for the question* of satisfying the Class A criteria in Operational Excellence (Class A criteria for operational excellence is/was documented in Oliver Wight's ABCD Checklist (4th and 5th editions) for Operational Excellence; see Figure 18.2a).[4]

---

[4] Oliver Wight International, Inc., *The Oliver Wight ABCD Checklist for Operational Excellence*, 4th and 5th editions (New York: John Wiley & Sons).

(a)   (b)

Figure 18.2   (a) Class A Checklists, 4th and 5th editions (criteria for Class A in operational excellence); (b) Class A Checklist, 6th edition and Standard, 7th edition (criteria for Class A in business excellence)

Note: Class A criteria for business excellence is documented in Oliver Wight's Class A Checklist (6th edition)/Standard (7th edition) for Business Excellence, Figure 18.2b.

This concludes the brief discussion on the overall *Proven Path* (2nd version) that was used (and sometimes is still used) to pursue operational excellence. Now let's focus our attention on where master planning and scheduling fits in this version of *The Proven Path* to operational excellence.

The Former Proven Path to Master Planning and Scheduling in a Class A Operational Excellence Environment

Presentation of the former essential activities on the Operational Excellence *Proven Path* to successful implementation is appropriate here because so many master planning and scheduling (MPS) issues must be addressed by the aspiring operational excellence company if it hopes to progress successfully along *The Proven Path*. In fact, an ERP/SCM system or systems will *not* work if MPS is not in place and operating correctly; quantities driven down through the ERP and SCM system will be too many, too few, too early, or too late if there is no master plan and/or schedule to connect production supply and market demand in an intelligent fashion.

Because master planning and scheduling is an integral part on *The Proven Path* (2nd version), we the authors decided to discuss the prior version of *The Proven Path* since so many companies used it (why, because it worked) to achieve Class A in Operational Excellence, *including sales and operations planning, demand planning, supply planning, master scheduling, rough cut capacity planning, material planning, production scheduling, supplier scheduling along with the item master, bills-of-material, process routings, work locations/centers, and inventory management.* So, let's take a look!

Master planning and scheduling issues appear frequently on *The Proven Path* (2nd version). For example, in first-cut education, the importance of MPS to the smooth functioning of operational excellence is made clear, often for the first time, to many participants. Again, in the development of accuracy and performance goals, goals for MPS are as relevant and important as are those for inventory record accuracy, quality, and management of the ERP and SCM system.

The importance of MPS to ERP and SCM is perhaps nowhere greater than in the planning, scheduling, and control area, where the defined methodology to balance demand and supply at the item mix level is implemented. If a company cannot effectively manage this balance, it will have trouble planning, scheduling, and controlling materials and capacities, and creation of a valid master plan and/or master schedule will be difficult.

The implementation of a solid MPS process has a path of its own, one that shares many of the characteristics of its operational excellence father or mother but also has several unique characteristics. These are schematically described in Figure 18.3. Implementation of master planning and scheduling takes place within three broad stages on *The Proven Path* (2nd version):

Stage 1 is the *evaluation and preparation* period in which key personnel in the company gain a general knowledge about MPS, determine where they currently stand with respect to best practices of MPS, analyze the benefits and costs of a state-of-the-art MPS process and system in their company, and decide what will have to happen to get a Class A MPS process up and running. At the end of this stage, a decision is made to either move forward with MPS, reject it, or go on hold; this point in time is again referred to as *point zero*.

Stage 2 is the *design and action* period devoted to the organizational issues required to launch and sustain a successful MPS process. This is a period of design and action. Like the previous stage, this one also features education and training. It features regular business meetings by the personnel charged with implementing and operating the process as well as the system and, to a lesser extent, others in the company who will be touched by MPS in important ways.

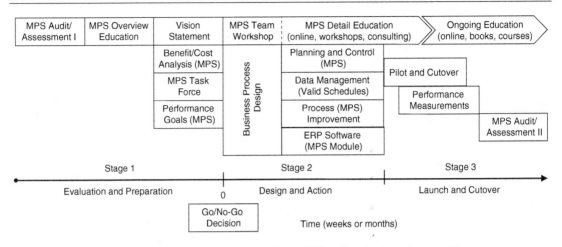

Figure 18.3   The Proven Path to Effectively Implementing Master Planning and Scheduling

Master planning and scheduling task force personnel must iron out the details with respect to demand management, supply management, integrated business planning or sales and operations planning, and the other features of master planning and scheduling discussed in earlier chapters. When this stage is over, it should be clear what is to be done, who will do it, and when.

Stage 3 is the *launch and cutover period*. This is when the company takes its first deliberate steps toward putting the processes in place (some processes may actually be implemented during stage 2) and bringing the MPS computer software system online. Because newly developed or redeveloped processes may not be fully understood and the chance that software bugs still may be present in a newly adopted or redesigned system, introduction is conducted in small steps.

Eventually, as the processes become familiar and the computer software is proved to work as designed and documented, and as personnel learn more about using their new policies, procedures, workflows, work instructions, accuracy and performance metrics, and tools, the master planning and scheduling system goes *on-the-air* company-wide.

It should be noted that when a company is pursuing *Oliver Wight Class A in Business Excellence* (7th edition) and following *The Proven Path* (3rd version), the initiative includes three phases (formerly referred to as stages)—those of Phase 1: Lead, Phase 2: Transform, and Phase 3: Own.

There you have it—a little *Proven Path* history along with a brief explanation of the predecessor to the latest Oliver Wight *Proven Path*. The remainder of this chapter concentrates on the current Lead Phase (the Transform Phase and Own Phase are covered in the next two chapters in this book) of the current *Proven Path* (3rd version) being used today by companies pursuing the Class A Milestone in Managing Internal Supply, which includes the master planning and scheduling (MPS) process.

The Journey to Excellence—Today and Tomorrow

The journey to excellence is tough and uncompromising. It is never-ending and is applied to every item and every process in the company. For such a journey to be sustained, it must continually deliver results and gains for all its stakeholders. The journey is a series of bite-sized projects with short timescales. These build into longer business improvement programs that assure success now and in the future.

Improvement activity must be prioritized to the current needs of stakeholders while delivering the firm foundations for future advanced work. As in building a house, the builder risks everything if he or she is not sure that the right foundations are firmly in place before he or she starts the walls, and that they are right before starting the roof and on to the finishing processes.

The Oliver Wight Business Maturity Map (see Figure 18.4a on page 681), supported by Maturity Transitions derived from *The Oliver Wight Class A Checklist for Business Excellence*, 6th edition, as well as the revised and enhanced succeeding edition, *The Oliver Wight Class A Standard for Business Excellence*, 7th edition, enables those within a company to understand the maturity of their business and the projects within their improvement program that will deliver the best real gain now. This is addressed in a Class A structured improvement program.

First things first! The company and its improvement teams must address the root causes of firefighting, dragon slaying, or event-driven management in its business. Unplanned events may be driven from the marketplace because the company's customers require more than the company and its standard processes can deliver; or they may arise from the company's own in-house lack of discipline in the way that it works and its behaviors as a total team.

Left unresolved, firefighting along with dragon slaying drain management of its time and energy in solving the same issues over and over. This questionable behavior prevents problem-solving and team-based initiatives gains from being sustained. Tackling the root causes of being event-driven constitutes Phase 1 of a company's journey toward excellence.

With the foundation of a well-planned and coordinated business in place, the improvement team members can expect sustainable gains from problem-solving initiatives. They may choose to accelerate the company's processes, make them more agile, or absolutely eliminate the root causes of failure in them.

By doing so, improvement team members will be capturing the knowledge and experience of people at all levels of the company into its processes and procedures so that it is not lost when people move on. Projects that eliminate the root causes form Phase 2 of a company's journey toward excellence. Both *The Oliver Wight Class A Checklist for Business Excellence*, 6th edition and *The Oliver Wight Class A Standard for Business Excellence*, 7th edition (refer back to Figure 18.2b on page 676) are benchmarked and expect that processes and behaviors of a Class A company will be in the top half of this Phase 2 maturity.

In Phase 3, a step change in productivity and effectiveness is sought by implanting this accumulated knowledge of the business into its systems and machines. Increasingly those systems become more intelligent and demand less and less human intervention in decision making. People play a more vital role at this time, focusing on the integrity and management of sophisticated processes rather than traditionally managing products and orders through processes. This phase is not about the number of computer terminals or computer-controlled machines in the company's operations. It is about the company's leadership and management teams' confidence that those systems will make the right decisions in all circumstances.

Phase 3 characteristics are *not* yet included in *The Oliver Wight Class A Standard for Business Excellence*. However, the standards Oliver Wight has included ensure that the reader and his or her company will be well prepared for this Phase 3 activity.

Finally, Phase 4 is getting the architecture of the entire company so that everyone and everything communicate with each other and each machine as one and give a seamless decision-making stream to the customer. This frees the company's people so they can work in small teams to develop and grow the business sectors and thereby develop and grow the entire business. As with Phase 3 activity, Phase 4 characteristics are *not* yet included in *The Oliver Wight Class A Standard for Business Excellence*.[5]

---

[5] Oliver Wight International, *The Oliver Wight Class A Standard for Business Excellence*, 6th and 7th editions (Hoboken, NJ:: John Wiley & Sons, 2005 and 2017). (Text extracted from both references with minor author modifications.)

Integrating the Business - Maturity

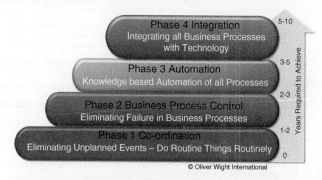

Figure 18.4a   The Oliver Wight Business Maturity Map

Oliver Wight's Class A Integrated Planning and Control Milestone

The purpose of the Class A Milestone for Integrated Planning and Control (available workbook) is to help companies to implement and drive valid and integrated product, demand, and supply chain plans along with their financial consequences to achieve the characteristics listed for a Class A company. *The Oliver Wight Class A Planning and Control Milestone Workbook*[6] is designed to guide a company and its improvement team on the journey to the top of Phase 1 maturity (see Figure 18.4b).

The planning and control milestone (of which master planning and scheduling is a critical part) recognizes that most companies go through a *maturity journey* in implementing and operating planning and control including master planning and scheduling practices. Achieving a Phase 1 level of business maturity is recognized as a primary milestone to sustained improvement and performance and may well initiate a journey to Business Excellence.

---

[6] *The Class A Planning and Control Milestone Workbook* is offered to Oliver Wight clients as an addendum to *The Class A Standard for Business Excellence* (Hoboken, NJ: John Wiley & Sons, 2017). At the time of this writing, the *Workbook* is not offered as a standalone product for sale.

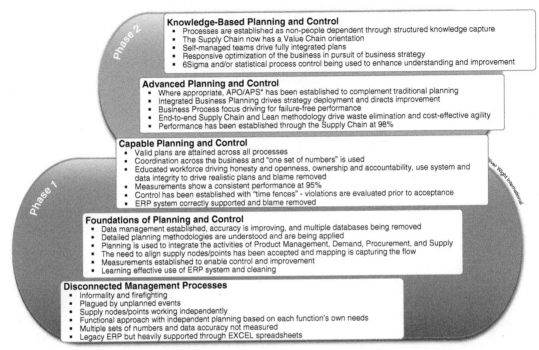

*APO/APS: Advanced Planning and Optimization/Scheduling

Figure 18.4b   The Oliver Wight Maturity Transition for Planning and Control

Figure 18.4b identifies the steps required to achieve *Capable* (the top of Phase 1 on the Planning and Control Maturity Chart) and *Advanced* (the middle of Phase 2 on the Planning and Control Maturity Chart) levels of maturity. The milestone is designed to help companies and their improvement teams identify its current *as is* status and then guide the improvement team or teams along the maturity journey. The Oliver Wight *Class A Planning and Control Milestone Workbook* is focused on getting a company to the top of Phase 1 maturity, which is often referred to as *Capable Planning and Control* in the Maturity Transition chart shown in Figure 18.4b.

The characteristics of *Advanced Planning and Control* are depicted in Phase 2 of the maturity transitions. The authors of this book along with the entire Oliver Wight team encourage companies to continue their improvement journey and further develop processes that operate at an advanced level. Criteria for the advanced level (full Class A standard) are shown in *The Oliver Wight Class A Standard for Business Excellence,* 7th edition.

Now that the characteristics of planning and control maturity have been discussed, we turn our attention to a *tried and proven* way for a company and its people to rise in their level of maturity. That tried and proven methodology is, one more time, referred to as *The Proven Path*. The remainder of this chapter discusses each step of Phase 1 on *The Oliver Wight Proven Path* to a successful planning and control implementation including the master planning and scheduling activities.

To avoid some confusion, the section just discussed referred to Phases 1 and 2 on the Maturity Transition Chart (Figure 18.4b on page 682) while the remainder of this chapter's discussion focuses on Phase 1 on *The Proven Path* (Figure 18.6 on page 685).

The Proven Path (3rd Version) to Successful Supply Chain Management and Master Planning and Scheduling Implementation

Following Darryl Landvater's early work on manufacturing resource planning, Oliver Wight the company developed an approach for managing change when implementing supply chain management processes and/or planning and control process improvements which, done correctly, will lead to business transformation. As noted several times in this chapter, Oliver Wight calls this approach *The Proven Path* (see Figure 18.5) because the change methodology has been used successfully for nearly 50 years.

This Proven Path change methodology encompasses:

- Executive commitment, involvement, and leadership—emphasized in Chapter 18;

- Creation of a journey and operational vision, business case for change, and return on investment—emphasized in Chapter 18;

- Implementation planning, preparation, execution, and control—emphasized in Chapter 18;

- Creating internal change agents, sometimes referred to as subject matter experts—emphasized in Chapter 19;

- Focus on structure (Class A Standard) and a structured approach (Proven Path) to ensure a successful implementation—emphasized in Chapter 19;

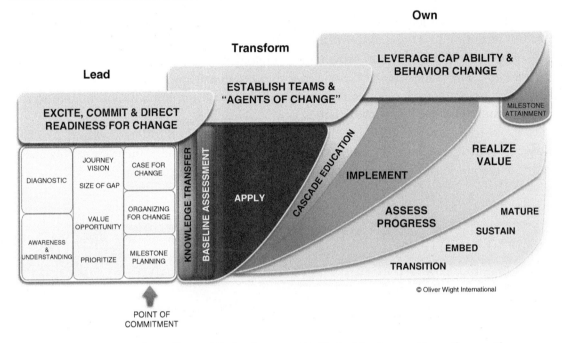

Figure 18.5 The Oliver Wight Proven Path to Business Transformation

- Education and training for all people within the company with a need to know—emphasized in Chapter 19;

- Ownership for policies (rules), process design (or redesign), and procedures (activities)—emphasized in Chapter 19;

- Behavior change, defined processes, and tool implementation—emphasized in Chapter 20;

- Strong foundation of data integrity—emphasized in Chapter 20;

- Measurement and reporting of results—emphasized in Chapter 20.

The Proven Path for each desired milestone concludes with transitioning the business to a new state, embedding the new behaviors and processes in the business culture, ensuring the sustaining of the new best practices over many years, and maturing the implementation to reach full process development, acceptance, and results.

Phase 1: Lead Phase (Understanding and Committing)

Implementing change and delivering true business transformation are challenging and many companies are unsuccessful in this quest. Oliver Wight has the experience of working with thousands of companies over its 50+-year history and our principals (educators as well as coaches) have created and refined our change management methodology. This change management methodology is called *The Proven Path for Business Transformation* (see Figure 18.6) and includes a step-by-step model for successful business transformation (it's truly a left-foot, right-foot, left-foot, right-foot, etc. approach).

The Proven Path is geared to a complete supply chain management initiative. While this and the following two chapters in this book discuss the overall *Proven Path*, emphasis is placed on the master planning and scheduling required activities. *The Proven Path* starts with the company and its players understanding how they are currently operating, how that stacks up to other companies in their industry, and how they might get better.

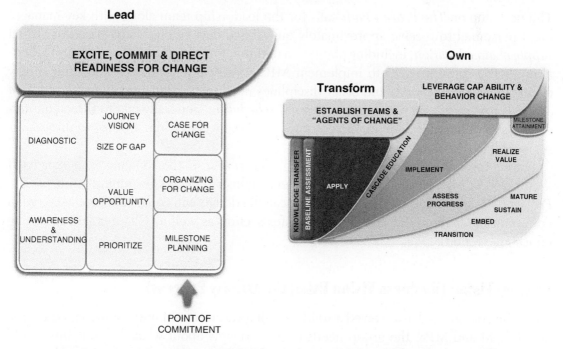

Figure 18.6   The Oliver Wight Proven Path Emphasizing Lead Phase

Diagnostic (Lay of the Land, Strengths, and Weaknesses)

The Lead Phase starts with a *diagnostic or business health check* to determine the *as-is* business practices and, hence, business maturity across a specified scope of the business. Observations and findings are reviewed with the leadership team (either in person or virtually) within a context of best-practice education to provide awareness and understanding to illustrate business gaps and opportunities. All supply chain management (planning and control) *diagnostics* include a section on master planning and scheduling.

Understanding the strengths and weaknesses of the business enables the improvement journey to be designed, approved, and implemented over a reasonable amount of time (design builds on strengths while changing/correcting weaknesses). Additionally, the *diagnostic* includes a set of initial recommendations required to move the company to Class A in business excellence and/or specified part of business excellence—that is, managing internal supply, which includes master planning and scheduling.

Awareness and Understanding (Initial Education and Learning)

The next step on *The Proven Path* calls for the leadership team along with key management personnel to receive approximately one to two days of classroom-based or virtual *supply chain education*, including about two to three hours of master planning and scheduling (MPS). In a program to implement MPS specifically, several people from supply chain management (SCM) and other disciplines need *more education and should take a concentrated course on master planning and scheduling*, generally two to three continuous days in duration if done in person or two to three weeks (done in two- to three-hour segments) in duration if done virtually.

During the *awareness and understanding education* step, the company is making itself aware of best MPS practices used throughout industry. At this beginning point on *The Proven Path*, the details of MPS are not critical; the details will come later (see MPS detail education in Chapter 19's knowledge transfer section as well as Chapter 20's cascading education section).

Journey Vision (Business Vision Using the Affinity Process)

Once the core group has received a solid base of awareness and understanding education about SCM and MPS, the group needs to think deeply about what the company would be like if (and when) Class A SCM, including MPS, was thoroughly integrated into its operations. From this thinking the group should develop a company *journey vision* (a series of bite-sized projects with reasonable and realistic timescales) as well as an *operational vision* (what will/does the supply chain including master planning and scheduling look like in say, two years?).

The *journey vision coupled with the operational vision* describes the way in which the company would be different and/or improved. Of course, some companies may want the *journey vision and/or operational vision* to really be a business excellence *journey vision and/or business vision*!

Since the typical company already has some form of vision and mission statement or is following a defined strategy that features an all-embracing focus for its business future, the business/operational vision statement that emerges from the MPS implementation process should logically address the central tenets of that primary mission or strategy. For example, if customer service is the strategic thrust of the company, the MPS part of the vision may describe how customer service regarding on-time delivery and reduced customer delivery lead times will be improved by the adoption of Class A master planning and scheduling.

Let's take a look at a real-company example of that vision of operations targeted at a planning and control improvement initiative. Key personnel from across this operation use master (planning and) scheduling and material requirements planning. The time frame to realize the vision was set at two years. Here is the executive summary (written in present tense as suggested during the Affinity process) of the vision of operations created.

COMPANY VISION OF OPERATIONS (A MODIFIED CLIENT EXAMPLE)

Company Comment

In developing this Vision of Operations (VOO), we recognize the substantial opportunity to improve our business processes by deploying an integrated set of processes and skills, enabled by our systems. As we pursue this vision, we also expect to measure it regularly, review it periodically, and adapt it as appropriate to the dynamics of our markets, customers, and suppliers.

Opening Statement

Our company is managed through an integrated business planning process known as business management. The company process provides a rolling 24-month operating plan that encompasses all businesses serviced by the global supply chain (GSC). Key decisions from the process are embedded into approved demand and supply plans in a timely manner so that demand and supply plans are aligned with the company's strategy and opportunities. This allows both the businesses and GSC to account for the necessary time-phased resources to support implementation of new initiatives. Rough cut capacity planning is used at the aggregate level to validate the supply plan.

Demand Planning

We have an approved demand plan that encompasses all sources of demand for the next 24 months including new products, sales promotions, product rationalizations, product transitions, and affiliate requirements. Where appropriate, the demand plan is disaggregated into smaller buckets to support master planning and scheduling activities.

The demand plan accuracy is continuously improving, which provides the basis for a stable environment for master planning and scheduling, material planning, capacity planning, supplier scheduling, and operations. Demand spikes are better anticipated, communicated to the supply organization, and accounted for in the master plan and/or master schedule. These demand planning improvements allow GSC to use our reserve capacity for new initiatives and permit the sales organization to be more aggressive in pursuing new opportunities.

Master Planning and Scheduling

We utilize a master planning and scheduling process that provides the linkage from the integrated business planning horizon to the operational planning horizon. The master plan coupled with the master schedule shows what we plan to produce, expressed in product groupings and/or specific configurations, quantities, and dates. In conjunction with available-to-promise (ATP) information, master planning and scheduling provides full visibility of our time-phased requirements and allows us to quantify our opportunities and potential service risks. We act on this information to achieve outstanding customer service, inventory management, and cost reduction goals.

Our master planning and scheduling process integrates the monthly supply plan with daily plant production scheduling. The process is based on a documented policy and associated procedures, designed to ensure that products are built in the right quantity at the right time in the right place. The process encourages feedback (top-down and bottom-up) regarding schedule content and accuracy. The master planning and scheduling process is enabled using the company's enterprise resource planning system.

The master plan and master schedule are the ***masters of all detailed plans and/ or schedules***. They account for all demand as well as planned inventory and/or desired backlog changes. The master plan and master schedule allow the production organization to proactively manage the required resources, including materials, staffing, and capacity. They provide the framework for the detailed production schedule, which authorizes work through manufacturing work orders.

The master schedule (driven by the master plan) drives the need for raw materials and intermediates using material requirements planning (MRP). The master schedule also provides the logistics organization with information to effectively plan warehouse and transportation resources. The master plan as well as the master schedule is continually validated by confirming capacity and material availability.

We have a process to approve changes to the master plan and/or master schedule and communicate changes to impacted areas. Changes are captured, measured, and analyzed for improvement opportunities. The master plan and/or master schedule is integrated with order management via the ATP demand control mechanism. This enables us to satisfy our established customer service level agreements. We have a process and a system capable of planning future changes to our network, including new products, sourcing changes, and customer changes.

Materials Management

We have a robust, global materials management system that provides real time on-hand and in-transit inventory at all locations. Material receipts are processed in the system immediately after raw materials arrive. Production work orders are fed directly from the process control systems into the enterprise resource planning system. We perform regular cycle counts; if discrepancies arise, we perform root cause analysis to review and correct the data. As a result, the inventory is highly accurate.

The materials management system enables multiple views of the working capital forecast so it can be reviewed and acted upon at all levels. Our flexible formulation strategy, which avoids single-sourced critical raw materials, allows us to optimize raw materials and finished goods to reduce inventory.

We utilize master planning and scheduling along with material requirements planning to plan/purchase finished goods and raw materials at all of our plants. All plants as well as the central planning organization follow one standard process for responding to material requirements planning, exception driven action messages. Our plants have accurate bills-of-material covering anticipated production for the next 12 months; additionally, the bills-of-material show future component and packaging revision changes for the 12-month horizon.

A valid master planning and scheduling process has improved supplier relationships and now allows for closer collaboration. Our enterprise resource planning system allows us to effectively and efficiently mine data and conduct analysis. This allows the planners to spend their time analyzing and not spending all their time generating the data. Responsibilities as well as accountabilities are clearly laid out in our RACI document. Our employees are well educated and trained on all business policies, process flows, procedures, work instructions, and metrics along with the functionality of our enterprise resource planning system.

Operations

The company's plants are recognized as efficient, reliable, and safe operations. Production lines are operated to optimize their availability and flexibility to meet demand. Common, consistent, and simple visual controls monitor performance of our sites.

Products are categorized and have appropriate run strategies that best meet operational targets and defined service levels. High-volume products are manufactured to minimize working capital by using a make-to-order (MTO) strategy. Lower-volume products are scheduled based on minimum run quantities, safety stocks, and available capacity. Production is managed using principles such as flow to the work for effective workforce utilization.

Third-party operations include daily communications to ensure alignment with the company's operations. These communications include, but are not limited to, safety, cost, key performance indicators, production schedule, inventory levels, customer service, and quality.

The master planning and scheduling process enables the company to effectively balance the stability of plant production with the flexibility to meet customer requirements. This allows optimization of productivity and working capital. Unplanned schedule events (e.g., unplanned overtime and holiday coverage) are minimized, contributing to a safe, clean, orderly, and efficient workplace.

Warehousing and Shipping

Our warehouse operations are best in class. All warehouses used by the company are organized on the same principles: right product, right quantity, right place, and right time. These principles provide a competitive advantage in storage and in pick/pack/ship activities.

Our competitive advantage is based on a highly accurate inventory, just-in-time production loaded directly into trucks, stored products located optimally for staging and shipment, efficient loading, and quick truck turnaround. Finished goods warehouses are neatly organized with sufficient space to manage demand variability. People have time to explore warehouse productivity and service enhancing projects. This optimizes manufacturing flexibility, inventory levels, and logistics cost.

Data Integrity

The importance of data integrity to the company is recognized and supported by people, processes, and tools. Adequate resources are in place to manage the integrity and accuracy of all master and supporting data. Master data records include item numbers, lead times, order quantities/lot sizes, safety stocks, and so on. Supporting data includes scheduled receipts (work orders, purchase orders), customer orders, firm planned orders, and so on.

Inventory records for finished goods, intermediates, and raw materials, including rebill locations and vendor-owned inventory, are highly accurate and visible in the system. Bills-of-material are accurate and support the generation of gross requirements at all planning levels. When planning bills are used for make-to-order products, their structure and content are accurate and visible. Percentages in these planning bills are provided by demand planning and represent the best estimate of the product mix needed to support customer orders.

We have a process to regularly review all item master data, do root cause analysis on errors detected, and correct any and all data as well as processing errors. The accountability for item master data is clearly assigned. All computer system users realize that the output of the enterprise resource planning system, which includes master planning and scheduling is unusable if best-practice data integrity is not maintained on a daily basis.

People

This company's vision recognizes that people are our most important asset. People have access to accurate and timely information and are empowered to make needed decisions. Long chaotic days, overflowing inboxes, constant firefighting, and surprises are things of the past. Meetings are collaborative, productive, and focused on the key assumptions, issues, opportunities, and risks.

Since people work in a less stressful environment, they have a better work-home life balance. Our people are self-directed and continually seek opportunities to improve their skills and capabilities. This is enabled by the discipline to follow defined policies and procedures, and leadership commitment to people wellness and development.

Closing Comments Regarding the VOO
(Again, Modified Client Example)

Our work over the past couple of years has led us to enjoying our workday as we satisfy our customers while safely making money and a profit for the company. The journey we have been on for this time has been very rewarding for each of us as well as for the company. All of us here at the company are quite proud of satisfying the requirements of Oliver Wight's Class A Milestone in Integrated Planning and Control (a milestone on our journey to Class A in Managing Internal Supply and Class A in Business Excellence).

* * *

While it may seem premature to develop a vision at this early stage, the core MPS group will have learned enough in the awareness and understanding education process to understand how MPS can improve operations, and optimism about that prospect is the normal result. The steps that follow are filled with hard work and constant reminders about the difficulties of fully integrating master planning and scheduling into company operations.

An unencumbered optimistic vision of operations along with a journey vision is needed during those difficult stages to remind everyone of the future value of their efforts. The one-day visioning workshop uses the Affinity process (an inherent similarity among things like demand management, supply management, master planning and scheduling, inventory management, backlog management, etc.) to drive the attendees to a completed vision draft by the end of the day's session (may well be a couple days when done virtually).

Size of Gap (Comparison between Vision and Diagnostic Findings)

Through the first three parts of the Lead Phase on *The Proven Path* (3rd version), the company and its supply chain improvement and master planning and scheduling team have created a journey vision, an operational or business vision, and documented the as-is business practices. The visionaries within the company have had enough awareness and understanding education to project their minds and thoughts into the future thereby creating and documenting the *vision of what they see (if they don't see it, they don't write it down).*

This sizing of the gap is made between the vision statement(s) and the diagnostic. To do this, the improvement team has a fundamental discussion regarding the vision and diagnostic gaps as well as the business value opportunity in closing the gap. Questions like "Can our company close the gap with just one step and/or one subproject or will it take several steps and/or several subprojects?" will arise. The answer to these and related questions are noted in the journey vision.

Value Opportunity (Benefit/Cost Analysis, ROI, Five-Year Cash Flow)

Implementing a master planning and scheduling system takes plenty of time spent by dozens of individuals in meetings, in doing analysis, and in writing reports. That time has a cost to the company. There are other direct costs as well—costs for computer hardware and software, education and training, achieving inventory record accuracy, getting the product and process definitions accurate, systems analysis, policy and procedure creation, programming, and coaching. The costs in time, effort, and direct outlays for implementing any new operating system are usually obvious to everyone. Less obvious are the benefits.

To win support for implementing a new master planning and scheduling process and possibly a new computer system or enhancing the current one, leaders and team members need to carry out a careful and unbiased analysis of the benefits and costs, which must be communicated to all parties concerned. There is no easier way to lose support for a good program than to fail to justify its costs to those who pay the bills and to those who do the work. The MPS task force also needs benefit/cost information to make informed decisions with respect to completing the implementation process.

Every company has its own set of implementation benefits and costs, and these need to be determined on an individual basis. In all cases, however, the categories of cost are *people, processes, tools*, and *data integrity*. Benefits invariably accrue to *sales* and various aspects of *material* and *labor* costs. Figure 18.7 itemizes the general categories of benefits and costs that implementers should include in their analysis.

The best sources to procure the benefits and costs are the individuals closest to the facts. For example, the sales vice president is in the best position to know what incremental increase in sales would result if the company always delivered customer product as promised and on time. The manufacturing vice president is in the best position to identify expected productivity improvements that would result from a valid, level-loaded schedule. The stockroom manager knows better than anyone the costs associated with bringing inventory record accuracy up to a Class A level needed to support a Class A MPS process.

BENEFITS			
Revenues	Increased Sales	$X,XXX,XXX	
People	Improved Order Promising	XXX,XXX	
	Increased Productivity	X,XXX,XXX	
	Unplanned Overtime Reductions	XXX,XXX	
	Fewer Underloaded Resources	XX,XXX	
	Expediting Cost Reductions	XX,XXX	
Materials	Purchase Cost Reductions	XXX,XXX	
	Inventory/Carrying Cost Reduction	X,XXX,XXX	
	Premium Charge Reductions	X,XXX	
Plant Productivity	Improved Utilization	X,XXX	
	Level-Loading	XX,XXX	
	Reduced Scrap	XX,XXX	
Freight	Load/Mode Optimization	XXX,XXX	
	Expediting Cost Reductions	XX,XXX	
		Total Benefits	$XX,XXX,XXX

COSTS			
People	Steering Committee	$XX,XXX	
	Project Team	XXX,XXX	
	Spin-Off Task Teams	XX,XXX	
	Education and Workshops	XX,XXX	
	Consulting	XX,XXX	
Data-Related	Inventory Record Accuracy	XX,XXX	
	Item Master Accuracy	X,XXX	
	Process Routing Accuracy	XX,XXX	
	Manufacturing Capacity Accuracy	X,XXX	
	Valid Schedules	X,XXX	
	Bill of Material Accuracy	XX,XXX	
Computer	Hardware and Software	XXX,XXX	
	Programming/Customization	XXX,XXX	
		Total Costs	$X,XXX,XXX

Figure 18.7   Benefit/Cost Analysis

The engineering department has the means to estimate the cost of improving the bills-of-material, recipes, or formulations it develops.

Using these individuals as sources for benefit and cost figures is also a way of enlisting their involvement and commitment to those benefits and costs when the program is fully implemented.

Prioritize (High Priority—Just Do It, Low Priority—Some Other Time)

By this time, the leadership team is getting a good picture painted in front of them. The current state including company strengths, weaknesses, and recommended improvements has been documented in the *diagnostic*. The leadership team has received some basic initial education to ensure their *awareness and understanding* of what operating in a Class A environment that uses best business practices in demand management, supply chain management, and master planning and scheduling is like. Of course, there are far more areas where improvements can be made and could be part of a business excellence and operational improvement initiative.

A vision of the company operating in a Class A manner has been created for the future. The improvement team has facilitated the preparation of the benefit and cost analysis (the people who will have their finger on the switch to deliver the benefits and control the costs are the ones who actually create the benefit/cost analysis). Using this data, a return-on-investment, the cost of a month's delay, and a five-year cash flow projection have been calculated by finance.

It's now time to establish the *priority* for this business improvement initiative. If the **priority assigned the initiative is 17**, Oliver Wight's recommendation is, "**Don't do it at this time!**" The risk of failure is "too high" and the company will not give the improvement initiative the attention it deserves and needs. However, if the **priority assigned is 2 or 3**, then the recommendation is, "**Let's move forward with this initiative!**" And when the company moves forward with the initiative, everyone including leadership should remember the high priority assigned to it and make sure the company's best people are assigned to the initiative.

Note: Any and all best-practice improvement initiative(s) will never be given a priority of one or top priority in the company; that honor belongs to shipping product and taking care of the customer. It is important for the steering committee, project team, and spin-off task teams (all defined later in this chapter) to be aware of this reality (*stuff happens* and when that *stuff happens* along the journey to Class A, the company and improvement team need to deal with it).

Case for Change (Diagnostic, Journey and Operational Vision, Gap Analysis, Benefit/Cost Analysis, Return-on-Investment, Five-Year Cash Flow, Recommended Company Priority)

Does the company really want to do this? The Journey to Excellence is tough and uncompromising. It is never-ending and is applied to every part of the business as well as every process within the company. For such a journey to be sustainable, it must continually deliver results and gains for all its stakeholders.

The journey is a series of bite-sized projects with reasonable and realistic timescales (repeating for author emphasis). These build into longer business improvement programs that ensure success now and in the future. Improvement activity must be prioritized (as stated earlier) to the current needs of stakeholders while delivering the firm foundations for future advanced work. As in building a house, you risk everything if the right foundation is not firmly in place before you continue the program to finish the house.

So, the next step on *The Proven Path* is to pull it all together into the case for change and how to organize for those upcoming changes. This will include (a) required resources—executive process owners as sponsors, project organization, and cross-functional design teams; (b) communication to articulate the case for change, to enroll and mobilize the critical mass of key influencers who will be active in the design/redesign; and (c) definition of the suite of measures by which success will be judged.

The case for change also should include the diagnostic summary, journey vision, business/operational vision, gaps between diagnostic and vision, benefit/cost analysis, recommended priority, organization model, and macro project plan. The project plan will define key milestone planning to drive early adoption and time-to-results. As these latter activities approach conclusion, the leadership team needs to make a formal decision to proceed or not to proceed. This point in time is referred to as the *Point of Commitment* on *The Proven Path*. Here is a client example of an executive summary taken from the company's case for change.

CASE FOR CHANGE (A MODIFIED EXCERPT FROM A CLIENT EXAMPLE)

Growth Strategy Requires Supply Chain Management Improvement

The company vision is to double sales by 20XX. This means that there will be increases in customer and supply expectations and complexity. To add additional layers of complexity to an already overburdened system without a solid foundation, there is a potential for monumental issues with customer service, which could in turn curtail the desired growth. In addition, there is a large risk of significant financial costs that could be avoided by capable people, solid business processes, and supporting systems in place.

We Are Not Delivering Operational Performance

The company is faced with the key challenges of providing excellent customer service while reducing the cost of goods sold and the investment required in the form of inventory. At the same time the company has the ambition to grow significantly over the next five years. On-time-in-full (OTIF) performance is 60 to 90 percent when best-in-class organizations are consistently delivering at 99 percent or greater. Inventory turns are below 4x when the minimum expected for a business of the same category as the company should be at least eight turns. Cost to manufacture is high due to frequent expediting, material shortages, poor use of labor, and last-minute changes to the production schedule.

Resources Are Overstretched and We Cannot Support Long-Term Growth

Our current supply planning processes between corporate-level supply chain planning and plant level production planning are not clearly defined, they are not synchronized, and they are not integrated to our integrated business planning (IBP) process. This causes confusion and inefficiencies, and hampers speed of execution. In a tight-capacity environment, our people are delivering through heroic efforts when execution should be seamless and unplanned customer demand changes managed with many fewer ups and downs. The consequence of this current state is that human resources are stretched. This condition is not sustainable for our long-term growth ambition.

Opportunity to Safely Make Money

The supply operations currently operate in a constant state of flux. We closely follow our strategy of being *customer focused on everything we do*. This means that we find a way to service the customer, *no matter what!"* This results in significant costs incurred in the manufacturing operations. We are reactive versus proactive and have no differentiation with our current customers with regard to supply that is not in line with our vertical integration strategy. We need to become proactive and leverage our different businesses with our customers.

Desire to Be One of the Best

In the marketplace we are currently perceived as a good supplier based on the relationships that our company has with our strategic customers. In order to really measure our differentiation, we have a huge opportunity to maximize our differentiation by leveraging our supply chain vertical integration and being proactive in delivering supply chain efficiencies to our customers. Improved effectiveness in supply chains across our entire portfolio will enable the up-sell strategy for our high-margin product customer base and down-sell strategy for our low-margin product customer base.

Organization for Change (Steering Committee, Project Team, Spinoff Task Forces)

The business of supply chain management and master planning and scheduling, as the preceding chapters have made clear, involves a broad set of disciplines, routines, policies, procedures, process flows, work instructions, accuracy metrics, and performance metrics. Additionally, a master planning and scheduling implementation requires strong supporting processes, such as integrated business planning or sales and operations planning, portfolio management, aggregate and detailed demand management, aggregate and detailed supply management, product (and sometimes option/attachment) definitions, process routings, inventory management, material and capacity planning, plant or site detailed production scheduling, capacity control, supplier scheduling, and material control, coupled with the use of computers and software, all of which are most important to truly experience a successful implementation.

In other words, disciplined good behaviors and linkages to other parts of the business are a must to ensure an effective and efficient master planning and scheduling sustained process. As part of the implementation process, each of these linkages and their associated tasks must be planned, staffed, and given a set of operational guidelines. The computer hardware and software requirements for MPS, for example, do not just appear. Someone must determine what capabilities are needed and how those capabilities would be used in the manufacturing facility.

Good implementations result when these assorted MPS disciplines, linkages, routines, policies, procedures, and so on are thought out by a number of task force members. The task force itself is staffed in part by members of the core group, which is dedicated to the implementation process, and in part by personnel likely to be involved in an up-and-running process using a computer hardware and software system for support. The task force is *not* immediately charged with developing the operational details required of a fully implemented MPS system. That would be premature, since the decision to go ahead with the implementation has not yet been made. Instead, the spinoff task team members' job is to determine what would have to be done and what resources would be required if a "go ahead" is the decision received.

In terms of computers and software, as just one example, the project team along with the master planning and scheduling task force would determine the dimensions of the requirements, who should be assigned to the job, and how much time would be required to get the computer software system into operation. Once questions like these have been answered by the project team and task force members, their findings should be compiled for the implementation group that is charged with the *"go/no-go"* decision. (These findings are useful later if a *"go"* decision is made; at that point they become the basis for operational planning in the next phase.)

If a *"go"* decision is made, the company's improvement initiative organization will be composed of an executive steering committee (make decisions, knock down obstacles), project team (generally small, all-encompassing activities such as information technology, standard operating policies/procedures formatting, project status reporting, budget control, etc.), and spinoff task forces (one per discipline, they do the work and are disbanded when their assigned tasks are done).

If a *"no-go"* decision is made, decisions will need to be made regarding the next steps; for example, leadership suggests that more work is required to improve the case for change, the benefit/cost analysis must be redone using leadership's input, the requested budget, resources, and timing need to be modified to align more with the company's strategy, possible disbandment of the teams as the company has decided to move in a different direction, and so on.

The leadership's *"go/no-go"* decision is made at the Point of Commitment noted on *The Proven Path* (still need a *macro implementation plan* to complete all planning elements of the Lead Phase, that of executive evaluation and overall planning). With that said, let's take a look at the final step in the Lead Phase.

Milestone Planning (Macro Project Plan—Tasks, Responsibility, Dates)

The last step of the evaluation and overall planning phase is for the core implementation group to consider what performance goals and what activities would be appropriate if a full SCM including MPS implementation were to be proposed and approved. *Business excellence* and *operational excellence* have many performance (as well as accuracy) goals and measurements; some key performance goals and measurements that pertain directly to MPS are that customer service, master schedule, production schedule, and supplier schedule must be 95 percent or better to be awarded Oliver Wight's Class A Milestone achievement in managing internal supply, which, again, includes master planning and scheduling.

All the Class A accuracy and performance criteria are defined in *The Oliver Wight Class A Checklist for Operational Excellence,* 4th and 5th editions (refer back to Figure 18.2a) as well as Class A Milestone in *The Oliver Wight Class A Checklist for Business Excellence*, 6th edition (refer back to Figure 18.2b) and Class A Milestone in *The Oliver Wight Class A Standard for Business Excellence*, 7th edition (refer back to

Figure 18.2b). Aggregate supply planning (volume) performance must be ± 2 percent to the approved supply plan.

Lead time reduction, inventory reduction, and throughput velocity improvement are other appropriate goals and measurements along the journey to Class A. Another important goal is to stabilize the master plan and/or master schedule; to do so requires discipline and a process that minimizes unnecessary master plan and/or master schedule changes.

At this point the company's leaders and management team have the information they need to make an informed decision with respect to fully implementing a formal SCM and/or MPS process supported by an up-to-date ERP and MPS software system. The core group of decision makers has been educated on the subject; the core group members have completed a diagnostic of the company with respect to Class A internal supply management, including master planning and scheduling performance; and it has formed a vision of how the company would look and how its ability to satisfy customers would be altered if it reached the heights of Class A performance.

A number of concrete facts would be laid alongside that mental image of the new company: benefit/cost analysis, a list of the resources and efforts, including potential task force members necessary for full implementation, and a set of performance goals that would be the company's new yardstick for future aggregate supply planning, master (supply) planning, master (supply) scheduling, detailed production scheduling, and supplier scheduling performance. With this information, leadership and the management team either decides to back off or go forward.

The decision to go forward must be articulated in a way that identifies the following points:

- This is where the company now stands with respect to its MPS practices (from diagnostic).

- This is where the company can go (from awareness, understanding, and vision statements).

- This is what it will take to consider the improvement initiative a success (from the size of the gap between vision and diagnostic).

- Moving forward with full MPS implementation will result in measurable benefits supported by defined costs (from value opportunity and priority setting).

- This is a task list of important activities that will need to be performed to reach full implementation—planning bills, inventory accuracy, computer system, and so on (from the case for change).

- Moving from the company's current practices to a Class A MPS environment will require this amount of time and this amount of staffing resources (from organization for change recommendations).

These are the kinds of performance achievements that will be expected under Class A MPS (from milestone planning as well as the design part of applying goal and measurement definitions).

Point of Commitment (Go/No-Go Decision)

Getting commitment is the first moment of truth in an implementation project. This is when the company turns thumbs up or thumbs down on Business Excellence in Managing Internal Supply and Master Planning and Scheduling. Oliver Wight refers to this time frame as the Point of Commitment.

As a result of the diagnostic, awareness and understanding education, visioning workshop, value opportunity, prioritizing the initiative, case for change, organization for change, and milestone planning, the executive team, demand management, supply chain management, operations management, and company key influencers should now know:

- What is supply chain management (SCM) and master planning and scheduling (MPS)?

- Is managing internal supply and master planning and scheduling to a Class A level right for the company?

- Is there a realistic possibility that the company can realize the defined journey vision and operational vision?

- What are the benefit opportunities, investment requirements, and return on investment?

- What is the cost-of-month's delay and what impact will such a delay have on the five-year cash flow projection?

- Does the improvement initiative carry a high priority within our company?

- Is the case for change strong enough that the company leaders as well as key influencers want to be involved?

- Are new products, sales and marketing, and financial organizations sold and onboard with this initiative?

- Are supply chain management, manufacturing operations, and master planning and scheduling, all-in?

- Is our company ready to start the journey to Class A in Business Excellence?

It's time for the decision! Is the executive steering committee ready to approve the project team moving into Phase 2, that of Design and Structure? To assist in that decision, let's review and spell out Class A:

C is for **Commitment** to following *The Proven Path* for a successful implementation.
L is for **Leadership** through the life of the improvement initiative.
A is for **Assisting** the project team and its members when help is requested.
S is for being a **Steering Committee Participant** all of the time, not just part of the time.
S is for the **Satisfaction** in knowing that the company is embarking on a game-changing initiative.
A (as in **Class A**) is for **Acceptance of the Accountability for the Success of the Class A Improvement Initiative!**

Segue to . . .

The Proven Path to a Successful MPS Implementation (Phase 2) Influencers Transform MPS Process Design and Structure

The Proven Path is a logical, straightforward implementation approach, based completely on demonstrated results. As stated earlier, it may be a lot of work, but virtually, it's at no risk. Even if a company is unsuccessful in its journey to full Class A in Business Excellence, its people will be more skilled and motivated, its processes will be more effective and efficient, its understanding and acceptance of technology will make all involved more productive and less stressed, and its data integrity will be more reliable and trustworthy. Now, if a company follows *The Proven Path* regarding supply chain management along with master planning and scheduling (no skipping steps) faithfully, sincerely, and vigorously, it will become Class A in Managing Internal Supply including Master Planning and Scheduling—and within one to two years.

With all that's been said in this chapter (and really this whole master planning and scheduling book), if the leadership team gives its approval and go ahead to move on to the next implementation phase, it's time to dive a little deeper into the supply chain management and master planning and scheduling detail. Chapter 19 deals with master planning and scheduling detailed education (initial education was two to three hours and this detailed education is generally two to three days of material that needs to be covered), initial detailed (facilitated) self-assessment using *The Oliver Wight Class A Standard for Business Excellence*, 7th edition (and any other *Oliver Wight Class A Standard for Business Excellence* edition or editions that may follow this 4th edition of the Master Planning and Scheduling book's), process design or redesign (high-level and detailed level), and mass education and training for those affected by the upcoming change. *This is when and where the heavy lifting takes place!*

19

The Proven Path to a Successful Master Planning and Scheduling Implementation (Phase 2)

Influencers Transform MPS Behavior and Process Design and Structure

You're never too old to set another goal or to dream a new dream!

Methodology for Implementing Change Revisited

The Proven Path for Business Transformation

As was stated in Chapter 18, Oliver Wight developed an approach for managing change when implementing processes and process improvement, which, done correctly, leads to business transformation. Again, Oliver Wight calls this approach *The Proven Path* because the change methodology has been used successfully for nearly 50 years.

To review, this *Proven Path* change methodology encompasses:

- Executive commitment, involvement, and leadership, which was discussed in the previous chapter;

- Creation of a journey and operational vision, the business case for change, and return on investment, which was discussed in the previous chapter;

- Implementation planning, preparation, execution, and control, which was discussed in the previous chapter;

- Creating internal change agents, sometimes referred to as subject matter experts, which is discussed in this chapter;

- Focus on structure (The Class A Standard) and a structured approach (*The Proven Path*) to ensure a successful implementation, which are discussed in this chapter;

- Ownership for policies (rules), process design (or redesign), and procedures (activities), which are discussed in this chapter;

- Education and training for all people within the company with a need to know, which are discussed in this chapter;

- Behavior change, defined processes, and tool implementation, which are discussed in the next chapter;

- Strong foundation of data integrity, which is discussed in the next chapter;

- Measurement and reporting of results, which are discussed in the next chapter;

- Transitioning to a new state, embedding in the culture, sustaining best practices over many years, and maturing the implementation that has reached full process development—acceptance and results as described in *The Oliver Wight Class A Planning and Control Milestone Workbook*.[1]

Again, as was stated in Chapter 18, implementing change and delivering true business transformation are challenging for sure. However, companies using the Oliver Wight Class A Standard for Business Excellence (refer back to Figure 18.2b on page 676) as a structure to keep focused on what needs to be done and following the Oliver Wight *Proven Path* (see the complete *Proven Path*, 3rd version, in Figure 19.1 on page 707)

---

[1] Oliver Wight International, Inc., *The Oliver Wight Class A Planning and Control Milestone Workbook*, 4th revision (New London, NH: Oliver Wight International, 2017).

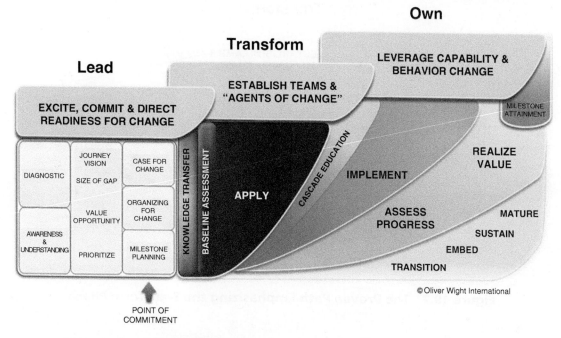

Figure 19.1   The Oliver Wight Proven Path for Business Excellence

as a structured approach to getting those things done will be successful in their implementation efforts.

The focus of this chapter is the Transform Phase, emphasizing the master planning and scheduling required activities. The overall planning has been done and the leadership team has approved the movement of the improvement initiative into the next phase, that of transforming the business along with master planning and scheduling into an industry best-practice state.

Phase 2: Transform Phase (Process Designing and Structuring)

Now, let's continue our discussion of *The Proven Path*, highlighting those master planning and scheduling required activities in the Transform Phase. The Transform Phase, shown in Figure 19.2 on page 708, starts with some in-depth *knowledge transfer* (detailed process education and training) followed by a *facilitated self-assessment* of the company's current

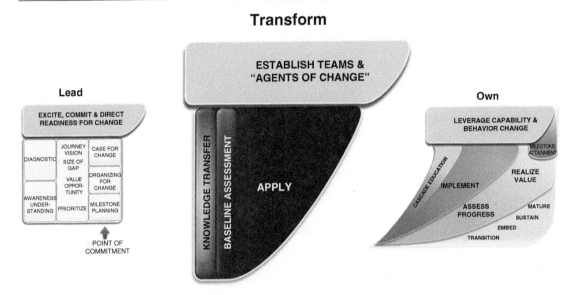

Figure 19.2 The Proven Path Emphasizing the Transform Phase

people behaviors, business process documentation as well as conformance, tool and technology usage, and data integrity using the Oliver Wight Class A Standard for Business Excellence. Once this initial assessment is completed, the defined (done as part of the Lead Phase) spinoff task teams move into the heavy lifting, that of *designing the new processes coupled with an education and training program* to spread the word as to how the company will operate in the future.

Knowledge Transfer (Business Process Education and Training Sessions)

Today and throughout the past several decades, education for integrated business planning, sales and operations planning, demand management, supply management, master planning and scheduling, material and capacity planning, procurement and supplier scheduling, logistics management, inventory management, backlog management, product definition management, process definition management, quality management, and financial management is/was seen as having a far broader mission than just installing new technology and software. People identified as users are today, and were in the past, expected to provide the inputs to the software, create and maintain accurate databases, fill in all the blanks in the databases, and do something with the software output to satisfy customers and safely make money and a profit for the company.

Since business education (i.e., integrated business planning (IBP) and master planning and scheduling (MPS) is so critical to a best-practice implementation, it is important for the implementors to recognize that there are two, not one, critically important education and training objectives: (1) *fact transfer*, which takes place when people learn the what(s), why(s), and how(s) (this is essential, but by itself, it's not nearly enough) and (2) *behavior change*, which occurs when people who have lived in the world of the informal system become convinced of the need to do their jobs differently (it's when they truly understand why and how they should use a formal system as a team to run the business more professionally, and how doing so will benefit them).

For example, fact transfer occurs when the sales and marketing people learn about the master plan and/or master schedule, how it should be used as the source of customer order promising, and how the available-to-promise (ATP) quantity is calculated. Behavior change takes place when the sales and marketing folks participate willingly in the sales forecasting and master planning and scheduling processes because they recognize it as the way to give better and faster service to their customers, increase sales volume, and make the company more competitive and profitable.

In this first step of the Transform Phase on *The Proven Path* (3rd version), detailed subject workshops are recommended for each spinoff task force. Looking at master planning and scheduling, a detailed two-day workshop is common for a company that only sells its product off the shelf (it only uses a make-to-stock strategy across the board). For all other companies (companies that use design-to-order, make-to-order, or multiple manufacturing strategies), a detailed three-day workshop is common.

Of course, other supporting detailed workshops on topics such as integrated business planning, inventory management, material and capacity planning, detailed production scheduling, data integrity, and so on are also required to ensure a successful implementation on the company's journey to Class A in business excellence and managing internal supply (one of the nine business processes called out in *The Oliver Wight Class A Standard for Business Excellence*). Class A criteria for master planning and scheduling is included in Managing Internal Supply Standard and Class A Planning and Control Milestone.

Baseline Assessment (Driving a Stake into the Ground Using Class A Standard)

The first step in preparing the company for the rather significant journey to Class A is to determine just where it currently is regarding the Class A criteria, the distance the company needs to travel to arrive at the Class A destination, and the time the company needs and has to get there. This is the initial purpose of the diagnostic, awareness education, visioning, and gaps between the journey and operational vision and diagnostic step.

The company needs to understand the current state of its master planning and scheduling (MPS) capabilities—supporting information foundation (data integrity), computer systems (tools and technology), practices (integrating business processes), and people behaviors (the skill level of its operating personnel). It needs to rate itself against some standard of good practice and, if the evaluation phase results in the decision to go forward with the newly designed/redesigned MPS implementation, a baseline of accuracy and performance against which future progress can be measured needs to be established (more detailed and defined criteria is now needed).

The Oliver Wight ABCD Checklist for Operational Excellence, 4th and 5th editions[2] (refer back to Figure 18.2a on page 676), contains a list of comprehensive criteria that companies can (and could) use to rate themselves on critical points in strategic planning, people and teams, new-product development, total quality management, planning and control, and continuous improvement. These Checklists included a rating system that defined Class A, B, C, and D companies. While these publications were written and published in the years 1993 and 2000 respectively to address the larger concerns of modern manufacturing, they *do* contain a section on master planning and scheduling (MPS) and its related disciplines. The criteria in that section can be (and has been) used to determine where the company stands in terms of Class A MPS process and performance.

The findings of any initial audit/assessment should be systematically recorded for comparison against future progress. However, time moves on and so do the Oliver Wight Class A criteria!

The Oliver Wight Class A Checklist for Business Excellence, 6th edition[3] contains a list of comprehensive criteria that companies can use (have used) to rate themselves on critical points in managing the strategic planning process, managing and leading people, driving business improvement, integrated business management, managing products and services, managing demand, managing the supply chain, managing internal supply, and managing external sourcing. This Checklist includes a rating system that defines Class A business excellence, business unit Class A accreditation, and Class A recognition award.

Class A business excellence is achieved when the entire business meets the requirements of all chapters in the checklist. Business-unit Class A accreditation is achieved when a stand-alone business within a multiunit business meets the requirements of its appropriate chapters. The Class A recognition award is achieved when predetermined

---

[2] Oliver Wight International, Inc., *The Oliver Wight ABCD Checklist for Operational Excellence*, 4th ed. (Essex Junction, VT: Oliver Wight Publications, Inc., 1993) and 5th ed. (New York: John Wiley & Sons, 2000).

[3] Oliver Wight International, Inc., *The Oliver Wight Class A Checklist for Business Excellence*, 6th ed. (Hoboken, NJ: John Wiley & Sons, 2005).

projects and milestones in a business improvement program have delivered their planned business gains on the journey to Class A business excellence.

The MPS criteria are defined in *The Oliver Wight Class A Checklist for Business Excellence* in the chapter "Managing the Internal Supply Chain" under the subject "Master Supply Planning and Capable People," which is supported by topics and definitions. However, time moves on and so do the Oliver Wight Class A criteria!

The Oliver Wight Class A Standard for Business Excellence, 7th edition[4] contains a list of comprehensive criteria that companies can use to *rate themselves on critical points* in managing the strategic planning process, managing and leading people, driving business improvement, integrated business management, managing products and services, managing demand, managing the supply chain, managing internal supply, and managing external sourcing (the same chapters as in *The Class A Checklist*, 6th edition, which has become *The Oliver Wight Class A Standard for Business Excellence*, 7th edition).

This Standard includes a rating system that defines Class A business excellence, business-unit Class A accreditation, and the Class A recognition award, as was the case in the previous published checklist. Again, Class A business excellence is achieved when the entire business meets the requirements of all chapters in The Standard.

Business-unit Class A accreditation is achieved when a stand-alone business within a multiunit business meets the requirements defined in *The Oliver Wight Class A Planning and Control Milestone Workbook*, 4th revision, copyrighted in 2017. The MPS criteria are defined in *The Oliver Wight Class A Standard for Business Excellence* in the chapter "Managing Internal Supply" under the subject "Internal Supply Planning," which is supported by topics and definitions (see Appendix A).

Apply (High-Level Process Design and Detailed Process Design)

The decision to go for a full supply chain management (SCM) implementation including master planning and scheduling (MPS) commits the company and many of its personnel to a somewhat long (18–24 months, which is long in today's times) but rewarding process. Organizationally, the SCM effort will be managed by an overall initiative project leader while the MPS effort will be managed by the project team's MPS spinoff task force leader. While some may think that this is an overwhelming job for someone who most likely works part-time, many of the operational responsibilities will be doled out to other specialized task forces.

---

[4] Oliver Wight International, Inc., *The Oliver Wight Class A Standard for Business Excellence*, 7th ed. (Hoboken, NJ: John Wiley & Sons, 2017).

The first part of that effort is to prepare the company and its personnel for the job of starting and operating a first-rate MPS process and computer system. This might be called the *design and action phase*, and its objective is to work out all the *operational details* that the MPS task force in the Lead Phase merely enumerated. In that Lead Phase (Phase One on *The Proven Path*) work, the task was to determine what would have to be done and what it would require to actually do it.

Here, a full-blown operational blueprint is developed. This blueprint will take the form of a detailed master planning and scheduling implementation plan. (See Appendix B for a sample detailed implementation task list; add to this task list responsibilities, commencement/start dates, and completion/stop dates and you have a detailed MPS implementation plan.)

As in the previous phase, education is an important part of the process. Members of the MPS spinoff task force of Phase One continue the education process begun earlier. Master planning and scheduling detailed education courses, facilitated workshops, web-based education, e-learning sessions, published books, and white (as in Oliver Wight) papers are valuable for this purpose. In this phase, accelerated learning is critical, and so members of the spin-off task force along with other members of the implementation team should convene every day or every other day for a series of highly structured, two-hour to four-hour meetings that review current progress, provide education on specific MPS techniques, and feature discussion on how those techniques can be implemented within the company. Discussion should account for fully half of the education session, or what might be called a business meeting. A sample of a typical meeting agenda is shown in Figure 19.3 on the following page.

The end result of each such meeting should be a list of action items that individuals must execute in order to implement the activities discussed. Responsibility for these items should be allocated to specific individuals, with specific dates for resolution. Progress on these action items should be discussed at future meetings, and their successful resolution should be rolled into the detailed MPS implementation plan.

Education at this stage must also be extended to personnel outside the core implementation group, to those individuals who will be dealing either directly or indirectly with the fully implemented MPS process and system. These sessions are more spread out and include discussion of the overall vision.

While this MPS education process continues, other implementation activities take place in parallel. Before considering these, however, we should look at how the core implementation group helps to define the company's new environment.

Meetings of task force members provide more than learning for a core group of associates or employees—they also serve as a format in which the important details of the company's emerging MPS process and system begin to surface. These details, as mentioned

Business Meeting Agenda (an Example)

Topic: Master Planning and Scheduling (MPS) Time Zones

Meeting Agenda (2 hours)

1. Review open action items list (10 minutes)

2. Education and fact transfer of master planning and scheduling methodology (30 minutes)

3. Discuss how to implement the methodology (70 minutes)

4. Create action items and assign responsibility (10 minutes)

Key Items to Be Addressed and Resolved

5. People behavior versus computer behavior and control

6. Approval policy needed for people behavior

7. System time fences needed for computer behavior

Applications

8. A policy is required defining who needs to approve changes by zone

9. The approvals required will be based on timing and cost impact

10. System time fences will be used to decouple demand and supply

11. Maintenance responsibility will be assigned

Action Items for MPS Implementation Plan

12. Write master planning and scheduling change approval policy

13. Write time fence setting and maintenance policy

14. Circulate policies for comments

15. Make modifications as appropriate

16. Secure approvals

17. Release and implement policies

Figure 19.3   Business Meeting Agenda (a Sample)

previously, must be captured in an implementation plan that defines the entire MPS process for the company.

Here the MPS process and system are transformed from the focus on what the process of Phase One *should* look like (as a reminder, Phase One on *The Proven Path* is known as the Lead Phase) to the question of what the process *will* look like in the near future. Central to this definition of the MPS process are manufacturing strategy, material flow and production process, customer order promising, establishing and releasing the schedule, policies, procedures, work instructions, defined metrics, and the assignment of responsibilities and accountabilities.

A good example of an important policy that must be determined at this point is the question of manufacturing strategy, or where the company should (and might want to) meet the customer. Will the company follow a product manufacturing strategy of make-to-order, with minimal inventory and moderate levels of customer delivery lead times, or will it pursue a product strategy of make-to-stock, characterized by aggressive levels of customer service and ample inventories to service demand? Or will yet another product strategy be followed, or will the company employ multiple manufacturing strategies depending upon the marketplace product strategy and the company's competition?

Choosing a product manufacturing strategy is a management issue of the first magnitude, and it requires input from all core functions of the company. As we will see shortly, the impact of the product manufacturing strategy that is accepted will spill over to the procedures area of the MPS implementation. For example, products using a make-to-stock strategy generally have different product definition schemes than do products using a make-to-order manufacturing strategy, which most likely uses different ones (product definition schemes) than does design-to-order or engineer-to-order (e.g., activity bills vs. engineering bills vs. manufacturing bills vs. planning bills vs. configuration bills).

Figure 19.4 on the following page considers primary areas within which policies, procedures, and work instructions must be developed and modified, as well as the individuals typically assigned responsibility for them. In essence, Figure 19.4 is a rough cut of what needs to be done. The level of detail in the development of policies, procedures, and work instructions and in the assigning of responsibility along with accountability is specified. The MPS implementation plan requirements are at a much higher level of detail.

For example, the policy and procedure for making changes to the master plan and/or master schedule—to pick just one area—requires full development of an approval process, naming those individuals authorized to approve changes, and describing the situations (by time period) in which they have that authority. For multiproduct companies, this may require an elaborate set of approvals. Figure 19.5 on page 716 suggests how such a set of approvals might appear. (This is a more specific set of guidelines than the discussion of time zones in Chapter 4.)

Policy and Procedure	Functions Involved
Manufacturing Strategy • Make-to-stock • Make-to-order • Design-to-order	President VP Sales and Marketing VP Manufacturing Controller
Service Levels/Order Promising • Fill rates, delivery to promise	VP Sales and Marketing VP Manufacturing
Backlog Levels • Customer lead time	VP Sales and Marketing VP Manufacturing
Inventory Levels • Finished goods • Intermediates, semi-finished • Bulks, raw materials • Supplier managed	VP Sales and Marketing VP Manufacturing Materials Manager Controller
Integrated Business Planning/S&OP • Portfolio planning • Sales planning • Production planning • Resource planning • Design planning • Financial planning	VP Sales and Marketing VP Manufacturing VP Portfolio/Product Management VP Engineering VP Finance VP Quality
Supply Management • Supply planning • Request for supply • Inventory management • Backlog management	VP Sales and Marketing VP Manufacturing VP Industrial Relations Materials Manager Manufacturing Manager Controller
Master Scheduling • Rough cut capacity planning • Order promising • Overplanning, safety stocks • Past dues	VP Manufacturing Materials Manager Master Scheduler Controller
Lead Times (Internal) • Finishing, final assembly • Intermediate, subassembly • Cumulative, strategic material	VP Sales and Marketing VP Manufacturing Purchasing Manager
Order Quantity • Lot size definition • Multiples, if used • Minimums, maximums	VP Manufacturing Materials Manager Purchasing Manager
Processes to Be Improved • Lead times to customers • Optimal schedules • Past-due condition	VP Manufacturing Manufacturing Manager Manufacturing Personnel

Figure 19.4   Areas That Require Policies and Procedures

MPS Change Approval Matrix			
	0–1 Week	**2–3 Weeks**	**4–6 Weeks**	**6–12 Weeks**
Product A	President General Manager	VP Sales VP Manufacturing	Sales Director Mfg. Director	Master Planner/ Scheduler
Product B	General Manager	General Manager	VP Sales Mfg. Manager	Master Planner/ Scheduler
Product C	VP Sales Mfg. Manager	Sales Director Mfg. Director	Sales Director Mfg. Director	Master Planner/ Scheduler
. . . .	. . . .	. . . .	. . . .	. . . .

Figure 19.5   Approval Policy for Master Planning and Scheduling Changes by Product Family and Time Zone (Example)

The definition of the MPS process and its implementation planning having been completed. It is time to move directly into the *functional areas where the detailed blueprint for its daily and weekly operation* must be drawn up and executed. These are planning and control, data management, process improvement, and software—all of which have been treated to some degree in previous chapters of this book. However, before we discuss these elements of the master planning and scheduling improvement initiative, let's take a look at the recommended workshop process for collecting data and information to include in both the high-level and detailed designs.

Master Planning and Scheduling High-Level Design Workshops Description

The master planning and scheduling (MPS) *high-level design (HLD)* workshops (the main workshops in MPS design are supply planning or master planning, master scheduling, rough cut capacity planning, and planning bills structure and use) are generally facilitated, private events that use tailored materials along with information and data collected during the company's diagnostic, initial education, visioning, gap analysis, value opportunity creation, priority setting, case for change, organization for success, macro planning, initial assessment, and master planning and scheduling detailed education. The education part of the HLD workshop explains the *what* (best practices for the company's industry) along with the *why* (addresses the change management and

Approval Policy for Master Planning and Scheduling Changes

Policy: Changes to the master plan and/or master schedule can be requested by sales, marketing, finance, supply chain planning, production, procurement, purchasing, quality, engineering, design, engineering, logistics, and/or distribution. All changes to the master plan and/or master schedule within an item's cumulative lead time must be approved by the person(s) identified.

Process: Requires planning, evaluating impact, and changing the master plan and/or master schedule. All changes to the master plan and/or master schedule are sanity checked using rough cut capacity planning before releasing the changed master plan and/or master schedule.

Initiator sends the master planner and/or master scheduler a written request for the change (includes reason change is being requested along with supporting documentation).

Master planner and/or master scheduler: Has a maximum of two working days to respond to the initiator with one of three answers:

1. Yes, the change can be made and is being implemented.

2. Yes, the change can be accommodated, but the following schedules are affected.

3. No, the change cannot be made for the following reason(s). The best alternative is _____ (fill in the blank).

Approvals: See Matrix

Measures:

1. Master Schedule Stability

2. Master Schedule Performance

	MPS Change Approval Matrix			
	0–1 Week	**2–3 Weeks**	**4–6 Weeks**	**6–12 Weeks**
Product A	President General Manager	VP Sales VP Manufacturing	Sales Director Mfg. Director	Master Planner / Scheduler
Product B	General Manager	General Manager	VP Sales Mfg. Manager	Master Planner / Scheduler
Product C	VP Sales Mfg. Manager	Sales Director Mfg. Director	Sales Director Mfg. Director	Master Planner / Scheduler
. . . .	. . . .	. . . .	. . . .	. . . .

motivation of the individual; i.e., benefits of following best practices and WIIFM [what's in it for me]).

This application workshop is designed to move the company forward at a faster pace (two to four times faster) than just coaching itself. The application workshop explains the *what* and *why* and then focuses on the *how to do it*. Education must be done in advance to avoid the risk that the company will develop a poor design. Typically, 33 to 50 percent of the workshop time is spent explaining master planning and scheduling concepts and practices while the balance of time is spent in applying those concepts and practices to the company's business. The HLD utilizes mind-mapping techniques to assist the design team in staying focused and organizing their thoughts (mind mapping in a workshop is explained in the next section).

At the conclusion of each workshop breakout session where a mind map has been created, the subteam that created the mind map presents its structure, including the main branches as well as integrating branches, to the full spinoff task force (sometimes to the entire project team if desired by the project leader). As input is received from the spinoff task force members, it is immediately added to the appropriate mind map. Since the mind-mapping process is a brainstorming technique, free rein is used during the creation of the mind map as well as the discussion session that follows the initial mind-map creation (the mind map will be subjected to scrubbing later in the HLD process in a similar manner as was done with the vision of operations).

Additional design aids such as preplanned flip charts, videos, and case studies can be used to enhance the workshop experience. Once the detailed topic education, initial assessment review, mind mapping, and group input is complete, the finale of the workshop is the creation of several work lists that are to be included in the *high-level design presentation and documentation.*

These lists consist of process boundaries, initiative schedule, process owner and coordinator, accuracy and performance metrics, system inputs and outputs, education and training, policies required, process flow diagrams required, procedures required, work instructions required, software needs, integration points, benefits/investment analysis, obstacles to successful implementation, and a parking lot of questions that need to be answered. These lists provide the basic makeup of the HLD package.

The Mind Mapping Process and How It Ties to High-Level Design

Mind mapping is a brainstorming technique to assist the master planning and scheduling (MPS) spinoff task force members in organizing their thoughts as ideas are put on the table or thrown into the air. The actual structure of the mind map is that branches are connected to the main topic and placed on the mind map as they are needed.

The authors have found that using a *structured* mind map at the beginning of the process allows the task force to be more focused and move at a faster pace. The structured mind map consists of, but is not limited to, process topic input (starting at 12 o'clock and moving clockwise), boundaries and schedules, process owner and coordinator, accuracy and performance metrics, process topic outputs, tools such as procedures and software, rules such as policies, and schools including education courses, seminars, books, and articles.

To review, once the mind map(s) is/are created and full team input received, multiple listings are created for the various sections included in the high-level design presentation and documentation. Three examples of mind maps are included in the next couple of pages: mind maps for master planning and scheduling (Figure 19.6 on page 720), rough cut capacity planning (Figure 19.8 on page 721), and material requirements planning (Figure 19.9 on page 722). They are provided as examples only (these mind maps are from a company that used *The Proven Path* during their journey to a successful master planning and scheduling implementation).

An example of the more detailed explosion of the capacity assumptions (under the inputs leg) and capacity plans (under the outputs leg) from the master planning and scheduling are show in Figure 19.7 on page 721. Each leg or *fishbone* is further appended and refined (represented by the dots; i.e., ". . ." in Figure 19.7) until all of the pertinent information is captured. Overall, the mind map examples have been trimmed and edited for the sake of readability but suffice it to say that they can get rather detailed given the space to capture the information.

Again, the mind mapping process is a technique to assist the master planning and scheduling task force/team members focus their attention on meaningful discussion topics and definitions as well as to organize their thoughts and inputs as they are identified and received. Figures 19.6 and 19.8 are examples of completed mind maps directly related to the MPS process. Figure 19.9 is a mind map example for time-phased material planning, which is a master planning and scheduling-driven process.

The mind mapping data along with the process lists created during the high-level design workshop provides the master planning and scheduling team with the information necessary to structure the *high-level design presentation* along with the supporting documentation (a presentation handout). So, let's take a look at the typical contents of the *high-level design presentation and documentation.*

Figure 19.6   Master Planning and Scheduling Mind Map Example

MPS High-Level Design Executive Presentation—Contents/Outline

Six of the more important elements on *The Proven Path* is when the initiative/project team, through its initiative/project champion and/or leader, *calls for the question*. In other words, the initiative/project team asks the executive steering committee (ESC) for approval to move to the next phase or subphase on *The Proven Path* of the new or improvement initiative journey.

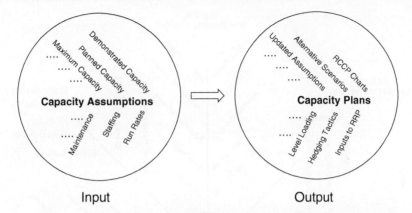

Figure 19.7 Master Planning and Scheduling Mind Map Explosion Example

Figure 19.8 Rough Cut Capacity Mind Map

Figure 19.9 Material Requirements Planning Mind Map

The six times the call for the question is put in front of the ESC are: (1) at the end of the awareness and understanding education, admitting a concern for the business and its future; (2) at the *point of commitment* to move from the Lead Phase to the Transform Phase; (3) as an acknowledgment that the high-level design (HLD) is taking the company in the right direction; (4) to express satisfaction with the *detailed design (DD)*, including all of its policies, process flows, procedures, work instructions, metrics, software, cascading education/training plan, and implementation plan to move from the Transform Phase to the Own Phase; (5) at the approval of the computer/software pilot, conference room pilot, and live pilot, and thereby ready to move to full site and/or company implementation; and (6) as recognition that all the "i's are dotted" and all the "t's are crossed" and the company receives Class A milestone recognition or full Class certification (refer to Appendix B for a Proven Path graphic with defined checkpoints displayed).

The HLD presentation is a critical part of the *approval to move on* process. This HLD presentation must make the ESC members comfortable with what has been done during the HLD work period. It's the HLD that sets up the *detailed design* work, which sets up the *pilots*, which sets up the *full company implementation*. Therefore, careful attention must be paid to the presentation materials as well as the accompanying documentation/presentation handout. A recommended agenda for the HLD presentation is as follows:

1. Presentation agenda (contents, presenter, timing);

2. Vision of operations along with journey vision (Affinity process used along with macro planning);

3. Transformation organization structure (Class A initiative leaders);

4. Scope of the initiative (what's *in* and what's *out*);

5. Class A benefits/investment analysis (return on investment, cost of a month's delay, cash flow, projection);

6. Class A facilitated self-assessment scores (radar chart);

7. *The Proven Path* (Lead, Transform, and Own Phases);

8. Class A workshops (pictures, examples, and results);

9. Master planning and scheduling process (business policies, process flows, business procedures, process work instructions, system work instructions, and metrics listings);

10. MPS spinoff task team members (leader, assistant leader, and task team members);

11. Master planning and scheduling charter (objectives, scope, key activities, and deliverables);

12. MPS process definition (inputs/outputs, boundaries/schedules, process owner/coordinator, metrics, schools, rules, tools—SRT[5]);

---

[5] **S**chools (education/training/books/white papers/podcasts), **R**ules (policies/guidelines/no-nos), **T**ools (process flow diagrams/business procedures/process work instructions/system work instructions/metrics).

13. Other supporting teams (demand, capacity management, scheduling, data integrity);

14. Definitions/glossary of terms (supply chain management as well as company terms);

15. Design RACI (responsibility, accountability, consulted, informed) example;

16. Software requirements (required vs. nice-to-have vs. wish list);

17. Mass education/training requirements (business as well as software changes);

18. Obstacles to remove (who's going to do this and what's the projected cost);

19. Next steps cross-referenced to *The Proven Path* (macro plan tied to the *Proven Path* journey);

20. Questions and answers (allow time in the agenda for this item);

21. Review parking lot items (response commitment made by responsibility party including due date);

22. Call for the question (approval to move to the next phase or subphase: return on investment (ROI), cost-of-month's-delay (COMD), five-year cash flow projection).

The high-level design generally takes about a half-day for most companies discussing supply chain management, which includes master planning and scheduling. For more complex environments, more time should be allowed, but the HLD presentation should not be less than two hours even for the smallest of companies; this is not the time to show lack of respect for the initiative/project team, who has probably worked very hard to ensure that they tell a good story regarding the company's new direction. Assuming that the ESC gives their approval to the team to move into the *detailed design* work, it's time for the heavy lifting.

Description of Master Planning and Scheduling Detailed Design Workshops

The master planning and scheduling process implementation and/or process improvement heavy lifting occurs during the detailed design work. It's during this detailed design initiative phase where all the identified elements of the high-level design start to come to life and where the identified policies (rules of the game) are written, tested, and approved.

Once the policies are documented and approved, the master planning and scheduling teams turns their attention to process flow creations, procedure writing, work-instruction creation, metrics definitions, software requirement definition, and so forth. The Oliver Wight company and its principals have found that using workshops to do this detailed work is the best and fastest way to get to the desired result.

Following is a listing of what an education workshop, application workshop, and facilitation methodology might look like. The authors recognize that meeting, education, and workshop environments have changed dramatically over the years, spurred on by the COVID-19 pandemic beginning in 2020. While virtual education/workshop methods and tools often differ from in-person methods and tools, the principles remain the same.

1. Educational Workshop
    a. An event (public or private or virtual)
    b. Uses tailored material (standard for public, tailored for private, either for virtual)
    c. Presented using best-practice teaching methodology (see 3 below)
    d. Explains *what*, such as best practices
    e. Explains *why*—addresses the change management and motivation of the individual, such as benefits of following best practices and WIIFM (what's in it for me)

2. Application Workshop
    a. A private event
    b. Tailored best-practice material
    c. Designed to move the company forward at a faster pace (two to four times faster) than just coaching by itself
    d. Explains the *why* and *what* and then focuses on *how to do it*
    e. Education must be done in advance to avoid the risk that the company will develop a poor design
    f. Typically, 33 to 50 percent of the time is explaining and the balance is applying
    g. Completes the application/task/decision and creates a plan for implementing them

3. Facilitation Methodology: Workshops
   a. Presenting: Uses PowerPoint material to introduce and explain key concepts
   b. Breakouts: Uses small group sessions to reinforce a specific point or enhance the learning during an education or application session
      i. Accomplished using preprinted posters and flip charts and slides
      ii. Provides first-hand experience in conducting the work process (e.g., being a master planner, master scheduler, or capacity planner)
      iii. Set up by identifying small breakout teams and providing the teams with objectives, available time, and report back requirements
      iv. Practical working examples where the participants get some hands-on experience (albeit simple) relative to the topic at hand
      v. A high-level view of current company gaps through self-assessments conducted in the workshop
   c. Plenary: A presenter-initiated discussion, at a predetermined point, to enhance the learning and sharing
   d. Discussion: Questions or opinions offered from the participants that broaden a specific point, to enhance learning and sharing, which the facilitator encourages and manages
   e. Flip charts: Spontaneous diagrams, discussion points being made, parking lot for open questions, and so on
   f. Public education workshops (in person or virtual)
      i. Explain or reinforce visuals already in the workbook
      ii. Answer questions from participants
      iii. Further explain a key point that the facilitator believes to be *added value* (caution—the facilitator needs to be careful when developing examples during the session and should prepare potential flip chart explanations in advance)
      iv. Not to be used to introduce *pet messages* or to artificially reinsert old visuals, as this would make public courses nonstandard
   g. Private education and application workshops (in person or virtual)
      i. Free rein to use whatever is necessary to ensure value-add for the company
      ii. Facilitate discussions around presented material as well as participants' real-world example(s)
   h. Video
      i. To illustrate a live example of a particular concept as an introduction to a workshop

    ii. Points made in the video are referred to during the workshop to reinforce specific points

    iii. Could be seen as an anchor for the workshop

4. Case Studies
   a. Issued as a preread
   b. Used to bring the subject matter to life and enhance learning
   c. Used as required through the workshop

It needs to be stressed here that the authors highly recommend the use of professional facilitators, educators, and coaches during the master planning and scheduling detailed workshops to ensure that a *best-practice design is the resulting output*. Since the time spent in the detailed design phase is roughly half of the total implementation time, a company needs to do what it can to increase the chances of success while decreasing the risks of failure.

So, what might the output of a successful detailed design workshop look like? What might the master planning and scheduling team expect? What success criteria are the project team and executive steering committee using? To assist the MPS design team in answering these questions, a master planning and scheduling workshop checklist might be helpful. Let's take a look:

Master Planning and Scheduling Workshop Checklist

- We understand the purpose of master planning and scheduling and the output required to operate in a Class A environment.

- We have determined and documented the master planning and scheduling required and optional participants.

- The key users have been identified and trained on the use of the enterprise resource planning system and/or other necessary tools.

- We have identified and documented the people and computer responsibilities of master planning and scheduling.

- We have established a weekly and daily process for developing a master plan and/or master schedule.

- We have defined product groupings and specific items required for supply chain planning as well as master planning and scheduling.

- We have established the integrated business planning or sales and operations planning, supply management/master planning, master scheduling, and detailed production scheduling planning horizons.

- We have determined and understand how to plan for where we meet the customer by product (design-to-order, buy-to-stock/make-to-order, buy-to-stock/finish-to-order, buy-to-stock/package-to-order, etc.).

- We have determined the unit of measure for master planning and scheduling (pieces, tons, pounds, etc.) as well as supply capabilities.

- The existing process for master planning and scheduling is documented as well as understood and the approved planning rules in forms of policies (including assumptions) have been written, approved, and implemented.

- We have established supply capabilities by plant or production line, utilization by production line, productivity by production line, products by plant or production line, new/retired production lines, and so forth.

- We have identified the key and/or critical resources for rough cut capacity planning at the mix level (supports master planning and scheduling).

- We have determined each resource's available capacity, productivity and load factors, demonstrated capacity in the recent past, planned capacity as we move forward, and maximum capacity.

- We have created resource/load profiles of required capacity by product groupings or specific items for each key and/or critical resource.

- Demand and supply planning lead times have been developed and agreed upon by the business leadership team.

- The supply management as well as the master planning and scheduling process includes scenario and contingency planning: Scenarios and contingency plans are forwarded to the monthly supply review, integrated reconciliation review, and management business review as required.

- The master planning and scheduling scenarios and contingency plans are submitted to the weekly integrated tactical planning meetings, with required execution discussions conducted each week as part of the ITP process.

- We have determined the master planning and scheduling inputs and timing during the month, week, and/or day—refer to flow diagrams, procedures, and work instructions.

- We have developed a process to identify and document master planning and scheduling's assumptions, opportunities, and/or risks.

- We have documented the role responsibilities and/or job descriptions for the master (supply) planner and master (supply) scheduler—a RACI (responsibility, accountability, consulted, and informed) matrix has been created.

- We have established accountability for the accumulation and review of the master (supply) plans and master (supply) schedules with the supply manager/master (supply) planner, and master (supply) scheduler.

- Timing for monthly/weekly master planning and weekly/daily master scheduling meetings and general agenda steps has been established and sent out to required participants.

- Agenda templates to be used at master (supply) planning and master (supply) scheduling meetings have been developed and documented.

- We establish the approved supply plan as an output of the supply review process (rolling 24–36 months).

- We have a process in place to handle near-term and long-term supply plan changes.

- We understand and manage anticipated, as well as firm, demand versus supply constraints and capabilities.

- We have a process to identify productive and preventive maintenance schedules and made them part of our supply planning as well as our master planning and scheduling processes.

- We have developed rules relative to the adjustment of production and procurement and purchasing to meet changes in demand within defined time fences (demand planner/master planner/master schedulers).

- We have defined and set safety stock levels where appropriate (in conjunction with demand and finance).

- We have a process in place on how we handle near- and long-term product development plan changes.

- We have created and use an *issues document* to communicate the status and actions from the latest master plan and/or master schedule.

- We have developed and documented our master planning and scheduling policy, procedures, and work instructions (tools).

- We have established communication links to demand management, product management, and finance.

- Existing actual key performance indicator (KPI) information has been collected and documented.

- Master planning and scheduling key performance indicators have been developed and documented (KPI dashboard—master plan and schedule performance by mix, productivity by production line, and so forth).

- We have established dashboard tolerances for green, yellow, and red status for each selected KPI (some businesses use a blue status indicator along with the green, yellow, and red).

- There is a process of continuous improvement and we have a plan to build a continuous improvement culture relative to KPIs.

- We have defined and documented a gap analysis process along with the corrective action planning rules (includes all assumptions).

- We understand the *silence is acceptance* concept and understand that we must communicate to those with a *need to know* any time we cannot meet our supply commitments.

- We embrace and practice the principle of *do what you say you are going to do*.

- We do what's necessary to satisfy the demand organization and the customer requirements while safely making money and a profit for the business and stakeholders.

Each task listed in the workshop checklist needs to be coupled with the person responsible for task management, task completion, start and expected completion dates, and progress status updates for the business MPS Steering Committee and Project Team!

Yes, doing the master planning and scheduling process design well is nothing short of a lot of work. However, the rewards of doing master planning and scheduling process design correctly and up to best practice standards is generally worth it. If the high-level and detailed design work is done right, the implementation or Own Phase generally goes smoothly.

Because the detailed design is so important to the actual implementation, it might be a good idea to spend a little more time discussing planning and control in general, data management, process improvement, and software before we conclude our discussion of the Transition Phase on *The Proven Path* and move to the next chapter, which discusses the third phase on *The Proven Path*, the Own Phase.

Policy, Flow Diagrams, Procedures, Work Instructions, and Metrics Defined

Highlighting Planning and Control

The previous activity of process definition created an inclusive set of policies, procedures, flow diagrams, work instructions, and metrics for all the MPS activities (see Appendix C for MPS policies, procedures, and flow diagrams improvement initiative suggestions). Here the policies, procedures, workflows, work instructions, and metrics are fleshed out in operational detail.

An analogy to the two different levels of detail is found in the federal government, where Congress passes legislation that establishes a set of rules. Once signed by the President, those rules are handed over to the appropriate agency, whose technical staff creates a much more detailed set of operational statutes, complete with dates, amounts, and so forth, all developed to reflect the intent of Congress. Here the intent of the higher-level policy makers is specified through written policies (the rules of the game) and implemented through written procedures (the responsibilities and activities required).

Planning and control must concentrate on integrated business planning (as stated earlier in this book, formerly sales and operations planning), new product introductions, demand management, supply management, master planning and scheduling, material and capacity planning, and material and capacity execution and control. A demand management policy and procedure need to be drawn up in detail, focusing on the role of the demand manager and/or demand planner (there needs to be one), sales and marketing personnel, and rules governing order promising.

Here, many of the MPS subpolicies and procedures described earlier have to be spelled out clearly: Exactly where will the planning time fences be placed? What safety stock policy will be followed? Who has the authority to make a change to the master (supply) plan and/or master (supply) schedule, and when?

**Master Schedule Policy
(a Sample)**

Manufacturing, supported by a valid master schedule, will maintain a performance level of 95 percent (Class A Milestone in Planning and Control) or better on meeting scheduled completion dates.

Rough cut capacity planning will be used to check that critical resource capacity is or will be available to satisfy the written master schedule before the master schedule is released for action.

The master schedule will be firmed up through the planning time fence using a combination of scheduled receipts such as campaigns, released orders in the form of work orders, and firm planned orders.

Note: A very detailed master scheduling policy example is shown in Appendix C of this book

---

Integrated business planning or sales and operations planning has to be institutionalized in company operations, with a regular schedule of reviews, a slate of attendees, and general agenda. For years, the Oliver Wight Companies have recommended that regular integrated business planning or sales and operations planning reviews begin several months prior to full implementation of enterprise resource planning and/or supply chain management, and the same advice applies here. This gives everyone a chance to develop the skills needed to hand the master (supply) planner and/or master (supply) scheduler a credible set of aggregate demand requirements and supply constraints.

Policies and procedures for MPS must be developed and disseminated to all who come into contact with the system. The following are just a couple examples of a policy and a procedure. The sample policy deals with a valid master *supply* schedule (could be a valid master *supply* plan) while the sample procedure deals with treatment of exception driven action messages. The sample procedure provided is not intended to be complete, but merely to provide an example.

Data Management

Like enterprise resource planning (ERP) and supply chain management (SCM), master planning and scheduling (MPS) will not be successful in the absence of data, or in the absence of *accurate* data. For ERP, SCM, and MPS purposes, data can be divided into two categories: forgiving data (in terms of accuracy) and unforgiving data.

**Master Schedule Procedure
Action Message Review (a Sample)**

Purpose: To establish a process that the master scheduler will follow to evaluate and initiate action as necessary after each master scheduling computer process run.

Scope: This procedure affects master scheduling, sales, marketing, manufacturing, material planning and control, production planning and control, detailed production scheduling, procurement and purchasing, supplier scheduling, inventory control, logistic planning, and engineering.

Definition: An action or exception message is an action that the master scheduling software system recommends that the master scheduler execute in order to correct an imbalance in demand and supply. Action messages may also be generated because of a past-due condition.

References:
Master scheduler's position description
Master schedule policy covering valid schedules
Reschedule time zone policy

Exhibits:
Master schedule time-phased screen
Master schedule action screen

Procedure:

Responsibility	Action
Master Scheduler	1. Receives the latest master scheduling computer output (exhibit 1). 2. Reviews action messages (exhibit 2). 3. Determines which action messages require action. 4. Asks the 6 (sometimes 7) questions to determine customer, market, material, capacity, cost, authorization, and morale impact (reference 1). 5. Determines appropriate changes to master schedule within supply plan guidelines (reference 2). 6. Makes changes as necessary. 7. Forwards change recommendations needing approval to approval authorities (reference 3).

Master Schedule Procedure
Action Message Review (a Sample) *(Continued)*

Procedure:

Responsibility	Action
Supply Vice President	8. Analyzes recommended changes to master schedule and supporting documentation.
	9. Approves or disapproves changes.
	10. Forwards change decision to Demand Vice-President, if necessary.
Demand Vice President	11. Determines if changes will satisfy customer requirements.
	12. Forwards approval or change recommendations back to Supply Vice President.
Supply Vice President	13. Forwards decision to Master Scheduler.
Master Scheduler	14. Receives decision; takes appropriate action.
	15. Informs appropriate parties when action is completed and what expected results will be.

Note: A very detailed master scheduling procedure example is shown in Appendix C of this book.

Forgiving data need not be extremely accurate; some margin for error is possible. From the MPS perspective, this includes lead times, safety stocks, order quantities, maximum capacities, and—of course—the demand forecast.

The unforgiving data can trip up ERP, SCM, and MPS without exception. This includes on-hand inventory balances, scheduled receipts, allocations (components reserved for scheduled receipts), product definition, process routings, and actual customer orders. Certainly, not all of these are the responsibility of the master planner and/or master scheduler, but without accuracy near 100 percent, the integrity of the company's game plan will come apart at the seams.

There is a point in the MPS implementation process at which a number of activities must be spelled out in detail. The listing that follows highlights some of the key actions required during the Transform Phase in a master planning and scheduling implementation:

- The items to be master planned and/or master scheduled are identified. If the inventory records for these items are not up to Class A standards, the process of making them so must be implemented. The same applies to product definition for the MPS items.

- The structuring of Class A planning bills, if required, has begun.

- The key resources needed for engineering and manufacturing jobs ahead are identified so that resource profiles and rough cut capacity planning can be effectively done.

- The company's approach to forecasting demand must be examined and steps outlined to improve its accuracy.

- The work location (work center, production line) database, including capacities of the key or critical resources, must be defined and required accuracy levels sustained.

- The models required to support advanced planning systems and finite capacity planning/scheduling must be identified along with the necessary data to run them.

Data used in master planning and scheduling includes, but is not limited to, new product plan, aggregate demand plan, aggregate supply plan, inventory, backlog, master (supply) plan and/or master (supply) schedule, detailed demand (forecast and/or customer orders—firm and pending), item master (lead time, lot size, safety stock/time, planning time fence, demand time fence, item description, unit of measure, master (supply) planner and/or master (supply) scheduler, lot size/order quantity, order multiples, etc.), demonstrated capacity, planned capacity, maximum capacity, available/gross capacity, work locations/centers, setup times, operational times, lead time offsets, load factors, pegging, bills-of-material, planning bills, mix percentages, resource profiles, and so forth.

Now, that's a lot of data that must be kept accurate and up to date if master planning and scheduling is to work for and at a company. Well, we do call this Class A for a reason. In fact, a good principle for companies to follow is, "Class A in everything that is done." This includes *all the data* in the systems supporting supply chain management including master planning and scheduling. If the reader needs to refresh his or her memory regarding data integrity, the authors suggest a review of Chapter 13 in this book.

Process Improvement

During the detailed design work, policies are developed and areas for process improvement are identified. At this point, detailed plans for making improvements in those areas are developed and assigned to individuals. For example, the use of planning bills and/or kanbans may have been articulated in the high-level design work as a company strategy along with the policy/policies and procedure/procedures that need to be followed. Here, the means to execute that policy (or those policies) using that procedure (or those procedures) must be spelled out in detail.

A policy dictating the use of planning bills would require a greater imagination and some free thinking among the users, in the demand organization as well as in the supply organization. As was discussed in planning make-to-order products (refer back to Chapters 8–10), the master (supply) planner and/or master (supply) scheduler does not know the final configuration of the product until the firm customer order is received.

Therefore, the company's manufacturing strategy of where it wants to meet its customer (what state the product must be in when the customer order is received; in other words, how much of the product purchase/build has been completed) is taken into account. Standard bills-of-material are replaced during the planning cycle by planning bills, which are referred to as pseudo bills or artificial bills-of-material (bills used only for planning, not for building).

A policy dictating the use of a kanban system would naturally require far-reaching process improvement in the manufacturing facility. Changeover times, a matter of concern for the master planner and/or master scheduler, would need to be dramatically reduced. This would not happen by itself but would succeed only with the help of a detailed plan for which an individual is accountable.

Software

An effective master planning and scheduling (MPS) process requires reliable software for five purposes: the MPS process itself, supply management, integrated business planning or sales and operations planning, rough cut capacity planning, and customer order management. Some software packages can handle all five purposes. Some can perform one function but not the others. In certain operations, integrated business planning or sales and operations planning may be handled on a personal computer using off-the-shelf software (*not* a recommendation, but a reality in today's world), while the master (supply) plan and/or master (supply) schedule, rough cut capacity planning, and finite scheduling (if used) jobs are handled on the company's main computer.

The first step in implementing the software requirements of an MPS system is to actually determine those requirements. This may require the hiring of outside expertise. Once the right software is acquired, a period of training for operational personnel is required, as is a shakeout period in which the software is debugged (freed of software errors) and any needed customization takes place.

Who's in Control of the Software?

Many off-the-shelf software packages for both enterprise resource planning and master planning and scheduling offer a maintenance service that provides for the "care and feeding" of the current system with periodic enhancements of the software. This practice is commonplace to most sectors of the software industry and is provided at an additional charge.

While it is reassuring to know that the expensive software being purchased or leased today is insured against obsolescence by such an offer, and that the company will be able to convert to newer versions as they become available, a caution should be observed. Some supply chain professionals think that reliance on an outside software supplier for such an important tool as manufacturing software is unwise. Regardless of the reader's thoughts, caution is the name of the game when the company makes this decision.

Thomas Wallace (a former Oliver Wight associate) makes this warning for MRPII software, and the same caution applies to ERP and MPS software packages. The noted dangers of this reliance are threefold:

1. In the fast-paced world of software development, your software supplier may not be in business tomorrow, leaving your company with a dead-end product.

2. Software firms may be committed to upgrading their products with new versions, but the timing of these improvements will be on their schedule, not yours. Thus, allowing an outside firm to control one of the most important management tools of your business is to allow an outsider to control the pace of your own continuous improvement. Management should never accede to that loss of control.

3. You cannot fully appreciate the capabilities, the limits, and the quirks of a software system if you do not fully understand how to alter and maintain it.

MPS Detailed Design Executive Presentation—Contents/Outline

The *detailed design (DD) presentation* is another critical part of the *approval to move on* process. This DD presentation must make the executive steering committee (ESC) members comfortable with what has been done during the detailed design work period.

It's the DD that sets up the implementation launch and measures' work still ahead on the company's Class A journey following *The Proven Path* to business excellence. Therefore, again, careful attention must be paid to the presentation materials as well as the accompanying documentation/presentation handout. A recommended agenda for the DD presentation is as follows:

1. Presentation agenda (contents, presenter, timing);

2. Vision of operations along with journey vision (review of where the company will be by a defined date);

3. Transformation organization structure (Class A initiative leaders, past and current);

4. Scope of the initiative (what's included in the DD and what's *not* included in the DD);

5. Class A benefits/investment review (update on opening numbers and the current numbers);

6. Class A facilitated self-assessment scores (radar charts showing progress to date—some improvement expected);

7. *The Proven Path* (Lead, Transform—where the improvement initiative is today, and Own Phases);

8. Class A workshops (pictures, examples, and results—time for some recognition);

9. Master planning and scheduling process (key policies, process flows, and Class A metrics);

10. MPS spinoff task force members (leader, assistant leader, and task team members, past and present);

11. Master planning and scheduling charter reviewed (status of key activities coupled with deliverables);

12. MPS process definition (what master planning and scheduling means to this company);

13. Supporting teams and process definitions (demand, capacity, material, scheduling, logistics, data integrity);

14. Review of key definitions/glossary of terms (supply chain management as well as company terms);

15. RACI documents for MPS and supporting functions (responsibility, accountability, consulted, informed);

16. Software requirements (required vs. nice-to-have vs. wish list);

17. Mass education/training program (business and software, including planned delivery schedule);

18. Obstacles still needing removal (who's going to do this and what's the projected cost);

19. Next steps cross-referenced to *The Proven Path* (macro plan tied to the *Proven Path* journey);

20. Questions and answers (allow time in the agenda for this item);

21. Review parking lot items (response commitment made by responsibility party, including due date);

22. Call for the question (approval to move to the Own Phase, which commences with mass education/training, which is followed by pilots, which is followed by full implementation, which is followed by measures/results).

The detailed design generally takes about one to two days for most companies discussing supply chain management, including master planning and scheduling. For more complex environments, more time should be allowed, but the DD presentation should not be less than six hours even for the smallest of companies; this is not the time to show lack of respect for the initiative/project team, who has probably worked very hard to ensure that they continue to tell a good story regarding the company's new direction. Assuming that the ESC gives their approval to the team to move on to the Own Phase work, it's time for the rubber to meet the road.

Cascading Education Responsibility Assigned, Created, Tested, and Approved

The final element of the Transform Phase is to ready the *education and training* for the people within the company with a need to know regarding the business transformation, including the *newly designed policies, process flows, procedures, work instructions, metrics, and software enhancements*. It is recommended that this education and training be done in the format of a business meeting. What that means is that more than half of the time in each of these *education and training* sessions is spent on *discussion, not* on one-way education and/or training.

These mass education and training sessions are conducted in six parts: (1) general concept education, (2) discussion on how the concept applies to the company's business, (3) introduction of design and documentation pertaining to the business concept being discussed in this session, (4) education and training on how the design and documentation presented will be used by the company following implementation, (5) action items (including responsibility and due dates) generated during the session discussions, and (6) questions and answers regarding the sessions contents. Each session should last one to two hours maximum; these are business meetings dealing with new structures, and the participants need time to digest and think about the impact to their areas as well as the impact on their own work.

The number of business meetings for the various company functions varies depending on the material to be covered, amount of change in each functional area, complexity of the functional area, impact of the change in business behaviors on current and future business, timing of the education and training relative to the cutover implementation schedule, and session facilitator availability. *It is recommended that the required functional education and training be completed entirely before the switch is thrown on the live pilot and/or full functional implementation.*

Keeping these objectives in mind, the spinoff task forces must create an education and training package that can be used to educate and train all those in the company with a need to know regarding the newly designed expected people behaviors, integrated business processes, tool and technology enhancements available, and new data integrity requirements. This education and training package must be created to be presented and facilitated in a very professional manner.

Remember, this education and training is to get everyone within the company to change how they view the business and how they do their work. Again, the delivery of this education and training is to get everyone prepared to put the rubber to the road!

Segue to . . .

The Proven Path to a Successful MPS Implementation (Phase 3) Users Own MPS Launch and Measures

As stated earlier in this chapter, the heavy lifting is done in the detailed design work as part of the Transform Phase on *The Proven Path* journey. So, in closing this chapter, the reader should now be familiar with what is done in the Lead Phase as well as in the Transform Phase. With Phases 1 and 2 behind us, let's move on to our final full chapter, that of Phase 3, Launch and Measures, or what Oliver Wight calls the Own Phase on *The Proven Path* journey. It's time for all to see the rubber meet the road!

20

The Proven Path to a Successful Master Planning and Scheduling Implementation (Phase 3)

Users Own MPS Behavior and Process

Launch and Measures

Don't let what you can't do stop you from doing what you can do!

Methodology for Implementing Change Revisited—Again!

The Proven Path for Business Transformation with Master Planning and Scheduling

As we stated in the previous two chapters, the Oliver Wight Companies developed an approach for managing change when implementing business processes and process improvements that, when done correctly, leads to business transformation. Again, as previously mentioned, Oliver Wight calls this approach *The Proven Path* because the change methodology has been used successfully for some 50 years. Let's quickly review a summary of that change methodology:

- Executive commitment, involvement, and leadership;
- Creation of a journey vision, business case for change, and return on investment;

- Implementation planning, preparation, execution, and control;

- Creating internal change agents, sometimes referred to as subject matter experts;

- Ownership for policies (rules), process design (or redesign), and procedures (activities);

- Behavior changes, defined processes, and tool implementation;

- Strong foundation of data integrity;

- Transition, embed, sustain, and mature;

- Measurement and reporting of results.

This chapter focuses on the last four change methodology components listed— (1) behavior changes, defined processes, and tool implementation, (2) strong foundation of data integrity, (3) transition, embed, sustain, and mature, and (4) measurement and reporting of results. Figure 20.1 graphically shows the three phases of *The Proven Path* while highlighting the Own Phase.

So, let's begin our discussion of Phase 3, the Own Phase. The supply chain management (SCM) and master planning and scheduling (MPS) teams have done the heavy lifting for

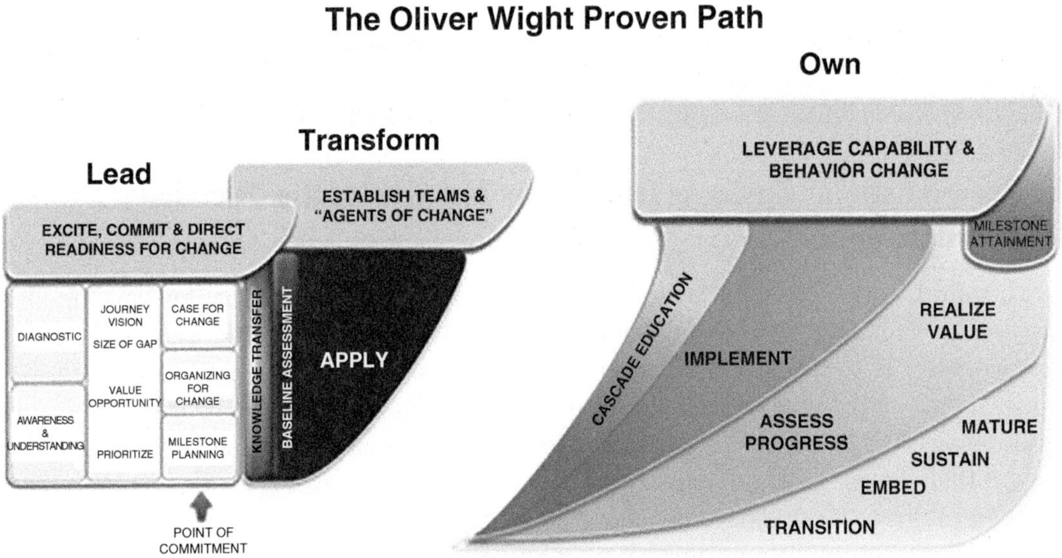

The Oliver Wight Proven Path

Figure 20.1   Highlighted Own Phase on The Proven Path

the supply improvement initiative and now it is time to reap the benefits of all that work. *Note: Words and how those words are put together is very important in this Own Phase. Therefore, the authors have included several word definitions throughout this chapter.*

Phase 3: Own Phase (Launching and Measuring)

A friend of John's tells the story of how he spent the better part of one Sunday connecting a new shower in his basement. First, he turned off the main water line; then he cut into nearby hot and cold feeder lines and, using a dozen or so copper elbows, Ts, and straight pipes, joined his new shower to the house water system. At 6:00 p.m. he soldered in the last connection using his very last piece of flux, then proudly surveyed all the bright new copper and the professional-looking fittings and angles that he—a mere amateur—had put together.

After inspecting all the soldering work, he called his wife from upstairs to observe the ceremony of turning on the new shower. He proudly turned on the main water valve and watched in disgust as fine streams of water sprayed out of at least half of his pipe fittings. The last of the soldering flux being used up, and the hardware store being closed for the day, my friend shut off the main water valve. He would call a plumber in the morning. The family would have no running water until then. My friend had done everything according to plan; he had even double-checked all of his fittings. Everything had seemed ready to go. But the only way to be sure was to actually turn on the water!

A company with fixed payroll expenses, customer promises to keep, and millions invested in plant and equipment cannot take a chance that its new operating system will spring a leak. Prudence dictates that any new system brought online in a complex business cannot be adopted cold turkey but must go through a trial period in which the system is debugged and tried out.

To fully cut over to the new process and computer system without this trial period would endanger the entire operation. This applies equally to a new telephone system, information system, ERP system, SCM system, or master planning and scheduling (MPS) system. Phase 3 of *The Proven Path* concerns itself with the final step in the implementation process—the switching on of the new policies, procedures, work instructions, system, and metrics of the improvement initiative including master planning and scheduling (MPS).

Cascading Education (Users Understand That Education and Training Never End)

Kicking off the final phase on *The Proven Path*, the launch and measurement phase, is *cascading education*. Just as the modern manufacturer understands that the road to success is paved with continuous process improvements, individuals close to the field of supply chain management and master planning and scheduling understand that knowledge and operational competence are among those important processes. Many months (most likely six to eight or more) have been spent on planning, diagnosing, educating, visioning, prioritizing, designing, and training preparation to ensure that the necessary behavior change, process improvement, and successful process and system cutover and implementation occurs.

The necessary behavior changes won't occur by just handing company associates new documented policies, workflows, procedures, work instructions, and required metric reporting. First of all, many of these people were *not* part of the design team, possibly receive *little or no* education, and possibly are *not* part of the improvement initiative at all. Therefore, these people (in fact, all the people with a need to know) must be educated and trained on supply chain management and master planning and scheduling as well as on the new way of doing business (policies or the rules, flow diagrams or the linkages among processes/decisions/actions, procedures or the actions required, work instructions or the how it's to be done, new or enhanced supporting systems such as ERP, MPS, Excel, and so forth).

Just because something is designed and understood by the improvement initiative team members doesn't mean that it can just be thrown over the fence and the implementation will magically happen. *No, no, no!* It just doesn't happen that way. Oliver Wight principals have long stressed that, when the project team gathers feedback and final lessons learned after an MPS improvement initiative, the practitioners will state that there should have been more education and training!

The Class A SCM and MPS company maintains an ongoing education program that continues to develop more MPS organizational expertise. This is done through outside-sponsored seminars (face-to-face or remotely conducted), web-based education sessions, technology-based education programs, internal business meetings (face-to-face or remotely conducted using current, state-of-art technology), hardbound or electronic books, paper or electronic articles, certification programs, and general MPS meetings (face-to-face or remotely conducted). Needless to say, education, training, and improvement never stop in a Class A company!

Now that all the company personnel affected by the supply chain management and master planning and scheduling improvement initiative are educated and trained on how the company expects to operate in the future, it's time to cautiously move into implementation. However, going back to our do-it-yourself plumber story, it might be prudent to mitigate the risk of something going wrong (even though all the plumbing and connections are carefully checked, Murphy might be at work during the implementation step). Let's take a look at the implementation step and the most-used approaches to that process and system implementation.

Implement (as the Old Saying Goes, It's Time to Jump into the Water)

The *implement* element of *The Proven Path's* Own Phase (see Figure 20.1, page 744) is when the company takes its first deliberate steps toward putting the processes in place (some processes, such as data integrity cleanup, may actually be implemented during the Transform Phase) and bringing the MPS computer hardware/software system online. Because newly developed or redeveloped processes may not be fully understood and there is a chance that software bugs still may be present in a newly adopted or redesigned system, introduction is conducted in small steps.

Eventually, as the processes become familiar and the computer hardware/software is proved to work as designed and documented, and as company personnel learn more about using their new policies, workflows, procedures, work instructions, accuracy and performance metrics, and tools/technology, the master planning and scheduling system goes on the air company-wide.

Now, *implement* is defined as putting something (in our case, a newly designed or enhanced master planning and scheduling process supported by technology/software; i.e., an enterprise resource planning system) into practical effect. There are three methods for switching on the new supply chain management (SCM) and enterprise resource planning (ERP) system including master planning and scheduling (MPS):

1. *The cold turkey approach.* Here, the old system is switched off and the new system is switched on. This is like jumping out of an airplane with a parachute packed by several unknown people—*not recommended*.

2. *The parallel approach.* Here, the new system is operated offline and its results and recommendations are compared to those of the existing system, which continues in operation. When the new system can consistently provide essentially the same

information as the old system, the old system is shut down and the new one continues online.

Problems with respect to the parallel approach are that (a) it is difficult to maintain and staff two different systems, and (b) the two process and computer systems should not be expected to have comparable results. The old process and computer system are being phased out because their performance and output were inadequate. *If we're upgrading our system, why would we want to duplicate the performance and output of the process and computer system we plan to retire?*

3. *The pilot approach.* This is the application of the cold-turkey approach to a small part of the company, ideally in a highly controlled environment. Here, the new SCM and MPS process and computer system can be tried out and monitored closely without too much risk of damage to the overall operations of the business.

4. If a company manufactured all sorts of writing instruments—ballpoint pens, felt-tipped pens, mechanical lead pencils, traditional wooden pencils, and so on—it might use its new SCM and MPS process and software system strictly in the wooden pencil operations, where a failure would not throw a wrench into the other parts of the business. The *pilot approach* accomplishes a number of things:

   - Policies, procedures, and work instructions developed earlier can be tried in a real-time (live pilot) exercise.

   - Personnel can learn to operate the system using real company data, *not* demonstration or testing data.

   - The hardware/software system can be tested and stressed in a live exercise (live pilot).

   - Design and creation problems can be identified and resolved.

   - The organization has an opportunity to gain confidence in the new system.

   - Company personnel can be trained in a workshop environment once the pilot is up and running.

Of these approaches, the pilot approach is recommended for reasons that should be obvious. Once a pilot testing of the new SCM and MPS system has been made in one area of the total manufacturing operation, the next step is the *cutover*, in which the new SCM and MPS process and computer system totally displace the old processes and system software.

A cutover can be accomplished in one stroke or by degrees. In a small operation, or one in which the results of a small pilot have been an overwhelming success, a total cutover may be feasible, but caution normally dictates a cutover *by degrees*—that is, the *gradual extension of the pilot to other operations*.

Assess Progress (Is the Company on Track to Achieving Documented Goals and Results?)

Once the MPS process and system are up and running, the company and its management team need to determine what is working and what is not. The comparison of performance results to the expected performance goals that were established in diagnostic, vision, and design is now done. Questions are asked: "Are we better off?" and "Where do we go from here?" Typical answers to these questions are "We're on the path of continuous improvement" and "Let's do more!"

Many executives believe that this is the *most important part* in the entire process. Certainly, it is a *very important* ingredient for success. There are four questions that need to be answered in order to assess an improvement initiative's progress:

1. How is the company doing in building on the company's strengths and eliminating the company's weaknesses that were documented in the initial diagnostic? What people behaviors, business processes, technology/tools, and data integrity changes have been made since the commencement of the improvement initiative?

2. How is the company doing regarding its original documented goals outlined in the benefit/cost analysis that was initially presented to the executive steering committee? Is the company tracking to the return-on-investment, cost-of-a-month's delay, and five-year projected cash flow?

3. How is the company doing in its improvement efforts regarding the initial (as well as ongoing) assessments, using the Oliver Wight Class A Standard for Business Excellence or Planning and Control Class A Milestone (or the criteria spelled out in the company's tailored Business Excellence Milestone) regarding master planning and scheduling? Are ongoing assessments showing improvements (by the numbers) in all defined criteria categories? If not, what is being done to move the needle in those areas where improvement is not being made as expected?

4. How is the company doing on delivering the documented tangible, as well as intangible, expected results (quick wins along with longer-term results)? Are real and

substantive benefits like increased productivity being realized? Are difficult-to-measure benefits like less planner and scheduler stress being felt within the company?

Supply chain management and master planning and scheduling improvements come in a couple flavors: being more accurate in one's work and performing better on the tasks that one is assigned. It might now be wise to spend some time discussing *accuracy and performance goals* along with *accuracy and performance measurements*.

Accuracy and Performance Goals

To get us started with an accuracy and performance discussion, a few definitions might be beneficial to get us all on the same page. Take a look!

- *Accuracy* is the condition or quality of being accurate—exactness and correctness. *Accurate* is defined as having no errors, correct, and conforming to or deviating only slightly from a standard or lying within a defined tolerance.

- *Performance* is defined as the act of performing or the condition of being performed, an act or style of performing a work or role before an audience, and the way in which someone or something functions (e.g., rating a machine's performance).

- *Perform* is defined as to begin and follow through to completion, to carry out in accordance with prescribed terms, and to accomplish something as promised or expected.

- *Goal* is defined as a desired result or purpose toward which one is working or an objective.

- *Measurement* is defined as the act or process of measuring, while *measure* has many definitions; measuring either accuracy or performance within a supply chain management environment is best thought of as the size, amount, capacity or degree of something determined by comparison with a standard or defined target.

- *Achievement* is defined as the act of accomplishing something or something that has been accomplished successfully, while the definition of *accomplish* states that there has been success in doing, reaching the end of, achieving, completing, and finishing.

With these definitions from *The American Heritage Desk Dictionary* (Houghton Mifflin Company, 1981), let's take a look at accuracy and performance goals along with accuracy and performance measurements.

Generally during the Lead Phase, an initiative core group considers which accuracy and performance goals would be appropriate for the company if a full master planning and scheduling (MPS) implementation were to take place. Oliver Wight's operational and business excellence standards and milestones have several accuracy and performance goals along with defined Class A measurement requirements and acceptable tolerances. Some of these key accuracy and performance goals and measurements pertain directly to MPS.

For instance, master schedule performance (intermediate-level groupings or stock-keeping unit/mix), and detailed manufacturing schedule performance (stock-keeping unit/work authorization—i.e., work order) need to be 95 percent or better, according to the Class A Planning and Control Milestone criteria as defined in *The Oliver Wight Class A Standard for Business Excellence,* 7th edition. It should also be noted that *full* Class A recognition in managing internal supply and master planning and scheduling requires the company to have schedule performance in the company's industry top quartile or at a minimum of 99.5 percent (within defined tolerances).

Aggregate supply plan (volume) performance needs to be plus or minus 2 percent to the last leadership-approved plan. Database accuracy across MPS-related elements (e.g., lead times, lot sizes, etc.) needs to be maintained at a minimum level of 95 percent (again, within defined tolerances). Accuracy also applies directly to the master plan as well as the master schedule.

The master plan along with the master schedule must be free of past-due work and be realistic and doable (refer to prior discussions on rough cut capacity planning and material planning). Lead-time reduction, inventory reduction, and throughput velocity improvement are other appropriate goals. Another important goal is stabilizing the master plan and schedule; to do so requires discipline and a process that minimizes unnecessary master plan and master schedule changes.

During the Lead Phase the company's leaders and management team had the information that they needed to make an informed decision with respect to fully implementing a formal MPS process supported by a reliable computer hardware/software system. The core group of decision makers was initially educated on best-practice master planning and scheduling processes; a diagnostic of the company with respect to Class A MPS accuracy and performance was done; and the master planning and scheduling team created a vision of how the company would look and how its ability to satisfy customers would be altered if (and when) it reached the heights of Class A accuracy and performance.

A number of concrete facts were laid alongside that mental image of the new company: benefit/cost analysis, a list of the resources and efforts including potential task force members necessary for full implementation, and a set of accuracy and performance goals that would be the company's new yardstick for future MPS and manufacturing data accuracy and performance.

It's during the progress assessments that the company determines how it is doing against the promises that were made many months earlier. Status reports relative to the following list need to be made monthly to the executive steering committee by the master planning and scheduling team leader and supply chain management improvement initiative project leader.

- This is where the company now stands with respect to its MPS practices (initially from the *diagnostic*).

- This is where the company can go (from the *vision statement*).

- These are the gaps that still need to be closed (from *vision to diagnostic gap analysis*).

- Continuing to move forward with full MPS implementation will result in these future measurable benefits and costs (from *benefit/cost analysis*).

- The priority of this improvement initiative was set and has or has not been honored (from *prioritizing* effort).

- The reason this improvement initiative continues to be so vital to this company (from *case for change* document).

- Moving from the company's current practices to a Class A MPS environment still requires this amount of time and this amount of staffing resources (from an updated detailed *project organization plan*).

- There is a checklist of important tasks that still need to be performed to reach full implementation (from the MPS *task force detailed project plan*).

- These are the accuracy and performance measurements implemented to date (from the *performance goal and measurement definitions*).

Okay, accuracy and performance goals are very important to a Class A initiative, but without accuracy and performance measurements a company can be breathing its own air, with comments like, "We think we are pretty good, but how do we really know?" This is where a solid accuracy and performance measurement process supported by a defined system becomes an integral part of the improvement initiative and implementation step.

Accuracy and Performance Measurements

As early as the evaluation and overall planning phase (refer back to Chapter 18 for a refresher), the master planning and scheduling implementation team develops a set of ideas about the kinds of goals the new processes and computer hardware/software system should have. To say it again, goals by themselves are *not* helpful unless they can be rendered into specific measurements. No one can tell how they are doing—and certainly cannot measure progress—unless accuracy and performance can be measured.

In developing a set of accuracy and performance goals and measures, there are 10 questions the authors believe need to be addressed:

1. What is being (or going to be) measured?

2. What is the purpose of the measurement?

3. Who does the measurement affect?

4. Who is accountable and responsible for the measurement?

5. What are the goals and measurement targets?

6. How are accuracy and performance calculated?

7. What and where is the data source?

8. What defined tolerances are (or will be) acceptable?

9. How is the measurement data secured?

10. Are there any general comments by those who are accountable, responsible, and/or impacted by the measurement being discussed?

Once measurements have been established, people today (machines in the future) must know what constitutes good and bad performance. This is accomplished by setting *accuracy and performance targets*. For example, master (supply) plan and/or master (supply) schedule performance may be defined as follows:

- Unacceptable accuracy and/or performance is less than 92 percent to plan and/or schedule (red);

- Minimal acceptable accuracy and/or performance is 92–94.9 percent to plan and/or schedule (yellow);

- Satisfactory accuracy and/or performance is 95–99.4 percent to plan and/or schedule (green);

- Outstanding accuracy and/or performance is 99.5 percent or better to plan and/or schedule (blue).

The reader may be wondering, percent to what plan and/or what schedule—how does that work? To answer this question, tolerances must first be determined (refer back to Figure 14.21 on page 488 for a review of the tolerance discussion). For example, we could say that manufacturing produced items within certain tolerances would be a success. Thus, production of the master scheduled item within plus or minus two days of scheduled completion date (e.g., up to two days early or no more than two days late) and plus or minus 4 percent of the scheduled quantities (e.g., up to a 4 percent overrun or no less than a 4 percent underrun) would be considered acceptable and therefore a *hit*, or good (numbers used in this example are arbitrary and do not constitute an authors' recommendation).

Production completions falling outside those specified ranges would be considered a *miss*, or bad. If performance to the master (supply) plan is within plus or minus 2 percent (if the master [supply] plan is the company's aggregate supply plan, otherwise it's measured to the 95–99.4 percent target) and/or master (supply) schedule is 95–99.4 percent (on a *hit-or-miss* basis), the company would be operating at a satisfactory or Class A milestone level of performance (as defined in *The Oliver Wight Planning and Control Milestone Workbook*, 7th edition).

Now that the master planning and scheduling team has defined the performance goals along with their associated measurements, and the overall project team along with the executive steering committee has approved these performance goals and measurements for each metric, it must be decided when an MPS item is to be earmarked for measurement. This time period is sometimes referred to as the *metric buy window*, or when the MPS planned and/or scheduled item is baselined for measurement.

For example, the company may decide that as master (supply) planned and/or master (supply) scheduled items move into the last month before the product being built is planned and/or scheduled to be completed (and shipped or moved into finished goods inventory) or the product being purchased is planned and/or scheduled to be received is considered to have entered the metric buy window and therefore baselined for performance measurement. The metric buy window is offered as a suggestion to ensure that everyone is doing what's right for the company and *not* just chasing a trophy!

To this point in our accuracy and performance measurement discussion, the company has defined the items to be master (supply) planned and/or master (supply) scheduled, the accuracy and performance goals and measurements have been established (documented and approved), the tolerances for each grouping and/or item have been identified (documented and approved), and the metric buy window has been determined (documented and approved). All the necessary ingredients for properly measuring MPS performance are now available to the master planning and scheduling team. The basic measurement is to determine if the MPS grouping and/or item was completed on time or within the defined tolerance; if it is determined that the grouping and/or item was completed on time or within the defined tolerance, it is considered a hit, otherwise a miss.

The last question regarding accuracy and performance measurement that needs to be answered is, "What is to be done with items that are past due and therefore cannot be completed to a valid due date?" In the spirit of encouraging master (supply) planners and/or master (supply) schedulers to do the right thing and behave in a Class A manner, any MPS grouping or stock-keeping unit that goes *past due* is subject to the company's *no past dues on the master (supply) plan and/or master (supply) schedule policy* and associated corrective guidelines.

An example of a *no past dues policy* is included in Appendix D of this book. It is strongly suggested that a company desiring to operate a Class A MPS process and system adopt the MPS performance measurement guideline that counts each day that an MPS item remains past due and is *not* rescheduled (to a valid and realistic date), as defined in the *no past dues policy* as a *miss* to performance (*yes, the authors are suggesting that every day an item on the master (supply) plan and/or master (supply) schedule remains in a past due state, it is counted as another miss to master (supply) plan and/or master (supply) schedule performance*).

Alright, that takes care of rescheduling past-due work. How about work that is not past due to its planned or scheduled completion date but is identified as "going to miss its completion date and going to enter a past due condition shortly"?

Again, in the spirit of encouraging Class A behavior in master planning and scheduling, MPS groupings and/or stock-keeping units that are rescheduled while in the metric buy window are counted as a performance *miss*, but the new due date assigned is now a *new due date* and, assuming the grouping and/or item is successfully completed by the new due date, it is given full credit; think about it—the grouping or item gets *one miss* for rescheduling an item while it was in the metric buy window and *one hit* for completing the item to its new due date, or a 50 percent overall credit—which is certainly better than getting no credit at all.

If the grouping and/or item needs to be rescheduled again (and its due date is within the metric buy window), its performance takes *another miss*; however, completion to the new due date is given full credit; again, think about it—the grouping and/or item gets *another miss* for rescheduling an item while it was in the metric buy window and *one hit* for completing the item to its new due date, or a 33 percent overall credit since it needed to be rescheduled twice within the defined metric buy window. Now back to the basic MPS metric calculation and reporting.

Calculating accuracy and performance measurements are generally the same; what changes in each calculation is the numerator and denominator. For instance, performance to the master (supply) plan and/or master (supply) schedule is the actual work completed for the measurement period divided by the planned work master (supply) planned and/or master (supply) scheduled for completion for the measurement period times 100 (to change the resultant fraction into a percentage).

A performance example: For a master (supply) planned and/or master (supply) scheduled product, grouping, or stock-keeping unit, let's say 200 units were planned and/or scheduled for completion in the current week and only 190 units were actually completed on time (or within the defined tolerance). The calculation is 190 completed units divided by 200 planned or scheduled units for completion times 100, equaling 95 percent performance to the master (supply) plan and/or master (supply) schedule. This master (supply) plan and/or master (supply) schedule performance would be colored green—good work, everyone!

Accuracy measurements for an audit are calculated by dividing the accurate records by the total records audited times 100, equaling audit accuracy. For a master (supply) planned and/or master (supply) scheduled product, grouping, or stock-keeping unit, let's say 50 records were audited in the current week and only 45 records were actually found to be accurate (or within the defined tolerance). The calculation is 45 accurate records divided by 50 audited records times 100, equaling 90 percent accuracy of the master plan or master schedule for the audit. This master (supply) plan and/or master (supply) schedule accuracy would be colored red—not so good, everyone!

A good metric system includes requirements that trigger action any time performance falls below specified levels (see Figure 20.2 on the following page). For example, any time

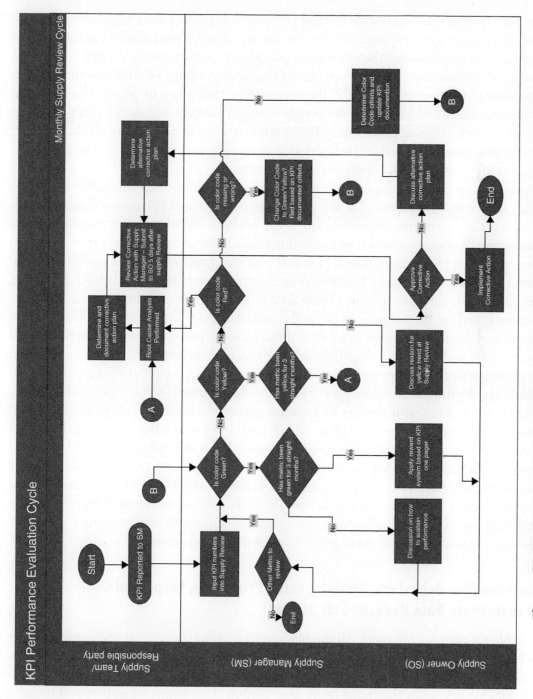

Figure 20.2 Accuracy and Performance Measurements Process Flow Example

the master (supply) plan and/or master (supply) schedule performance slips below the minimum, the people with responsibility for the master (supply) plan and/or master (supply) schedule performance—say, the master (supply) planner and/or master (supply) scheduler (input) and manufacturing and/or operations manager (output)—would submit a written explanation of what went wrong and the corrective action taken or planned to be taken; that explanation would be due on the supply manager's and/or supply director's (or other authority's) desk within approximately 48–72 hours (the authors recommend that the corrective action plan be created and submitted to the supply owner for approval *no more than 120 hours* after the monthly supply review adjournment).

Figure 20.2 on page 757 displays an example of the key performance evaluation cycle for a typical manufacturing company. The key performance indicator (KPI) process flow starts with the accuracy and performance calculation of the previous month's results (monitoring and reporting can be done on a weekly and sometimes daily basis) and reporting of those results to the company's supply manager. The KPI numbers are analyzed and receive a colored (green, yellow, red) notation reflecting where the company stands regarding the KPI under discussion.

As the process flow example in Figure 20.2 indicates, different directions and actions are taken based on the color code given the metric. Again, Figure 20.2 is offered as an example and should be treated as such; it should also be noted that some companies use a fourth color such as blue to highlight accuracy and/or performance that exceeds green or is considered outstanding (refer to the earlier paragraph example defining a color code example highlighting red, yellow, green, and blue designations).

This level of detail with respect to accuracy and performance needs to be developed before the pilot and cutover take place—back in the process definition phase. However, the accuracy and performance plan should be revisited frequently even as the pilot and cutover are taking place. Accuracy and performance to the master plan and/or master schedule notifies leadership and management just how well the pilot is performing and where corrective interventions may be required. As cutover to the new MPS system is completed, accuracy and performance measures become matters of ongoing importance to the operation and continuous improvement of the MPS process.

Transition (Old Behaviors, Nonintegrated Processes, Inept Tools, and Inaccurate Data Records Left Behind)

The *rubber is meeting the road*! All the planning, visioning, designing, and implementing is behind the implementors. The new and/or enhanced processes along with the new and/or enhanced hardware/software system are up and running. People are trading in their old habits for new ones that have been described in the various education and training sessions. All data residing in the company's data files is expected to be trustworthy, no questions asked. It's most likely a time when people's nerves and stress levels are tested—"Hey, it's bringing a new life into the company's world," is how one implementor put it.

The transition element is where the company and its people see their environment really changing. However, the company is in a transition from the old way of doing business to a new one. Things, such as people behaviors, must change if the improvement initiative is to be successful.

Transition is defined as the process of changing from one state (of performance and doing business) to another state. As long as the up-front work is or was done in a Class A manner, the transition or transitions (assuming multiple parallel/serial cutovers) is expected to go down the road smoothly.

Embed (Business Is Operating Using the Newly Implemented Approach)

As the transition element on *The Proven Path* progresses, the improvement implementers turn their attention to embedding the newly designed people and machine behaviors, business processes (i.e., master planning and scheduling), technology/tools (i.e., use of the ERP system), and data integrity requirements into the company's culture. This element is not to be taken lightly.

People, in general, do not like change itself even though the current way of doing things is not embraced or working well. What many people like to do is talk about change, but when push comes to shove, one can hear voices in the supply chain management community shouting, "Please do not take away my Excel spreadsheet; that new system sure is a step backward!"

So, with this possibility in mind, the improvement initiative team should create and run trial scenarios dealing with various anticipated inputs and comments that were heard during the implement and transition stages (it's a good idea to get ready in advance of the pushback that most likely will surface along the implementation path). Of course, an effective education and training program prior to the implement and transition phase will pay dividends. Time to move to the next element, that of sustaining the changes within the company.

Sustain (Behaviors Changed, Processes Solid, Tools Working, Integrity in Data)

Sustaining is defined as keeping in existence and maintaining the newly implemented way of doing business. This is another *Proven Path* element to which the implementors must pay attention. In fact, the sustaining part of the improvement initiative may well go on for several weeks, months, and possibly years. Oliver Wight once said, "The informal system is always waiting in the wings." Care is to be taken so the informal way of doing business from the past is not allowed to reenter and take center stage.

To ensure that the embedded processes are sustained, encouragement for those using the formal master planning and scheduling process and doing it right are heard from management as well as leadership. If something goes wrong, care should be taken to not shoot the messenger.

What must be done is to analyze what needs to be done to correct the wrong turn, formulate a corrective action plan to get back on track, and implement the corrective action plan to get back on the road to where the master (supply) planner and/or master (supply) scheduler is directing the company. Once the wrong has been made right, then do root cause analysis to identify what went wrong and why the wrong turn was made followed by ensuring a fail-safe (capable of compensating automatically for a failure) process so that the same (wrong) turn cannot be taken in the future.

Mature (Continuous Improvement Ensures Implementation Accepted)

A principle of those professionals working in a Class A supply chain management environment is to do routine things routinely. That's one of the improvement goals set during the Lead Phase of the improvement initiative and certainly one of the initial goals that leadership and management expect following a supply chain management (SCM) including master planning and scheduling (MPS) implementation. For this *handling routine things routinely* principle to become reality, the improvement initiative implementation must pass through the elements of transition, embedment, sustainability, and maturity.

The past three sections have discussed transitioning the MPS process into the company's supply chain management process, embedding the MPS process into the company's supply chain management process and culture, and ensuring the sustainability of the MPS process as part of the company's supply chain management process. What's now needed is time for the master planning and scheduling process to mature.

Maturity is defined as the condition or quality of being mature, especially having full growth. So, for the newly implemented master planning and scheduling process to be considered mature means that the MPS process has reached full development, implementation, and acceptance as "just the way we do business around here"! Is it time for benefits and rewards?

Realize Value (Comparison to Initial Benefit/Cost Analysis, Return-on-Investment, Five-Year Cash Flow, and Class A Milestone Attainment and/or Class A Recognition)

Most likely, the company and its people will not have to wait until this point on its master planning and scheduling journey to realize some benefits and value. As the authors have mentioned a few times in this master planning and scheduling (MPS) book, successful implementation of a Class A master planning and scheduling process using The Oliver Wight Class A Standard for Business Excellence and/or The Class A Planning and Control Milestone Workbook and following *The Proven Path is truly a journey, not a destination!*

Of course, arriving at this point in a company's MPS improvement initiative is achievement of a major milestone. And when the company and its MPS implementation team arrive at a major (or even minor) milestone, benefits and paybacks are anticipated and expected by the leadership and management teams.

Realizing value says that real and actual results are being felt by all those involved in the MPS improvement initiative. During the Lead Phase, a benefit/cost analysis was prepared and presented to the executive steering committee. Additionally, a return-on-investment analysis was created and also presented to the executive steering committee. Along with these two documents (which were approved and established as improvement initiative goals), a five-year cash flow projection was initialized (this projection is used throughout all phases of the improvement project or initiative).

It is normal business for the supply chain management improvement initiative project leader, supported by finance and the master planning and scheduling team leader, to present to the executive steering committee what benefits and value have been realized, what benefits and value have *not* been realized, what areas have showed a return on the investment, what areas have *not* showed a return on the investment, and how the improvement initiative is currently tracking to the five-year cash flow projection.

Although real results are what separates an Oliver Wight Class A implementation from many other defined improvement initiatives, the various spinoff task teams have remained focused on the goal of achieving the Class A milestone in master planning and scheduling. Oliver Wight has defined what it refers to as Class A for the past 40-plus years (*The Oliver Wight ABCD Checklist*; *ABCD Checklist for Operational Excellence*; *Class A Standard for Business Excellence*, now in its 7th edition; and several Class A Milestone workbooks, one of which is the *Planning and Control Milestone Workbook*, revision 4). To refresh the reader's memory, the master planning and scheduling process is part of the Oliver Wight Class A Standard for Business Excellence Managing Internal Supply, as well as the Class A Planning and Control Milestone.

There are four levels of maturity regarding a company's planning and control processes (refer back to Figure 18.4b on page 682 in this master planning and scheduling book for a review of the four levels of planning and control maturity). Within the first two phases of maturity, there are three transitions (Ts) in Phase 1 (T1–T3) on the maturity chart and two transitions in Phase 2 (T4 and T5) on the maturity chart.

Full Class A in Planning and Control is targeted at T4, or in the middle of Phase 2 Maturity. Class A Milestone recognition in Planning and Control is targeted at T3, or at the top of Phase 1 Maturity. It is the authors' recommendation that companies desiring to achieve Full Class A in Planning and Control pass through the T3 (Capable Planning and Control) Milestone on its way to T4 (Advanced Planning and Control) and possibly on to T5 (Knowledge-Based Planning and Control).

It's during this *Proven Path* step that the leadership, supply management, and master planning and scheduling team call for the question, "Are we confident in our master planning and scheduling (MPS) people behaviors, business processes, tools and technology being used, and integrity in our data to ask Oliver Wight to recognize our company in achieving the T3 Class A Milestone in Managing Internal Supply and/or Master Planning and Scheduling or to certify our company as T4 Class A in Managing Internal Supply and/or Master Planning and Scheduling?" Class A in managing internal supply and master planning and scheduling sure does sound *good*! It sounds a lot better than Class C or Class D!

With that said, all those currently involved in a Class A improvement initiative or expecting to be involved in a Class A improvement initiative in the future need to understand that *not* all companies that start toward Class A remain on *The Proven Path* and actually realize the Class A lofty goal. It's just a fact of master planning and scheduling implementations. To help the reader understand some of the things that can derail a master planning and scheduling successful implementation as defined by the Class A standard criteria and actual company expected results, the next section discusses some obstacles and barriers to watch out for along the improvement initiative road.

Deterrents to Successful Implementation of the Master Planning and Scheduling Process and Supporting System Technology

As was just said in the previous section, not every company that attempts to implement master planning and scheduling (MPS) will be successful. Fewer still will succeed in reaching Class A status. These are some of the typical problems that get in the way:

- *Ignorance:* People do not know how to do things right because they do not understand the principles and the details of MPS. The antidote: *Educate key people*.

- *Not all of the important people are on board:* It is easy to believe that MPS is only a production issue. But if sales and marketing people do not understand the issues involved, and if they do not participate in the demand management, supply management, and integrated business planning or sales and operations planning process, problems with demand, plant overloading, overpromising, and so forth will persist. Solution: *Get marketing and sales involved.*

- *Company direction is unknown:* This is where the executive team gets into the game. Master planning and scheduling is absolutely reliant upon a well-functioning, integrated business planning or sales and operations planning process, and the early involvement of the leaders in this process sends a clear signal to the rest of the company that it means business. Recommendation: *Do integrated business planning early. You cannot start soon enough.*

- *Capacities and capabilities are not planned:* A quick sanity check on the demand plan and supply plan as well as the master (supply) plan and/or master (supply) schedule can prevent an unrealistic master (supply) plan and/or master (supply) schedule from getting into the plant. *Start rough cut capacity planning this coming Monday.*

- *An overloaded master (supply) plan and/or master (supply) schedule.* If a friend asked your advice about learning how to swim, you would not suggest that he or she start by putting on a 10-pound weight belt and jumping into a fast-moving river. This would only lead to disaster. Your friend would do better to start with the least encumbrance and in a calm pool. Nevertheless, many MPS implementation programs start with schedules that are so overloaded and overpromised that they quickly sink and never come up for air. Word to the wise: *Give your new process and computer system every opportunity for success by starting with a clean slate.*

- *Organizational responsibilities are unclear:* Many failures can be traced to the simple problem of key people not understanding their responsibilities. *Clarify accountabilities and responsibilities. Be sure that everyone understands the goal and his or her part in reaching it.*

- *A lack of written rules (policies) and "how-to" guidelines (procedures and work instructions):* Each policy, flow diagram, procedure, work instruction, and metric should be documented; each policy, procedure, and work instruction should be implemented, followed, and enforced. *Needed: A list of required policies, flow diagrams procedures, and work instructions along with responsibility assignments, expected completion dates, and execution requirements.*

- *No accuracy or performance measurements:* Accuracy and performance goals and measurements are keys to success. The goals as well as the measurements themselves must be clearly defined so that everyone understands them. *Advice: Use master planning and scheduling accuracy and performance measurements as an improvement tool, not as a report card.*

The Master Planner's and Master Scheduler's List of Responsibilities

It is only fitting that the last three chapters in this book on effective implementation (indeed, the entire book) should end with some discussion of the individuals at the center of the processes: the master (supply) planner and master (supply) scheduler. In the end, he or she must implement the business policies, flow diagrams, business procedures, work instructions, and identified metrics that the president or managing director, various vice presidents or directors, financial officer or controller, demand and supply manager, and others had a hand in crafting.

It is the master (supply) planner and/or master (supply) scheduler who must be the artful leader and manager, responsible on a monthly, weekly, and daily basis for the fine balance between what the customers have ordered or intend to order and what the company can deliver or intends to deliver. If the responsibilities of these positions were distilled into a list of responsibilities, they would appear as follows:

Master (Supply) Planner List of Responsibilities or Position Description

OBJECTIVE OF THE MASTER (SUPPLY) PLANNING FUNCTION (LEVEL 2 PLANNING; REFER TO FIGURE 14.10 ON PAGE 469) Create and maintain a valid master (supply) plan (product subfamily, mix level, weeks/months) for material and capacity by effectively balancing demand and supply for a planned product build and/or purchase; a valid master (supply) plan is one in which priority due dates equal need dates and planned capacity equals required capacity.

Specific Responsibilities of a Master (Supply) Planner

1. Disaggregate the leadership's approved supply plan (output of the integrate business planning process) into product subfamilies, anticipated product mix, and weekly requirements for the short-term and monthly requirements for the intermediate- to long-term time periods.

2. Work closely with the demand manager to establish a master supply plan consistent with company strategies and supply/manufacturing policies.

3. Optimize the performance of the company's manufacturing facilities while satisfying firm demand and putting the company in a position to satisfy anticipated demand when it surfaces.

4. Evaluate current supply capabilities relative to the company-approved supply plan and recommend production changes as required.

5. Coordinate the aggregation of current and planned production information and incorporate that information into the company master (supply) plan.

6. Coordinate intermediate- to long-term raw material supply requirements with procurement and/or purchasing and plant production to ensure their availability with respect to the company's master (supply) plan and master (supply) schedule(s).

7. Ensure that the master (supply) planner's monthly *requests for supply* are reflected in actual plant's planned and actual output.

8. Advise the demand manager regarding changes in plant capabilities, particularly as they may affect the ability to satisfy customers.

9. Communicate regularly with plant-level master (supply) schedulers to determine demonstrated plant capacities and the impact of production changes on the master (supply) plan and on individual master (supply) schedules.

10. Ensure that inventory levels fall within approved ranges.

11. Ensure that backlogs are managed to competitive and approved levels.

12. Work closely with each manufacturing facility's master (supply) scheduler to ensure that the company's master (supply) plan is communicated accurately and timely and the plant's part of the company's master (supply) plan becomes a formal *request for product* as well as the constraints to the plant's master (supply) schedule!

Master (Supply) Scheduler's List of Responsibilities or Position Description

OBJECTIVE OF THE MASTER (SUPPLY) SCHEDULING FUNCTION (LEVEL 3 PLANNING; REFER BACK TO FIGURE 14.10 ON PAGE 469) Create and maintain a valid master (supply) schedule (grouping or stock-keeping unit, mix level, days/weeks) for material and capacity by effectively balancing demand and supply for planned product build and/or purchase; a valid master (supply) schedule is one in which priority due dates equal need dates and planned capacity equals required capacity.

Specific Responsibilities of a Master (Supply) Scheduler

1. Develop a working knowledge of the company's products and processes to ensure optimal master (supply) schedule stability, order creation, rescheduling, load leveling, and so forth.

2. Analyze the demand and supply balance at the product subfamily (act as another set of eyes for the master supply planner) and master levels, determining out-of-balance conditions, identifying alternatives, and recommending action(s) for approval.

3. Work with sales, marketing, and manufacturing to better understand competitive lead times for master scheduled items.

4. Seek ways to reduce internal lead times as well as lead times to the customer.

5. Challenge current manufacturing strategies for all product lines to be sure that the best and most customer-oriented strategy is being used.

6. Look for ways to move company make-to-stock products into using a make-to-order manufacturing strategy while remaining competitive in the marketplace regarding delivery lead times.

7. Conduct rough cut capacity planning prior to publishing a master (supply) schedule in which significant changes have occurred.

8. Summarize daily and weekly master (supply) schedules for released and firm planned orders and compare these to the (approved) master (supply) plan to ensure that the master (supply) schedule is within the integrated business planning (IBP) or sales and operations planning (S&OP) policy.

9. Work within policy guidelines pertaining to master (supply) scheduling.

10. Observe and follow all stated master planning and scheduling approved policies, process flows, procedures, and work instructions.

11. Respond in a timely manner to significant action messages generated by the master planning and scheduling software system.

12. Act as an internal educator and coach on master (supply) scheduling issues, providing education and training throughout the company to improve company-wide understanding of master planning and scheduling functions.

13. Identify, negotiate, and resolve conflicts with respect to material and capacity availability as well as order-promising integrity.

14. Maintain a master (supply) schedule following the company policy of permitting *no* master (supply) schedule item to have a released or firm planned order date less than the current date (no past dues at the master [supply] schedule level);

15. Create a monthly (it might be weekly) financial summary of overplanned stock to ensure that it is within the approved master (supply) scheduling budget.

16. Integrate master (supply) scheduling with other company functions as needed.

17. Maintain planned (supply) scheduling parameters, such as manufacturing lead times, lot sizes, supply order multiples, safety stock minimum level, delivery lead times, and order file data for all master (supply) schedule items.

18. Review each master (supply) scheduled item at least weekly (some companies may require daily reviews).

19. Create a master (supply) schedule that satisfies customer demand (both firm and anticipated) with optimum inventory/backlog levels and resource utilization as dictated by company (manufacturing) strategy and master planning and scheduling policy.

20. Ensure that a common master schedule is used to drive all company priorities in sales, marketing, research, engineering, manufacturing support, production, and finance.

21. Create a master (supply) schedule that can be used for detailed material/capacity planning as well as financial planning.

22. Ensure that master (supply) scheduling operational data is the basis of a single set of books.

23. Establish a working line of communication with all company functions.

24. Assist demand management in the identification of abnormal demand entering the system.

25. Assist demand management in setting priorities when demand outstrips the company's supply of products or the resources necessary to build the requested product.

26. Maintain planning bill structures, as required (but not being responsible for setting the option forecast probability factors within the planning bill structure).

27. Assist demand management in setting the probability mix factors, which belong to marketing and sales.

28. Inform management when demand cannot be met and recommend alternatives on how the requested demand could be satisfied.

29. Create a master (supply) schedule that levels work being released to manufacturing and at the same time satisfies customer demand.

30. Work with all company functions to create a stress-free environment and fun/rewarding place to work!

It takes an extraordinary person (or possibly several extraordinary people) to meet each of these position descriptions and requirements, but these challenging duties merely underscore the importance of effective master planning and scheduling to the (business) success of a supply (not to ignore new product, demand, and finance contributions) organization.

Putting It All Together to Ensure Success—Guaranteed

For a company to enjoy a *guaranteed* successful master planning and scheduling implementation requires three things: (1) a *structure* such as Oliver Wight's Class A Standard for Business Excellence to ensure a master planning and scheduling team focus; (2) a *structured approach* such as Oliver Wight's *Proven Path* to ensure that all master planning and scheduling required improvement steps are taken and no steps are skipped; and (3) a dedicated team consisting of leaders who lead, management who manage, planners who plan, designers who design, educators who educate, trainers who train, implementors who implement, supporters who support, and users who use! No quitters are allowed in this Class A improvement initiative. That's a lot said, but there you, the reader, have it. *Follow Oliver Wight's Proven Path step by step and ultimate success is (all but) guaranteed!*

The Oliver Wight recommended improvement initiative structure (Class A Standard for Business Excellence) was discussed earlier in Chapter 18 and is reviewed here in Figure 20.3. Master planning and scheduling implementation's structure is supported by two documents, that of full Class A ("Managing Internal Supply," Chapter 8 of *The Oliver Wight Class A Standard*, 7th edition, and Class A Planning and Control Milestones, 4th revision, sections 8.3, 8.4, 8.14, and 8.15, which are directly related to master planning and scheduling), while sections 8.5–8.22 are indirectly related to master planning and scheduling.

The Class A Standard for a Successful Master Planning and Scheduling Implementation

So, there's the *structure*; now for the *structured approach*. Again, Oliver Wight's *Proven Path* was discussed earlier in Chapter 18 and reviewed here in Figure 20.4 on the following page. Master planning and scheduling implementation *structured approach* is supported basically by two diagrams, that of the full Class A *Proven Path*, 3rd edition (discussed in the last 3 chapters in this book) and *Quick Slice Class A Proven Path*, 3rd edition (a slightly modified version of *The Proven Path* consisting of a series of small and fast implementations below the master planning and scheduling level in supply chain management).

Figure 20.3   Oliver Wight's Class A Criteria to Class A Results

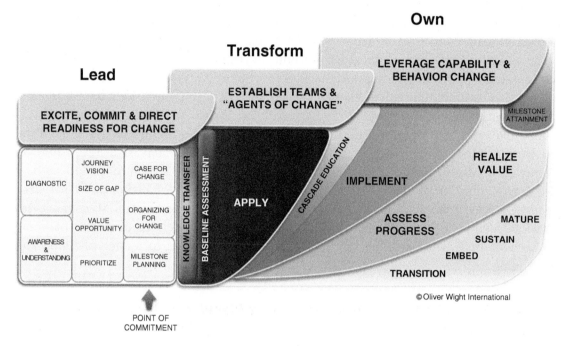

Figure 20.4   Oliver Wight's Proven Path to Class A Results

The Proven Path for a Successful Master Planning and Scheduling Implementation

Alright, there's the *structured approach*; now for the *dedicated team*. Throughout this master planning and scheduling book, the authors have discussed the MPS improvement initiative team as well as the people who support this all-important planning, designing, and implementing team. The company leadership and management teams must be onboard and involved from the initiative planning, approval process, support when needed, knock down obstacles when they appear, and financial and resource assignment as promised during the initial initiative planning and approval cycle. Figure 20.5 on the next page shows a typical supply chain management (including master planning and scheduling) improvement initiative organization that has worked well in the past and most likely will work well in the future.

The Dedicated Teams for a Successful Master Planning and Scheduling Implementation

So, there's a *structure* (Class A Standard, Figure 20.3, page 769), a *structured approach* (*Proven Path*, Figure 20.4), and a *dedicated team* (subject matter experts, Figure 20.5) that

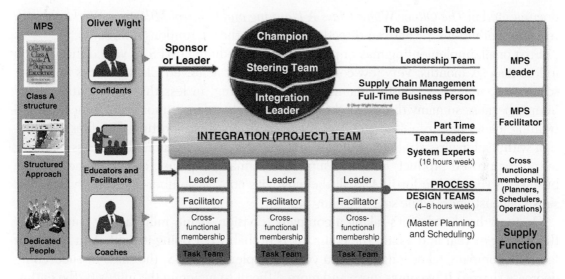

Figure 20.5   Oliver Wight's Recommended Organization Structure to Class A Results

can be used to successfully change current business behaviors from questionable behaviors to good behaviors to best-practice behaviors, poor business practices to effective and efficient business practices, outdated master planning and scheduling tools and technology to state-of-the-art (and affordable) tools and technology, and suspicious and unusable data to accurate and trustworthy data across the board. That, our friends and readers, is Class A, a Class A business environment, a stress-free workplace where many folks spend a good part of their adult life, and a very rewarding and fun place to work!

An Aggressive Master Plan and Schedule for the MPS Implementation

The question arises: "How long should it take to implement master planning and scheduling as part of supply chain management from our starting position until we reach Class A status in master planning and scheduling (based on The Oliver Wight Class A Standard for Business Excellence, 7th edition, Chapter 8, "Managing Internal Supply," in the "Internal Supply Planning" section definitions 5 and 6 directly plus some other definitions indirectly)?" Additionally, master planning and scheduling Class A criteria are also documented in *The Oliver Wight Class A Planning and Control Milestone Workbook*, 4th revision (definitions 8.3 and 8.4 directly plus some other definitions indirectly).

First of all, implementing master planning and scheduling (MPS) is very difficult to do in less than six months. Very few companies have ever achieved Class A status in master scheduling, much less master planning and scheduling, in less than six months. Why? Simply because so many things need to be done, such as large amounts of education and training, data integrity raised to Class A standards on all supporting data files, integration with leadership's strategic direction expressed in their integrated business planning output (approved product, demand, supply, and financial plans), changing the way the business is run, and so forth. And all the while, it's not the number-one priority, which is satisfying customers while safely making a profit.

On the other hand, if it's taking a company (division, plant, mill, factory, unit) longer than a year or year and a half, the company is probably *not* doing it right. As a matter of fact, if a company takes longer than a year to implement MPS, the odds of succeeding decrease sharply. It becomes more and more difficult to maintain the intensity, the enthusiasm, the drive and dedication necessary, and to keep master planning and scheduling pegged as a high-number priority (like 2, 3, . . . 5).

Therefore, plan on it taking a minimum of six months and, for best results, less than a year (taking more than a year may reduce the chance for a successful MPS implementation). For purposes of simplicity and consistency, let's pick the midpoint and routinely refer to a nine-month time frame as somewhat aggressive and ambitious, but not overly cautious and lethargic.

Next question is, Does nine months seem unrealistic to implement the MPS process described in this book? No, it's not! It's very practical and it's also necessary. Here's why:

- *Intensity and enthusiasm:* MPS will be implemented by users, the people running supply chain management and the business. Their first priority must be running the supply chain as well as the business, a full-time job in itself. Now, their responsibility for implementing MPS will require more work and more hours, above and beyond running supply chain management and the business.

  With a long, extended improvement initiative, these people become discouraged. The payoff is too far in the future. There's no light at the end of the tunnel.

  However, with an aggressive schedule, these people can see progress being made early on. They can expect that things will start to improve substantially within six months or so. In our experience, the operating people—master planners, master schedulers, production schedulers, material planners, capacity planners, operations, logistics planners, and so on—respond favorably to this environment.

- *Priority:* The MPS improvement initiative must be given a very high priority, right behind running supply chain management and the business, which includes making shipments. However, it's quite likely that MPS can hold such a high priority over one or two years. (Companies are like people; their attention spans are limited.) As the improvement initiative priority drops, so do the odds of success.

    The best approach is to establish MPS as a very high priority; implement it quickly and successfully. And then capitalize on it. Build on it. Use it to help run supply chain management and the business better and better.

- *Change:* Change comes in two forms: changes in people, and changes in operating environment. Each type represents a threat to the MPS improvement initiative.

    Regarding people changes, take the case of a division whose supply chain manager is MPS-knowledgeable, enthusiastic, and leading the implementation effort. Suppose this person is suddenly promoted to the corporate office. The new supply manager is an unknown quantity.

    That person's reaction to MPS will have a major impact on the improvement initiative's chances for success. He or she may oppose MPS for some reason and the entire implementation effort will be at risk. Environmental changes include factors such as a sharp increase in business (*we're too busy to work on MPS*), a sharp decrease in business (*we can't afford MPS*), competitive pressures, new government regulations, and so forth.

    While such changes can certainly occur during a six- to nine-month improvement initiative, they're twice as likely to occur in a one- to two-year improvement initiative.

- *Schedule slippage:* In a major improvement initiative like implementing MPS, it's easy for schedules to slip. Throughout this book, we have discussed a few ways to minimize slippage or implementing master planning and scheduling incorrectly (or said another way, implementing MPS with the wrong objectives and expectations). For now, let us just point out an interesting phenomenon: In many cases, tight aggressive schedules are actually less likely to slip than loose, casual, nonaggressive schedules.

- *Benefits:* Taking longer than necessary to implement defers getting the benefits. The lost opportunity cost of a delay of only one month can, for many U.S. companies, exceed $50,000–$100,000. A delay of six months to one year could easily range into the million-dollar range for a U.S.-based company.

An aggressive implementation schedule, therefore, is very desirable. But is it practical? *Yes, almost always!* To understand how, we need to understand the concept of the *three gears* (sometimes referred to as three knobs) in our figure on the following page.

The Variables of a Master Planning and Scheduling Implementation

In project management, there are three primary variables: (1) the amount of work to be done, (2) the amount of time to do the work, and (3) the amount of resources available to accomplish the work. Think of these variables as three adjustable control dials that are integrated (by some gearing) with each other and with an output dial that indicates the chance of success of the project (see Figure 20.6).

Once the work, time, and resources have been *dialed in* for a successful project plan (i.e., the dials are in balance), one cannot adjust a single dial without adjusting at least one of the other two dials if one desires to keep the same or similar chance of project success (it's possible that both of the other two dials might be adjusted to ensure a chance of success).

One also must recognize that there are inherent, reasonable limits to the adjustments of any dial. If leadership wants the improvement initiative to be successfully done faster

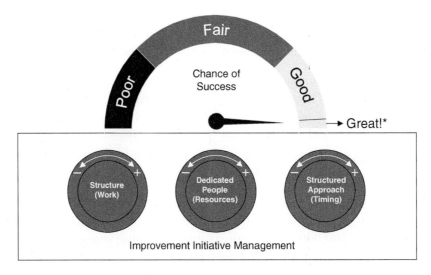

*The authors consider this 100 percent of the dedicated people following *The Proven Path* as a step-by-step structured approach and using *The Oliver Wight Class A Standard for Business Excellence* as a focused structure as guidance.

Figure 20.6   The Working Gears of a Successful MPS Implementation

(turning the *timing* dial clockwise in the "+" direction), then they must either add more *resources* (+) or reduce the scope of *work* (−) or a combination of the two.

If the leadership team wishes to increase the scope of *work* (+), then they must either add more *resources* (+) to keep the *timing* the same or extend the *timing* (+) to do the project with the same *resources*, or a combination of the two. Finally, if the leadership team wants to increase the *resources* (+) on the initiative, the *timing* may be reduced (−), or the scope of *work* may be increased (+), or a combination of the two.

In Chapters 18–20, the authors defined the *work* of implementing master planning and scheduling as a constant using *The Class A Standard structure*. The authors have also defined the *timing* of a master planning and scheduling implementation as a constant through the step-by-step process as defined by *The Proven Path structured approach*, fixed at about nine months (again, completing it earlier is typically difficult and stretching the project out too far introduces other risks of failure).

Therefore, leadership and the steering team must manage the resources gear accordingly to complete the ideal scope of work in the ideal timeframe and provide the greatest chance of success. *This is the right way to do it!*

Managing Work, Timing, and Resources for a Successful Master Planning and Scheduling Implementation

The wrong approach, when *planning* for the improvement initiative, is to accept resources as fixed and constant. This may lead to either the time dial being increased, resulting in a longer improvement initiative than originally planned, or the work dial being decreased, increasing the risk of a complete and unsuccessful improvement initiative. Developing a proper benefit/cost justification can put the resource issue into clearer focus.

Even though managing and adjusting the *resources* dial is the recommended path forward, management does have the right and capability to adjust *work* and *timing* dials at some risk. The message here is that during a master planning and scheduling implementation, work scope, initiative timing, and available resources must be managed on a weekly basis (it is recommended that the master planning and scheduling team leads meet at least weekly).

It is also recommended that the supply chain management improvement initiative team meet at least weekly (MPS team meets prior to SCM weekly team review). These implementation reviews should have as their objective that of securing what each team member needs to be successful, *not* wasting everyone's time listening to status updates.

Concluding this chapter on implementation, some people ask about existing Class A companies. Did they all do it in nine months? *Certainly not!* Many of them took much longer (a few in less than nine months), because their implementations were in the late 1970s through 2000. In those days, the body of knowledge about how to implement was more limited and technology support was also more limited.

However, in the twenty-first century, more and more companies have achieved Class A MPS results in less than one year. We think there's a form of learning curve here. As the number of successful MPS implementations doubles (or even triples), it takes half the time to successfully implement master planning and scheduling. Several companies these days are saying, *"Just do it and do it right the first time!"*

A Book Summary

Let's conclude the 20 chapters of this book with a look at some down-to-earth principles that may be helpful during a company's journey to Class A. Oliver Wight Principals have practiced these *eight principles* since the founding of the company some 50 years ago (it's actually *seven original principles* since the founding of the Oliver Companies—the last principle was added several years after the original seven principles were identified).

These principles have not only guided Oliver Wight Principals to successful implementations as users and through rewarding careers in educating and coaching thousands of companies to Class A status and results in business excellence but have also had a never-ending effect on the people who work in those Class A companies (and probably many people who weren't fortunate enough to be part of a Class A implementation, but maybe achieved Class B or even Class C status and results). Figure 20.7 on the following page is a list of the *eight principles*, not in any particular order of importance (all *eight principles* are equally important).

Additional principles offered by this book's authors may include the following: (1) there is a respect for the company and its business; (2) each associate cares not only for the company's customers, but also for the company's all-important suppliers; (3) company associates care for each other and they cover each other's back as necessary (it's a family, etc.); (4) company associates continue to earn the right to be part of the company's culture and legacy; and (5) there is no fear of failure, as failure in one component can present an opportunity for success in another component or even the entire initiative.

This book's reader most likely can add other principles that might be beneficial to include in their company's master planning and scheduling improvement initiative charter. The authors have used the Oliver Wight eight principles along with the five additional principles added in these closing remarks and called upon some of their past experiences to create the *magic dozen (principles)* that have been added to the back cover of this book.

Oliver Wight Principals' Principles

A Passion for Our Customers' Success (Customers are Reason for Business*)

Respect for the Individual (Everyone's Opinion Counts*)

Class A in Everything We Do (Don't Settle for Second Best*)

Commitment to Teamwork (Team Consensus Betters Individual Opinion*)

Trust Among All Members of Our Team (Need We Say More*)

Open and Honest Communication (Tell Yourself the Truth as You Know It*)

Enthusiasm for Our Mission (Make the Class A Journey One to Remember*)

Do What You Say You're Going to Do (Secret to Business Success*)

---

*Authors' Additional Comments to the Key Principles in the Parenthesis

Figure 20.7   Principles to Practice During a Class A Implementation

As the reader nears the conclusion of this final chapter, the authors encourage him or her to put into practice all these principles during their Class A improvement implementation. By doing so, the company's improvement teams will find their efforts more rewarding as well as feeling a greater sense of accomplishment for the company's customers, stakeholders, leadership, management, and co-workers (the authors' experience from the 50 years or so that Oliver Wight Principals have worked with companies pursuing Class A goals and results).

Our concluding comments are to convey to all those who find themselves in the master planning and scheduling (MPS) profession and possibly part of a master planning and scheduling (MPS) improvement initiative best wishes for a successful Class A career and implementation. Both feats (an MPS career and MPS Class A implementation) are noteworthy accomplishments!

Epilogue

Order from Chaos

May the best day of your past be the worst day of your future.

This book began with a parable about a manufacturing company whose production floor on the last business day of the month was out of control. Partially completed products waited on skids for delayed material. Frustration and frayed nerves were commonplace among managers and associates.

Customers were calling to complain about late shipments. Expediters ran around the plant with hot sheets. Instead of being channeled into problem resolution and customer-oriented production, the company's energy was being dissipated through finger pointing and internal conflict.

"Is this the manufacturer from hell?" some might ask. Hardly! It is still symptomatic of too many manufacturing situations today. Hopefully, this nightmarish parable will become a quaint fairy tale, an artifact of the industrial past, as master planning and scheduling practices become more professional and as those practices diffuse through the industry. In the case of our fictional company, we can hypothesize that change will eventually come because the company could not survive and prosper if it did not.

The Place: The executive vice president's office in a typical North American manufacturing company

The Time: 9:00 A.M.

The Date: The first day of a new month

Present: The plant manager, the sales and marketing director, the manufacturing vice president, the supply chain management director, the master supply planner, the master supply scheduler, and the executive vice president. "I've had enough of this!" exclaimed the executive vice president. "And I hope that you've had enough of it, too. I am sick and tired of what we went through the other day. What we have on our hands is a situation in which we are incurring higher costs, production disruptions, and frayed nerves."

The others in the room nodded their agreement. "Worse, there seem to be no winners for all this trouble on our manufacturing floor. Everyone is the loser!"

"It's starting to hurt us in the field, too," the sales and marketing director interjected. "I got a call from one of our better Florida accounts warning me that one more late shipment and they'll find a new supplier."

"I agree," said the manufacturing vice president. "Something has to change. Our people on the line are tired of every week and every month being a race against the clock, of stealing materials from one order to take care of another. It's getting hard to hold on to our best people and harder to motivate the rest."

"Then change is the thing, isn't it?" said the supply chain management director along with a node from the plant manager. "Something has to change. Something fundamental. We need to see a change in the way our plant looks and acts. No more queues, no more hot lists, no more stockouts or late deliveries. It's all of our responsibility to ensure that our united team makes it happen."

Few companies undertake fundamental change as a natural step in the road to progress. It usually takes some extraordinary event, such as the threat of failure, to motivate the leadership to undertake a serious campaign of change.

Ford Motor Company and Xerox Corporation underwent a course of internally generated change in the period 1978–1983 because both sensed that they were in a serious downward trajectory in their respective industries. General Motors, IBM, and DEC faced the same stage of awareness and change in the mid-1990s. Not to be outdone (tongue in cheek), Apple, Amazon, and Best Buy saw and implemented new ways of doing business in the first two decades of this century.

And reacting to the 2020 COVID-19 pandemic, more companies have decided to change the way that they plan and control demand and supply in this twenty-first century.

Our fictional company appears to have reached the point where something like a deathbed conversion is taking place with respect to its managing demand and supply.

If we were to fast-forward in time, we might see this company entering that period of self-assessment that leads to the effective implementation of a master planning and scheduling program, as laid out in this book. Over a period of 6 to 12 months, the company would develop the internal competencies and sets of guidelines that make a full changeover to master planning and scheduling possible.

From that point, through a period of adjustment and improvement, the company would experience steady incremental increases in manufacturing effectiveness and efficiency as measured by the absence of production-floor disruptions, delayed shipments, hot lists, past dues, the dreaded end-of-the-month crunch, and the other ills that motivated the supply chain management director and plant manager to recommend a course of change.

The ills of the past would eventually be replaced by the rewards that accrue to a Class A Business Excellence company, the foremost of these being measurable improvements in company's profits and associates' morale and high levels of customer satisfaction.

People and Process and Profession

*Success is not guaranteed, but **opportunity** in supply chain management is;
the opportunities will just be different than they were in the past decade or so!*

*Remembering the Past, but not obsessed with it!
Living the Present, but not stuck on it!
Realizing the Future, but not comfortable with it!*

The authors began Chapter 14 of this book by comparing a business to an army on the battlefield. On the battlefield, armies that fail to coordinate the movement of infantry with support from artillery, air, sea, and armor typically are defeated by opponents whose main force and support functions operate as one. In business, the company whose sales force (demand management) is out booking orders and promising delivery dates without the concurrence of manufacturing (supply management), design/engineering (product management), and cost accounting (financial management) is likewise imperiled.

Coordination among business functions does not just happen; it needs a formal mechanism to ensure that it occurs. For most Class A companies, that mechanism is integrated business planning (IBP) and master planning and scheduling (MPS).

Integrated business planning is a formal process for managing aggregate change, integrating product, demand, supply, and financial plans for the next 24 to 36+ months and ensuring that the business strategy is being deployed, as described in Chapters 14–17 of this master planning and scheduling book. Master planning and scheduling is a formal process for managing detailed mix-level change related to product, demand, and supply as described in Chapters 2–12 of this book.

Chapter 1 sets the stage for designing and implementing a master planning and scheduling improvement initiative, while Chapters 18–20 educate and coach the reader on how to do just that, implement an effective and efficient master planning and scheduling process, run by skilled and knowledgeable people and supported by technology. As professional supply chain management personnel will tell you, none of this is possible without data integrity, which is addressed in Chapter 13.

Finally, the Epilogue describes how it feels when a fictitious manufacturing company moves from a chaotic environment to a well-managed, best-practice one. There's something to be said about running and/or working in a Class A company!

WHY THESE FINAL THOUGHTS NEEDED TO BE WRITTEN IN THE FOURTH EDITION OF THIS MPS BOOK

With all that has been said in the previous pages of this book behind us, the authors' attention is now turned to the future of master planning and scheduling, focusing on the *people and process and profession*. The comments that follow are the authors' opinions based on what they see happening around them every day. So, what is going on around us today?

Well, to start that conversation, all of us are somewhat married to our smartphones (a recent statement heard by one author was that the smartphone is now people's number-one possession, replacing the automobile as well as the refrigerator). If we're *not* engaged with someone verbally through our smartphone, we are most likely communicating with others via e-mail, text, or web-based virtual meetings. To some, face-to-face meetings are a thing of the past, especially in the work environment.

That was all true even before the coronavirus pandemic of 2020 hit. As of the writing of this master planning and scheduling book revision, many people in the workforce are working remotely and physical interaction is limited to that which is absolutely necessary.

Over many years, supply chain management and master planning and scheduling professionals worked at their company's facility, whether that be a mill, factory, plant, distribution center, and so forth. In fact, these supply chain professionals were encouraged to get out on the production floor where the action was happening; don't be caught sitting at your desk in an office or a cubical. That way of working, my friends, is changing or, better said, has changed!

To set the stage for the next 20 years or so, let's look back at the past 70 years, breaking them down into the 50 years preceding the year 2000, followed by the 20 years from year 2000 through 2020. Since this book is based on the master planning and scheduling people and process and profession, we will concentrate our discussion on what supply chain management (SCM) and master planning and scheduling (MPS) innovations came onto the scene through these important years and decades.

PLANNING ADVANCEMENTS IN THE LAST 50 YEARS OF THE PAST CENTURY

What did we ever do without computers? That's a question today that many people might ask. The older generation might ask, "How did Mom and Pop ever survive without a television, refrigerator, microware, and so forth?" The answer is, "If you don't know about them, you don't know about them! You just use what's available to you. But many of us dream about using something that seems just out-of-reach."

Those dreamers did a great deal for the supply chain management profession over the past 70 years. In the 1950s, a dreamer asked why products and materials were not available when they were needed for sale or to build something. They thought, *there must be a better way of doing what needs to be done (planning in the manufacturing world) than the way we are currently doing it.*

Finance and payroll seem to be using that thing called a computer to help in their world—*why not me in my world?* Enter the order point and reorder point systems (see Figure FT.1).

Reorder point systems were coupled with work order *launch and expedite* methods within the planning and control functions. Although computer software support was limited for inventory planning and the production control planner, hope was on the horizon. During the 1960s, Oliver Wight and a couple of friends (namely Joe Orlicky and George Plossl) thought of and defined a way to use the computer and bill-of-material to do time-phased material planning. Orlicky's book on material requirements planning (little mrp) was published in 1975.[1]

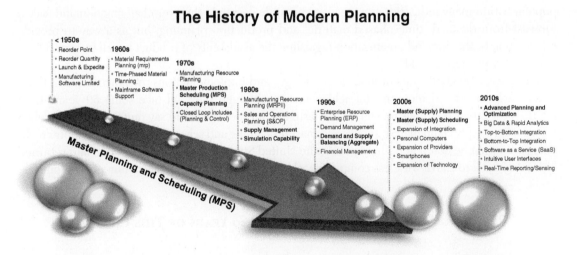

The History of Modern Planning

Figure FT.1   Seventy Years of Supply Chain Planning and Control

---

[1] Joseph Orlicky, *Material Requirements Planning* (New York: McGraw-Hill Book Company, 1975).

It didn't stop there. During the 1970s, material requirements planning expanded to manufacturing resource planning (big MRP), which included not only material planning and control, but capacity planning and control (*the big breakthrough, as was the next event*).

During the mid- to late 1970s, although traction was not really realized until the 1980s, a small company in the southeastern United States designed and commenced selling software that was called *master production scheduling* (and the first original use of the acronym MPS). This process sat/sits between the demand (sales) forecasting process and the material requirements planning process. *The MPS process introduced the first thought that demand and supply can and should be uncoupled; a company can sell product at a different rate than it builds product; and that company can also choose to build product at a different rate than it sells product!*

Another breakthrough occurred in the 1980s that greatly affected the supply chain management and master scheduling professions; that breakthrough was the Oliver Wight Company's pioneering development of the sales and operations planning process, originally called *marketing manufacturing resource planning*, or MMRP. However, four-letter acronyms such as MMRP were not in style then, so S&OP was accepted throughout industry. As we neared the end of the 1980s, simulations using computer technology were getting some press, along with the writing of the *first definitive book covering the subject of master scheduling, published in 1994.*[2]

Quite a bit happened in the 1990s. Besides the release of the master scheduling book (now in its 27+-year history through four editions, including this one), along came enterprise resource planning (ERP), demand management, improvement in demand and supply balancing at the aggregate level, and enhanced financial management. Additionally, master scheduling was becoming more popular within many industries as a means to not only decouple the ever-changing demand (sales) forecast from detailed, time-phased material and production planning, but as a way to provide information to the demand organization regarding the availability of product to sell (referred to as available-to-promise or ATP).

Those were 50 good years of innovation, design, and implementations. Advancements in those years were considered monumental achievements, although they did take some 50 years. During the next 20 years, things moved a little faster, or maybe we should say quite a bit faster, when referencing supply chain management's and master planning and scheduling's use of computer technology. It might be noted here that in 1969, the United States put a man on the moon and returned him safely back to Earth with less computer technology than we have today in our smartphones!

PLANNING ADVANCEMENTS IN THE PAST 20 YEARS OF THIS CENTURY

Continuing our discussion regarding past supply chain management and master planning and scheduling people behaviors, business processes, technology enhancements, and data integrity improvements, we look at the past 20 years through a careful, observant eye as to what was

[2] John F. Proud, *Master Scheduling—A Practical Guide to Competitive Manufacturing* (New York: John Wiley & Sons, 1994).

happening and at what speed it was happening. From the 2000s through the 2010s, we saw master planning and scheduling (a new, better reference for the acronym MPS) come to the forefront along with an expansion of functional and system integration, the use of personal computers and of smartphones, and the expansion of technology throughout the world.

The first decade of the twenty-first century set the stage for what was about to happen in the second decade of the twenty-first century. Planning, both at the aggregate level and detailed level, got a facelift. With computer technology moving at jet engine speed (prior years had moved at propeller and automobile speeds), advanced planning and optimization systems entered the supply chain management arena.

New to the scene was that of big data, rapid analysis, top-to-bottom automated integration, bottom-to-top automated integration, side-to-side integration, and real-time reporting. And that wasn't all; software was being offered as a service, intuitive user interfaces were being offered, and information/data sensing became more popular. Again, all this was done at jet engine speed and the world of supply chain management (SCM) and master planning and scheduling (MPS) was truly changing, or certainly about to change, in many manufacturing businesses!

With that said, let's take a closer look at some additional advancements in SCM and MPS during the past couple of decades, especially the last decade. Remember, all that follows was/is happening at jet engine speeds!

A Look at Master Planning and Scheduling in the Past Two Decades

Here are a few examples of where technology enhancements in supply chain management and master planning and scheduling happened just yesterday, are happening today, and may be happening in the future. This is only a selected few, but it's a start.

The authors know that even if you read this book the day it is published, some of this information will be dated. With that risk, we still want to expose the reader to some of the technology that is available today (and was available in the past decade or so). These technology advancements are not limited to material planning, capacity planning, production scheduling, and so forth, but are geared directly to master planning and scheduling (MPS) as well as integrated business planning (IBP).

Raw Data

Historically, enterprise resource planning (ERP) solutions have been very high-touch, requiring workers to manually enter information regarding inventory, bills-of-material, operational routings, work authorizations, and customer shipments. Workers had to enter almost everything that they did in order to provide accurate information to the planning, control, and execution systems to ensure that a valid plan (realistic and achievable) was in place. Those plans provided operational direction to meet customer demand in the most economical way possible and at the same time provided visibility to cross-functional leaders.

The manual entry of this data did or can create latency and accuracy issues in the ERP system. If the data in the ERP system is not accurate, then the plans are invalid, which means that operations is now working on the wrong items and customer service and profitability can or will be adversely affected.

If the worker mistakenly enters the wrong information or enters the right information but uses the wrong transaction type, again an invalid schedule may be created, and if so, the *churn* starts. In each case the ERP system has bad data and will not accurately reflect what the real customer needs are or what the real supply requirements are and most likely will drive inefficiencies.

A new generation of solutions is emerging that applies sensor fusion technology to automatically provide accurate inventory, bills-of-material, operational routings and movement of material through the manufacturing process, customer shipments, and even delivery to the customer. That is, rather than having the human workers manually enter this information into the ERP system, the data is collected and entered by sensor fusion technology. Sensor fusion technology includes radio-frequency identification (RFID) tags, computer vision, weight sensors, and many other data-collecting sensor technologies.

This solution provides complete real-time visibility into the operation, enabling real-time accurate data to support the ERP system with valid plans at a low cost. With these solutions, operational leaders receive real-time alerts and notifications when the plan is out of balance (not valid) so that proper corrective action can be taken. Using this technology, there is confidence in the plan and people can focus on its execution.

Sensor fusion technology can help in the following areas to significantly improve data accuracy and provide needed information in order to have a valid plan (realistic and achievable).[3]

Planning Data

- **Scrap Percentage:** *What was the percent of scrap on the last order compared to the scrap percent in the ERP system?* The addition of scrap factors into the ERP system addresses the reality of scrap in the manufacturing environment, but if it is not monitored regularly, the real amount of scrap is not put in the system.

- If manufacturing solves the problem, the system needs to be kept up to date. This allows exception-driven action messages to be sent to the supply planner and/or scheduler every time a supply order is run so that the scrap factor can be analyzed.

- **Rework Percentage:** *What was the percent of rework on the last order as compared to the expected rework on file?* Like scrap, rework has to be analyzed.

- **Lead Time:** *What was the actual lead time compared to the planned lead time in the ERP system?* One would not expect them to be the same because from the time the supply order

---

[3] James G. Correll, Lloyd Snowden, and James Bentzley, *Supercharged Supply Chains* (Hoboken, NJ: John Wiley & Sons, 2021). (Slightly modified in order to tie and support these MPS Final Thoughts.)

was/is released, the timing of the supply order can be changed either to an expedite or de-expedite status in the ERP system (chances are the times are somewhat close).

- If there is a large variation or consistent variations are occurring, these variations and the cause of the variations need to be investigated. It is not unusual for planners and/or schedulers to perform root cause analysis to identify the real problem or problems (just not the symptom or symptoms of each problem).

Inventory Records

- ***Receiving into a Facility:*** Raw materials and other inventory are tagged and onboarded into the system, enabling it to be tracked throughout its lifecycle. The RFID tags could be put on at the supplier and on-time shipment and transportation can be tracked.

- ***Receiving into a Specific Location:*** Once the product is received and put into a receiving location, it then goes into a specific location such a 12-6-B-C (aisle 12, rack 6, height B, slot C), which is used to quickly find the product.

- ***Stock-to-Stock Transfers:*** If stock has to be moved to another location, the new location is automatically updated.

- ***Issuing from a Specific Location to a Work Order:*** When the product is taken from the location, it is automatically issued to a work order in the ERP system.

- ***Back Flushing:*** Back flushing at each station on the line, instead of the end of the line, is done quickly and efficiently.

- ***Scrapped Items on a Work Order:*** Once a work order is released to manufacturing, losses can occur because some of the product can be scrapped, which should be recorded in the system but often is not done! As soon as the product is moved to the next operation, a signal is sent that the quantity isn't correct, and the work order quantity can be immediately adjusted.

- ***Issued to Work Order:*** When material for a work order is pulled, the material is automatically scanned and checked against the bill-of-material to see if all the raw materials and components including the correct quantity have been issued. An automatic issue does or can occur. A highlighted deficiency report is or can be generated and sent to the supply planner and/or scheduler for action to resolve the issue now and prevent future problems.

- ***Completed Work Order:*** Is everything there that needs to be there? What is missing? When an order or product is completed, scanning the item determines if everything according to the bill-of-material is present and/or if anything additional is present. This ensures product conformance and allows the supply planner and/or scheduler to investigate issues at the moment identified.

Operational Routings

- **Work Location:** Is the work location (also referred to as work center) that was scanned the same as the work location on the operational routing? An example: One company's general manager was pushing to get the productivity up when through an audit found out that many times jobs were being run on alternate machines, lowering the productivity.

- A nine-point improvement in productivity was achieved when capacity planning was put into place and permission to run on an alternate machine was acquired from industrial engineering. By the way, the on-time delivery in this company example went from 31 percent to 97 percent.

- **Setup/Run Time:** Was the setup time reported within a preestablished tolerance? Reported through a cell phone, the production supervisors can immediately see if the time spent was within the tolerance, which gives them an opportunity to immediately talk to the operator to get at the root cause of any problem so that an identified problem can be resolved quickly.

- **Operation Sequence:** Was the operation sequence in which the work was run the sequence defined in the routing on file? This can be a great opportunity to ensure the quality of the work. Often, the defined operation sequence is changed because it delivers a higher-quality product, but no one takes the time to change the operation routing.

Work Authorization Tracking by Operation

- **Scrap:** *Was the scrap reported the same as the actual count?* This gives the supply planner and/or supply scheduler the opportunity to see problems coming if large quantities of scrap on supply orders aren't reported. The supply planner and/or supply scheduler can then start another supply order at lead time to avoid shortages due to the product scrappage.

- **Rework:** *Was the rework reported the same as the actual count?* When rework is identified, it can be scheduled so that the missing items can be scheduled for the reworked item in order to satisfy the demand for the rework item or items.

- **On-Time Release:** *Was the supply order released on time?* Ninety-five percent of the supply orders need to be released on time if purchasing and manufacturing are to meet their due dates. If *on-time release* is *not* occurring, the root cause is investigated.

- **On-Time Operation Started/Completed:** *Was the operation started/completed on time?* This gives the production supervisor real-time information to solve potential missed order due dates.

- **On-Time Order Completion:** *Was the order completed on time?* On-time order completion is what ERP systems rely on. Monitoring the operation due dates is what ensures on-time order completion.

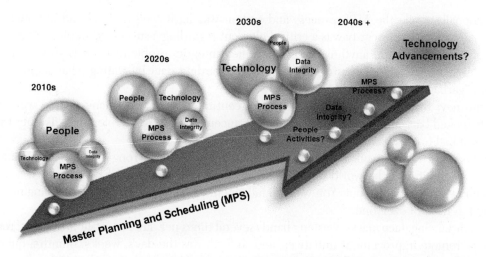

Figure FT.2   Master Planning and Scheduling in the Next Two Decades

- ***Time Constraint Alert:*** If there is a time constraint on an operation, an alert is/can be sent to notify those with a need to know that the operation time constraint is in jeopardy of being missed.

With all that said regarding the past 70 years, it's time to raise the high bar to rocket speed as we discuss the third decade of the twenty-first century (see Figure FT.2). Automation and technology advancements are *not* going to stop! In fact, most people believe that these technology advancements will be coming at us at an even faster pace than they came at us during the past couple of decades (take a breath, if you dare).

A Look at Supply Chain Management Today and Tomorrow (Emphasis on MPS)

Oliver Wight (the man) *educated and coached* (referred to as *trained and consulted* in the early years of inventory planning and production scheduling) that educated and trained people were the missing component in failed implementations. Ollie would say that it's not the computer and its functionality that caused the inventory planning and production scheduling implementation to go astray. It's the people who make any implementation successful and it's the people who cause any failed implementation. And for many years, Oliver Wight principals have educated and coached following Ollie's footprints.

However, the times, they are *a-changin'*, as the Bob Dylan song goes! During the 2010s through the 2020s, people remained the *heartbeat* of a supply chain management (SCM) system's implementation success, including master planning and scheduling (MPS). Tools and technology were important, but if the project team paid too much attention to the software itself or relied too heavily on the software to do the job, disastrous results were generally waiting in the wings.

Additionally, while the MPS process and system was fairly well defined and although most people knew that data integrity was a critical element regarding a successful implementation, *not* many of those people did anything about identified integrity problems. And ERP system users coined and commenced expressing their feelings regarding data by stating what seemed to be obvious, "garbage in, garbage out."

As the new third decade of the twenty-first century approached, many people working in industry looked back at a decade of successful advancements and profitable times. Twenty-twenty (2020) just had to be a banner year. *Oops!*

The year started out well, but soon something went awfully wrong—the novel coronavirus (SARS-CoV-2) hit, and the world found itself in a pandemic the likes of which few (if any) had ever seen or lived to talk about. You want to talk about a changing world; well, a changing world was right in front of everyone.

Social distancing, face masks, washing hands several times per day, stay-at-home orders, remote meetings, remote improvement initiatives, and so forth was the day's, week's, month's, quarter's, and year's agenda for everyone! Yes, Bob Dylan, times really were changing! *And the change was not and is not short-term.*

What was going to happen in the next decade was now right in front of many people, and certainly right in front of master planners and master schedulers. The movement to remote planning and scheduling was already underway, but now it was given a sense of urgency.

The outbreak of COVID-19 required a quick response to developing a vaccine to protect people from the deadly virus. The outbreak also highlighted the fact that the business processes required for a company to satisfy customer demand, while safely making money and a profit, were vulnerable when people did not attend to those business processes or were unable to perform the activities and tasks required to make those processes properly function.

An old, but sometimes treated as a new, problem had surfaced. That problem, witnessed by many, many people over many, many years, was that people were a key part of the equation. If one really thinks about it, many of the problems we see or hear about every day are caused by people, directly or indirectly.

Supply chain management and master planning and scheduling professionals have been taught for years to ask *why* five times when a problem arises so that the root cause of the problem can be identified and fixed. If this root cause analysis is not done or is done improperly, many fixes are directed at the symptoms of the problem and never really fix the real problem.

So, ask *why* five times as to the reason or reasons *why* customers weren't buying product, manufacturers weren't making product, suppliers weren't shipping product, planners weren't ordering materials, schedulers weren't scheduling production, and so forth when these were not occurring during the pandemic (or for at least the first few months).

Chances are that *people* were in the equation somewhere (people get sick, people have injuries, people lack discipline, people miss work). Oh, by the way, *machines* don't get sick, machines don't have injuries, machines don't lack discipline, and machines don't miss work!

The point being made here is that the root cause of many supply chain management and master planning and scheduling problems is simply *people being in the equation*. There can be direct causes—lack of discipline, lack of knowledge, or even blatant sabotage—or indirect causes like normal human error, even with the best of intentions.

Take, for instance, the previous section, which discussed record accuracy and current advancements in that arena. How does a company's item or material master get messed up or corrupted with bad data? A person generally is responsible to input master and supporting parameter data. How does a company's bill-of-material get messed up? A person is generally responsible to input the bill's items, unit of measures, quantities, and so on.

How does an operational routing get messed up? A person is generally responsible to input the routing's operation number, work location, setup time, operation time, and so on. How does the work location, work center, or production line data get messed up? Many times, a person is responsible to input operation start, operation completion, available capacity, load factors, and so on.

Finally, how do the inventory records get messed up? Well, again, *people* are responsible for processing receiving transactions, picking transactions, transfer transactions, and so on in many companies, but not all. Some companies have totally automated the inventory planning, storage, movement, housekeeping, and security of their warehouse(s) and distribution center(s); *no people, just machines* (robots, computer- or technology-controlled lift trucks or straddle trucks, etc.).

Some of these companies have completely automated the movement of inventory (to and from their locations). Good examples of this automation are up-to-date, sophisticated warehouse piers and the movement (unloading, storing, picking, loading) of containers off and on marine vessels.

Do you think those warehouse piers have an inventory record accuracy problem? *Probably not!* Why? *Because they removed people from the equation.* In other words, these companies now have machines doing the tasks that people once did.

Can and/or does this change in a distribution network apply or work in the manufacturing environment? And, more importantly, can it or does it have application in the master planning and scheduling world of material planning, capacity planning, and production scheduling?

Figure FT.2 on page 791 shows technology becoming a bigger and bigger piece of supply chain management and master planning and scheduling in the next decade as well as the one following that third decade. And highly accurate data integrity is coming right along with that technology advancement.

Robots don't think (at least, not today); computers and robots take large volumes of data, process it very quickly, and make decisions based on its programming and findings. Additionally, computers and robots don't really have a vision of the future (at least, not today); again, computers and robots take large volumes of data, process it very quickly, and visualize the future based on the past and what it knows regarding the future.

Yes, people are still in the equation; it's people who are doing the machine/software/robot design and programming (at least, today). Notice that new professions related to supply chain management and master planning and scheduling are being created every day at rocket speeds!

ANTICIPATED TECHNOLOGY ADVANCEMENTS IN THE
NEXT 10 TO 20 YEARS

Blockchain

Blockchain is a way of validating, recording, and distributing records of transactions across a decentralized network of databases. Because the transactions are duplicated and stored by independent participants across the network, it makes it nearly impossible to falsify or change records of transactions.

Blockchain technology is another potential driver of data accuracy across the supply chain, including upstream to suppliers and downstream to the end consumer. This technology is most widely known for its use with cryptocurrencies, such as Bitcoin. The strength of the technology is due to its base nature; it is essentially a distributed ledger of data. This provides for some real benefits within the supply chain such as:[4]

- **Transparency:** All partners across the supply chain will have a common picture.

- **Truth:** By its distributed nature, there will be only one set of numbers, since every transaction must pass stringent approvals as set by the participants.

- **Traceability:** Supply chains that require lot and batch traceability will benefit by recording the full history of every transaction, from raw material at the country and supplier of origin through the finished product at the end consumer.

- **Real-Time Monitoring:** Partners can monitor the real-time status of goods moving through the supply chain to address issues faster when there are still multiple courses of action available to fix them.

- **Insights:** Availability of information from the end of the supply chain, like changes in demand, can be leveraged immediately at the beginning of the supply chain to better balance demand and supply.

At the time of this publication, data standards are still being developed to support the use of this technology within the supply chain, but the benefits look incredibly promising. As blockchain technology expands, its usefulness in supply chain management and master planning and scheduling will surely be affected.

Let's say it again, *times are a-changin'!* What else is going on within the supply chain management and master planning and scheduling world? Meet *Another Interesting* thought, *Artificial Intelligence*.

---

[4] James G. Correll, Lloyd Snowden, and James Bentzley, *Supercharged Supply Chains* (Hoboken, NJ: John Wiley & Sons, 2021). (Slightly modified in order to tie and support these MPS Final Thoughts.)

The Role of Artificial Intelligence in Supply Chain Management in the 2020s and 2030s

Artificial intelligence (AI) exists in several forms. For over 50 years, planning and scheduling systems have existed and attempted to solve material shortage and capacity overload/underload problems. This is a form of artificial intelligence. Most of these planning and scheduling systems used *if/then* logic, also called *rules-based* logic.

For example, if the required capacity exceeds the planned capacity, then first look at using overtime (within the constraints of some rules like no more than 10 percent, no more than two weekends in the summer, and so on). If that does not solve the problem, the system then looks to see if the work can be done on an alternate work center that might have available capacity. Dependent upon the data and programmed system logic, the item under analysis is rescheduled to where it fits within the planned capacity.

These capacity planning and scheduling systems are generally called *finite loaders*. One of the biggest problems through the past years with *finite loading or finite scheduling systems* is that when the system's logic starts to reschedule, it either has to move the load into a future time period or push it back into a previous time period.

This movement was done without people's input at the time; it was all based on previous input and system logic. Remember Oliver Wight's concern? Well, Ollie was on record saying that it generally wasn't the system, but the uneducated and untrained people in the equation. And he was right all those years ago!

Fast-forward 50 years. System technology has certainly come a long way. We're not even sure what the military technology looks like; it's probably 10–20 years ahead in technology advancements than our master planning and scheduling computer technology. However, through the past 50 years, one thing has remained constant: people remain in the equation and supply chain management (SCM) and master planning and scheduling (MPS) problems are still contributed to by uneducated and untrained people!

What if the system/machine was taught today's SCM/MPS thinking and it made decisions using today's SCM/MPS thinking; would a company really need people in the supply chain management (SCM) and master planning and scheduling (MPS) function? *In time, the answer will likely be no!* But how is this going to occur? The answer to this question is the topic of the next section, but let's first complete our short discussion regarding artificial intelligence.

A newer form of artificial intelligence includes neural nets, deep learning, and machine learning. These types of artificial intelligence work quite differently from if/then, rules-based logic. Basically, they are similar to how human brains work. This means they need a good deal of training. For simplicity, these will be referred to as neural net AI. This training comes in two forms: supervised and unsupervised.

Unsupervised learning is where the AI algorithm learns on its own. This works, for example, when an AI algorithm learns to play a game such as *Go*. Once the rules of the game are put into the algorithm, the machine tries something and, using the rules of the game, can determine on its own whether what it tried was successful or not. Doing this over and over gradually trains the algorithm, and computers are capable doing this type of training millions or billions of times.

Supervised learning requires outside help. For example, an image recognition AI algorithm needs to know if the picture is, for example, a tiger or not a tiger. It cannot learn this on its own. Instead, it needs to be fed labeled pictures of tigers and labeled pictures that are not tigers. After being fed millions of pictures of tigers and not tigers, the algorithm is capable of determining if a picture is a tiger or not. This tiger example is a simple illustration intended to explain the concept; actual image recognition AI algorithms are more general and are not restricted to one type of image.

With that as background, will neural net AI provide significant benefits to master planning and scheduling systems? Possibly, but some fairly serious limitations exist at the current time. One concern is the massive amount of data required for training.

Consider, for example, a neural net AI algorithm designed to automatically handle exception-driven action messages recommending that a supply order (i.e., an MPS firm planned order) be rescheduled to an earlier date. If the item is a manufactured item, how many remaining operations need to be completed? How long will they take? Can the work be done on other equipment? Is there available capacity at an earlier date? Is there move and queue time that can be compressed? Are other supply orders also having their move and queue times compressed? Are there limitations in skilled operators? The list of questions goes on and on.

The combinations of all these variables becomes a large number. For the algorithm to learn what to do, it would need to be exposed to quite a few of these different combinations of variables. At any one company, there just may not be enough training data. So the question is, can we use training data from many companies to train this exception-driven action message AI algorithm?

Possibly, but the situations in the companies would need to be similar. For example, one company might operate on small margins, and so its management might be willing to make a customer wait rather than incur a large cost to reschedule an order to an earlier date and therefore deliver a finished item earlier.

A second company may produce low-volume, high-margin products and they would be willing to incur higher costs to reschedule an order to an earlier date and therefore deliver a finished item to a customer earlier. Most people would not want to confuse this exception-driven action message AI algorithm with this type of inconsistent training data. Again, people and their thoughts are in the equation.

If, at some point in the future, these neural net AI algorithms are capable of learning from much smaller training sets of data, then it might be feasible for an algorithm to be trained on a single company's data. That assumes the company does not have too many different types of products—in this example, some high-margin products, some low-margin products, and so forth. It also assumes that the business has not changed in a significant way, so what a master planner and/or master scheduler would do to handle a situation in the past is also how they should handle it in the future.

For example, if a business has been disrupted by a new technology, such as electric cars, then the way someone dealt with a particular master planning and/or master scheduling situation in the past may not be how they would deal with it in the future. In such a case, it would be necessary to train the AI algorithm on the new realities of the business to prevent the algorithm from blindly taking actions that would be appropriate for internal combustion–powered cars but not appropriate for electric cars. *People, people, people!*

The basic issue is that judgment and creativity are things people do fairly well, and computers do not – at least, not *at this time*. So, if there is a significant amount of judgment and/or creativity in a situation, and there is not a huge amount of training data, then that is probably not a good opportunity for a neural net AI algorithm.

A more reasonable case could be made for categorizing abnormal demands using a neural net AI algorithm. Looking at a pattern of sales and identifying outliers is something that could possibly be similar across many companies and many products. Image recognition is a skill that deep learning neural nets have been proven to do well, and a sales pattern is a type of image. If/then rules-based logic has been used for years to identify outliers and so it would be interesting to see if an AI algorithm trained across many companies and many products would give better results.

A second basic issue with neural net AI algorithms is accountability. This is also an issue with if/then rules-based artificial intelligence. If it's not clear how an artificial intelligence algorithm came up with an action or recommendation, then it's hard to hold someone accountable for any problems that result. In some of the capacity planning and scheduling systems that use if/then rules-based logic, the results of the algorithm are displayed in a Gantt chart.

Someone (person) or something (machine) could look at the chart and decide if the plan looked good or not. While the logic used to come up with the plan was not visible, the plan itself was visible in a way that someone could either approve it or not.

For neural net AI algorithms, accountability is limiting their use in a number of situations. For example, an AI algorithm recommending parole for prisoners was accused of racial basis. The parolee's lawyer demanded to know how the algorithm came up with the parole ruling, insisting it was biased against his client. Since this is not visible within the algorithm, the parole board was unable to defend against the claim of bias.

Similarly, an artificial intelligence algorithm that recommends purchasing material, scheduling overtime, subcontracting work, and other expenditures of the company's money will need some way to justify the expense. *As mentioned before, many of these decisions involve elements of judgment and/or creativity, and so, because the algorithm is not infallible in these situations, some method of maintaining accountability will need to be developed.*

All this means that using artificial intelligence algorithms to manage a master planning and scheduling (MPS) system is mostly in the future (sometime later this decade or, at the latest, early next decade). However, progress has been rapid recently, so there may be some breakthroughs.

The general view within the AI community is that the current AI capabilities are fairly narrow and require a large amount of training data. These algorithms are quite effective in uses like image recognition, natural language processing (including sentiment analysis), and general pattern recognition such as what other items may interest a buyer, what other movies may be good recommendations for a viewer, what time of day to increase electrical power production, and so forth. So it's likely that these fairly narrow situations will dominate AI use in the near term of this third decade of the twenty-first century.

One obvious type of pattern analysis is demand or sales forecasting. There is a pattern of sales activity and a number of factors, some or all of which may have an effect on demand and/or sales. For example, what is the effect of price, different types of advertising, time of year, competitive prices and advertising, other products that cannibalize sales, and so on? If enough training data were available, a neural net AI algorithm should be able to make predictions accounting for all these different factors.

As mentioned earlier in the explanation of using a neural net AI algorithm to handle exception-driven action messages, the question is whether a company has enough suitable data for training (both the amount of data and data that is consistent and not confusing, such as grouping items that behave differently into the same training set) and if the results are visible enough to hold someone accountable if they choose to accept the AI forecast. It's important to note that such a demand forecast assumes that the future will be like the past, and in any demand forecast it's necessary to also consider why the future would be different from the past and apply these assumptions to the AI-generated forecast.[5]

MACHINES (COMPUTERS AND ROBOTS) DOING TASKS PEOPLE ONCE DID

There is really nothing new about what is going on during the latest technology explosion. People for hundreds and hundreds of years have looked for ways to get machines to do the activities and tasks that they had to do. Before the invention of the wheel, people tied a line or rope around a rock and dragged it to its destination using pure muscle power. When the wheel came along, this form of people power was no longer necessary. Of course, today machines are not only being used to do physical labor, but are being designed and programmed to do some of the thinking a person did or is now doing.

Again, for years and years, people have looked to have machines/computers do the tasks that people do! As time passes, machines (technology/robots/computers) have been improved to do just that (log splitter, microwave, automobile, elevator, medical implants, telephone, bicycle, wheel, driverless car, skiing tow rope, skiing lift chair, baby swing, art, scripture, and so forth). And what about chisel and hammer versus molds, manufacturing using all people versus people using machines versus only machines (lights out factory), communications via hard letters/notes versus wired devices versus wireless devices, and so forth.

---

[5] James G. Correll, Lloyd Snowden, and James Bentzley, *Supercharged Supply Chains* (Hoboken, NJ: John Wiley & Sons, 2021). (Slightly modified in order to tie and support these MPS Final Thoughts.)

Let's be sure we all understand that machines haven't replaced jobs in the past; what they did was replace activities and tasks that people once did with machine power! So, machines/computers/robots don't replace *people*; machines/computers/robots use technology advancements to do the *activities and tasks* people are doing today or that people used to do yesterday!

Moving our attention to the people within a service and/or manufacturing company, one might ask, "What are the people tasks being replaced by machines?" and "What companies are doing the people task replacements?" These certainly are very fair questions. Let's address each question, starting with functions that were once done by people, are no longer done by people, and where it all goes from here. Figure FT.3 shows a migration from bottom to top.

Manufacturing companies for years have experienced manufacturing operations on the manufacturing floor once done by people being replaced by machines, robots, and computer technology. This all started at the bottom (refer to Figure FT.3) and is working its way to the top, moving from the manufacturing floor to manufacturing supporting operations, activities, and tasks that people currently do.

Operations management, production scheduling, warehousing management, and logistics planning and scheduling and accounting functions are the next primary targets (and are already being done in many if not all of those areas). It is worth noting that this isn't entirely a serial process. Several tasks and activities in demand management, marketing, product/project management, and finance are performed by software in parallel.

Technology Doing Tasks People Once Did!*

Financial Management, Tactical and Strategic Planning	⬆?
Product Management, New Product Development	⬆
Demand Management, Master Planning, Selling, Marketing	⬆
Supply Management, Master Scheduling, Online Ordering, Transportation	⬆
Operations Management, Production, Warehousing, Logistics, Accounting	⬆

* It starts/started at the bottom and works its way up the chain

Figure FT.3 Technology Advancements' Impact on Master Planning and Scheduling

Following machine technology of operations management, production scheduling, warehouse operations, logistics planning, and scheduling and financial accounting, the automation movement will commence being done in supply management, master scheduling, online ordering, and transportation. This is not to imply that nothing has been done in these areas; *no, lots of work has already been implemented at many distribution and manufacturing sites*. Again, a good example is evident in many marine loading/unloading piers and warehouses.

Containers are offloaded from ships by computer automation, satellite-guided lift trucks move the containers to their stocking location, satellite-guided lift trucks find inventory in the warehouse, computer-programmed robots pick the inventory required, satellite-guided lift trucks move the inventory (the container) to the pier where the ship is anchored, and computer-controlled winches load the ship—*no people, just machines!*

There were people who dreamed that it could be done and guess what, it was done! Fear of failure could have prevented these types of operations from identifying the opportunity for success. Those who fear going too far will never know how far they can go!

Next in line is demand management, master planning, selling, and marketing (in fact, activities like statistical demand forecasting and sensing, algorithm-based targeted marketing/advertising on social media, etc. have been around for several years). Following these are product management and new product development (in fact, there are many current examples of drug discovery and development being driven by software algorithms). Finally, financial management and tactical and strategic planning is automated and/or heavily supported by technology.

Now, whether this progression is accurate or not, the point being made is that computer technology is advancing faster than any of us thought we would ever see. One might think, *Hey, progress doesn't stop to rest or take a breather!* No, progress just keeps moving forward.

Now let's turn our discussion to which businesses and/or companies are or will be participating in this movement. Figure FT.4 on page 801 takes a run at answering this question. Here it starts at the top and works its way to the bottom.

What this is saying is that the businesses and companies that have all the money and resources move first. These are the Fortune 100 to 500 companies that have the money, knowledge, and skill needed to make it happen. Following closely behind these business and companies is large companies with multiple facilities (competitive pressures push these businesses and companies in this direction in order to stay competitive).

Large businesses and companies are followed by medium-sized businesses and companies with multiple facilities (as well as medium-sized businesses and companies with a single facility), which are followed by small businesses and companies with a single facility as well as multiple facilities. Finally, sometime in the next decade, the very small businesses and companies will move forward with automation (the do-it-yourself mentality will be dead).

Technology advancements over the next decade or two will be at a speed never seen by those of us who, over the past several years, worked in various supply chain management and/or master planning and scheduling functions. However, supply chain management *functions*, as well as the

Technology Doing Master Planning and Scheduling*

| Fortune 100 to 500 Companies (Money, Knowledge, Skill) | ⬇ |

| Large Sized Companies with Multiple Facilities (Competitive Pressure) | ⬇ |

| Medium Sized Companies with Multiple Facilities / Single Facility (Slowly) | ⬇ |

| Small Sized Companies with Single Facility / Multiple Facilities (Some Day) | ⬇ |

| Mom and Pop Companies with Single Facility (Do It Yourself Mindset) | ⬇? |

* It starts/started at the top and works its way down the chain

Figure FT.4   Technology Advancements' Impact on Master Planning and Scheduling

master planning and scheduling *function* (although enhanced), will continue to exist in this new world of tomorrow.

People will continue to be involved in these functions, but they will be doing activities and tasks that many leaders and managers have not even thought of today. Repeating the words of the movie *Moneyball* (the story of turning the Oakland Athletics baseball team's complete failure to success on a very limited budget during the 1970s), "Real change comes from bottom up, not the top down! Machines calculate and people implement."

The message here is that people and their experiences and thinking were initially in the way; if you want to solve the problem, get those people out of the equation during the initial analysis! Again, this was taking place 40–50 years ago.

INTEGRATING THE SUPPLY CHAIN

In retail, a completely integrated supply chain would extend from point-of-sale at stores or e-commerce fulfillment centers back through the distribution network, manufacturing plants, and raw material suppliers. This is accomplished using distribution resource planning (DRP) at the store level and integrating with DRP at the retailer's distribution centers, the manufacturer's distribution centers, manufacturing plants, and suppliers. Distribution resource planning and its tie to master planning and scheduling was briefly discussed in Chapter 17.

Work with retailers and manufacturers has shown that this works well in improving customer service, reducing inventory, and increasing productivity. These improvements happen not only for the retailer but also help the manufacturer since manufacturers no longer must guess as to what the retailer is planning to buy from them.

One of the major obstacles to this integration has been the enormous stock-keeping unit (SKU) count at the retail store level. For example, a small retailer might have several hundred or thousand or million SKUs and a large retailer can have several hundred thousand or hundred million SKUs.

To effectively manage these data volumes, software needs to be designed to reduce the labor hours per SKU as well as the computer processing cost per SKU. The good news is that software does exist that has been tested and proven in both areas. Labor hours to run the system are at levels equal to or below the labor needed to run the prior generation of reorder point systems, and the computer processing costs are economical and, on a scale, similar to the cost to run the prior generation of reorder point systems.

However, it is worth mentioning that some retailers have attempted to use software designed for manufacturing distribution centers at the store level. The results have been mixed since this software was not designed for store-level data volumes and the resulting labor hours and computer hardware costs are high.[6]

MASTER PLANNING AND SCHEDULING: PEOPLE AND PROCESS AND PROFESSION

So, where does it all go from here? Prior to this book's chapter discussions, the authors opened by highlighting a few *initial thoughts* regarding supply chain management (SCM) as a complete planning, control, and execution function, including master planning and scheduling (MPS) as a subprocess of that SCM function. Brief discussions centered around *behaviors* (as in *people behaviors* within a SCM/MPS environment), *breakthroughs* (as in *breakthrough processes* within a SCM/MPS environment), and *business* (as in *business professional* within a SCM/MPS environment).

As stated in this book's initial thoughts, *there have been many changes in the supply chain management and master planning and scheduling world over the past 50 or so years*. For instance, people were originally left out of the equation when material requirements planning hit the manufacturing floor; inventory and production control people were told to just buy this MRP system and then sit back and watch all their material shortage problems disappear. Well, that didn't happen!

Over the next 10 years, production scheduling professionals were told to just buy this shop dispatching software, sit back, and watch all their missed production due dates disappear. Well, that didn't happen, again! And so, the story goes for many years thereafter.

---

[6] James G. Correll, Lloyd Snowden, and James Bentzley, *Supercharged Supply Chains* (Hoboken, NJ: John Wiley & Sons, 2021). (Slightly modified in order to tie and support these MPS Final Thoughts.)

Enter Oliver Wight and his team of professionals with the *recipe* and key ingredients that all manufacturing companies had to adopt in order to be successful: (1) plan material, (2) plan capacity, (3) control material, and (4) control capacity. In other words, just planning material using an MRP system was not enough.

Besides planning material, the company had to control the flow of that material. Along with materials, the company had to plan and control capacity and workflow. But you know what? Companies using MRP systems still weren't successful. They needed the secret (at the time) ingredient, and that secret ingredient was educated and trained *people*!

Without the workforce becoming *educated on the whys* and *trained on the hows* of an MRP system environment, there would be no success. And Ollie was so right; all one seemed to hear 50 years ago was that another company was failing as it tried to implement an MRP software package.

A couple of other problems that surfaced early in the last half-century or so was allowing the inaccurate forecast to drive the material requirements planning logic (prior to master scheduling being implemented), data integrity issues (prior to auditing and root cause analysis), and people *not* buying into the new formal way of doing business (Why change? We've always done it this way!). What was going on was described in Chapter 1 of this book, "Chaos in Manufacturing."

Oliver Wight and the Oliver Wight Companies set out to guide companies on a path so that they would truly experience the success that they had been promised by so many software companies. In the late 1970s a structure (the original Class A Checklist) and structured approach (the original Proven Path, called the Implementation Plan at the time) to something called Class A in inventory and production control was developed.

These two breakthroughs were coupled with education and training courses and programs to ensure that the people with a need to know *did know* what had to be done and *how* to do it. *And Ollie was right a second time; people started to hear (some 30–40 years ago) that some companies were actually reaching the lofty status of Class A (the initial ABCD Checklist was a list of 20 questions, some regarding people but many questions, referred to today as criteria, targeted at system software).*

The evolution of manufacturing support software continued with the release of manufacturing resource planning (MRP), manufacturing resource planning with financial interfaces (MRPII), and enterprise resource planning (ERP) packages. Again, all the implementations using these software systems relied heavily on *people*. Let's now fast-forward 20–30 years.

Technology has continued to advance and instead of the advancement curve being slow to rise, it seems that it is turning straight up. In other words, technology advancements in the supply chain management environment are becoming more relied on than ever before. Where *people* were the key ingredient to a successful master planning and scheduling implementation 20, 30, 40, and 50 years ago, *machines and computers and robots* are increasingly becoming the key to successful master planning and scheduling implementations today and will continue to be that key ingredient throughout this decade. *What Ollie saw 50 years ago has changed and will continue to change!* (Authors' opinion)

MULTITASKING SUPPORTED BY TECHNOLOGY IS THE NEW MASTER PLANNING AND SCHEDULING ROLE

Again, where does it all go from here? With regard to *people*, master planning and scheduling as we know it today and as we have known it for years is drastically changed. By 2025–2030, p*eople* will no longer be the key ingredient to successful MPS implementations (see Figure FT.5). *The new MPS key ingredient will be technology and machines/computers.*

If MPS is separated into master planning (referred to as level 2 planning, Figure 2.17a on page 69 and 2.18 on page 74) and master scheduling (level 3 planning, Figure 2.17b on page 72 and 2.18), turning the workload over to technology will be done first at the master scheduling level followed closely by the master planning level (refer to Figures FT.3 on page 799 and FT.4 on page 801). Ollie was right for the past 50–60 years, but *times are a-changing!* As Steve Jobs (of Apple Computer) once said, *"People who are crazy enough to think they can change the world, **DO**!"* And those technology designers are doing just that.

The computer doesn't think; it's not innovative! It only learns and doesn't forget what it's learned. It takes data, analyzes it, and comes to a conclusion. The computer is an extension of people and what people do.

So what happens to people when the machine/computer learns the activities and/or tasks that those people currently do? *People learn new things using their thinking and innovative skills and then the computer learns how to do these things. As time moves on, so does the innovative nature of people.*

Fast forward to 2025–2030. Where are the people associated with master planning and scheduling and what are these people doing? They're doing other and different activities than they did

This Century at a Glance
Master Planning and Scheduling

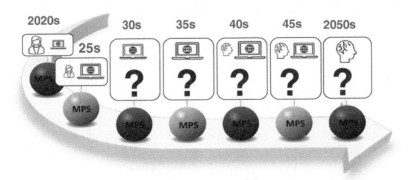

Figure FT.5   The Path Forward for Master Planning and Scheduling

in the past; what they're doing may be associated with master planning and scheduling or possibly some activity not even thought of today. Let's call those activities "Imlac" and "Zoolig" (these are nonsense terms the authors made up for effect and don't stand for anything, YET).

In other words, the authors are like everyone else; we don't know at this time, but if the reader ever hears or reads about something called "Imlac" or "Zoolig," remember that it was the authors (said with a smile on our faces) who created those noted activities! Another saying the authors picked up in their past is, "You can dance in the rain or watch (the rain) through the window!" The authors want all master planners and schedulers to dance in the rain to ensure that they all know how it feels.

What about the master planning and scheduling process? A review of all the chapter quotes paints a clear picture that the MPS process is here to stay.

Sayings like "If you don't know where you are going, any road will get you there"; "Success in business is easy if you do two things well: plan your work and work your plan"; "When you think you have all the answers, it may be time to reask the question"; "Without data you are just another person with an opinion"; "Rolling delivery promises gather no reorders"; "Don't change the schedule faster than the real world can respond"; and "If you always do what you've always done, you will always get what you've always gotten" indicate that an effective and efficient planning and scheduling process is essential to making it all work in manufacturing.

Finally, let's take a look at master planning and scheduling as a profession. Well, if the MPS process is alive and well, people are no longer the key ingredient to a successful MPS implementation, and technology is playing a much larger role in master planning and scheduling than ever before, the MPS profession as we know it today is gone.

However, the MPS profession as redefined is one of the places to be within a service and/or manufacturing operation. The age of scheduling specialists will continue to become history as we move through the next decade or so. People in supply chain management will increasingly communicate with technology and perhaps even think using mind-computer interfaces (if Elon Musk has his way).

Chances are that we are only scratching the surface. As professional supply chain management and master planning and scheduling people, we might ask, "What technological capability does the military have that hasn't surfaced in the service and manufacturing world yet?"

As stated earlier, there's a good chance that the military might be 10–20 years ahead of people on the street when it comes to technology advancements. Someday (10 years is *not* that far into the future), that technology will be available to master planning and scheduling personnel or computers or machines or robots.

WHY THESE FINAL THOUGHTS WERE NECESSARY TO PUT ON THE MPS TABLE

Repeating what was said earlier, the question put on the table is, where does it all go from here? Prior to this book's chapter discussions, the authors opened by highlighting a few initial thoughts regarding supply chain management (SCM) as a complete planning, control, and execution function, including master planning and scheduling (MPS) as a subprocess of that SCM function. Discussions centered around *behaviors* (as in *people behaviors* within a SCM/MPS environment), *breakthroughs* (as in *breakthrough processes* within a SCM/MPS environment), and *business* (as in *business professional* within a SCM/MPS environment).

Many people throughout time have enjoyed working directly in the areas of inventory and production control, supply chain management, and master planning and scheduling. There's still another group of people who have enjoyed (most of the time) working indirectly in the mentioned areas or functions. These people (expediters working with planners and schedulers) have seen many changes in these functional areas over the years. As changes were happening, these people changed how they did their work and performed the activities necessary to satisfy sales and the customer while helping their company make money and a profit (MPS bookend objectives).

That passion for getting things done must not stop. Technology advancements are being made available to master planning and scheduling professionals every day. It would be wrong for any of these MPS professionals to turn their back on what's going on around them. The world around us and the technology advancements that are happening as this paragraph is being written answer the questions people have not yet learned to ask! The authors once heard someone say, "Humans are the least effective and efficient animal on earth. However, give them a machine and they become the best." Yes, yes, yes!

Expediters learned many years ago that when they understood the situation, even though they had antiquated (certainly by today's standards) technology and tools available they could *make it happen* and *make it happen quickly*. It's basically the same thing now, just at a more formal and professional level using better technology (not only better but *lights out* better).

Again, it would be wrong for any SCM and/or MPS professional to turn their back on what's going on around them or to put their heads in the sand and *not* acknowledge that the master planning and scheduling landscape is changing, and it's starting to change faster and faster. *It's time to fully embrace technology, not run away from it, and acknowledge that machines such as computers and robots are going to take over the role (as we know it today) of master planning and scheduling!*

Why? Robots and computers don't get tired; robots and computers don't have to eat; don't need mandatory breaks; don't have to sleep; don't make errors; don't get sick; don't miss work; don't have to think (in fact, they can't think today)! Robots and computers do things faster with better quality while *not* making errors (unless a mechanical breakdown occurs or there is human intervention). In the future, robots and people will be more closely aligned than ever before.

Yesterday, people thought and talked, and robots and computers picked up the sounds. Today, people think and talk, and robots and computers pick up their sounds as well as (some) of their thoughts. Tomorrow, people will think and talk, and robots and computers will pick up the sounds and (all) of their thoughts.

Make people the robots (that might be where it's going)! Take, for instance, what is today, now, a reality (available to the public, not just the military).

- Today: Drones in the sky controlled by computers (all at once—form letters, change colors, change shapes)!

- Tomorrow: Drones in the sky controlled by people's thoughts (make people the robots and/ or computers)!

- Future: Drones in the sky controlled by computer thoughts (people as robots and/or computers?)!

People need to harness automation (e.g., automate driverless automobiles, flying automobiles); automation is *not* going to stop. Cell phone technology to children today is like refrigerators were to those children's parents when they were kids, and the icebox were to their parents' parents when they were kids. How about the breadbox, dishwasher, air conditioning, automatic transmission, microwave, garbage disposal, LED lights, wireless home security systems, and the list goes on and on!

Take hold of the future or the future will take hold of you. People today beginning a master planning and scheduling career should endeavor to live in the 2050s and see tomorrow (as in 2025 and 2030) as history. As we will see, in the years ahead, company board debates about the future will not be so much about trends, which will often be obvious, but about timing, which will be absolutely critical. For example, by when will most new cars sold in Paris be electric powered?[7]

Alright! Let's get back to discussing people and master planning and scheduling. Again, what will the people in master planning and scheduling today do tomorrow? And what will the next generation of would-be master planners and schedulers be doing in the future? These again are very good questions and might not truly be answered until this master planning and scheduling book is released in a fifth edition.

What the authors believe they do know today is that these would-be master planners and/or master schedulers will be doing different activities and tasks than those being done by master planners and/or master schedulers today (just like what best-practice master planners and master schedulers do today is totally or somewhat different than what the reorder point analyst did yesterday, or the expediter did yesterday).

Most likely, the skill set required in tomorrow's master planning and scheduling world resolves around information technology, financial understanding, and remote planning and scheduling. The future (or death) of SCM and MPS is on its own clock. The job world of today and, more so, tomorrow will involve/require technology!

Although somewhat risky, the authors have tried to remain true to our beliefs in open and honest communication (the future of master planning and scheduling *process* and *supporting system*) along with respect for the individual (*people* in master planning and scheduling as a *profession*). Someone once said, it's only worth it if one can enjoy it!

---

[7] Patrick Dixon, *The Future of (Almost) Everything* (London: Profile Books Ltd., 2019).

Master planning and scheduling, as a place where people and machines work together to get things done, as a process that really works and works really well, and as a profession that is drastically changing right before our eyes, still might be a place where innovators, rational thinkers, problem solvers, and doers want to be in (or associated with) the future!

Authors' Note: There are those who like to coach the already achieved result. Oliver Wight principals don't coach the result; Oliver Wight principals coach getting to the result!

You are never too old to set another goal or dream a new dream. You can do whatever you want to do. You can choose how you want to live the rest of your life. It doesn't matter whether you win or lose as long as you put it all out there. You can choose to follow the principle Class A in everything that you do. Go for it!

The future of master planning and scheduling is on its own clock!

Appendix A

Master Planning and Scheduling Process and Performance Standards

Nothing is worse than ignorance in action.

The Oliver Wight Class A Standard for Business Excellence, 7th edition[1] (*current structure used for Class A focus*) and The Oliver Wight ABCD Checklist for Operational Excellence, preceding editions (*original structure used for Class A focus*) were published to help companies become the best they can be in business planning, control, and execution. Being the best of the best is what Class A is all about. Many companies take pride in achieving Class A status and the results that come along with this lofty accomplishment.

However, most companies that attain Class A status tend not to be completely satisfied. In fact, they tend to become more aggressive in pushing forward, knowing they can do even better. "Yes, we are good and probably better than our competition, but we all know that we can be even better with just a little more effort" is a comment commonly heard from Class A companies. Responding to this need, Oliver Wight International initially created *The Oliver Wight ABCD Checklist for Operational Excellence* followed by *The Oliver Wight Class A Standard for Business Excellence*.

While the *Class A Standard for Business Excellence* was written to address the larger concern of modern service and manufacturing, it does contain a section on master planning and scheduling and

---

[1] *The Oliver Wight Class A **Standard for Business Excellence*** was originally adopted and published in 2007 as a sixth edition and updated to the seventh edition in 2017. Prior to 2007, Oliver Wight referred to (*what was to become the standard*) as just the *ABCD **Checklist*** in eighties and the *ABCD **Checklist for Operational Excellence***, published in 2000.

its related disciplines. The criteria in that section can be pulled together and addressed to determine where a company stands in terms of Class A master planning and scheduling processes and performance. The criteria related to master planning and scheduling are shown in this appendix.

Master planning and scheduling is defined as a process that perpetually manages demand and supply in order to ensure a balance of stability and responsiveness. The master (supply) plan and/or master (supply) schedule is continually reconciled with the aggregate, approved supply plan resulting from the integrated business planning or sales and operations planning process.

If a company relies on both a master (supply) plan (level 2 planning) and a master (supply) schedule (level 3 planning), the master plan (level 2) is reconciled with the approved, aggregate supply plan (level 1) while the master (supply) schedule (level 3) is reconciled with the master (supply) plan (level 2).

Working in conjunction with the master planning and scheduling processes just defined, a Class A company in master planning and scheduling must satisfy performance measurements directly and indirectly related to master planning and scheduling. The master planning and scheduling performance measurement itself states that accountability for master planning and/or master scheduling has been established and the goals and method of measurement agreed upon. The performance criteria further state that all goals, metrics, and performance results are communicated to appropriate company functions.

Full Class A (Transition 4 on the Supply Chain Maturity Chart) standards (milestone recognition is at Transition 3 on the Supply Chain Maturity Chart) have been set for performance in supply planning, control, and execution. The standard for each performance measurement is either the upper quartile for the company's industry, a minimum standard of 99.5 percent, or attainment of the business plan objectives.

The five main performance measurements related to master planning and scheduling are customer service (on-time-in-full delivery to customer promise), the aggregate supply plan (monthly achievement of the supply plan approved through the integrated business planning process), the master (supply) plan (monthly and/or weekly achievement of the master plan released during the master planning process), the master (supply) schedule (weekly achievement of the master schedule released during the master scheduling process), and the detailed production schedule (daily achievement of the daily production schedule released during the production scheduling process).

Milestone recognition in master plan and/or master schedule performance must be 95–100 percent of the defined (and baselined for measurement) plan or schedule (see MPS Class A criteria as well as MPS milestone criteria in coming sections). Graphs or charts showing actual performance versus planned performance are maintained along with the appropriate analysis, highlighting the primary causes of all deviations from established and management approved tolerances.

MASTER PLANNING AND SCHEDULING AS PART OF BUSINESS EXCELLENCE

Although past users of the Oliver Wight checklists may find the standard a little different, the main features remain unchanged. The standard is direct and practical. The contents of the standard are not theoretical, but rather a collection of best practices that really good companies do every day.

The standards' chapters continue to be divided into two parts: those processes and practices that are common throughout the entire business (Managing the Strategic Planning Process, Managing and Leading People, and Driving Business Improvements), and those that enable the entire business to be successful (Integrated Business Planning, Managing Product and Services, Managing Demand, Managing the Supply Chain, Managing Internal Supply, and Managing External Sourcing). Master planning and scheduling as part of business excellence standard items were taken directly from *The Oliver Wight Class A Standard for Business Excellence*, 7th edition (John Wiley & Sons, 2017).

As stated earlier, master planning and scheduling is addressed in the Managing Internal Supply chapter. Today's business is focused on improving the supply chain, from customers to suppliers. However, a company will serve itself well if it gets its own house in order before worrying about the outside. Since this book covers master planning and scheduling, let's take a more detailed look at the contents of Managing Internal Supply.

The Managing Internal Supply chapter is divided into nine subjects, one of which is internal supply planning. The internal supply planning section is supported by two definitions and several topics. The two definitions, along with their related topics, are shown in the following list (definitions and topics are taken directly from *The Oliver Wight Class A Standard for Business Excellence*).

MANAGING INTERNAL SUPPLY (CHAPTER 8 IN THE OLIVER WIGHT CLASS A STANDARD FOR BUSINESS EXCELLENCE)

Internal Supply Planning (Definitions 5 and 6)

Definition 5: Master Supply Planning has evolved to include Advanced Planning techniques. Master Supply Planning is knowledge based, and that knowledge is embedded in technology.

a. *The Supply Planner:* The key role of the supply planner is to develop opportunities and improvements to deliver the internal supply roadmap. The supply planner is accountable for the rule-based supply plan.

b. *Plans:* The supply plan is aligned to the internal supply roadmap to provide a segmented supply response. It demonstrates the required capability and agility with a financial and operational view of planned activities.

c. *Translation of Plans:* There is clear alignment across all planning horizons, which are customer-focused, are integrated, and use appropriate management and planning techniques.

d. *Resource Planning:* Critical resources are managed, and goals are set to optimize those resources, both internally and externally.

e. *Systems, Tools, and Data:* There is a seamless suite of tools to provide rule-based automation of the supply plan. The knowledge behind the plan is managed, maintained, and improved by the supply planner. There is tool-based integration with adjacent supply plans.

f. *Planning and Scheduling Techniques:* The supply model provides clear direction on appropriate planning and scheduling techniques using the planning parameters, available capacity, and agility requirements/capabilities.

g. *Linkages to the Master Supply Schedule:* The internal supply plan is managed at the appropriate level of granularity over the entire planning horizon. Time zones within the planning horizon are segment-/product-specific and enable planned agility.

Definition 6: The impact of agility on internal supply is understood, is modeled, and provides a cost-effective and planned response to anticipated and unanticipated demands.

a. *Agility Planning:* The requirement for agility is known, planned, and modeled through the planning horizon. Constraints and improvements are resolved through integrated business planning. There is a commitment to maintaining agility as a competitive advantage.

b. *Agility Execution:* The short-term utilization of agility is measured. The amount of unutilized agility is known, is stated as an opportunity, and is appropriately utilized.

c. *Cost of Agility:* The cost of planning and utilizing agility is known and modeled.

d. *Lean:* The process of deriving agility is initially from existing resources. Where resources have been exhausted, resources are added in line with the internal supply roadmap.

Note: Certification to the Class A Standard for Master Planning and Scheduling (MPS) as part of Managing Internal Supply has additional criteria within The Oliver Wight Class A Standard for Business Excellence that must be satisfied for full certification.

MASTER PLANNING AND SCHEDULING AS PART OF PLANNING AND CONTROL INTERNAL SUPPLY MODEL (DEFINITIONS 8.3 AND 8.4 IN *THE OLIVER WIGHT CLASS A PLANNING AND CONTROL MILESTONE WORKBOOK*)

Definition 8.3: Master Supply Planning (Minimum Score 3.5)—The master supply schedule is perpetually managed in order to ensure a balance of stability and responsiveness. The master supply schedule is reconciled monthly with the aggregate supply plan resulting from the integrated business planning process.

a. *The Supply Planner*—The supply planner manages the supply plan to ensure that commitments to customers are met in full and to optimize both inventory and the efficiency of the business. The supply planner understands the product, manufacturing/purchasing constraints, and application to the ERP system. The supply planner operates within current policies and is a major contributor to their improvement and uses them to develop the supply plan for the integrated business planning process.

b. *Rough Cut Capacity Planning*—A formal process defines key resources and indicates their criticality to changing business conditions. Critical resources are managed, both internally and externally.

c. *Accountability*—Accountability for maintaining a valid master supply schedule is clear. The importance of master supply planning is reflected in the organization and reporting relationship within the company.

d. *Master Supply Planning Policy*—A written master supply planning policy is followed to monitor stability and responsiveness; goals are established, and performance is measured.

e. *All Demands*—The master supply schedule takes into account all demands, including forecasts, contracts, customer orders, samples, specials, prototypes, spares, interplant, and so forth. It directs and drives all manufacturing, purchasing, and internal product-related activities.

f. *Firm Planned Order Capability*—The system has a firm planned order (FPO) capability that is used to take control of the master supply schedule covering the horizon within the planning time fence (PTF).

g. *Use of Planning Bill*—A formal process is in place that defines how planning bills (if appropriate) are used to plan material and capacity, and to direct the finishing/final assembly operations. Planning bills-of-material are maintained jointly by supply planning, demand management, sales, and marketing. The alternative approaches used with planning bills to develop options and production forecasts are well understood and maintained.

h. *Planning Time Fence*—The master supply schedule is "firmed up" over a sufficient horizon to enable stability of operations. Guidelines for this firmed horizon include cumulative lead time (CLT), lead time to plan and adjust capacity, and lead time to establish and maintain supplier agreements.

i. *Managing Schedule Changes*—Master supply schedule changes within the emergency and trading time zones are managed and monitored; changes are authorized by the appropriate people, measured, and reviewed for cause.

j. *Reconciliation of Master Supply Schedule to IBP*—The master supply schedule is summarized and reconciled with the agreed-to aggregate supply plan from the integrated business planning process.

k. *No Past Dues*—The master supply schedule is expressed in weekly, daily, or smaller time periods. No items on the master supply schedule are past due. All action messages are reviewed, analyzed, and acted upon daily.

l. *Weekly Schedule Review*—A weekly schedule review meeting exists to communicate exceptions and coordinate actions. It is attended by all affected functions.

Definition 8.4: Capable People (Minimum Score 3.5)—Capable people are managing all supply plans.

a. *Planner Competence and Accountability*—Those responsible for planning and scheduling are educated and trained to operate at best-practice standards. They understand supply and material processes and systems and are held accountable for creating and maintaining valid plans to support business goals. Planners are responsible for creating, maintaining, reviewing, and analyzing the validity of planning rules.

b. *Managing Change with Decision Points (Time Fences)*—Time fences have been identified, recognized, and actively used to manage change. Supplier time fences are known, and rules are recognized, to ensure that promises or changes are not made that cannot be honored.

c. *What-If Analysis and the Impact of Change*—Requests for change are modeled within the formal planning and scheduling system to determine their overall effect, such as their impact on customer service, all supply plans, and costs.

d. *Driving Improvements*—Those responsible for planning and scheduling understand performance measures and proactively use root cause analysis to identify improvement opportunities. Challenging the status quo is common behavior with documented improvements in many areas such as reduced lead times, order quantities, and reduced reliance on safety buffers.

e. *Policies, Process, and Procedures*—Formal documentation addresses all policy, process, procedure, and work instruction requirements for supply planning and scheduling. The planning process is not reliant on key individuals whose absence may inhibit best practice and attaining excellent results.

Note: Recognition to the Class A Milestone for Master Planning and Scheduling (MPS) as part of Integrated Planning and Control has additional Class A criteria within The Oliver Wight Class A Standard for Business Excellence that must be satisfied for full recognition.

Appendix B

Master Planning and Scheduling Improvement Initiative Task Listing

If you don't know where you are going, any road will get you there.

The *Oliver Wight Proven Path* (shown in Figure B.1) to a successful implementation or reimplementation was described in detail in Chapters 18 (covering the *Lead Phase*), 19 (covering the *Transform Phase*), and 20 (covering the *Own Phase*). In this appendix, a sample detailed activities or task list (see Figure B.2) is offered as an *example* to assist the master planning and scheduling spinoff task team in charting their journey to attaining Class A recognition (T3 on the Planning and Control maturity chart) and/or Class A certification (T4 on the Planning and Control maturity chart).

All milestones called out on *The Proven Path* are highlighted in the detailed activities or task listing. Additionally, other possible activities and tasks are listed that the MPS initiative improvement team may want to include as landmarks or milestones that the company will pass during its journey to a better way of doing planning and scheduling and control.

Again, the reader is cautioned that the activities or task list shown in this appendix is only an *example* and should *not* be used as is and without tailoring it to the company implementing (or reimplementing) a master planning and scheduling improvement initiative. However, the *example* should provide the MPS initiative improvement team with a starting position in creating the all-important project plan.

The Oliver Wight Proven Path

Understandings and Approvals and Commitments

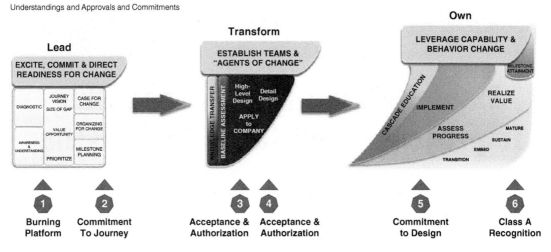

Figure B.1   The Proven Path Highlighting Approval Milestones

(1) Suspect Change Is Needed   (3) HDL Approved / Move to DD   (5) Pilot Approved / Move to Implementation
(2) Case for Change Accepted   (4) DD Approved / Move to Pilot   (6) Class A Criteria Achieved and Accepted by OW

Master Planning and Scheduling Project Plan as a Part of a Class A Journey (Example)

Task Number	Task Description (Each task must have an Owner, Start Date, and Complete Date)
0010	**Master Planning and Scheduling (MPS) Journey to Class A via *The Proven Path***
0020	MPS Improvement Initiative Planning
0030	Process Owner Identified
0040	Process Coordinator Identified
0050	Process Coordinator in Place
0060	Create MPS Team Reference Binder
0070	Master Planning and Scheduling Team Leader(s) Named
0080	Select Initial Subteam Members
0090	Subteam Members in Place
0100	Team Initial Roles and Responsibilities Defined
0110	Team Roles and Responsibilities Assigned
0120	Weekly Meetings Scheduled and Conducted
0130	Master Planning and Scheduling Team Charter
0140	Identify MPS Activities (Draft)—Opening Bid
0150	Identify MPS Deliverables (Draft)—Opening Bid
0160	Write Initial MPS Charter (Draft)—Opening Bid
0170	Charter (Draft) Submitted to Project Team (PT)

MPS Class A Project Plan continued

Task Number	Task Description (Each task must have an Owner, Start Date, and Complete Date)
0180	Charter (Draft) Reviewed with Project Team (PT) and Executive Steering Committee (ESC)
0190	MPS (Draft) Charter Updated with PT and ESC Requirements
0200	MPS Charter Approved and Initial Funding Authorized
0210	Commence *MPS Proven Path Lead Phase, Planning Future*
0220	**Diagnostic** Related to Master Planning and Scheduling
0230	Determine How Diagnostic Will Be Accomplished (Onsite or Virtual)
0240	Schedule Diagnostic Including Facilitator(s) and Participant(s)
0250	Conduct Diagnostic Through Interviews (Walkthrough is Questionable)
0260	Observations and Findings Documented and Presented to PT and ESC
0270	**Awareness and Understanding** Initial Education
0280	Integrated Supply Chain Management Course (Public, Private, Virtual)
0290	Key Influencers to Public/Virtual Master Planning and Scheduling Course
0300	Determine If Private MPS Course Needed (Onsite or Virtual)
0310	Schedule Private MPS Course (Onsite or Virtual)
0320	Conduct Master Planning and Scheduling Course
0330	Document Parking Lot Notes and Pass to MPS Task Team Leader
0340	Secure Approval to Complete Proven Path Phase 1 and Move to Phase 2
0350	*Stop and Check #1—Approval to Proceed in Completing Lead Phase*
0360	**Vision Statement(s)** for Master Planning and Scheduling
0370	Affinity Process Session for Journey and Operational Vision
0380	Create MPS Visions (Drafts) for Categories Identified
0390	Rework Individual Team (Drafts) Visions
0400	Tie Vision (Draft) for Master Planning and Scheduling Together
0410	Final Draft of Master Planning and Scheduling Vision
0420	Submit MPS Vision (Draft) to Project Team
0430	Rework Vision (Draft) with Project Team Feedback
0440	Submit Vision for Executive Steering Committee Approval
0450	Publish (or Include in HLD) Master Planning and Scheduling Vision
0460	**Size of the Gap** Between MPS Vision and MPS Diagnostic
0470	Identify Strengths (S) of Current MPS Process Using Diagnostic
0480	Identify Weaknesses (W) of Current MPS Process Using Diagnostic
0490	Compare MPS Process S/W to MPS Vision Statement
0500	Prepare Gap Analysis Report
0510	Submit Gap Analysis to Project Team
0520	Gap Analysis is Submitted to ESC by Project Team Leader
0530	**Value Opportunity** Attributed to Master Planning and Scheduling
0540	List of Master Planning and Scheduling Benefits/Cost Developed
0550	Master Planning and Scheduling Benefits/Cost Statement (Draft)
0560	Master Planning and Scheduling Task Teams Discussion
0570	MPS Benefits/Cost Statement Final Team Draft
0580	Submit Benefits/Cost Statement to Project Team Leader

MPS Class A Project Plan continued

Task Number	Task Description (Each task must have an Owner, Start Date, and Complete Date)
0590	Rework Benefits/Cost Statement with Project Team Feedback
0600	Resubmit Benefits/Cost Statement for ESC Approval
0610	Publish (or include in HLD) MPS Benefits/Cost Analysis
0620	**Prioritization** of Master Planning and Scheduling
0630	Compare Value Opportunity Against Other Company Initiatives
0640	Secure Priority for MPS Improvement Initiative
0650	Determine Whether MPS Initiative Is Within Top Five Company Initiatives
0660	Top Five, Move On—Otherwise, More Work to Be Done
0670	Enter MPS Priority into *Case for Change* Document
0680	**Case For Change (CFC)**
0690	Pull Diagnostic, Vision, Gap Analysis, Value Opportunity, Priority Together
0700	Prepare CFC Document Including All **Lead Phase** Gathered Data
0710	Submit CFC to Overall Project Team
0720	Case for Change (CFC) Submitted to ESC by Project Team Leader
0730	**Organizing for Change**
0740	Create Macro Master Planning and Scheduling Task Improvement Plan
0750	Identify Anticipated Resources Required (External and Internal)
0760	Create Resource Matrix for MPS Initiative (Rough Cut Capacity Plan)
0770	Summarize People Hours Required by Function and Task
0780	Submit Resource Matrix to Overall Project Team
0790	**Milestone Planning**
0800	Review Macro MPS Task Improvement Plan
0810	Add/Change/Delete Tasks as Appropriate
0820	Tie Macro MPS Task Plan to Proven Path
0830	Make Macro Plan Part of Case for Change
0840	Submit Macro MPS Task Improvement Plan to Project Team
0850	Secure Approval to Move to Proven Path Phase 2
0860	***Stop and Check #2—Approval to Proceed to Transform Phase***
0870	**Point of Commitment** Reached
0880	Present Case For Change to Project Team
0890	Present CFC to ESC Seeking Approval to Proceed to **Transform Phase**
0900	Receive Approval to Move to **Phase 2 on Proven Path, Designing Future**
0910	**Knowledge Transfer** for Master Planning and Scheduling
0920	Determine How MPS Task Team Will Be Educated
0930	MPS Education/Training Plan Created
0940	MPS Education/Training Plan Approved
0950	MPS Sessions Schedule Created and Approved
0960	Broadcast of MPS Education and Training Sessions
0970	MPS Sessions Run (Education and Training)
0980	Supply Chain Management Library Established with MPS Book

MPS Class A Project Plan continued

Task Number	Task Description (Each task must have an Owner, Start Date, and Complete Date)
0990	**Baseline Assessment** for Master Planning and Scheduling
1000	Assess MPS/RCCP Using Planning and Control Milestone Workbook
1010	Assessment One Report for Master Planning and Scheduling
1020	MPS Assessment One Reviewed with Project Team (Detail)
1030	MPS Assessment One Submitted (or Included in HLD) to ESC (Overview)
1040	**Apply—High-Level Design (HLD)** Workshops and Design Sessions
1050	Review MPS Concepts Taught in MPS Detailed Education Session(s)
1060	Mind Map Master Planning (MP) Process
1070	Mind Map Master Scheduling (MS) Process
1080	Mind Map Rough Cut Capacity Planning (RCCP) Process
1090	Mind Map Data Integrity (DI) to Support MPS Process
1100	Document MPS Design Using Mind Maps (MP and MS)
1110	Document MPS/RCCP Design Using Mind Map (RCCP)
1120	Document MPS/DI Design Using Mind Map (DI)
1130	Create Listing of MPS/RCCP Policies Required
1140	Create Listing of MPS/RCCP Process Flow Diagrams Required
1150	Create Listing of MPS/RCCP Procedures Required
1160	Create Listing of MPS/RCCP Work Instructions Required
1170	Create Listing of MPS Goals and Metrics Required
1180	Create Listing of MPS/RCCP Software Requirements
1190	Create Listing of MPS Education and Training Requirements for Rollout
1200	Identify Obstacles to Success to Be Removed
1210	Identify Main MPS/RCCP Reporting Requirements
1220	Highlight Master Planner's and Master Scheduler's Role Responsibilities
1230	Initialize Master Planning and Scheduling Glossary of Terms
1240	Integrate Diagnostic, Vision, Gaps, Benefits, Investment, Organization, Key Goals, Defined Measurements, Education, Training, Mind Maps, MPS Policies, Flow Diagrams, MPS Procedures, Work Instructions into Master Planning and Scheduling High-Level Design (HDL)
1250	Submit High-Level Design (HLD) to Project Team for Feedback
1260	Rework High-Level Design (HLD) with Project Team Feedback
1270	Prepare High-Level Design (HDL) Executive Presentation
1280	Present HLD to ESC and Invited Guest
1290	Document ESC and Management Feedback from Presentation
1300	Create Action Plan for ESC and Management Feedback
1310	Secure Approval to Move to Detailed Design Work (Heavy Lifting)
1320	***Stop and Check #3—Approval to Proceed to Detailed Design (DD)***
1330	Detailed Design Workshops and Design Sessions Planned and Scheduled
1340	Review Master Planning and Scheduling Process Flows Required
1350	Create Detailed Master Planning and Scheduling Process Flows

MPS Class A Project Plan continued

Task Number	Task Description (Each task must have an Owner, Start Date, and Complete Date)
1360	Update List of MPS Policies and Procedures Required
1370	Assign Responsibilities for MPS Policies and Procedures Creation
1380	Identify Policy and Procedure Format to Be Used
1390	Write Key MPS/RCCP Policies (See List in Appendix C)
1400	Submit Key Master Planning and Scheduling Policies to Project Team
1410	Rework MPS/RCCP Policies with Project Team Feedback
1420	Resubmit MPS/RCCP Policies for Executive Steering Committee Approval
1430	Identify Key MPS/RCCP Decisions That Need to Be Made
1440	Integrate Vision, Organization, Metrics, MPS/RCCP Flow Diagrams, MPS/RCCP Policies, MPS/RCCP Procedures, Obstacles, Decisions Needed, and Implementation Implications into MPS/RCCP DD
1450	Submit Detailed Design (DD) to Project Team for Feedback
1460	Rework Detailed Design (DD) with Project Team Feedback
1470	Prepare Detailed Design (DD) Presentation
1480	Present Detailed Design to ESC and Invited Guests
1490	Document Feedback from Detailed Design (DD) Presentation
1500	Create Action Plan Using ESC and Management Feedback
1510	Secure Approval to Move to Proven Path Phase 3
1520	***Stop and Check #4—Approval to Proceed to Own Phase***
1530	**Cascade Education** (and Training) for Master Planning and Scheduling
1540	Review MPS Education and Training Plan (Need-to-Know Personnel)
1550	Schedule E&T Rollout for Service, Distribution, and Manufacturing Sites
1560	Conduct Rollout Education and Training (Policies, Procedures, System, . . .)
1570	**Rollout Implementation Planning**
1580	Determine MPS Rollout Sequence (Live Pilot to Full Cutover)
1590	Broadcast MPS Rollout Plan and Resources/Time Required
1600	**Implementation**
1610	Review Where and What to Master Plan and Master Schedule
1620	Review Typical Product Profiles
1630	Discuss Where to Meet the Customer by Product Family/Subfamily
1640	Generate Indented Bill-of-Material (BOM) for MPS Pilot Product Family
1650	Add Lead Times to Indented Bill-of-Material (BOM)
1660	Create Time-Phased Bill-of-Material for Pilot Products
1670	Secure Customer and Marketplace Lead Time Expectations
1680	Overlay Customer/Marketplace Expectations on Indented BOM
1690	Identify Point on Indented BOM to Meet the Customer
1700	Define Where and What to Master Plan and Schedule for Pilot Product Family
1710	Repeat Steps Above for All Product Families
1720	Master Planning and Scheduling Full Rollout Preparation
1730	Assign the Master Planner(s) and Master Scheduler(s) to Implementation
1740	Review Roles/Responsibilities of the Master Planner and Master Scheduler

MPS Class A Project Plan continued

Task Number	Task Description (Each task must have an Owner, Start Date, and Complete Date)
1750	Review MPS Planning Horizons Length
1760	Review Master Planning and Scheduling Period (Bucket) Size
1770	Review Where to Place the Planning Time Fences (by Groupings and Items)
1780	Assign Responsibility for Maintaining Planning Time Fences
1790	Determine How to Use Firm Planned Orders (FPOs)
1800	Create Planning Bills to Support Disaggregation of Product Families
1810	Develop Long-Term MPS Requirements for Software
1820	Complete Master Planning and Scheduling Policies Creation
1830	Submit All Master Planning and Scheduling Policies to Management
1840	Rework Master Planning and Scheduling Policies with Feedback
1850	Resubmit MPS/RCCP Policies for PT and ESC for Approval
1860	Publish Master Planning and Scheduling Policies
1870	Write/Complete MPS/RCCP Procedures Identified in Design Documents
1880	Submit to Project Team for Feedback
1890	Rework Procedures with Project Team Feedback
1900	Resubmit Procedures to PT and ESC for Approval
1910	Publish Master Planning and Scheduling Procedures
1920	Conduct Refresher on MPS/RCCP Policies, Process Flows, Procedures, ...
1930	Data Integrity Requirements in Support of Master Planning and Scheduling
1940	Create/Review Listing of Planning Parameters Used in MPS Process
1950	Assign Responsibility for MPS/RCCP Related Data Cleanup
1960	Clean Up Database Planning Parameters (Lead Times, Lot Sizes, etc.)
1970	Print Report Showing Database Changes (MPS-Related Data)
1980	Review All Changes Made to Database (MPS-Related Data)
1990	Update Database Parameters as Required (Based on Review)
2000	Database Ready for Use
2010	Audit Bills-of-Material for Accuracy (Sample Size)
2020	Audit Planning Bills for Accuracy (Sample Size)
2030	Bills-of-Material Data Base Ready for Usage
2040	Cycle Count Inventory (Master Planning and Scheduling Items Sample)
2050	Audit MPS/RCCP Finished-Goods Locations
2060	Inventory Records Database Ready for Use
2070	Performance Goals and Measurements for MPS-Related Areas
2080	List of Accuracy and Performance Goals Developed/Reviewed
2090	Accuracy/Performance Measurements Defined/Reviewed
2100	One-Page Definition Documents Created/Reviewed (One-Pagers)
2110	Master Planning and Scheduling Task Team Discussions (As Needed)
2120	One-Pagers Final Draft for All MPS Goals and Measurements
2130	Submit/Resubmit One-Pagers to PT and ESC
2140	Rework One-Pagers with ESC and Management Feedback
2150	Resubmit One-Pagers for ESC Approval

MPS Class A Project Plan continued

Task Number	Task Description (Each task must have an Owner, Start Date, and Complete Date)
2160	Publish One-Pagers to All with a Need-to-Know
2170	Software Selection for Master Planning and Scheduling (If Required)
2180	Complete MPS/RCCP Software Requirements Document
2190	Review and Critique Master Planning and Scheduling Software Solutions
2200	Select Master Planning and Scheduling Software (If Required)
2210	Information Technology Computer Pilot
2220	Conversion Checklist Defined and Delivered
2230	Identify All Systems That Need Interfaces
2240	Create All Interfaces/Conversion Tools
2250	Interface Architecture and Methodology Complete
2260	Interfaces Developed and Delivered
2270	Master Planning and Scheduling Software Tool Configuration Complete
2280	Master Planning and Scheduling Hierarchy Designed
2290	MPS Process Tied to Integrated Business Planning (IBP) Process
2300	MPS Process Tied to Product/Portfolio Management Process
2310	MPS Process Tied to Demand and Supply Management Processes
2320	MPS Process Tied to Integrated Tactical Planning (ITP) Process
2330	MPS Process Tied to Detailed Production Scheduling (DPS) Process
2340	MPS Process Tied to Financial Management Process
2350	Product and Materials and Capacity Required Configuration in Place
2360	Running the MPS Computer Test System
2370	Input Planning Bills (A/R) into Master Planning and Scheduling System
2380	Create Master Plan and/or Master Schedule for Test Product Family
2390	Run Computer Test Case Using Planning Bills (IF Designed in Process)
2400	Document Results from Computer Test
2410	Enter Customer Order(s) to Test Demand Input
2420	Determine Forecast Consumption Rules to Use
2430	Review Forecast Consumption Results
2440	Determine Available-to-Promise (ATP) and Abnormal Demand Rules to Use
2450	Update Available-to-Promise (ATP) and Check Results
2460	Document Results from Computer Test
2470	All Policies and Procedures in Place (Checkpoint)
2480	All Personnel Trained on Policies, Procedures, and System (Checkpoint)
2490	**Additional Implementation Preparation**
2500	Determine Safety Stock Level (Demand and Financial Management)
2510	Input Safety Stock Levels by Item Number into System
2520	Use Planning Bills to Create Unit Demand at the MPS Level
2530	Tie Master Planning and Scheduling to Integrated Business Planning Output
2540	Create Program to Aggregate MPS and Tie to IBP Output
2550	Tie Master Plan and/or Master Schedule to Demand Management
2560	Tie Master Schedule to Detailed Daily Plant/Mill/Factory Schedule

MPS Class A Project Plan continued

Task Number	Task Description (Each task must have an Owner, Start Date, and Complete Date)
2570	Finalize ATP and Abnormal Demand Rules to Be Used
2580	Finalize Forecast Consumption Rules to Be Used
2590	Scheduling in MPS Software Tool Configuration
2600	Computer Testing Procedures and Guidelines Available
2610	Changes Requested (As Needed)
2620	Modify MPS Software as a Result of Computer Pilot Test
2630	Conference Room Pilot
2640	Master Planning and Scheduling Process Modeled in MPS Software
2650	MPS/RCCP Software Refined (As Necessary)
2660	Reports/Screens Modified (If Necessary)
2670	MPS Task Team Ensures MPS/RCCP Process Is Working
2680	MPS/RCCP Model Is Demonstrated to Broader Group
2690	Master Planning and Scheduling Conference Room Pilot Testing Is Complete
2700	Modify MPS/RCCP Model as a Result of Conference Room Pilot
2710	MPS/RCCP Conference Room Pilot Is Complete
2720	Update Master Planning and Scheduling Implementation Plan
2730	Refine MPS/RCCP Implementation (As Necessary)
2740	Accountability for Master Planning and Scheduling System Assigned
2750	Software MPS/RCCP Tool Training Program
2760	Master Planning and Scheduling Software Overview to All Users
2770	Master Planning and Scheduling Software Detail to All Key Users
	Implementation of Master Planning and Scheduling Designed Processes
2780	Live MPS/RCCP Pilot
2790	Live Pilot Site Selected
2800	MPS/RCCP Pilot Cutover Date Established and Approved
2810	Commitment to MPS Design
2820	MPS/RCCP *Go/No-Go Checklist* Reviewed
2830	Secure Authorization to Move to Pilot Site Implementation(s)
2840	Commence Master Planning and Scheduling (MPS) with Pilot Items
2850	Master Planning and Scheduling Pilot Results Reviewed
2860	MPS/RCCP Process Modifications Made (as Necessary)
2870	Master Planning and Scheduling Live Pilot Complete
2882	Secure Approval to Move to All Site Cutovers
2890	*Stop and Check #5—Approval to Proceed to Full Cutover*
2900	Determine Product and/or Site Cutover Schedule
2910	Publish Product and/or Site Cutover Schedule
2920	Cutover Products/Sites to *New* Master Planning and Scheduling Processes
2930	Information Technology Support for Users (As Required)
2940	Cutover Remaining MPS Related Accuracy and Performance Measurements
2950	Post-Cutover Analysis of Master Planning and Scheduling Implementation
2960	Master Scheduling Is Driving Material and Production and Logistics Planning

MPS Class A Project Plan continued

Task Number	Task Description (Each task must have an Owner, Start Date, and Complete Date)
2970	Available-to-Promise (ATP) Is Functioning
2980	Master Planning and Scheduling is Running within IBP and MPS Policy
2990	Assess Progress Toward MPS Vision and Goals
3000	Monthly Progress Assessment (Time to Get Serious During Assessment)
3010	Assessment Forwarded to Project Team and Executive Steering Committee
3020	**Realize Value** Outlined and Committed in Value Opportunity
3030	Document Benefit Realized and Benefits Not Realized
3040	Document Return-on-Investment (ROI) to Date
3050	Initiative Tracking to Five-Year Cash Flow Projection (Financial Input)
3060	Movement to Satisfy Class A Milestone Criteria
3070	**Transition**
3080	Out with the Old and In with the New
3090	People Behaviors Are Changing
3100	Old Process and System Is Replaced
3110	**Embed**
3120	Talking Is Done and the Company Is Accepting the Change
3130	Anticipated Pushbacks Are Being Addressed Privately as Well as Publicly
3140	Refresher Education and Training Are Conducted on an As-Needed Basis
3150	**Sustain**
3160	Leadership and Management Sending Positive Vibes to Implementers
3170	No One Is Shooting the Messengers
3180	As Problems Occur, Corrective Actions Are Put into Place
3190	MPS Process Is Being Fail-Safed from Problems Using Root Cause Analysis
3200	**Mature**
3210	Routine Things Are Being Done Routinely
3220	MPS Has Reached Full Development and Implementation Status
3230	MPS Is Accepted as an Integral Part of the Business
3240	Comments Like "It's Just the Way We Do Things Around Here" Are Common
3250	**Milestone Attainment**
3260	Assess MPS Using Class A Planning and Control Milestone Workbook
3270	Self-Assessment Using Oliver Wight Class A Standard and Workbook
3280	Weaknesses of Master Planning and Scheduling Process Identified
3290	MPS/RCCP Process Improvements in Identified Weak Areas
3300	All MPS/RCCP Processes Are Defined as Strengths
3310	Master Planning and Scheduling Self-Audit Shows Class A Results
3320	Oliver Wight Class A Audit of Master Planning and Scheduling
3330	Class A MPS Milestone Recognition for Master Planning and Scheduling
3340	Class A MPS Full Certification for Master Planning and Scheduling
3350	Now What? Class A in Managing Internal Supply? Class A in Operational Excellence? Class A in Business Excellence? Class A in Everything We do?

Figure B.2 Master Planning and Scheduling Improvement Initiative Task Plan

Appendix C

Master Planning and Scheduling Policy, Procedure, and Flow Diagram

A company can do what it wants to do and therefore, it can choose how it wants to operate its supply chain!

This appendix provides three somewhat complete listings of the master planning and scheduling suggested policies (rules that need to be implemented), suggested procedures (what action needs to take place and how to do it), and suggested process flow diagrams (the ins and outs of process steps including decision points along the way). The listings are in alphabetic order so as not to imply that one suggestion is better than another.

It is recommended that the master planning and scheduling initiative improvement team go through each list (line by line) and discuss the merits of including the suggested element as part of their improvement implementation.

It is *not* the authors' intention that every line contains a *must-have* requirement for a successful and effective MPS process. Choosing the ones that matter to the company and business is left for each project team to decide whether to include or not include in their implementation.

POLICY LISTING FOR CONSIDERATION (ALPHABETICAL ORDER)

Abnormal Demand Identification and Handling
Abnormal Supply Identification and Handling
Aggregating the Master Plan and Tying to Approved Supply Plan
Aggregating the Master Schedule and Tying to Master (Supply) Plan
Aggregating the Production Schedule and Tying to Master Schedule

POLICY LISTING FOR CONSIDERATION   (CONTINUED)

Available-to-Promise (ATP) Usage and Violation Consequences
Backlog Levels Acceptable Using Upper and Lower Limits
Booking Customer Orders (Consumption of Forecast and ATP Usage)
Changing the Master Plan and/or Master Schedule (Approvals)
Class A Certification and Milestone Recognition in Master Planning and Scheduling
Communications with Master Planner and/or Master Scheduler
Customer Service Levels Including Measurement and Reporting
Data Accuracy Requirements to Support Master Planning and Scheduling
Determining the Product Manufacturing Strategy (Product Family and Item)
Demand Time Fence (DTF) Settings and Maintenance
Disaggregating the Approved Supply Plan (Volume) into Master (Supply) Plan (Mix)
Disaggregating the Master Plan into Facility Master Schedules (Request for Supply)
Disaggregating the Master (Supply) Schedule into Facility Detailed Production Schedule
Dollarizing the Master Plan and/or Master Schedule
Education and Training Requirements to Support Effective MPS
Exception-Driven Action Messages (Working the Recommended Actions)
Forecast Consumption Rules for Normal versus Abnormal Customer Order Bookings
Integrated Business Planning Tie to Master Planning and Scheduling Requirements
Integrated Tactical Planning Tie to Master Planning and Scheduling Requirements
Inventory Levels Acceptable Using Upper and Lower Limits
Master Planning and Scheduling Overall Rules
Metrics Definitions for MPS Accuracy and Performance
Overplanning the Master Plan and/or Master Schedule
Past Dues on Master Plan and/or Master Schedule (Handling of These Past-Due Orders)
Performance as well as Accuracy Periodic Reporting
Planning Bills (Creation and Maintenance and Use)
Planning Time Fence (PTF) Settings and Maintenance
Planning Time Horizon Establishment and Maintenance
Request for Supply (RFS) as Notification Corporate Planning to Manufacturing Sites
Rough Cut Capacity Planning (Sanity Checks Required for MPS)
Safety Stocks (Establishing and Approving the Acceptable Levels)
Silver Bullets Between Product Portfolio, Demand, Supply, and Financial Management
Tying the Master Plan to the Approved Supply Plan (IBP/S&OP Output)
Tying the Master Plan to the Master Schedule (Master Scheduling Output)
Tying the Master Schedule to the Detailed Production Schedule (Production Output)
Tying the Master Schedule to the Master Plan (Master Planning Output)

PROCEDURE LISTING FOR CONSIDERATION (ALPHABETICAL ORDER)

Assessing the Master Planning and Scheduling Process
Booking Customer Orders Using Available-to-Promise Information
Buy Window (MPS Performance) Usage in Master Planning and Scheduling Environment
Calculating Master Plan and/or Master Schedule Accuracy and Performance Metrics
Changing the Master (Supply) Plan and/or Master (Supply) Schedule
Communicating Changes to/from Demand Management Organization
Communicating Changes to/from Master Planner and/or Master Scheduler
Communicating Changes to/from Supply Chain Management Owner
Creating and Maintaining the Product Family Planning Bill
Determining Product Manufacturing Strategy (Product Family and Subfamily and Item)
Disaggregating Approved, Aggregate Supply Plan into Master (Supply) Plan
Disaggregating Master (Supply) Plan into Master (Supply) Schedule
Establishing and Maintaining Demand Time Fence (DTF)
Establishing and Maintaining Planning Time Fence (PTF)
Establishing/Changing Inventory Targets and Upper/Lower Limits
Establishing/Changing Option Overplanning Levels
Establishing/Changing Safety Stock Levels
Evaluating Rough Cut Capacity Planning Output Before Releasing MPS
Identification and Handling Abnormal Demand
Identification and Handling Abnormal Supply
Integrated Tactical Planning and Master Planning and Scheduling Working Together
Maintaining Resource Profiles and Capacity Data
Making Promises to Customers to Satisfy Unplanned Demand
Penalty for Supply Orders Remaining Past Due (Grace Period)
Requesting Approval (When Required) to Change Master Plan and/or Master Schedule
Releasing the Master Plan and/or Master Schedule
Reporting Accuracy of the Master Plan and/or Master Schedule
Reporting Performance to Master Plan and/or Master Schedule
Requesting Changes to Master Plan and/or Master Schedule
Requesting Education and Training Related to Master Planning and Scheduling
Rescheduling Past Due Work to Valid and Realistic Due Date
Running Rough Cut Capacity Planning (RCCP)
Running the Master Plan and/or Master Schedule
Setting/Changing the Planning Horizon
Setting/Changing the Demand and/or Supply Planning Time Fences
Summarizing/Comparing Detailed Production Schedule to Master (Supply) Schedule
Summarizing/Comparing Master (Supply) Schedule to Master (Supply) Plan

Procedure Listing for Consideration   (*Continued*)

Summarizing/Comparing Master (Supply) Plan to Approved, Aggregate Supply Plan
Updating Capacity Data Used in Rough Cut Capacity Planning Process
Use of Silver Bullets by Product Portfolio, Demand, Supply, and Financial Management
Working System-Generated Action Messages

Flow Diagrams Listing for Consideration (Alphabetical Order)

Abnormal Demand and Supply (Handling)
Action Message Review (Continuous)
Aggregating Detailed Production Schedule and Tying to Master (Supply) Schedule
Aggregating Master (Supply) Schedule and Tying to Master (Supply) Plan
Available-to-Promise (Using to Promise Customer Deliveries)
Changing/Maintaining the Master (Supply) Plan and/or Master (Supply) Schedule
Driving Capacity Requirements Planning (Time-Phased CRP)
Driving Material Requirements Planning (Time-Phased MRP and Other Techniques)
Forecast Changes (Channel of Communications)
Inputs to Pre-Integrated Business Planning or Sales and Operations Planning Process
Integrated Tactical Planning (ITP) and Master Planning and Scheduling (MPS) Integration
Master Planning and Scheduling Main Flow (Continuous)
Master Planning and Scheduling Monthly Process
Master Planning and Scheduling Weekly Process
Past Dues (Identification and Resolution and Rescheduling)
Recording and Publishing Accuracy and Performance Metrics
Receiving Requirements from IBP/S&OP Supply and MBR Reviews (Master Planning)
Rough Cut Capacity Planning (RCCP)
Updating System with Demand Forecast
Updating System with Material and Resource Availability

Again, the reader is cautioned *not* to just accept everything contained on each listing. These listings are provided as a jump starter for the initiative improvement team to create the project's own listings (these listings should be part of the master planning and scheduling high-level design [HLD] and HDL executive presentation). The actual creation of each policy, procedure, and flow diagram selected is accomplished during the detail design (DD) activity and shared with the executives and steering committee during (or before) the DD executive presentation.

Appendix D

Master Planning and Scheduling
MPS Overall Policy and MPS Past Due Policy Examples

Please tell me the rules of the game—it just makes it easier to understand and avoid penalties!

MASTER PLANNING AND SCHEDULING POLICY INCLUDING SUBPOLICIES (AN EXAMPLE)

1. *Purpose*
   1.1 To establish master planning and scheduling (MPS), rough cut capacity planning (RCCP), monthly disaggregation of request for supply (RFS) to plant build quantities, monthly aggregation of build schedule (plant production schedule to plant master schedule and plant master schedule to master planning RFS), and key performance indicators (KPIs) rules and best practices and ensure that the master planning and scheduling process is aligned, synchronized, and integrated with overall company supply objectives as well as maintaining Class A status.

2. *Scope*
   2.1 This policy applies to all master planning and scheduling processes and practices for all company locations (corporate and plants).

3. *Function Responsible for Implementation and Training*
   3.1 Master Planning/Master Scheduling/Plant Operations
   3.2 Document control (policies, flow diagrams, procedures, work instructions, KPI one-pagers)
   3.3 Applicable training programs/presentations/documents
   3.4 Information technology (IT) for software

4. *Policy and Subpolicies*
   4.1 Opening Statements: Master planning and scheduling is the process that the company uses to develop tactical and operational plans based on setting the manufacturing site/plant level of manufacturing output (master plan and master schedule) and other activities to best satisfy the current planned levels of demand (sales plan/anticipated demand or forecast), while meeting general business objectives of profitability, productivity, competitive customer lead times, product available-to-promise or available-to-sell, and so on, as expressed in the overall approved supply plan.
   4.1.1 Supply management establishes supply rates that achieve management's objectives of satisfying customer demand by maintaining, raising, or lowering inventories or backlogs, while attempting to keep the work force relatively stable and to safely make money.
   4.1.2 The demand and supply capabilities at the mix level are compared, and various manufacturing strategies that include make-to-stock (MTS), make-to-order (MTO), and design-to-order (DTO), along with supporting plans for materials and work force requirements, and so on, are developed.
   4.1.3 The master plan and/or master schedule is prepared with information from new product, demand, and finance and coordinated with the functions of logistics, quality assurance, manufacturing support, production, procurement, and purchasing.
   4.1.4 It is expected that all members of the company's supply organization understand these policies and abide by each of them.
   4.2 An integrated software tool is used to support the master planning and scheduling process, as well as other processes within the supply planning and control monthly processes.
   4.3 All integrated software tool exception-driven action messages are reviewed, analyzed, and cleared/handled in an appropriate manner—at a minimum, weekly.
   4.4 The master (supply) planning (corporate—level 2 planning), planning horizon is 12 months while the master (supply) schedule (plants—level 3 planning) planning horizon is set at 6 months.
   4.5 The master (supply) plan (corporate—level 2 planning) is by product grouping and fiscal time period while the master (supply) schedule (plants—level 3 planning) is by stock-keeping unit (SKU), weekly time periods for months 2 through 6 (mix planning), and daily for month 1 (mix planning).

4.6 Communications between the demand manager, master (supply) planner, plant manager, and master (supply) scheduler are routine and expected by the company's leadership team.

4.7 The supply manager and/or master (supply) planner is responsible to inform each manufacturing site/plant master scheduler when the approved supply plan (ASP)/ request for supply (RFS) is ready for execution. ASP/RFP will be released within three business days from management business review (MBR) approval.

4.8 Each manufacturing site's/plant's master scheduler, supported by his or her plant management team, is responsible for accepting and/or declining the monthly RFP from the company's master (supply) planner within two business days of receipt (the *silence is acceptance* principle is practiced during this monthly process).

4.9 The master (supply) planner is approved to modify the RFP during the month; the manufacturing site/plant weekly/monthly master schedule key performance indicator (KPI) is also modified as appropriate.

4.10 Planning bills are used by the company to disaggregate the approved supply plans (ASP volume plans) into requests for production (RFP mix plans).

4.11 Planning bill structures are maintained by the supply organization whereas the planning bill percentages are maintained by the demand organization.

4.12 The manufacturing site master schedulers, supported by the company's master (supply) planner, ensure that planned customer lead times are monitored and met.

4.13 The plant master schedulers, supported by the company's master (supply) planner, are responsible to optimize product loading across plant production lines while satisfying firm and anticipated demand.

4.14 The company's master planning and scheduling change matrix outlines a hierarchy of approval, to be used before any changes to the respective plant's master schedule, are implemented. Changes to the master schedule are measured via a *master schedule changes* KPI (see KPI one-pager).

4.15 The master plan and/or master schedule performance goal is 95–100 percent weekly for each business unit and/or plant, aggregated monthly (using weighted averages, as appropriate) for supply management reporting in the supply review (SR) and management business review (MBR).

4.16 The master schedulers (plants) support the company's master (supply) planner and supply manager during the integrated business planning (IBP), supply review (SR), master planning (MP), and request for supply (RFS) processes.

4.17 The master schedulers, supported by the master (supply) planner, ensure that customer backlogs are managed to competitive and approved levels.

4.18 Rough cut capacity planning (RCCP) is done on all key or critical resources to validate the master plan and/or master schedule before releasing the master plan and/or master schedule for further action.

4.19 Rough cut capacity planning (RCCP) is used to validate all significant changes to the master plan and/or master schedule prior to the master plan and/or master schedule being released for detailed production scheduling (DPS) and material planning (MP) (i.e., time-phased MRP).

4.20 Past-due supply work orders or firm planned orders are prohibited on a plant's master schedule (a grace period of 24 hours is granted to the master scheduler to analyze and reschedule any supply work order or firm planned order with a past-due date— each day beyond the grace period is counted as another miss when calculating master schedule performance).

4.22 The master schedulers supported by the master (supply) planner ensure sufficient production volume/mix to meet business/region/plant demand.

4.23 All changes to a plant's master schedule must be authorized according to company's master planning and scheduling change policy.

4.24 Manufacturing sites/plants are authorized to produce approved supply plan (ASP)/ request for supply (RFS) quantities plus or minus the defined percentage tolerance (there can be different tolerances between product families and/or product subfamilies).

4.25 Plant master scheduling is responsible to measure its performance to the master schedule weekly, report weekly performance to the plant manager as well as the master (supply) planner, and to aggregate the weekly performance for each month by averaging (weighted averages are used as directed by the supply manager) the weekly performances (monthly performances are reported to the plant manager and master supply planner).

4.26 Excel usage in master planning and scheduling as well as supply chain management is limited; Excel usage to override the master plan and/or master schedule (and/or company's planning system calculations) is prohibited.

4.27 All customer orders booked by the sales organization honor the available-to-promise (ATP) created as part of the master planning and scheduling process (it is a violation of this policy to book customer orders that drive the ATP into the RED).

4.28 The integrated master planning and scheduling system's planning time fence (PTF) capability is used to decouple demand and supply on the master plan and/or master schedule.

4.29 The PTF for each master plan's and/or master schedule's item will be set at or greater than the item's cumulative lead time unless defined material strategies are being used to shorten the actual item's lead time.

4.30 The integrated master planning and scheduling system's demand time fence (DTF) capability is used at the discretion of the demand and supply managers (use of the DTF instructs the integrated system software to ignore demand forecast inside the DTF and only use firm customer orders when calculating the master plan's and/or master schedule's projected available balance or projected on-hand balance).

4.31 Safety stocks at the master planning and scheduling (MPS) level or option overplanning at the MPS level must be approved by the supply manager or vice president of supply chain management.

4.32 The firm planned order (FPO) capability in the integrated master planning and scheduling system is used to create, maintain, and state the plant's master schedule.

4.33 The master plan as well as the master schedule is dollarized prior to its release to detailed production scheduling and material planning (the dollarized master plan and master schedule is sanity checked for any abnormal conditions before the final master plan and/or master schedule is released).

4.34 The master schedule (plant) is the driver of the company's material plans—all items that are made in the company's manufacturing facilities must be included on the plant's master schedule.

4.35 The plant's detailed production schedule(s) (DPS) is/are driven by the plant's master schedule—no work orders, trials, and/or design tests are created and/or forwarded to the manufacturing floor for any item, quantity, or due date that's not included on the plant's master schedule.

4.37 Master planning and scheduling, as a member of the supply management organization, maintains Class A Milestone recognition (and Full Class A when achieved) status in master planning and scheduling functional areas.

4.38 Supply management is responsible (along with logistics, manufacturing support, production, quality assurance, procurement, and purchasing) to satisfy Class A master planning and scheduling accuracy and performance targets week after week after week and approved supply plan accuracy and performance targets month after month after month.

4.39 Supply management, in conjunction with prestage, shipping, production, purchasing, procurement, quality assurance, and information technology, support the master data integrity program regarding the item or material master records (lead times, lot sizes, safety stocks), inventory records, and planning bills (structures, quantities, and probability percentages provided by the demand organization, usually marketing) for items that are master planned and/or master scheduled.

5. *Guiding Principles*
    5.1 Master planning is conducted at the subfamily/group level (corporate—level 2 planning).
    5.2 Master scheduling is conducted at the group/SKU level (plant—level 3 planning).
    5.3 Performance indicators exist to measure and drive improvements in the master planning and scheduling process.

5.4   Integration and feedback loops are formalized and part of the weekly and daily supply management processes.

5.5   Approved and implemented policies, flow diagrams, procedures, and work instructions are followed by everyone.

5.6   The *silence is acceptance* principle is practiced at the company.

5.7   The master planning and scheduling team understands that its members must communicate to those with a need to know any time the manufacturing site/plant cannot meet its supply requirements and/or commitments.

5.8   The master planning and scheduling team embraces and practices the principle of *do what you say you are going to do*.

5.9   The master planning and scheduling team will do what is necessary to satisfy both demand and customer requirements while safely making money and a profit for the company.

5.10 System data is accurate and trusted by all.

5.11 Master planning and scheduling is committed to achieving and maintaining Class A accuracy and performance at the MPS Milestone recognition level (initial goal) and Full Certification (the ultimate goal) level (when achieved).

5.12 The master planning and scheduling team is on the same team as new product management, demand management, supply chain management, and financial management.

6. *Records*
   a. Demand charts (aggregate and detailed) and customer orders
   b. Master plan alignment and synchronization of demand and supply charts
   c. Rough cut capacity charts (volume and mix)
   d. Financial charts tied to IBP process tool
   e. Request for supply (RFS) to plant computer records
   f. Manufacturing site/plant master schedules
   g. Detailed production schedules and material plans
   h. Supplier schedules and purchase orders

7. *Forms*
   a. Policies (company rules supported by individual policies)
   b. Flow diagrams (main flows supported by subflow diagrams)
   c. Procedures defining the *how-tos*
   d. Work instructions tied to supporting software
   e. Performance and accuracy metrics (one-pagers)

8. *Definitions*
   Available-to-Promise (ATP): The uncommitted portion of a company's inventory and planned production, maintained in the master plan and/or master schedule to support customer

order promising. The ATP quantity is the uncommitted inventory balance in the first period and is normally calculated for each period in which a master planned and/or master scheduled receipt is scheduled. In the first period, ATP equals on-hand inventory plus any master planned and/or master scheduled receipt in the first period less customer orders that are currently due and overdue.

In any time period other than the first period containing master scheduled receipts, ATP equals the master planned and/or master scheduled quantity less customer orders in this period and all subsequent periods before the next master planned and/or master scheduled receipt. A negative ATP in one period generally reduces the ATP of the prior period(s).

Demand Planning (Aggregate): Demand planning at the aggregate level is the process of planning all demands for products and services to support the marketplace over at least a 24-month horizon. This process involves updating the product, brand, marketing, and sales plans and assumption each month and reaching consensus on an updated demand plan.

Detail Capacity Planning (Capacity Requirements Planning): The process of determining the amount of capacity required to produce product in the future and the resources needed to produce the projected level of work required from a facility over a time horizon. Capacity requirements are usually expressed in terms of hours of work or, when units consume similar resources at the same rate, units of production (e.g., pounds).

Integrated Business Planning (IBP): A process to develop tactical plans that provides leadership the ability to strategically direct its business to achieve competitive advantage on a continuous basis by integrating customer-focused sales and marketing plans for new and existing product with the management of the supply chain. The process brings together all the plans for the business (sales, marketing, development, manufacturing, sourcing, and financial) into one integrated set of plans.

It is performed at least once a month and is reviewed by leadership at an aggregate (product family) level. The process must reconcile all new product, demand, and supply plans at the aggregate level and tie to the business plan.

It is the definitive statement of the company's plans for the intermediate- to long-range term covering a horizon sufficient to plan for resources and to support the annual business planning process. Executed properly, the IBP process links the strategic plans for the business with its execution and reviews performance measurements for continuous improvement. Integrated business planning (IBP) is sometimes referred to as advanced sales and operations planning (S&OP).

Master Planning and Scheduling (MPS): A group of the business processes that may include the following activities: demand management (forecasting and customer order servicing), supply chain management or master supply planning (manufacturing and resource planning), and master scheduling (finishing/packaging scheduling, master supply scheduling, and rough cut capacity planning).

Master Schedule: A format that includes time periods (dates), the forecast, customer orders, projected available balance, available-to-promise, and the master schedule itself. The master schedule line on the master schedule grid reflects the anticipated build schedule for those items assigned to the master scheduler. The master scheduler maintains this schedule, and, in turn, becomes a set of planning numbers that drives material requirements planning. The master schedule represents what the company plans to produce expressed in specific configurations, quantities, and dates. The master schedule is not a sales forecast that represents a statement of demand. The master schedule is a statement of supply that takes into account the approved demand plan (forecast in some cases), the approved supply plan, and other important considerations such as backlog, availability of material, availability of capacity, and management policies and goals.

Master Scheduling: The process where the master schedule is generated, reviewed, and analyzed for balance, feasibility, and completeness. Adjustments (if necessary) are made to the master schedule to ensure consistency with the approved supply plan. The master schedule (the line on the grid) is the primary input to the material requirements planning (MRP) process. The sum of the master schedules for the items within the product family must equal (within defined tolerances) the approved supply plan for that family.

Material Requirements Planning (MRP): A set of techniques that uses bills-of-material, inventory data, and the master schedule to calculate requirements for materials. It makes recommendations to release replenishment orders for materials. Further, since it is time phased, it makes recommendations to reschedule open orders when due dates and need dates are not in phase.

Time-phased MRP begins with the items listed on the master schedule and determines (1) the quantity of all items and materials required to produce those items and (2) the date that the items and materials are required. Time-phased MRP is accomplished by exploding the master schedule through the bills-of-materials, adjusting for inventory quantities on hand or on order, and offsetting the net requirements by the appropriate lead times.

Production Schedule (Detailed Schedule): A plan that authorizes the manufacturing plant to take raw material and convert that raw material into a product or, said another way, to manufacture a certain quantity of a specific item. The sum of the daily detailed production schedules for an item must equal (within defined tolerances) the manufacturing site's weekly master schedule.

Production Scheduling (Detailed Scheduling): The process of developing the manufacturing site's detailed production schedule. Generally, while manufacturing is working the weekly or daily (defined in days, shifts, hours, minutes) production schedule, plant planning is creating the following week's detailed production schedule (days, shifts, hours, minutes) using the plant's master schedule.

Rough Cut Capacity Planning (RCCP): The process of converting the master plan and/or master schedule into requirements for key resources, often including labor, machinery, warehouse/cooler space, loading doors, suppliers' capabilities, and, in some cases, money. Comparison to planned capacity (demonstrated capacity plus or minus planned changes to the process) is usually done for each key or critical resource. This comparison assists the master planner and/or master scheduler in establishing a doable master plan and/or master schedule.

Supplier Scheduling: A procurement/purchasing approach that provides suppliers with schedules rather than individual purchase orders. Generally, a supplier scheduling program includes buyers who negotiate business agreements (contracts) for each supplier (among other responsibilities), a weekly (or more frequent) schedule for each supplier extending for some time into the future (schedule broken into three zones of commitment), and supplier schedulers who release against the supplier agreements (among other responsibilities). Also required is a formal priority planning system that works well, because it is essential in this arrangement to provide the supplier with valid quantities and due dates for all items on the supplier schedule.

Supply Chain Planning (Corporate): This process is responsible to ensure that the approved demand plan from IBP is satisfied with product and the approved supply plan is optimally assigned to the manufacturing facility (or facilities in a multi-plant environment). The corporate supply chain planning function does not schedule any of the company's manufacturing facilities (plants); instead, it requests certain types and quantities of products to be built in order to meet anticipated demand. Additionally, the supply chain planning function monitors projected inventory and backlogs to ensure that neither gets out of IBP tolerances. Thus, the corporate supply manager supported by the master supply planner act/s as a corporate-level balancer of demand and supply using many of the same techniques used by the plant-level master schedulers.

Supply Point Management: This is the internal part of the supply chain. The basic supply chain in the business world consists of customers (part of the external supply chain), suppliers (part of the external supply chain), and the company's owned facilities (e.g., manufacturing facilities, product development labs, etc.—part of the internal supply chain). Best practices suggest that a company get its own house in order before extending ties to the external supply chain.

Supply Review: The step in the IBP process where the submitted demand plan or request-for-product is received, analyzed, and accepted, which means that the request can be met in terms of inventory and/or capacity at an economical cost. Alternative supply plans are developed as needed to support demand where supply capabilities are lacking.

9. *Reference Documents*
    a. RACI for master (supply) scheduling as well as master (supply) planning
    b. Master planning and scheduling process flows and procedures as well as supply chain management procedures
    c. Work instructions for the enterprise resource planning (ERP) tool—integrated system tool

   d. One-pagers for metric definitions (performance and accuracy)
   e. RACI for master (supply) scheduling as well as master (supply) planning
   f. Master planning and scheduling process flows and procedures as well as supply chain management procedures
   g. Work instructions for the enterprise resource planning (ERP) tool—integrated system tool
   h. One-pagers for metric definitions (performance and accuracy)

MASTER PLANNING AND SCHEDULING PAST-DUE SUPPLY POLICY (AN EXAMPLE)

1. *Purpose*
   The purpose of this policy is to set the standard regarding past-due supply on the master plan and/or master schedule.

2. *Scope*
   This policy applies to all supply planners and schedulers managing make and/or buy items.

3. *Policy Statement*
   There will be **NO** past dues on the supply line of the master plan and/or master schedule.
   Past-due supply orders can trigger a downstream effect to all points (materials and capacity) feeding into the company's supply stream, thereby making everything that goes into the past-due item that is *not* already in that past-due item *past due*. This has a negative effect on the entire supply chain, both internal and external.
   The master plan and/or schedule is the master of all schedules. (All demand must pass through the master plan and master schedule.)
   It is the responsibility of the master planner and/or master scheduler to keep the master plan and/or master schedule valid and realistic so that supply chain partners and the company's partners can trust the master plan and/or master schedule as well as the company's performance against it.
   Demand management (sales and marketing) determine customer priorities. Supply management (master planning and scheduling) determine how to satisfy those customer priorities.

4. *Compliance*
   If there is a *past due* on the supply line of the master plan and/or master schedule, the master planner and/or master scheduler will have 48 hours to analyze and resolve the past due. On January 1, 20xx, master planners and/or master schedulers will have 24 hours to resolve and analyze the *past due*.
   (Note: This change is dependent upon the company reaching Class A status.)

During the 48 or 24 hours, the master planner and/or master scheduler must either make the supply materialize (expediting freight, increase production, fix a machine, etc.) or reschedule the work to a realistic, valid, and doable date. Rescheduling is the only approach to resolve a past due when all other options fail and must be set to an achievable date that requires no additional rescheduling.

5. *References and Associated Documents*
   Policy: All demand must pass through the master plan and/or master schedule.

Approved By

Supply Chain Director and/or Supply Manager (Master Planner) and/or Master Scheduler (Approvals to be determined in high-level design work)

Appendix E

Supply Chain Management Overall Process Flow Diagram (An Example)

The computer is an extension of people and what people do!

Here's an example of an integrated demand-driven supply management process flow that highlights the master (planning and) scheduling process and its integration points. The diagram was put together with the help of Jimmie White, Class A ERP Project Leader and Materials Manager for a West Coast company.

Jimmie White and the authors hope that this diagram helps the reader understand where master (planning and) scheduling fits into the total demand and supply planning process. Again, the flow diagram is only an example of the supply chain process at one company and therefore the reader is cautioned not to use it without the modifications needed to reflect the readers' and/or users' company.

This process flow was put together before *Master Scheduling: A Practical Guide to Competitive Manufacturing*, 3rd edition, was published and released in 2008. The authors chose to include the figure in this *Master Planning and Scheduling: An Essential Guide to Competitive Manufacturing*, 4th edition because it's still valid and required in a Class A supply chain management and master planning and scheduling environment.

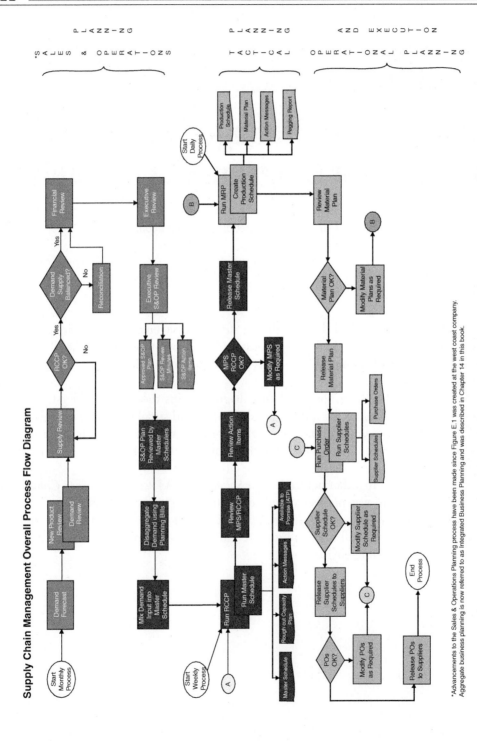

Figure E.1 Supply Chain Management Highlighting Master (Planning and) Scheduling (Darker Boxes)

*Advancements to the Sales & Operations Planning process have been made since Figure E.1 was created at the west coast company. Aggregate business planning is now referred to as Integrated Business Planning and was described in Chapter 14 in this book.

Appendix F

Master Planning and Scheduling Process Flow Diagram Examples

It doesn't matter whether you win or lose as long as you put it all out there!

An effective master planning and scheduling (MPS) process is comprised of master (supply) planning, master (supply) scheduling, and rough cut capacity planning. As has been detailed in this book, many companies have four levels of planning, of which level 2 is referred to as master planning (also called supply management or master supply planning) and level 3 is referred to as master scheduling (also called master supply scheduling).

Displayed in this appendix are four sample flow diagrams to enhance the readers' understanding of these two (master planning and master scheduling) all-important supply chain processes. The first and fourth flow diagrams (see Figures F.1 and F.4) describe what might happen on a *monthly* basis while the second (see Figure F.2) and third (see Figure F.3) flow diagrams describe what might happen on a *weekly* basis.

Again, all four of these master planning and scheduling flow diagrams are offered as examples to assist an initiative improvement team in getting started during the detailed design activity required to implement an effective and efficient MPS process. Although it is expected that these sample flow diagrams do and will fit most company environments, the reader is cautioned on just using them without the modifications necessary to make them company-specific.

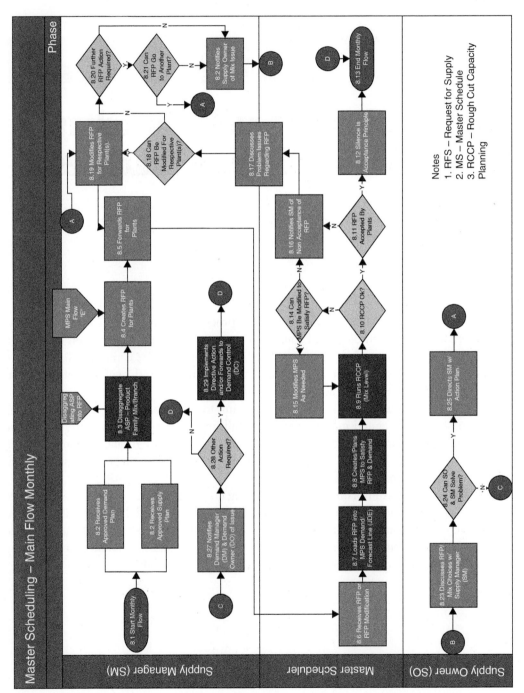

Figure F.1 Master Scheduling—Main Flow Monthly (an Example)

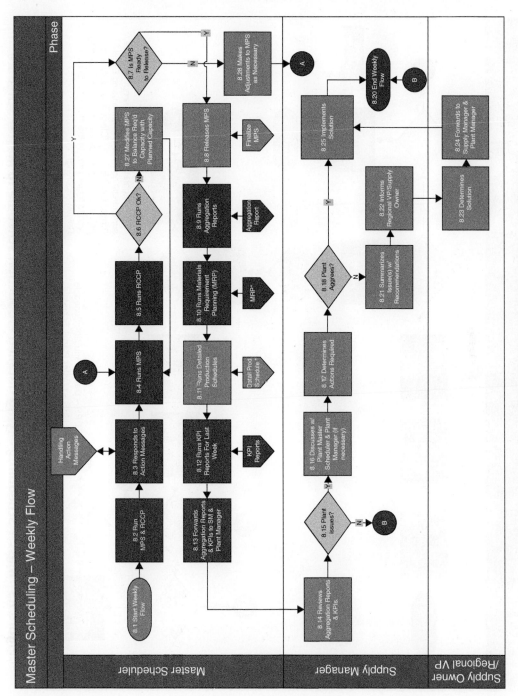

Figure F.2   Master Scheduling—Weekly Flow (an Example)

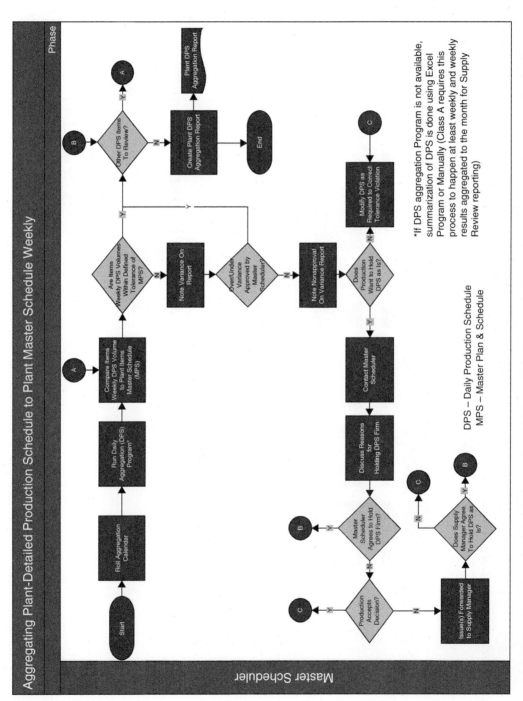

Figure F.3   Master Scheduling—Tying Detailed Production Schedule to Master Schedule

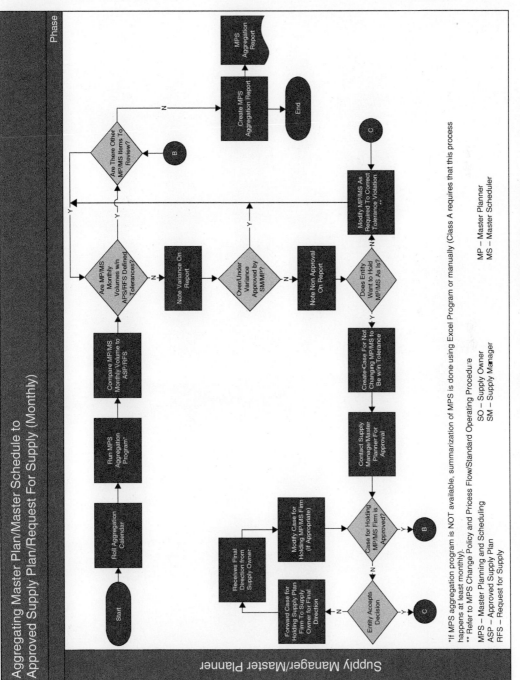

Figure F.4 Master Planning—Tying Master Plan and/or Master Schedule to Integrated Business Plan

Appendix G

Master Planning and Scheduling RACI Examples

It's only worth it if you enjoy it!

A successful master planning and scheduling (including rough cut capacity planning) process requires policies/rules, procedures/how-to's, flow diagrams, work instructions, accuracy/performance metrics, root cause analysis, and data integrity. Coupled with these behaviors and documents, responsibility and accountability must be laid out in a clear and understandable manner.

Enter the RACI template and format for identifying the functions responsible (R) and accountable (A) for various activities tied to the master planning and scheduling process. Additionally, the RACI matrix identifies the functions that should (need to) be consulted (C) as well as the functions that should be informed (I) during the execution of the activities listed. Figure G.1 displayed in this appendix is an example of a RACI for master planning and scheduling (MPS) along with Figure G.2 which is an example of a RACI for rough cut capacity planning (RCCP).

Once again, the reader is cautioned that the RACI matrices included in this appendix are only shared as *examples*. Each master planning and scheduling (including rough cut capacity planning) improvement initiative should create RACI matrices for these processes that are tied directly to the company and improvement initiative. These examples should *not* be picked up and used as they are presented in this book; tailoring for the company and MPS/RCCP improvement initiative must be done.

Function or Role	Sales	Supply Owner	Supply Manager	Plant Managers	Plant Master Scheduler	Demand Manager	Demand Owner	Customer Service Mgr	Customer Service Rep	Financial Lead
Create RFS for plants			C	A/R	C	C	C			
Disaggregate PF ASP to mix				A/R	I	I	C		C	
Forwards RFS to plants			I	A/R	I	C	C/I			
Reviews exception-driven action messages					I	A	R	C/I	I/C	I
Add/Change Resource Profile			A	R	C	C	C			
Aggregate Plant Master Schedules (MPS)			I	C	A	R	I			
Balance Demand & Supply			I	C	A	R	C	I	C	C
Calculate Mfg. Site Productivity (Efficiency & Utilization)			I	I	A	C	I	I		
Calculate MPS Performance by Branch Plant (BP)			I	C	A	R	I	I	I	I
Change Master Scheduling Assumptions			I	A	C	R	C	I	I	I
Change RFS			C	A/R	C	C	C			
Change sales order	R					I	C	A	C	C
Changes approved demand plan	C	I	I			R	A	C	C	C
Changes approved supply plan			A	R	C	C				
Changes prior customer order commitments	R			I	I	I	C	A	C	I
Compare MPS to RFS to ASP			I	I	A	R				
Confirm abnormal demand	R				I	I	I	A	C	C
Confirm or deny order				C	I	I	R	A	C	C
Create Planning Bills for Disaggregation Process	C	A	R	I	C	C	I	C	C	
Creates initial available to promise information	I	I	A	I	R		I	I	I	I
Creates MS to satisfy RFS demand			I	C	A	R				
Determine abnormal demand	R				I		I	A	R	R
Determine Available, Demonstrated, Planned & Maximum Capacity for RCCP			I	C	A	C				
Determine if RFS can be modified				A/R	C	C	C	C		
Determine Required Capacity for RCCP			I	C	A	R				
Determines actions needed to modify RFS			C	A/R	C	C	I			
Determines MS readiness for release	I			I	A	R		I	I	
Disaggregate Approved Supply Plan (ASP)				A/R			C/I	C/I		
Discusses problems/issues with RFS		C	A/R	C	C	C	I	I	C	I
Enter sales order	A/R						I	I	C	C
Execute RCCP at mix level				C	A	R				
Forwards aggregation / supply KPI reports to SM and Plant Manager		I		C	A	R	I			
Identify Gaps Between Demand & Supply		A	R	R	R	R	A	C	C	I
Implements KPI corrective action as necessary		I		C	A	R	C	I	I	
Informs Supply Manager of plant operation issues					I	A	R			I
Loads RFS into MS demand forecast line (JDE)				C	A	R				
Maintain Planning Bill Percentages for Disaggregation Process	R						R	A	C	C
Maintain Planning Bills for Disaggregation Process				A/R		C	C		C	
Maintains planning bill structure				A/R		C	C		C	
Manages planning time fence				I	A	R				
Modify MPS				C	A	R				
Modify MS as needed				C	A	R	C		C	C
Modify MS to balance req'd capacity with planned capacity				C	A	R				
Monitors data accuracy	R	I		A	R	R	R	I	R	I
Monitors available to promise use				I	R		I	R	A	I
Notify CS of order confirmation	R							A	I	
Notify Supply Management of non-acceptance of RFS		I		I	A	R		I	I	
Practice Silence is acceptance principal	R	A	R	R	R	R	A	I	I	I
Receive customer purchase order	R							A	C	C
Receive RFS /RFS Modification				C	A	R				
Receives modified or changed demand plan	I	I	I				R	A		
Receives modified or changed supply plan		A		R	I	I	I			
Releases MS				I	A	R				
Request to change demand plan	R	C	C	C	C	C	A	R	R	C
Request to change supply plan		C	A/R	R	R	R	R	C		
Reschedules past dues			I	C	A	R	C		C	C
Respond to RFS				C	A	R				
Responds to action messages				C	A	R	C			
RFS accepted or denied			I	C	A	R	I			
Run MS aggregations reports			I	C	A	R	I	I		
Runs detailed production schedules				I	A/C					
Runs Master Schedule				I	A	R				
Runs material planning						A				
Runs MS performance report			I	I	A	R	I	I	I	I
Supports Supply Manager during IBP process		A			R	R	I	I		C
Updates planning bill with probability percentages	R			I				R	A	
Uses pegging report when dealing with action messages				C	A	R	C		I	I
Validates ATP	C	C	R	C	R	R	R	A	C	I
Verifies MS is valid and realistic		I	C	C	R	C	I			

Figure G.1   Master Planning and Scheduling RACI (An Example)

Function or Role	Supply Owner	Supply Manager	Operations Directors	Procurement/ Purchasing	Engineering	Plant Managers	Master Scheduler	Demand Manager
Calculate Mfg. Site Productivity (Efficiency & Utilization)	A	R	C		I	C	I	
Determine Demonstrated Capacity for RCCP	A	R	C	I	C	C	I	
Determine Available/Gross Capacity for RCCP	A	R	C	I	C	C	I	
Determine Planned Capacity for RCCP	A	R	C	I	C	C	I	
Determine Maximum Capacity for RCCP	A	R	C	I	C	C	I	
Structure/Change Resource Profile	A	R	C	I	C	C	I	I
Determine Required Capacity for RCCP	A	R	C	C		C		I

Figure G.2   Rough Cut Capacity Planning RACI (An Example)

Appendix H

Master Planning and Scheduling Spinoff Task Team Charter

It doesn't matter whether you win or lose as long as you put it all out there!

This appendix highlights a master planning and scheduling spinoff task team charter. The idea behind creating a team charter is that all members of the task team agree to the major activities listed along with their defined deliverables. Additionally, all team members commit to being part of the MPS improvement initiative until all major activities are completed and the defined deliverables are met.

Once the spinoff task team completes the major activities defined in the team charter and ensures that all defined deliverables have been met, the spinoff task team is disbanded. Along with approving the MPS charter, the executive steering committee is committing that a job equal to or greater than the one left by each MPS task team member is awaiting each team member when the MPS task force is disbanded.

Figure H.1 is an example of a master planning and scheduling (MPS) spinoff task team charter. The example is offered to the reader as an example only. Each deliverable needs to have an accountable owner and associated due date.

Once again, the reader is cautioned on just picking up this MPS charter example and using it as is in their master planning and scheduling improvement initiative. The way to use this example is to carefully read it, discuss it, decide on what makes sense to the team, add other elements that make sense to the team, add due dates for each deliverable, package the tailored charter, submit to overall project team, submit to executive steering committee, and receive ESC approval for the charter contents.

Master Planning and Scheduling (MPS) Spinoff Task Team Charter

Activities	Deliverables
1. Detailed MPS Education	1. Attend/ Participate in MPS Education Workshop

2. High Level Design (MPS)
 	
(D-Document, P-Presentation,
PA-Presentation/Approval)
CFQ – Call for Questions
MP – Master Planning
MS – Master Scheduling
ESC – Executive
Steering Committee
	2. MPS High Level Design (HLD) Deliverables:
	   a. High Level Design Package Created for MP and MS
	   b. HDL Presentation Material Created and Presenter Note
	   c. High Level Design (HDL) Presented to ESC
	   d. High Level Design (HDL) Approved by ESC
	   e. ESC Authorizes Moving to Detailed Design Cadence to Be Followed

3. Obstacles to Remove
 	
Master Planning and
Scheduling (MPS)
Team and/or Project Team and/or
Executive Steering Committee
	3. Obstacle Regarding MPS Deliverables:
	   a. Listing of MPS Implementation Obstacles Identified
	   b. Obstacles/Show Stoppers Eliminated by MPS Task

4. Create MPS Task Plan (Create, Review, Enhance, Approve, Implement)	4. Approved MPS Task Plan by Project Leader (Project Leader, Working with MPS Team Leader, Creates a Summary for Executive Steering Committee)

5. Detailed Design (MPS)
 	
(D, P, PA, CFQ) – Rollout
MP – Master Planning
MS – Master Scheduling
ESC – Executive
Steering Committee
	5. MPS Detail Design (DD) Deliverables:
	   a. Detailed Design Documents Created for MP and MS
	   b. DD Presentation Material Created and Presenter Noted
	   c. Detailed Design (DD) Presented to ESC
	   d. Detailed Design (DD) Approved by ESC
	   e. ESC Authorized Moving to Own Phase on Proven Path

6. Create MPS Policies	6. All MPS Policies Noted in HDL Policy listing Created, Reviewed, Approved, and Implemented

Master Planning and Scheduling (MPS) Spinoff Task Team Charter *(Continued)*

Activities	Deliverables
7. Create MPS Process Flows	7. All MPS Process Flows Noted in HLD Process Flow Diagrams Listing Created, Reviewed, Approved, and Implemented
8. Create MPS Procedures	8. All MPS Procedures Noted in HLD Procedures Listing Created, Reviewed, Approved, and Implemented
9. Create MPS Work Instructions	9. All MPS Work Instructions Noted in HLD Work Instructions Listing Created, Reviewed, Approved, and Implemented

10. Create MPS Metrics	10. MPS Metric Deliverables:
	    a. All MPS Metrics Identified in High Level Design Defined Using One Pager Template
	    b. All MPS Metrics Defined on One Pagers Implemented, and Reporting Is Standard Process

11. Create Roles and Responsibilities for Master Planner and Master Scheduler	11. All Required Functional MPS Job Descriptions Complete and Approved by Executive Steering Committee (ESC) and Human Resources (HR)

12. Software Requirements to Support Master Planning and Scheduling (MPS)	12. MPS Software Deliverables:
	    a. All Required Software Changes/Enhancements Identified
	    b. MPS Software Changes/Enhancements Approved/Rejected

13. MPS Pilots – Computer, Conference Room, Live	13. MPS Pilot Testing and Implementation
	    a. MPS Computer Pilot Successful
	    b. MPS Conference Room Pilot Successful
	    c. MPS Live Pilot Successful

14. MPS Rollout Schedule (Site Implementations)	14. Master Planning and Scheduling Rollout Schedule Prepared, Reviewed, Modified, Accepted, and Approved
15. Company Sites Inform of MPS Implementations via Newsletter	15. Newsletter Sent to All Employees Announcing Master Planning and Scheduling (MPS) Site Rollout Plan

Master Planning and Scheduling (MPS) Spinoff Task Team Charter *(Continued)*

Activities	Deliverables
16. MPS Software (Support Software Installed and Implementation)	16. MPS Support Software Reviewed, Tested, Selected, Approved, Installed, and Implemented

17. MPS Integration Points Implemented	17. Required MPS Integrations with Other Process/Systems
	    a. Supply Management to Master Planning
	    b. Demand Management to Master Planning and Scheduling
	    c. Master Scheduling to Material Requirements Planning
	    d. Master Scheduling to Detailed Production Scheduling
	    e. Master Scheduling to Logistics Planning and Execution

18. Post Cutover Analysis	18. Post Cutover Analysis Deliverables:
	    a. Lessons Learned Discussed and Documented
	    b. Document Made Ready for MPS Task Team
	    c. Lessons Learned Forwarded to Overall Project Team and Executive Steering Committee

19. Team Final Assessment and Benefit Analysis	19. Final Assessment and Benefit Deliverables:
	    a. Final MPS Class A Self-Assessment Milestone Recognition
	    b. Formal Oliver Wight Audit Requested for T3 Milestone
	    c. Final MPS Class A Self-Assessment Full Certification
	    d. Formal Oliver Wight Audit Requested for T4 Certification

20. Oliver Wight Class A MPS (Capable) Criteria Assessment (T3)	20. Oliver Wight Class A MPS Capable Assessment Documented, Packaged, Presented, Approved, and Recognized
21. Oliver Wight Class A MPS (Advanced) Criteria Assessment (T4)	21. Oliver Wight Class A MPS Capable Milestone Recognition from Oliver Wight Received for MPS Milestones within Managing Internal Supply

Figure H.1   Master Planning and Scheduling Improvement Initiative Team Charter (An Example)

Appendix I

Master Planning and Scheduling Oliver Wight International Offerings Founders' and Co-Authors' Biographies

The secret to change is not on fighting the old but building on the new!

Sustainable business improvement can only be achieved by your own people. Unlike other consultancy firms, Oliver Wight Principals transfer to our clients our knowledge of how to operate to best practices and Class A standards.

Your executives will develop a clear understanding of corporate strategy and objectives, priorities, and compelling business needs. Oliver Wight Principals educate, coach, and mentor you to define your company's vision as well as your team's and/or your personal vision in addition to driving change throughout the business in order to achieve tangible (and nontangible) sustainable results.

Oliver Wight provides a series of offerings available throughout the world. Figure I.1 is a table highlighting several offerings along with pointing out other reasons why Oliver Wight and its Principals is the first choice of many companies looking to improve their value chains and/or supply chain management capabilities.

Oliver Wight works leadership, management, and tactical team members as they design, implement, and operate the new way, with a single, agreed-upon agenda for success. The reader and his or her company can gain a competitive advantage and achieve key company goals by tapping the Oliver Wight knowledge base, thought leadership, and global hands-on experience.

About Oliver Wight
Together We Make a Difference

People Skills	Process Knowledge	Tools Available	Delivery Methodology	Trusted Advisors
Educators Facilitators	Product/Portfolio Management	Class A Standard	Public Courses	Leadership Confidant
Coaches Mentors	Demand Management	Proven Path	Private Courses	Credible Communicator
Innovators Thought Leaders	Supply Management	IBP-Accelerator Accelerator	Facilitated Workshops	Reliable High Integrity
Authors Problem Solvers	Financial Management	Licensed Packages	Virtual Education	Passionate Enthusiastic
Change Management	Business Management	Book Series Wight Papers	On-Site/Virtual Coaching	Commitment Team Players

Figure I.1   Oliver Wight's Offerings and Capabilities

OLIVER WIGHT BIOGRAPHY
(FOUNDER OF OLIVER WIGHT EDUCATION ASSOCIATES)

Oliver Wight was a pioneer in planning processes. Ollie recognized the problems faced by companies and had a clear understanding of their needs. He was always looking to the future and finding things to improve. Oliver Wight had three great gifts: (1) He could take complicated subjects, unravel them, and make them simple, (2) He had a sensitivity to people that broke down barriers, and (3) He had innovative ideas and could communicate them in a way that gained acceptance, commitment, and enthusiasm.

Somehow, in the early years of the computer revolution, the role of people was misplaced. Ollie made it his personal mission to put people back where they belong and to give them the understanding they need to use their new tools.

Among his many enduring tenets is "Computers are *not* the key to success, people are (the key to success)." This remains a core philosophy of the Oliver Wight Companies. (*Authors' Note: Oliver Wight's quote and the Oliver Wight Companies philosophy are still true today as we enter the third decade of the twenty-first century. Please see "Final Thoughts" (following the Epilogue), which discusses master planning and scheduling in the future, that of moving thru the third (and maybe some of fourth) decade of the twenty-first century.)*

Oliver Wight used his gifts to build an enduring legacy in business processes. Nearly every company using planning processes and Ollie's philosophies, passed on through teaching, writing, and consulting, experienced significant increases in productivity, inventory turnover, customer service, and growth. His emphasis on the people side of business solutions earned him a reputation as a leading thinker in business education.

Ollie once said, quite modestly, "I've left some footprints." Those who have chosen to follow them are better off both personally and professionally. Oliver Wight was 53 years old when he passed away in 1983. The current Oliver Wight Principals have been following Ollie's footprints for 50 years now and (you know what) those Principals (including John and Eric) also have left several footprints.

WALT GODDARD BIOGRAPHY
(OLIVER WIGHT'S PARTNER AND CONFIDANT)

*A Person Ollie Could Trust**

Walt E. Goddard was Oliver Wight's partner until Ollie's death in 1983. Walt then became President of Oliver Wight Education Associates until 1998 when he retired and sold the company to the then-existing Oliver Wight Company Associates.

The Oliver Wight Companies were and remain the leaders in the field of educating servicing and manufacturing entities to improving their competitive position through better planning and scheduling. Since joining Ollie in 1970 and through 1998, Walt conducted courses for executives in top management, as well as for the designers and users of manufacturing resource planning with financial integration (MRPII) systems.

In addition to his many years of manufacturing experience, Walt worked as a consultant and educator with many of the companies featured in the Oliver Wight book series. He helped those companies improve their planning and scheduling processes and systems bringing sizeable benefits to the bottom line.

Walt dedicated his professional life to making servicing and manufacturing companies more competitive. He graduated from Rensselaer Polytechnic Institute with a Bachelor of Science degree in Management Engineering and was a well-known writer and speaker in the field.

Together Oliver Wight and Walt Goddard made a difference! The making a difference tradition continues today and is planned to continue tomorrow!

*Ollie's chosen words when Walt asked why Ollie chose him to be his Partner – "Because I can trust you!"

JOHN F. PROUD BIOGRAPHY
(CO-AUTHOR OF MASTER PLANNING AND SCHEDULING)

John Proud has been an Oliver Wight Principal for 33 plus years. During John's time with Oliver Wight Americas, Inc., he has educated, coached, mentored, advised, and authored on supply chain management principles and techniques. To be specific, John taught master planning and scheduling publicly for 17 years (privately for 30 plus years), integrated supply chain management publicly for 14 years (privately for 30 plus years), and all other Oliver Wight offered educational and workshop engagements privately during his total time with the company. He is a past member of Oliver Wight America's Board of Directors.

Regarding John's coaching assignments, he worked with a variety of companies as they pursued the lofty goal of Class A in Business Excellence, Class A in Operational Excellence, and Class A in Integrated Planning and Control. Through the years, he has mentored many supply chain management and manufacturing professionals in best-practice people behaviors, business processes, tools and technology, and data integrity requirements.

Prior to joining Oliver Wight in 1988, John held several positions with manufacturing companies. Those positions included manager of just-in-time manufacturing, customer service manager, customer education manager, information systems manager, systems analyst, industry marketing analyst, service parts scheduler, production control specialist, and captured consultant. Most of John's industry experience was developed at Xerox Corporation, Century Data Systems, and Burroughs Corporation (now Unisys).

Additionally, John has owned and been a partner/president of his California corporation since 1967. Proud Corporation has been involved in a number of businesses (service industry unrelated to manufacturing) over the years as well as supply chain management and master planning and scheduling educating, consulting, and mentoring. John holds a Bachelor of Science degree in mathematics from California Polytechnic State University (Cal Poly) and a Master of Science degree in management sciences from West Coast University.

As an author, he co-authored the books *Master Planning and Scheduling: An Essential Guide to Competitive Manufacturing* (4th edition), *The Oliver Wight ABCD Checklist for Operational Excellence* (5th edition), and *The Oliver Wight Proven Path* (2nd and 3rd editions). He also is the sole author of *Master Scheduling: A Practical Guide to Competitive Manufacturing* (1st through 3rd editions), the predecessor to this book. John was a contributing author to the Computers in Manufacturing series published by Auerbach Publishers, Inc. as well as the volume 2 reviewer (Master Production Scheduling). Not to be overlooked, Proud has authored several articles published by Oliver Wight, Auerbach, and APICS (ASCM).

During John's 50-plus year career in supply chain management, he spent 35 years as a member of APICS serving in a variety of capacities. He served as APICS Orange County Executive Advisor, Chapter President, President-Elect, and Vice-President Programs. John was the 1995 International Conference Chairperson, member of 1987 and 1992 International Conference Committees, and participated three years as a member of the Forecasting and Production Planning Certification Committee (creating the certification examinations) He is lifetime-certified in production and inventory management at the fellow level by the Association of Supply Chain Management (formerly APICS).

John is a Albert Nelson Marquis Lifetime Achievement Award recipient, an honor reserved for Marquis Biographees who have achieved career longevity and demonstrated unwavering excellence in their chosen fields. Prior to receiving this 2021 award, John was honored to be recognized in Who's Who in California and Who's Who in the West as well as being a recipient of The Golden State Award from Who's Who Historical Society. As his professional career nears an end, John has been notified that his biography and lifetime achievements will be published in Who's Who in America in 2022!

Eric Deutsch Biography
(Co-Author of Master Planning and Scheduling)

Eric Deutsch has been an Oliver Wight Principal for 10 plus years. During Eric's time with Oliver Wight Americas, Inc., he has educated, coached, mentored, advised, and authored on supply chain management and integrated business planning principles and techniques. At the time this book was published, Eric instructed the public Master Planning and Scheduling course and was a member of the Oliver Wight America's Board of Directors.

Eric has worked with diverse industries, including government (Department of Defense), apparel, food, furniture, sporting goods, chemical, pharmaceutical, and biotech. He has spent his Oliver Wight career assessing client's current practices, coaching and facilitating the design of best-practice future states, and providing shoulder-to-shoulder support for practitioners while implementing integrated business planning, master planning and scheduling, and supply chain planning processes.

Prior to joining Oliver Wight, Eric held several leadership positions in supply chain, manufacturing, and distribution with Merck, KGaA (EMD Chemicals) in North America. His experience includes transformational business process improvements, ERP system implementations (including SAP), and managing teams through several mergers and major corporate restructuring.

As project manager, Eric led the integrated business planning (advanced S&OP) implementation at EMD across four diverse business units simultaneously. The divisions achieved significant operational and financial performance results through IBP (see the EMD Chemicals case study at www.oliverwight-americas.com). In addition to leading the IBP implementation, Eric led supporting improvements in demand management, master scheduling, and supply chain planning, and execution.

As an author, he co-authored the book *The Oliver Wight Class A Standard for Business Excellence* (7th edition) and this fourth edition of *Master Planning and Scheduling: An Essential Guide to Competitive Manufacturing*, as well as several white papers to be found at www.oliverwight-americas.com.

Eric holds a Bachelor of Science degree in Bacteriology from the University of Wisconsin–Madison.

You are never too old to set another goal or dream a new dream! You can do whatever you want to do! You can choose how you want to live the rest of your life! It doesn't matter whether you win or lose as long as you put it all out there! You can also choose to follow the principle Class A in everything that you do! Go for it!

Glossary

Any body of knowledge be it accounting, engineering, manufacturing, law, medicine, and/or value chain management acquires a vocabulary of its own. Integrated business planning, sales and operations planning, product/portfolio management, demand management, supply management, financial management, master planning and scheduling, supply chain management, and enterprise resource planning are no exceptions. Jargon and acronyms notwithstanding, the need to use specific terminology remains.

Hence, this glossary is provided to help the reader with terms that may not be totally familiar. The definitions in this glossary have been taken from the *APICS Dictionary,* published by the Association for Supply Chain Management, the *Arista Manufacturing Systems Glossary of Terms*, and the authors' creativity and experience.

ABC Classification   The classification of a group of items in decreasing order of annual dollar volume (price multiplied by projected volume) or other criteria. This array is then split into three classes, called A, B, and C. The A group usually represents 10 to 20 percent by number of items and 50 to 70 percent by projected dollar volume. The C class contains 60 to 70 percent of the items and represents about 10 to 30 percent of the dollar volume. The ABC principle states that effort and money can be saved through applying looser controls to the low-dollar volume class items than will be applied to high-dollar class items. The ABC principle is applicable to inventories, purchasing, sales, and so on. *Syn:* ABC analysis, distribution by value. *See* Pareto Principle.

Abnormal Demand   Demand in any period that is outside the limits established by management policy. This demand may come from a new customer or from existing customers whose own demand is increasing or decreasing. Care must be taken in evaluating the nature of the demand: Is it a volume change, is it a change in product mix, or is it related to the timing of the order? *See* outlier.

Action Message   An output of a system that identifies the need for and the type of action to be taken to correct a current or potential problem. Examples of action messages in an MRP system include release order, reschedule in, reschedule out, and cancel. *Syn:* exception message, action report.

Actual Demand   Customer orders (and often allocations of items/ingredients/raw materials to production or distribution). Actual demand nets against, or "consumes," the forecast, depending on rules chosen over a time horizon. For example, actual demand will totally replace forecast inside the "sold-out" zone and partially replaces the forecast between the "sold-out" and "no order" zones (known as the "partially-sold-out" zone).

Actual Volume   Actual output expressed as a volume of capacity. It is used in the calculation of variances when compared to demonstrated capacity (practical capacity) or budgeted capacity.

Advanced Planning and Scheduling (APS)   Techniques that deal with analysis and planning of logistics and manufacturing over the short-, intermediate-, and long-term time periods. APS describes any computer program that uses advanced mathematical algorithms or logic to perform optimization or simulation on finite-capacity scheduling, sourcing, capital planning, resource planning, forecasting, demand management, and others. These techniques simultaneously consider a range of constraints and business rules to provide real-time planning and scheduling, decision support, available-to-promise, and capable-to-promise capabilities. APS often generates and evaluates multiple scenarios; management then selects one scenario to use as the official plan. The five main components of APS are demand planning, production (supply) planning, production scheduling, distribution planning, and transportation planning.

Affinity Diagram A total quality management tool whereby employees working in silence generate ideas and later categorize these ideas.

Aggregate Forecast An estimate of sales, often time-phased, for a grouping of products or product families produced by a manufacturing facility or firm. Stated in terms of units or dollars or both, the aggregate forecast is used for sales and planning (or for sales and operations planning) purposes.

Aggregate Planning A process to develop tactical plans to support the organization's business plan. Aggregate planning usually includes the development, analysis, and maintenance of plans for total sales, total production, targeted inventory, and target customer backlog for families of products. The production plan is the result of the aggregate planning process.

Anticipated Delay Report A report, normally issued by both manufacturing and purchasing to the material planning function, regarding jobs or purchase orders that will not be completed on time, giving the reasons why and stating when they will be completed. This report is an essential ingredient of the closed-loop MRP system.

APICS *See* Association for Supply Chain Management (ASCM).

Arista Manufacturing Systems Where MPS got its start. A small North Carolina company that recognized the need to decouple demand and supply (for example, sales forecast to material requirements planning) and inserted the master production schedule into the planning process for the first time. This initial MPS has evolved through the years into master scheduling and then into master planning and scheduling.

Assemble-to-Order The production environment where a good or service can be assembled after receipt of a customer's order. The key components (bulk, semifinished, intermediate, subassembly, fabricated, purchased, packaging, etc.) used in the assembly or finishing process are planned and usually stocked in anticipation of a customer order. Receipt of an order initiates assembly of the customized product. This strategy is useful where a large number of end products (based on the selection of options and accessories) can be assembled from common components. *Syn:* finish-to-order.

Assembly Lead Time The time that normally elapses between the issuance of a work order to the assembly floor and work completion.

ASCM Founded in 1957 as the American Production and Inventory Control Society (APICS), the Association for Operations Management builds operations management excellence in individuals and enterprises through superior education and training, internationally recognized certifications, comprehensive resources, and a worldwide network of accomplished industry professionals.

Automatic Rescheduling Rescheduling done by the computer to automatically change due dates on scheduled receipts when it detects that the due dates and need dates are out of phase. *Ant:* manual rescheduling.

Available Capacity The highest reasonable output rate that can be achieved with a given product mix, product specifications, workforce, plant, and equipment.

Available Inventory The on-hand balance minus allocations, reservations, back orders, and (usually) quantities held for quality problems. Often called *beginning available balance. Syn:* beginning available balance, net inventory.

Available-to-Promise (ATP) The uncommitted portion of a company's inventory and planned production, maintained in the master plan and/or master schedule to support customer order promising. The ATP quantity is the uncommitted inventory balance in the first period and is normally calculated for each period in which a master planned and/or master scheduled receipt is scheduled. In the first period, ATP equals on-hand inventory plus any master planned and/or master scheduled receipt in the first period less customer orders that are currently due and overdue. In any time period other than the first period containing master scheduled receipts, ATP equals the master planned and/or master scheduled quantity less customer orders in this period and all subsequent periods before the next master planned and/or master scheduled receipt. A negative ATP in one period generally reduces the ATP of the prior period(s).

Backlog　All of the customer orders received but not yet shipped. Sometimes referred to as *open orders* or the *order board. Syn:* order backlog.

Backorder　An unfilled customer order or commitment. It is an immediate (or past-due) demand against an item whose inventory is insufficient to satisfy the demand.

Back Scheduling　A technique for calculating operation start and due dates. The schedule is computed by starting with the due date for the order and working backward to determine the required start date and/or due dates for each operation.

Baseline Measures　A set of measurements (or metrics) that seek to establish the current or starting level of performance of a process, function, product, firm, and so on. Baseline measures are usually established before the implementation of improvement activities and programs.

Batch Manufacturing　A manufacturing facility whose resources or work centers are organized around particular types of equipment or operations, such as drilling, forging, spinning, mixing, compressing, blending, and the like. Products move through departments by individual work orders. *Syn:* job shop.

Bill-of-Material (BOM)　(1) A listing of all the subassemblies, intermediates, parts, and raw materials that go into a parent assembly showing the quantity of each required to make an assembly. It is used in conjunction with the master production schedule to determine the items for which purchase requisitions and production orders must be released. A variety of display formats exist for bills-of-material, including the single-level bill-of-material, indented bill-of-material, modular (planning) bill-of-material, transient bill-of-material, matrix bill-of-material, and costed bill-of-material. (2) A list of all the materials needed to make one production run of a product, by a contract manufacturer, of piece parts/components for its customers. The bill-of-material may also be called the *formula, recipe,* or *ingredients list* in certain process industries.

Bill-of-Material Explosion　The process of determining component identities, quantities per assembly, and other parent/component relationship data for a parent item. Explosion may be single-level, indented, or summarized.

Bill of Resources　A listing of the required capacity and key resources needed to manufacture one unit of a selected item or family. Rough cut capacity planning uses these bills to calculate the approximate capacity requirements of the master production schedule. Resource planning may use a form of this bill. *Syn:* bill of capacity. *See* bill of labor, capacity planning using overall factors, product load profile, resource profile, rough cut capacity planning, routing.

Block Scheduling　An operation scheduling technique wherein each operation is allowed a block of time, such as a day or a week.

Blow-Through　The computer technique for passing requirements through pseudo and phantom bill-of-material items. This process creates requirements for the component materials needed to manufacture higher-level items.

Bottleneck　A facility, function, department, or resource whose capacity is equal to or less than the demand placed upon it. For example, a bottleneck machine or work center exists where jobs are processed at a slower rate than they are demanded.

Bottom-Up Replanning　In MRP, the process of using pegging data to solve material availability and/or problems. This process is accomplished by the planner (not the computer system), who evaluates the effects of possible solutions. Potential solutions include compressing lead time, cutting order quantity, substituting material, and changing the master schedule.

Bucketed System   An MRP, DRP, or other time-phased system in which all time-phased data is accumulated into time periods, or "buckets." If the period of accumulation is one week, then the system is said to have weekly buckets.

Bucketless System   An MRP, DRP, or other time-phased system in which all time-phased data is processed, stored, and displayed using dated records rather than defined time periods, or buckets.

Bulk Issue   Parts issued from stores to work-in-process inventory, but not based on a job order. They are issued in quantities estimated to cover requirements of individual work centers and production lines. The issue may be used to cover a period of time or to fill a fixed-size container.

Business Plan   A statement of long-range strategy and revenue cost, and profit objectives usually accompanied by budgets, a projected balance sheet, and a cash flow (source and application of funds) statement. A business plan is usually stated in terms of dollars and grouped by product family. The business plan is then translated into synchronized tactical functional plans through the production planning process (or the sales and operations planning process). Although frequently stated in different terms (dollars versus units), these tactical plans should agree with each other and with the business plan.

By-Product   A material of value produced as a residual of or incidental to the production process. The ratio of by-product to primary product is usually predictable. By-products may be recycled, sold as is, or used for other purposes. *See* coproduct.

Capable-to-Promise (CTP)   The process of committing orders against available capacity as well as inventory. This process may involve multiple manufacturing or distribution sites. Capable-to-promise is used to determine when a new or unscheduled customer order can be delivered. Capable-to-promise employs a finite-scheduling model of the manufacturing system to determine when an item can be delivered. It includes any constraints that might restrict the production, such as availability of resources, lead times for raw materials or purchased parts, and requirements for lower-level components or subassemblies. The resulting delivery date takes into consideration production capacity, the current manufacturing environment, and future order commitments. The objective is to reduce the time spent by production planners in expediting orders and adjusting plans because of inaccurate delivery-date promises.

Capacity   (1) The capability of a system to perform its expected function. (2) The capability of a worker, machine, work center, plant, or organization to produce output per time period. Capacity required represents the capability needed to make a given product mix (assuming technology, product specification, etc.). As a planning function, both capacity available and capacity required can be measured in the short term (capacity requirements planning), intermediate term (rough cut capacity plan), and long term (resource plan). Capacity control is the execution through the input/output control report of the short-term plan. Capacity can be classified as budgeted, dedicated, demonstrated, productive, rated, safety, standing, theoretical, or maximum.

Capacity Available   The capability of a system or resource to produce a quantity of output in a particular time period.

Capacity Management   The function of establishing, measuring, monitoring, and adjusting limits or levels of capacity in order to execute all manufacturing schedules—that is, the production plan, master schedule, material requirements plan, and dispatch list. Capacity management is executed at four levels: resource planning, rough cut capacity planning, capacity requirements planning, and input/output control.

Capacity Planning   The process of determining the amount of capacity required to produce in the future. This process may be performed at an aggregate or product-line level (resource requirements planning), at the master scheduling level (rough cut capacity planning), and at the material requirements planning (capacity requirements planning) level.

Capacity Required   The capacity of a system or resource needed to produce a desired output in a particular time period. *See* capacity.

Capacity Requirements   The resources needed to produce the projected level of work required from a facility over a time horizon. Capacity requirements are usually expressed in terms of hours of work or, when units consume similar resources at the same rate, units of production.

Capacity Requirements Planning   *See* detailed capacity planning.

Cash Cow   A highly profitable product in a low-growth market.

Cell   A manufacturing or service unit consisting of a number of workstations and the materials transport mechanisms and storage buffers that interconnect them.

Cellular Manufacturing   A manufacturing process that produces families of parts within a single line or cell of machines operated by machinists who work only within the line or cell.

Class A   The zenith of business performance, achieved by operating a completely integrated business with excellence at all organization levels across all functions. It reflects a strong focus on deploying and achieving the strategic plans and objectives of the business, while maximizing rewards for stakeholders.

Common-Items Bill (-of-Material)   A type of planning bill that groups common components or ingredients for a product or family or products into one bill-of-material, structured to a pseudo parent item number. *Syn:* common-parts bill.

Component   The raw material, part, or subassembly that goes into a higher-level assembly, compound, or other item. This term may also include packaging materials for finished items. *See* ingredient, intermediate part.

Configuration   The arrangements of components as specified to produce an assembly.

Constraint   Any element or factor that prevents a system from achieving a higher level of performance with respect to its goal. Constraints can be physical, such as a machine center or lack of material, but they can also be managerial, such as a policy or procedure.

Continuous Flow (Production)   Lotless production in which products flow continuously rather than being divided.

Continuous Production   A production system in which the productive equipment is organized and sequenced according to the steps involved in producing the product. This term denotes that material flow is continuous during the production process. The routing of the jobs is fixed, and setups are seldom changed. *See* mass production, project management.

Coproduct   Product that is usually manufactured together or sequentially because of product or process similarities. *See* by-product.

Cumulative Lead Time   The longest planned length of time involved to accomplish the activity in question. For any item planned through MRP, it is found by reviewing the lead time for each bill-of-material path below the item; whichever path adds up to the greatest number defines cumulative lead time. *Syn:* aggregate lead time, combined lead time, composite lead time, critical path lead time, stacked lead time.

Cumulative Manufacturing Lead Time   The cumulative planned lead time when all purchased items are assumed to be in stock. *Syn:* composite manufacturing lead time.

Customer Order   An order from a customer for a particular product or a number of products. It is often referred to as an *actual demand* to distinguish it from a forecasted demand.

Customer Service   The ability of a company to address the needs, inquiries, and requests of customers. A measure of the delivery of a product to the customer at the time the customer specified.

Cycle Time   In industrial engineering, the time between completion of two discrete units of production. For example, the cycle time of motors assembled at a rate of 120 per hour would be 30 seconds. In materials management, it refers to the length of time from when material enters a production facility until it exits. *Syn:* throughput time.

Database   A data-processing file management approach designed to establish the independence of computer programs from data files. Redundancy is minimized, and data elements can be added to, or deleted from, the file designs without necessitating changes to existing computer programs.

Data Integrity   The accuracy and consistency of stored data, supported by standard rules and procedures that ensure that data has not been changed accidentally or deliberately without authority, and that it is accurate, complete, and on time.

Delivery Lead Time   The time from the receipt of a customer order to the delivery of the product. *Syn:* delivery cycle.

Demand   A need for a particular product or component. The demand could come from any number of sources: for example, customer order or forecast, an interplant requirement, or a request from a branch warehouse for a service part or for manufacturing another product. At the finished-goods level, demand data is usually different from sales data because demand does not necessarily result in sales; that is, if there is no stock, there will be no sale.

Demand Management   The function of recognizing and managing all of the demands for products to ensure that the master scheduler is aware of them. It encompasses the activities of forecasting, order entry, order promising, branch warehouse requirements, interplant orders, and service parts requirements.

Demand Plan   The set of activities and drivers that need to be actioned to deliver the forecast numbers. *See* forecast.

Demand Planning (Aggregate)   Demand planning at the aggregate level is the process of planning all demands for products and services to support the marketplace over at least a 24-month horizon. This process involves updating the product, brand, marketing, and sales plans and assumptions each month and reaching consensus on an updated demand plan.

Demand Pull   The triggering of material movement to a work center only when that work center is out of work and/or ready to begin the next job. It in effect eliminates the queue from in front of a work center, but it can cause a queue at the end of a previous work center.

Demand Rate   A statement of requirements in terms of quantity per unit of time (hour, day, week, month, etc.).

Demand Time Fence (DTF)   (1) That point in time inside of which the forecast is no longer included in total demand and projected available inventory calculations; inside this point, only customer orders are considered. Beyond this point, total demand is a combination of actual orders and forecasts, depending on the forecast consumption technique chosen. (2) In some contexts, the demand time fence may correspond to that point in the future inside which changes to the master schedule must be approved by an authority higher than the master scheduler. Note, however, that customer orders may still be promised inside the demand time fence without higher authority approval if there are quantities available-to-promise (ATP). Beyond the demand time fence, the master scheduler may change the MPS within the limits of established rescheduling rules, without the approval of higher authority. *See* option overplanning, planning time fence, time fence.

Demonstrated Capacity   Proven capacity calculated from actual performance data, usually expressed as the average number of items produced multiplied by the standard hours per item.

Dependent Demand   Demand that is directly related to or derived from the bill-of-material structure for other items or end products. Such demands are therefore calculated and need not and should not be forecast. A given inventory item may have both dependent and independent demand at any given time. For example, a part may simultaneously be the component of an assembly and also sold as a service part.

Derived Demand   Demand for components that arises from the demand for final design products. For example, the demand for steel is derived from the demand for automobiles.

Design for Manufacturability (DFM)   A rigorous, structured method of new-product design and introduction that intensively involves people from manufacturing, marketing, and suppliers in the development process.

Done effectively, DFM can dramatically enhance a company's ability to bring new products to market quickly, at lower costs, and with fewer downstream engineering changes.

Detail Capacity Planning (Capacity Requirements Planning)   The process of determining the amount of capacity required to produce product in the future and the resources needed to produce the projected level of work required from a facility over a time horizon. Capacity requirements are usually expressed in terms of hours of work or, when units consume similar resources at the same rate, units of production (e.g., pounds).

Detail Schedule   *See* production schedule.

Detailed Scheduling   *See* production scheduling.

Discrete Order Quantity   An order quantity that represents an integer number of periods of demand. Most MRP systems employ discrete order quantities. *See* fixed-period requirements, lot-for-lot, period order quantity.

Dispatch List   A listing of manufacturing orders in priority sequence. The dispatch list, which is usually communicated to the manufacturing floor via hard copy or CRT display, contains detailed information on priority, location, quantity, and the capacity requirements of the manufacturing order by operation. Dispatch lists are normally generated daily and oriented by work center.

Distribution Center   A warehouse with finished goods and/or service items. A company, for example, might have a manufacturing facility in Philadelphia and distribution centers in Atlanta, Dallas, Los Angeles, San Francisco, and Chicago. "Distribution center" is synonymous with the term "branch warehouse," although the former has become more commonly used recently. When there is a warehouse that serves a group of satellite warehouses, it is usually called a regional distribution center. *Syn:* field warehouse.

Distribution Requirements Planning   The function of determining the needs to replenish inventory at branch warehouses. A time-phased order-point approach is used where the planned orders at the branch warehouse level are "exploded" via MRP logic to become gross requirements on the supplying source. In the case of multilevel distribution networks, this explosion process can continue down through the various levels of regional warehouses, master warehouse, factory warehouse, and so on, and become input to the master schedule. Demand on the supplying source(s) is recognized as dependent, and standard MRP logic applies.

Distribution Resource Planning (DRP)   The extension of distribution requirements planning into the planning of the key resources contained in a distribution system: warehouse space, workforce, money, trucks, freight cars, and the like.

Dog   A slang term used to refer to a low-growth, low-market-share product.

Due Date   The date when purchased material or production material is due to be available for use. *Syn:* arrival date, expected receipt date.

Dynamic Data   A term used to describe data that change as a result of ongoing business transactions, such as inventory movement, as opposed to static data, which is data that are changed only as the rules of the business change, such as batch quantities or bills-of-material. *See* master data, static data.

Electronic Data Interchange (EDI)   The paperless (electronic) exchange of trading documents, such as purchase orders, shipment authorizations, advanced shipment notices, and invoices, using standardized document formats.

End Item   A product sold as a completed item or repair part; any item subject to a customer order or sales forecast. *Syn:* end product, finished good, finished product.

Engineering Change   A revision to a drawing or design released by engineering to modify or correct a part. The request for the change can be from a customer or from production, quality control, another department, or a supplier.

Engineer-to-Order (ETO)   Product whose customer specifications require unique engineering design, significant customization, or new purchased material. Each customer order results in a unique set of part numbers, bills-of-material, and routings. *Syn:* design-to-order.

Enterprise Resource Planning (ERP)   Framework for organizing, defining, and standardizing the business processes necessary to effectively plan and control an organization so the organization can use its internal knowledge to seek external advantage.

Enterprise Resource Planning (ERP) System   An accounting-oriented information system for identifying and planning the enterprise-wide resources needed to take, make, ship, and account for customer orders. An ERP system differs from the typical MRPII system in technical requirements such as graphical user interface, relational database, use of fourth-generation language, and computer-aided software engineering tools in development, client-server architecture, and open-system portability. *Syn:* customer-oriented manufacturing management system.

Exception Message   Also referred to as an exception driven action message. *Syn:* action message.

Exception Report   A report that lists or flags only those items that deviate from the plan.

Excess Capacity   A situation in which the output capabilities at a non-constraint resource exceed the amount of productive and protective capacity required to achieve a given level of throughput at the constraint.

Excess Inventory   Any inventory in the system that exceeds the minimum amount necessary to achieve the desired throughput rate at the constraint or that exceeds the minimum amount necessary to achieve the desired due date performance.

Expedite   To rush or chase production or purchase orders that are needed in less than the normal lead time; to take extraordinary action because of an increase in relative priority. *Syn:* stock chase.

Expediter   A production control person whose primary duties are expediting.

Fabrication   Manufacturing operations for making components, as opposed to assembly operations.

Fabrication/Assembly Plant   A manufacturing facility in which a configuration or geometric change is the majority of activity.

Family   A group of end items whose similarity of design and manufacture facilities is planned in aggregate, whose sales performance is monitored together, and, occasionally, whose cost is aggregated at this level.

Feedback   The flow of information back into the control system so that actual performance can be compared with planned performance.

Final Assembly   The highest-level assembled product, as it is shipped to customers.

Final Assembly Schedule (FAS)   A schedule of end items to finish the product for specific customers' orders in a make-to-order or assemble-to-order environment. It is also referred to as the *finishing schedule* because it may involve operations other than just the final assembly; also, it may not involve assembly, but simply final mixing, cutting, packaging, and the like. The FAS is prepared after receipt of a customer order as constrained by the availability of material and capacity, and it schedules the operations required to complete the product from the level where it is stocked (or master scheduled) to the end-item level.

Financial Appraisal   The process (occasionally a formal process step review) within the integrated business planning (IBP) process wherein operational (e.g., volume) plans and scenarios are assessed for their financial impact to the company. The process results in financial projections across the IBP planning horizon and pro-forma financial statements.

Finishing Lead Time   The time that is necessary to finish manufacturing a product after receipt of a customer order. The time allowed for completing the product based on the final assembly schedule.

Finish-to-Order (FTO)   A completing process that is very similar to assemble-to-order but usually is done near the end of the building cycle. *Syn:* assemble-to-order.

Finite Forward Scheduling An equipment scheduling technique that builds a schedule by proceeding sequentially from the initial period to the final period while observing capacity limits. A Gantt chart may be used with this technique.

Finite Loading Assigning no more work to a work center than the work center can be expected to execute in a given time period. The specific term usually refers to a computer technique that involves calculating shop priority revisions in order to level-load operation by operation.

Firm Planned Order (FPO) A planned order that can be frozen in quantity and time. The computer is not allowed to change it automatically; this is the responsibility of the scheduler in charge of the item that is being planned. This technique can aid schedulers working with master scheduling systems to respond to material and capacity problems by firming up selected planned orders. Firm planned orders are the normal method of stating the master schedule.

Fixed Order Quantity A lot-sizing technique in MRP or inventory management that will always cause planned or actual orders to be generated for a predetermined fixed quantity, or multiples thereof, if net requirements for the period exceed the fixed order quantity.

Fixed-Period Quantity An MRP lot-sizing technique that sets the lot size equal to the net requirements for a given number of periods.

Fixed-Period Requirements A lot-sizing technique that sets the order quantity to the demand for a given number of periods. *See* discrete order quantity.

Flexibility The ability of the manufacturing system to respond quickly, in terms of range and time, to external or internal changes. Six different categories of flexibility can be considered: mix flexibility, design changeover flexibility, modification flexibility, volume flexibility, rerouting flexibility, and material flexibility (see individual terms for a more detailed discussion). In addition, flexibility involves concerns of product flexibility. Flexibility can be useful in coping with various types of uncertainty (regarding mix, volume, etc.).

Flexibility Responsiveness The ability of the firm and its management to change rapidly in response to changes in the marketplace.

Flexible Automation Automation that provides short setup times and the ability to switch quickly from one product to another.

Flexible Capacity The ability to operate manufacturing equipment at different production rates by varying staffing levels and operating hours or starting and stopping at will.

Flowchart The output of a flowcharting process; a chart that shows the operations, transportation, storages, delays, inspections, and so on related to a process. Flowcharts are drawn to better understand processes. The flowchart is one of the seven tools of quality.

Flowcharting A systems analysis tool that graphically presents a procedure. Symbols are used to represent operations, transportation, inspections, storages, delays, and equipment.

Flow Order An order filled not by moving material through production as an integral lot but by production made over time and checked by cumulative count until the flow-order quantity is complete.

Flow Shop A form of manufacturing organization in which machines and operators handle a standard, usually uninterrupted, material flow. The operators generally perform the same operations for each production run. A flow shop is often referred to as a mass production shop or is said to have a continuous manufacturing layout. The plant layout (arrangement of machines, benches, assembly lines, etc.) is designed to facilitate product flow. Some process industries (chemicals, oil, paint, etc.) are extreme examples of flow shops. Each product, though variable in material specifications, uses the same flow pattern through the shop. Production is set at a given rate, and the products are generally manufactured in bulk. *Syn:* flow line, flow manufacturing, flow plant.

Forecast An estimate of future demand. A forecast can be determined by mathematical means using historical data; it can be created subjectively by using estimates from informal sources; or it can represent a combination of both techniques. The sum of the unconsumed forecast and the booked customer orders should remain constant unless an intentional change to the forecast is desired. Abnormal demands should not consume the forecast. *See* demand plan.

Forecast Bias The tendency of a forecast to systematically miss the actual demand (consistently being either high or low).

Forecast Consumption The process of reducing the forecast by customer orders or other types of actual demands as they are received. The adjustments yield the value of the remaining forecast for each period.

Forecast Error The difference between actual demand and forecast demand, stated as an absolute value or as a percentage.

Formula A statement of ingredient requirements. A formula may also include processing instructions and ingredient sequencing directions. *Syn:* formulation, recipe

Formulation *Syn:* formula.

Forward Scheduling A scheduling technique where the scheduler proceeds from a known start date and computes the completion date for an order, usually proceeding from the first operation to the last. Dates generated by this technique are generally the earliest start dates (ESDs) for operations. *Ant:* backward scheduling.

Four Ps (Sales/Marketing) A set of marketing tools to direct the business offering to the customer. The four Ps are product, price, place, and promotion.

Full Pegging The ability of a system to automatically trace requirements for a given component all the way to its ultimate end item, customer, or contract number. *Syn:* contract pegging.

Gross Requirement The total of independent and dependent demand for an item or an assembly prior to the netting of on-hand inventory and scheduled receipts.

Hardware (1) In manufacturing, relatively standard items such as nuts, bolts, washers, or clips. (2) In data processing, the computer and its peripherals.

Hedge In master scheduling, a quantity of stock used to protect against uncertainty in demand. The hedge is similar to safety stock, except that a hedge has the dimension of timing as well as amount. In purchasing, any purchase or sale transaction intended to eliminate the negative aspects of price fluctuations.

Horizontal Display A method of displaying output from a master scheduling or other time-phased system in which requirements, scheduled receipts, projected balance, and so on are displayed across the document. Horizontal displays routinely summarize data into time periods or buckets.

Housekeeping The manufacturing activity of identifying and maintaining an orderly environment for preventing errors and contamination in the manufacturing process.

Implementation The act of installing a system into operation. It concludes the system project, with the exception of appropriate follow-up or post-installation review.

Indented Bill-of-Material A form of multilevel bill-of-material. It exhibits the highest-level parents closest to the left-side margin, and all the components going into these parents are shown indented to the right. All subsequent levels of components are indented further to the right. If a component is used in more than one parent within a given product structure, it will appear more than once, under every subassembly in which it is used.

Independent Demand The demand for an item that is unrelated to the demand for other items. Demand for finished goods, parts required for destructive testing, and service parts requirements are examples of independent demand. *See* dependent demand.

Infinite Loading Calculation of the capacity required at work centers in the time periods required regardless of the capacity available to perform this work.

Information System Interrelated computer hardware and software along with people and processes designed for the collection, processing, and dissemination of information for planning, decision making, and control.

Information Technology The technology of computers, telecommunications, and other devices that integrate data, equipment, personnel, and problem-solving methods in planning and controlling business activities. Information technology provides the means for collecting, storing, encoding, processing, analyzing, transmitting, receiving, and printing text, audio, or video information.

Ingredient In the process industries, the raw material or component of a mixture. *See* component.

Integrated Business Planning (IBP) A monthly management process comprised of five key elements: product management review, demand review, supply review, integrated reconciliation review, and management business review. The process is led by senior management and evaluates and revises time-phased projections for demand, supply, portfolio, and strategic projects and the resulting financial plans. This is done on a 24-month (minimum) rolling planning horizon. It is a decision-making process that realigns the tactical plans for all business functions in all geographies to support the company's business goals, strategies, and targets. A primary objective of the process is to reach consensus on a single operating plan, to which executives of the management team hold themselves accountable and allocates the critical resources of people, equipment, inventory, materials, time, and money to most effectively satisfy customers in a profitable way.

Integrated Tactical Planning (ITP) A weekly cross-functional replanning process designed to ensure that the business stays on track to deliver the first three months of the signed-off integrated business planning process plans, thereby releasing time for senior management to spend on strategy and business plan development and deployment through the integrated business planning process.

Intermediate Part Material processed beyond raw material and used in higher-level items. *See* component.

Intermittent Production A form of manufacturing in which the jobs pass through the functional departments in lots, and each lot may have a different routing. *See* job shop.

Interplant Demand One plant's need for a part or product that is produced by another plant or division within the same organization. Although it is not a customer order, it is usually handled by the master production scheduling system in a similar manner.

Inventory Those stocks or items used to support production (raw materials and work-in-process items), supporting activities (maintenance, repair, and operating supplies), and customer service (finished goods and spare parts). Demand for inventory is dependent and independent. Inventory functions are anticipation, hedge, cycle (lot size), fluctuation (safety, buffer, or reserve), transportation (pipeline), and service parts.

Inventory Management The branch of business management concerned with planning and controlling inventories.

Item Any unique manufactured or purchased part, material, intermediate, subassembly, or product.

Item Record The master record for an item. Typically, it contains identifying and descriptive data and control values (lead times, lot sizes, etc.), and may contain data on inventory status, requirements, planned orders, and costs. Item records are linked together by bill-of-material records (or product structure records), thus identifying the bill-of-material. *Syn:* item master record, part master record, part record.

Job Order *Syn:* manufacturing order.

Job Shop (1) An organization in which similar equipment is organized by function. Each job follows a distinct routing through the shop. (2) A type of manufacturing process used to produce items to each customer's specifications.

Production operations are designed to handle a wide range of product designs and are performed at fixed plant locations using general-purpose equipment. *Syn:* jobbing. *See* intermittent production.

Job Shop Scheduling   The production planning and control techniques used to sequence and prioritize production quantities across operations in a job shop.

Just-in-Time (JIT)   A philosophy of manufacturing based on planned elimination of all waste and continuous improvement of productivity. It encompasses the successful execution of all manufacturing activities required to produce a final product, from design engineering to delivery and including all stages of conversion from raw material onward. The primary elements of zero inventories are to have only the required inventory when needed; to improve quality to zero defects; to reduce lead times by reducing setup times, queue lengths, and lot sizes; to incrementally revise the operations themselves; and to accomplish these things at minimum cost. In the broad sense it applies to all forms of manufacturing, job shop, and process as well as repetitive. *Syn:* short-cycle manufacturing, stockless production, zero inventories.

Kanban   A method of just-in-time production that uses standard containers or lot sizes with a single card attached to each. It is a pull system in which work centers signal with a card that they wish to withdraw parts from feeding operations or suppliers. The Japanese word *kanban,* loosely translated, means *card, billboard,* or *sign.* The term is often used synonymously for the specific scheduling system developed and used by the Toyota Corporation in Japan.

Latest Start Date   The latest date at which an operation order can be started in order to meet the due date of the order.

Lead Time   (1) A span of time required to perform a process (or series of operations). (2) In a logistics context, the time between recognition of the need for an order and the receipt of goods. Individual components of lead time can include order preparation time, queue time, processing time, move or transportation time, and receiving and inspection time. *Syn:* total lead time. *See* manufacturing lead time, purchasing lead time.

Lead-Time Offset   A technique used in MRP wherein a planned order receipt in one time period will require the release of that order in an earlier time period based on the lead time for the item. *Syn:* component lead-time offsetting, offsetting.

Lean Manufacturing   A philosophy of production that emphasizes the minimization of the amount of all the resources (including time) used in the various activities of the enterprise. It involves identifying and eliminating non-value-adding activities in design, production, supply chain management, and dealing with the customers. Lean producers employ teams of multiskilled workers at all levels of the organization and use highly flexible, increasingly automated machines to produce volumes of products in potentially enormous variety.

Level   Every part or assembly in a product structure is assigned a level code signifying the relative level in which that part or assembly is used within the product structure. Oftentimes the end items are assigned level 0 with the components/subassemblies going into it assigned to level 1 and so on. The MRP explosion process starts from level 0 and proceeds downward one level at a time.

Level-Loading   *Syn:* level schedule, load-leveling.

Level Schedule   (1) In traditional management, a production schedule or master production schedule that generates material and labor requirements that are as evenly spread over time as possible. Finished-goods inventories buffer the production system against seasonal demand. *See* level production method. (2) In just-in-time production, a level schedule (usually constructed monthly) ideally means scheduling each day's customer demand to be built on the day it will be shipped. A level schedule is the output of the load-leveling process. *See* load-leveling.

Line   (1) A specific physical space for the manufacture of a product that in a flow shop layout is represented by a straight line. In actuality, this may be a series of pieces of equipment connected by piping or conveyor systems. (2) A type of manufacturing process used to produce a narrow range of standard items with identical or highly similar designs. Production volumes are high, production and material handling equipment is specialized, and all products typically pass through the same sequence of operations. *See* assembly line.

Linearity (1) Production at a constant quantity. (2) Use of resources at a level rate, typically measured daily or more frequently.

Line Balancing (1) The balancing of the assignment of the tasks to workstations in a manner that minimizes the number of workstations and minimizes the total amount of idle time at all stations for a given output level. In balancing these tasks, the specified time requirement per unit of product for each task and its sequential relationship with the other tasks must be considered. (2) A technique for determining the product mix that can be run down an assembly line to provide a fairly consistent flow of work through that assembly line at the planned line rate.

Line Loading The loading of a production line by multiplying the total pieces by the rate per piece for each item to come up with a finished schedule for the line.

Load The amount of planned work scheduled, and actual work released for a facility, work center, or operation for a specific span of time. Usually expressed in terms of standard hours of work or, when items consume similar resources at the same rate, units of production.

Load-Leveling Spreading orders out in time or rescheduling operations so that the amount of work to be done in sequential time periods tends to be distributed evenly and is achievable. Although both material and labor are ideally level-loaded, specific businesses and industries may load to one or the other exclusively (e.g., service industries). *Syn:* capacity smoothing, level-loading. *See* level schedule.

Load Profile A display of future capacity requirements based on released and/or planned orders over a given span of time. *Syn:* load projection. *See* capacity requirements plan.

Logistics (1) In an industrial context, the art and science of obtaining, producing, and distributing material and product in the proper place and in proper quantities. (2) In a military sense (where it has greater usage), its meaning can also include the movement of personnel.

Lot A quantity produced together and sharing the same production costs and specifications.

Lot-for-Lot A lot-sizing technique that generates planned orders in quantities equal to the net requirements in each time period. *Syn:* discrete order quantity.

Lot Number A unique identification assigned to a homogeneous quantity of material.

Lot Size The amount of a particular item that is ordered from the plant or a supplier or issued as a standard quantity to the production process. *Syn:* order quantity.

Lot Sizing The process of, or techniques used in, determining lot size. *See* order policy.

Lot Splitting Dividing a lot into two or more sublots and simultaneously processing each sublot on identical (or very similar) facilities as separate lots, usually to compress lead time or to expedite a small quantity. *Syn:* operation splitting.

Make-to-Order (MTO) A production environment where a good or service can be made after receipt of a customer's order. The final product is usually a combination of standard items and items custom-designed to meet the special needs of the customer. Where options or accessories are stocked before customer orders arrive, the term *assemble-to-order* is frequently used. *See* assemble-to-order, make-to-stock.

Make-to-Stock (MTS) A production environment where products can be and usually are finished before receipt of a customer order. Customer orders are typically filled from existing stocks, and production orders used to replenish those stocks. *See* assemble-to-order, make-to-order.

Manufacturability A measure of the design of a product or process in terms of its ability to be produced easily, consistently, and with high quality.

Manufacturing   A series of interrelated activities and operations involving the design, material selection, planning, production, quality assurance, management, and marketing of discrete consumer and durable goods.

Manufacturing Calendar   A calendar used in inventory and production planning functions that consecutively numbers only the working days so that the component and work order scheduling may be done based on the actual number of workdays available.

Manufacturing Environment   The framework in which manufacturing strategy is developed and implemented. Elements of the manufacturing environment include external environmental forces, corporate strategy, business unit strategy, other functional strategies (marketing, engineering, finance, etc.), product selection, product/process design, product/process technology, and management competencies. Often refers to whether a company, plant, product, or service is make-to-stock, make-to-order, or assemble-to-order.

Manufacturing Lead Time   The total time required to manufacture an item, exclusive of lower-level purchasing lead time. For make-to-order products, it is the length of time between the release of an order to the production process and shipment to the final customer. For make-to-stock products, it is the length of time between the release of an order to the production process and receipt into finished-goods inventory. Included here are order preparation time, queue time, setup time, run time, move time, inspection time, and put-away time. *Syn:* manufacturing cycle, production cycle, production lead time. *See* lead time.

Manufacturing Order   A document, group of documents, or schedule conveying authority for the manufacture of specified parts of products in specified quantities. *Syn:* job order, manufacturing authorization, production order, production release, run order, shop order, work order.

Manufacturing Process   The series of operations performed upon material to convert it from the raw material or a semifinished state to a state of further completion. Manufacturing processes can be arranged in a process layout, product layout, cellular layout, or fixed-position layout. Manufacturing processes can be planned to support make-to-stock, make-to-order, assemble-to-order, and so on, based on the strategic use and placement of inventories. *See* production process, transformation process.

Manufacturing Resource Planning (MRPII)   A method for the effective planning of all resources of a manufacturing company. Ideally, it addresses operational planning in units, financial planning in dollars, and has simulation capability to answer what-if questions. It is made up of a variety of functions, each linked together: business planning, sales and operations planning, master scheduling, material requirements planning, capacity requirements planning, and the execution support systems for capacity and material. Output from these systems is integrated with financial reports such as the business plan, purchase commitment report, shipping budget, inventory projections in dollars, and so on. Manufacturing resource planning is a direct outgrowth and extension of closed-loop MRP.

Manufacturing Strategy   A collective pattern of decisions that acts upon the formulation and deployment of manufacturing resources. To be most effective, the manufacturing strategy should act in support of the overall strategic direction of the business and provide for competitive advantages.

Marketing Strategy   The basic plan marketing expects to use to achieve its business and marketing objectives in a particular market. This plan includes marketing expenditures, marketing mix, and marketing allocation.

Mass Production   High-quantity production characterized by specialization of equipment and labor. *See* continuous production.

Master Data   The data that are being used in a planning system to manage the business through the software system in a formal manner. Examples of common master data are bills-of-material, routings, work center files, and item (material) master.

Master Planning and Scheduling (MPS)   A group of the business processes that may include the following activities: demand management (forecasting and customer order servicing), supply chain management or master supply planning (manufacturing and resource planning), and master scheduling (finishing/packaging scheduling, master supply scheduling, and rough cut capacity planning).

Master Plan   The master plan is a format that includes time periods (dates), projected customer requirement groupings (e.g., key accounts), projected available balance by product subfamily/grouping, available-to-promise by group, and the master plan itself. The master plan reflects the anticipated build plan for those subfamilies/groupings assigned to the master planner. The master planner maintains this plan, and in turn, it becomes a request for production to the supplying site(s). The master plan represents what the company plans to supply expressed in subfamilies or groupings, quantities, and dates. The master plan is not a demand plan that represents a statement of demand. The master plan is a statement of supply that takes into account the approved demand plan, the approved supply plan, and other important considerations such as backlog, availability of capacity, and management policies and goals.

Master Planner   Often the job title of the person charged with the responsibility of managing, establishing, reviewing, and maintaining a master plan at the subfamily or grouping level (level 2 planning). Ideally, the person should have substantial product, plant, process, and market knowledge because the consequences of this individual's actions often have a great impact on customer service, material, and capacity planning. *See* master plan.

Master (Supply) Planning   A grouping of the business processes that includes the following activities: demand management (which includes forecasting and order servicing); production and resource planning; and master scheduling (which includes the final assembly schedule, the master schedule, and the rough cut capacity plan).

Master Schedule   The master schedule is a format that includes time periods (dates), the forecast, customer orders, projected available balance, available-to-promise, and the master schedule itself. The master schedule line on the master schedule grid reflects the anticipated build schedule for those items assigned to the master scheduler. The master scheduler maintains this schedule, which, in turn, becomes a set of planning numbers that drives material requirements planning. The master schedule represents what the company plans to produce expressed in specific configurations, quantities, and dates. The master schedule is not a sales forecast that represents a statement of demand. The master schedule is a statement of supply that takes into account the approved demand plan (forecast in some cases), the approved supply plan, and other important considerations such as backlog, availability of material, availability of capacity, and management policies and goals.

Master Schedule Item   A part (item) number selected to be planned by the master scheduler. The item is deemed critical in terms of its impact on lower-level components and/or resources such as skilled labor, key machines, dollars, and the like. Therefore, the master scheduler, not the computer, maintains the plan for these items. A master schedule item may be an end item, a component, a pseudo number, or a planning bill-of-material (an event).

Master Schedule Process   A time-phased planning activity using firm and planned quantities of demand, supply, and inventory balances for each item. Its primary use is to help in developing the master schedule, and it contains lines for forecast and customer order demands, the MPS supply, and the available-to-promise and projected available inventory balances. Most computer systems use logic to assist the master scheduler in establishing MPS quantities and due dates that meet lead time, safety stock, and lot-size policies established for the item.

Master Scheduler   Often the job title of the person charged with the responsibility of managing, establishing, reviewing, and maintaining a master schedule for select items. Ideally, the person should have substantial product, plant, process, and market knowledge because the consequences of this individual's actions often have a great impact on customer service, material, and capacity planning.

Master Scheduling   The process where the master schedule is generated, reviewed, and analyzed for balance, feasibility, and completeness. Adjustments (if necessary) are made to the master schedule to ensure consistency with the approved supply plan. The master schedule (the line on the grid) is the primary input to the material requirements planning (MRP) process. The sum of the master schedules for the items within the product family must equal (within defined tolerances) the approved supply plan for that family.

Material Requirements Planning (MRP)   A set of techniques that uses bills-of-material, inventory data, and the master schedule to calculate requirements for materials. It makes recommendations to release replenishment orders for materials. Further, since it is time-phased, it makes recommendations to reschedule open orders when due dates and need dates are not in phase. Time-phased MRP begins with the items listed on the master schedule and determines (1) the quantity of all items and materials required to produce those items and (2) the date that the items and materials are required. Time-phased MRP is accomplished by exploding the master schedule through the bills-of-materials, adjusting for inventory quantities on hand or on order, and offsetting the net requirements by the appropriate lead times.

Materials Management   The grouping of management functions supporting the complete cycle of material flow, from the purchase and internal control of production materials to the planning and control of work-in-process to the warehousing, shipping, and distribution of the finished product.

Matrix   A mathematical array having one, two, and sometimes more dimensions, into which collections of data may be stored and processed.

Maximum Capacity   The highest amount of actual output produced in the past when all efforts have been made to "optimize" the resource; for instance, overtime, additional personnel, extra hours, extra shifts, reassignment of personnel, or use of any related equipment. Maximum capacity is the most one could ever expect to produce in a short period of time but represents a rate that cannot be maintained over a long period of time.

Mixed-Model Master Schedule   The technique of setting and maintaining the master schedule to support mixed-model production.

Mixed-Model Production   Making several different parts of products in varying lot sizes so that a factory is making close to the same mix of products that will be sold that day. The mixed-model schedule governs the making and the delivery of component parts, including those provided by outside suppliers. The goal is to build every model, every day, according to daily demand.

Mixed-Model Scheduling   The process of developing one or more schedules to enable mixed-model production. The goal is to achieve a day's production each day. *See* mixed-model production.

Mix Forecast   Forecast of the proportion of products that will be sold within a given product family, or the proportion of options offered within a product line. Product and option mix must be forecasted as well as aggregate product families. Even though the appropriate level of units is forecasted for a given product line, an inaccurate mix forecast can create material shortages and inventory problems.

Modular Bill-of-Material   A type of planning bill that is arranged in product modules or options. It is often used in companies where the product has many optional features—for example, assemble-to-order companies such as automobile manufacturers. *See* pseudo bill-of-material.

Move Card   In the just-in-time context, a card or other signal indicating that a specific number of units of a particular item are to be taken from a source (usually outbound stock point) and taken to the point of use (usually inbound stock point). It authorizes the movement of one part number between a single pair of work centers. The card circulates between the outbound stock point of the supplying work center and the inbound stock point of the using work center. *Syn:* move signal. *See* kanban.

Multilevel Bill-of-Material   A display of all the components directly or indirectly used in a parent, together with the quantity required with each component. If a component is a subassembly, blend, intermediate, or the like, all of its components and all their components also will be exhibited, down to purchase parts and materials.

Multilevel Master Schedule   A master scheduling technique that allows any level in an end item's bill-of-material to be master scheduled. To accomplish this, MPS items must receive requirements from independent and dependent demand sources.

Need Date   The date when an item is required for its intended use. In an MRP system, this date is calculated by a bill-of-material explosion of a schedule and the netting of available inventory against that requirement.

Net Change MRP   An approach in which the material requirements plan is continually retained in the computer. Whenever a change is needed in requirements, open order inventory status, or bill-of-material, a partial explosion and netting is made for only those parts affected by the change.

Net Requirements   In MRP, the net requirements for a part or an assembly are derived by applying gross requirements and allocations against inventory on hand, scheduled receipts, and safety stock. Net requirements, lot-sized and offset for lead time, become planned orders.

Netting   The process of calculating net requirements.

New Product Introduction (NPI)   Defines processes for creating and introducing a new product or new service that the firm has not marketed previously. It usually excludes products or services that are minor modifications, line extensions, or changes in promotions.

Non-Value-Added   An activity that does not add value to a product; for example, moving the product from one work center to another inside a facility. One aspect of continuous improvement is the elimination or reduction of non-value-added activities.

Offload   To reschedule or use alternate routings to reduce the workload on a machine, work center, or facility.

Offsetting   *Syn:* lead-time offset

On-Hand Balance   The quantity shown in the inventory records as being physically in stock.

On-Time Schedule Performance   A measure (percentage) of meeting the customer's originally negotiated delivery request date. Performance can be expressed as a percentage based on the number of orders, line items, or dollar value shipped on time.

Open Order   (1) A released manufacturing order or purchase order. *Syn:* released order. (2) An unfilled customer order.

Operation   (1) A job or task, consisting of one or more work elements, usually done essentially in one location. (2) The performance of any planned work or method associated with an individual, machine, process, department, or inspection. (3) One or more elements that involve one of the following: the intentional changing of an object in any of its physical or chemical characteristics; the assembly or disassembly of parts or objects; the preparation of an object for another operation, transportation, inspection, or storage; planning, calculating, or giving or receiving information.

Operation Number   A sequential number, usually two, three, or four digits long, such as 010, 020, or 030, that indicates the sequence in which operations are to be performed within an item's routing.

Operations Scheduling   The actual assignment of starting or completion dates to operations or groups of operations to show when these operations must be done if the manufacturing order is to be completed on time. These dates are used in the dispatching function. *Syn:* detailed scheduling, order scheduling, shop scheduling.

Operations Sequence   The sequential steps for an item to follow in its flow through the plant. For instance: operation 1, cut bar stock; operation 2, grind bar stock; operation 3, shape; operation 4, polish; operation 5, inspect and send to stock. This information is normally maintained in the routing file.

Operations Sequencing   A technique for short-term planning of actual jobs to be run in each work center based upon capacity (i.e., existing workforce and machine availability) and priorities. The result is a set of projected completion times for the operations and simulated queue levels for facilities.

Optimization   Achieving the best possible solution to a problem in terms of a specified objective function.

Option A choice that must be made by the customer or company when customizing the end product. In many companies, the term *option* means a mandatory choice from a limited selection.

Option Overplanning Typically, scheduling extra quantities of a master schedule option greater than the expected sales for that option to protect against unanticipated demand. This schedule quantity may only be planned in the time period where new customer orders are currently being accepted, typically just after the demand time fence. This technique is usually used on the second level of a two-level master scheduling approach to create a situation where more of the individual options are available than of the overall family.

Order A general term that may refer to such diverse items as a purchase order, shop order, customer order, planned order, or schedule.

Order Entry The process of accepting and translating what a customer wants into terms used by the manufacturer or distributor. This can be as simple as creating shipping documents for a finished-goods product, or it might be a more complicated series of activities, including engineering efforts for make-to-order products.

Order Management The planning, directing, monitoring, and controlling of the processes related to customer orders, manufacturing orders, and purchase orders. Regarding customer orders, order management includes order promising, order entry, order pick, pack and ship, billing, and reconciliation of the customer account. Regarding manufacturing orders, order management includes order release, routing, manufacture, monitoring, and receipt into stores or finished-goods inventories. Regarding purchasing orders, order management includes order placement, monitoring, receiving, acceptance, and payment of supplier.

Order Promising The process of making a delivery commitment—that is, answering the question "When can you ship?" For make-to-order products, this usually involves a check of uncommitted material and availability of capacity, often as represented by the master schedule available-to-promise. *Syn:* customer order promising, order dating. *See* available-to-promise, order service.

Order Quantity The amount of an item to be ordered. *Syn:* lot size.

Order Release The activity of releasing materials to a production process to support a manufacturing order.

Outbound Stock Point The designated locations near the point of use on a plant floor to which material produced is taken until it is pulled to the next operation.

Overload A condition when the total hours of work outstanding at a work center exceed that work center's capacity.

Overloaded Master Schedule A schedule that includes either past-due quantities or quantities that are greater than the ability to produce, given current capacity and material availability. An overloaded master schedule should be made feasible before MRP is run.

Overtime Work beyond normal established working hours that usually requires that a premium be paid to the workers.

Package-to-Order A production environment in which a good or service can be packaged after receipt of a customer order. The item is common across many different customers; packaging determines the end product.

Parent Item The item produced from one or more components.

Pareto Principle A theory developed by Vilfredo Pareto, an Italian economist, that states that a small percentage of a group accounts for the largest fraction of the impact, value, and so on. In an ABC classification, for example, 20 percent of the inventory items may constitute 80 percent of the inventory value.

Part Generally, a material item that is used as a component and is not an assembly, subassembly, blend, intermediate, or the like.

Part Family A collection of parts grouped for some managerial purpose.

Part Number *Syn:* item number.

Past-Due Order   A line item on an open customer order that has an original scheduled ship date that is earlier than the current date. *Syn:* delinquent order, late order. *See* backlog, order backlog.

Payback   A method of evaluating an investment opportunity that provides a measure of the time required to recover the initial amount invested in a project.

Pegged Requirement   A requirement that shows the next-level parent item (or customer order) as the source of the demand.

Pegging   In MRP and MPS, the capability to identify for a given item the sources of its gross requirements and/or allocations. Pegging can be thought of as "live where-used" information.

Performance Measure   In a performance measurement system, the actual value measured for the criterion. *See* performance criterion, performance measurement system, performance standard.

Performance Measurement System   A system for collecting, measuring, and comparing a measure to a standard for a specific criterion for an operation, item, good, service, business, or the like. A performance measurement system consists of a criterion, a standard, and a measure.

Performance Standard   In a performance measurement system, the accepted, targeted, or expected value for the criterion.

Period Capacity   The number of standard hours of work that can be performed at a facility or work center in a given time period.

Period Order Quantity   A lot-sizing technique under which the lot size is equal to the net requirements for a given number of time periods, for example, a week into the future.

Phantom   An intermediate or assembly that is manufactured but is immediately consumed in the manufacture of its parent. Phantoms are "blow-through" items.

Phantom Bill-of-Material   A bill-of-material coding and structuring technique used primarily for transient (non-stocked) subassemblies. For the transient item, lead time is set to zero and the order quantity to lot-for-lot. This permits MRP logic to drive requirements straight through the phantom item to its components, but the MRP system usually retains its ability to net against any occasional inventories of the item. This technique also facilitates the use of common bills-of-material for engineering and manufacturing. *Syn:* blow-through, transient bill-of-material. *See* pseudo bill-of-material.

Plan   A predetermined course of action over a specified period of time that represents a projected response to an anticipated environment to accomplish a specific set of adaptive objectives.

Planned Capacity   Demonstrated capacity plus or minus anticipated adjustments to that capacity in the future. Adjustments might include the addition of equipment or people, or reductions in machines or staff.

Planned Order   A suggested order quantity, release date, and due date created by the planning system's logic when it encounters net requirements in processing MRP. In some cases, it can also be created by a master scheduling module. Planned orders are created by the computer, exist only within the computer, and may be changed or deleted by the computer during subsequent processing if conditions change. Planned orders at one level will be exploded into gross requirements for components at the next level. Planned orders, along with released orders, serve as input to capacity requirements planning to show the total capacity requirements by work center in future time periods. *See* planning time fence.

Planned Receipt   An anticipated receipt against an open purchase order or open production order. *Syn:* planned order receipt.

Planning Bill-of-Material   An artificial grouping of items and/or events in the bill-of-material format, used to facilitate master scheduling and material planning. It may include the historical average of demand expressed as a percentage of total demand for all options within a feature or for a specific end item within a product family and is used as the quantity per in the planning bill-of-material. *Syn:* planning bill.

Planning Fence   *Syn:* planning time fence.

Planning Horizon   The amount of time a plan extends into the future. For a master schedule, this is normally set to cover a minimum of cumulative lead time plus time for lot sizing low-level components and for capacity changes of primary work centers or of key suppliers. For longer-term plans the planning horizon must be long enough to permit any needed additions to capacity. *See* cumulative lead time, planning time fence.

Planning Time Fence (PTF)   A point in time denoted in the planning horizon of the master scheduling process that marks a boundary inside of which changes to the schedule may adversely affect component schedules, capacity plans, customer deliveries, and cost. Planned orders outside the planning time fence can be changed by system planning logic. Changes inside the planning time fence must be manually changed by the master scheduler. *Syn:* planning fence. *See* cumulative lead time, demand time fence, firm planned order, planned order, planning horizon, time fence.

Point-of-Use Delivery   Direct delivery of material to a specified location on a plant floor near the operation where it is to be used.

Policies   Definitive statements of what should be done in the business (rules of the game).

Postponement   A product design strategy that shifts product differentiation closer to the consumer by postponing identity changes, such as assembly or packaging, to the last possible supply chain location.

Prediction   An intuitive estimate of demand taking into account changes and new factors influencing the market, as opposed to a forecast, which is an objective projection of the past into the future.

Priority   In a general sense, the relative importance of jobs; that is, the sequence in which jobs should be worked on. It is a separate concept from capacity.

Priority Planning   The function of determining what material is needed and when. Master scheduling and material requirements planning are the elements used for the planning and replanning process in order to maintain proper due dates on required materials.

Probability   Mathematically, a number between 0 and 1 that estimates the fraction of experiments (if the same experiment were being repeated many times) in which a particular result would occur. This number can be either subjective or based upon the empirical results of experimentation. It can also be derived for a process to give the probable outcome of experimentation.

Procedures   Definitions of approved methods used to accomplish tasks (script of how things are to be done).

Process   (1) A planned series of actions or operations (e.g., mechanical, electrical, chemical, inspection, test) that advances a material or procedure from one stage of completion to another. (2) A planned and controlled treatment that subjects materials or procedures to the influence of one or more types of energy (e.g., human, mechanical, electrical, chemical, thermal) for the time required to bring about the desired reactions or results.

Process Flow Production   A production approach with minimal interruptions in the actual processing in any one production run or between production runs of similar products. Queue time is virtually eliminated by integrating the movement of the product into the actual operation of the resource performing the work.

Process Flow Scheduling   A generalized method for planning equipment usage and material requirements that uses the process structure to guide scheduling calculations. It is used in flow environments common in process industries.

Process Manufacturing   Production that adds value by mixing, separating, forming, and/or performing chemical reactions. It may be done in either batch or continuous mode.

Process Plant   A manufacturing facility in which a chemical or compositional change is the majority of activity.

Process Sheet   Detailed manufacturing instructions issued to the plant. The instructions may include specifications on speeds, feeds, temperatures, tools, fixtures, and machines and sketches of setups and semifinished dimensions.

Process Steps   The operations or stages within the manufacturing cycle required to transform components into intermediates or finished goods. From a larger perspective, the operations or stages within any business required to turn inputs into outputs.

Product Configurator   A system generally rule based, to be used in design-to-order, engineer-to-order, or make-to-order environments where numerous product variations exist. Product configurators perform intelligent modeling of the part of product attributes and often create solid models, drawings, bills-of-material, and cost estimates that can be integrated into CAD/CAM and MRPII systems as well as sales order entry systems.

Product Differentiation   A strategy of making a product distinct from the competition on a nonprice basis—for example, in availability, durability, quality, reliability, and the like.

Product Portfolio Management   A business management process that helps managers assess the product portfolio process now and relative to a future position.

Product Management Review   A monthly meeting focused on reaching consensus on the product portfolio plan over a typical horizon of 24 to 36 months. It is an integral element of the integrated business planning process.

Production   The conversion of inputs into finished products.

Production and Inventory Management   General term referring to the body of knowledge and activities concerned with planning and controlling rates of purchasing, production, distribution, and related capacity resources to achieve target levels of customer service, backlogs, operating costs, inventory investment, manufacturing efficiency, and ultimately, profit and return on investment.

Production Capability   (1) The highest sustainable output rate that can be achieved for a given product mix, raw materials, worker effort, plant, and equipment. (2) The collection of personnel, equipment, material, and process segment capabilities. (3) The total of the current committed, available, and unattainable capability of the production facility. The capability includes the capacity of the resource.

Production Control   The function of directing or regulating the movement of goods through the entire manufacturing cycle from the requesting of raw material to the delivery of the finished products.

Production Forecast   A projected level of customer demand for a feature (option, accessory, etc.) of a make-to-order or an assemble-to-order product. Used in two-level master scheduling, it is calculated by netting customer backlog against an overall family or product line master production schedule and then factoring this product's available-to-promise by the option percentage in a planning bill-of-material. *Syn:* option forecast.

Production Process   The activities involved in converting inputs into finished goods.

Production Rate   The rate of production, usually expressed in units, cases, or some other broad measure, expressed by a period of time, for example, per hour, shift, day, or week.

Production Schedule (Detailed Schedule)   A plan that authorizes the manufacturing plant to take raw material and convert that raw material into a product, or said another way, to manufacture a certain quantity of a specific item. The sum of the daily detailed production schedules for an item must equal (within defined tolerances) the manufacturing site's weekly master schedule.

Production Scheduling (Detailed Scheduling)   The process of developing the manufacturing site's detailed production schedule. Generally, while manufacturing is working the weekly or daily (defined in days, shifts, hours, minutes) production schedule, plant planning is creating the following week's detailed production schedule (days, shifts, hours, minutes) using the plant's master schedule.

Product Life Cycle   The stages a new product idea goes through from beginning to end; that is, the stages that a product passes through from introduction through growth, maturity, and decline. The time from initial research and development to the time at which sales and support of the product to customers are withdrawn. The period of time during which a product can be produced and marketed profitably.

Product Line   A group of products whose similarity in manufacturing procedures, marketing characteristics, or specifications enables them to be aggregated for planning, marketing, or, occasionally, costing.

Product Load Profile   A listing of the required capacity and key resources needed to manufacture one unit of a selected item or family. The resource requirements are further defined by a lead-time offset to predict the impact of the product on the load of the key resources by a specific time period. The product load profile can be used for rough cut capacity planning to calculate the approximate capacity requirements of the master production schedule. *See* bill of resources, resource profile, rough cut capacity planning.

Product Mix   The proportion of individual products that make up the total production or sales volume. Changes in the product mix can mean drastic changes in the manufacturing requirements for certain types of labor and material.

Product Structure   The sequence that components follow during their manufacturing into a product. A typical product structure would show raw material converted into fabricated components, components put together to make subassemblies, subassemblies going into assemblies, and so on.

Production Line   A series of pieces of equipment dedicated to the manufacture of a specific number of products or families.

Production Order   *Syn:* manufacturing order.

Production Process   The activities involved in converting inputs into finished goods. *See* manufacturing process, transformation process.

Productivity   An overall measure of the ability to produce a good or a service. It is the actual output of production compared to the actual input of resources. Productivity is a relative measure across time or against common entities. In the production literature, attempts have been made to define total productivity where the effects of labor and capital are combined and divided into the output. One example is a ratio that is calculated by adding the standard hours of labor actually produced plus the standard machine hours actually produced in a given time period divided by the actual hours available for both labor and machines in the time period.

Projected Available Balance   The inventory balance projected into the future. It is the running sum of on-hand inventory minus requirements plus scheduled receipts and planned orders.

Prototype   (1) A product model constructed for testing and evaluation to see how the product performs before releasing the product to manufacture. (2) A model consisting of all files and programs needed for a business application.

Proven Path   The Oliver Wight Proven Path is an implementation and change management methodology, developed over 50-plus years of Oliver Wight Principals working with some of the world's most successful companies. It provides a roadmap for a company's journey to business excellence.

Pseudo Bill-of-Material   An artificial grouping of items that facilitates planning. *See* modular bill-of-material, phantom bill-of-material, planning bill-of-material, super bill-of-material.

Pull (System)   (1) In production, the production of items only as demanded for use or to replace those taken for use. (2) In material control, the withdrawal of inventory as demanded by the using operations. Material is not issued until a signal comes from the user. (3) In distribution, a system for replenishing field warehouse inventories where replenishment decisions are made at the field warehouse itself, not at the central warehouse or plant.

Push (System)   (1) In production, the production of items at times required by a given schedule planned in advance. (2) In material control, the issuing of material according to a given schedule or issuing material to a job order at its start time. (3) In distribution, a system for replenishing field warehouse inventories where replenishment decision making is centralized, usually at the manufacturing site or central supply facility.

Rate-Based Scheduling   A method for scheduling and producing based on a periodic rate, for example, daily, weekly, or monthly. Traditionally, this method has been applied to high-volume and process industries. The concept has been recently applied within job shops using cellular layouts and mixed-model level schedules where the production rate is matched to the selling rate.

Rated Capacity   The expected output capability of a resource or system. Capacity is traditionally calculated from such data as planned hours, efficiency, and utilization. The rated capacity is equal to hours available × efficiency × utilization. *Syn:* calculated capacity, effective capacity, nominal capacity, standing capacity

Raw Material   Purchased items or extracted materials that are converted via the manufacturing process into components and products.

Raw Materials Inventory   Inventory of material that has not undergone processing at a facility.

Real Time   The technique of coordinating data processing with external related physical events as they occur, thereby permitting prompt reporting of conditions.

Receipt   (1) The physical acceptance of an item into a stocking location. (2) Often, the transaction reporting of this activity.

Recipe   *Syn:* formula.

Regeneration MRP   An MRP processing approach where the master production schedule is totally re-exploded down through all bills-of-material to maintain valid priorities. New requirements and planned orders are completely recalculated or "regenerated" at that time.

Release   The authorization to produce or ship material that has already been ordered.

Remanufacturing   (1) An industrial process in which worn-out products are restored to like-new condition. In contrast, a repaired or rebuilt product normally retains its identity, and only those parts that have failed or are badly worn are replaced or serviced. (2) The manufacturing environment where worn-out products are restored to like-new condition.

Repetitive Manufacturing   The repeated production of the same discrete products or families of products. Repetitive methodology minimizes setups, inventory, and manufacturing lead times by using production lines, assembly lines, or cells. Work orders are no longer necessary; production scheduling and control is based on production rates. Products may be standard or assembled from modules. Repetitive is not a function of speed or volume. *Syn:* repetitive process

Required Capacity   *Syn:* capacity required.

Requirements Explosion   The process of calculating the demand for the components of a parent item by multiplying the parent item requirements by the component usage quantity specified in the bill-of-material. *Syn:* explosion.

Rescheduling   The process of changing order or operation due dates, usually as a result of their being out of phase when they are needed.

Rescheduling Assumption   A fundamental piece of MRP logic that assumes that existing open orders can be rescheduled in nearer time periods far more easily than new orders can be released and received. As a result, planned order receipts are not created until all scheduled receipts have been applied to cover gross requirements.

Resource   Anything that adds value to a product or service in its creation, production, and delivery.

Resource Profile   The standard hours of load placed on a resource by time period. Production lead-time data is taken into account to provide time-phased projections of the capacity requirements for individual production facilities. *See* bill-of-resources, capacity planning using overall factors, product load profile, rough cut capacity planning.

Resource Requirements Planning (RRP)   The process of converting the aggregate supply plan and/or master plan into requirements for critical resources, often including groups of labor, machinery, and so on. Comparison to planned capacity is usually done for each critical resource. This comparison assists the master (supply) planner in establishing an achievable master (supply) plan.

Rough Cut Capacity Planning (RCCP)   The process of converting the master plan and/or master schedule into requirements for key resources, often including labor, machinery, warehouse/cooler space, loading doors, suppliers' capabilities, and, in some cases, money. Comparison to planned capacity (demonstrated capacity plus or minus planned changes to the process) is usually done for each key or critical resource. This comparison assists the master planner and/or master scheduler in establishing a doable master plan and/or master schedule.

Route Sheet   *Syn:* routing.

Routing   (1) Information detailing the method of manufacture of a particular item. It includes the operations to be performed, their sequence, the various work centers involved, and the standards for setup and run. In some companies, the routing also includes information on tooling, operator skill levels, inspection operations, and testing requirements, and the like. *Syn:* bill-of-operations, instruction sheet, manufacturing data sheet, operation chart, operation list, operation sheet, route sheet, routing sheet. *See* bill-of-labor, bill-of-resources. (2) In information systems, the process of defining the path a message will take from one computer to another computer.

Safety Capacity   The planned amount by which the available capacity exceeds current productive capacity. This capacity provides protection from planned activities such as resource contention, preventive maintenance, and so on, and unplanned activities such as resource breakdown, poor quality, rework, lateness, and the like. Safety capacity plus productive capacity plus idle or excess capacity is equal to 100 percent of capacity. *Syn:* protective capacity.

Safety Lead Time   An element of time added to normal lead time for the purpose of completing an order in advance of its real need date to protect against fluctuations in lead time. When used, the MRP system, in offsetting for lead time, will plan both order release and order completion for earlier dates than it would otherwise.

Safety Stock   (1) In general, a quantity of stock planned to be in inventory to protect against fluctuations in demand and/or supply. (2) In the context of master production scheduling, the additional inventory and/or capacity planned as protection against forecast errors and/or short-term changes in the backlog. Overplanning can be used to create safety stock. *Syn:* buffer stock, reserve stock.

Safety Time   *Syn:* safety lead time.

Sales and Operations Planning (S&OP)   The progenitor of integrated business planning, consisting largely of monthly demand, supply, inventory and capacity planning, and balancing at the aggregate level. Industry has adopted the term *integrated business planning* (advanced S&OP) to more accurately describe the evolved process. *See* integrated business planning, aggregate planning, supply planning, demand planning, integrated tactical planning.

Sales Forecast   *Syn:* forecast.

Sales Plan   *See* demand plan.

Sales Planning   *See* demand planning.

Scenario Planning   The process of developing alternative future plans and predictions using multiple data sets and assumptions, typically supported by specialized advanced planning and optimization software. Scenario planning supports contingency plans at both the strategic and tactical levels, ensuring that plans, resources, and capabilities are in place for potential future events and variables.

Schedule   A timetable for planned occurrences; for example, shipping schedule, master production schedule, maintenance schedule, supplier schedule. Some schedules (e.g., project schedules) include the starting and ending times for activities.

Schedule Board   *Syn:* control board.

Scheduled Receipt   An open order that has an assigned due date. *See* open order.

Scheduling   The act of creating a schedule, such as a master schedule, shop schedule, maintenance schedule, supplier schedule, and so on.

Scrap Factor   A factor that expresses the quantity of a particular component that is expected to be scrapped upon receipt from a vendor, completion of production, or while that component is being built into a given assembly. *Syn:* scrap rate.

Seasonality   A repetitive pattern of demand from year to year (or other repeating time interval) with some periods considerably higher than others. *See* base series.

Semifinished Goods   Products that have been stored uncompleted awaiting final operations that adapt them to different uses or customer specifications.

Sequencing   Determining the order in which a manufacturing facility is to process a number of different jobs in order to achieve certain objectives.

Service Parts   Those modules, components, and elements that are planned to be used without modification to replace an original part. *Syn:* repair parts.

Service Parts Demand   The need or requirement for a component to be sold by itself, as opposed to being used in production to make a higher-level product. *Syn:* repair parts demand.

Setup Time   The time required for a specific machine, resource, work center, or line to convert from the production of the last good piece of lot A to the first good piece of lot B. *Syn:* setup lead time.

Shelf Life   The amount of time an item may be held in inventory before it becomes unusable.

Shipping   The function that performs tasks for the outgoing shipment of parts, components, and products. It includes packaging, marking, weighing, and loading for shipment.

Shipping Lead Time   The number of working days in transit normally required for goods to move between a shipping and receiving point, plus acceptance time in days at the receiving point.

Shop Packet   A package of documents used to plan and control the shop floor movement of an order. The packet may include a manufacturing order, operations sheets, engineering blueprints, picking lists, move tickets, inspection tickets, time tickets, and others.

Significant Part Number   A part number that is intended to convey certain information, such as the source of the part, the material in the part, the shape of the part, and the like. These usually make part numbers longer. *Ant:* nonsignificant part number.

Simulation   (1) The technique of using representative or artificial data to reproduce in a model various conditions that are likely to occur in the actual performance of a system. It is frequently used to test the behavior of a system under different operating policies. (2) Within MRPII, using the operational data to perform what-if evaluations of alternative plans to answer the question, Can we do it? If yes, the simulation can then be run in the financial mode to help answer the question, Do we really want to? *Syn:* scenario planning.

Single-Level Bill-of-Material   A display of components that are directly used in a parent item. It shows only the relationship one level down.

Single-Level Where-Used   Single-level where-used for a component lists each parent in which that component is directly used and in what quantity. This information is usually made available through the technique known as implosion.

Software   The programs and documentation necessary to make use of a computer.

Spare Parts   *Syn:* service parts.

Spare Parts Demand   *Syn:* service parts demand.

Split Lot   A manufacturing order quantity that has been divided into two or more smaller quantities, usually after the order has been released. The quantities of a split lot may be worked on in parallel or a portion of the original quantity may be sent ahead to a subsequent operation to be worked on while work on the remainder of the quantity is being completed at the current operation. The purpose of splitting a lot is to reduce the lead time of part of the order.

Standard   (1) An established norm against which measurements are compared. (2) An established norm of productivity defined in terms of units of output per set time (units per hour) or in standard time (minutes per unit). (3) The time allowed to perform a specific job including quantity of work to be produced.

Standard Costs   The target costs of an operation, process, or product, including direct material, direct labor, and overhead charges.

Standard Time   The length of time that should be required to (1) set up a given machine or operation and (2) run one batch or one or more parts, assemblies, or end products through that operation. This time is used in determining machine requirements and labor requirements. Standard time assumes an average worker following prescribed methods and allows time for personal rest to overcome fatigue and unavoidable delays. It is also frequently used as a basis for incentive pay systems and as a basis of allocating overhead in cost accounting systems. *Syn:* standard hours.

Star   A slang term for a high-growth, high-profit-margin product.

Static Data   Data that remain relatively unchanged over time and are changed only as the rules of the business change, as opposed to dynamic data that change as a result of ongoing business transactions. Examples of static data include lead-time parameters, inventory parameters, routing and work center parameters, logistics parameters, and bills-of-material. *See* master data, dynamic data.

Strategic Planning   The process of developing a strategic plan.

Strategy   The strategy of an enterprise identifies how a company will function in its environment. The strategy specifies how to satisfy customers, how to grow the business, how to compete in its environment, how to manage the organization and develop capabilities within the business, and how to achieve financial objectives.

Structure   *See The Oliver Wight Class A Standard for Business Excellence*, 7th edition.

Structured Approach   *See* Oliver Wight's *Proven Path: A Roadmap to Class A Success—The Integrated Approach to MPRII, JIT/TQC, and DRP*, 2nd edition, and *The Proven Path to a Successful (MPS) Implementation*, 3rd edition.

Subassembly   An assembly that is used at a higher level to build another assembly.

Subcontracting   Sending production work outside to another manufacturer.

Suboptimization   A solution to a problem that is best from a narrow point of view but not from a higher or overall company point of view. For example, a department manager who would not have employees work overtime to minimize the department's operating expense may cause lost sales and a reduction in overall company profitability.

Supply   (1) The quantity of goods available for use. (2) The actual or planned replenishment of a product or component. The replenishment quantities are created in response to a demand for the product or component or in anticipation of such a demand.

Supply Chain   The global network used to deliver products and services from raw materials to end customers through an engineered flow of information, physical distribution, and cash.

Supply Chain Management   The design, planning, execution, control, and monitoring of supply chain activities with the objective of creating net value, building a competitive infrastructure, leveraging worldwide logistics, synchronizing supply with demand, and measuring performance globally.

Supply Chain Planning (Corporate)   This process is responsible for ensuring that the approved demand plan from IBP is satisfied with product and the approved supply plan is optimally assigned to the manufacturing facility (or facilities in a multi-plant environment). The corporate supply chain planning function does not schedule any of the company's manufacturing facilities (plants); instead, it requests certain types and quantities of products to be built in order to meet anticipated demand. Additionally, the supply chain planning function monitors projected inventory and backlogs to ensure that neither gets out of IBP tolerances. Thus, the corporate supply manager, supported by the master supply planner, acts as a corporate-level balancer of demand and supply using many of the same techniques used by the plant-level master schedulers.

Supply Plan   The agreed-upon plan that comes from the supply planning (integrated business planning) process, specifically the overall level of supply output planned to be produced and/or procured, usually stated as a monthly rate for each product family (group of products). Various units of measurement can be used to express the plan: units, tonnage, standard hours, number of workers, and so on. The supply plan is management's authorization for the master planner and/or master scheduler to convert it into a more detailed plan—that is, the master plan and/or master schedule.

Supply Planning   A process to develop tactical plans based on setting the overall level of supply output (manufacturing and/or procurement plan) and other activities to best satisfy the current planned levels of demand, while meeting general business objectives as expressed in the overall business plan.

Supply Point Management   This is the internal part of the supply chain. The basic supply chain in the business world consists of customers (part of the external supply chain), suppliers (part of the external supply chain), and the company's owned facilities (e.g., manufacturing facilities, product development labs, etc.—part of the internal supply chain). Best practices suggest that a company get its own house in order before extending ties to the external supply chain.

Supply Review   The step in the IBP process where the submitted demand plan or request-for-product is received, analyzed, and accepted, which means that the request can be met in terms of inventory and/or capacity at an economical cost. Alternative supply plans are developed as needed to support demand where supply capabilities are lacking.

Synchronized Production   A manufacturing management philosophy that includes a consistent set of principles, procedures, and techniques where every action is evaluated in terms of the global goal of the system. Both kanban, which is part of the just-in-time and lean manufacturing philosophy, and drum-buffer-rope, which is a part of the theory of constraints philosophy, represent synchronized production control approaches. *Syn:* just-in-time, theory of constraints.

Tactical Planning   The process of developing a set of tactical plans (e.g., production plan, sales plan, marketing plan, etc.). Two approaches to tactical planning exist for linking tactical plans to strategic plans—production planning and sales and operations planning. *See* operational planning, strategic planning.

Time Bucket   A number of days of data summarized into one columnar display. A weekly time bucket in MRP would contain all of the relevant data summarized for an entire week. Weekly time buckets are considered to be the largest possible (at least in the near and medium term) to permit effective MRP.

Time Fence   A policy or guideline established to note where various restrictions or changes in operating procedures take place. For example, changes to the master production schedule can be accomplished easily beyond the cumulative lead time, while changes inside the cumulative lead time become increasingly more difficult to a point where changes should be resisted. Time fences can be used to define these points. *See* demand time fence, hedge, planning time fence.

Time Phasing   The technique of expressing future demand, supply, and inventories by time period. Time phasing is one of the key elements of material requirements planning.

Time Standard   The predetermined times allowed for the performance of a specific job. The standard will often consist of two parts, that for machine setup and that for actual running. The standard can be developed through observation of the actual work (time study), summation of standard micromotion times (predetermined or synthetic time standards), or approximation (historical job times).

Time-to-Market   The total time required to design, build, and deliver a product (timed from concept to delivery).

Tolerance   Allowable departure from a nominal value established by design engineers that is deemed acceptable for the functioning of the good or service over its life cycle.

Total Lead Time   *Syn:* lead time.

Transit Time   A standard allowance that is assumed on any given order for the movement of items from one operation to the next. *Syn:* travel time.

Transportation   The function of planning, scheduling, and controlling activities related to mode, vendor, and movement of inventories into and out of an organization.

Two-Level Master Production Schedule   A master scheduling approach in which a planning bill-of-material is used to master schedule an end product or family, along with selected key features (options and accessories). *See* hedge, multilevel master production schedule, production forecast.

U-Lines   Production lines shaped like the letter U. The shape allows workers to easily perform several nonsequential tasks without much walk time. The number of workstations in a U-line is usually determined by line balancing. U-lines promote communication.

Unit of Measure   The unit in which the quantity of an item is managed; for example, pounds, each, box of 12, package of 20, case of 144.

Value Added   (1) In accounting, the addition of direct labor, direct material, and allocated overhead assigned at an operation. It is the cost roll-up as a part goes through a manufacturing process to finished inventory. (2) In current manufacturing terms, the actual increase of utility from the viewpoint of the customer as a part is transformed from raw material to finished inventory. It is the contribution made by an operation or a plant to the final usefulness and value of a product, as seen by the customer. The objective is to eliminate all non-value-added activities in producing and providing a good or service.

Value Chain   The functions within a company that add value to the goods or services that the organization sells to customers and for which it receives payment.

Velocity   (1) The rate of change of an item with respect to time. (2) In supply chain management, a term used to indicate the relative speed of all transactions, collectively, within a supply chain community. A maximum velocity is most desirable because it indicates higher asset turnover for stockholders and faster order-to-delivery response for customers.

Vertical Display   A method of displaying or printing output from a master scheduling system where requirements, scheduled receipts, projected balance, and so on, are displayed vertically, that is, down the page. Vertical displays are often used in conjunction with bucketless systems. *Ant:* horizontal display

Vision   The shared perception of the organization's future—what the organization will achieve and a supporting philosophy. This shared vision must be supported by strategic objectives, strategies, and action plans to move it in the desired direction. *See* vision statement.

Vision Statement   An organization's statement of its vision. *See* vision.

Warehouse Demand   The need for an item to replenish stock at a branch warehouse. *Syn:* branch warehouse demand.

What-If Simulation   *See* scenario planning.

Work Cell   Dissimilar machines grouped together into a production unit to produce a family of parts having similar routings.

Work Center   A specific production facility, consisting of one or more people and/or machines with identical capabilities, that can be considered as one unit for purposes of capacity requirements planning and detailed scheduling. *Syn:* load center.

Work-in-Process (WIP)   A good or goods in various stages of completion throughout the plant, including all material from raw material that has been released for initial processing up to completely processed material awaiting final inspection and acceptance as finished-goods inventory. Many accounting systems also include the value of semifinished stock and components in this category. *Syn:* in-process inventory.

Work Order   (1) An order to the machine shop for tool manufacture or equipment maintenance, not to be confused with a manufacturing order. *Syn:* work ticket. (2) An authorization to start work on an activity (e.g., maintenance) or product. *See* manufacturing order.

Workstation   The assigned location where a worker performs the job; it could be a machine or a workbench.

Yield   The amount of good or acceptable material available after the completion of a process.

Zamboni (because we needed a Z definition)   An ice resurfacer (vehicle or hand-pushed device) used to clean and smooth the surface of a sheet of ice, usually in an ice rink. The first ice resurfacer was developed by American inventor and engineer Frank Zamboni in 1949 in the city of Paramount, California. As such, an ice resurfacer is often referred to as a Zamboni regardless of brand or manufacturer.

Zamboni MPS   A professional hockey team needs clean and refreshed ice to perform at the highest level. A Class A company uses clean (error free) and refreshed (no past dues) master plans and/or master schedules to plan, control, and execute all (and we do mean all) detailed supply plans and schedules to win the game!

Index